FIFTH EDITION

Software
Engineering

INTERNATIONAL COMPUTER SCIENCE SERIES

Consulting Editor **A D McGettrick** University of Strathclyde

SELECTED TITLES IN THE SERIES

Software Development with Z   *J Wordsworth*

Program Verification   *N Francez*

Performance Modelling of Communication Networks   *P Harrison and N Patel*

Concurrent Systems: An Integrated Approach to Operating Systems, Database, and Distributed Systems   *J Bacon*

Introduction to Parallel Processing   *B Codenotti and M Leoncini*

Concurrent Programming   *A Burns and G Davies*

Comparative Programming Languages (2nd edn)   *L Wilson and R Clark*

Functional Programming   *R Plasmeijer and M van Eekelen*

Object-Oriented Database Systems: Concepts and Architectures   *E Bertino and L D Martino*

Programming in Ada (4th edn)   *J Barnes*

Software Design   *D Budgen*

Ada from the Beginning (2nd edn)   *J Skansholm*

Programming Language Essentials   *H E Bal and D Grune*

Human–Computer Interaction   *J Preece et al.*

Distributed Systems: Concepts and Design (2nd edn)   *G Coulouris, J Dollimore and T Kindberg*

Fortran 90 Programming   *T M R Ellis, I Philips and T Lahey*

Parallel Processing: The Transputer and its Applications   *E Hull, D Crookes and P Sweeney*

Foundations of Computing: System Development with Set Theory and Logic   *T Scheurer*

FIFTH EDITION

Software
Engineering

Ian Sommerville
Lancaster University

ADDISON-WESLEY PUBLISHING COMPANY

WOKINGHAM, ENGLAND • READING, MASSACHUSETTS • MENLO PARK, CALIFORNIA • NEW YORK
DON MILLS, ONTARIO • AMSTERDAM • BONN • SYDNEY • SINGAPORE
TOKYO • MADRID • SAN JUAN • MILAN • PARIS • MEXICO CITY • SEOUL • TAIPEI

Cover designed by Designers & Partners of Oxford
Typeset by Meridian Phototypesetting Limited, Pangbourne
Printed in the United States of America

First edition published 1982. Reprinted 1983 and 1984.
Second edition published 1984. Reprinted 1985, 1986, 1987 and 1988.
Third edition published 1989. Reprinted 1989, 1990 (twice) and 1991.
Fourth edition published 1992. Reprinted 1993 and 1994.
Fifth edition printed 1995.

ISBN 0-201-42765-6

British Library Cataloguing-in-Publication Data
A catalogue record for this book is available from the British Library.

Library of Congress Cataloging-in-Publication Data is available

Preface

Software systems are now ubiquitous. Virtually all electrical equipment now includes some kind of software; software is used to help run manufacturing industry, schools and universities, health care, finance and government; many people now use software of different kinds for entertainment and education. The specification, development, management and evolution of these software systems make up the discipline of *software engineering*.

Even simple software systems have a high inherent complexity so engineering principles have to be used in their development. Software engineering is therefore an engineering discipline where software engineers use methods and theory from computer science and apply this cost-effectively to solve difficult problems. These difficult problems have meant that many software development projects have not been successful. However, most modern software provides good service to its users; we should not let high-profile failures obscure the real successes of software engineers over the past 30 years.

Books inevitably reflect the opinions and prejudices of their authors. Some readers will inevitably disagree with my opinions and with the choice of material which I include. Such disagreement is a healthy reflection of the diversity of the discipline and is essential for its evolution. Nevertheless, I hope that all software engineers and software engineering students can find something of interest here.

Although the book is intended as a general introduction to software engineering, it is biased, to some extent, towards my own interests in system requirements engineering and critical systems. I think these are particularly important for software engineering in the 21st century where the challenge we face is to ensure that our software meets the real needs of its users without causing damage to them or to the environment.

I dislike zealots of any kind, whether they are academics preaching the benefits of formal methods or salesmen trying to convince me that some tool or method is the answer to software development problems. There are no simple solutions to the problems of software engineering and we need a wide spectrum of tools and techniques to solve software engineering problems. I therefore don't describe commercial design methods or CASE systems but paint a broad picture of software engineering methods and tools.

Software engineering research has made tremendous strides over the past 15 years but there has been a relatively slow diffusion of this research into industrial practice. The principal challenge which we now face is not the development of new techniques and methods but the transfer of advanced software engineering research into everyday use. I see this book as a contributor to this process. I therefore discuss some techniques, such as viewpoints for requirements engineering, which are reasonably well developed but which are not yet widely used in industry.

Finally, it is impossible to over-emphasize the importance of people in the software engineering process. People specify, design and implement systems which help other people with their work. Most of the difficulties of very large system engineering are not technical problems but are the problems of managing large numbers of people with diverse priorities, abilities and interests. Software engineering techniques and tools are only effective when applied in a context which respects these different skills and abilities.

Changes from the fourth edition

Like many software systems, this book has grown and changed since its first edition was published in 1982. This latest edition started as a relatively minor update of the fourth edition but, in the course of writing the book, I decided that more significant revision and re-engineering was necessary. Although much of the material in the fourth edition has been retained, the following changes have been made:

- There are five completely new chapters covering computer-based system engineering, requirements analysis, architectural design, process improvement and software re-engineering.

- The book has been restructured into eight parts covering an introduction to software engineering, requirements and specification, design, dependable systems development, verification and validation, CASE, management, and software evolution.

- There have been radical revisions of the material on requirements engineering, object-oriented and functional design, and CASE.

- Project management is introduced in the first part of the book then covered in more detail in a separate section which incorporates previous material on human factors. There is more emphasis on quality management.

In previous editions, I have presented program examples in Ada as I consider this an excellent language for large-scale software engineering. However, Ada has not become as widely used as was once predicted. C or C++ are the programming languages of choice for most personal computer and workstation applications. Because of this wide use, I have included C++ as well as Ada versions of most of the program examples in the book. For safety-critical systems, however, I think it unwise to use a language which includes potentially unsafe constructs. Those examples are, therefore, only presented in Ada.

I considered for a long time whether it would be appropriate to include a new chapter on professional and ethical issues. I decided not to do so because the topic is so subjective that it is difficult to present in a balanced way in a single chapter. There are no absolutes in this area and it is best addressed in an interactive context rather than as a chapter of a book. However, I have included a brief discussion of these issues in the introduction to the book. I have also included possible ethical and professional topics for discussion as exercises in many chapters. Links to WWW pages on this topic are included in the Web page whose URL is given below.

The further reading associated with each chapter has been updated from previous editions. However, in many cases, articles written in the 1980s are still the best introduction to some topics. As new articles which are useful become available, I will include them on the Web page. The author index in previous editions has been removed. Rather, each entry in the References section includes the page numbers where it has been referenced.

Readership

The book is aimed at students in undergraduate and graduate courses and at software engineers in commerce and industry. It may be used in general software engineering courses or in courses such as advanced programming, software specification, software design or management. Practitioners may find the book useful as general reading and as a means of updating their knowledge on particular topics such as requirements engineering, architectural design, dependable systems development and process improvement. Wherever practicable, the examples in the text have been given a practical bias to reflect the type of applications which software engineers must develop.

I assume that readers have a basic familiarity with programming and modern computer systems. Some examples rely on knowledge of basic data structures such as stacks, lists and queues. The chapters on formal specification assume knowledge of very elementary set theory. No other mathematical background is required.

Using the book as a course text

There are three main types of software engineering courses where this book can be used:

(1) General introductory courses in software engineering. For students who have no previous software engineering experience, you can start with the introductory section then pick and choose the introductory chapters from the different sections of the book. This will give students a general overview of the subject with the opportunity of more detailed study for those students who are interested.

(2)   Introductory or intermediate courses on specific topics in software engineering such as software specification, design or dependable systems development. Each of the parts in the book can serve as a text in its own right for an introductory or intermediate course on that topic.

(3)   More advanced courses in specific software engineering topics. In this case, the chapters in the book form a foundation for the course which must be supplemented with further reading which explores the topic in more detail. All chapters include my suggestions for further reading.

The benefit of a general text like this is that it can be used in several different related courses. At Lancaster, we use the text in an introductory software engineering course, in courses on specification, design and critical systems and in a software management course where it is supplemented with further reading. With a single text, students are presented with a consistent view of the subject. They also like the extensive coverage because they don't have to buy several different books.

This book covers all suggested material in Units SE2 to SE5 in the ACM/IEEE 1991 Curriculum. It also includes material to supplement an introductory programming text which would normally cover Unit SE1 and all material in the suggested course entitled 'Advanced Software Engineering'.

Supplements

The following supplements are available:

- An instructor's guide including hints on teaching the material in each chapter, class and term project suggestions, and solutions to some of the exercises. This is available in Postscript or on paper from Addison-Wesley.

- A set of overhead projector transparencies for each chapter. These are available in Postscript and in Microsoft Powerpoint format.

- Source code for most of the individual program examples including supplementary code required for compilation.

- An introduction to the Ada programming language.

- Information on course presentation using electronically mediated communication and links to material for that approach to teaching.

These are available, free of charge, over the Internet at URL:

http://www.comp.lancs.ac.uk/computing/resources/ser/

This page also includes links to other software engineering resources which you may find useful. If you have any problems, you can contact me by E-mail (is@comp.lancs.ac.uk).

Acknowledgements

I am indebted to a number of reviewers who provided helpful and constructive criticism of early drafts of this book. Many thanks to Leonor Barocca of the Open University, Stewart Green of the University of the West of England, Andrew McGettrick of the University of Strathclyde, Philip Morrow of the University of Ulster and Ray Welland of the University of Glasgow. Thanks also to Rodney L. Bown, University of Houston-Clear Lake, Charles P. Howerton, Metropolitan State College of Denver, Josephine DeGuzman Mendoza of California State University, San Bernardino and David C. Rine of George Mason University.

Thanks also to all users of previous editions who have provided me with comments and constructive criticism and to my colleagues in the Cooperative Systems Engineering Group and Lancaster University.

Finally, a big thank-you to my wife Anne and daughters, Ali and Jay. They have provided coffee, encouragement and occasional inspiration during the long hours I spent writing this book.

Ian Sommerville
August 1995

Contents

Part One
Introduction

The chapters in this introductory part introduce the topic of software engineering and place it in the context of a system engineering process. They emphasize that software engineering is a managed process by including discussions of software and system engineering process models and a short introduction to fundamentals of project management. Project management is also discussed in more detail later in Part 7.

Contents

Introduction

Objectives

- To define software engineering and to explain why it is important.

- To introduce the concept of a software product and the attributes of well-engineered software.

- To describe the basic activities of the software engineering process and to illustrate a number of generic software process models.

- To explain why software process visibility is essential for process management.

- To explain why software engineers must consider their responsibilities to the engineering profession.

Contents

3

In all industrialized countries, and increasingly in developing countries, computer systems are economically critical. More and more products incorporate computers in some form. Educational, administrative and health care systems are dependent on computer systems. The software in these systems represents a large and increasing proportion of the total system costs. The effective functioning of modern economic and political systems therefore depends on our ability to produce software in a cost-effective way.

Software engineering is concerned with the theories, methods and tools which are needed to develop the software for these computers. In most cases, the software systems which must be developed are large and complex systems. They are also abstract in that they do not have any physical form. Software engineering is therefore different from other engineering disciplines. It is not constrained by materials governed by physical laws or by manufacturing processes.

Software engineers model parts of the real world in software. These models are large, abstract and complex so they must be made visible in documents such as system designs, user manuals, and so on. Producing these documents is as much part of the software engineering process as programming. As the real world which is modelled changes, so too must the software. Therefore, software engineering is also concerned with evolving these models to meet changing needs and requirements.

The notion of 'software engineering' was proposed in the late 1960s at a conference held to discuss what was then called the 'software crisis'. This software crisis resulted directly from the introduction of third-generation computer hardware. These machines were orders of magnitude more powerful than second-generation machines. Their power made hitherto unrealizable applications a feasible proposition. The implementation of these applications required large software systems to be built.

Early experience in building large software systems showed that existing methods of software development were not good enough. Techniques applicable to small systems could not be scaled up. Major projects were sometimes years late. They cost much more than originally predicted, were unreliable, difficult to maintain and performed poorly. Software development was in crisis. Hardware costs were tumbling while software costs were rising rapidly. New techniques and methods were needed to control the complexity inherent in large software systems.

After almost 30 years of development, we have made enormous progress in software engineering. Productivity improvements are hard to quantify but there is no doubt that our ability to produce efficient and dependable software has markedly improved. We have a much better understanding of the activities involved in software development. We have developed methods of software specification, design and implementation. New notations and tools reduce the effort required to produce large and complex systems.

Nevertheless, many large software projects are still late and over-budget. Software is delivered and installed which does not meet the real needs of the customers buying that software. New technologies resulting from the convergence of computers and communication systems place new demands on software engineers.

Software engineering has come far in its short lifetime; it still has far to go.

1.1 Software products

The objective of software engineering is to produce software products. Software products are software systems delivered to a customer with the documentation which describes how to install and use the system. In some cases, software products will be part of systems products where hardware as well as software is delivered to a customer.

Software products fall into two broad classes:

(1) *Generic products*   These are stand-alone systems which are produced by a development organization and sold on the open market to any customer who is able to buy them.

(2) *Bespoke (customized) products*   These are systems which are commissioned by a particular customer. The software is developed specially for that customer by some contractor.

Until the 1980s, the vast majority of software systems which were sold were bespoke, specially designed systems which ran on large computers. They were expensive because all the development cost had to be met by a single client.

Since the development of personal computers, this situation has completely changed. The personal computer market is totally dominated by software products produced by companies such as Microsoft. These account for the vast majority of software sales. These are usually relatively cheap because their development cost is spread across hundreds or thousands of different customers.

However, there is still a large market for specially designed systems. Hardware control always requires some kind of special-purpose system. As computers are embedded in more and more devices, there is an increasing demand for software controllers. Consequently, most software development effort is still probably devoted to producing bespoke systems rather than shrink-wrapped software products.

The problems of software development and the software engineering methods which may be used are the same for software products and bespoke systems. The most significant difference is that generic product specifications are produced internally by the marketing department of the product company. They reflect what they think will sell. They are usually flexible and non-prescriptive. By contrast, specifications for bespoke systems are often the basis for the contract between customer and contractor. They are usually defined in detail and changes have to be negotiated and carefully costed.

1.1.2 Software product attributes

Like all engineering, software engineering is not just about producing products but involves producing products in a cost-effective way. Given unlimited resources, the majority of software problems can probably be solved. The challenge for software engineers is to produce high-quality software with a finite amount of resources and to a predicted schedule.

The attributes of a software product are the characteristics displayed by the product once it is installed and put into use. These are not the services provided by the product. Rather, they are concerned with the product's dynamic behaviour and the use made of the product. Examples of these attributes are therefore efficiency, reliability, maintainability, robustness, portability, and so on.

The relative importance of these characteristics obviously varies from system to system. However, I think the characteristics shown in Figure 1.1 are critical quality attributes which are the essence of well-engineered software.

Optimizing all of these attributes is difficult as some are exclusive. For example, providing a better user interface may reduce system efficiency. All are subject to the law of diminishing returns. The relationship between cost and improvements in each of these attributes is not a linear one. Small improvements in any of the attributes can be expensive. A great deal of effort must be devoted to optimizing a particular attribute.

As an example of this, Figure 1.2 shows how costs may rise exponentially as efficiency improvements are required.

For some kinds of system, such as avionic systems, efficiency is a prime consideration. The software may have to run on a computer where weight and size considerations restrict the power of the hardware which can be used. It may have to run in a relatively small memory with no associated disks. It may be necessary to optimize efficiency at the expense of the other system attributes. Where this is necessary, the design decisions for efficiency should be explicit and the consequences of these decisions carefully analysed.

In this book, I concentrate on methods, strategies, tools and policies which lead to dependable and maintainable software. Almost all software, irrespective of application domain, must have these characteristics. Usability is discussed in Chapter 17 which introduces user interface design. I don't discuss methods of making software efficient in this book as these usually rely on detailed characteristics of algorithms or hardware.

Product characteristic	Description
Maintainability	It should be possible to evolve software to meet the changing needs of customers.
Dependability	Software dependability includes a range of characteristics including reliability, security and safety. Dependable software should not cause physical or economic damage in the event of system failure.
Efficiency	Software should not make wasteful use of system resources such as memory and processor cycles.
Usability	Software should have an appropriate user interface and adequate documentation.

Figure 1.1
Essential attributes of well-engineered software.

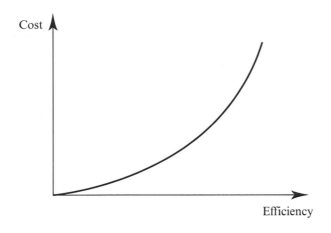

Figure 1.2
Costs vs efficiency.

1.2 The software process

The software process is the set of activities and associated results which produce a software product. These activities are mostly carried out by software engineers. CASE (computer-aided software engineering) tools may be used to help with some process activities.

There are four fundamental process activities (covered later in the book) which are common to all software processes. The activities are:

(1)   *Software specification*   The functionality of the software and constraints on its operation must be defined.

(2)   *Software development*   The software to meet the specification must be produced.

(3)   *Software validation*   The software must be validated to ensure that it does what the customer wants.

(4)   *Software evolution*   The software must evolve to meet changing customer needs.

There is no such thing as a 'right' or a 'wrong' software process. Different software processes decompose these activities in different ways. The timing of the activities varies as does the results of each activity. Different organizations use different processes to produce the same type of product. Different types of product may be produced by an organization using different processes. However, some processes are more suitable than others for some types of application. If the wrong process is used, this will probably reduce the quality or the usefulness of the software product to be developed.

Because there are a variety of different process models used, it is impossible to produce reliable figures for cost distribution across these activities. However, we do know that modifying software usually takes up more than 60% of total software costs. This percentage is increasing as more and more software is produced and has to be maintained. Designing software for change is therefore essential.

Software processes (like most business processes) are complex and involve a very large number of activities. Like products, processes also have attributes or characteristics such as those shown in Figure 1.3.

It is not possible to optimize all process attributes simultaneously. For example, if a rapid development process is required then it may be necessary to reduce the process visibility. Making a process visible means producing documents at regular intervals. This will slow down the process.

Detailed software process models are still the subject of research but it is now clear that there are a number of different general models or paradigms of software development:

(1) *The waterfall approach*   This takes the above activities and represents them as separate process phases such as requirements specification, software design, implementation, testing and so on. After each stage is defined it is 'signed-off' and development goes on to the following stage.

(2) *Evolutionary development*   This approach interleaves the activities of specification, development and validation. An initial system is rapidly developed from very abstract specifications. This is then refined with customer input to produce a system which satisfies the customer's needs. The system may then be delivered. Alternatively, it may be re-implemented using a more structured approach to produce a more robust and maintainable system.

(3) *Formal transformation*   This approach is based on producing a formal mathematical system specification and transforming this specification, using mathematical methods, to a program. These transformations are 'correctness-preserving'. This means that you can be sure that the developed program meets its specification.

(4) *System assembly from reusable components*   This technique assumes that parts of the system already exist. The system development process focuses on integrating these parts rather than developing them from scratch.

The first two of these approaches, namely the waterfall approach and evolutionary development, are now widely used for practical systems development. Some systems have been built using correctness-preserving transformations but this is still an experimental process. It is discussed in more detail in Chapter 9.

A reuse-oriented process is commonplace in Japan (Cusamano, 1989). The potential of this approach is slowly being recognized in Europe and North America. In the US, a major reuse initiative with a budget of $150 million started in 1995. However, reuse is still experimental in most companies so it is too early to comment on the effectiveness of a reuse-driven process. I discuss reuse issues in Chapter 20.

Process characteristic	Description
Understandability	To what extent is the process explicitly defined and how easy is it to understand the process definition?
Visibility	Do the process activities culminate in clear results so that the progress of the process is externally visible?
Supportability	To what extent can the process activities be supported by CASE tools?
Acceptability	Is the defined process acceptable to and usable by the engineers responsible for producing the software product?
Reliability	Is the process designed in such a way that process errors are avoided or trapped before they result in product errors?
Robustness	Can the process continue in spite of unexpected problems?
Maintainability	Can the process evolve to reflect changing organizational requirements or identified process improvements?
Rapidity	How fast can the process of delivering a system from a given specification be completed?

Figure 1.3
Process characteristics.

1.2.1 The 'waterfall' model

The first explicit model of the software development process was derived from other engineering processes (Royce, 1970). This was enthusiastically accepted by software project management. It offered a means of making the development process more visible. Because of the cascade from one phase to another, this model is known as the 'waterfall model' (Figure 1.4).

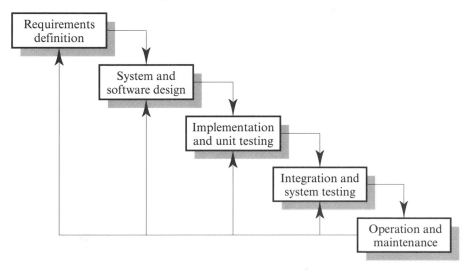

Figure 1.4
The software life cycle.

There are numerous variations of this process model (which is sometimes called the software life cycle). The principal stages of the model map onto the fundamental development activities:

(1) *Requirements analysis and definition* The system's services, constraints and goals are established by consultation with system users. They are then defined in a manner which is understandable by both users and development staff.

(2) *System and software design* The systems design process partitions the requirements to either hardware or software systems. It establishes an overall system architecture. Software design involves representing the software system functions in a form that may be transformed into one or more executable programs.

(3) *Implementation and unit testing* During this stage, the software design is realized as a set of programs or program units. Unit testing involves verifying that each unit meets its specification.

(4) *Integration and system testing* The individual program units or programs are integrated and tested as a complete system to ensure that the software requirements have been met. After testing, the software system is delivered to the customer.

(5) *Operation and maintenance* Normally (although not necessarily) this is the longest life cycle phase. The system is installed and put into practical use. Maintenance involves correcting errors which were not discovered in earlier stages of the life cycle, improving the implementation of system units and enhancing the system's services as new requirements are discovered.

In practice, these stages overlap and feed information to each other. During design, problems with requirements are identified; during coding, design problems are found and so on. The software process is not a simple linear model but involves a sequence of iterations of the development activities.

During the final life cycle phase (operation and maintenance) the software is put into use. Errors and omissions in the original software requirements are discovered. Program and design errors emerge and the need for new functionality is identified. Modifications become necessary for the software to remain useful. Making these changes (software maintenance) may involve repeating some or all previous process stages.

Unfortunately, a model which includes frequent iterations makes it difficult to identify definite management checkpoints for planning and reporting. Therefore, after a small number of iterations, it is normal to freeze parts of the development, such as the specification, and to continue with the later development stages. Problems are left for later resolution, ignored or are programmed around. This premature freezing of requirements may mean that the system won't do what the user wants. It may also lead to badly structured systems as design problems are circumvented by implementation tricks.

The problem with the waterfall model is its inflexible partitioning of the project into these distinct stages. Delivered systems are sometimes unusable as they do not meet the customer's real requirements. Nevertheless, the waterfall model reflects engineering practice. Consequently, it is likely that software process models based on this approach will remain the norm for large hardware–software systems development.

1.2.2 Evolutionary development

Evolutionary development is based on the idea of developing an initial implementation, exposing this to user comment and refining this through many versions until an adequate system has been developed (Figure 1.5). Rather than have separate specification, development and validation activities, these are carried out concurrently with rapid feedback across these activities.

There are two types of evolutionary development:

(1)   *Exploratory programming* where the objective of the process is to work with the customer to explore their requirements and deliver a final system. The development starts with the parts of the system which are understood. The system evolves by adding new features as they are proposed by the customer.

(2)   *Throw-away prototyping* where the objective of the evolutionary development process is to understand the customer's requirements and hence develop a better requirements definition for the system. The prototype concentrates on experimenting with those parts of the customer requirements which are poorly understood.

Exploratory programming is essential when it is difficult (or impossible) to establish a detailed system specification. Some people might argue that all systems fall into

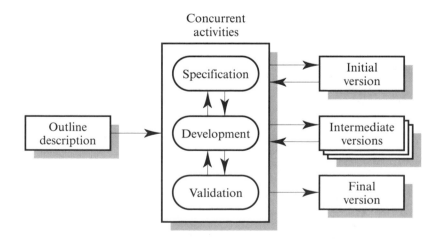

Figure 1.5
Evolutionary
development.

this class. However, exploratory programming is mostly used for the development of AI systems which attempt to emulate some human capabilities. As we don't understand how humans carry out tasks, setting out a detailed specification for software to imitate humans is impossible.

The evolutionary approach to software development is usually more effective than the waterfall approach in producing systems which meet the immediate needs of customers. However, from an engineering and management perspective, it has three basic problems:

(1) *The process is not visible*   Managers need regular deliverables to measure progress. If systems are developed quickly, it is not cost-effective to produce documents which reflect every version of the system.

(2) *Systems are usually poorly structured*   Continual change tends to corrupt the software structure. Software evolution is therefore likely to be difficult and costly.

(3) *Special skills are often required*   It is not clear how the range of skills which is normal in software engineering teams can be used effectively for this mode of development. Most available systems developed in this way have been implemented by small teams of highly skilled and motivated individuals.

To resolve these problems, the objective of evolutionary development is sometimes the development of a system prototype. This is used to understand and validate the system specifications. Here, the evolutionary development process is part of some wider process (such as the waterfall process).

Because of these problems, large-scale systems are not usually developed in this way. Evolutionary development is more appropriate for:

(1) The development of relatively small systems. The problems of changing the existing system are avoided by re-implementing the system in its entirety whenever significant changes are required. If prototyping tools are used, this need not be too expensive.

(2) The development of systems with a short lifetime. Here, the system is developed to support some activity which is bounded in time. For example, a system may be developed specifically for the launch of a new product.

(3) The development of systems or parts of larger systems where it is impossible to express detailed specifications in advance. Examples of this type of system are artificial intelligence (AI) systems and user interfaces.

I discuss the evolutionary development process and support for this process in more detail in Chapter 8 where various prototyping techniques are described.

1.3 Boehm's spiral model

A document-oriented, visible waterfall process model has been adopted as a general standard by many government agencies and large software procurers. Thus, it cannot simply be wished away in spite of its difficulties. We need an improved process model for management which can subsume all the generic models discussed in the previous section. It must also satisfy the requirements of software procurers. An alternative approach was proposed by Boehm (1988). He suggested that a model which explicitly recognized risk may form the basis of a generic process model.

Boehm's model takes the form of a spiral (Figure 1.6). Each loop in the spiral represents a phase (as defined by management) of the software process. Thus, the innermost loop might be concerned with system feasibility, the next loop with system requirements definition, the next loop with system design and so on.

There are no fixed phases in this model; the phases shown in Figure 1.6 are merely examples. Management must decide how to structure the project into phases. Organizations will usually work on some generic phase model with extra phases added for specific projects or when problems are identified during a project.

Figure 1.6
Boehm's spiral model of the software process.

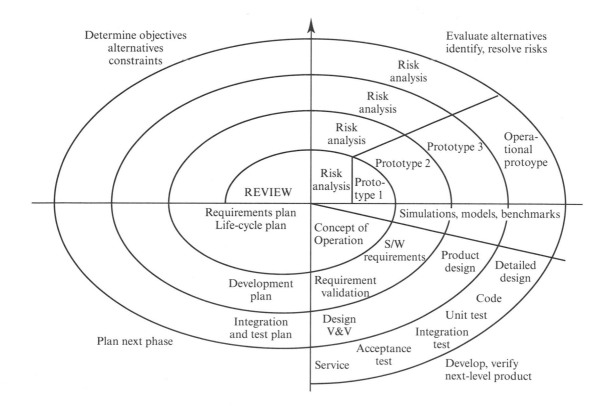

Each loop in the spiral is split into four sectors:

(1)   *Objective setting*   Specific objectives for the phase of the project are defined. Constraints on the process and the product are identified and a detailed management plan is drawn up. Project risks are identified. Alternative strategies, depending on these risks, may be planned.

(2)   *Risk assessment and reduction*   For each of the identified project risks, a detailed analysis is carried out. Steps are taken to reduce the risk. For example, if there is a risk that the requirements are inappropriate, a prototype system may be developed.

(3)   *Development and validation*   After risk evaluation, a development model for the system is then chosen. For example, if user interface risks are dominant, an appropriate development model might be evolutionary prototyping. If safety risks are the main consideration, development based on formal transformations may be the most appropriate and so on. The waterfall model may be the most appropriate development model if the main identified risk is sub-system integration.

(4)   *Planning*   The project is reviewed and a decision made whether to continue with a further loop of the spiral. If it is decided to continue, plans are drawn up for the next phase of the project.

There is no need to adopt a single model in each cycle of the spiral or, indeed, for the whole of one software system. The spiral model encompasses other process models. Prototyping may be used in one spiral to resolve requirements risk. This may be followed by a conventional waterfall development. Formal transformation may be used to develop those parts of the system with high security requirements and a reuse-oriented approach used for implementing the other parts of the data management system.

1.3.1 Risk management

The most important distinction between the spiral model and other software process models is the explicit consideration of risk in the spiral model. Risk is a concept that is difficult to define precisely. Informally, it is simply something which can go wrong. For example, if the intention is to use a new programming language, a risk is that the available compilers are unreliable or do not produce sufficiently efficient object code.

Risks are a consequence of inadequate information. They are resolved by initiating some actions which discover information that reduces uncertainty. In the above example, the risk would be resolved by a market survey to find out which compilers were available and how good they were. If no suitable system was discovered, the decision to use a new language must be changed.

A cycle of the spiral begins by elaborating objectives such as performance, functionality, and so on. Alternative ways of achieving these objectives and the constraints imposed on each of these alternatives are then enumerated. Each alternative is assessed against each objective. This usually results in the identification of sources of project risk. The next step is to evaluate these risks by activities such as more detailed analysis, prototyping, simulation, and so on.

To use the spiral model, Boehm suggests a standard form which is filled in for each round of the spiral. This may be completed at an abstract level or may be a fairly detailed assessment of a software product development. The fields of the form are:

- *Objectives*   The aims of the analysis.
- *Constraints*   Factors which limit the possibilities.
- *Alternatives*   Different possible ways of achieving the objectives.
- *Risks*   Possible risks with identified alternatives.
- *Risk resolution*   Strategies used to reduce the identified risks.
- *Results*   The outcomes of the risk resolution strategies.
- *Plans*   How to tackle the next phase of the analysis.
- *Commitment*   Management decisions on how to continue.

To illustrate this approach, consider an organization that has an overall objective of significantly improving the quality of the software it produces. Figure 1.7 uses the standard form structure to set out objectives, risks and plans for software quality improvement.

Objectives	Significantly improve software quality
Constraints	Within a three-year timescale Without large-scale capital investment Without radical change to company standards
Alternatives	Reuse existing certified software Introduce formal specification and verification Invest in testing and validation tools
Risks	No cost-effective quality improvement possible Quality improvements may increase costs excessively New methods might cause existing staff to leave
Risk resolution	Literature survey Pilot project Survey of potential reusable components Assessment of available tool support Staff training and motivation seminars
Results	Experience of formal methods is limited Hard to quantify improvements Limited tool support available for company standard development system Reusable components available but little reuse tool support
Plans	Explore reuse option in more detail Develop prototype reuse support tools Explore component certification scheme
Commitment	Fund further 12 month development

Figure 1.7
Risks and risk resolution for quality improvement.

Objectives	Procure software component catalogue
Constraints	Within a year
	Must support existing component types
	Total cost must be less than $100,000
Alternatives	Buy existing information retrieval software
	Buy a database and develop the catalogue using a 4GL
	Develop a special-purpose cataloging system integrated with CASE tools
Risks	May be impossible to procure within the existing constraints
	Catalogue specifications are unclear
Risk resolution	Develop prototype catalogue to clarify requirements
	Commission consultant's report on existing information retrieval systems
	Relax time constraints
Results	Information retrieval systems are inflexible and difficult to adapt to local needs
	Special-purpose catalogue development is not cost-effective
	Prototype may be enhanced to provide complete functionality
Plans	Develop catalogue by using a 4GL and a database system. The existing prototype should be enhanced
Commitment	Fund further 12 month development

Figure 1.8
Risks and risk resolution for catalogue procurement.

The form is filled in progressively as a spiral proceeds. Clearly Figure 1.7 is at an abstract level. However, it makes the choices and risks explicit and forces managers to consider all possibilities. The same format can be used at a more detailed level when a particular software system (say a reusable components catalogue) is to be developed. Figure 1.8 shows the form for this system. As part of risk resolution, a prototype catalogue is developed. After evaluation, the future plans are to continue development of this system using an evolutionary prototyping approach.

The risk assessment for the catalogue can then be developed in more detail, examining, say, the user interface requirements for the catalogue. As Figure 1.8 shows, this risk-driven approach to the software process can accommodate different development process models such as evolutionary prototyping.

1.4 Process visibility

Because of the intangible nature of software systems, software process managers need documents, reports and reviews to keep track of what is going on. Consequently, most organizations involved in large system development use a 'deliverable-oriented' process. Each activity must end with the production of some document. These documents make the software process visible.

However, regular document production has some drawbacks:

(1) *Management needs regular deliverables to assess project progress* The timing of management requirements may not correspond with the time needed to complete an activity. Extra documents may have to be produced adding to the cost of the process.

(2) *The need to approve documents constrains process iteration* The costs of going back and adapting a completed deliverable are high. If problems are discovered during the process, inelegant solutions are sometimes adopted to avoid the need to change 'accepted' project deliverables.

(3) *The time required to review and approve a document is significant* There is rarely a smooth transition from one phase of the process to the next. In reality, formal procedures are sometimes ignored. Development may continue before the previous phase document has been completed.

The waterfall process model is still the most widely adopted 'deliverable' model. Figure 1.9 shows one possible way of splitting it into stages and the deliverables which might be produced at each stage. Another view of this model is in Chapter 22, Figure 22.5, which shows how documents produced during development feeds into validation activities. This is sometimes known as the V-model of development.

Activity	Output documents
Requirements analysis	Feasibility study Outline requirements
Requirements definition	Requirements document
System specification	Functional specification Acceptance test plan Draft user manual
Architectural design	Architectural specification System test plan
Interface design	Interface specification Integration test plan
Detailed design	Design specification Unit test plan
Coding	Program code
Unit testing	Unit test report
Module testing	Module test report
Integration testing	Integration test report Final user manual
System testing	System test report
Acceptance testing	Final system plus documentation

Figure 1.9
Documents from the waterfall model.

Process model	Process visibility
Waterfall model	Good visibility. Each activity produces some deliverable
Evolutionary development	Poor visibility. Uneconomic to produce documents during rapid iteration
Formal transformations	Good visibility. Documents must be produced from each phase for the process to continue
Reuse-oriented development	Moderate visibility. It may be artificial to produce documents describing reuse and reusable components
Spiral model	Good visibility. Each segment and each ring of the spiral should produce some document

Figure 1.10
Process model
visibility.

Figure 1.10 summarizes the visibility of the generic software process models introduced in Section 1.2. You can see that the waterfall model, the formal transformation model and the spiral model all have reasonable process visibility.

1.5 Professional responsibility

Like other engineers, software engineers must accept that their job involves wider responsibilities than simply the application of technical skills. Their work is carried out within a legal and social framework. Software engineering is obviously bounded by local, national and international laws. Software engineers must behave in an ethical and morally responsible way if they are to be respected as professionals.

In this respect, professional societies and institutions have an important role to play. Organizations such as the ACM and the British Computer Society publish a code of professional conduct. Members of these organizations undertake to follow that code.

It goes without saying that engineers should uphold normal standards of honesty and integrity. They should not use their skills and abilities to behave in a dishonest way or in a way that will bring disrepute to the software engineering profession. However, there are areas where standards of acceptable behaviour are not bounded by laws but by the more tenuous notion of professional responsibility. Some of these are:

(1) *Confidentiality* Engineers should normally respect the confidentiality of their employers or clients irrespective of whether or not a formal confidentiality agreement has been signed.

(2) *Competence* Engineers should not misrepresent their level of competence. They should not knowingly accept work which is beyond their competence.

(3)   *Intellectual property rights*   Engineers should be aware of local laws governing the use of intellectual property such as patents, copyright, and so on. They should be careful to ensure that the intellectual property of employers and clients is protected.

(4)   *Computer misuse*   Software engineers should not use their technical skills to misuse other people's computers. Computer misuse ranges from relatively trivial (game-playing on an employer's machine, say) to extremely serious (dissemination of viruses).

A difficult situation for professional engineers arises when their employer acts in an unethical way. Say a company is responsible for developing a safety-critical system and because of time-pressure falsifies the safety validation records. Is the engineer's responsibility to maintain confidentiality or to alert the customer or publicize, in some way, that the delivered system may be unsafe?

Engineers must make up their own mind in these matters. In this case, clearly the potential for damage, the extent of the damage and the people affected by the damage must influence the decision. If the situation is very dangerous, it may be justified to publicize it using the national press, for example. However, engineers should first try to resolve the situation while respecting the rights of employers.

Another ethical issue is the participation of engineers in the development of military and nuclear systems. Some people feel strongly about these issues. They do not wish to participate in any way in this class of system development. These wishes should be respected. Employers should make clear to prospective employees if participation in such development projects is expected. If this is not done, employees should not be coerced into working on systems with which they feel uncomfortable.

I have neither the space nor the qualifications to go into ethical issues in any detail in this book. However, where appropriate, I suggest possible ethical issues to discuss in the exercises associated with each chapter.

Further reading

Managing the Software Process. This is a general text on software management which is oriented around the concept of a software process. It is good general background for this chapter. (W. S. Humphrey, 1989, Addison-Wesley.)

'A spiral model of software development and enhancement'. This paper introduces the spiral model and risk management. It discusses practical experience in using the model to develop a software engineering environment. (B.W. Boehm, *IEEE Computer*, **21** (5), May 1988.)

'No silver bullet: Essence and accidents of software engineering'. This paper is a good general introduction to the problems of software engineering. (F.P. Brooks, *IEEE Computer*, **20** (4), April 1987.)

Professional Issues in Software Engineering. This is an excellent book discussing legal and professional issues as well as ethics. (F. Bott, A. Coleman, J. Eaton and D. Rowland, 1995, UCL Press.)

KEY POINTS

■ Software engineering is concerned with methods, tools, and techniques for developing and managing the process of creating and evolving software products.

■ Software products consist of developed programs and associated documentation. Essential product attributes are maintainability, dependability, efficiency and usability.

■ The software process consists of activities which are involved in developing software products. Basic activities are software specification, development, validation and evolution.

■ The waterfall model of the software process considers each process activity as a separate and discrete phase.

■ The evolutionary development model of the software process treats specification, development and validation as concurrent activities.

■ A risk-oriented spiral model of process management forces the consideration of all alternatives and risks. It can accommodate all other models of development.

■ Process visibility is achieved through the creation of deliverable documents which are a result of process activities.

■ Software engineers have responsibilities to the engineering profession and society. They should not simply be concerned with technical issues.

EXERCISES

1.1   What are four important attributes which all software products should have? Suggest four other attributes which may be significant.

1.2   Explain why the waterfall model of the software process is not an accurate reflection of software development activities.

1.3   Giving reasons for your answer based on the type of system being developed, suggest the most appropriate generic software process model which might be used as a basis for managing the development of the following systems:

(a) a system to control anti-lock braking in a car;

(b) a virtual reality system to support software maintenance;

(c) a university accounting system which is intended to replace an existing system;

(d) an interactive system which allows railway passengers to find train times from terminals installed in stations.

1.4   Explain why programs which are developed using evolutionary development are likely to be difficult to maintain.

1.5   Explain how both the waterfall model of the software process and the prototyping model can be accommodated in the spiral process model.

1.6   A university intends to procure an integrated student management system holding all details of registered students including personal information, courses taken and examination marks achieved. The alternative approaches to be adopted are either:

(a) buy a database management system and develop an in-house system based on this database;

(b) buy a system from another university and modify it to local requirements;

(c) join a consortium of other universities, establish a common set of requirements and contract a software house to develop a single system for all of the universities in the consortium.

Identify two possible risks in each of these strategies and suggest techniques for risk resolution which would help in deciding which approach to adopt.

1.7   Discuss whether professional engineers should be certified in the same way as doctors or lawyers.

1.8   Discuss why it is important that professional societies should have a code of professional conduct which members should follow.

2

Computer-based System Engineering

Objectives

- To provide software engineers with an awareness of broader system engineering concepts.

- To illustrate the problems of developing computer-based systems which include hardware, software and people.

- To explain why systems must have a close relationship with the environment in which they are installed.

- To describe the system procurement and system engineering processes.

- To explain why overall system reliability depends on all system components.

Contents

23

Software on its own is completely useless. Until software (merely a string of symbols) is combined with some processor and other hardware to form a *system,* it cannot do anything at all. Software engineers must understand that there are more general problems of system engineering. These concern the interactions between software and hardware system components and the human users of the system.

System engineering is the activity of specifying, designing, implementing, validating, installing and maintaining systems *as a whole.* System engineers must take a broad view of a system. They must think about the services that the system provides, the constraints under which the system must be built and operated, the interactions of the system with its environment and so on.

There are many possible definitions of a system from the very abstract to the concrete but I believe a useful working definition is:

> *A system is a collection of interrelated components that work together to achieve some objective.*

This very general definition embraces a vast range of systems. For example, a very simple system such as a pen may be composed of three or four hardware components. By contrast, an air traffic control system is made up of thousands of hardware and software components plus human users which carry out a large number of different tasks. In this book, I am only interested in computer-based systems which include hardware and software and which offer an interface to human users. These systems usually incorporate a great deal of software so software engineering is an essential part of computer-based system engineering (CBSE).

A characteristic of systems is that the properties and the behaviour of the system components are inextricably intermingled. The successful functioning of each system component depends on the functioning of some other components. Thus, software can only operate if the processor is operational. The processor can only carry out computations if the software system defining these computations has been successfully installed.

Some system components can operate as independent systems. However, when they are incorporated into a system, their behaviour depends on interactions with other system components. For example, consider a security camera that is part of some computer-controlled security system. The camera may be able to operate in an autonomous way. When it is embedded in the system, the timing of its pictures and the angle of the camera is controlled by other system components.

The complex relationships between the components in a system means that the system is more than simply the sum of its parts. It has properties that are properties of the whole. They cannot be attributed to any specific part. These are sometimes called *emergent properties* (Checkland, 1981). This means that they only emerge when the system as a whole is considered. Some of these properties can be derived directly from comparable component properties. Other emergent properties, however, cannot be derived from the properties of individual components.

Emergent properties are usually non-functional properties. Some examples of these properties are:

(1)   *The overall weight of the system*   This is an example of an emergent property which can be computed from individual component properties.

(2)   *The reliability of the system*   This depends on the reliability of system components and the relationships between the components. This is covered in Section 2.6.

(3)   *The usability of a system*   This is a very complex property which is not simply dependent on the system hardware and software but also depends on the system operators and the way in which it is used in a particular environment.

2.1 Systems and their environment

Systems are not independent entities but exist in an environment. This environment affects the functioning and the performance of the system. The environment may be thought of as a system in its own right. When a system is part of another system (the containing system), it is called a *sub-system*. Sub-systems may themselves be decomposed hierarchically until it is not useful to consider the components as independent systems.

Figure 2.1 shows some of the systems that might be incorporated in an office building. The heating system, the power system, the lighting system, the plumbing system, the waste system and the security system are all sub-systems within the building which is itself a system. The building is located in a street that is in a town, and so on. The local environment of a system is the systems at the same level. The overall environment is composed of the local environment plus the environment of the containing system.

Consider the security system shown in Figure 2.1. The local environment of that security system is the other systems within the building. The overall environ-

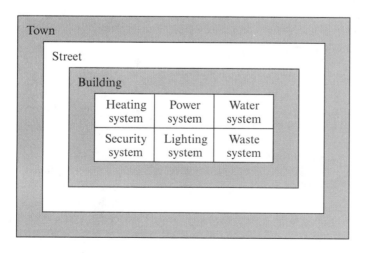

Figure 2.1
System hierarchies.

ment includes all other systems outside of the building in the street and the town as well as natural systems such as the weather system.

There are two main reasons why the environment of a system must be understood by system engineers:

(1)   In many cases, the reason for the existence of a system is to make some changes in its environment. Therefore, a heating system changes its environment by increasing or decreasing the temperature of the environment. The functioning of a system, therefore, depends to some extent on the environment.

(2)   There are many relationships between a system and its environment and some of these are indirect rather than direct relationships. The functioning of a system can be affected by changes in the system's environment in ways which can be very difficult to predict. For example, the electrical system in a building may be affected by environmental changes that take place outside the building. Works in the street outside may cut a power cable and the electrical system is thus disabled. More subtly, a lighting storm can induce currents in the electrical system which affect its normal functioning.

As well as the physical environment shown in Figure 2.1, systems are also situated in an organizational environment. This is made up of organizational policies and procedures that are themselves governed by wider political, economic, social and environmental issues. If this organizational environment is not properly understood, systems may be inappropriate and rejected by users and organizational managers. Checkland (1981; Checkland and Scholes, 1990) describes an approach called Soft Systems Methodology which takes account of these environmental factors when designing systems.

System engineers, therefore, should not consider systems as completely self-contained entities but must have knowledge of the environment where the system is to be installed. In principle, all such environmental knowledge should be included in the system specification. In reality, this is impossible. The engineer must make some environmental assumptions based on other comparable systems and on common sense. If these assumptions are incorrect (for example, if the system is not designed to survive a lightning strike) the system may malfunction in unpredictable ways.

2.2 System procurement

System procurement is the process of acquiring a system for an organization to meet some identified need. The system may be bought as a whole, may be bought as separate parts that are then integrated or may be specially designed and developed. For large systems, deciding which of these procurement options to choose can take several months or years. It may be necessary to complete some system specification and architectural design before procurement decisions are made.

There are two main reasons for this:

(1)   To buy or let a contract to design and build a system, a high-level specifica-
       tion of what that system should do must be completed.

(2)   It is almost always cheaper to buy a system than to design, manufacture and
       build it as a separate project. Some architectural design is necessary to iden-
       tify those sub-systems that can be bought rather than specially designed and
       manufactured.

It is very rare for any one organization to specify, design, manufacture and test
all the components of a large complex system. More normally, a user organization
will buy the system from a supplier organization. This supplier, who is usually called
the principal contractor, may contract out the development of different sub-systems
to a number of sub-contractors. The model of procurement is illustrated in
Figure 2.2.

This contractor/sub-contractor model minimizes the number of organizations
which the procurer must deal with. The sub-contractors design and build parts
of the system to a specification produced by the principal contractor. Once
completed, these different parts are integrated by the principal contractor. They
are then delivered to the customer buying the system. Depending on the contract,
the procurer may allow the principal contractor a free choice of sub-contractors
or may require the principal contractor to choose sub-contractors from an approved
list.

Large complex systems usually consist of a mixture of off-the-shelf components and specially built components. One reason why more and more software is
included in systems is that it allows more use of existing hardware components with
the software acting as a 'glue' to make these different pieces of hardware work
together effectively.

Figure 2.3 shows the procurement process for off-the-shelf systems and
bespoke systems.

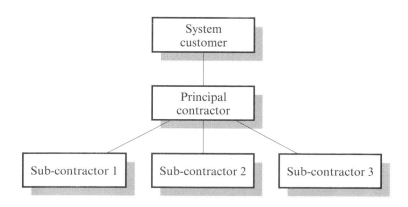

Figure 2.2
The contractor/
sub-contractor model.

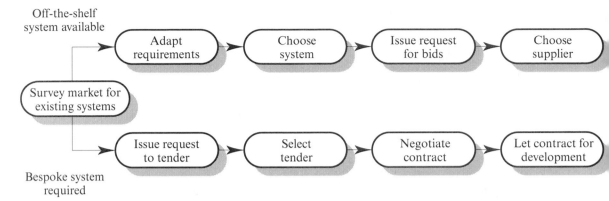

Figure 2.3
The system
procurement process.

Some important points about the process shown in Figure 2.3 are:

(1)   It is rare for existing components to match requirements exactly, unless the requirements have been written with these components in mind. Therefore, choosing a system means finding the closest match between the system requirements and the facilities offered by off-the-shelf systems. The requirements then have to be modified. This can have knock-on effects on other sub-systems.

(2)   When a system is to be built specially, the specification of requirements acts as the basis of a contract for the system procurement. It is therefore a legal as well as a technical document.

(3)   After a contractor to build a system has been selected, there is a further contract negotiation period in which further changes to the requirements may be agreed and issues such as the cost of change discussed.

The majority of hardware sub-systems and, increasingly, software sub-systems such as database management systems are not developed specially when they are included in some larger system. The term COTS (commercial off-the-shelf) systems is sometimes used to refer to this class of system. Software is used to tailor such systems to the needs of an organization and to integrate them with other sub-systems.

2.3 The system engineering process

System engineering is an interdisciplinary activity involving teams drawn from different backgrounds. System engineering teams are needed because it is unlikely that any single engineer has sufficient knowledge and understanding to consider all the implications of system design decisions.

Consider an air traffic control (ATC) system that uses radars and other sensors to determine aircraft position. Figure 2.4 shows some of the many different disciplines that may be involved in the system engineering team.

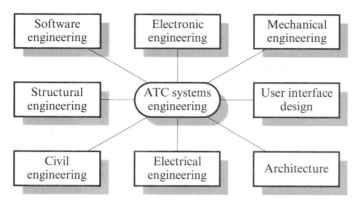

Figure 2.4
Interdisciplinary
involvement in system
engineering.

For many systems, there are almost infinite possibilities for trade-offs between different types of sub-system. Different engineering disciplines must negotiate to decide how functionality should be provided. Often there is no 'correct' decision on how a system should be decomposed. Rather, there is a range of possible alternatives. The selection of one of these alternatives need not necessarily be made for technical reasons. For example, say one alternative in an air traffic control system is to build new radars rather than refit existing installations. If the civil engineers involved in this process do not have much other work, they may favour this alternative because it allows them to keep their jobs. They may then rationalize this choice using technical arguments.

The phases of the system engineering process are shown in Figure 2.5. The 'waterfall' model of the software process was derived directly from this design process.

There are important distinctions between the system engineering process and this software process:

(1)   *Interdisciplinary involvement*   This requires long periods of negotiation between the different engineers. There is immense scope for misunderstanding because of the different terminology used in different engineering disciplines.

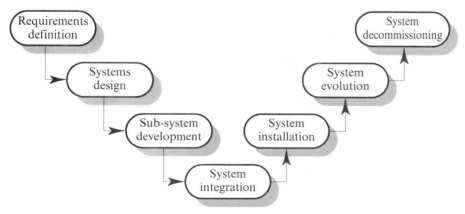

Figure 2.5
The system
engineering process.

(2)   *Reduced scope for iteration between phases*   Once some system engineering decisions have been made (for example, the siting of radars in an ATC system), it is extremely expensive to change them if unanticipated problems arise. System re-design is often impossible. Problems which arise may have to be solved within each sub-system rather than by changing the overall system design.

In reality, because software is inherently flexible, many unexpected problems are left to software engineers to solve. For example, say the site of a radar is such that some image ghosting occurs. It is impractical to move the radar, so some other way of removing this ghosting is required. The solution may be to enhance the image-processing capabilities of the software to remove the ghost images. Of course, this may then require increased processor power in the system which again may be impossible to provide.

Software engineers are left with the problem of enhancing the software capabilities without increasing the hardware cost. Many so-called 'software failures' were not a consequence of inherent software problems. They were the result of trying to change the software to accommodate modified system engineering requirements.

2.3.1 System requirements definition

The system requirements definition activity is intended to discover the requirements for the system as a whole. As with software requirements analysis, the process involves consultations with system customers and end-users. This requirements definition phase usually concentrates on deriving three types of requirement:

(1)   *Coarse-grain functional requirements*   The basic functions that the system must provide must be defined. These are set out at an abstract level rather than in detail. Detailed functional requirements specification takes place at the sub-system level. For example, in the air traffic control system, this requirements activity would probably identify the need for a flight-plan database. The flight plans of all aircraft entering the controlled space are entered in this database. However, the details of the database probably do not affect the functioning of other sub-systems.

(2)   *System properties*   These are the non-functional emergent system properties as discussed above. These may be properties such as availability, performance, safety, and so on. These non-functional system properties affect the requirements for all sub-systems.

(3)   *Characteristics which the system must not exhibit*   It is sometimes as important to specify what the system must not do as it is to specify what the system should do. For example, in an air traffic control system, it might be specified that the system should not present the controller with too much information. This requirement implies that tests for information overload should be carried out.

An important part of the requirements definition phase is to establish a set of overall objectives which the system should meet. These should not be expressed in terms
of the system's functionality but should define why the system is being procured for
a particular environment.

To illustrate the distinction between these, consider a system that is to be procured for an office building to provide for fire protection and for intruder detection.
A statement of objectives which is based around the system functionality might be:

> *To provide a fire and intruder alarm system for the building which will
> provide internal and external warning of fire or unauthorized intrusion.*

This objective states explicitly that there needs to be an alarm system which provides
some warnings of undesired events. By contrast, a broader statement of objectives
might be:

> *To ensure that the normal functioning of the work carried out in the building
> is not seriously disrupted by events such as fire and unauthorized intrusion.*

Stating the objective in this way both broadens and limits some design choices. It
allows for intruder protection using sophisticated locking technology without any
internal alarms. It may exclude the use of sprinklers for fire protection. These may
affect the electrical systems in the building and seriously disrupt the work that is
going on.

A fundamental difficulty in establishing system requirements is that the problems which complex systems are usually built to help tackle are usually 'wicked
problems' (Rittel and Webber, 1973). A 'wicked problem' is a problem which is so
complex and in which there are so many related entities that there is no definitive
problem specification. The true nature of the problem only emerges as a solution is
developed. An extreme example of a 'wicked problem' is earthquake planning. No
one can accurately predict where the epicentre of an earthquake will be, what time
it will occur, what effect it will have on the local environment and so on. We cannot
therefore completely specify how to deal with a major earthquake. The problem can
only be tackled after the earthquake has happened.

2.3.2 System design

System design (Figure 2.6) is concerned with how the system functionality is to be
provided by the different components of the system. The activities involved in this
process are:

(1) *Partition requirements*   During this phase, the requirements are analysed
    and collected into related groups. There are usually several possible parti-
    tioning options and a number of alternatives may be produced at this stage of
    the process.

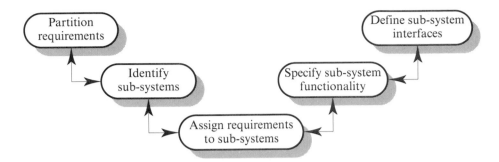

Figure 2.6
The system design
process.

(2)   *Identify sub-systems*   This activity is concerned with identifying the different sub-systems that can, individually or collectively, meet the requirements.
Groups of requirements are usually related to sub-systems so this activity and
requirements partitioning may be carried out together. However, the sub-
system identification may not simply be driven by the system requirements.
It may also be influenced by other organizational or environmental factors.
Because of the time required for manufacturing, it is particularly important to
identify hardware that has to be built at this stage.

(3)   *Assign requirements to sub-systems*   In this phase, the requirements are
assigned to sub-systems. In principle, this should be straightforward if the
requirements partitioning is used to drive the sub-system identification. In
practice, there is never a clean match between requirements partitions and
identified sub-systems. Limitations of COTS sub-systems may mean that
requirements have to be modified.

(4)   *Specify sub-system functionality*   This may be seen as part of the system
design phase or, if the sub-system is a software system, part of the requirements specification activity for that system. Therefore, there is not a clear
division between system design and sub-system development.

(5)   *Define sub-system interfaces*   This critical activity involves defining the
interfaces that are provided and expected by each sub-system. Once these
interfaces have been agreed, parallel development of the sub-systems
becomes possible.

As the double-ended arrows in Figure 2.6 imply, there is a great deal of feedback and
iteration from one stage to another in this process.

For almost all systems, there are many possible designs that may be
developed. These cover a range of solutions with different combinations of hardware, software and human operations. The solution chosen for further development
may be the most appropriate technical solution which meets the requirements.
However, in many cases wider organizational and political influences influence the
choice of solution. For example, if the system is a government system, national
rather than foreign suppliers may be preferred even if the national product is
technically inferior.

2.3.3 Sub-system development

The sub-system development activity involves developing each of the sub-systems identified during system design. This may involve entering another system engineering process for the sub-system itself. Where a sub-system is a software system, a software process involving requirements, design, implementation and so on may be started.

Occasionally, the development process will develop all sub-systems from scratch. More normally, however, some of the sub-systems are COTS systems that are procured for integration into the system. It is difficult to predict what off-the-shelf components will be available for development during the design phase. Sometimes the design activity must be re-entered during development to accommodate a bought-in component. It is usually much cheaper to buy existing products rather than develop special-purpose components. If off-the-shelf products are available, it is usually worth the expense of re-thinking the design.

The different sub-systems are usually developed in parallel. When problems are encountered which cut across sub-system boundaries, a system modification request must be made. Where systems involve extensive hardware engineering, making modifications after manufacturing has started is usually very expensive. Often 'work-arounds' which compensate for the problem must be found. These 'work-arounds' often involve software changes because of the software's inherent flexibility. This emphasizes the need, discussed in Chapter 1, to build software that is designed for change.

2.3.4 System integration

System integration involves taking independently developed sub-systems and putting them together to make up a complete system. This is often a complex and expensive activity. Sub-system faults that are a consequence of invalid assumptions about other sub-systems are often revealed at this stage.

Integration can be done using a 'big bang' approach where all the sub-systems are integrated at the same time. However, for both technical and managerial reasons, an incremental integration process in which sub-systems are integrated one at a time is the best approach to adopt.

This incremental process is the most appropriate approach for two reasons:

(1)   It is usually impossible to schedule all the different sub-system developments so that all development is completed at the same time.

(2)   Incremental integration reduces the cost of error location. If many sub-systems are simultaneously integrated, an error that arises during testing may be located in any of these sub-systems. When a single sub-system is integrated with an already working system, errors which occur are probably in the newly integrated sub-system or in the interactions between the existing sub-systems and the new sub-system.

There may be disputes between the various contractors responsible for the different sub-systems because of system integration difficulties. When problems are discovered in sub-system interaction, the different contractors may argue about who is responsible for the problem. The negotiations to resolve the problems may take several weeks or months.

2.3.5 System installation

System installation is the activity of installing a system in the environment in which it is intended to operate. While this may appear to be a simple process, there are many different problems that can arise which mean that the installation of a complex system can take many months or even years.

Problems that can arise during system installation are:

(1)   The environment in which the system is to be installed is not the same as the environment that has been assumed by the developers of the system. This is a common problem when software systems are installed. For example, the system may make use of facilities provided by a specific version of the operating system. These may not be identical in the operating system version in the installation environment. Thus, when the system is installed, it may not work at all or may operate in a way that was not anticipated by its developers.

(2)   There may be human resistance to the introduction of a new system. Not everyone sees computer systems as beneficial. Potential users of the system may be hostile to the introduction of the system. It may reduce their responsibility or the number of jobs in an organization. People may therefore deliberately refuse to cooperate with the system installers. They may actively work to ensure that the system installation will fail. For example, they may refuse to participate in operator training or may deny access to information that is essential for system installation.

(3)   A new system may have to coexist with an existing system for some time before the organization is satisfied that the new system works properly. This causes particular installation problems if the systems are not completely independent but share some components. It may be impossible to install the new system without de-installing the old system. Trials of the new system can only take place at times when the existing system is not required. They therefore may take a long time.

(4)   There may be physical installation problems. The majority of the world's buildings were erected before widespread computer system networking. There may be very real difficulties in fitting a new system into an existing building as there may not be enough room in existing ducts for cabling. If the installation is to take place in a historic building, building modifications may be completely forbidden.

2.3.6 System operation

Once the system has been installed, it is put into operation. Operating the system may involve organizing training sessions for operators and changing the normal work process to make effective use of the new system. Undetected problems may arise at this stage because the system specification may contain errors or omissions. While the system may perform to specification, its functions may not meet real operational needs. Consequently, the mode of use of the system may not be as anticipated by the system designers.

A problem that may only emerge after the system goes into operation is that of operating the new system with existing systems. There may be physical problems of incompatibility. It may be difficult to transfer data from one system to another. More subtle problems might be radically different user interfaces offered by different systems. Introducing a new system may increase the operator error rate for existing systems as operators mix up user interface commands.

2.3.7 System evolution

Large and complex systems have a very long lifetime. It is inevitable that, during their lifetime, some system evolution will take place. This may be due to errors in the original system requirements or construction. It may be as a result of new requirements which arise after the system is in operation. The system computers may have to be replaced with new, cheaper machines. The organization that uses the system may re-organize itself and hence use the system in a different way. The external environment of the system may change thus forcing changes to the system.

System evolution, like software evolution (discussed in Part 8), is inherently very costly for a number of reasons:

(1)   Proposed changes have to be analysed very carefully both from a business and a technical perspective. They must be approved by a range of people before being put into effect.

(2)   Because sub-systems are never independent, changes to one sub-system may adversely affect the performance of another sub-system. This can be a particular problem when changes affect the timing behaviour of sub-systems. Timing problems are particularly difficult to find and correct.

(3)   The reasons for original design decisions are often unrecorded. Those responsible for the system evolution have to work out why particular design decisions were made.

(4)   As systems age, their structure typically becomes corrupted by change so the costs of additional changes increase.

Although system evolution is very expensive, as society becomes increasingly dependent on systems of various types, the amount of effort devoted to evolution rather than new system development will tend to increase. These existing systems that must be retained are now sometimes called *legacy systems*.

2.3.8 System decommissioning

System decommissioning means taking the system out of service after the end of its useful operational lifetime. For some classes of system this is straightforward but some systems contain materials which are potentially damaging to the environment. The system engineering activity should anticipate decommissioning and take the problems of disposing of the materials into account during the design phase. For example, the use of toxic chemicals might be confined to sealed modules which can be removed as a single unit and reprocessed.

As far as software is concerned there are, of course, no physical decommissioning problems. However, some software functionality may be incorporated in a system to assist with the decommissioning process. For example, software may be used to monitor the state of other system components. When the system is decommissioned, components which are not worn can therefore be identified and reused in other systems.

If the data in the system that is being decommissioned must be retained by the organization, it must be converted for use by some other system. This can often involve significant costs as the data structure may be implicitly defined in the software itself. I cover some of these problems of data re-engineering in Chapter 34.

2.4 System architecture modelling

As part of the systems requirements and design activity, the system has to be modelled as a set of components and relationships between these components. These are normally illustrated graphically in a system architecture model.

The system architecture is usually depicted as a block diagram showing the major sub-systems and the interconnections between these sub-systems. Figure 2.7 illustrates the architecture of a (hypothetical) air traffic control system. There are several major sub-systems (shown in boxes) which, in this case, are themselves large systems. Information flow between these sub-systems is shown by the arrowed lines connecting these systems.

At this level of detail, the system is decomposed into sub-systems. Each sub-system can be represented in a similar way until the system is decomposed into functional components. Functional components are components that, when viewed from the perspective of the sub-system, provide a single function. By contrast, a sub-system is usually multi-functional. Of course, when viewed from another perspective (say, that of the component manufacturer), a functional component may itself be a system in its own right.

Conventionally, the system architecture model has identified hardware and software components. These components can then be developed in parallel. While it is essential that the hardware which has to be bought or built is identified, this simplistic hardware/software separation is only relevant at a detailed level. Given the

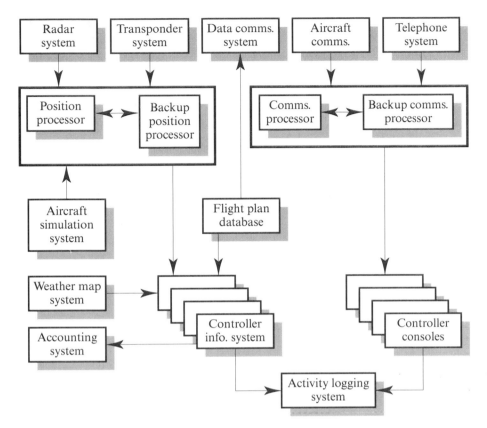

Figure 2.7
The architecture of
an air traffic control
system.

relatively low cost of computers, many hardware components now include embedded computing capabilities. Components incorporate one or more computers plus associated software. For example, a network linking machines will consist of physical cables plus repeaters and network gateways. The repeaters and the gateways include processors and software to drive these processors as well as specialized electronic components.

I think that, at the architectural level, it is more appropriate to identify functional components before making decisions about hardware/software trade-offs. The decision whether a function should be provided in hardware or software may be governed by non-technical factors such as the availability of COTS components or the time required to develop the component.

2.4.1 Functional system components

The functional components in a system can be classified under a number of different functional headings.

(1)   *Sensor components* collect information from a system's environment. Examples of sensor components are radars in an air traffic control system, paper position sensors in a laser printer and a thermocouple in a steel furnace.

(2)   *Actuator components* cause some change in the system's environment. Examples of actuators are valves which open and close to increase or decrease the flow rate of liquid in a pipe, the flight surfaces on an aircraft which control the angle of flight and the paper feed mechanism on a laser printer which moves the paper across the scanning beam.

(3)   *Computation components* are components which, given some input, carry out some computations on that input and produce some output. An example of a computation component is a floating-point processor which carries out computations on real numbers.

(4)   *Communication components* are components that allow other system components to communicate with each other. An example of a communication component is an Ethernet linking different computers in a building.

(5)   *Coordination components* are system components that coordinate the operation of other components. An example of a coordination component is a scheduler in a real-time system. This decides when the different processes should be scheduled to run on a processor.

(6)   *Interface components* are components that transform the representation used by one system component into the representation used by another component. An obvious example is a human interface component which takes some system model and displays it for the human operator. Another example of an interface component is an analog–digital converter that converts an analog input into a digital output.

This classification of components is, of course, approximate. There is no hard and fast division between the different component types. A characteristic of these component types is that they cannot normally be classed as exclusively hardware or exclusively software components. In the types of systems in which software engineers are likely to be involved, most components will include embedded software. Software will be used to control the overall system.

Figure 2.8 shows some of these component types in a simple intruder alarm system. Figure 2.9 explains which of the different functional component types are used in this alarm system.

2.5 Human factors

All systems have human users who use the system in a social and organizational environment with other social and technical systems. Appropriate user interface design is critical for successful system operation. However, there are also other human factors that must be taken into account by system engineers. Some points that must be taken into consideration are:

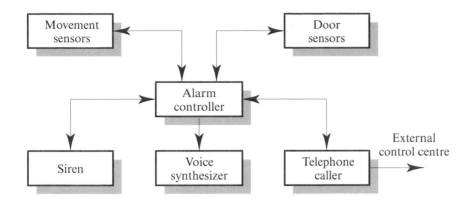

Figure 2.8
A simple intruder
alarm system.

Component type	Components	Function
Sensor	Movement sensor, Door sensor	Detect movement in a protected space, detect protected door opening
Actuator	Siren	Audible warning of intrusion
Communication	Telephone caller	Call external control centre to issue warning of intrusion. Receive commands from control centre
Coordination	Alarm controller	Coordinate all system components. Act on commands from control panel and control centre
Interface	Voice synthesizer	Synthesize message giving location of intrusion

Figure 2.9
Component types
in the intruder
alarm system.

(1)   Does the system require changes to the work processes in the environment? If so, training will certainly be required. If changes are significant, or if they involve people losing their jobs, there is a danger that the system will be resisted by the users.

(2)   Does the system de-skill the users in an environment? If so, they may actively resist the introduction of the system into the organization.

(3)   Does the system change the political power structure in an organization? For example, if an organization is dependent on a complex system, those who know how to operate the system have a great deal of political power.

(4)   Does the system require users to change the way they work? This can be a problem if it involves users undertaking tasks that are normally seen as lower-status tasks. For example, lawyers may resist the introduction of a computer system because it requires them to learn to type. They may think that typing should be done by secretaries.

These factors are often very significant. They may be critical in determining whether or not a system successfully meets its objectives. Unfortunately, predicting which factors will be significant is very difficult. This is especially true for engineers who have little experience of social or cultural studies. As a consequence, there is increasing recognition that social scientists may have a useful role to play in the system design process. This is briefly discussed in Chapter 5.

2.6 System reliability engineering

Reliability is a complex concept which must always be considered at the system level rather than the individual component level. Because the components in a system are interdependent, faults in one component can be propagated through the system and affect the operation of other components. Most disasters occur in situations where different components fail simultaneously. System designers often cannot anticipate how the consequences of these failures propagate through the system.

It can be argued that it is impossible to anticipate all the consequences of component failure in complex systems. As well as anticipated component dependencies, there may also be unanticipated dependencies which may differ from one installation of the system to another. Furthermore, the designers of a system do not know what other systems will be installed. There may be further unpredictable relationships between all the systems in an environment. It is therefore impossible to produce a system that is guaranteed never to fail.

For example, say a system is designed to operate at normal room temperatures. To allow for variations and exceptional conditions, the electronic components of a system should be designed to operate within a certain range of temperature, say from 0 degrees to 45 degrees. Outside this temperature range, the components will behave in an unpredictable way. Now assume that this system is installed close to an air conditioner. If this air conditioner fails and vents hot gas over the electronic components, these components and hence the whole system may then fail.

If this system had been installed elsewhere in that environment there would have been no problems. When the air conditioner worked normally there were no problems. However, because of the physical closeness of these machines, an unanticipated relationship existed between them that caused system failure.

In a system, there are three closely related influences on the overall reliability:

(1)   *Hardware reliability*   What is the probability of a hardware component failing and how long does it take to repair that component?

(2)   *Software reliability*   How likely is it that a software component will produce an incorrect output? Software failure is usually distinct from hardware failure in that software does not wear out. It can continue in operation even after an incorrect result has been produced.

(3)   *Operator reliability*   How likely is it that the operator of a system will make an error?

All of these are closely linked. Hardware failure can cause spurious signals to be generated which are outside the range of inputs expected by software. The software can then behave unpredictably. Operator error is most likely in conditions of stress. These conditions arise when system failures are occurring. Operator errors may further stress the hardware, causing more failures and so on. Therefore, a situation can occur in which a single sub-system failure that is recoverable can rapidly develop into a serious problem requiring complete system shutdown.

The ability of a system to continue in operation with one or more component failures is called the *resilience* of the system. The required resilience is an important factor in the system design process. Systems in which failure poses a danger to people or to the system's environment rather than causing inconvenience must be particularly resilient.

The design of the user interface is absolutely critical in avoiding operator error. For complex systems, the principal objectives of the user interface design process must be to produce safe and resilient interfaces. This involves finding answers to questions such as:

(1) What, in the system's operating context, should be considered as an operator error?

(2) How can the system be designed so that mistakes are avoided? That is, should it be impossible for the operator to give the system incorrect input?

(3) What information does the operator need from the system? How can it be presented so that, under stressful conditions, the operator will not misread the information?

(4) How can hardware and software errors be detected and reported to the operator?

(5) What degree of operator overriding should be allowed? That is, under what circumstances should the operator be able to override checks built into the system?

I return to the topic of reliability and dependable systems development in Part 4 of the book.

Further reading

'The systems approach'. This is a classic paper which presents a succinct summary of the need to take a broad perspective when building systems. (G.M. Jenkins, *J. Sys. Eng.,* **1** (1), 1969.)

'System engineering of computer-based systems'. This paper gives a good overview of computer-based system engineering and calls for the establishment of a discipline of ECBS, that is, the engineering of computer-based systems. (S. White *et al., IEEE Computer,* **26** (11), November 1993.)

Systems Engineering: Principles and Practice of Computer-based Systems Engineering. Covers various aspects of CBSE including the development process, project management and system design methods. (B. Thomé (ed.), 1993, John Wiley and Sons.)

KEY POINTS

- System engineering is a complex and difficult process which requires input from a range of engineering disciplines.

- The cheapest way to procure a system is to buy it off-the-shelf. However, almost all large systems require some tailored sub-systems. Software may be required to act as the 'glue' between off-the-shelf hardware components.

- The system engineering process consists of the same activities as the 'water-fall' model of the software process introduced in Chapter 1. The integration activity is particularly critical. Sub-systems from different suppliers must be made to work together.

- System architectures are usually best described using block diagrams showing the major sub-systems and their interconnections.

- Types of functional system component include sensor components, actuator components, computation components, coordination components, communication components and interface components.

- The reliability of a system depends on hardware, software and operator reliability. The software and its user interface should be designed to avoid user interface errors and to be resilient when errors occur.

EXERCISES

2.1   Explain why other systems within a system's environment can have unanticipated effects on the functioning of a system.

2.2   Modify Figure 2.6 to incorporate an explicit procurement activity once the sub-systems have been identified. Show, in your diagram, the feedback that results from the incorporation of this activity.

2.3   Explain why specifying a system to be used by emergency services for disaster management is an inherently wicked problem.

2.4   Suggest how the software systems used in a car can help with the decommissioning (scrapping) of the overall system.

2.5   Describe five different types of functional components that might be part of a large-scale hardware/software system.

2.6   Explain why it is important to produce an overall description of a system architecture at an early stage in the system specification process.

2.7   Figure 2.1 shows a range of systems in a building. The security system is a much-extended version of the system shown in Figure 2.8 that is intended to protect against intrusion and to detect fire. It incorporates smoke sensors, movement sensors and door sensors, video cameras (under computer control) located at various places in the building, an operator console where the system status is reported, and external communication facilities to call the appropriate services such as police, fire, and so on. Draw a block diagram of a possible design for such a system.

2.8   A flood warning system is to be procured which will give early warning of possible flood dangers to sites that are threatened by floods. The system will include a set of sensors to monitor the rate of change of river levels, links to a meteorological system giving weather forecasts, links to the communication systems of emergency services (police, coastguard and so on), video monitors installed at selected locations, and a control room equipped with operator consoles and video monitors.

Controllers can access database information and switch video displays. The system database includes information about the sensors, the location of sites at risk and the threat conditions for these sites (for example, high tide, south-westerly winds), tide tables for coastal sites, the inventory and location of flood control equipment, contact details for emergency services, local radio stations, and so on.

Draw a block diagram of a possible architecture for such a system. You should identify the principal sub-systems and the links between them.

2.9   Assuming that some system that has been ordered meets its specification, describe, using associated examples, three problems which might arise when it is installed in an organization.

2.10   What are the arguments for and against considering system engineering as a profession in its own right such as electrical engineering, software engineering, and so on?

2.11   You are an engineer involved in the development of a financial system. During installation, you discover that this system will make a significant number of people redundant. The people in the environment deny you access to essential information to complete the system installation. To what extent should you, as a system engineer, become involved in this? Is it your professional responsibility to complete the installation as contracted? Should you simply abandon the work until the procuring organization has sorted out the problem?

3

Project Management

Objectives

- To introduce software project management and to distinguish it from other types of engineering project management.

- To describe, in outline, the job of a software manager.

- To introduce the task of project planning and to suggest a structure for a project plan.

- To illustrate the use of graphical representations (activity charts and bar charts) used to describe project schedules.

Contents

Professional software engineering is always subject to budget and schedule constraints. These are set by the organization developing the software. Project managers ensure that the software development is consistent with the organization's policies, goals and requirements. This chapter is an introduction to project management. It introduces the main tasks of a project manager and discusses project planning in more detail. Other management topics are covered in Part 7 of the book.

The failure of many large software projects in the 1960s and early 1970s highlighted the problems of software management. The delivered software was late, unreliable, cost several times the original estimates and often exhibited poor performance characteristics (Brooks, 1975). These projects did not fail because managers or programmers were incompetent. These large, challenging projects attracted people of above-average ability. The fault lay in the approach to management that was used. Management techniques derived from small-scale projects did not scale up to large systems development.

Software managers are responsible for planning and scheduling project development. They supervise the work to ensure that it is carried out to the required standards. They monitor progress to check that the development is on time and within budget. Good management cannot guarantee project success. However, bad management usually results in project failure. The software is delivered late, costs more than originally estimated and fails to meet its requirements.

Software managers do the same kind of job as other engineering project managers. However, software engineering is distinct from other types of engineering in a number of ways which can make software management particularly difficult. Some of the differences are:

(1) *The product is intangible*   The manager of a shipbuilding project or of a civil engineering project can see the product being developed. If a schedule slips the effect on the product is visible. Parts of the structure are obviously unfinished. Software is intangible. It cannot be seen or touched. Software project managers cannot see progress. They rely on others to produce the documentation needed to review progress.

(2) *There is no standard process*   We do not have a clear understanding of the relationships between the software process and product types. In engineering disciplines with a long history, the process is tried and tested. The engineering process for particular types of system, such as a bridge, is well understood. Our understanding of the software process has developed significantly in the past few years. However, we still cannot predict with certainty when a particular software process is likely to cause development problems.

(3) *Large software projects are often 'one-off' projects*   New systems that are different from previous projects are common. We don't have a large body of previous experience which can be used to reduce uncertainty in plans. It is consequently more difficult to anticipate problems. Rapid technological changes in computers and communications outdate previous experience. Lessons learned from that experience may not be transferable to new projects.

Because of these problems, it is not surprising that some software projects are late, over-budget and behind schedule. Software systems are often new and technically innovative. Engineering projects (such as new transport systems) which are innovative often also have schedule problems. Given the difficulties involved, it is perhaps remarkable that so many software projects are delivered on time and to budget!

3.1 Management activities

It is impossible to write a standard job description for a software manager. The job varies tremendously depending on the organization and on the software product being developed. However, most managers take responsibility at some stage for some or all of the following activities:

- proposal writing
- project costing
- project planning and scheduling
- project monitoring and reviews
- personnel selection and evaluation
- report writing and presentations

The first stage in a software project may involve writing a proposal to carry out that project. The proposal describes the objectives of the project and how it will be carried out. It usually includes cost and schedule estimates. It may justify why the project contract should be awarded to a particular organization or team.

Proposal writing is a critical task as the existence of many software organizations depends on having enough proposals accepted and contracts awarded. There can be no set guidelines for this task; proposal writing is a skill which is acquired by experience. Aron (1983) includes a discussion of proposal writing which is recommended to interested readers.

Project planning is concerned with identifying the activities, milestones and deliverables produced by a project. A plan must then be drawn up to guide the development towards the project goals. Software estimation is a related activity that is concerned with estimating the resources required to accomplish the project plan. Planning is covered later in this chapter; estimation is covered in Chapter 29.

Project monitoring is a continuing project activity. The manager must keep track of the progress of the project and compare actual and planned progress and costs. Although most organizations have formal mechanisms for monitoring, a skilled manager can often form a clear picture of what is going on by informal discussion with project staff.

Informal monitoring can often predict potential project problems as they may reveal difficulties as they occur. For example, daily discussions with project staff might reveal a particular problem in finding some software fault. Rather than waiting for a schedule slippage to be reported, the software manager might assign some expert to the problem or might decide that it should be programmed around.

During a project, it is normal to have a number of formal, project management reviews. They are concerned with reviewing overall progress and technical development of the project and considering the project's status against the aims of the organization commissioning the software.

The development time for a large software project may be many years. During that time, organizational objectives are almost certain to change. These changes may mean that the software is no longer required or that the original project requirements are inappropriate. Management may decide to stop software development or to change the project to accommodate the changes to the organization's objectives.

Project managers usually have to select people to work on their project. Ideally, skilled staff with appropriate experience will be available to work on the project. However, in most cases, managers have to settle for a less than ideal project team. The reasons for this are:

(1)   The project budget may not cover the use of highly paid staff. Less experienced, less well-paid staff may have to be used.

(2)   Staff with the appropriate experience may not be available either within an organization or externally. It may be impossible to recruit new staff to the project. Within the organization, the best people may already be allocated to other projects.

(3)   The organization may wish to develop the skills of its employees. Inexperienced staff may be assigned to a project to learn and to gain experience.

The software manager has to work within these constraints when selecting project staff. However, problems are likely unless at least one project member has some experience of the type of system being developed. Without this experience, many simple mistakes are likely to be made. In Chapter 28, I discuss team building and staff selection.

The project manager is usually responsible for reporting on the project to both the client and contractor organizations. Project managers must write concise, coherent documents which abstract critical information from detailed project reports. They must be able to present this information during progress reviews.

3.2 Project planning

Effective management of a software project depends on thoroughly planning the progress of the project. The project manager must anticipate problems which might arise and prepare tentative solutions to those problems. A plan, drawn up at the start of a project, should be used as the driver for the project. This initial plan is not static but must be modified as the project progresses and better information becomes available.

Plan	Description
Quality plan	Describes the quality procedures and standards that will be used in a project
Validation plan	Describes the approach, resources and schedule used for system validation
Configuration management plan	Describes the configuration management procedures and structures to be used
Maintenance plan	Predicts the maintenance requirements of the system, maintenance costs and effort required
Staff development plan	Describes how the skills and experience of the project team members will be developed

Figure 3.1
Types of plan.

Project planning is probably the activity that takes most management time. Planning is required for development activities from specification through to delivery of the system. Organizations must, of course, have longer-term business and strategic plans. These will be used to guide choices on which projects have the highest priority and to assess whether or not software systems are needed.

A structure for a software development plan is described in Section 3.2.1. As well as a project plan, managers may also have to draw up other types of plan. These are briefly described in Figure 3.1 and covered in more detail in the relevant chapter elsewhere in the book.

The pseudo-code shown in Figure 3.2 describes the project planning process for software development. It shows that planning is an iterative process which is only complete when the project itself is complete. As project information becomes available during the project, the plan must be regularly revised.

The planning process starts with an assessment of the constraints (required delivery date, staff available, overall budget, and so on) affecting the project. This

```
Establish the project constraints
Make initial assessments of the project parameters
Define project milestones and deliverables
while project has not been completed or cancelled loop
        Draw up project schedule
        Initiate activities according to schedule
        Wait ( for a while )
        Review project progress
        Revise estimates of project parameters
        Update the project schedule
        Re-negotiate project constraints and deliverables
        if ( problems arise ) then
                Initiate technical review and possible revision
        end if
end loop
```

Figure 3.2
Project planning.

is carried out in conjunction with an estimation of project parameters such as its structure, size and distribution of functions. The progress milestones and deliverables are then defined.

The process then enters a loop. A schedule for the project is drawn up and the activities defined in the schedule are initiated or given permission to continue. After some time (usually about 2–3 weeks), progress is reviewed and discrepancies noted. Because initial estimates of project parameters are tentative, the plan will always need to be modified.

Project managers revise the assumptions about the project as more information becomes available. They re-plan the project schedule. If the project is delayed, they may have to re-negotiate the project constraints and deliverables with the customer. If this re-negotiation is unsuccessful and the schedule cannot be met, a project technical review may be held. The objective of this review is to find some alternative approach to development which falls within the project constraints and meets the schedule.

Of course, wise project managers do not assume that all will go well. Problems of some description nearly always arise during a project. The initial assumptions and scheduling should be pessimistic rather than optimistic. There should be sufficient contingency built into the plan so that the project constraints and milestones need not be re-negotiated every time round the planning loop.

3.2.1 The project plan

The project plan sets out the resources available to the project, the work breakdown and a schedule for carrying out the work. In some organizations, the project plan is a single document including all the different types of plan introduced above. In other cases, the project plan is solely concerned with the development process. References to these other plans are included but the plans themselves are separate.

The plan structure which I describe here is for this latter type of plan. The details of the project plan vary depending on the type of project and organization. However, most plans should include the following sections:

(1) *Introduction* This briefly describes the objectives of the project and sets out the constraints (such as budget, time, and so on) which affect the project management.

(2) *Project organization* This describes the way in which the development team is organized, the people involved and their roles in the team.

(3) *Risk analysis* This describes possible project risks, the likelihood of these risks arising and the risk reduction strategies which are proposed.

(4) *Hardware and software resource requirements* This describes the hardware and the support software required to carry out the development. If hardware has to be bought, estimates of the prices and the delivery schedule should be included.

(5)   *Work breakdown*   This describes the breakdown of the project into activities and identifies the milestones and deliverables associated with each activity.

(6)   *Project schedule*   This describes the dependencies between activities, the estimated time required to reach each milestone and the allocation of people to activities.

(7)   *Monitoring and reporting mechanisms*   This describes the management reports which should be produced, when these should be produced and the project monitoring mechanisms used.

The project plan should be regularly revised during the project. Some parts, such as the project schedule, will change frequently; other parts will be more stable. A document organization which allows for the replacement of sections should be used.

3.3 Activity organization

Managers need information. As software is intangible, this information can only be provided as documents describing the work that has been carried out. Without this information, it is impossible to judge progress, and cost estimates and schedules cannot be updated.

When planning a project, a series of *milestones* should be established where a milestone is an end-point of some software process *activity*. At each milestone, a formal progress report should be presented to management. These milestones should represent the end of a distinct stage in the project. Indefinite milestones such as 'coding 80% complete', where it is impossible to decide unequivocally if the milestone has been reached, are useless for project management. Milestones need not be large documents. They may simply be a short report of achievements in a project activity.

A *deliverable* is a project result which is delivered to the customer. It is usually delivered at the end of some major project phase such as specification, design, and so on. Deliverables are usually milestones. However, milestones are not necessarily deliverables. They may simply be used to check project progress and need not be given to the customer.

To establish milestones, the software process which is being followed for a particular project must be broken down into activities. An output should be associated with each of these activities. For example, Figure 3.3 shows activities involved in requirements specification when prototyping is used to help validate requirements. The principal milestones for each activity are shown. Depending on the project size, subsidiary milestones for each of these may also be defined. The deliverables are the requirements definition and the requirements specification.

It is not necessary for all activities to end at a milestone. If milestones are too frequent, the project team spend all their time preparing milestones which may not be essential for the progress of the project. If they are infrequent, progress problems

ACTIVITIES

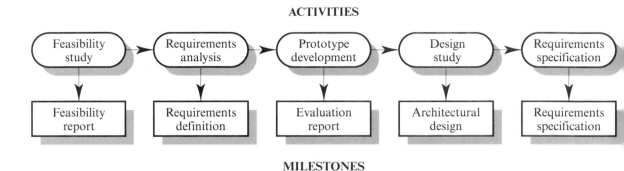

MILESTONES

Figure 3.3
Milestones in the
requirements process.

may lie undetected for some time. It may then be difficult to recover from these problems.

One reason for the widespread adoption of the 'waterfall' model of the software process is that it allows for the straightforward definition of milestones throughout a project. Alternative approaches, such as exploratory programming, are such that milestone definition is a more difficult and a less certain process. Consequently, in spite of its known deficiencies, some variant of the 'waterfall' model will probably continue to be the process model used in most large software projects.

3.4 Project scheduling

Project scheduling is a particularly demanding task for software managers. Managers estimate the time and resources required to complete activities and organize them in a coherent sequence. Unless the project being scheduled is similar to a previous project, previous estimates are an uncertain basis for new project scheduling. Schedule estimation is further complicated by the fact that different projects may use different design methods and implementation languages.

If the project is technically advanced, initial estimates will almost certainly be optimistic even when managers try to consider all eventualities. In this respect, software scheduling is no different from scheduling any other type of large advanced project. New aircraft, bridges and even cars are frequently late because of unanticipated problems. Schedules, therefore, must be continually updated as better progress information becomes available.

Project scheduling involves separating the total work involved in a project into separate activities and judging the time required to complete these activities. Usually, some of these activities are carried out in parallel. Project schedulers must coordinate these parallel activities and organize the work so that the workforce is used optimally. They must avoid a situation where the whole project is delayed because a critical task is unfinished.

In estimating schedules, managers should not assume that every stage of the project will be problem-free. Individuals working on a project may fall ill or may leave, hardware may break down and essential support software or hardware may be delivered late. If the project is new and technically advanced, certain parts of it may turn out to be more difficult and take longer than originally anticipated.

As well as calendar time, managers must also estimate the resources needed to complete each task. The principal resource is the human effort required. Other resources may be the disk space required, the time required on specialized hardware, such as a simulator, and the travel budget required for project staff. Estimation methods are covered in Chapter 29.

A guideline for estimating is to estimate as if nothing will go wrong then increase that estimate to cover anticipated problems. A further contingency factor to cover unanticipated problems may also be added to the estimate. This extra contingency factor depends on the type of project, the process parameters (deadline, standards, and so on), and the quality and experience of the software engineers working on the project.

The project schedule is usually represented as a set of charts showing the work breakdown, activity dependencies and staff allocations. These are discussed in the following section. Software management tools, running on PCs or workstations, are now generally used to automate chart production.

3.4.1 Bar charts and activity networks

Bar charts and activity networks are graphical notations which are used to illustrate the project schedule. Bar charts show who is responsible for each activity and when the activity is scheduled to begin and end. Activity networks show the dependencies between the different activities making up a project. Bar charts and activity charts can be generated automatically from a database of project information using a project management tool.

Consider the set of activities shown in Figure 3.4. This table shows activities, their duration, and activity inter-dependencies. From Figure 3.4, we can see that Task T3 is dependent on Task T1. This means that T1 must be completed before T3 starts. For example, T1 might be the preparation of a component design and T3, the implementation of that design. Before implementation starts, the design should be complete.

Given dependency and estimated duration of activities, an activity chart which shows activity sequences may be generated (Figure 3.5). It shows which activities can be carried out in parallel and which must be executed in sequence because of a dependency on an earlier activity. Activities are represented as rectangles. Milestones are shown with rounded corners. Dates in this diagram are written in British style where the day precedes the month.

It is not useful to subdivide activities into units which take less than a week or two to execute. Finer subdivision means that a disproportionate amount of time must be spent on estimating and chart revision. It is also useful to set a maximum amount of time for any task on the chart of about eight to ten weeks.

Task	Duration (days)	Dependencies
T1	8	
T2	15	
T3	15	T1
T4	10	
T5	10	T2, T4
T6	5	T1, T2
T7	20	T1
T8	25	T4
T9	15	T3, T6
T10	15	T5, T7
T11	7	T9
T12	10	T11

Figure 3.4
Task durations and
dependencies.

Before progress can be made from one milestone to another, all paths leading
to it must be complete. For example, task T9, shown in Figure 3.5, cannot be started
until tasks T3 and T6 are finished. The arrival at milestone M4 shows that these tasks
have been completed.

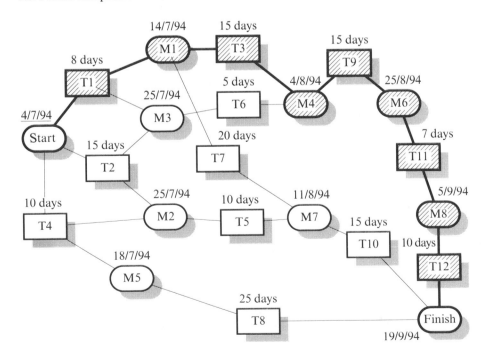

Figure 3.5
An activity network.

The minimum time required to finish the project can be estimated by considering the longest path in the activity graph (the critical path). In Figure 3.5 the critical path is shown as a sequence of shaded boxes. The overall schedule of the project depends on the critical path. Any slippage in the completion in any critical activity causes project delays.

Delays in activities which do not lie on the critical path, however, need not cause an overall schedule slippage. So long as the delays do not extend these activities so much that the total time exceeds the critical path, the project schedule will not be affected. For example, from the bar chart shown as Figure 3.6, we can see that T8 could be delayed by up to four weeks without affecting the schedule.

PERT charts are a more sophisticated form of activity chart in which, instead of making a single estimate for each task, pessimistic, likely and optimistic estimates are made. There are therefore many potential critical paths. These depend on the permutation of estimates for each activity. Critical path analysis in PERT charts is therefore very complex. Specialized tools for chart analysis are required.

Managers also use activity charts when allocating project work. They can provide insights into activity dependencies which are not intuitively obvious. It may be possible to modify the system design so that the critical path is shortened. The project schedule may be shortened because of the reduced amount of time spent waiting for activities to finish.

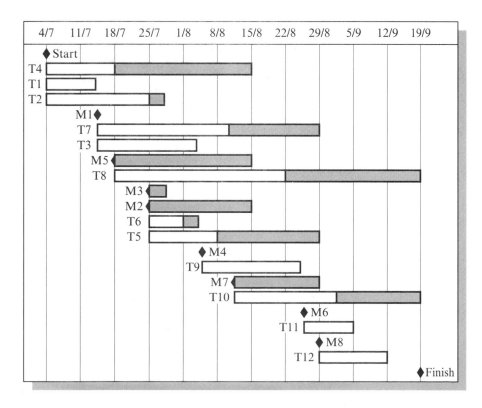

Figure 3.6
Activity bar chart.

Figure 3.6 is an alternative way of representing project schedule information. It is a bar chart (sometimes called a Gantt chart, after their inventor) showing a project calendar and how activities start and finish at various dates.

Some of the activities in Figure 3.6 are followed by a shaded bar, the length of which is computed by the scheduling tool. This shows that there is some flexibility in the completion date of these activities. If an activity does not complete on time, the critical path will not be affected until the end of the period marked by the shaded bar. Activities which lie on the critical path have no margin of error.

As well as considering schedules, project managers must also consider resource allocation and, in particular, the allocation of staff to project activities. Figure 3.7 suggests an allocation of staff to the activities illustrated in Figure 3.6.

Staff allocations can also be processed by project management support tools. A bar chart can be generated which shows the time periods when staff are employed on the project (Figure 3.8).

Staff don't have to be assigned to a project at all times. During intervening periods they may be on holiday, working on other projects, attending training courses or some other activity.

Large organizations usually employ a number of specialists who work on a project as required. This can cause scheduling problems. If one project is delayed while a specialist is working on it, this may have a knock-on effect on other projects. They may also be delayed because the specialist is not available.

Inevitably, initial project schedules will be incorrect. As a project develops, estimates should be compared with actual elapsed time. This comparison can be used as a basis for revising the schedule for later parts of the project. When actual figures are known, the activity chart should be reviewed. Later project activities may be reorganized to reduce the length of the critical path.

Task	Engineer
T1	Jane
T2	Anne
T3	Jane
T4	Fred
T5	Mary
T6	Anne
T7	Jim
T8	Fred
T9	Jane
T10	Anne
T11	Fred
T12	Fred

Figure 3.7
Allocation of people to activities.

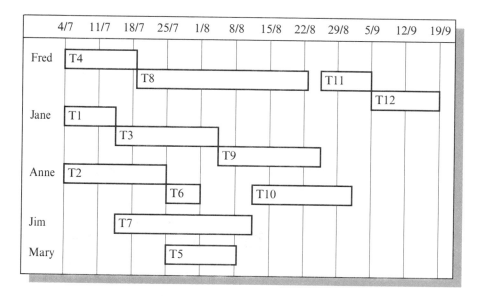

Figure 3.8
Staff allocation vs time chart.

Further reading

The problems of software management have been unchanged since the 1960s so reading on this subject does not date in the same way as technical literature. See Part 7 for other readings on management.

IEE/BCS Software Engineering J. **1** (1), January 1986. This special issue includes several papers on the management of software projects. The paper by Rook is particularly recommended.

The Mythical Man Month. An interesting and readable account of the management of one of the first very large software projects, the IBM OS/360 operating system. (F.P. Brooks, 1975, Addison-Wesley.)

Principles of Software Engineering Management. This is an idiosyncratic account of software management but it contains good advice. It is written in an easy-to-read way. (T. Gilb, 1988, Addison-Wesley.)

Managing the Software Process. Chapter 6 in this book is a good description of project planning, although it is not particularly detailed. (W.S. Humphrey, 1989, Addison-Wesley.)

KEY POINTS

- Good software project management is essential if software engineering projects are to be developed on schedule and within budget.
- Software management is distinct from other engineering management. Software is intangible. Projects may be novel or innovative so there is no

body of experience to guide their management. Software processes are not well understood.

■ Software managers have diverse roles. Their most significant activities are project planning, estimating and scheduling.

■ Planning and estimating are iterative processes. They continue throughout a project. As more information becomes available, plans and schedules must be revised.

■ A project milestone is a predictable outcome of an activity in which some formal report of progress should be presented to management. Milestones should occur regularly throughout a software project. A deliverable is a milestone which is delivered to the project customer.

■ Project scheduling involves the creation of various graphical plan representations of part of the project plan. These include activity charts showing the interrelationships of project activities and bar charts showing activity durations. These charts are usually produced automatically using project management tools.

EXERCISES

3.1 Explain why the intangibility of software systems poses special problems for software project management.

3.2 Explain why the best programmers do not always make the best software managers. You may find it helpful to base your answer on the list of management activities given in Section 3.1.

3.3 Explain why the process of project planning is an iterative one and why a plan must be continually reviewed during a software project.

3.4 Briefly explain the purpose of each of the sections in a software project plan.

3.5 What is the critical distinction between a milestone and a deliverable?

3.6 Figure 3.9 sets out a number of activities, durations and dependencies. Draw an activity chart and a bar chart showing the project schedule.

3.7 Figure 3.9 gives task durations for software project activities. Assume that a serious, unanticipated setback occurs and, instead of taking 10 days, task T5 takes 40 days. Revise the activity chart accordingly, highlighting the new critical path. Draw up new bar charts showing how the project might be re-organized.

Task	Duration (days)	Dependencies
T1	10	
T2	15	T1
T3	10	T1, T2
T4	20	
T5	10	
T6	15	T3, T4
T7	20	T3
T8	35	T7
T9	15	T3, T6
T10	5	T5, T9
T11	10	T9
T12	20	T10
T13	35	T3, T4
T14	10	T8, T9
T15	20	T9, T14
T16	10	T15

Figure 3.9
Task durations and
dependencies.

3.8   Using reported instances of project problems in the literature, list management difficulties which occurred in these failed programming projects. (Start with Brooks's book, as suggested in Further Reading.)

3.9   You are asked by your manager to deliver software to a schedule which you know can only be met by asking your project team to work unpaid overtime. All team members have young children. Discuss whether you should accept this demand from your manager or whether you should persuade your team to give their time to the organization rather than their families. What factors might be significant in your decision?

3.10   As a programmer, you are offered promotion to project management but you feel that you can make a more effective contribution in a technical rather than a managerial role. Discuss whether you should accept the promotion.

Part Two

Requirements and Specification

This part of the book is concerned with the introductory phases of the software process in which the requirements for the software are established and specified in detail for further development. Chapter 4 introduces the process of requirements engineering and this is explained in more detail in Chapters 5 to 7. Chapter 8 covers prototyping as a means of requirements validation. Chapters 9 to 11 introduce the specification of software using formal mathematical methods.

Contents

4

Requirements Engineering

Objectives

- To introduce requirements engineering, the first phase of large-scale software system development.

- To explain why system requirements must be written at different levels of detail for different types of reader.

- To describe how system requirements may be organized for presentation to customers, users and engineers.

- To explain what is involved in validating that requirements meet the needs of the system customer.

- To explain why requirements always change during the lifetime of a system and to suggest a classification system for changing requirements.

Contents

63

The problems which software engineers are called upon to solve are often immensely complex. Understanding the nature of the problem can be very difficult. If the system is new, there is no existing system to help understand the nature of the problem. Consequently, it is difficult to establish exactly what the system should do. The process of establishing the services the system should provide and the constraints under which it must operate is called *requirements engineering*. The term 'engineering' is used rather loosely in this respect. It means that a systematic process is used to derive a definition of the software system which is to be developed.

System requirements should set out *what* the system should do rather than *how* this is done. A requirement may be a *functional requirement,* that is, it describes a system service or function. Alternatively, it may be a *non-functional requirement.* A non-functional requirement is a constraint placed on the system (for instance, the required response time) or on the development process (such as the use of a specific language standard).

Unfortunately, the term *requirement* is not used throughout the software industry in a consistent way. In some cases, a requirement is seen as a high-level, abstract statement of a service that the system should provide or a constraint on the system. At the other extreme, it is a detailed, mathematically formal definition of a system function. The example below, suggested by Davis (1993), is a good illustration of why these differences exist.

> If a company wishes to let a contract for a large software development project, it must define its needs in a sufficiently abstract way that a solution is not pre-defined. The requirements must be written so that several contractors can bid for the contract, offering, perhaps, different ways of meeting the client organisation's needs. Once a contract has been awarded, the contractor must write a system definition for the client in more detail so that the client understands and can validate what the software will do. Both of these documents may be called the *requirements document* for the system.

Some of the problems that arise during the requirements engineering process are a result of failing to make a clear separation between these different levels of description. I make this separation by using the term *requirements definition* to mean the high-level abstract description of requirements and *requirements specification* to mean the detailed description of what the system should do. As well as these two levels of detail, a further, even more detailed description (a software specification) may be produced to bridge the requirements engineering and design activities. Requirements definition, requirements specification and software specification may be defined as follows:

(1)   A *requirements definition* is a statement, in a natural language plus diagrams, of what services the system is expected to provide and the constraints under which it must operate. It is generated using customer-supplied information.

(2)   A *requirements specification* is a structured document which sets out the system services in detail. This document, which is sometimes called a functional

specification, should be precise. It may serve as a contract between the system buyer and software developer.

(3)   A *software specification* is an abstract description of the software which is a basis for design and implementation. This specification may add further detail to the requirements specification.

This chapter, with Chapters 5 to 8, discusses the development of the requirements definition and specification. The software specification is a document for the design team rather than the system customer. It may be expressed in a formal notation or in some design language. I discuss the use of formal notations to express the software specification in Chapters 9, 10 and 11. Software specifications may not be written during the specification process. Rather, the design is based directly on the requirements specification.

The requirements engineering process should normally involve writing a requirements definition then expanding this into a requirements specification. Figure 4.1 illustrates how a definition of a requirement may be expanded in more detail as a requirements specification.

Different levels of system specification are useful because they communicate information about the system to different types of reader. Figure 4.2 shows the classes of reader that may be concerned with the different levels of specification.

The requirements definition should be targeted at a managerial level. It must be understandable by both client and contractor management who will not have a detailed technical knowledge of the system. The requirements specification should be targeted at senior technical staff and project managers. Again, it will be used by staff from both the client and the contractor. System end-users may read both of these documents. Finally, the software specification is an implementation-oriented

Requirements definition

> 1. The software must provide a means of representing and
>   accessing external files created by other tools.

Requirements specification

> 1.1 The user should be provided with facilities to define the type of
>   external files.
> 1.2 Each external file type may have an associated tool which may be
>   applied to the file.
> 1.3 Each external file type may be represented as a specific icon on
>   the user's display.
> 1.4 Facilities should be provided for the icon representing an
>   external file type to be defined by the user.
> 1.5 When a user selects an icon representing an external file, the
>   effect of that selection is to apply the tool associated with the type of
>   the external file to the file represented by the selected icon.

Figure 4.1
Requirements definitions and requirements specifications.

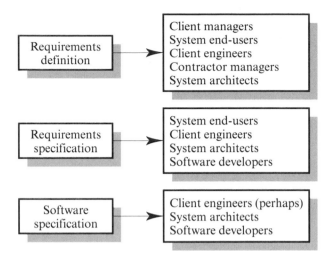

Figure 4.2
Readers of different
types of specification.

document. It should be written for the software engineers who will be involved in developing the system.

Large software systems are usually developed to address 'wicked' problems (as discussed in Chapter 2). This makes the formulation of requirements very difficult. Because the problem cannot be fully defined, the software requirements are bound to be incomplete. During the software process, the developer's understanding of the problem is constantly changing. This naturally leads to volatile system requirements.

There are several reasons why it is virtually impossible to define a complete and consistent set of requirements to address a problem:

(1) Large software systems are usually required to improve upon the *status quo*. The existing system may be manual or an out-of-date computer system. Although difficulties with the current system may be known, it is hard to anticipate what effects the 'improved' system will have on the organization.

(2) Large systems usually have a diverse user community. Different users have different requirements and priorities. These may be conflicting or contradictory. The final system requirements are inevitably a compromise between them.

(3) The people who pay for a system and the users of a system are rarely the same people. System customers impose requirements because of organizational and budgetary constraints. These may conflict with end-user requirements.

Sometimes, formulating outline requirements for a project is difficult as the application domain is poorly understood. In such cases, it is unrealistic to expect a definitive requirements definition before system development begins. A process model based on system prototyping (see Chapter 8) is more appropriate than the classical 'waterfall' model in these cases.

4.1 The requirements engineering process

The requirements engineering process is shown in Figure 4.3. This process is the set of activities that lead to the production of the requirements definition and requirements specification. Other information, such as a report on the feasibility of the system and a software specification, may also be produced in this process. These are illustrated in Figure 4.3 which also shows that the requirements definition and the requirements specification may be presented in a single requirements document.

There are four principal stages in this process:

(1)   *Feasibility study*   An estimate is made of whether the identified user needs may be satisfied using current software and hardware technologies. The study will decide if the proposed system will be cost-effective from a business point of view and if it can be developed given existing budgetary constraints: A feasibility study should be relatively cheap and quick. The result should inform the decision of whether to go ahead with a more detailed analysis.

(2)   *Requirements analysis*   This is the process of deriving the system requirements through observation of existing systems, discussions with potential users and procurers, task analysis and so on. This may involve the development of one or more different system models. These help the analyst understand the system to be specified. System prototypes may also be developed to help understand the requirements.

(3)   *Requirements definition*   Requirements definition is the activity of translating the information gathered during the analysis activity into a document that defines a set of requirements. These should accurately reflect what the customer wants. This document must be written so that it can be understood by the end-user and the system customer.

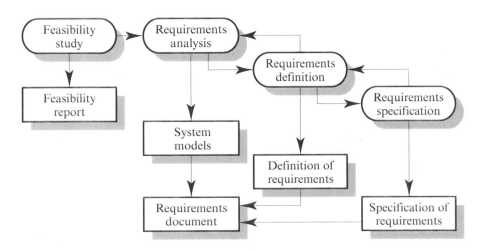

Figure 4.3
The requirements
engineering process.

(4) *Requirements specification* A detailed and precise description of the system requirements is set out to act as a basis for a contract between client and software developer. The creation of this document is usually carried out in parallel with some high-level design. The design and requirements activities influence each other as they develop. During the creation of this document, errors in the requirements definition are inevitably discovered. It must be modified to correct these problems.

Of course, the activities in the requirements process are not simply carried out in sequence but are iterated. The requirements analysis continues during definition and specification and new requirements arise during the process. Thus, the documents are subject to frequent change and should be placed under the control of a configuration management system (see Chapter 33).

4.2 The software requirements document

System requirements are expressed in a software requirements document. The software requirements document (sometimes called the software requirements specification or SRS) is the official statement of what is required of the system developers.

This requirements document includes the requirements definition and the requirements specification. In some cases, these may not be presented separately but integrated into a single description. Sometimes, the requirements definition is presented as an introduction to the requirements specification. In my view, however, the most effective approach is to present the detailed specification as an appendix to the requirements definition. Depending on the size of the document, this may be bound with the requirements definition or presented in a separate volume.

The software requirements document is not a design document. It should set out what the system should do without specifying how it should be done. The requirements should be stated so that there is traceability between these requirements and the final system design. This means that it should be possible to take each specified requirement and map it onto the part of the system design that implements that requirement. If the services, constraints and properties specified in the software requirements document are satisfied by the software design then that design is an acceptable solution to the problem.

In principle, the requirements set out in this document ought to be complete and consistent. All system functions should be specified and requirements should not conflict. As discussed above, this is difficult to achieve. Errors and omissions will inevitably exist in the document so it should be structured to be easy to change. The document should therefore be split into chapters and sections. Cross-references from one requirement to another should be kept to a minimum.

Heninger (1980) suggests that there are six requirements which a software requirements document should satisfy:

- It should only specify external system behaviour.
- It should specify constraints on the implementation.
- It should be easy to change.
- It should serve as a reference tool for system maintainers.
- It should record forethought about the life cycle of the system.
- It should characterize acceptable responses to undesired events.

The requirements document is a combination of requirements definition and requirements specification. The best organization is as a series of chapters with the detailed specification perhaps presented as an appendix to the document. A possible generic structure for a requirements document is shown in Figure 4.4.

Chapter	Description
Introduction	This should describe the need for the system. It should briefly describe its functions and explain how it will work with other systems. It should describe how the system fits into the overall business or strategic objectives of the organization commissioning the software.
Glossary	This should define the technical terms used in the document. No assumptions should be made about the experience or expertise of the reader.
System models	This should set out one or more system models showing the relationships between the system components and the system and its environment. These might include object models, data-flow models and semantic data models.
Functional requirements definition	The services provided for the user should be described in this section. This description may use natural language, diagrams or other notations that are understandable by customers.
Non-functional requirements definition	The constraints imposed on the software and restrictions on the freedom of the designer should be described here and related to the functional requirements. This might include details of specific data representation, response time and memory requirements, and so on. Product and process standards which must be followed should be specified.
System evolution	This should describe the fundamental assumptions on which the system is based and anticipated changes due to hardware evolution, changing user needs, and so on.
Requirements specification	This should describe the functional requirements in more detail. If necessary, further detail may also be added to the non-functional requirements, for example interfaces to other systems may be defined.

Figure 4.4
The structure of a requirements document.

It is particularly important to relate the system to the business objectives of the organization and the business rationale for the system. It must be clear to those responsible for paying for the system that there is a case for buying it.

The requirements document may also include, either in separate chapters in the document or as appendices, the following information:

(1)   *Hardware* If the system is to be implemented on special hardware, this hardware and its interfaces should be described. If off-the-shelf hardware is to be used, the minimal and optimal configurations for the system should be defined.

(2)   *Database requirements* The logical organization of the data used by the system and its interrelationships should be described. Data modelling techniques such as entity-relational modelling (covered in Chapter 6) may be used to describe the database requirements.

(3)   *Index* More than one kind of index to the document may be provided. As well as a normal alphabetic index, there may be an index per chapter, an index of functions and so on.

This generic structure must, of course, be instantiated in a form that is appropriate for the organization sponsoring the software development. Examples of some standards for requirements documents include the US DoD standard DI-MCCR-80025A for a software requirements specification and IEEE standard 830-1984 for requirements documents. Davis (1990) discusses these and other standards and compares their contents.

The requirements document is a reference tool. It should record forethought about the system life cycle. It will be used by maintenance engineers to find out what the system is supposed to do. They will have to find information quickly so the document should have a detailed table of contents, plus one or more indexes. Terminology differences can be minimized by including a glossary of terms used. Evolution is also simplified if the document includes a definition of the changes anticipated and the system provision for these changes.

4.3 Requirements validation

Requirements validation is concerned with showing that the requirements actually define the system that the customer wants. If this validation is inadequate, errors in the requirements will be propagated to the system design and implementation. Expensive system modifications may be required at a later stage to correct problems with the requirements.

The cost of errors in requirements is particularly high if these errors are not discovered until the system is implemented. The cost of making a system change resulting from a requirements problem is much greater than repairing design or coding errors. A requirements change implies that the design and implementation must also be changed. The system testing and validation processes must be repeated. The cost of changing a system after delivery because of a requirements change can therefore be up to 100 times more than the cost of repairing a programming error.

There are several aspects of the requirements which must be checked:

(1) *Validity*   A user may think that a system is needed to perform certain functions. However, further thought and analysis may identify additional or different functions that are required. Systems have diverse users with different needs and any set of requirements is inevitably a compromise across the user community.

(2) *Consistency*   Any one requirement should not conflict with any other.

(3) *Completeness*   The definition should include all functions and constraints intended by the system user.

(4) *Realism*   There is no point in specifying requirements that are unrealizable. It may be acceptable to anticipate some hardware developments but developments in software technology are much less predictable.

Demonstrating that a set of requirements meets a user's needs is difficult if an abstract approach is adopted. By reading a definition and specification, users must picture the system in operation. They must imagine how that system would fit into their work. It is hard for skilled computer professionals to perform this type of abstract analysis; it is almost impossible for system users. As a result, many systems are delivered which do not meet the user's needs and which are simply discarded after delivery.

Prototyping, whereby an executable model of the system is demonstrated to users, is an important requirements validation technique. It is useful because it gives users hands-on experience with a system. They can see how it actually supports their work. Prototyping is an important subject in its own right which is discussed in Chapter 8.

Validation should not be seen as a process to be carried out after the requirements document has been completed. Regular requirements reviews involving both users and software engineers are essential while the requirements definition is being formulated.

A requirements review is a manual process which involves multiple readers from both client and contractor staff checking the requirements document for anomalies and omissions. The review process may be managed in the same way as design reviews (see Chapter 30). Alternatively, it may be organized on a larger scale with many participants involved in checking different parts of the document.

Requirements reviews can be informal or formal. Informal reviews simply involve contractors discussing requirements with clients. It is surprising how often communication between system developers and potential system users is limited. Many problems can be detected easily by talking about the system to these users.

In a formal requirements review, the development team should 'walk' the client through the system requirements explaining the implications of each requirement. The review team should check each requirement for consistency and should check the requirements as a whole for completeness. They might also check for:

- *Verifiability*   Is the requirement as stated realistically testable?
- *Comprehensibility*   Is the requirement properly understood by the procurers or end-users of the system?
- *Traceability*   Is the origin of the requirement clearly stated? This is particularly important when requirements evolve. It may be necessary to go back to the source of the requirement to assess the impact of change. Traceability is a particularly important issue as it allows the impact of change to be assessed. I discuss it in more detail in Chapter 7.
- *Adaptability*   Is the requirement adaptable? That is, can the requirement be changed without large-scale effects on other system requirements?

Conflicts, contradictions, errors and omissions in the requirements should be pointed out during the review and formally recorded. It is then up to the users, the system procurer and the system developer to negotiate a solution to these identified problems.

Requirements reviews are generally successful in detecting many errors in the requirements definition. They are really the only approach that can check the completeness of requirements. However, the consistency of the requirements can be checked, to some extent, using automated tools. This is only possible when the requirements are expressed in a special-purpose language with defined syntax and semantics (Figure 4.5).

Automated consistency checking involves processing the requirements definition and building a requirements database where the links between different requirements are stored. This database may then be analysed by a separate tool which reports potential inconsistencies and omissions.

Expressing the requirements in a formal or structured language (see Chapter 7) allows interface inconsistencies to be detected. These are often particularly crucial in any large system specification. If this is supplemented by a precise description of the system expressed using a logic-based notation, behavioural inconsistencies can also be identified using checking tools.

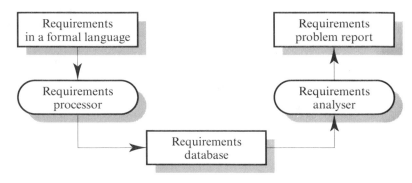

Figure 4.5
Automated consistency checking of requirements.

In situations where the non-functional requirements are critical, these requirements may be validated by constructing a simulator which simulates the timing behaviour of the system. One of the tools used in conjunction with the requirements statement language RSL (Alford, 1985) is a simulator generator. This tool analyses an RSL definition and automatically generates a system simulator in Pascal. Procedures which simulate each functional definition are provided by the specifier as part of the requirements definition.

4.4 Requirements evolution

Developing software requirements focuses attention on software capabilities, business objectives and other business systems. As the requirements definition is developed, a better understanding of users' needs is achieved. This feeds information back to the user which causes the requirements to be changed (Figure 4.6). Furthermore, the time required to analyse requirements and to develop a large system may be several years. Over that time, the system's environment and the business objectives will almost certainly change. The requirements must therefore be changed to reflect this.

The inevitability of change should be recognized and anticipated when producing a requirements document. It is unwise to prematurely freeze requirements. Although this is attractive as far as system development is concerned, it leads to systems that are unlikely to meet the real business needs of the system procurer.

From an evolution perspective, requirements fall into two classes:

(1) *Enduring requirements* These are relatively stable requirements which derive from the core activity of the organization and which relate directly to the domain of the system. For example, in a hospital there will always be requirements concerned with patients, doctors, nurses, treatments, and so on.

(2) *Volatile requirements* These are requirements which are likely to change during the system development or after the system has been put into operation. Examples of volatile requirements are requirements resulting from government health-care policies.

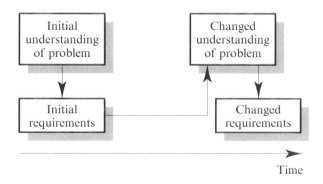

Figure 4.6
Requirements
evolution.

Enduring requirements can sometimes be derived from domain models (Prieto-Díaz and Arango, 1991). These models are abstract representations of the entities and relations which characterize an application domain. Domain analysis and modelling is now an important research topic in requirements engineering (Easterbrook, 1993). However, the use of explicit domain models is still relatively uncommon in industrial software engineering.

Harker *et al.* (1993) have suggested that volatile requirements fall into five classes. However, I think that two of their classes are closely related. I prefer a classification as shown in Figure 4.7.

Non-functional requirements are particularly affected by changes in hardware technology. The development time for a large system may be several years so the power of the hardware available will increase during the development process. Furthermore, the hardware will continue to improve throughout the lifetime of the developed software. The non-functional requirements will have to be modified while the software is in use.

Hardware improvements while the software is being developed can be anticipated. Hardware-dependent non-functional requirements can be specified which assume hardware capability will be available when the software is delivered. However, changes during the project's lifetime should not be assumed. The specifier of requirements should avoid, as far as possible, detailed hardware dependencies.

The software requirements document should be organized so that changes can be accommodated without extensive rewriting. If changing the document is difficult, changes in the requirements may be directly implemented without recording these changes in the requirements document. The system and its specification therefore become inconsistent. This is illustrated in Figure 4.8. This diagram also shows

Requirement type	Description
Mutable requirements	Requirements that change because of changes to the environment in which the organization is operating. For example, in hospital systems, the funding of patient care may change and thus require different treatment information to be collected.
Emergent requirements	Requirements that emerge as the customer's understanding of the system develops during the system development. The design process may reveal new emergent requirements.
Consequential requirements	Requirements that result from the introduction of the computer system. Introducing the computer system may change the organization's processes and open up new ways of working which generate new system requirements.
Compatibility requirements	Requirements that depend on the particular systems or business processes within an organization. As these change, the compatibility requirements on the commissioned or delivered system may also have to evolve.

Figure 4.7
Classification of volatile requirements.

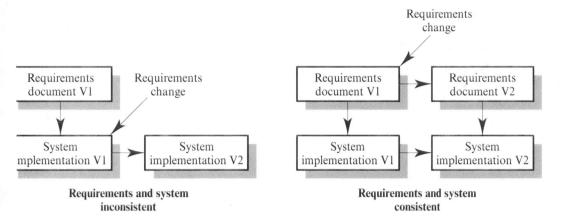

Figure 4.8
Uncontrolled
and controlled
requirements
evolution.

that the requirements document should always be updated so that it is an accurate reflection of the system implementation.

As with programs, changeability in documents is achieved by minimizing external references and making the document sections as modular as possible. A change management process, supported by a configuration management system, should be established for the requirements.

The problems of change are, of course, exacerbated because paper-based documents are normally used as the means of communication between client and contractor. A requirements document is presented as a book. It may not be available in machine-readable form to the system developer. Changes must be managed using the unwieldy system of change control forms and replacement pages. It is only immediately after the delivery of a document that all the requirements are summarized in one place.

The answer to this problem is more extensive use of electronic documentation and automatic consolidation of change requests and original requirements. However, the diversity of different word and text processing systems still makes document exchange inconvenient. The problem will only be solved when a standard for electronic document architecture is established.

Further reading

System and Software Requirements Engineering. This is an excellent volume in the IEEE's Tutorial Series. It contains a lot of new material by some of the most established researchers and practitioners in this area. (R.H. Thayer and M. Dorfman (eds), 1990, IEEE Press.)

Software Requirements: Objects, Functions and States. This book surveys various techniques for requirements specification and definition. It is a good general text on software requirements. (A.M. Davis, 1993, Prentice-Hall.)

IEEE Software, **11** (2), March 1994. This is a special issue covering requirements engineering. The paper by Potts *et al.* is particularly recommended.

KEY POINTS

- It is very difficult to formulate a complete and consistent requirements specification for large software systems.

- A requirements definition, a requirements specification and a software specification are all ways of describing specifications at different levels of detail. They are intended for different types of reader.

- The software requirements document is a description of the system requirements for both system customers and developers.

- Requirements inevitably change. The requirements document should be designed so that it may be easily modified.

- Requirements errors are usually very expensive to correct after system delivery. Requirements validation is therefore a critical requirements engineering activity.

- Reviews involving both client and contractor are used to validate system requirements.

- Stable requirements are requirements which are related to the core activities of a software customer. Volatile requirements are those requirements which are dependent on the environment where the delivered system is to be used. Organizational, political or technical changes may mean that requirements must change.

EXERCISES

4.1   Suggest four 'wicked' problems in which it might be very difficult to define the requirements for software systems to help tackle these problems.

4.2   Explain why it is useful to draw a distinction between a requirements definition and a requirements specification.

4.3   Explain why it is very difficult to produce a complete and consistent set of requirements.

4.4   You have been given the task of producing guidelines for creating a requirements document which can be readily modified. Write a report setting out standards for the organization of a requirements document which will ensure its maintainability.

4.5   Who should be involved in a requirements review? Draw a process model showing how such a review might be organized.

4.6   Rewrite the following requirements so that they may be objectively validated. You may make any reasonable assumptions about the requirements.

(a) The software system should provide acceptable performance under maximum load conditions.

(b) The system interface should use a character set as available on a standard terminal.

(c) If the system should fail in operation, there should be minimal loss of data.

(d) The software development process used should ensure that all of the required reviews have been carried out.

(e) Structured programming should be used for program development.

(f) The software must be developed in such a way that it can be used by inexperienced users.

4.7   When emergency changes have to be made to systems, the system software may have to be modified before changes to the requirements have been approved. Suggest a model of a process for making these modifications which ensures that the requirements document and the system implementation do not become inconsistent.

4.8   Using systems that you know, give examples of the different classes of volatile requirements identified in Figure 4.6.

4.9   While studying a requirements document, you discover a significant requirements conflict which you know would be expensive to correct after the system has been implemented. You point this out to the system customer who rejects your arguments after what you think is a superficial analysis. You are confident that your technical decision is correct. Discuss what you should do in such a situation.

5

Requirements Analysis

Objectives

- To describe a number of different approaches which help to discover end-user and organizational requirements.

- To explain why it is important to consider the analysis of a system from different perspectives or viewpoints.

- To illustrate a structured approach to requirements analysis based on a defined method with associated notations and rules.

- To explain the importance of social and organizational factors which influence system requirements.

Contents

After initial feasibility studies, the first major stage of the requirements engineering process is requirements analysis or elicitation. Technical software development staff work with customers and system end-users to find out about the application domain, what services the system should provide, the required performance of the system, hardware constraints, and so on.

Requirements analysis is an important process. The acceptability of the system after it has been delivered depends on how well it meets the customer's needs and supports the work to be automated. If the analyst does not discover the customer's real requirements, the delivered system is unlikely to meet their expectations.

Requirements analysis may involve a variety of different kinds of people in an organization. These include system end-users who will ultimately interact with the system and their managers. It should involve others in an organization who will be affected by the installation of the system. Engineers who are developing or maintaining other related systems, domain experts, trade union representatives and so on may also be consulted. The term *stakeholder* is used to refer to everyone who may have some direct or indirect influence on the system requirements.

Requirements analysis is a difficult process for a number of reasons:

(1)   Stakeholders often don't really know what they want from the computer system except in the most general terms. Even when they have a clear idea of what they would like the system to do, they may find this difficult to articulate. They may make unrealistic demands because they are unaware of the costs of their requests.

(2)   Stakeholders in a system naturally express requirements in their own terms and with implicit knowledge of their own work. Engineers, without much experience in the customer's domain, must understand these requirements and translate them to an agreed form.

(3)   Different stakeholders have different requirements and they may express these in quite different ways. Engineers must discover all potential sources of requirements and discover commonalities and conflict.

(4)   Analysis takes place in an organizational context. Political factors may influence the requirements of the system. These factors may not be obvious to the system end-users. They may come from higher management influencing the system procurement in ways that satisfy their personal agenda.

(5)   The economic and business environment in which the analysis takes place is dynamic. It inevitably changes during the analysis process. Hence the importance of particular requirements may change. New requirements may emerge from new stakeholders who were not originally consulted.

To carry out a requirements analysis, analysts must develop an understanding of the problem domain. The actual process used is often domain-dependent. Models of the process are inevitably simplifications. However, the process model shown in Figure 5.1 illustrates a number of important requirements analysis activities.

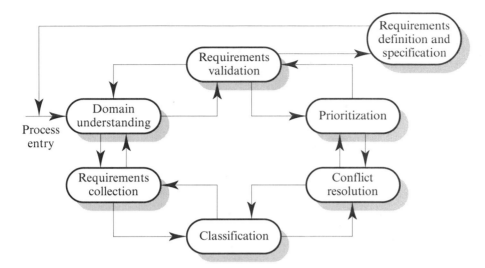

Figure 5.1
The requirements
analysis process.

The activities shown in Figure 5.1 are highly iterative with continual feed-back from each activity to other activities. The process can be viewed as a cycle, starting with domain understanding and ending with requirements validation. The analyst's understanding of the requirements improves with each round of the cycle. The process activities are:

(1) *Domain understanding* Analysts must develop their understanding of the application domain. Therefore, if a system for a supermarket is required, the analyst must find out as much as possible about supermarkets.

(2) *Requirements collection* This is the process of interacting with stakeholders in the system to discover their requirements. Obviously, domain understanding will also develop during this activity.

(3) *Classification* This activity takes the unstructured collection of requirements and organizes them into coherent clusters.

(4) *Conflict resolution* Inevitably, where multiple stakeholders are involved, requirements will conflict. This activity is concerned with finding and resolving these conflicts.

(5) *Prioritization* In any set of requirements, some will be more important than others. This stage involves interaction with stakeholders to discover the most important requirements.

(6) *Requirements validation* The identified requirements are checked to discover if they are complete, consistent and in accordance with what stakeholders really want from the system.

Several different system models may be produced during requirements analysis. A model is an abstract view of the system and the different models express different kinds of information, perhaps derived from different sources, about the required services and constraints. The form and expression of some types of these system models is covered in the following chapter.

It was suggested in Chapter 4 that the process of requirements capture and analysis was separate from requirements definition and specification. This is an artificial separation which was introduced simply to allow the process to be discussed. In fact, the activities of requirements analysis, system modelling, requirements definition and requirements specification are very difficult to separate. In Figure 5.1, you can see there is a feedback loop from definition and specification back into the analysis process.

Davis (1990) suggests that the analysis process must always include three important structuring activities. These are partitioning, abstraction and projection. Partitioning is concerned with identifying the structural ('part-of') relationships between entities so that one entity can be described in terms of its parts. Abstraction is concerned with identifying generalities among entities (for example, the abstraction wheeled-vehicle might represent bicycles, cars, trucks, and so on). Projection is concerned with identifying different ways of looking at a problem.

Partitioning and abstraction result in different models of a system. The 'part of' model is often represented as an entity-attribute-relation model. The abstraction relation may be shown as an object model. Both of these are covered in the next chapter. Projection is discussed in the next section.

5.1 Viewpoint-oriented analysis

For any medium-sized or large system, there are usually different types of end-user. Different people in an organization all have some kind of interest in the system requirements. For example, say an auto-teller system is to be developed for a bank. Examples of the people who may be stakeholders in such a system include:

- *Current bank customers*   They will receive services from the system.
- *Representatives from other banks who cooperate with the bank installing the auto-teller system*   They may have reciprocal agreements which allow each other's machines to be used.
- *Managers of bank branches where the system is to be installed*   They will be interested in obtaining management information from the system.
- *Counter staff at bank branches where the system is to be installed*   They will be involved in the day-to-day running of the system, handling customer complaints, and so on.
- *Database administrators*   They will be responsible for integrating the system with the bank's customer database.
- *Bank security managers*   They will be interested in ensuring that the system will not pose a security hazard of some kind.

- *Communications engineers* They will be responsible for implementing communications between the auto-teller and other machines.

- *The bank's marketing department* They will be interested in selling the system to customers and using any innovative characteristics as a means of marketing the bank.

- *Hardware and software maintenance engineers* They will be responsible for keeping the system working and upgrading it with new versions of the software.

- *The bank's personnel department* They may have to handle changes in staffing policies which result from automation.

Of course, some of these people have a more direct interest in the requirements of the system than others. There may be no real need to consult all of these people. However, the list shows that, for even a relatively simple system, there are many different *viewpoints* that should be considered. The most important viewpoints may be identified and used as a basis for structuring the requirements analysis.

The different viewpoints on a problem see it in different ways (Figure 5.2). However, their perspectives are not completely independent but usually partially overlap. A key strength of viewpoint-oriented analysis is recognizing these overlaps. An important activity is discovering conflicts across the different viewpoints.

The initial ideas for requirements viewpoints were proposed in the 1970s. However, it is only relatively recently that there has been a more detailed analysis of viewpoints and their role in requirements analysis. All approaches recognize that the idea of top-down analysis with a single system representation is simplistic. Real systems have many 'tops'. It is important to consider all of them during the requirements analysis.

Viewpoints are implicitly recognized in analysis methods such as SRD (Orr, 1981) and SADT (Ross, 1977; Schoman and Ross, 1977). Viewpoints were first proposed as an explicit mechanism for requirements analysis in the CORE method (Mullery, 1979). Since then, there have been several other proposals for viewpoint-oriented analysis (Finkelstein *et al.*, 1990; Leite, 1989; Fickas *et al.*, 1991). These are compared by Kotonya and Sommerville (1992).

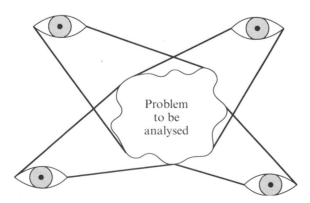

Problem
to be
analysed

Figure 5.2
Multiple viewpoints on a problem.

Different methods have different ideas of what is meant by a 'viewpoint'. A viewpoint may be considered as:

(1) *A data source or sink*   In this case, viewpoints are responsible for producing or consuming data. The analysis involves identifying all such viewpoints, identifying what data is produced or consumed and what processing is carried out. The analysis for each viewpoint can be cross-checked to discover if data is being produced but not consumed or vice versa. The CORE method uses this notion of a viewpoint.

(2) *A representation framework*   In this case, a viewpoint is considered to be a particular type of system model. For example, different engineers might develop an entity-relational model, a state-machine model and so on. Each approach to analysis discovers different things about the system being analysed. These may be compared to discover requirements that would be missed by using a single representation. The VOSE method (Finkelstein *et al.,* 1990) uses this notion of a viewpoint.

(3) *A receiver of services*   In this case, viewpoints are external to the system and receive services from the system. Viewpoints may provide data for these services or control signals. The analysis involves examining the services received by different viewpoints, collecting these and resolving conflicts. This approach is used in the VORD method (Kotonya and Sommerville, 1992) and in the SOS approach (Greenspan and Feblowitz, 1993).

Each of these models of a viewpoint has different strengths and weaknesses. Viewpoints as data sources or sinks and viewpoints as representations are particularly valuable for discovering detailed conflicts between requirements. They are also fairly universally applicable. However, they are less useful for structuring the requirements analysis process. There is not a simple relationship between viewpoints and system stakeholders.

In my opinion, the most effective viewpoint-oriented approach for analysis is based on external viewpoints. Viewpoints interact with the system by receiving services from it and providing data and control signals to the system.

The advantages of this type of viewpoint are:

(1) In the majority of interactive systems, it is natural to think of end-users as receivers of system services.

(2) Because they are external to the system, viewpoints are a natural way to structure the requirements elicitation process.

(3) It is relatively easy to decide if some agent is or is not a valid viewpoint. If there is no interaction with the system, it is clearly not a viewpoint.

(4) Viewpoints and services are a useful way of structuring non-functional requirements. Each service may have associated non-functional requirements. The same service, however, may have different non-functional requirements in different viewpoints.

The service-oriented approach is most suitable for interactive systems where services are delivered to people. Some classes of real-time system don't have much user interaction. The viewpoints required are therefore less intuitive. Furthermore, the service-oriented approach is fairly abstract. While service conflicts can be detected, it does not allow for the detection of conflicts between different system models. At this level, the VOSE method is more effective.

I continue the discussion of viewpoints for requirements analysis in the next section. I use a viewpoint-oriented method to describe a general approach to requirements analysis based on structured methods.

5.2 Method-based analysis

Method-based analysis is probably the most widely used approach to requirements analysis. It depends on the application of some structured method to understand the system. The results of the analysis are expressed as a set of system models defined by whatever method is being used. Analysis methods have different emphases. Some are exclusively designed for requirements elicitation and analysis; others are very close to design methods.

Structured methods usually include some or all of the following:

- *A process model* This defines the activities in the method. Examples of activities are data-flow analysis, control scenario identification, and so on. The process model usually presents activities as a sequence. However, in practice, the analysis iterates between activities.

- *System modelling notations* These notations may be diagrammatic, form-based or linguistic. Examples of diagram types are data-flow diagrams, entity-relation diagrams, object structure diagrams, and such like.

- *Rules applied to the system model* Rules may hold within a single model (for example, every entity in a diagram must have a name) or across models (for example, input and output items in a data-flow diagram must be documented using an entity-relation diagram).

- *Design guidelines* These are not enforceable rules but are intended to avoid poor design. An example of such a guideline might be that an object should normally have no more than five sub-objects.

- *Report templates* These define how the information collected during the analysis should be presented. Information in diagrams is normally supplemented by other textual information. This can be combined with the diagrams into a report for the analyst.

Without exception, structured methods collect vast amounts of information and generate a large volume of documentation. The information management problem posed by methods was a significant factor in the development of CASE toolsets (see

Chapters 25 to 27). Indeed, for many people, the term *CASE tool* means a tool to help with the application of an analysis or design method.

Object-oriented analysis (Coad and Yourdon, 1990; Rumbaugh *et al.,* 1991), and data-flow based methods (DeMarco, 1978; Ward and Mellor, 1985; Hatley and Pirbhai, 1987) are fairly widely used. Because they develop models of the system that are based on computational concepts, I think both of these approaches are more suited to design than analysis.

The reason for this is that structured methods based on computational models are incomplete. End-users and their managers do not think of their work as object-oriented. Nor are data flows and associated data structures central to their concerns. People are interested in how systems can help them with their work. Most structured methods either ignore user interaction or consider people to be computational agents. It cannot be emphasized strongly enough that people are not agents. They are much smarter than computers and they don't always respond to the same stimulus in the same way.

Neither object-oriented nor functional methods address the essence of requirements analysis, which is the capture of information from many different stakeholders. I therefore use a viewpoint-oriented method here to illustrate a methodical approach to requirements analysis and to explain, in more detail, the notion of a viewpoint as introduced in the following section.

The method which I use is called VORD (Kotonya and Sommerville, 1992). The principal activities of this method are shown in Figure 5.3.

This method is principally intended for requirements discovery and analysis. It also includes steps to help translate this analysis into an object-oriented system model. This takes place in the last activity shown in Figure 5.3, namely viewpoint–system mapping. Information collected from the different viewpoints is systematically transformed to an object-oriented design. However, as space is limited and this activity is not central to requirements analysis, I shall not discuss it any further here.

The first three stages of the VORD method are concerned with viewpoint and service identification, viewpoint structuring and documentation:

(1) *Viewpoint identification* involves discovering viewpoints which receive system services and identifying the specific services provided to each viewpoint.

(2) *Viewpoint structuring* involves grouping related viewpoints into a hierarchy. Common services are provided at higher levels in the hierarchy and are inherited by lower-level viewpoints.

(3) *Viewpoint documentation* involves refining the description of the identified viewpoints and services.

Figure 5.3
The VORD method of requirements analysis.

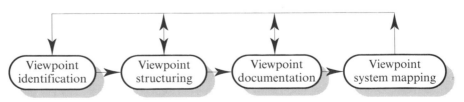

Viewpoint and service information in VORD is collected using standard forms. The forms used for viewpoint information (the viewpoint template) and service information (the service template) are shown in Figure 5.4. VORD also uses various diagrammatic notations including viewpoint hierarchy diagrams (see example in Figure 5.8), and data/control charts (see example in Figure 5.10).

The viewpoint and service templates, the viewpoint hierarchy diagram and the data/control charts are developed during the first three activities shown in Figure 5.3. The forms are used to structure the information collected during the analysis. In general, a form cannot be completely filled in from a single activity. This is typical of method-based analysis. Information about the system emerges during all stages. Only at the end of the analysis is the information complete.

I illustrate the application of this method by applying the first three steps in the analysis of requirements for a bank auto-teller (ATM) control system. Automated teller machines are now common outside banks. They have an embedded software system to drive the machine hardware and to communicate with the bank's central account database.

The ATM system accepts customer requests and delivers cash, account information, database updates and so on. Customers may send standard messages to their bank branch requesting an account statement, cheque book, and so forth. Facilities for customers to initiate an electronic funds transfer may be available. The machines provided by a particular bank may allow customers of other banks to use a subset (typically cash withdrawal and account balance querying) of their facilities.

The first step in viewpoint analysis is to identify possible viewpoints. In all methods, this initial identification is probably the most difficult stage. One approach is a brainstorming approach where potential services and entities which interact with the system are identified. Figure 5.5 shows part of the output of this brainstorming process for the auto-teller system.

Figure 5.4
Viewpoint and service templates.

Viewpoint template			**Service template**	
Reference	The viewpoint name		**Reference**	The service name
Attributes	Attributes providing viewpoint information		**Rationale**	Reason why the service is provided
Events	A reference to a set of event scenarios describing how the system reacts to viewpoint events		**Specification**	Reference to a list of service specifications. These may be expressed in different notations
			Viewpoints	List of viewpoint names receiving the service
Services	A reference to a set of service descriptions		**Non-functional requirements**	Reference to a set of non-functional requirements which constrain the service
Sub-VPs	The names of sub-viewpoints		**Provider**	Reference to a list of system objects which provide the service

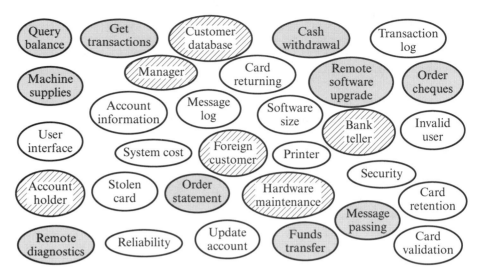

Figure 5.5
Brainstorming for
viewpoint identification
for an ATM system.

When brainstorming, you should try to identify potential viewpoints, system services, data inputs, non-functional requirements, control events and exceptions. At this stage of the analysis, you should not try to impose a structure on the diagram. Any possible way of looking at the system should be written down. Sources of information which may be used in creating this initial view of the system may be documents setting out the high-level goals of the system, knowledge of software engineers from previous projects or, in this case, experience as bank customers. More formally, interviews may be held with bank managers, counter staff, consultants, engineers and customers.

The next stage of the process is to identify viewpoints (shown as hatched bubbles in Figure 5.5) and services (shown as shaded bubbles). The services should be allocated to viewpoints. Unallocated services can suggest viewpoints that have not been identified in the initial brainstorming session. For example, the 'Remote software upgrade' and 'Remote diagnostics' services in Figure 5.5 imply that there may be a need for a software maintenance viewpoint.

Figure 5.6 illustrates, for some of the viewpoints identified in Figure 5.5, the allocation of services. The same service may be allocated to several viewpoints.

As well as receiving services, viewpoints supply data required to provide these services. For example, auto-teller users must specify the amount of money they want when they withdraw cash. Viewpoints also provide control information to determine if and when services are delivered.

During this early stage of the process, this data and control information is simply identified by name. Figure 5.7 shows this information for the account holder viewpoint, the services of which are identified in Figure 5.6.

The viewpoint information is used to fill in viewpoint template forms and to organize the viewpoints into an inheritance hierarchy. To show viewpoint commonalities and to reuse viewpoint information, the inheritance hierarchy factors out viewpoints which provide common services. These services are inherited by lower-level viewpoints. Data and control information are also inherited.

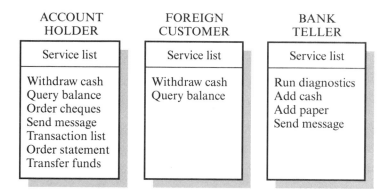

Figure 5.6
Viewpoint service information.

Figure 5.8 shows part of the viewpoint hierarchy for the ATM system. To avoid clutter, I have only shown the services associated with two viewpoints and I have left out a number of bank staff viewpoints.

The viewpoint hierarchy shows the services delivered to each viewpoint. Services are inherited down the hierarchy. Therefore, the services associated with the 'Customer' viewpoint are inherited by 'Account holder' and 'Foreign customer'. The lower-level viewpoints may change the non-functional requirements with these inherited services.

The viewpoint hierarchy is also a useful management tool. It represents the first real breakdown of a system into its components. It can be used as a basis for drawing up initial plans and estimates for the remainder of the requirements derivation activity. It allows a prioritization of requirements. The inherited requirements usually have the highest priority. Different priorities can be associated with each viewpoint's requirements.

The next process stage is to discover more detailed information about the services provided, the data that they require and how they are controlled. This involves using the viewpoints to structure the elicitation process. The service needs of each viewpoint are discussed with either end-users or with viewpoint experts if the viewpoint is another automated system. Figure 5.9 shows an example of a completed viewpoint template for the customer viewpoint and a template for the cash withdrawal service.

One of the fields in the viewpoint template is used to refer to event scenarios which illustrate the system's response to various events. Event scenarios document

ACCOUNT HOLDER	Control input	Data input
	Start transaction	Card details
	Cancel transaction	PIN
	End transaction	Amount required
	Select service	Message

Figure 5.7
Viewpoint data and control information.

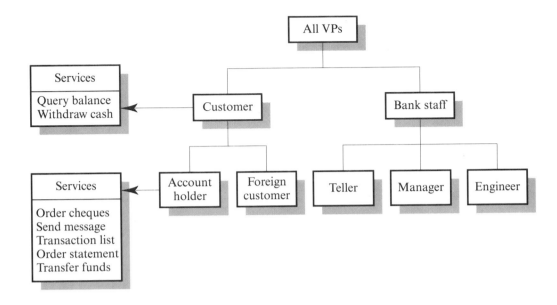

Figure 5.8
Viewpoint structuring.

the system behaviour when presented with specific events. They include a description of data flows and the actions of the system. An important feature of these event scenarios is the documentation of exceptions which can arise. Many requirements problems result because exceptions are not adequately addressed by the analysis method.

Figure 5.10 shows the scenario to a 'Start transaction' event which is initiated by a customer inserting their card into the machine.

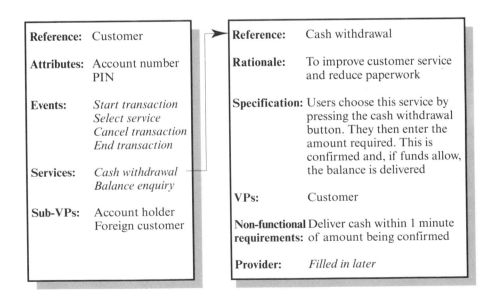

Figure 5.9
Customer viewpoint
and cash withdrawal
templates.

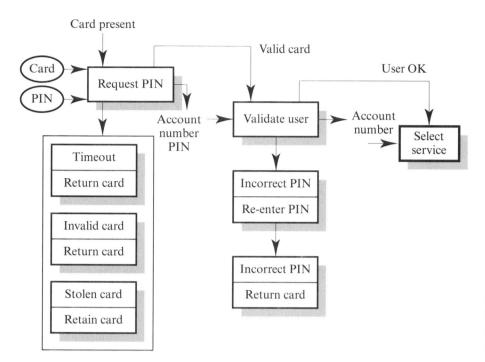

Figure 5.10
Data and control analysis – Start transaction.

The diagrammatic conventions used in these data/control charts are:

(1)   Data provided from a viewpoint or delivered to a viewpoint is shown in ellipses.

(2)   Control information enters and leaves at the top of each box.

(3)   Data leaves from the right of each box. If it is not enclosed, this means that it is internal to the system.

(4)   Exceptions are shown at the bottom of the box. Where there are several possible exceptions, these are enclosed in a box as shown on the left of Figure 5.10.

(5)   The name of the next expected event after completion of the scenario is shown in a box with thick edges.

Figure 5.10 shows that when a card is entered, the customer's personal identification number (PIN) is requested. The customer inputs his or her card (the card must be present to trigger the request) and PIN. If the card is a valid card which can be processed by the machine, control can move to the next stage, which is concerned with checking that the PIN is associated with the customer's account number.

In the first stage, there are three possible exceptions:

(1)   *Timeout*   The customer may fail to enter a PIN within the allowed time limit. The card is returned.

(2)   *Invalid card*   The card is not recognized and is returned.

(3) *Stolen card* The card is recognized as a stolen card and is retained by the machine.

Each exception must be defined in more detail by constructing a separate data and control analysis diagram.

The 'Validate user' stage checks that the PIN is associated with the customer's account number in which case it can trigger the next stage (service selection) with the 'User OK' event. The account number is also output from this stage. Possible exceptions are the input of an incorrect PIN in which case the PIN is requested again. The diagram shows that this repeated request can also have an exception. If an incorrect PIN is again input, the card is returned.

Viewpoint and service templates, and control and data charts are developed for all viewpoints and services. Errors in the analysis and conflicts where the same service is defined in different ways can be found by cross-checking the information collected. Obviously, all of this generates a great deal of information. VORD, like other analysis methods, is only practically usable with CASE tool support.

Methods naturally impose structure on the requirements analysis process. Standard documentation is produced for the system. Methods may be supported by CASE toolsets which automate system documentation and provide some checking capabilities. Finally, analysis methods can result in system models that lead naturally to design, so simplifying later stages of the software process.

Method-based analysis has the advantage that it can be applied reasonably systematically. It has the disadvantage that it forces the modelling of a system into a computational framework which may be artificial. Furthermore, few, if any, methods allow for the description of users as part of a system.

Different analysis methods with different activities may be best suited to different domains. Because of the costs of adopting a method, organizations usually standardize on one method. They apply it whether or not it is appropriate for analysing a particular domain. If a method is unsuited to a domain, its use will almost certainly result in requirements which are less likely to meet customer needs than an informal analysis process.

5.3 System contexts

Early in the analysis process, the boundaries of the system have to be established. The system customer must work with requirements analysts to distinguish what is the system and what is the system's environment. This decision has to be made early in the process to limit the system costs and the time needed for analysis. It may be necessary so that other associated systems in the environment can be specified and costed.

In some cases, the boundary between a system and its environment is relatively clear. For example, where an automated system is replacing an existing manual or computerized system, the environment of the new system is usually the same as the existing system's environment. In other cases, a fairly arbitrary distinction must be made between a system and its environment.

For example, the environment of a CASE toolset may include an existing database whose services are used by the system or the toolset may define its own internal database. Given that a database already exists, the positioning of the boundary between these systems may be a difficult technical and managerial problem. It is only possible to make a decision about what is and what is not part of the system after some analysis.

Once some decisions on the boundaries of the system have been made, part of the analysis activity is to define that context and the dependencies which a system has on its environment. Normally, producing a simple block diagram is the first step in this activity.

Figure 5.11 is a diagram of the context of the ATM system. From it we see that an auto-teller is connected to an account database, a local branch accounting system, a security system and a system to support machine maintenance. The system is also connected to a usage database which monitors how the network of ATMs is used and to a local branch counter system. This counter system provides services such as backup and printing. These, therefore, need not be included in the auto-teller itself.

This diagram identifies the environment of the auto-teller system. It does not show the relationships between the other systems in the environment and the system which is being specified. External systems might produce data for or consume data from the system. They might share data with the system, they might be connected directly, through a network, or not connected at all. They might be physically co-located or located in separate buildings. All of these relations might affect the requirements of the system being defined and must be taken into account.

Therefore, the simple block diagrams should be expanded into one or more environmental models that might also be developed during the requirements analysis process. These may be based on the types of system model which I discuss in the following chapter.

The definition of a system context is not, of course, a value-free judgement. Social and organizational factors may mean that the position of a system boundary may be determined by non-technical factors. For example, a system boundary may be positioned so that the analysis process can all be carried out on one site; it may

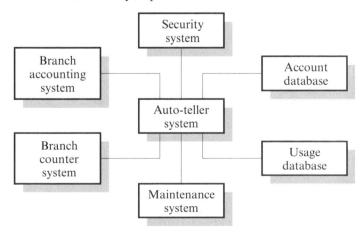

Figure 5.11
The auto-teller system context.

be positioned so that a particularly difficult manager need not be consulted; it may be positioned so that the system cost is increased and the system development division must therefore expand to design and implement the system.

5.4 Social and organizational factors

Software systems do not exist in isolation. Rather, they are used in a social and organizational context. That context can influence or even dominate both the requirements for the system and the requirements analysis process. A significant weakness of most methods of analysis is that they have no mechanisms for taking such factors into account. As I said above, there are few if any methods which include steps to analyse and document the human interaction requirements.

The social and organizational factors which influence a system's requirements cannot really be considered as a single viewpoint. Rather, they are potential influences on all viewpoints. Good requirements analysts must be sensitive to the human and business factors affecting the process. However, because these factors are not well defined, there is no systematic way of tackling their analysis.

As an example of how social and organizational factors can be important, imagine that a software system is proposed which will allow senior management in a company to access information directly without the intervention of middle management. Those senior managers do not normally interact directly with computers. Rather, they interact with the computer through a secretary or some other assistant.

Factors which might affect the requirements for this system are:

- *The manager's status* Senior managers may feel that they are too important to use a keyboard themselves. Furthermore, they may not be able to type quickly and would not like secretaries to see them hunting for keys. Therefore, systems in which the user interface relies on a command line interface may well be unacceptable.

- *The manager's responsibilities* Managers may simply not have long, uninterrupted periods where they can learn to use the new computer. Therefore, systems that need even a short training period may not be acceptable.

In this case, an organizational factor which may affect the requirements analysis process is the intention of the organization to reduce the number of middle managers. These middle managers have a vested interest in the system failing. They are, however, very important sources of information about the system requirements. They may refuse to cooperate in the analysis process or they may deliberately withhold information so that the system will not be successful.

There have been some research projects which have investigated how to take such factors into account when formulating system requirements. Sociologists and social anthropologists participated in the requirements engineering process to analyse relevant human, social and organizational factors.

This social analysis is based on a technique called ethnography, whereby a sociologist spends a considerable amount of time in the working environment. The day-to-day work is observed and notes made of the actual tasks in which participants are involved.

The value of ethnography is that it does not involve people trying to explain what they are doing. People find it very difficult to articulate details of their work because it is second nature to them. They understand their own work but may not understand its relationship with other work in the organization. Social and organizational factors which affect the work but which are not obvious to individuals may only become clear when noticed by an unbiased observer.

All of these factors make it difficult for participants to explain their real requirements for software support. Ethnographers should be able to discover the actual rather than the formal organizational processes. They can therefore suggest requirements which will allow effective support software to be written.

The role that ethnography can play in studies of automation was first demonstrated by Suchman (1983). She studied office work and found that the actual work practices were far richer, more complex and more dynamic than the relatively simplistic models assumed by office automation systems. The difference between the assumed and the actual work was the most important reason why these office systems had no significant effect on productivity.

Other studies have involved studies of the police (Ackroyd *et al.*, 1992), underground railway control rooms (Heath and Luff, 1991) and air-traffic control (Bentley *et al.*, 1992; Hughes *et al.*, 1992). I was involved in the studies of air-traffic controllers. This ethnographic study discovered that there was a very important but implicit interaction between controllers which had not been recognized in previous analyses. Previous systems automating part of the controllers' interface with a flight data system had been rejected by the controllers because they made this implicit interaction impossible. As this was a critical part of the process of safety assurance, these systems were rejected by the controllers.

Classical ethnography involves a social scientist spending a period in observation then reporting the results. To be effective in requirements analysis, the ethnography must be more focused. The model of interaction which we devised (Sommerville *et al.*, 1993) and which worked reasonably successfully is shown in Figure 5.12.

We found that ethnography was effective when combined with prototyping (see Chapter 8). The ethnography informed the development of the prototype so that fewer prototype refinement cycles were required. Furthermore, the prototyping

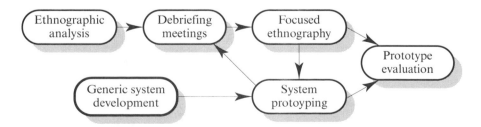

Figure 5.12
Ethnography and prototyping for requirements analysis.

focused the ethnography by identifying problems and questions which were discussed with the ethnographer. He looked for the answers to these questions during the next phase of the system study.

Of course there is a danger of simply studying existing work, particularly if that work is already supported by imperfect systems. Weinberg (1982) calls this the railroad paradox. The railroad paradox (derived from the fact that US railways are little used for passengers) can be summarized as follows:

> A service isn't good so users complain about it. They find alternatives to the service (e.g. cars) so it isn't used much. In response to the complaints, analysts examine how the system is used, find it isn't popular so decide that it isn't necessary.

If we simply look at the superficial features of a system, we may get the wrong impression of it. An example of this can be found in air-traffic control systems that provide an audible warning (conflict alert) when aircraft are placed onto potentially intersecting flight paths. However, conflict alert systems can't tell the difference between controller errors and deliberate controller decisions. Sometimes, air-traffic controllers deliberately place aircraft on conflicting paths. They know that they will relocate these aircraft before any problems arise. When they do this, however, the conflict alert alarm keeps going off. Many controllers therefore switch it off.

A superficial analysis of the system might therefore suggest that there is no need for a conflict alert system because so few controllers use it. In fact, such a system may be useful. However, it must be designed carefully so that it doesn't detect intersecting flight paths too early causing unnecessary alarms. Prolonged ethnography allows deep knowledge of work to be developed. The ethnographer can discover why it is switched off and not simply observe that it isn't used.

Ethnographic studies can contribute to an analysis process but are not, in themselves, the complete answer. They can be used with other methods of requirements analysis (Figure 5.13) to provide a deeper understanding of how the system fits into an existing organization and work practices.

Further research is required to discover how to integrate these with structured methods of analysis so that the costs can be reduced and multiple viewpoints can be handled more effectively. Nevertheless, as the human and organizational influences on computer systems become more widely recognized, the role of ethnography in the analysis process is likely to become more important.

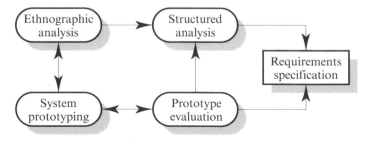

Figure 5.13
Ethnography,
prototyping and
structured analysis.

Further reading

Software Requirements: Objects, Functions and States. This book has a reasonable chapter on analysis in general and includes a good survey of methods of requirements analysis. However, it does not cover approaches to analysis based on multiple viewpoints. (A.M. Davis, 1993, Prentice-Hall.)

'Integrating ethnography into the requirements engineering process'. This paper discusses how ethnography was used in the requirements analysis for an air traffic control system. (T. Rodden *et al.*, *Proc. RE'93: 1st International Symposium on Requirements Engineering*, 1993, IEEE Press.)

Comm. *ACM*, **38** (5). A special issue of this journal which is concerned with human factors in requirements engineering. (May, 1995.)

Other books which cover specific analysis methods are suggested in the further reading section of Chapter 6.

KEY POINTS

- Requirements analysis is an iterative process which involves domain under-standing, requirements collection, classification, structuring, prioritization and validation.

- Different stakeholders in the system have different requirements. All complex systems should therefore be analysed from a number of different viewpoints.

- Viewpoints may be based on sources or sinks of data, different models of the system expressed using different notations or external interaction with the system.

- Methods for requirements analysis should include a set of activities, associated notations, rules governing the use of these notations, guidelines defining good practice and standard forms or reports used to document the analysis.

- The viewpoint-oriented method used here is based on viewpoints which are external to the system and the services delivered to these viewpoints. Data and control requirements for these services are also defined.

- It is important to define the boundaries between a system and its environ-ment. Consequently, as part of the analysis process, the system's environment or context should be studied and described.

- Social and organizational factors have a strong influence on system require-ments and may be critical in determining whether the software is actually used.

EXERCISES

5.1 Suggest who might be stakeholders in a university student records system. Explain why it is almost inevitable that the requirements of different stakeholders will conflict in some ways.

5.2 Explain why requirements analysts need to develop knowledge of the application domain of the system which is being specified.

5.3 Briefly describe the different notions of a viewpoint which are used in viewpoint-oriented analysis methods. Suggest advantages and disadvantages of each viewpoint type.

5.4 A software system is to be developed to automate a library catalogue. This system will contain information about all the books in a library and will be usable by library staff and by book borrowers and readers. The system should support catalogue browsing, querying, and should provide facilities allowing users to send messages to library staff reserving a book that is on loan. Identify the principal viewpoints which might be taken into account in the specification of this system. Show their relationships using a viewpoint hierarchy diagram.

5.5 For one or more of the viewpoints identified in the libary cataloguing system, suggest services which might be provided to that viewpoint, data which the viewpoint might provide and events which control the provision of these services.

5.6 For the services identified in Exercise 5.4, identify what might be the most important non-functional constraints.

5.7 Discuss an example of a type of system in which social and political factors might strongly influence the system requirements. Explain why these factors are important in your example.

5.8 Your company uses a standard analysis method which is normally applied to all requirements analysis. In your work, you find that this method cannot represent social factors which are significant in the system you are analysing. You point this out to your manager who makes clear that the standard should be followed. Discuss what you should do in such a situation.

6

System Models

Objectives

- To explain the role of system models in the requirements analysis process.

- To show how a number of different types of model can present complementary information about a system.

- To describe different types of system model.

- To introduce the idea of a data dictionary as a supplement to system models.

Contents

One of the outputs of the requirements analysis process is a set of system models that present abstract descriptions of the system to be developed. Method-based approaches to analysis are systematic ways of producing these system models. In general, these system models are based on computational concepts such as objects or functions rather than application domain concepts. They are therefore an important bridge between the analysis and design processes.

The most important thing to realize about a system model is that it leaves things out. A system model is an abstraction of the system being studied rather than an alternative representation of that system. Ideally, a *representation* of a system should maintain all the information about the entity being represented. An *abstraction* deliberately simplifies and picks out the most salient characteristics. For example, in the unlikely event of this book being summarized in the *Reader's Digest,* the presentation there would be an abstraction of the key points. If it was translated into Swedish, this would be an alternative representation. The translator's intention would be to maintain all the information as it was presented in English.

The proponents of particular methods of analysis (such as object-oriented analysis) choose a set of system models as part of the method. They claim, usually without any justification, that these models are all you need to represent the system. I completely disagree with such assertions. Different types of system model contribute in different ways to our understanding of the system. There is no ideal system model; nor is there an ideal method for developing such models. Good analysts develop several kinds of system model. They then include those which reflect the most relevant features of the system as far as further software development is concerned in the requirements document.

Different types of system model are based on different approaches to abstraction. A data-flow model (for example) concentrates on the flow of data and the functional transformations on that data. It leaves out details of the data structures. By contrast, an entity-relation model is intended to document the system data and its relationships without concern for the functions in the system.

Examples of the different types of system model which might be produced as part of the analysis process and the notations used to represent these models are:

- A *data-processing model*   Data-flow diagrams may be used to show how data is processed at different stages in the system.
- A *composition model*   Entity-relation diagrams may be used to show how some entities in the system are composed of other entities.
- A *classification model*   Object class/inheritance diagrams may be used to show how entities have common characteristics.
- A *stimulus-response model*   State transition diagrams may be used to show how the system reacts to internal and external events.
- A *process model*   Process models may be used to show the principal activities and deliverables involved in carrying out some process.

In this chapter, I discuss some types of model that may be developed during requirements analysis. Remember that analysts don't have to restrict themselves to the models proposed in any particular method. For example, object-oriented methods which develop various object models rarely suggest that data-flow models should be developed. However, in my experience, such models are sometimes useful as part of an object-oriented analysis process. They often reflect the end-user's understanding of the system. They also may contribute directly to object identification (the data which flows) and the identification of operations on these objects.

I describe three widely used types of system model. These are data-flow models, semantic data models and object models. I also cover data dictionaries which can be used to support all kinds of system model. State machine models, which are particularly important in real-time systems analysis, are covered in Chapter 16. Process models, which document some of the human activities which may be automated, are covered in Chapter 31. There are many examples of process models throughout the book.

6.1 Data-flow models

Data-flow models are an intuitive way of showing how data is processed by a system. At the analysis level, they should be used to model the way in which data is processed in the existing system. The notation used in these models represents functional processing, data stores and data movements between functions. The use of data-flow models for analysis became widespread after the publication of DeMarco's book (1978) on structured systems analysis. They are an intrinsic part of methods that have been developed from this work.

Data-flow models are used to show how data flows through a sequence of processing steps. The data is transformed at each step before moving on to the next stage. These processing steps or transformations are program functions when data-flow diagrams are used to document a software design (see Chapter 15). When used for analysis, the processing may be carried out by people or computers.

This is illustrated in Figure 6.1 which shows the steps involved in processing an order for goods (such as computer equipment) in an organization. The model shows how the order for the goods moves from process to process. It also shows the data stores that are involved in this process.

There are various notations used for data-flow diagrams. In Figure 6.1, rounded rectangles represent processing steps, arrows annotated with the data name represent flows and rectangles represent data stores (or data sources).

Data-flow models are valuable because tracking and documenting how the data associated with a particular process moves through the system helps analysts understand what is going on. Data-flow diagrams have the advantage that, unlike some other modelling notations, they are simple and intuitive. It is usually possible to explain them to potential system users who can therefore participate in validating the analysis.

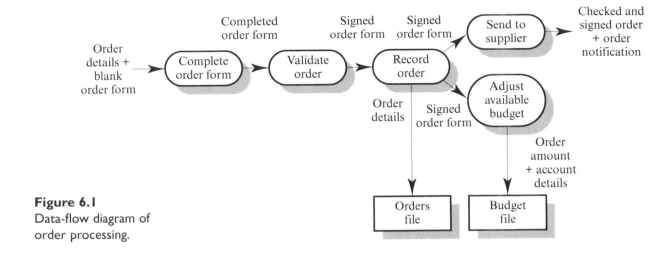

Figure 6.1
Data-flow diagram of
order processing.

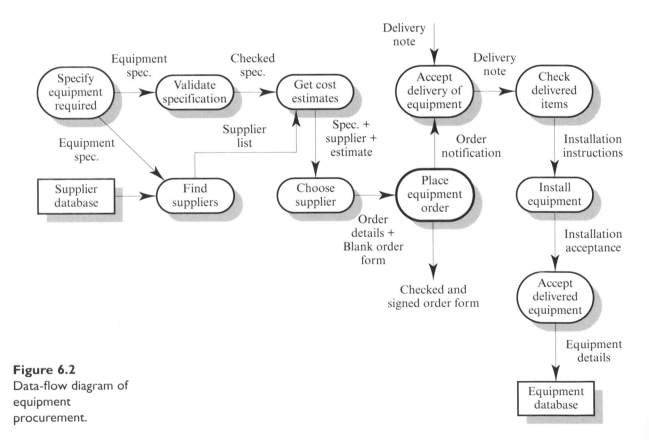

Figure 6.2
Data-flow diagram of
equipment
procurement.

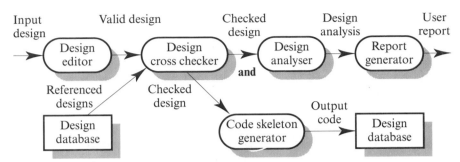

Figure 6.3
Data-flow diagram of a CASE toolset.

Data-flow diagrams can be expressed at a number of different levels of abstraction. Figure 6.2 is a higher-level model which illustrates the process of procuring and installing an item of equipment. The bubble named 'Place equipment order' might be expanded to the diagram shown in Figure 6.1.

In principle, the development of models such as data-flow models should be a 'top-down' process. In this example, this would imply that the overall procurement process should be analysed first. The analysis of the parts of that process, such as ordering, should then be carried out. In practice, analysis is never like that. Information about the system is normally acquired about several different levels at the same time. Lower-level models may be developed first then abstracted to create a more general model.

Data-flow models show a functional perspective whereby each transformation represents a single function. When used to describe system models however, it is sometimes useful to use data-flow descriptions at an architectural level. At this level, various sub-systems may have been identified. The data-flow model can show how these sub-systems exchange information. These sub-systems need not be single functions. For example, one sub-system might be a storage server with a fairly complex interface.

Figure 6.3 shows an example of a data-flow diagram used in this way. In this example, the rounded rectangles represent sub-systems that may themselves be complete programs. Rectangles are used to represent data stores and circles mean user interactions.

Data-flow diagrams are not a good way to describe sub-systems with complex interfaces. A separate diagram is required for each possible input data item. The overall picture of the interface can only be gained by integrating these models. Object models as discussed in Section 6.3 are more suitable for this type of description.

6.2 Semantic data models

Most large software systems make use of a large database of information. In some cases, this database exists independently of the software system. In others, it is created for the system being developed. An important part of systems modelling is to define the logical form of the data processed by the system.

One way of defining the logical form of data is to use a relational model (Codd, 1970; Date, 1990). Using the relational model, the logical data structure is specified as a set of tables, with some tables having common keys. This model allows the relationships between data items to be defined without considering the physical database organization.

However, the relational approach has two main disadvantages:

(1)   *Implicit data typing*   There is no way to define a type and associate it with relations. The only mechanism is to infer the type from the relation names.

(2)   *Inadequate modelling of relations*   Logical relations (such as PART-OF, DERIVED-FROM, and so on) between data items are 'second-class citizens'. They are represented implicitly, rather than explicitly, through shared values in a table. The relationships cannot be named or given attributes.

An alternative approach to data modelling which includes information about the semantics of the data allows a better abstract model to be produced. Semantic data models always identify the entities in a database, their attributes and explicit relationships between them. Approaches to semantic data modelling include entity-relation (E-R) modelling (Chen, 1976), SDM (Hammer and McLeod, 1981), and Codd's own extension of the relational model, RM/T (Codd, 1979).

I don't have space to describe these approaches in detail here. Briefly, the E-R model sets out data entities (which, in programming language terms, roughly correspond to record data types) and relations between these entities. Entities can have attributes (fields of records) as can relations (in programming language terms, private data values). Attributes are usually atomic and are not decomposed. However, they need not correspond to base types in a programming language.

The model used here to illustrate this approach is based on an extension of Chen's entity-relation (E-R) model as discussed by Hull and King (1987). This involves adding sub- and super-typing to the basic entity and relation primitives originally proposed by Chen. Types may have sub-types so a special type of relation called an inheritance relation has been introduced to extend the basic E-R model. Sub-types inherit the attributes of their super-type. Additional private attributes may be added to the sub-type entity. Inheritance is supported directly in object-oriented programming languages.

Semantic data models are invariably described using graphical notations. These graphical notations are readily understandable by management and users so they can participate in data modelling. The notation used here is set out in Figure 6.4. There are a variety of other notations for describing E-R diagrams, some of which are supported by commercially available CASE tools.

Relations between entities may be 1:1, which means one entity instance participates in a relation with one other entity instance. Alternatively, they may be 1:M, where an entity instance participates in a relationship with more than one other entity instance, or M:N where several entity instances participate in a relation with several others.

Data models are often used to supplement the information provided on data-flow diagrams. As a simple illustration of data modelling, consider Figure 6.5 which

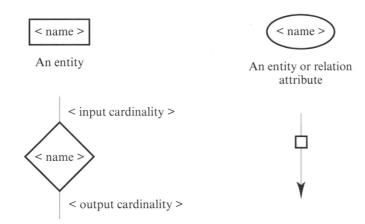

A relation between entities.
The number of input entity instances
is the input cardinality. The number
of output instances is the output
cardinality.

An inheritance relation.
An entity inherits the attributes of its
related entity. The sub-type is referenced
by the arrow.

Figure 6.4
Notation for semantic
data models.

shows how a design (as exchanged in the data-flow model in Figure 6.3) may be represented.

Designs may be thought of as directed graphs. They consist of a set of nodes of different types connected by links representing the relationships between design nodes. There is a screen representation of this graph which is a design diagram and a corresponding database representation. The editing system performs a mapping from the database representation to the screen representation every time it draws a diagram. The information produced by the editor for other design analysis tools should include the logical representation of the design graph. However, these analysis tools are not interested in the details of the physical screen representation. They process the entities, their logical attributes (such as their names) and their relationships.

The logical organization of this design graph which might be exchanged by CASE tools is shown in Figure 6.5. A design has attributes, the values of which are the design name, a design description, a creation date (C-date) and a modification date (M-date). The design is composed of a set of nodes and a set of links. Nodes have associated links between them. Nodes and links have name and type attributes. They may have a set of associated labels which store other descriptive information. Each label has a name and a type. It can either be a text label or an icon. A text label has a text attribute and an icon has a bitmap attribute.

On the left of Figure 6.5, a relation 'is-a' is shown which shows that a node can be related to a whole design. Rather than introduce a loop in the model and complicate the layout, the entity named 'Design' is repeated. To indicate that this is the same entity as the root node in this model, the name is emboldened and the node box is shown with a thick enclosing line.

Entity-relationship models have been widely used in database design. Barker (1989) shows that they can be readily implemented using relational databases. The database schemas derived from these models are naturally in third normal form

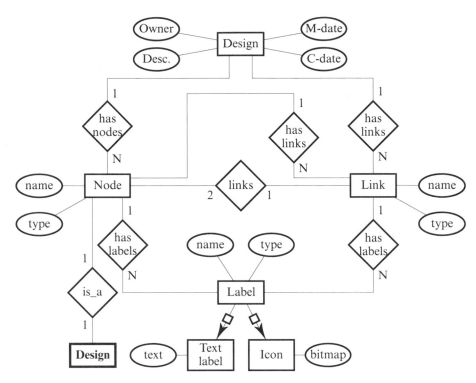

Figure 6.5
Semantic data model of
a software design.

which is a desirable characteristic of relational schemas. Because of the explicit typing and the recognition of sub- and super-types, it is also straightforward to map these models onto object-oriented databases.

6.3 Object models

An object-oriented approach to programming was first proposed in 1967 with the development of the Simula-67 language. However, it is only since the late 1980s that this method of development has been widely adopted in industry. To support object-oriented programming, an object-oriented development approach may be adopted. This means expressing the system requirements using an object model, designing using an object-oriented approach and developing the system in an object-oriented programming language such as C++.

Object models developed during requirements analysis may be used to represent both system data and its processing. In this respect, they combine some of the uses of data-flow and semantic data models. They are also useful for showing how entities in the system may be classified and composed of other entities.

Object models of systems which are developed during requirements analysis should not include details of the individual objects in the system. This is a design consideration. Rather, they should model classes of objects representing real-world entities. An object class is an abstraction over a set of objects which identifies common attributes (as in a semantic data model) and the services or operations which are provided by each object.

Various types of object models can be produced showing how object classes are related to each other, how objects are aggregated to form other objects, how objects use the services provided by other objects and so on. All of these can add to our understanding of a system which is being specified.

For some classes of system, object models are natural ways of reflecting the real-world entities that are manipulated by the system. This is particularly true where the system is concerned with processing of information about concrete entities such as cars, aircraft, books and so on, which have clearly identifiable attributes. More abstract, higher-level entities, such as the concept of a library, a medical record system or a word processor are harder to model as object classes. They do not necessarily have a simple interface consisting of independent attributes and operations.

The analysis process for identifying objects and object classes is recognized as one of the most difficult areas of object-oriented development. Object identification is basically the same for analysis and design. The methods of object identification covered in Chapter 14, which discusses object-oriented design, may be used. I concentrate here on some of the object models which might be generated during the analysis process.

There have been various notations used to represent object models (Booch, 1994; Coad and Yourdon, 1990; Rumbaugh *et al.,* 1991). These are semantically equivalent. Any of these notations may be used for model description.

Figure 6.6 shows the notation which I use to represent an object class. There are three parts to this. The object class name has its obvious meaning and the attributes section lists the attributes of that object class. When objects are created using the class as a template, all created objects acquire these attributes. They may then be assigned values that are conformant with the attribute type declared in the object class. The service section shows the operations associated with the object. These operations may modify attribute values and may be activated from other object classes.

An object class is similar to an abstract data type in that it can be used as a basis for creating objects which are executable entities with the attributes and services of the object class. The specification of an object class is an interface specification in which the visible parts of the entity are set out. The created object may, of course, have other attributes and procedures which are private to that object. These do not appear in the class specification.

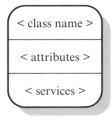

Figure 6.6
Notation to represent
an object class.

6.3.1 Inheritance models

Object-oriented modelling involves identifying the classes of object which are important in the domain being studied. These are then organized into a taxonomy. A taxonomy is a classification scheme which shows how an object class is related to other classes through common attributes and services.

To display this taxonomy, we usually organize the classes into an inheritance or class hierarchy where the most general object classes are presented at the top of the hierarchy. More specialized objects inherit their attributes and services. These specialized objects may have their own attributes and services.

Figure 6.7 illustrates part of a simplified class hierarchy that might be developed when modelling a library system. This hierarchy gives information about the items held in the library. I assume that the library does not simply hold books but also other types of item such as music, recordings of films, magazines, newspapers, and so on.

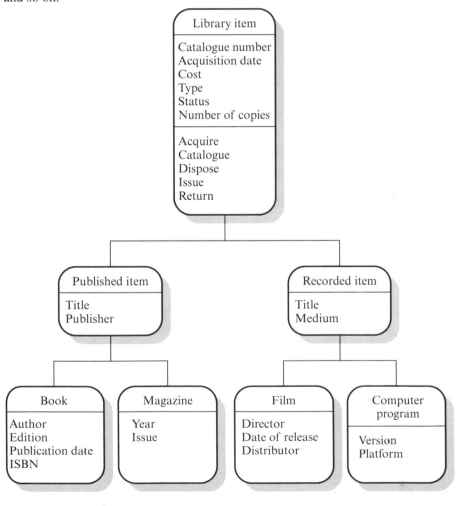

Figure 6.7
Part of a class hierarchy for a library system.

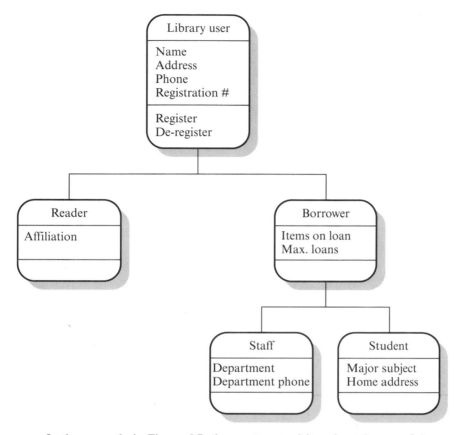

Figure 6.8
User class hierarchy.

In the example in Figure 6.7, the most general item is at the top of the tree and has a set of attributes and services which are common to all library items. These are inherited by the classes ('Published item' and 'Recorded item') which add their own attributes and pass these on to lower-level items.

Figure 6.8 is an example of another inheritance hierarchy which might be part of a library model. In this case, the users of a library are shown. There are two classes of user: those who are allowed to borrow books and those who may only read books in the library without taking them away.

Figures 6.7 and 6.8 show class inheritance hierarchies where every class has only a single parent class from which it inherits its attributes and services. Multiple inheritance models may also be constructed in which a class has several parents. Its inherited attributes and services are a conjunction of those inherited from each super-class. Figure 6.9 shows an example of a multiple inheritance model which might also be part of a library model.

In Figure 6.9, the object 'Talking book', which is a voice recording of a published book, inherits attributes from both 'Book' and from 'Voice recording'. The object class 'Talking book' inherits all of the attributes of its parent classes including those which are inherited by the parent classes themselves. It also adds a specific attribute which records the number of tapes in the recording.

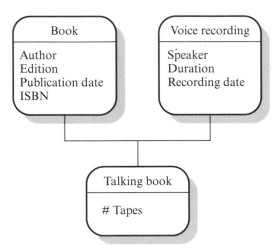

Figure 6.9
Multiple inheritance.

The principal problem with multiple inheritance is designing an inheritance graph in which objects do not inherit unnecessary attributes. Other problems include the difficulty of re-organizing the inheritance graph when changes are required and resolving name clashes where two or more super-classes have attributes with the same name but different meanings. At the system modelling level, such clashes are relatively easy to resolve by manually altering the object model. They cause more problems in object-oriented programming.

The design of class hierarchies is not a simple process. One advantage of developing such models is that the analyst needs to understand, in detail, the domain in which the system is to be installed. As an example of the subtlety of the problems which arise in practice, consider the library item hierarchy. It would seem that the attribute 'Title' could be held in the most general item, then inherited by all lower-level items.

However, while everything in a library must have some kind of identifier or registration number, it does not follow that everything must have a title. For example, a library may hold the personal papers of a retired politician. Many of these items may not be explicitly titled. These will be classified using some other class (not shown here) which has a different set of attributes.

6.3.2 Object aggregation

As well as acquiring attributes and services through an inheritance relationship with other objects, some objects are aggregations of other objects. The classes representing these objects may be modelled using an aggregation model as shown in Figure 6.10. In this example, I have modelled a potential library item which is the material for a particular class given in a university. This does not consist of a single item but includes lecture notes, assignments, sample solutions, copies of transparencies used in lectures, videotapes and so on.

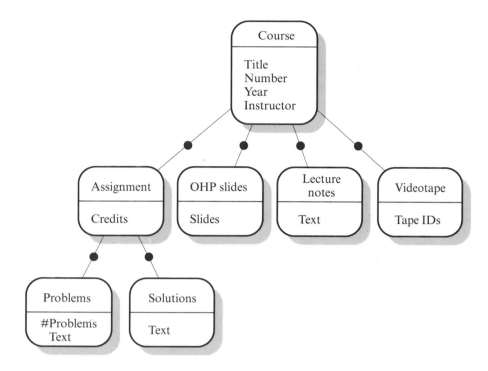

Figure 6.10
An aggregate object
representing a course.

Notice the use of the different symbol for links in this hierarchy. Adding a black blob to a link means that the relationship between objects is a 'part-of' relationship rather than an inheritance relationship.

6.3.3 Service usage models

The hierarchical models which I have covered show object classes and the services associated with each object. They do not give any information about how object classes use the services provided by other classes. As well as these hierarchical models, a model showing how one class is related to other classes through the operations used is also useful. Figure 6.11 shows some of the classes from the library model. It illustrates that the class 'Library user' makes use of the services 'Issue' and 'Return' associated with 'Library item'. The class 'Library staff' uses the 'Acquire', 'Catalogue' and 'Dispose' services associated with 'Library item' and the 'Register' and 'De-register' services associated with 'Library user'.

Further examples of service usage models are shown in Chapter 15, which covers object-oriented design. These models are fairly detailed and it may not be necessary to develop them for all object interactions.

Object models developed during requirements analysis simplify the transition to object-oriented design and programming. In spite of claims to the contrary by some of their advocates, end-users of a system often find object models difficult to understand. They may prefer to adopt a more functional, data-processing view.

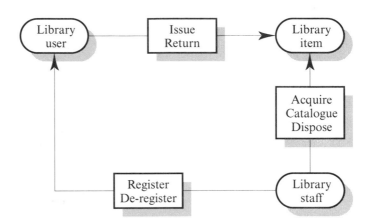

Figure 6.11
Service usage.

6.4 Data dictionaries

As a system data model is derived, many named entities, relationships and so forth will be identified. The names given to the entities should be chosen to give the reader some clues to their meaning. However, further description of the named entities is usually needed to make the model understandable. This description can be informal or formal. Whatever approach is used, it is always worth collecting all descriptions in a single repository or *data dictionary*.

A data dictionary is, simplistically, a list of names used by the system, arranged alphabetically. As well as the name, the dictionary should include a description of the named entity and, if the name represents a composite object, there may be a description of the composition. Other information such as the date of creation, the creator, and the representation of the entity may also be included depending on the type of model which is being developed.

The advantages of using a data dictionary are:

(1)   It is a mechanism for name management. A large system model may be developed by many different people who have to invent names for entities and relationships. These names should be used consistently and should not clash. The data dictionary software can check for name uniqueness and tell requirements analysts of name duplications.

(2)   It serves as a store of organizational information which can link analysis, design, implementation and evolution. As the system is developed, information is taken to inform the development. New information is added to it. All information about an entity is in one place.

All system names, whether they be names of entities, types, relations, attributes or services, should be entered in the dictionary. Support software should be available to create, maintain and interrogate the dictionary. This software might be integrated with other tools so that dictionary creation is partially automated.

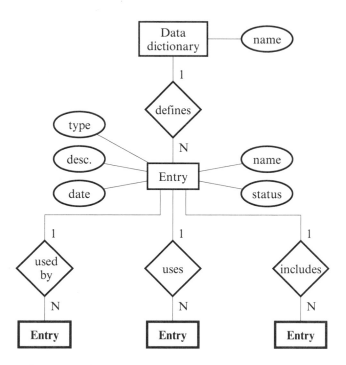

Figure 6.12
Semantic data model of
a data dictionary.

A possible semantic data model for a data dictionary is shown in Figure 6.12. This specifies that a data dictionary is made up of a number of entries, each of which has a name, a type, a description, a creation date and a status (which allows for an entry to become obsolete). Each entry participates in three relations with other entries. These show which entities use that entity, which entities are used by that entity and which entities are included in the entity (for example, operation entities are included in abstract data type entities).

Examples of fragments of data dictionary entries are shown in Figure 6.13. To simplify the presentation of this example, I have deliberately excluded some attribute values and the links to the other entries as shown in Figure 6.12. The names in the dictionary are taken from the semantic data model of the software design.

Further Reading

Structured Analysis and System Specification. This was perhaps the first and is certainly the best-known description of data-flow modelling. This topic is also covered in many more modern books but they have not necessarily improved on the original. (T. DeMarco, 1978, Yourdon Press.)

'Semantic database modeling: Survey, applications and research issues'. This is a good survey paper covering the various approaches which have been developed for developing semantic data models. (R. Hull and R. King, *ACM Computing Surveys*, **19** (3), 1987.)

Object-oriented Analysis and Design with Applications (2nd edition). There is now a vast number of books on object-oriented analysis, design and programming. There is not a great deal to choose between them. I like Booch's book because of its good examples. (G. Booch, 1994, Benjamin Cummings.)

Name	Description	Type	Date
has_labels	1:N relation between entities of type Node or Link and entities of type Label.	Relation	5.10.93
Label	Holds structured or unstructured information about nodes or links. Labels can be text or can be an icon.	Entity	8.12.93
Link	Represents a relation between design entities represented as nodes. Links are typed and may be named.	Relation	8.12.93
name (label)	Each label has a name which identifies the type of label. The name must be unique within the set of label types used in a design.	Attribute	8.12.93
name (node)	Each node has a name which must be unique within a design. The name may be up to 64 characters long.	Attribute	15.11.93

Figure 6.13
Examples of data dictionary entries.

KEY POINTS

- A model is an abstract view of a system which ignores some system details. Complementary system models can be developed which present different information about the system.

- Data-flow diagrams may be used to model the data processing carried out by a system. The system is modelled as a set of data transformations with functions acting on the data.

- Semantic data models describe the logical structure of the data which is imported to and exported by the system. These models show system entities, their attributes and the relationships in which they participate.

- Object models describe the logical system entities and their classification and aggregation. They combine a data model with a processing model. Possible object models which may be developed include inheritance models, aggregation models and service-use models.

■ Object models are particularly valuable for modelling system interfaces in an abstract way. However, end-users sometimes find object models difficult to understand.

■ A data dictionary is an important tool for maintaining information about system entities throughout the lifetime of a project. It can support any kind of system model. Entries may be added at any time during analysis and design.

EXERCISES

6.1   Suggest why data-flow diagrams are intuitive and easy-to-understand by non-technical staff.

6.2   Based on your experience with a bank ATM, draw a data-flow diagram modelling the data processing involved when a customer withdraws cash from the machine.

6.3   Model the data processing which might take place in an electronic mail system that can send and receive messages from remote computers. You should model the mail-sending and mail-receiving processing separately.

6.4   Extend the model of a software design shown in Figure 6.5 to include physical layout information. Nodes may be represented by composite symbols which are a combination of simpler symbols such as rectangle, line and so on, and are displayed at a particular coordinate. Links are made up of a number of line segments which may be solid or dotted lines. Text is displayed in a specified font. The name associated with a node, link or label is positioned inside or near to the named item.

6.5   Model the object classes which might be used in an electronic mail system. If you have tried Exercise 6.3, describe the similarities and differences between the data processing model and the object model.

6.6   Using an entity-relation approach, describe a possible data model for the library cataloguing system described in Exercise 5.4. Assume that the items in the library are those modelled in Figure 6.7.

6.7   Develop an object model including a class hierarchy diagram and an aggregation diagram showing the principal components of a personal computer system and its system software.

6.8   Using the model of the data dictionary shown in Figure 6.12, design plausible data dictionary entries for the names, relations and attributes shown in the model of the data dictionary and/or the extended version of the editor model which you have designed in completing Exercise 6.4.

7

Requirements Definition and Specification

Objectives

- To illustrate a forms-based method of writing precise definitions of system requirements.

- To describe ways of writing requirements specifications which are the basis of a system design and which may be part of a system development contract.

- To explain the importance of non-functional requirements which constrain the system being developed and the development process.

- To describe different types of non-functional requirement and how these can be written.

Contents

General principles of requirements engineering were introduced in Chapter 4 where I made a distinction between requirements definitions and requirements specifications. Requirements definitions are customer-oriented descriptions of what the system should do. They should be written in the customer's language. This usually means that they should be written using natural language and easy-to-understand diagrams.

Requirements specifications are more precise descriptions of the system's functionality and the constraints on its operation. They are intended to specify the system for software designers so they are sometimes called functional specifications. A requirements specification may be the basis of a contract between the system developer and customer. It should not be ambiguous or informal as this may lead to misinterpretation by the customer or system developer.

Many of the problems of software engineering are difficulties with the requirements specification. It is natural for a system developer to interpret an ambiguous requirement so that its realization is as cheap as possible. Often, however, this is not what the customer wants. New requirements have to be established and changes made to the system. Of course, this delays system delivery and increases costs.

To reduce the potential for dispute between customer and contractor, system requirements should always be written so that they are verifiable. This means that, using the requirement, a set of checks can be designed which will show if the delivered system meets that requirement. These checks may be tests of the delivered program. Alternatively, they may define what a reviewer should look for in the system documentation.

This chapter is concerned with ways of writing both requirements definitions and requirements specifications so that the requirements are precise and unambiguous, understandable by the people for whom they are written, verifiable and not unduly expensive to write. Various notations for writing functional and non-functional requirements are covered.

7.1 Requirements definition

A software requirements definition is an abstract description of the services which the system should provide and the constraints under which the system must operate. It should only specify the external behaviour of the system. It should not be concerned with system design characteristics. Consequently, the requirements should not be defined using an implementation model. The definition should be written in such a way that it is understandable by customers without knowledge of specialized notations. The notations used for requirements definition must therefore be based on natural language, forms and simple intuitive diagrams.

System requirements may be either functional or non-functional requirements:

- *Functional requirements* These are statements of services the system should provide, how the system should react to particular inputs and how the system should behave in particular situations. In some cases, the functional requirements may also explicitly state what the system should not do.

● *Non-functional requirements*   These are constraints on the services or functions offered by the system. They include timing constraints, constraints on the development process, standards and so on.

In principle, the functional requirements definition of a system should be both complete and consistent. Completeness means that all services required by the user should be defined. Consistency means that requirements should not have contradictory definitions. In practice, for large, complex systems, it is practically impossible to achieve requirements consistency and completeness. The reason for this is partly because of the inherent system complexity and partly because different viewpoints (see Chapter 5) have inconsistent needs. These inconsistencies may not be obvious when the requirements are first specified. The problems only emerge after deeper analysis. As problems are discovered during reviews or in later life cycle phases, the problems in requirements documents must be corrected.

There are three types of major problem with requirements definitions written in natural language:

(1)   *Lack of clarity*   It is very difficult to use language in a precise and unambiguous way without making the document wordy and difficult to read.

(2)   *Requirements confusion*   Functional requirements, non-functional requirements, system goals and design information may not be clearly distinguished.

(3)   *Requirements amalgamation*   Several different requirements may be expressed together as a single requirement.

Few requirements documents are in the public domain so it is difficult to find examples that may be freely quoted. One document that is available is the Stoneman document (Buxton, 1980) which sets out requirements for an Ada programming support environment (APSE). Although this document is now rather old, requirements are largely still written in the same way.

In general, this definition is not badly written but it does contain some examples of the above problems. For example, requirement 4.A.5 from the Stoneman document is shown in Figure 7.1. This is an example of requirements amalgamation.

4.A.5   The database shall support the generation and control of configuration objects; that is, objects which are themselves groupings of other objects in the database. The configuration control facilities shall allow access to the objects in a version group by the use of an incomplete name.

Figure 7.1
A requirement on a database for an Ada support environment.

This requirement includes both conceptual and detailed information. It expresses the concept that there should be configuration control facilities provided as an inherent part of the APSE. However, it also includes the detail that those facilities should allow access to the objects in a version group by use of an incomplete name. This detail would have been better left to a section in which the configuration control requirements were specified more fully.

Some organizations try to produce a single specification to act as both a requirements definition and a requirements specification. When a requirements definition (for non-technical readers) is combined with a specification (for technicians) there is often confusion between concepts and details. Figure 7.2 illustrates this confusion. This example is taken from the requirements definition for a CASE tool (a design editing system) whose system model is shown in Figure 6.3. The user of the design editor may specify that a grid should be displayed so that diagram entities may be accurately positioned.

The first sentence in this requirement mixes up three different kinds of requirement.

(1)   A conceptual, functional requirement states that the editing system should provide a grid. It presents a rationale for this.

(2)   A non-functional requirement giving detailed information about the grid units (centimetres or inches).

(3)   A non-functional user interface requirement which defines how that grid is switched on and off by the user.

The requirement in Figure 7.2 also gives some but not all initialization information. It defines that the grid is initially off. However, it does not define its units when turned on. It provides some detailed information, namely that the user may toggle between units but not the spacing between grid lines.

It is easy to criticize but much more difficult to write a requirements definition. The first version of a requirements definition is inevitably unstructured as a natural authoring tendency is to include information as it comes to mind. To produce a good specification, you have to reorganize and restructure the document to make it more readable and usable.

Perhaps the most useful approach to writing a readable requirements definition is to invent a standard format and to ensure that all requirements definitions

Figure 7.2
A requirements definition for an editor grid.

> **2.6 Grid facilities**   To assist in the positioning of entities on a diagram, the user may turn on a grid in either centimetres or inches, via an option on the control panel. Initially, the grid is off. The grid may be turned on and off at any time during an editing session and can be toggled between inches and centimetres at any time. A grid option will be provided on the reduce-to-fit view but the number of grid lines shown will be reduced to avoid filling the smaller diagram with grid lines.

adhere to that format. The use of a standard format means that omissions are less likely. It also simplifies cross-checking of requirements.

Figure 7.3 illustrates this method of presentation. It restates the requirement for an editor grid. It is written in a stylized way, in which a requirement is stated followed by its rationale and a reference to a more detailed specification.

Text highlighting (bold and italic) adds structure to sentences and paragraphs. Closely related requirements are grouped and enclosed in a frame to emphasize their relationship. The principal requirement is presented in a short sentence which is emboldened. The remaining text adds information to this principal requirement.

The rationale associated with a requirements definition is important. Without it, some facilities may appear arbitrary and their importance may not be understood by engineers developing a more detailed specification or maintaining the system. For example, in Figure 7.3, the rationale recognizes that an active grid where positioned objects automatically 'snap to' a grid line can be useful. However, it deliberately rejects this option in favour of manual positioning. If a change to this is proposed at some later stage, it is then clear that the decision to have a passive grid was a deliberate one.

A further example of this stylized format, which also defines part of the editing system, is shown in Figure 7.4. This is a more detailed specification of a function. It illustrates another facet of a standardized format for requirements definitions. In this case, the definition includes a list of user actions. This is sometimes necessary so that all functions can be provided in a consistent way. Implementation details should not be included in this additional information. Therefore, the definition does not set out how the cursor and the symbol are moved, or how the type is selected.

2.6   Grid facilities

2.6.1   The editor shall provide a grid facility where a matrix of horizontal and vertical lines provide a background to the editor window. This grid shall be a passive grid where the alignment of entities is the user's responsibility.

Rationale: A grid helps the user to create a tidy diagram with well-spaced entities. Although an active grid, where entities 'snap-to' grid lines can be useful, the positioning is imprecise. The user is the best person to decide where entities should be positioned.

2.6.2   When used in 'reduce-to-fit' mode (see 2.1), the number of units separating grid lines must be increased.

Rationale: If line spacing is not increased, the background will be very cluttered with grid lines.

Specification: ECLIPSE/WS/Tools/DE/FS Section 5.6

Figure 7.3
A definition of an editor grid facility.

> **3.5.1**   **Adding nodes to a design**
>
> 3.5.1.1   **The editor shall provide a facility where users can add nodes of a specified type to a design.** Nodes are selected (see 3.4) when they are added to the design.
>
> 3.5.1.2   The sequence of actions to add a node should be as follows:
>
>   (1) The user should select the type of node to be added.
>
>   (2) The user moves the cursor to the approximate node position in the diagram and indicates that the node symbol should be added at that point.
>
>   (3) The symbol may then be dragged to its final position.
>
>   *Rationale:* The user is the best person to decide where to position a node on the diagram. This approach gives the user direct control over node type selection and positioning.
>
> *Specification:* ECLIPSE/WS/Tools/DE/FS. Section 3.5.1

Figure 7.4
The requirements definition for node creation.

7.2 Requirements specification

Requirements specifications add further information to the requirements definition. The requirements specification is usually presented with the system models developed during requirements analysis. The specification plus the model should describe the system to be designed and implemented. It should include all necessary information about what the system must do and all constraints on its operation.

Natural language is often used to write requirements specifications. However, a natural language specification is not a particularly good basis for either a design or a contract between customer and system developer. There are several reasons for this:

(1)   Natural language understanding relies on the specification readers and writers using the same words for the same concept. This leads to misunderstandings because of the inherent ambiguity of natural language words. Jackson (1995) gives an excellent example of this when he discusses signs displayed by an escalator. These said 'Shoes must be worn' and 'Dogs must be carried'. There are many conflicting interpretations of these phrases.

(2)   A natural language requirements specification is over-flexible. You can say the same thing in completely different ways. It is up to the reader to find out when requirements are the same and when they are distinct. This is a very error-prone process.

(3)   Requirements are not partitioned effectively by the language itself. It is difficult to find all related requirements. To discover the consequence of a change, you may have to look at every requirement rather than just a group of related requirements.

Because of these problems, requirements specifications written in natural language are prone to misunderstandings. These are often not discovered until the design or the implementation phases of the software process. As discussed in Chapter 4, the problems may then be very expensive to resolve. There is, therefore, a good case for using alternative notations that avoid some of the problems of unrestricted natural language.

There are various alternatives to the use of natural language which add structure to the specification and which should reduce ambiguity. These are:

(1) *Structured natural language* This approach depends on defining standard forms or templates to express the requirements specification. This is an extended, more detailed form of the structured definitions discussed in the first part of this chapter. Decision tables (Moret, 1982) are a form of structured language.

(2) *Design description languages* This approach relies on using a language which is like a programming language but with more abstract features to specify the requirements by defining an operational model of the system.

(3) *Requirements specification languages* Various special-purpose languages have been designed to express software requirements, such as PSL/PSA (Teichrow and Hershey, 1977) and RSL (Alford, 1977; Bell *et al.*, 1977; Alford, 1985). The advantage of this approach is that special-purpose tool support can be developed.

(4) *Graphical notations* Perhaps the best known graphical notation for requirements is SADT (Ross, 1977; Schoman and Ross, 1977). SADT has a fairly complex graphical vocabulary so is mostly used by specialists. It has been fairly widely used for analysis and requirements specification.

(5) *Mathematical specifications* These are notations based on a formal mathematical concept such as finite-state machines, Petri nets (Peterson, 1977) or more basic concepts such as sets. These unambiguous specifications reduce the arguments between customer and contractor about system functionality. However, most customers don't understand a formal mathematical specification. They are therefore reluctant to accept it as a system contract. Hall (1990a) suggests that the way to tackle this problem is to develop a formal specification then paraphrase this in a way that is more understandable to the customer.

Davis (1990) summarizes and compares some of these different approaches to requirements specification. In this chapter, I focus on the first two of these approaches, namely structured natural language and the use of design description languages. Specialized requirements languages have never become widely known or used. Graphical notations are similar to the notations used to define system models, discussed in Chapter 6. Formal specifications are discussed in Chapters 9 to 11.

When requirements specifications are written, it is important that related requirements should be cross-referenced. When requirements have to be changed, other requirements which may be affected can be found by following the cross-references. Traceability is a property of a requirements specification which reflects the ease of finding related requirements.

Sometimes the relationships between requirements can be very subtle. It is therefore impossible to be definitive about how to write traceable requirements. However, there are some simple methods of traceability that may be applied to any requirements definition or specification:

(1)   All requirements should be assigned a unique number.

(2)   Requirements should explicitly identify related requirements by referring to their number.

(3)   Each requirement document should contain a cross-reference matrix showing related requirements. Different matrices may be developed for different types of relationship.

As well as these simple techniques, CASE tools which are used to support requirements analysis and specification may include support for traceability. Some tools include simple facilities which find requirements that use the same terms. The underlying assumption is that these requirements are therefore related in some way. Linking facilities allowing navigation from one requirement to related requirements may also be supported.

7.2.1 Structured language specifications

Structured natural language is a restricted form of natural language for requirements specification. Structured language notations may limit the terminology used and may use templates to specify system requirements. They may incorporate control constructs derived from programming languages and graphical highlighting to partition the specification. The advantage of this approach is that it maintains most of the expressiveness and understandability of natural language. It does, however, ensure that some degree of uniformity is imposed on the specification.

A project which used structured natural language for requirements specification is described by Heninger (1980). Special-purpose forms were designed to describe the input, output and functions of an aircraft software system. The system requirements were specified using these forms. Although the system described by Heninger is a manual one, a forms-based approach can be supported with computer-based tools.

A forms-based approach to requirements specification relies on defining one or more standard forms or templates to express the requirements. The specification may be structured around the objects manipulated by the system, the functions performed by the system or the events processed by the system. The form structure will vary depending on the requirements structuring technique used. Functionally oriented specifications are probably the most common.

An example of such a specification for part of the CASE tool editing system is shown in Figure 7.5. This is a more detailed definition of the function defined in Figure 7.4.

If a standard form is used for specification, the following information should be included:

(1)   The description of the function or entity being specified.

(2)   A description of its inputs and where these come from.

(3)   A description of its outputs and where these go to.

(4)   An indication of what other entities are used (the *requires* part).

(5)   If a functional approach is used, a pre-condition setting out what must be true before the function is called and a post-condition specifying what is true after the function is called.

(6)   A description of the side-effects (if any) of the operation.

ECLIPSE/Workstation/Tools/DE/FS/3.5.1	
Function	Add node
Description	Adds a node to an existing design. The user selects the type of node, and its position. When added to the design, the node becomes the current selection. The user chooses the node position by moving the cursor to the area where the node is added.
Inputs	Node type, Node position, Design identifier.
Source	Node type and Node position are input by the user, Design identifier from the database.
Outputs	Design identifier.
Destination	The design database. The design is committed to the database on completion of the operation.
Requires	Design graph rooted at input design identifier.
Pre-condition	The design is open and displayed on the user's screen.
Post-condition	The design is unchanged apart from the addition of a node of the specified type at the given position.
Side-effects	None
Definition: ECLIPSE/Workstation/Tools/DE/RD/3.5.1	

Figure 7.5
Requirements specification using a standard form.

The form-based approach to specification may be used with formal mathematical specifications. A formal specification can be defined and paraphrased in a set of forms. These should be understandable by customers and can serve as a system contract. Alternatively, the structured forms can be used as the first stage in the design process. Where appropriate, fields in the form can be filled in using a mathematically formal notation.

Using formatted specifications removes some of the problems of natural language specification in that there is less variability in the specification and requirements are partitioned more effectively. However, some ambiguity may remain in the specification. Alternative methods which use more structured notations such as PDL (described below) go some way towards tackling the problem of specification ambiguity. However, non-specialists find them harder to understand.

7.2.2 Requirements specification using a PDL

To counter the inherent ambiguities in natural language specification, it is possible to describe requirements operationally using a program description language or PDL. A PDL is a language derived from a programming language like Ada. It may contain additional, more abstract, constructs to increase its expressive power. The advantage of using a PDL is that it may be checked syntactically and semantically by software tools. Requirements omissions and inconsistencies may be inferred from the results of these checks.

Using a PDL to specify requirements involves annotating the system model with further information that adds to the information provided by the modelling notation. Using a PDL may be the best way to provide this information in two situations:

(1)   When an operation is specified as a sequence of simpler actions and the order of execution is important. Descriptions of such sequences in natural language are sometimes confusing, particularly if nested conditionals and loops are involved.

(2)   When hardware and software interfaces have to be specified. In many cases, the interfaces between sub-systems are defined in the requirements specification, particularly if these sub-systems already exist. This allows these systems to be developed independently. The PDL usually allows more detail about interface objects and types to be specified.

If the reader of a requirements specification is familiar with the PDL used, specifying the requirements in this way can make them less ambiguous and easier to understand. If the PDL is based on the implementation language, there is a natural transition from requirements to design. The possibility of misinterpretation is reduced. Specifiers need not be trained in another description language.

Of course, there are disadvantages to this approach to requirements specification:

- The language used to write the specification may not be sufficiently expressive to describe application domain concepts in an understandable way. In particular, customer staff who are unfamiliar with programming languages may be intimidated by the notation.

- The specification will be seen as an abstract design rather than a model to help the user understand the system. Design decisions may be made too early in the software process and this can restrict the freedom of designers to meet other, non-functional, system requirements.

Figure 7.6 shows how a PDL may be used in a situation where the sequence of actions in a system is significant. This describes the bank ATM, introduced in Chapter 5. A form-based specification cannot convey this sequential information in such a concise way.

The PDL description shows that, in this case, customers must have a valid card then input a valid PIN. They may then select one or more services. After completion, their card is returned to them. The use of meaningful names in this situation is very important. The specification should not be cluttered with detailed type or procedure declarations.

```
— ATM/RS/CONT/1 Control specification for an ATM
procedure ATM is
        PIN: Pin_no ;
        Acc_no: Account_number ;
        Balance: Amount ;
        Service: Available_services ;
        Valid_card, Valid_PIN: Boolean ;
begin
        loop
            Get_card ( Acc_no, PIN, Valid_card) ;
            if Valid_card then
                Validate_PIN (PIN, Valid_PIN) ;
                if Valid_PIN then
                    Get_account (Acc_no, Balance) ;
                    Get_service (Service) ;
                    while a service is selected loop
                        Deliver_selected_service ;
                        Get_service (Service) ;
                    end loop ;
                    Return_card ;
                end if ;
            end if ;
        end loop ;
    end ATM ;
```

Figure 7.6
A PDL description of
ATM operation.

In principle, PDLs may be based on any programming language. In practice, programming languages such as C or C++ are rarely used as the basis for PDLs. Their notation is fairly cryptic and difficult for non-specialists to understand. Ada, a standard high-level language in the defence industry, was designed for readability. It is therefore a good choice as a base language for a PDL.

An effective way to use this approach to specification is to combine it with the use of structured natural language. A forms-based approach may be used to specify the overall system. Where it is necessary to define control sequences or interfaces in more detail, a PDL may be used.

The vast majority of software systems must operate with other systems which have already been implemented and installed in an environment. If the new system and the existing systems must work together, the interfaces of existing systems must be precisely specified. These specifications should be defined early in the process and included (perhaps as an appendix) in the requirements specification.

There are three types of interface which may have to be defined:

(1)   Procedural interfaces where existing sub-systems offer a range of services which are accessed by calling interface procedures.

(2)   Data structures which are passed from one sub-system to another.

(3)   Representations of data which have been established for an existing sub-system.

Figure 7.7 is an example of a definition of the first of these interface types. In this case, the interface is the procedural interface offered by a print server. This manages a queue of requests to print files on different printers. Users may examine the queue associated with a printer and may remove their print jobs from that queue. They may also switch jobs from one printer to another.

The specification in Figure 7.7 provides an abstract model of the print server without revealing any interface details. In some cases, it is important to have a more detailed structural description of data which is passed across interfaces. Figure 7.8 shows the description of a message that may be exchanged as part of some communication system. Ada type definitions are a particularly suitable means of expressing this type of interface.

At a more detailed level, it may be necessary to specify the precise representation of elements in the interface. Ada has a built-in facility that allows the values used to represent type elements to be specified and the arrangement of type elements

Figure 7.7
The PDL description of a print server.

```
package Print_server is
    procedure Initialize (P: PRINTER) ;
    procedure Print (P: PRINTER ; F: PRINT_FILE ) ;
    procedure Display_print_queue (P: PRINTER ) ;
    procedure Cancel_print_job (P: PRINTER; N: PRINT_ID) ;
    procedure Switch_printer (P1, P2: PRINTER; N: PRINT_ID) ;
end Print_server ;
```

```
type MESSAGE is record
    Sender : SYSTEM_ID;
    Receiver : SYSTEM_ID;
    Dispatch_time : DATE;
    Length: MESSAGE_LENGTH ;
    Terminator: CHARACTER ;
    Message : TEXT;
end record;

type SYSTEM_ID is range 20_000..30_000 ;
type YEAR_TYPE is range 1980..2080 ;
type DATE is record
    Seconds: NATURAL ;
    Year: YEAR_TYPE ;
end record ;
type MESSAGE_LENGTH is range 0..10_000 ;
type TEXT is array (MESSAGE_LENGTH) of CHARACTER ;
```

Figure 7.8
Representation of an
interchange format.

```
for SYSTEM_ID'SIZE use 2*BYTE ;
for YEAR_TYPE'SIZE use 2*BYTE ;
for MESSAGE_LENGTH'SIZE use 2*BYTE ;
```

Figure 7.9
Size representation.

```
type STATE is (Halted, Waiting, Ready, Running);
for STATE use (Halted => 1, Waiting => 4, Ready => 16,
                Running => 256);
```

Figure 7.10
Representation
of shared state
information.

in memory. Figure 7.9 shows how some of the types defined in Figure 7.8 are represented. The SIZE attribute is used to specify the number of bytes used by entities of that type.

Figure 7.10 shows how values may be associated with identifiers in an enumerated type. In this case, the system being specified exchanges information about the state of processes.

As discussed in Chapters 9 to 11, formal mathematical notations may also be used for interface specification. Their formal nature means that they are unambiguous and precise. However, the specialized nature of formal specifications means that they are not understandable without special training. Although less formal, PDL interface descriptions are a compromise between comprehensibility and precision. Non-technical managers and users may be intimidated by them but they should be understandable by most engineers with some programming experience.

7.3 Non-functional requirements

Non-functional requirements define system properties and constraints. Examples of system properties are reliability, response time and store occupancy. Examples of constraints are the capabilities of the I/O devices attached to the system and the data representations used by other systems connected to the required system.

Non-functional requirements are sometimes more critical than functional requirements. For example, if a system to be installed in an aircraft is not certified as safe by national and international aviation authorities, it cannot be used. If a real-time system does not meet its performance requirements, it may be completely useless. Therefore, non-functional requirements are as important as functional requirements.

Some non-functional requirements may be process rather than product requirements. These constrain the process which may be used to develop the system. Examples of process requirements include a specification of the quality standards which must be used in the process, a specification that the design must be produced with a specified CASE toolset and a description of the process model which should be followed. Customers impose these process requirements for two reasons:

(1) *System quality* In general, a good process leads to a good product. This is discussed in Chapters 30 and 31.

(2) *System maintainability* Process requirements may be imposed so that the development methods used to design and implement the system are compatible with those to be used for system maintenance.

Non-functional requirements arise through user needs, because of budget constraints, because of organizational policies, because of the need for interoperability with other software or hardware systems or because of external factors such as safety regulations, privacy legislation, and so on. There are, therefore, many different types of non-functional requirement.

Figure 7.11 shows different types of non-functional requirements. I have classified these non-functional requirements depending on how they have been derived:

- *Product requirements* These are requirements which result from the need for the delivered product to behave in a particular way. Examples include requirements on how fast the system must execute and how much memory it requires; reliability requirements that set out the acceptable failure rate; portability requirements and usability requirements. This type of non-functional requirement may be derived directly from user needs.

- *Organizational requirements* These are requirements which are a consequence of organizational policies and procedures. Examples include process standards which must be used; implementation requirements such as the programming language or design method used and delivery requirements

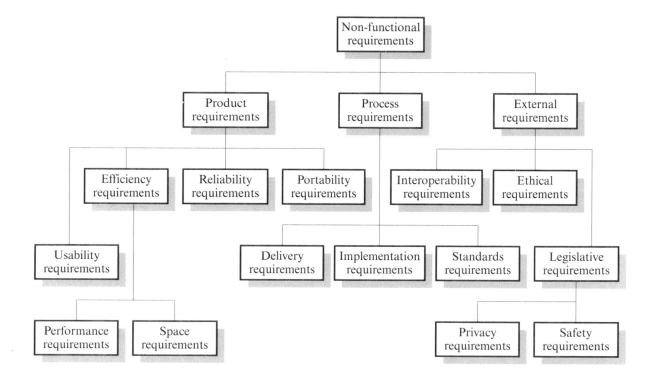

Figure 7.11
Types of non-functional
requirement.

which specify when the product and its documentation are to be delivered. Organizational requirements may be derived from both the customer's and the developer's organization.

- *External requirements*   This broad heading covers all requirements which arise from factors external to the system and its development process. These include interoperability requirements which define how the system interacts with systems in other organizations; legislative requirements which must be followed to ensure that the system operates within the law; and ethical requirements. Ethical requirements are requirements placed on a system to ensure that it will be acceptable to its users and the general public.

Figure 7.12 shows examples of each of these different types of non-functional requirement.

The product requirement restricts the freedom of APSE designers in their choice of symbols used in the APSE user interface. It says nothing about the functionality of the APSE and clearly identifies a system constraint rather than a function. The process requirement specifies that the system must be developed according to a company standard process defined as XYZCo-SP-STAN-95. The external requirement is derived from the need for the system to conform to privacy legislation. Users must be able to inspect and correct personal data that is maintained in the system.

Figure 7.12
Examples of
non-functional
requirements.

> **Product requirement**
> 4.C.8 It shall be possible for all necessary communication between the APSE and the user to be expressed in the standard Ada character set.
> **Organizational requirement**
> 9.3.2 The system development process and deliverable documents shall conform to the process and deliverables defined in XYZCo-SP-STAN-95.
> **External requirement**
> 7.6.5 The system shall provide facilities that allow any user to check if personal data is maintained on the system. A procedure must be defined and supported in the software that will allow users to inspect personal data and to correct any errors in that data.

A very common error in requirements specifications is to confuse non-functional requirements with general goals of the system customer. For example, a goal might be that the system should be 'user friendly'. This is not verifiable, as 'friendliness' is a subjective attribute. An associated requirement (which can be verified) might be that all user command selection should take place using command menus.

For example, Figure 7.13 is a typical example of a product 'requirement' concerning system usability. Leaving aside the fact that there might be two requirements expressed in Figure 7.13 (easy to use and tolerant of error), this requirement cannot be objectively verified. The notions of ease of use and error minimization are subjective. Requirements statements of this type are the cause of a great deal of customer dissatisfaction in delivered software systems.

A better expression of this requirement might define the time required to learn to use the system and the number of errors expected over a given time period (Figure 7.14). This requirement assumes that ease of use and short training time are closely related. It can be verified by objective testing, unlike the requirement shown in Figure 7.13.

The best way to ensure that non-functional requirements are verifiable is to express them quantitatively. This relies on measuring some characteristic of the software that is related in some way to a desirable system property such as its ease of use. I deliberately avoid using the term *metric* here. As Fenton (1991) points out, this term is used to mean different things by different people in the software engineering community. Rather, a *measure* is some quantifiable attribute of a system.

Figure 7.13
An unverifiable
non-functional
requirement.

> The system should be easy to use by experienced controllers and should be organized in such a way that user errors are minimized.

Experienced controllers should be able to use all the system functions after a total of two hours training. After this training, the average number of errors made by experienced users should not exceed
two per day.

Figure 7.14
A verifiable non-
functional requirement.

Figure 7.15 shows a number of possible measures which may be used to
specify non-functional system properties.

Non-functional requirements often conflict and interact with other system
functional requirements. For example, it may be a requirement that the maximum
store occupied by a system should be 256K because the entire system has to be fitted into read-only memory and installed on a spacecraft. A further requirement
might be that the system should be written in Ada. However, it may not be possible
to compile an Ada program with the required functionality into less than 256K.
Some trade-off between these requirements must be made. An alternative development language may be used or increased ROM added to the system.

In principle, functional and non-functional requirements should be differen-
tiated in a requirements specification. This is difficult because individual non-
functional requirements may be expressed as system requirements rather than
requirements on any specific system functions. These system-level requirements are
often expressed in a very abstract way, particularly if they are derived from organizational or external sources. Figure 7.16 is an example of such a requirement which
relates to the learnability of the system.

If the non-functional requirements are stated separately from the functional
requirements, it is sometimes difficult to see the relationships between them. If
stated with the functional requirements, it may be difficult to separate functional and
non-functional considerations and to identify these system requirements.

Property	Measure
Speed	Processed transactions/second
	User/event response time
	Screen refresh time
Size	Kbytes
	Number of RAM chips
Ease of use	Training time
	Number of help frames
Reliability	Mean time to failure
	Probability of unavailability
	Rate of failure occurrence
	Availability
Robustness	Time to restart after failure
	Percentage of events causing failure
	Probability of data corruption on failure
Portability	Percentage of target-dependent statements
	Number of target systems

Figure 7.15
Requirements
measures.

Figure 7.16
A system-level non-functional requirement.

> The time required for training a system operator to be proficient in
> the use of the system must not exceed two working days.

Further reading

The further reading suggested in Chapter 4 is relevant to this chapter.

KEY POINTS

- A requirements definition is intended for use by people involved in using and procuring the system. It should be written using natural language, tables and diagrams so that they can understand it. Requirements definitions should be structured so that they are easier to understand and manage.

- Rationale should always be included in a requirements definition. Without rationale, it is difficult to understand the consequences of changes to the system.

- Requirements should always be written so that they are verifiable. This means that there can be no argument over whether or not the system satisfies the requirement.

- Requirements specifications are intended to communicate, in a precise way, the functions which the system must provide. To reduce ambiguity, they may be written in a structured language of some kind. This may be a structured form of natural language, a language based on a high-level programming language or a special language for requirements specification.

- The three principal classes of non-functional requirement are product requirements which constrain the system being developed, process requirements which apply to the development process and external requirements. External requirements may affect both product and process.

- Non-functional requirements tend to be so varied and complex that natural language must be used for their expression. An exception to this is the specification of interface requirements where an interface definition language may be used.

EXERCISES

7.1   Discuss the problems of using natural language for requirements specification and show, using small examples, how structuring natural language into forms can help avoid some of these difficulties.

7.2   Discover ambiguities or omissions in the following statement of requirements for part of a ticket issuing system.

A ticket issuing system is intended to automate the sale of rail tickets. Users select their destination, and input a credit card and a personal identification number. The rail ticket is issued and their credit card account charged with its cost. When the user presses the start button, a menu display of potential destinations is activated along with a message to the user to select a destination. Once a destination has been selected, users are requested to input their credit card. Its validity is checked and the user is then requested to input a personal identifier. When the credit transaction has been validated, the ticket is issued.

7.3   Rewrite the above description using the structured approach described in this chapter. Resolve the identified ambiguities in some appropriate way.

7.4   Produce a requirements specification of the above system using an Ada-based notation. You may make any reasonable assumptions about the system. Pay particular attention to specifying user errors.

7.5   Using the technique suggested here where natural language is presented in a standard way, write a plausible requirements definition for the following functions:

(a) an unattended petrol (gas) pump system which includes a credit card reader. The customer swipes the card through the reader then specifies the amount of fuel required. The fuel is delivered and the customer's account debited;

(b) the cash dispensing function in a bank auto-teller machine;

(c) the spell checking and correcting function in a word processor.

7.6   Describe three different types of non-functional requirement which may be placed on a system. Give examples of each of these different types of requirement.

7.7   Write a set of non-functional requirements for the ticket issuing system described above, setting out its expected reliability and its response time.

7.8   What are the characteristics of programming languages which might be used as a basis for defining interface specifications? Comment on the suitability of C, C++ and Ada for this purpose.

7.9   Suggest how an engineer responsible for drawing up a requirements specification might keep track of the relationships between functional and non-functional requirements.

7.10   You have taken a job with a software user who has contracted your previous employer to develop a system for them. You discover that your company's interpretation of the requirements is different from the interpretation taken by your previous employer. Discuss what you should do in such a situation. You know that the costs to your current employer will increase if the ambiguities are not resolved. You also have a responsibility of confidentiality to your previous employer.

Software Prototyping

Objectives

- To describe how a prototype software system may be useful in validating the system requirements.

- To discuss evolutionary and exploratory prototyping and to explain the critical differences between these approaches.

- To introduce a number of techniques which may be used for the rapid development of a prototype system.

- To explain why it is necessary to develop prototypes of user interface designs.

Contents

Software customers and end-users usually find it very difficult to express their real requirements. It is almost impossible to predict how a system will affect working practices, how it will interact with other systems and what user operations should be automated. Careful requirements analysis along with systematic reviews of the requirements help to reduce the uncertainty about what the system should do. However, there is no real substitute for trying out a requirement before committing to it. This is possible if a prototype of the system to be developed is available.

A function described in a specification may seem useful and well defined. However, when that function is used with others, users often find that their initial view was incorrect or incomplete. System prototypes allow users to experiment with requirements and to see how the system supports their work. Prototyping is therefore a means of requirements validation. Users discover requirements errors or omissions early in the software process.

Software prototyping and hardware prototyping have different objectives. When developing hardware systems, a prototype is normally used to validate the system design. An electronic system prototype may be developed using off-the-shelf components before investment is made in expensive, special-purpose integrated circuits to implement the production version of the system. A software prototype is not normally intended for design validation but to help develop and check the real requirements of the system. The prototype design is often quite different from that of the final system.

The benefits of developing a prototype early in the software process are:

(1)   Misunderstandings between software developers and users may be identified as the system functions are demonstrated.

(2)   Missing user services may be detected.

(3)   Difficult-to-use or confusing user services may be identified and refined.

(4)   Software development staff may find incomplete and/or inconsistent requirements as the prototype is developed.

(5)   A working, albeit limited, system is available quickly to demonstrate the feasibility and usefulness of the application to management.

(6)   The prototype serves as a basis for writing the specification for a production quality system.

Although the principal purpose of prototyping is to validate software requirements, software prototypes also have other uses (Ince and Hekmatpour, 1987):

(1)   *User training*   A prototype system can be used for training users before the final system has been delivered.

(2)   *System testing*   Prototypes can run 'back-to-back' tests. This reduces the need for tedious manual checking of test runs. The same test cases are submitted to both the prototype and the system under test. If both systems give the same result, the test case has not detected a fault. If the results are

different, this implies that the tester should look in more detail at the reasons for the difference. Back-to-back testing is discussed in Chapter 22.

One way to view prototyping is as a technique of risk reduction. A significant risk in software development is requirements errors and omissions. The costs of fixing requirements errors at later stages in the process can be very high. Experiments have shown (Boehm *et al.,* 1984) that prototyping reduces the number of problems with the requirements specification and the overall development costs may be lower if a prototype is developed.

A process model for prototype development is shown in Figure 8.1. The objectives of prototyping should be made explicit from the start of the process. The objective may be to develop a system to prototype the user interface; it may be to develop a system to validate functional system requirements; it may be to develop a system to demonstrate the feasibility of the application to management and so on. The same prototype cannot meet all objectives. If objectives are left implicit, management or end-users may misunderstand the function of the prototype. Consequently, they may not get the benefits that they expected from the prototype development.

The next stage in the process to is decide what to put into and, perhaps more importantly, what to leave out of the prototype system. Software prototyping is expensive if the prototype is implemented using the same tools and to the same standards as the final system. Thus, it may be decided to prototype all system functions but at a reduced level. Alternatively a subset of system functions may be included in the prototype. Normal practice in prototype development is to relax non-functional requirements such as response time and memory utilization. Error handling and management may be ignored or may be rudimentary unless the objective of the prototype is to establish a user interface. Standards of reliability and program quality may be reduced.

The final stage of the process is prototype evaluation. Ince and Hekmatpour suggest that this is the most important stage of prototyping. Provision must be made during this stage for user training and the prototype objectives should be used to derive a plan for evaluation. Users need time to become comfortable with a new system and to settle into a normal pattern of usage. Once they are using the system normally, they then discover requirements errors and omissions.

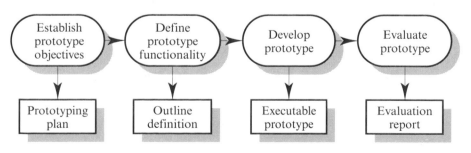

Figure 8.1
The process of prototype development.

The major technical problems associated with prototyping revolve around the need for rapid software development. However, there are non-technical, managerial problems which may make it difficult to use prototyping in some organizations:

● Planning, costing and estimating a prototyping project is outside the experience of many software project managers.

● Procedures for change and configuration management may be unsuitable for controlling the rapid change inherent in prototyping. However, if there are no change management procedures, evaluation is difficult; the evaluators are trying to assess a constantly changing system.

● Managers may exert pressure on prototype evaluators to reach swift conclusions about the prototype. These may result in inappropriate requirements.

A common argument against prototyping is that the cost of prototyping represents an unacceptably large fraction of the total development costs. It may be more economic to modify a finished system to meet unperceived needs than to provide an opportunity for users to understand and refine their needs before the final system is built.

This may be true for some systems but effective prototyping increases software quality. It can give software developers a competitive edge over their competitors. In the 1960s and 1970s, the US and European automobile industries did not invest in quality procedures. They lost a great deal of their market share to higher-quality Japanese automobiles. This is a telling illustration of how a 'build it cheap and fix it later' philosophy can be extremely expensive in the long term.

Although prototyping is now a well-established approach, there is little reported information about the costs of prototyping and its influence on total system costs. An early study was reported by Gomaa (1983) who describes the advantages of developing a prototype for a process management and information system. Prototype development costs were less than 10% of the total system costs. In the development of the production-quality system, there were no requirements definition problems. The project was completed on time and the system was well received by users. User satisfaction and a reduction in development time of 40% have also been reported more recently by Bernstein (1993).

As discussed in Chapter 1, prototyping is a key technique in the spiral process model for risk evaluation. By developing a prototype, requirements and design risks can be reduced. Short-term additional costs may result in long-term savings as requirements and design decisions are clarified during the prototyping process.

8.1 Prototyping in the software process

As I have already discussed, it is very difficult for end-users to anticipate how they will use new software systems to support their everyday work. If these systems are large and complex, it is probably impossible to make this assessment before the system is built and put into use.

One way of tackling this difficulty is to use an evolutionary approach to systems development. This means giving the user a system which is incomplete and then modifying and augmenting it as the user requirements become clear. Alternatively, a deliberate decision might be made to build a 'throw-away' prototype to help requirements analysis and validation. After evaluation, the prototype is discarded and a production-quality system built.

The distinction between these two approaches is that evolutionary prototyping starts out with a limited understanding of the system requirements and the system is augmented and changed as new requirements are discovered. There may never be a system specification. In fact, systems developed by this approach may be unspecifiable because we do not understand the process which they are trying to automate. For example, it is impossible to specify many types of AI system because we don't understand how people solve problems.

By contrast, the throw-away prototyping approach is intended to discover the system specification so that the output of the prototype development phase is that specification. Figure 8.2 illustrates both these approaches to prototype development.

There is an important difference between the objectives of evolutionary and throw-away programming:

- The objective of evolutionary prototyping is to deliver a working system to end-users.

- The objective of throw-away prototyping is to validate or derive the system requirements.

In the first case, the first priority is to incorporate well-understood requirements in the prototype then move on to those requirements which are unclear. In throw-away prototyping, the priority is to understand requirements that are unclear. You therefore start with those requirements that are not well understood. Requirements which are straightforward may never need to be prototyped.

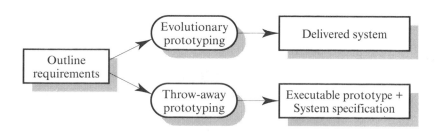

Figure 8.2
Evolutionary and throw-away prototyping.

8.1.1 Evolutionary prototyping

Evolutionary prototyping is based on the idea of developing an initial implementation, exposing this to user comment and refining this through many stages until an adequate system has been developed (Figure 8.3).

Evolutionary prototyping is the only realistic way to develop systems where it is difficult (or impossible) to establish a detailed system specification. Some might argue that all systems fall into this class but this approach has mostly been used for the development of AI systems that attempt to emulate some human capabilities.

The key to success in this approach is to use techniques which allow for rapid system iterations. Suggested changes may be incorporated and demonstrated as quickly as possible. As discussed in the following section, this may mean using a very high level programming language such as Lisp or Prolog for software development. Special-purpose environments and integrated software tools may be used to support the development process.

An important difference between evolutionary prototyping and a specification-based approach to development is in verification and validation. Verification is only meaningful when a program is compared to its specification. If there is no specification, verification is impossible. The validation process should demonstrate that the program is suitable for its intended purpose rather than its conformance to a specification.

Adequacy, of course, is not readily measurable and only subjective judgements of a program's adequacy can be made. This does not invalidate its usefulness; human performance cannot be guaranteed to be correct but we are satisfied if performance is adequate for the task in hand.

There are three main problems with evolutionary prototyping which are particularly important when large, long-lifetime systems are to be developed:

(1)   Existing software management structures are set up to deal with a software process model that generates regular deliverables to assess progress. Prototypes usually evolve so quickly that it is not cost-effective to produce a great deal of system documentation.

(2)   Continual change tends to corrupt the structure of the prototype system. Maintenance is therefore likely to be difficult and costly. This is particularly

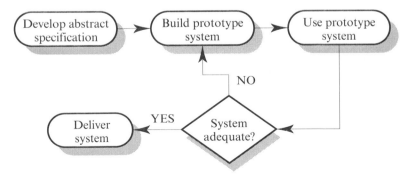

Figure 8.3
Evolutionary
prototyping.

likely when the system maintainers are not the original developers. As I discuss in Chapter 32, development teams are hardly ever responsible for system maintenance.

(3)   It is not clear how the range of skills which is normal in software engineering teams can be used effectively for this mode of development. Most available systems developed in this way have been implemented by small teams of highly skilled and motivated individuals.

These difficulties do not mean that evolutionary prototyping should be rejected. It allows systems to be developed and delivered rapidly. System development costs are reduced. If users are involved in the development, it is likely to be appropriate for their real needs. However, organizations that use this approach must accept that the lifetime of the system will be relatively short. As its structure becomes unmaintainable, it must be completely rewritten.

8.1.2 Throw-away prototyping

A software process model based on an initial throw-away prototyping stage is illustrated in Figure 8.4. This approach extends the requirements analysis process with the intention of reducing overall life cycle costs. The principal function of the prototype is to clarify requirements and provide additional information for managers to assess process risks. After evaluation, the prototype is thrown away. It is not used as a basis for further system development.

The process model in Figure 8.4 assumes that the prototype is developed from an outline system specification, delivered for experiment and modified until the client is satisfied with its functionality. At this stage, a conventional software process model is entered, a specification is derived from the prototype and the system re-implemented in a final production version. Components from the prototype may be reused in the production-quality system.

Customers and end-users should resist the temptation to turn the throw-away prototype into a delivered system that is put into use. The reasons for this are:

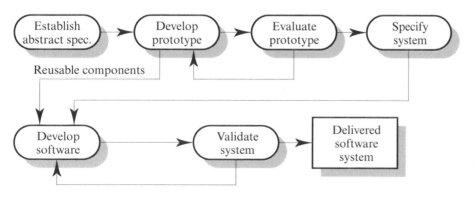

Figure 8.4
A software process with throw-away prototyping.

(1)   Important system characteristics such as performance, security, robustness and reliability may have been ignored during prototype development so that a rapid implementation could be developed. It may be impossible to tune the prototype to meet these non-functional requirements.

(2)   During the prototype development, the prototype will have been changed to reflect user needs. It is likely that these changes will have been made in an uncontrolled way. The only design specification is the prototype code. This is not good enough for long-term maintenance.

(3)   The changes made during prototype development will probably have degraded the system structure. The system will be difficult and expensive to maintain.

Rather than derive a specification from the prototype, it is sometimes suggested that the system specification should be the prototype implementation itself. The instruction to the software contractor should simply be 'write a system like this one'. There are also several problems with this approach:

(1)   Important features may have been left out of the prototype to simplify rapid implementation. In fact, it may not be possible to prototype some of the most important parts of the system such as safety-critical functions.

(2)   An implementation has no legal standing as a contract between customer and contractor.

(3)   Non-functional requirements such as those concerning reliability, robustness and safety cannot be adequately tested in a prototype implementation.

A general problem with throw-away prototyping is that the mode of use of the prototype may not correspond with the way that the final delivered system is used. The tester of the prototype may be particularly interested in the system and may not be typical of system users. The training time during prototype evaluation may be insufficient. If the prototype is slow, the evaluators may adjust their way of working and avoid those system features which have slow response times. When provided with better response in the final system, they may use it in a different way.

8.1.3 Incremental development

An alternative process model which combines the advantages of evolutionary prototyping with the control required for large-scale development has been suggested by Mills *et al.* (1980). This incremental development model (Figure 8.5) involves developing the requirements and delivering the system in an incremental fashion. Thus, as a part of the system is delivered, the user may experiment with it and provide feedback to later parts of the system. Incremental development is a key part of the Cleanroom development process, discussed in Chapter 24.

Incremental development avoids the problems of constant change which characterize evolutionary prototyping. An overall system architecture is established

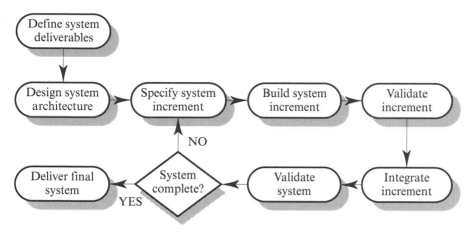

Figure 8.5
An incremental
development process.

early in the process to act as a framework. System components are incrementally developed and delivered within this framework. Once these have been validated and delivered, neither the framework nor the components are changed unless errors are discovered. User feedback from delivered components, however, can influence the design of components scheduled for later delivery.

Incremental development is more manageable than evolutionary prototyping as the normal software process standards are followed. Plans and documentation must be produced for each system increment. It allows some user feedback early in the process and limits system errors as the development team is not concerned with interactions between quite different parts of the software system. Once an increment has been delivered, its interfaces are frozen. Later increments must adapt to these interfaces and can be tested against them.

A problem with incremental development is that the system architecture has to be established before the requirements are complete. This means that the requirements tend to be constrained by the architecture that is established. Another, non-technical problem is that this approach to development does not fit well with established contractual models for software developers. Contracts for the development must be flexible and established before the requirements are fixed. Many organizations that use traditional engineering models for software procurement find it impossible to adapt to the form of contract which this approach requires.

8.2 Prototyping techniques

System prototyping techniques should allow the rapid development of a prototype system. As staff costs are the principal software cost, rapid development means that prototype costs are minimized. It also means that feedback from users can be obtained early in the overall software process.

There are a number of techniques which have been used for system prototyping. These include:

- executable specification languages,
- very high level languages,
- application generators and fourth-generation languages,
- composition of reusable components.

All of these approaches are discussed below. Of course, these prototyping techniques are not mutually exclusive. They can be used in combination. For example, one part of the system may be generated using an application generator and linked to reusable components that have been taken from existing systems. Luqi (1992) describes this mixed approach which was used to create a prototype of a command and control system.

8.2.1 Executable specification languages

If a system specification is expressed in a formal, mathematical language, it may be possible to animate that specification to provide a system prototype. A number of executable formal specification languages have been developed (Lee and Sluizer, 1985; Henderson and Minkowitz, 1986; Gallimore *et al.,* 1989). Diller (1994) discusses techniques of animating formal specifications written in Z, the specification language covered in Chapter 11.

Developing a prototype from a formal specification is attractive in some ways as it combines an unambiguous specification with a prototype. There are no additional costs in prototype development after the specification has been written. However, there are practical difficulties in applying this approach:

(1) Graphical user interfaces cannot be prototyped using this technique. Although models of a graphical interface can be formally specified (Took, 1986), these cannot be systematically animated using current windowing systems.

(2) Prototype development may not be particularly rapid. Formal specification requires a detailed system analysis and much time may be devoted to the detailed modelling of system functions which are rejected after prototype evaluation.

(3) The executable system is usually slow and inefficient. Users may get a false impression of the system and compensate for this slowness during evaluation. They may not use the system in the same way they would use a more efficient version. Users may therefore define a different set of requirements from those which would be suggested if a faster prototype was available.

(4) Executable specifications only test functional requirements. In many cases, the non-functional characteristics of the system are particularly important so the value of the prototype is limited.

Some of these problems have been addressed by the developers of functional languages which have been integrated with graphical user interface libraries and which allow rapid program development.

A functional language is a formal language where the system is defined as a mathematical function. Evaluation of that function (which is obviously decomposed into many other functions) is equivalent to executing a procedural program. Miranda (Turner, 1985) and ML (Wikstrom, 1988) are practical functional languages which have been used for the development of non-trivial prototypes.

Functional languages might also be classed as very high level languages as discussed in the following section. They allow a very concise expression of the problem to be solved. Because of their mathematical basis, a functional program can also be viewed as a formal system specification. However, the execution speed of functional programs on sequential hardware is typically several orders of magnitude slower than conventional programs. This means that they cannot be used for prototyping large software systems.

8.2.2 Very high level languages

Very high level languages are programming languages which include powerful data management facilities. These simplify program development because they reduce many problems of storage allocation and management. The language system includes many facilities which normally have to be built from more primitive constructs in languages like Pascal or Ada. Examples of very high level languages are Lisp (based on list structures), Prolog (based on logic), Smalltalk (based on objects), APL (based on vectors) and SETL (based on sets).

Very high level dynamic languages are not normally used for large system development because they need a large run-time support system. This run-time support increases the storage needs and reduces the execution speeds of programs written in the language. If performance requirements can be relaxed for the prototype, then the overhead of the run-time support is acceptable.

Figure 8.6 lists a number of prototype programming languages. Different languages are suited to different types of system. I therefore also suggest the most appropriate application domain in Figure 8.6.

As well as the application domain, there are other factors which should influence the choice of prototyping language:

Language	Type	Application domain
Smalltalk	Object-oriented	Interactive systems
LOOPS	Wide spectrum	Interactive systems
Prolog	Logic	Symbolic processing
Lisp	List-based	Symbolic processing
Miranda	Functional	Symbolic processing
SETL	Set-based	Symbolic processing
APL	Mathematical	Scientific systems
4GLs	Database	Business DP
CASE tools	Graphical	Business DP

Figure 8.6
Languages for rapid prototyping.

(1)   *The interactive features of the system to be prototyped*   Some languages, such as Smalltalk and 4GLs, have better support for user interaction than others.

(2)   *The support environment that is provided with the language*   In this respect, Lisp and Smalltalk have far better environments than alternative languages. Outside the business domain, where 4GLs are common, these have been the most widely used prototyping languages.

One of the most powerful prototyping systems for interactive systems is the Smalltalk system (Goldberg and Robson, 1983). Smalltalk is an object-oriented programming language which is tightly integrated with its environment. It is an excellent prototyping language for three reasons:

(1)   The language is object-oriented so systems are resilient to change. Rapid modifications of a Smalltalk system are possible without unforeseen effects on the rest of the system. Indeed, Smalltalk is only suitable for this style of development.

(2)   The Smalltalk system and environment is an inherent part of the language. All the objects defined in the environment are available to the Smalltalk programmer. Thus, a large number of reusable components are available that may be incorporated in the prototype under development.

(3)   Some versions of the language are now packaged with a support system (Visualworks) which partially automates the construction of user interfaces for interactive systems. This is a screen drawing package for graphical interfaces such as those supported by user interface management systems (see Section 8.3).

A class of programming languages which have been proposed as prototyping languages are so-called multi-paradigm or wide-spectrum programming languages. Examples of wide-spectrum languages are REFINE (Smith *et al.,* 1985), EPROL (Hekmatpour, 1988), and LOOPS (Stefik *et al.,* 1986).

A wide-spectrum language is a programming language which combines a number of paradigms. Most languages are based on a single paradigm. Pascal is an imperative language, Lisp is based on functions and lists, Prolog is based on facts and logic and so on. By contrast, a wide-spectrum language may include objects, logic programming, imperative constructs and so on. However, the practical problems of developing efficient implementations of wide-spectrum languages have meant that few commercial language products are available. LOOPS is the only language in this category that is widely used.

As an alternative to using a wide-spectrum language, you can use a mixed-language approach to prototype development. Different parts of the system may be programmed in different languages and a communication framework established between the parts. Zave (1989) describes this approach to development in the prototyping of a telephone network system. Four different languages were used: Prolog for database prototyping, Awk (Aho *et al.,* 1988) for billing, CSP (Hoare, 1985) for protocol specification and PAISLey (Zave and Schell, 1986) for performance simulation.

There is never an ideal language for prototyping large systems as different parts of the system are so diverse. The advantage of a mixed-language approach is that the most appropriate language for a logical part of the application can be chosen, thus speeding up prototype development. The disadvantage is that it may be difficult to establish a communication framework which will allow multiple languages to communicate. The entities used in the different languages are very diverse. Consequently, lengthy code sections may be needed to translate an entity from one language to another.

8.2.3 Fourth-generation languages

Evolutionary prototyping is now fairly commonly used for developing applications in the business system domain. These rely on the use of *fourth-generation languages* (4GLs) for system development. There are many 4GLs and their use usually reduces the time needed for system development.

Fourth-generation languages are successful because there is a great deal of commonality across data processing applications. In essence, these applications are concerned with updating a database and producing reports from the information held in the database. Standard forms are used for input and output.

At their simplest, 4GLs are database query languages such as SQL (Date and Darwen, 1993). 4GLs may also package a report generator and a screen form design package with the query language to provide a powerful interactive facility for application generation (Figure 8.7). Some spreadsheet-type facilities may also be included. 4GLs rely on software reuse where common abstractions have been identified and parameterized. Routines to access a database and produce reports are provided. The programmer need only describe how these routines are tailored and controlled.

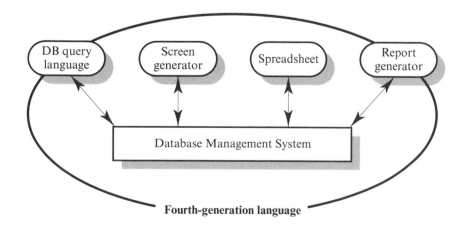

Figure 8.7
Fourth-generation languages.

Fourth-generation languages are generally used, often in conjunction with CASE tools, for the development of small to medium-sized systems. The end-users may be involved in the development or may even act as developers. Of course, this can result in systems which are poorly structured and difficult to change.

The vendors of 4GL products accept that this is the case. However, they claim that system maintenance is simpler because application development time is rapid. The developed applications are usually much smaller than the equivalent COBOL programs. Rather than worry about structuring the system for maintenance, requirements changes are implemented by a complete system rewrite.

Using 4GLs for developing data processing systems is cost-effective in some cases, particularly for relatively small systems. However, 4GLs are slower than conventional programming languages and require much more memory. In an experiment in which I was involved, rewriting a 4GL program in C++ resulted in a 50% reduction in memory requirements. The program also ran 10 times faster than before.

There is no standardization or uniformity across fourth-generation languages. This means that users may incur future costs rewriting programs because the language in which they were originally written is obsolete. Although they clearly reduce systems development costs, the effect of 4GLs on overall life-cycle costs for large DP systems is not yet clear. They are obviously to be recommended for prototyping but the lack of standardization may mean that total life-cycle cost savings may be less than anticipated.

Some CASE toolsets are closely integrated with 4GLs. Using such systems has the advantage that documentation is produced at the same time as the prototype system. The generated system should be more structured and easier to maintain. These tools may generate 4GL code or may generate code in a lower-level language such as COBOL. Forte (1992) describes a number of tools of this type in a brief survey of fourth-generation languages.

4GL-based development can be used either for evolutionary prototyping or may be used in conjunction with a method-based analysis where system models are used to generate the prototype system. The structure which CASE tools impose on the application means that evolutionary prototypes developed using this approach should be maintainable.

8.2.4 Composition of reusable components

The time needed to develop a system can be reduced if many parts of that system can be reused rather than designed and implemented. Prototypes can be constructed quickly if you have a library of reusable components and some mechanism to compose these components into systems. The composition mechanism must include control facilities and a way of interconnecting components. This approach is illustrated in Figure 8.8.

Prototyping with reusable components involves developing a system specification by taking account of what reusable components are available. These

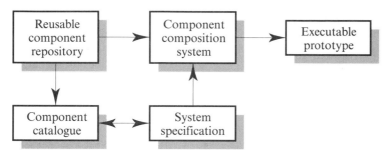

Figure 8.8
Reusable component composition.

components are then taken from a repository and put together to form the prototype system. This approach is usually most suitable for throw-away prototyping as the specification may not be exactly what is required. The prototype simply demonstrates what is possible. Of course, the reusable components may also be used in the final system thus reducing its development cost.

Perhaps the best example of this approach to prototyping is found in the Unix operating system. The features of Unix which make it particularly suitable for prototyping with reusable components include:

- Various shell programming languages (Rosenberg, 1991) which may be used as the composition mechanism for reusable components. Unix shells are command languages which include looping and decision constructs. They provide facilities for combining commands which operate on files, integers and character strings.

- A set of functions that have been designed so that they can be combined in various ways. Functions usually rely on simple character stream interfaces which means that they are easy to connect. Examples of these functions are *grep* (a pattern matcher), *sort* (a sorting program), and *wc* (a word counter).

- Its command interconnection mechanism (pipes) combined with its model of files and I/O devices as character streams. This makes it easy to connect functions to each other and to files and peripherals.

However, prototyping using Unix is limited because the granularity of the software components is relatively coarse. The function of the individual components is often too general-purpose to combine effectively with other components. Furthermore, user interface prototyping using the shell is limited because of the simple I/O model adopted by the Unix system.

Prototyping using reusable components is often combined with other approaches using very high level or fourth-generation languages. The success of Smalltalk and Lisp as prototyping languages is as much due to their reusable component libraries as to their inbuilt language facilities.

8.3 User interface prototyping

Graphical or forms-based user interfaces have now become the norm for interactive systems. The effort involved in specifying, designing and implementing a user interface represents a very significant part of application development costs. As discussed in Chapter 17, it is not acceptable for designers simply to impose their view of an acceptable user interface on users. The user must take part in the interface design process. This realization has led to an approach to design called user-centred design (Norman and Draper, 1986) which depends on interface prototyping and user involvement throughout the interface design stage.

Design here does not mean, of course, the software design but is rather the 'look and feel' of the user interface. Evolutionary prototyping is used in the process. An initial interface is produced, evaluated with users and revised until the user is satisfied with the system. After an acceptable interface has been agreed on, it then may be re-implemented, although if interface generators are used this may not be necessary. Interface generators allow interfaces to be specified and a well-structured program is generated from that specification. Thus the iterations inherent in exploratory programming do not degrade the software structure and re-implementation is not required.

Interface generation systems may be based around user interface management systems (Myers, 1988) which provide basic user interface functionality such as menu selection, object display and so on. They are placed between the application and the user interface (Figure 8.9) and provide facilities for screen definition and dialogue specification. These facilities may be based on state transition diagrams for command specification (Jacob, 1986) or on formal grammars for dialogue design (Browne, 1986). A survey of tools for user interface design is given by Myers (1989).

Some of the languages described in Section 8.2 are appropriate for user interface prototyping. Very high level languages like Smalltalk and Lisp have many user interface components as part of the system. These can often be modified to develop the particular application interface required. Fourth-generation language systems usually include screen definition facilities whereby screen templates can be defined by picking and positioning form fields. Increasingly, comparable facilities are being developed (Harbert *et al.*, 1990) for use with graphical user interfaces such as Motif. Some of these go further than simply providing screen definition facilities. They generate the majority of an application with only limited end-user input (Colebourne *et al.*, 1993).

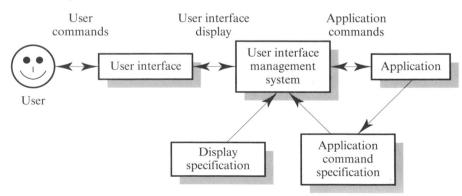

Figure 8.9
User interface
management system.

From a software engineering point of view, it is important to realize that user interface prototyping is an essential part of the process. Unlike the prototyping of system functionality, it is usually acceptable to present an interface prototype as a system specification. Because of the dynamic nature of user interfaces, paper specifications are not good enough for expressing the user interface requirements.

Further reading

Software Prototyping, Formal Methods and VDM. Unlike many prototyping books, this book is not solely concerned with data processing systems. The authors' approach to prototyping is based around executable formal specifications but the first few chapters are an excellent general introduction to prototyping. (S. Hekmatpour and D. Ince, 1988, Addison-Wesley.)

IEEE Computer, **22** (5), September 1989. This is a special issue of the journal devoted to rapid prototyping. Apart from data processing system prototyping, the papers cover a wide area from real-time systems prototyping to user interface development.

'Status report: Computer-aided prototyping'. This is a short, readable article which succinctly communicates approaches to prototyping and the advantages of using prototyping in the development process. (Luqi, *IEEE Software*, **9** (6), November 1992.)

'User-Interface Software Tools.' An updated version of Myers's 1989 survey of user-interface development systems. (B.A. Myers, *ACM Trans. on CHI,* **2** (1), March 1995.)

KEY POINTS

- A system prototype can be developed to give end-users a concrete impression of the system capabilities. The prototype may therefore help in establishing and validating system requirements.

- Prototyping in the software process may involve 'throw-away' prototyping in which a prototype is developed to understand the system requirements, or evolutionary prototyping in which a prototype evolves through a number of versions to the final system.

- The principal problem with evolutionary prototyping is that the system structure becomes corrupted by constant change. Further changes to the system become increasingly difficult to make.

- When implementing a throw-away prototype, you first develop the parts of the system you understand least; in an evolutionary prototype, you develop the parts of the system you understand best.

- Prototyping techniques include the use of executable specification languages, very high level languages, fourth-generation languages and prototype construction from reusable components.

- Rapid development is important for prototype systems. To deliver a prototype quickly, you may have to leave out some system functionality or relax non-functional constraints such as response speed and reliability.

- For some applications or application fragments such as the user interface, it is essential to use prototyping to derive the requirements as an abstract analysis is unlikely to yield an acceptable result.

EXERCISES

8.1   You have been asked to investigate the feasibility of prototyping as a standard part of the software development process in your organization. Write a report for your manager discussing the classes of project where prototyping should be used and setting out the expected costs and benefits from using prototyping.

8.2   Explain why, for large systems development, it is recommended that prototypes should be 'throw-away' prototypes.

8.3   What features of languages like Smalltalk and Lisp contribute to their support of rapid prototyping?

8.4   Under what circumstances would you recommend that prototyping should be used as a means of validating system requirements?

8.5   There are particular difficulties in prototyping real-time embedded computer systems. Suggest what these might be and propose ways of resolving the difficulties.

8.6   A software manager is involved in a project development of a software design support system which is intended to assist with the translation of software requirements to a formal software specification. The system must run on a personal computer but may be developed on another system and ported to that machine. Three possible development strategies are:

(a) Develop a throw-away prototype using a prototyping language such as Smalltalk. Evaluate this prototype then review requirements. Develop the final system using C and X-windows.

(b) Develop the system from the existing requirements using C and X-windows then modify it to adapt to any changed user requirements.

(c) Develop the system using evolutionary prototyping with a prototyping language such as Smalltalk. Modify the system according to the user's requests and deliver the modified prototype.

Comment on the advantages and disadvantages of each of these development strategies.

8.7 Discuss prototyping using reusable components and explain the problems which arise using this approach (you may find it useful to read Chapter 20).

8.8 Using examples, explain how the Unix shell may be used as a prototyping system. What are the difficulties of using the shell approach with reusable components which are not functions?

8.9 Using the Unix shell, develop a prototype for the data dictionary system whose data model was defined in Chapter 6. (Hint: use different files for each field in the dictionary.)

8.10 You have developed a throw-away prototype system for a client who is very happy with it. However, she suggests that there is no need to develop another system but that you should deliver the prototype and offer an excellent price for it. You know that there may be future problems with maintaining the system. Discuss how you might respond to this customer.

9

Formal Specification

Objectives

- To explain the place of formal software specification in the software process.

- To discuss the pros and cons of formal specifications and to explain when formal specification is cost-effective.

- To describe a process model based on the transformation of formal specifications to an executable system.

- To introduce a very simple approach to formal specification based on specifying function pre- and post-conditions as predicates.

Contents

Detailed software specifications used to be written using flowcharts or PDL. They were not expressed at a level of abstraction which could usefully feed back information to the system requirements specification. However, as implementation languages have become more abstract, the need for this level of specification has almost disappeared. Detailed specifications can now be expressed in an abstract way which can influence the requirements specification. The most precise way of expressing a detailed specification is to use a formal mathematical notation.

The development of a formal specification of the software may be part of the software specification activity introduced in Chapter 5. During software specification, the requirements specification is analysed in detail to see exactly what it means. An abstract statement of the program's functionality may be produced to clarify the requirements.

The involvement of the client for the software decreases and the involvement of the contractor increases as the specification is developed. In the early stages of the process, it is essential that the specification is 'customer-oriented'. It should be written so that it is understandable to the client and should make as few assumptions as possible about the software design. However, the final stage of the process, which is the construction of a complete, consistent and precise specification, is principally intended for the software contractor. It serves as a basis for the system implementation.

Figure 9.1 shows the stages of software specification and its interface with the design process. The specification stages shown in Figure 9.1 are not independent nor are they necessarily carried out in sequence. Figure 9.2 shows that specification and design activities may be carried out in parallel streams. There is a two-way relation between each stage in the process. Information is fed from the specification to the design process and vice versa.

As a specification is developed in detail, the specifier's understanding of that specification increases. Creating a formal specification forces a detailed systems analysis that usually reveals errors and inconsistencies in the informal specification. These are fed back to allow earlier specifications to be modified. Error detection is the most potent argument for developing a formal specification. Requirements prob-

Figure 9.1
Specification and design.

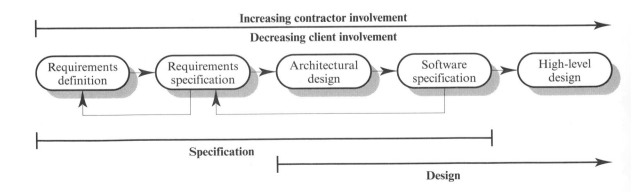

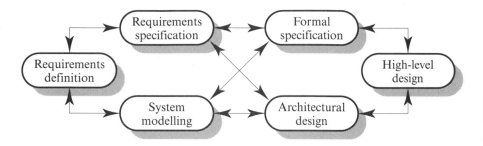

Figure 9.2
Formal specification in the software process.

lems which remain undetected until later stages of the software process are usually expensive to correct.

Depending on the process used, these might be fed back to the requirements specification if this has not already been agreed. If the requirements specification has been accepted as the basis of a contract, the problems which have been discovered should be raised with the customer for resolution before starting on the system design.

9.1 Formal specification on trial

A formal software specification is a specification expressed in a language whose vocabulary, syntax and semantics are formally defined. The need for a formal semantic definition means that the specification languages cannot be based on natural languages. They must be based on mathematics.

If we consider the development of 'traditional' engineering disciplines such as electrical and civil engineering, we can see that progress in these disciplines has usually gone hand-in-hand with better mathematical techniques. The engineering industry has had no difficulty accepting the need for mathematical analysis and in incorporating mathematical analysis into its processes.

However, software engineering has not followed the same path. Formal specification techniques are not widely used in industrial software development. The specification process model in Figure 9.1 is an idealized one. Many organizations start design after the definition of the detailed requirements or functional specification. There is great reluctance in the software industry to accept mathematically based methods of software development.

In this section, I discuss why this attitude is so common and put forward the case for and against the use of formal specification. In the final part, I put forward my views on where formal software development methods can be used cost-effectively and how these methods will become used for some types of application.

9.1.1 The case against formal specification

There is widespread reluctance in the software industry to accept the use of mathematics to support the system development process. Although evangelists such as

Hall (1990) and Zave (1989) have discussed successes with the use of formal methods, these have had little real impact on industrial practice.

There have been various reasons put forward as to why formal specification and formal development methods have not been widely used:

- Software management is inherently conservative and is unwilling to adopt new techniques for which payoff is not obvious. It is difficult to demonstrate that the relatively high cost of developing a formal system specification will reduce overall software development costs. In this respect, the use of mathematics in software engineering is different from in other engineering disciplines. Mathematical analysis of structures can result in cost savings in materials and allows cheaper designs to be used.

- Many software engineers, particularly those in senior positions, have not been trained in the techniques required to develop formal software specifications. Developing specifications requires a familiarity with discrete mathematics and logic. Inexperience of these techniques makes specification development appear to be difficult.

- System customers are unlikely to be familiar with formal specification techniques. They may be unwilling to fund development activities that they cannot easily monitor.

- Some classes of software system are difficult to specify using existing techniques. In particular, current techniques can't be used for the specification of the interactive components of user interfaces. Some classes of parallel processing system, such as interrupt-driven systems, are difficult to specify.

- There is widespread ignorance of the practicality of current specification techniques and their applicability. The technique has been used successfully in a significant number of non-trivial development projects.

- Most of the effort in specification research has been concerned with the development of languages and their theoretical underpinnings. Relatively little effort has been devoted to method and tool support. Fraser *et al.* (1994) discuss this and suggest it is an important reason for the non-acceptance of formal methods.

9.1.2 The case for formal specification

The reasons set out above for the lack of use of formal methods are mostly based on the problems of introducing formal specifications into current software processes. By contrast, proponents of formal methods tend to base their arguments on the potential technical advantages of this approach. Some of these advantages are:

- The development of a formal specification provides insights into and an understanding of the software requirements and the software design. This reduces requirements errors and omissions. It provides a basis for an elegant software design.

- Formal software specifications are mathematical entities and may be analysed using mathematical methods. In particular it may be possible to prove specification consistency and completeness. It may also be possible to prove that an implementation conforms to its specification. The absence of certain classes of error may be demonstrated. However, program verification is expensive and the ability to reason about the specification itself is probably more significant.

- Formal specifications may be automatically processed. Software tools can be built to assist with their development, understanding and debugging. As discussed in Chapter 8, it may be possible to animate a formal specification to provide a prototype system.

- Formal specifications may be used as a guide to the tester of a component in identifying appropriate test cases. The use of formal specifications for this purpose is discussed by Hayes (1986).

In an excellent article, Hall (1990) directly refutes some of the arguments against the use of formal methods where he presents 'seven myths of formal methods'. These myths, and the arguments against them, are:

(1)　*Perfect software results from the use of formal methods*　This view is clearly nonsense. A formal specification is a model of the real world and it may incorporate misunderstandings about the real world, specification errors and omissions. Its translation into an executable program is limited by the computer hardware, operating system and compilers. However, a formal approach is effective because it makes specification errors easier to detect. It provides an unambiguous basis for system design.

(2)　*Formal methods mean program proving*　Program proving is just one approach to the use of formal methods. More significant benefits probably accrue from the specification analysis.

(3)　*Formal methods are so expensive that their use can only be justified in safety-critical systems*　Hall says that his company's experience is that development costs for all classes of system are reduced by using formal specifications.

(4)　*Formal methods require a high level of mathematical skill*　This is simply untrue. As we shall see in the following chapters, formal specification uses simple mathematics. Only elementary mathematical skills are required.

(5)　*Formal methods increase development costs*　Hall's experience suggests that this is not the case although the development cost profile is altered with more costs incurred at the early stages in the software process.

(6)　*Customers cannot understand formal specifications*　Hall suggests that specifications can be understood by customers by paraphrasing them in natural language and by specification animation. The development of a formal specification allows a better, easier-to-understand requirements specification to be produced.

(7)   *Formal methods have only been used for trivial system development* As we
have already discussed, this is incorrect. For example, Earl *et al.* (1986)
describe the formal specification of a software engineering environment.
Spivey (1990) discusses the specification of a kernel for a real-time system.
Delisle and Garlan (1990) show how an oscilloscope may be formally specified and Wordsworth (1990) describes part of IBM's CICS system specification.

Figure 9.3 shows how software process costs are affected by the use of formal specification. When a conventional process is used, validation costs are about 50% of
development costs and implementation and design costs are about twice the costs of
specification. With formal specification, specification and implementation costs are
comparable and system validation costs are significantly reduced.

9.1.3 The verdict

The arguments for and against the use of formal specifications are usually expressed
using different criteria. This makes it difficult to arrive at any conclusive verdict
about the cost-effectiveness and future usefulness of this approach. The arguments
against the use of formal methods are not technical but question whether they are
worth the high cost involved. The arguments for this approach tend to stress the technical improvements that derive from formal specification.

Unfortunately, a number of people have taken extreme positions on the use of
formal methods for software development. This has clouded the issue of how and

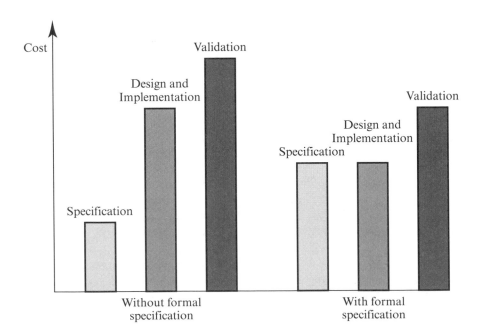

Figure 9.3
Software development
costs with formal
specification.

when this approach can be used cost-effectively. Some members of the computer science community (not all academics!) who are active in the development of formal methods have suggested that software engineering means using formal methods of software development. Understandably, such nonsense makes pragmatic software engineers wary of their proposed solutions.

The reasons presented above for the lack of use of formal specifications are all valid. However, changes to the market and to software engineering practice have probably been more significant in the rejection of formal methods by large sections of the software engineering community. These changes are:

(1)   *The move to interactive systems*   There has been an increasing acceptance of the need for prototyping to understand the requirements for interactive systems. It is difficult to integrate a rapid prototyping process with a formal development process. Hekmatpour and Ince (1988) suggest that prototypes can be generated from formal specification. However, the inability of most formal specification languages to cope with interactive graphical interfaces means that such prototypes are of limited use.

(2)   *Successful software engineering*   The use of software engineering methods in the design and development processes have resulted in improvement in software quality. This contradicts some of the predictions of early proponents of formal methods that program proofs were essential for quality improvement. In short, we have made great improvements without the use of mathematical methods; why should they be introduced now?

The demand for interactive systems is growing rapidly and there is still a great deal of potential for improvement in industrial software engineering practice without the use of formal methods. For interactive systems particularly, it is almost certainly more cost-effective to devote resources to other process improvements such as object-oriented development or better program inspections rather than formal specification. It is unlikely that formal methods will be widely used for interactive and business system development in the foreseeable future.

However, where system dependability is critical, I believe that the industrial use of formal development methods will become common. For system applications where safety, reliability or security is paramount, formal specification and analysis are effective ways of increasing confidence that the system meets its requirements. It may be the case that critical parts of these systems are developed using formal methods with other interactive parts developed informally.

Another area where the use of formal specifications is likely to develop is in the area of standards definition (Blyth *et al.*, 1990). Standards must be unambiguous and precise. The best way to do this is to specify them formally with an associated natural language explanation.

The verdict on formal specifications and associated methods is therefore not clear-cut. For a large class of systems, their use probably isn't cost-effective. However, for a smaller but very important class of systems, it is probably essential to use these methods if software engineering practice is to improve. This has been recognized in UK defence standards for safety-critical systems (MOD, 1995) where the use of formal methods of specification and verification is mandated.

9.2 Transformational development

In Chapter 1, a software process based on formal transformations was briefly described. A formal system specification is a prerequisite for this process. The specification is transformed through a series of correctness-preserving steps to a finished program (Figure 9.4).

Each transformation is sufficiently close to the previous description that the effort of verifying the transformation is not excessive. It can therefore be guaranteed, assuming there are no verification errors, that the program is a true implementation of the specification.

The advantage of the transformational approach compared to proving that a program meets its specification is that the distance between each transformation is less than the distance between a specification and a program. Program proofs are very long and impractical for large-scale systems. However, a transformational approach made up of a sequence of smaller steps may be more effective. However, the process is not easy. Choosing which transformation to apply is a skilled task and proving the correspondence of transformations is difficult.

Few (if any) large-scale systems have been developed using the transformational model of the software process. It is unlikely that a purely transformational approach will ever be adopted for large systems development. Nevertheless, the incorporation of this model into other process models (such as the spiral model) offers the opportunity to improve the process of critical systems development.

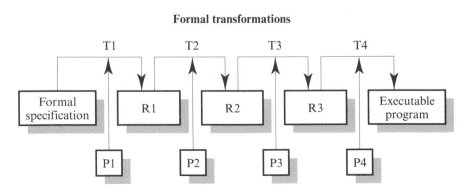

Figure 9.4
Transformational
software development.

9.3 Specifying functional abstractions

As an introduction to formal specification, I discuss a simple technique that can be used to specify functions. Functions accept inputs and return a result but are stateless. Previous inputs do not affect the result which they return. Functions may be specified using pre- and post-conditions. A pre-condition is a specification of a condition which always holds for the function's inputs. A post-condition is a specification of the corresponding condition for the function's outputs. The difference between them defines how the function transforms its inputs to its outputs.

Paradoxically, perhaps, the approach that I use to introduce formal specification is an informal one. This is partly for space reasons as a formal treatment of the subject requires a book to itself. Of equal importance, however, is the fact that readers without a mathematical background are alienated by formality. They tend to reject such material as beyond their abilities. In fact, the practical advantages which result from using formal specification can be achieved without an extensive understanding of the underlying mathematics. An informal approach can illustrate the techniques to readers who are not mathematicians.

Software engineers have been reluctant to make use of formal specification techniques because many of them are intimidated by the specialized notations used. Notations such as VDM (Jones, 1980) and Z (Spivey, 1992) require specialized symbols invented by the authors of the notation. This leads to precision but involves a significant learning effort before reading or writing specifications.

An alternative approach is used in the Larch specification language (Guttag *et al.,* 1985). Larch uses a mnemonic notation rather than specialized symbols. This is less alien to many software engineers and has the further advantage that it may be typed using a standard keyboard. I use a mnemonic notation in this chapter that should be intuitively understandable. I also use graphical highlighting to separate the formal specification from surrounding text. This improves the readability of a specification. It also encourages the specifier to develop the specification in an incremental way.

Pre- and post-conditions are predicates over the inputs and outputs of a function. A predicate is a Boolean expression which is true or false and whose variables are the parameters of the function being specified. Examples of predicates are shown in Figure 9.5.

As well as operators such as =, >=, <=, **not**, **and**, **or** and so on, predicates may also include quantifiers which allow the predicate to be applied to all members of a collection (**for_all**) and to a particular member of a collection (**exists**). These are the universal and existential quantifiers ($\forall$ and $\exists$) used in set theory. The operator **in** is used to select the range over which the quantifier applies. It is analogous to the operator $\in$ used in set theory but, in the simple examples used here, may be applied to arrays as well as sets.

The development of a specification of a function using pre- and post-conditions involves a number of stages:

All variables referenced are of type INTEGER

1 The value of variable A is greater than the value of B and the value of variable C is greater than D

A > B **and** C > D

2. This predicate illustrates the use of the **exists** quantifier. The predicate is true if there are values of i, j and k between M and N such that $i^2 = j^2 + k^2$. Thus, if M is 1 and N is 5, the predicate is true as $3^2 + 4^2 = 5^2$. If M is 6 and N is 9, the predicate is false. There are no values of i, j and k between 6 and 9 which satisfy the condition.

exists i, j, k **in** M..N: $i^2 = j^2 + k^2$

3 This predicate illustrates the use of the universal quantifier **for_all.** It concerns the values of an array called Squares. It is true if the first ten values in the array take a value which is the square of an integer between 1 and 10.

for_all i **in** 1..10, **exists** j **in** 1..10: Squares (i) = j^2

Figure 9.5
Examples of predicates.

(1)   Establish the range of the input parameters over which the function should behave correctly. Specify the input parameter constraints as a predicate.

(2)   Specify a predicate defining a condition which must hold on the output of the function if it behaves correctly.

(3)   Establish what changes (if any) are made to the function's input parameters and specify these. Of course, a pure mathematical function shouldn't change its inputs but programming languages usually allow function inputs to be modified by passing them by reference.

(4)   Combine these into pre- and post-conditions for the function.

As an example, consider the function Search (Figure 9.6) which accepts an array of integers and an integer key as its parameters. The function returns the array index of the member of the array whose value is equal to the key. The original input array is unchanged.

The post-condition must refer to the value returned by the function. I use the normal convention that the name of the function refers to the value returned by the function.

Figure 9.6
The specification of a search function.

function Search (X: **in** INTEGER_ARRAY ; Key: INTEGER)
       return INTEGER ;
Pre: exists i **in** X'FIRST..X'LAST: X(i) = Key
Post: X" (Search (X, Key)) = Key and X = X"

(1)   *Pre-condition*   **exists** i **in** (X'FIRST..X'LAST): X (i) = Key

If Search is to work properly, one of the array elements must match the key. The pre-condition therefore states that there must exist some element (called i here) whose value matches an element in the array. Assume that the attributes FIRST and LAST refer to the lower and upper bounds of the array.

(2)   *Post-condition*   X" (Search (X, Key)) = Key

Search should return the value of the index of the element equal to the key. This can be expressed as a predicate using the function name to refer to the returned value. The notation X" refers to the value of the array X after the function has been evaluated.

(3)   *Post-condition*   X = X"

It is not enough to specify that a particular value of the array matches the key if that can be achieved by modifying the input array. The specifier must also state that the input is unchanged by the function. In many programming languages (like Ada or Pascal) this is achieved by passing the function parameters by value rather than by reference.

The function pre-condition states the condition which must hold if the post-condition is to be valid. A specification should also set out the behaviour of a component if it is presented with unexpected input. How should the function Search behave if there are no array elements which match the input key?

The number of possible types of error and whether the error action depends on the error type affects the approach used for error specification. In the case of Search, there is only a single type of error and a single action to be taken. If the pre-condition is not satisfied, an error predicate can be included. This sets out the post-condition that holds if the pre-condition is false (Figure 9.7).

In Figure 9.7, the error is indicated by returning a value which is greater than the value of the upper bound of the array. Thus, the user of Search can test the value returned to see if the operation has been successful.

This form of error indication is possible in some cases but is not generally satisfactory. The type signature of Search specifies that it must evaluate to an integer. Alternatively, the function could be defined so that it evaluates to a tuple. One value is an integer setting out the key matching the index and the error is a Boolean error state indicator. This is true if the pre-condition is satisfied. Furthermore, it is

---

function Search (X: **in** INTEGER_ARRAY ; Key: INTEGER)
                          return INTEGER ;
Pre: exists i **in** X'FIRST..X'LAST: X (i) = Key
Post: X" (Search (X, Key)) = Key and X = X"
Error: Search (X, Key) = X'LAST + 1

Figure 9.7
The specification of Search with error predicate.

	Sequential	**Concurrent**
Algebraic	Larch (Guttag *et al.,* 1985), OBJ (Futatsugi *et al.,* 1985)	Lotos (Bolognesi and Brinksma, 1987)
Model-based	Z (Spivey, 1992) VDM (Jones, 1980)	CSP (Hoare, 1985) Petri nets (Peterson, 1981)

Figure 9.8
Formal specification languages.

sometimes necessary to have a separate specification for each type of error. This problem is discussed in the following chapters.

The notion of pre- and post-conditions is a fundamental one in formal specification. It is possible to describe large systems as a number of functions but this is unnatural and leads to a complex specification. More powerful approaches to specification have been developed which are simpler to use for large specifications.

There are two approaches to formal specification that have been used to develop relatively complex systems. These are:

(1)   An algebraic approach whereby the system is described in terms of operations and their relationships.

(2)   A model-based approach whereby a model of the system is constructed using well-understood mathematical entities such as sets and sequences.

Different languages in these families have been developed to specify sequential and concurrent systems. Figure 9.8 shows examples of the languages in each class.

In the next two chapters, I introduce the algebraic and model-based specification of sequential systems. The specification of concurrent systems is more specialized and complex and I don't cover it in this book.

Further reading

IEEE Software, **7** (5), September 1990. This special issue of the journal contains a series of readable, tutorial articles discussing different aspects of formal methods. The article by Hall is particularly recommended.

'A specifier's introduction to formal methods'. This is a good survey article which describes the principles of formal specification and introduces a number of different approaches. (J.M. Wing, *IEEE Computer,* **23** (9), September 1990.)

'Strategies for incorporating formal specifications in software development'. Again an overview but the authors pay more attention to classifying different approaches to formal specification. They suggest that the lack of methodological and tool support is a significant factor in the non-use of formal methods. (M.D. Fraser, K. Kumar and V. Vaishnavi, *Comm. ACM,* **37** (10), October 1994.)

KEY POINTS

- Formal system specification is complementary to informal specification techniques.

- Formal specifications are precise and unambiguous. They remove areas of doubt in a specification.

- The principal value of using formal specification techniques in the software process is that it forces an analysis of the system requirements at an early stage. Correcting errors at this stage is cheaper than modifying a delivered system.

- Formal specification techniques are unlikely to be cost-effective in the fore-seeable future for the development of interactive systems. The area where they are most applicable is in the development of safety-critical systems and standards.

- Functions can be specified by setting out pre- and post-conditions for the function. Pre- and post-conditions state what is true before and after the function is evaluated.

- Specifications based on pre- and post-conditions do not scale up to large or medium-sized systems. The reason for this is the inherent complexity of the pre- and post-conditions when system state is considered.

EXERCISES

9.1 Suggest why the architectural design of a system should precede the development of a formal specification.

9.2 You have been given the task of 'selling' formal specification techniques to a software development organization. Outline how you would go about explaining the advantages of formal specifications and countering the reservations of practising software engineers.

9.3 Write predicates to express the following English language statements.

(a) There exists an array of 100 sensors and associated control valves. Sensors can take the values high and low and the control valves can be in state open or closed. If a sensor reading is high, the state of the control valve is closed.

(b) In an array of integers, there is at least one value in that array which is negative.

(c) In a collection of natural numbers, the lowest number is 20 and the largest number is greater than 250.

(d) Given a collection of processes which have an integer attribute called **DELAY** and which may be in states running, waiting or stopped, there is no process which is waiting and whose value of **DELAY** exceeds 2.

9.4 Write pre- and post-conditions for a function that finds the minimum value in an array of integers.

9.5 Write pre- and post-conditions to define a function called **Run_process** which acts on a process which may be running, waiting or stopped. **Run_process** takes a process identifier as an example and, if the process is waiting, changes its state to running and modifies the **DELAY** attribute accordingly.

9.6 Write pre- and post-conditions for a function which sorts an array. You may assume the existence of a predicate called **PERM** that takes two arrays as its parameters and returns true if one is a permutation of the other.

9.7 Explain why there may be problems in the specification of erroneous conditions when a function returns a single value. Using an example, show how these can be tackled by redefining the function to return a tuple (record).

9.8 You are a systems engineer and you are asked to suggest the best way to develop a small safety-critical system for a heart pacemaker. You suggest formally specifying the system but your suggestion is rejected by your manager. You think his reasons are weak and based on prejudice. Is it ethical to develop the system using methods which you think are not the most effective?

10

Algebraic Specification

Objectives

- To explain the role of formal specifications in the definition of interfaces between sub-systems.

- To introduce the algebraic approach to formal specification where abstract data types or object classes are specified by defining the properties of their associated operations.

- To describe a systematic way to write an algebraic specification.

- To illustrate a number of incremental ways to construct algebraic specifications from simpler specifications.

Contents

Large systems are usually decomposed into sub-systems which are developed independently. Sub-systems obviously make use of other sub-systems so an essential part of the specification process is to define sub-system interfaces. Once the interfaces are agreed and defined, the sub-systems can be developed independently.

Sub-system interfaces are often defined as a set of abstract data types or objects (Figure 10.1). Each sub-system implements these interfaces and all sub-system access is through the interfaces. It is therefore essential that the sub-system interface is clearly and unambiguously specified. This reduces the chances of misunderstandings between the sub-system providing a facility and the sub-system using that facility.

The starting point for the specification is an informal interface specification, expressed as a set of abstract data types or object classes, that has been negotiated by the sub-system designers. The algebraic approach is particularly suitable for the definition of sub-system interfaces. This method of formal specification defines an object class or abstract data type in terms of the relationships between the type operations.

Guttag (1977) first discussed this approach in the specification of abstract data types. Cohen *et al.* (1986) show how the technique can be extended to complete system specification using an example of a document retrieval system. Liskov and Guttag (1986) also cover the algebraic specification of abstract data types. Several languages for algebraic specification have been developed including OBJ (Futatsugi *et al.,* 1985) and Larch (Guttag *et al.,* 1985).

It is sometimes difficult to prove that algebraic specifications are mathematically complete and consistent. Van Vliet (1993) discusses some of the reasons for this in a way which is understandable by non-mathematicians. These problems do not, however, detract from their usefulness in supporting the critical process of interface specification. However, an incomplete formal specification may be more precise than informal interface definitions. Theoretical limitations of the algebraic approach do not necessarily detract from its practical utility.

As I discussed in Chapter 9, there are good reasons for developing a formal specification even if no mathematical manipulation of the specification is carried out. Developing a formal specification forces an analysis of an informal interface description. It therefore may reveal potential inconsistencies and ambiguities in that description. The formal specification supplements the informal description. It reduces communication problems between the developers and the users of the sub-system interface.

Interface objects

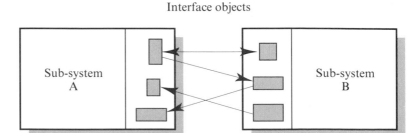

Figure 10.1
Sub-system interface objects.

In the notation which I use here, each specification has a name and an optional generic parameter list. By allowing generic parameters, abstract types which are collections of other types (arrays, lists, and so on) may be specified without concern for the types in the collection. The generic type may be instantiated to create a more specific specification. For example, an array with a generic parameter could be instantiated to an array of integers, an array of strings, an array of arrays and so on. As part of this generic type specification, operations which must be defined over the generic type may be specified.

Figure 10.2 illustrates how algebraic specifications are presented in this chapter. The body of the specification has four components:

(1)   An introduction that declares the sort (the type name) of the entity being specified. A sort is the name of a set of objects. It is usually implemented as a type. The introduction may also include an imports declaration where the names of specifications (not the sort names) defining other sorts are declared. Importing a specification makes these sorts available for use.

(2)   A description part in which the operations are described informally. This makes the formal specification easier to understand. The formal specification complements this description by providing an unambiguous syntax and semantics for the type operations.

(3)   The signature part defines the syntax of the interface to the object class or abstract data type. The names of the operations that are defined, the number and sorts of their parameters and the sort of operation results are described in the signature.

(4)   The axioms part defines the semantics of the operations by defining a set of axioms which characterize the behaviour of the abstract data type. These axioms relate the operations used to construct entities of the defined sort with operations used to inspect its values.

To illustrate the parts of an abstract data type specification, consider the specification of an array (Figure 10.3). This is a generic abstract data type provided in almost all programming languages. It is an *abstract* data type (although it is not defined as such in Ada, C or C++) because it has a restricted set of allowed operations. It is a

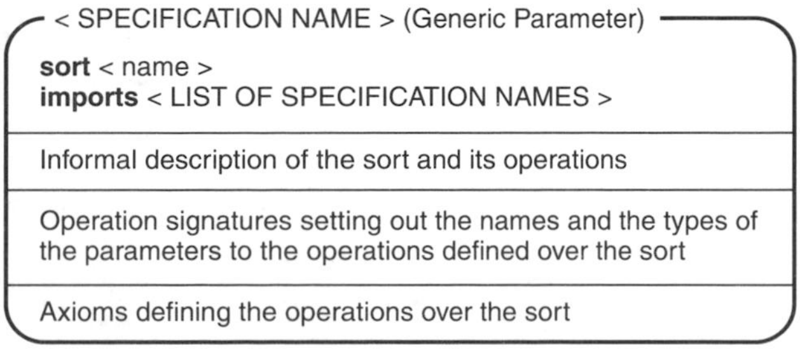

< SPECIFICATION NAME > (Generic Parameter)

sort < name >
imports < LIST OF SPECIFICATION NAMES >

Informal description of the sort and its operations

Operation signatures setting out the names and the types of the parameters to the operations defined over the sort

Axioms defining the operations over the sort

Figure 10.2
The format of an algebraic specification.

```
┌─ ARRAY ( Elem: [Undefined → Elem] ) ──────────────────┐
│                                                         │
│  sort Array                                             │
│  imports INTEGER                                        │
│  ┌───────────────────────────────────────────────────┐ │
│  │ Arrays are collections of elements of generic type │ │
│  │ Elem. They have a lower and upper bound (discovered │ │
│  │ by the operations First and Last). Individual       │ │
│  │ elements are accessed via their numeric index.      │ │
│  │        Create takes the array bounds as parameters  │ │
│  │ and creates the array, initializing its values to   │ │
│  │ Undefined. Assign creates a new array which is the  │ │
│  │ same as its input with the specified element        │ │
│  │ assigned the given value. Eval reveals the value of │ │
│  │ a specified element. If an attempt is made to access│ │
│  │ a value outside the bounds of the array, the value  │ │
│  │ is undefined.                                       │ │
│  ├───────────────────────────────────────────────────┤ │
│  │ Create (Integer, Integer) → Array                  │ │
│  │ Assign (Array, Integer, Elem) → Array              │ │
│  │ First (Array) → Integer                            │ │
│  │ Last (Array) → Integer                             │ │
│  │ Eval (Array, Integer) → Elem                       │ │
│  ├───────────────────────────────────────────────────┤ │
│  │ First (Create (x, y)) = x                          │ │
│  │ First (Assign (a, n, v)) = First (a)               │ │
│  │ Last (Create (x, y)) = y                           │ │
│  │ Last (Assign (a, n, v)) = Last (a)                 │ │
│  │ Eval (Create (x, y), n) = Undefined                │ │
│  │ Eval (Assign (a, n, v), m) =                       │ │
│  │     if m < First (a) or m > Last (a) then Undefined│ │
│  │       else                                         │ │
│  │         if m = n then v else Eval (a, m)           │ │
│  └───────────────────────────────────────────────────┘ │
└─────────────────────────────────────────────────────────┘
```

Figure 10.3
The specification of
sort Array.

generic type because the elements of an array can usually be of any other type. The defined operations create the array, discover the lower and upper bounds, find the value of an array element and assign a value to an array element.

I use the notation suggested by Cohen *et al.* (1986) to introduce generic parameters. The name of the generic parameter is Elem meaning any element type. Any operations which must be defined for the instantiated parameter must also be specified with the generic parameter. In the array specification, this means that the sort which instantiates Elem must have an operation called Undefined associated with it. Undefined is a special value whose type is Elem. It indicates that the evaluation of some operation has resulted in an error. For example, the result of the operation is Undefined when an attempt is made to access an element which has not been given a value.

10.1 Systematic algebraic specification

In this section, I describe a systematic approach that may be used to define an algebraic specification of an abstract data type or object class. This is illustrated by specifying an abstract data type representing a very simple linked list. There are six stages in this approach. These are not necessarily carried out in sequence. As the specification is developed, the specifier refines the results of earlier stages in the process.

The stages in developing an algebraic specification are:

(1) *Specification structuring*   The informal interface specification must be structured into a set of abstract data types or object classes. Operations should be proposed for each interface entity.

(2) *Specification naming*   Establish a name for the specification, decide whether or not it requires generic parameters and decide on a name for the sorts identified.

(3) *Operation selection*   Choose a set of operations on these entities based on the identified interface functionality. This should include operations to create instances of the sort, to modify the value of instances and to inspect the instance values. You may have to add functions to those initially identified in the informal interface definition.

(4) *Informal operation specification*   Write an informal specification of each operation. This should describe how the operations affect the defined sort.

(5) *Syntax definition*   Define the syntax of the operations and the parameters to each operation. This represents the signature part of the formal specification. Update the informal specification at this stage if necessary.

(6) *Axiom definition*   Define the semantics of the operations. This is described in Section 10.1.1.

To develop the example of the list specification, assume that the first stage, namely specification structuring, has been carried out and that the need for a list has been identified. The name of the specification and the name of the sort can be the same although it is useful to distinguish between these by using some convention. I use upper case for the specification name (LIST) and lower case with an initial capital for the sort name (List). As lists are collections of other types, the specification has a generic parameter (Elem).

In general, for each abstract type, the required operations must include an operation to bring instances of the type into existence (Create) and to construct the type from its elements (Cons). In the case of lists, we need an operation to evaluate the first list element (Head), an operation which returns the list created by removing the first element (Tail) and an operation to count the number of list elements (Length). We shall see in Section 10.2 how to add more operations to this set.

To define the syntax of each of these operations, you must decide which parameters are required for the operation and the results of the operation. In general, input parameters are either the sort being defined (List) or the generic sort. Results of operations may be either of those sorts or some other sort such as integer or Boolean. In the list example, the Length operation returns an integer. An imports declaration declaring that the specification of integer is used should therefore be included in the specification. Finally, the semantics are defined as a set of equations as explained in Section 10.1.1. The final specification is shown in Figure 10.4.

LIST (Elem: [Undefined → Elem])

sort List
imports INTEGER

Defines a list where elements are added at the end and removed from the front. The operations are Create, which brings an empty list into existence, Cons, which creates a new list with an added member, Length, which evaluates the list size, Head, which evaluates the front element of the list, and Tail, which creates a list by removing the head from its input list.

Create → List
Cons (List, Elem) → List
Tail (List) → List
Head (List) → Elem
Length (List) → Integer

Head (Create) = Undefined -- Error to evaluate an empty list
Head (Cons (L, v)) = **if** L = Create **then** v **else** Head (L)
Length (Create) = 0
Length (Cons (L, v)) = Length (L) + 1
Tail (Create) = Create
Tail (Cons (L, v)) = **if** L = Create **then** Create **else** Cons (Tail (L), v)

Figure 10.4
The specification of
sort List.

10.1.1 Defining axioms

The axioms which define the semantics of an abstract data type are written using the operations defined in the signature part. They specify the semantics by setting out what is always true about the behaviour of entities with that abstract type.

Operations on an abstract data type usually fall into two classes:

(1) *Constructor operations* which create or modify entities of the sort defined in the specification. Typically, these are given names such as Create, Update, Add and so on.

(2) *Inspection operations* which evaluate attributes of the sort defined in the specification. Typically, these are given names which correspond to attribute names or names such as Eval, Get and so on.

A good rule of thumb for writing an algebraic specification is to establish the constructor operations and write down an axiom for each inspection operation over each constructor. This suggests that if there are m constructor operations and n inspection operations there should be $m*n$ axioms defined.

However, the constructor operations associated with an abstract type may not be primitive constructors. Primitive constructors are operations which can't be expressed using other constructors. If a constructor operation can be defined using other constructors, it is only necessary to define the inspection operations using the primitive constructors.

An example of this is given in the specification of a list shown in Figure 10.4. The constructor operations are Create, Cons and Tail, which build lists. The access operations are Head and Length, which are used to discover list attributes. The Tail operation is not a primitive constructor as it can be defined using Cons and Create. There is therefore no need to define axioms over the Tail operation for Head and Length operations. These would include redundant information that could be derived from other axioms.

Evaluating the head of an empty list results in an undefined value. The specifications of Head and Tail show that Head evaluates the front of the list and Tail evaluates to the input list with its head removed. The specification of Head states that the head of a list created using Cons is either the value added to the list (if the initial list is empty) or is the same as the head of the initial list parameter to Cons. Adding an element to a list does not affect its head unless the list is empty.

The value of the Tail operation is the list which is formed by taking the input list and removing its head. The definition of Tail shows how recursion is used in constructing algebraic specifications. The operation is defined on empty lists then recursively on non-empty lists with the recursion terminating when the empty list results. This is a very common technique to use when writing algebraic specifications.

It is sometimes easier to understand recursive specifications by developing a short example. Say we have a list [5, 7] where 5 is the front of the list and 7 the end of the list. The operation Cons ([5, 7], 9) should return a list [5, 7, 9] and a Tail operation applied to this should return the list [7, 9]. The sequence of equations which results from substituting the parameters in the above specification with these values is:

```
Tail ([5, 7, 9]) =
 Tail (Cons ( [5, 7], 9)) =
  Cons (Tail ([5, 7]), 9) =
   Cons (Tail (Cons ([5], 7)), 9) =
    Cons (Cons (Tail ([5]), 7), 9) =
     Cons (Cons (Tail (Cons ([], 5)), 7), 9) =
      Cons (Cons ([Create], 7), 9) =
       Cons ([7], 9) =
        [7, 9]
```

The systematic rewriting of the axiom for Tail illustrates that it does indeed produce the anticipated result. The axiom for Head can be verified using a similar approach.

10.1.2 Primitive constructor operations

When developing an algebraic specification, it is sometimes necessary to introduce additional constructor operations in addition to those identified as part of the interface specification. The interface constructors are then defined in terms of these more primitive operations.

These additional primitive constructors may be required because it is difficult or impossible to define the inspection functions in terms of the interface functions.

Operation	Description
Create	Creates an empty tree.
Add (Binary_tree, Elem)	Adds a node to the binary tree using the usual ordering principles, that is, if it is less than the current node it is entered in the left sub-tree; if it is greater than or equal to the current node, it is entered in the right sub-tree.
Left (Binary_tree)	Returns the left sub-tree of the top of the tree.
Data (Binary_tree)	Returns the value of the data element at the top of the tree.
Right (Binary_tree)	Returns the right sub-tree of the top of the tree.
Is_empty (Binary_tree)	Returns true if the tree does not contain any elements.
Contains (Binary_tree, Elem)	Returns true if the tree contains the given element.

Figure 10.5
Operations on a binary tree.

We can see an example of this in a binary tree specification with the identified interface functions as shown in Figure 10.5.

It is impossible to specify the inspection operations (Left, Data, Right, Is_empty, Contains) in terms of the Add function. An extra function (Build) is therefore added to the specification to simplify their definition. There is no easy or automatic way to identify these functions. If you find it very difficult to specify inspection functions in terms of the identified constructors, this may mean that you have to think about the problem and try to identify a more primitive constructor operation.

The specification for Binary_tree with the Add constructor defined in terms of the Build constructor and other functions is shown in Figure 10.6.

The notation .=. (Elem, Elem) means that the equality operator '=' is an infix operator with operands of type Elem. The precise notion of equality depends on the sort of the entities to which the operator is applied. It must therefore be defined for each abstract type which may be used to instantiate Elem.

10.2 Structured specification

Writing formal specifications is time-consuming and is an expensive software process activity. A good strategy to minimize the amount of effort needed to develop a specification is to reuse specifications which have already been developed. To do

```
┌─ BINTREE ( Elem: [Undefined → Elem, .=. → Bool, .<. → Bool] ) ─┐
│                                                                 │
│  sort Binary_tree                                               │
│  imports BOOLEAN                                                │
├─────────────────────────────────────────────────────────────── │
│  Defines a binary tree where the data is of generic type Elem.  │
│  See Figure 10.5 for interface operation description.           │
│  Build is an additional primitive constructor operation which is│
│  introduced to simplify the specification. It builds a tree given│
│  the value of a node and the left and right sub-trees.          │
├─────────────────────────────────────────────────────────────── │
│  Create → Binary_tree                                           │
│  Add (Binary_tree, Elem) → Binary_tree                          │
│  Left (Binary_tree) → Binary_tree                               │
│  Data (Binary_tree) → Elem                                      │
│  Right (Binary_tree) → Binary_tree                              │
│  Is_empty (Binary_tree) → Boolean                               │
│  Contains (Binary_tree, Elem) → Boolean                         │
│  Build (Binary_tree, Elem,Binary_tree) → Binary_tree            │
├─────────────────────────────────────────────────────────────── │
│  Add (Create, E) = Build (Create, E, Create)                    │
│  Add (B, E) = if E < Data (B) then Add (Left (B), E)            │
│                            else Add (Right (B), E)              │
│  Left (Create) = Create                                         │
│  Right (Create) = Create                                        │
│  Data (Create) = Undefined                                      │
│  Left (Build (L, D, R)) = L                                     │
│  Right (Build (L, D, R)) = R                                    │
│  Data (Build (L, D, R)) = D                                     │
│  Is_empty (Create) = true                                       │
│  Is_empty (Build (L, D, R)) = false                             │
│  Contains (Create, E) = false                                   │
│  Contains (Build (L, D, R), E) = if E = D then true else if E < D then│
│                            Contains (L, D) else Contains (R,D)  │
└─────────────────────────────────────────────────────────────── ┘
```

Figure 10.6
The specification of
sort Binary_tree.

this, you need to derive specifications in an incremental way. Simple specifications then serve as building blocks for more complex specifications.

There are a number of different ways in which specifications can be reused. I shall discuss three of these here, namely:

(1)   The instantiation of generic specifications.

(2)   The incremental development of specifications.

(3)   The enrichment of specifications.

10.2.1   Specification instantiation

The simplest form of reuse is to take an existing specification which has been specified with a generic parameter and instantiate this with some other sort. Figure 10.7 shows an example of how the array specification given in Figure 10.3 can be instantiated to create the specification of an array of characters. I assume that the sort Char has been defined in a separate specification. It must have a constant operation called

Figure 10.7
The specification of a
character array.

```
┌─ CHAR_ARRAY: ARRAY ──────────────────────────────
│  sort Char_array instantiates Array (Elem:=Char)
│  imports INTEGER
└──────────────────────────────────────────────────
```

Undefined associated with it. This could be implemented using some reserved bit
pattern.

　　　　To instantiate a specification, the name of the generic specification is given
along with the name of the specification being defined. The new sort name is defined
by instantiating it with the name of the generic sort and the element type. When
specifications are instantiated, the set of operations available is the same as the set
of operations in the generic specification.

10.2.2 Incremental development

The incremental development of specifications involves developing simple specifications then using these to specify more complex entities. The simple specifications
are imported into the more complex specifications. This means the operations which
are defined on the imported specifications are available for use in the importing
specification.

　　　　Figure 10.8 is an example of a general-purpose specification building block.
A basic building block for a graphical system is an object class representing a
Cartesian coordinate. Figure 10.8 shows an example of a simple algebraic specification of a sort called Coord. The operations are create a coordinate, test coordinates
for equality and access the X and Y components.

　　　　The specification of Coord can be used in the specification of a cursor in a
graphical user interface (Figure 10.9). Cursors can be moved around the screen to
point at a particular screen element. They have an associated representation (such as
an arrow) which may change depending on the area of the screen where the cursor
is positioned. This is supported in the specification by importing the specification of

Figure 10.8
The specification of
sort Coord.

```
┌─ COORD ──────────────────────────────────────────────────┐
│  sort Coord                                               │
│  imports INTEGER, BOOLEAN                                 │
├───────────────────────────────────────────────────────────┤
│  Defines a sort representing a Cartesian coordinate. The  │
│  operations defined on Coord are X and Y which evaluate the│
│  x and y attributes of an entity of this sort and Eq which │
│  compares two entities of sort Coord for equality.        │
├───────────────────────────────────────────────────────────┤
│  Create (Integer, Integer) → Coord ;                      │
│  X (Coord) → Integer ;                                    │
│  Y (Coord) → Integer ;                                    │
│  Eq (Coord, Coord) → Boolean ;                            │
├───────────────────────────────────────────────────────────┤
│  X (Create (x, y)) = x                                    │
│  Y (Create (x, y)) = y                                    │
│  Eq (Create (x1, y1), Create (x2, y2)) = ((x1 = x2) and (y1 = y2)) │
└───────────────────────────────────────────────────────────┘
```

---- CURSOR ----

sort Cursor
imports INTEGER, COORD, BITMAP

A cursor is a representation of a screen position. Defined
operations are Create which associates an icon with the cursor at a
screen position, Position which returns the current coordinate of the
cursor, Translate which moves the cursor a given amount in the x
and y directions and Change_Icon which causes the cursor icon to
be switched.

The Display operation is not defined formally. Informally, it causes
the icon associated with the cursor to be displayed so that the
top-left corner of the icon represents the cursor's position. When
displayed, the 'clear' parts of the cursor bitmap should not obscure
the underlying objects.

Create (Coord, Bitmap) → Cursor
Translate (Cursor, Integer, Integer) → Cursor
Position (Cursor) → Coord
Change_Icon (Cursor, Bitmap) → Cursor
Dispaly (Cursor) → Cursor

Translate (Create (C, Icon), xd, yd) =
     Create (COORD.Create (X(C)+xd, Y(C)+yd), Icon)
Position (Create (C, Icon)) = C
Position (Translate (C, xd, yd)) = COORD.Create (X(C)+xd, Y(C)+yd)
Change_Icon (Create (C, Icon), Icon 2) = Create (C, Icon2)

Figure 10.9
The specification of
sort Cursor.

a bitmap (not defined here). Assume that the change of cursor is invoked by some
event handler which detects the cursor position with respect to other displayed
objects. Note that the operations defined in COORD may be accessed directly if their
name is distinct from names defined in CURSOR. If the names clash, the operation
name in the imported specification must be preceded by the specification name.

The specification of a cursor class illustrates a problem with algebraic specification. It is difficult to use this approach to specify input and output operations.
Most formal specification techniques are deficient in this respect. However, the algebraic approach is particularly inconvenient because it is difficult to specify global
state changes which are the side-effects of operations.

It is good design practice in an object-oriented system for each object class to
include an operation which displays objects. In the case of cursors, the icon associated with the cursor is displayed in such a way that the 'clear' parts of the cursor
icon does not obscure other display objects. In general, cursor icons occupy a group
of coordinates, only one of which is the cursor 'hot spot'. The specification must
establish the position of this hot spot with respect to the cursor icon.

This is an example of an informal specification which is shorter and more
readable than a formal specification. When formal specifications are developed as
part of the software specification process, it is always important to keep in mind that
formality is usually intended to clarify the specification. It is not an objective in
its own right. You should not insist on formality when it does not have any real

benefits. In the specification of Cursor given in Figure 10.9, I have therefore excluded the Display operation from the formal part of the specification.

10.2.3 Specification enrichment

The enrichment of a specification is like inheritance in object-oriented development. The operations and axioms on the base sort are inherited and become part of the specification. New operations in the specification may overwrite operations with the same name in the base sort, operations may be added to the base specification or removed from it.

Enrichment is not the same as importing a specification. When a specification is imported, the sort and its operations defined in the imported specification are made accessible to (or, in programming terms, brought into the scope of) the specification being defined. They do not become part of that specification.

As an illustration of enrichment, consider the list specification defined in Figure 10.4. A list with additional functionality is needed where elements can be added to either end and an operation to test for list membership is included. Figure 10.10 summarizes the operations on the List sort. The Add operation adds an element to the front of the list and the Member operation tests if a given value is contained in the list.

Figure 10.11 shows the basic definition of List may be used as a component in the definition of a sort New_List which is an enriched version of the sort List. New_List inherits the operations and axioms defined on List so that these also apply to that sort. In effect, they could be written into the specification NEW_LIST with the name List replaced by New_List.

To complete the specification the access operations Head, Tail and Member must be defined over the new constructor (Add) and Member must be specified over previously defined constructor operations.

When a sort is created by enrichment, the names of the generic parameters of the base sort are inherited. The generic parameters in an enriched specification must

Figure 10.10
The operations on sort New_List.

Operation	Description
Create	Brings a list into existence.
Cons (New_List, Elem)	Adds an element to the end of the list
Add (New_List, Elem)	Adds an element to the front of the list
Head (New_List)	Returns the first element in the list
Tail (New_List)	Returns the list with the first element removed
Member (New_List, Elem)	Returns true if an element of the list matches Elem
Length (New_List)	Returns the number of elements in the list

NEW_LIST (Elem: [Undefined → Elem; .==. → Boolean])

sort New_List **enrich** List
imports INTEGER, BOOLEAN

Defines an extended form of list which inherits the operations
and properties of the simpler specification of List and which adds
new operations (Add and Member) to these.
See Figure 10.10 for a description of the list operations.

Add (New_List, Elem) → New_List
Member (New_List, Elem) → Boolean

Add (Create, v) = Cons (Create, v)
Member (Create, v) = FALSE
Member (Add (L, v), v1) = ((v == v1) **or** Member (L, v1))
Member (Cons (L, v), v1) = ((v == v1) **or** Member (L, v1))
Head (Add (L, v)) = v
Tail (Add (L, v)) = L
Length (Add (L, v)) = Length (L) + 1

Figure 10.11
The specification of
sort List.

include the operations from the base sort. In NEW_LIST, the parameters of LIST are extended with an additional equality operation ("==").

In the above examples of array and list specifications, the operations on a sort have been shown as functions which evaluate to a single atomic value. In many cases, this is a reasonable model of the system which is being specified. However, there are some classes of operation which, when implemented, involve modifying more than one entity. For example, the familiar stack pop operation returns a value from a stack and also removes the top element from the stack.

It is possible to model such operations using multiple simpler operations which take the top value from the stack and which remove the top stack element. However, a more natural approach is to define operations which return a tuple rather than a single value. Rather than returning a single value, the function has multiple output values. Thus, the stack pop operation might have the signature:

Pop (Stack) → (Elem, Stack)

Operations which evaluate to a tuple are used in a specification of a queue which can be specified as an enrichment of lists. An operation is added which evaluates to a pair consisting of the first item on the queue and the queue minus its head. The operations on sort Queue are shown in Figure 10.12 and the queue specification in Figure 10.13.

10.3 Error specification

A problem which faces the developer of a specification is how to indicate errors and exceptional conditions. The basic problem is that, under normal conditions, the result of an operation may be of some sort X but under exceptional conditions an

Operation	Description
Create	Brings a queue into existence
Cons (Queue, Elem)	Adds an element to the end of the queue
Head (Queue)	Returns the element at the front of the queue
Tail (Queue)	Returns the queue minus its front element
Length (Queue)	Returns the number of elements in the queue
Get (Queue)	Returns a tuple composed of the element at the head of the queue and the queue with the front element removed

Figure 10.12
The operations on sort Queue.

QUEUE (Elem: [Undefined → Elem])

sort Queue **enrich** List
imports INTEGER

This specification defines a queue which is a first-in, first-out data structure. It can therefore be specified as a List where the insert operation adds a member to the end of the queue.
See Figure 10.12 for a description of queue operations.

Get (Queue) → (Elem, Queue)

Get (Create) = (Undefined, Create)
Get (Cons (Q, v)) = (Head (Q), Tail (Cons (Q, v)))

Figure 10.13
The specification of a queue.

error should be indicated. The appropriate error indicator may not be of the same sort as the normal result so a type clash occurs.

There are several ways of tackling this problem. Three possibilities are:

(1) A special distinguished, constant operation such as Undefined may be defined. In exceptional cases, the operation evaluates to Undefined. We have already seen examples of this technique in the array specification in Figure 10.3. The Eval operation evaluates to Undefined if the index is out of bounds. The value Undefined is untyped so can be the result of any specification operation.

(2) The operation may evaluate to a tuple where one component of the tuple indicates whether or not the operation has evaluated successfully. The specification of a queue shown in Figure 10.13 illustrated how a tuple could be the result of an operation. The examples in Chapter 20 which is concerned with software reuse illustrate how this approach can be implemented.

(3) The specification may include an exceptions section which defines conditions under which the axioms do not hold.

Figure 10.14 illustrates how an exceptions section can be added to the specification of a list which was introduced in Figure 10.4. In this case, the exceptions part

```
┌─ LIST ( Elem ) ──────────────────────────────────────┐
│  sort List                                            │
│  imports INTEGER                                      │
├───────────────────────────────────────────────────────┤
│  See Figure 10.4                                      │
├───────────────────────────────────────────────────────┤
│  Create → List                                        │
│  Cons (List, Elem) → List                             │
│  Tail (List) → List                                   │
│  Head (List) → Elem                                   │
│  Length (List) → Integer                              │
├───────────────────────────────────────────────────────┤
│  Head (Cons (L, v)) = if L = Create then v else Head (L) │
│  Length (Create) = 0                                  │
│  Length (Cons (L, v)) = Length (L) + 1                │
│  Tail (Create ) = Create                              │
│  Tail (Cons (L, v)) = if L = Create then Create else Cons (Tail (L), v) │
│                                                       │
│  exceptions                                           │
│       Length (L) = 0 ⇒ failure (Head (L))             │
└───────────────────────────────────────────────────────┘
```

Figure 10.14
The specification of List with an exception part.

specifies that if the length of the list L is 0 then the Head operation, applied to L, fails. Notice that this means that no operations need be associated with the generic specification parameter. Guttag (1980) discusses this approach to error specification in more detail.

Further reading

Recent books on algebraic specification have concentrated on describing the method on its own without placing it in the context of a wider software development process. I have therefore suggested these older references which should be available in libraries. They are better for understanding how this technique can be used.

The Specification of Complex Systems. This excellent introductory text contains a good chapter discussing algebraic specification. A simple electronic mail system is used as an example. (B. Cohen, W.T. Harwood and M.I. Jackson, 1986, Addison-Wesley.)

'Formal specification as a design tool'. This paper is included in a collection of papers on specification which includes other papers on algebraic specification. I think this paper is particularly useful as it illustrates the practical use of formal specification. (J.V. Guttag and J.J. Horning, in *Software Specification Techniques,* Gehani, N. and McGettrick, A.D. (eds), 1986, Addison-Wesley.)

Abstraction and Specification in Program Development. This is a general text on systems development with good chapters on algebraic specification. (B. Liskov and J. Guttag, 1986, MIT Press.)

KEY POINTS

- Algebraic specification is a particularly appropriate technique when interfaces between software systems must be specified.

- Algebraic specification involves designing the operations on an abstract data type or object and specifying them in terms of their interrelationships.

- An algebraic specification consists of two formal parts: a signature part in which the operations and their parameters are set out, and an axioms part in which the relationships between these operations are defined.

- Formal specifications should always have an associated informal description to make the formal semantics more understandable.

- Algebraic specifications should be constructed by identifying constructor operations, which create instances of the type or class, and inspection operations which inspect the values of these instances. The semantics of each inspection operation should be defined for each constructor.

- Complex formal specifications may be constructed from simple building blocks. Specifications can be developed from simpler specifications by instantiating a generic specification, incremental specification development and specification enrichment.

- Errors in operations can be specified by identifying distinguished 'error values', by associating an error indicator with the value of an operation or by incorporating a special section in a specification which defines values for exceptional situations.

EXERCISES

10.1 Explain why formal specification is a valuable technique for defining the interfaces between sub-systems.

10.2 An abstract data type representing a stack has the following operations associated with it:

New: Bring a stack into existence
Push: Add an element to the top of the stack
Top: Evaluate the element on top of the stack
Retract: Remove the top element from the stack and return the modified stack
Empty: True if there are no elements on the stack

Write an algebraic specification of this stack. Make reasonable assumptions about the syntax and semantics of the stack operations.

10.3 Modify the example presented in Figure 10.3 (array specification) by adding a new operation called **ArrayAssign** which assigns all the values of one array to another array given that the arrays have the same number of elements.

10.4   An abstract data type called **Set** has a signature defined as follows:

New → Set
Add (Set, Elem) → Set
Size (Set) → Integer
Remove (Set) → Elem
Contains (Set, Elem) → Boolean
Delete (Set, Elem) → Set

Explain informally what these operations are likely to do. Write axioms which formally define your informal English specification.

10.5   Using the equation rewriting approach as used in Example 10.4, verify that the operation **Add** ([10, 7, 4], 8) on the list defined in Figure 10.11 causes the list [8, 10, 7, 4] to be built. (Hint: Show the head of the list is 8 and the tail is [10, 7, 4].)

10.6   Write a formal algebraic specification of a sort **Symbol_table** whose operations are informally defined as follows:

Create: Bring a symbol table into existence
Enter: Enter a symbol and its type into the table.
Lookup: Return the type associated with a name in the table.
Delete: Remove a name, type pair from the table, given a name as a parameter.
Replace: Replace the type associated with a given name with the type specified as a parameter.

The **Enter** operation fails if the name is in the table. The **Lookup, Delete** and **Replace** operations fail if the name is not in the table.

10.7   Discuss how your specification would have to be modified if a block-structured symbol table was required. A block-structured symbol table is one used in compiling a language with block structure like Pascal where declarations in an inner block override the outer block declarations if the same name is used.

10.8   Enrich the specification of **List** (Figure 10.11) with further operations to implement an ordered list. Add a new operation called **Insert** which inserts an element in the correct place to maintain the ordering and an operation **Remove** which, given an element value, removes the element with that value from the list.

10.9   For all of the abstract data types you have specified, write Ada or C++ package specifications defining a package to implement the abstract type. Pay particular attention to error handling in the implementation.

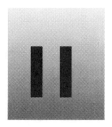

Model-based
Specification

Objectives

- To introduce an approach to formal specification which is based on developing a mathematical model of a software system.
- To present some features of the Z specification language which is used to specify formal state models of a system and operations on that state.
- To illustrate the Z specification process using several small examples.
- To show how incremental specifications can be developed using Z schemas.

Contents

Model-based specification is an approach to formal specification where the system specification is expressed as a system state model. This state model is constructed using well-understood mathematical entities such as sets and functions. System operations are specified by defining how they affect the state of the system model.

The most widely used notations for developing model-based specifications are VDM (Jones, 1980, 1986) and Z (Hayes, 1987; Spivey, 1992). I use Z (pronounced Zed, not Zee) for describing this approach here. This notation is based on typed set theory. Systems are therefore modelled using sets and relations between sets. However, Z has augmented these mathematical concepts with constructs which specifically support formal software specification.

Formal specifications can be difficult and tedious to read especially when they are presented as large mathematical formulae. Understandably, this has inhibited many software engineers from investigating their potential in systems development. The designers of Z have paid particular attention to this problem. Specifications are presented as informal text supplemented with formal descriptions. The formal description is included as small, easy-to-read chunks (called schemas) which are distinguished from associated text using graphical highlighting.

In an introduction to model-based specification, I can only give an overview of how a specification can be developed. It is not even possible to introduce all of Z. A complete description of the Z notation would be longer than this chapter. Rather, I present some small examples to illustrate the technique and introduce notation as it is required. A full description of the Z notation is given in textbooks such as those by Diller (1994) and Wordsworth (1992). Hayes (1987) describes a number of case studies where Z has been used and a reference manual for the language has been published (Spivey, 1992).

11.1 Z schemas

In Chapter 10, I introduced the notion of incremental specification where formal specifications are constructed from simpler specifications. Z incorporates excellent support for incremental specification. Specifications are built from components called *schemas*. Schemas are used to introduce state variables and to define constraints and operations on the state. Schema operations include schema composition, schema renaming and schema hiding. These operations allow schemas to be manipulated. They are a powerful mechanism for system specification.

To be most effective, a formal specification must be supplemented by supporting, informal description. The Z schema presentation has been designed so that it stands out from surrounding text (Figure 11.1).

The schema is given a meaningful name which is used to refer to it in other parts of the specification. The schema signature declares the names and types of the entities introduced in the schema. In Figure 11.1 the signature introduces two state variables. These are contents and capacity which are modelled as natural numbers (indicated by $\mathbb{N}$). A natural number is an integer that is greater than or equal to

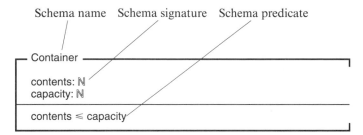

Schema name   Schema signature   Schema predicate

┌─ Container ──┐
│ contents: ℕ   │
│ capacity: ℕ   │
├──┤
│ contents ≤ capacity   │
└──┘

Figure 11.1
A Z schema specifying
a container.

zero. These partially define a container which can hold a discrete quantity of something.

The schema predicate defines relationships between the entities in the signature by stating a logical expression which must always be true (an invariant). The predicate states the obvious fact that the contents of the container cannot exceed its capacity. This specification says nothing about the size of the container or what the container is intended to hold. The definition of contents and capacity as natural numbers states that the container must hold a discrete amount of contents.

The specification in Figure 11.1 is a building block which can be used in further specifications. Figure 11.2 shows a specification of another building block that might be associated with a container to provide information about its contents.

The indicator specified in Figure 11.2 introduces three entities, namely light (modelled by the values off and on), reading and danger_level (modelled as natural numbers). Both light and reading would have some physical manifestation in the real system (a warning lamp and a dial, perhaps) which provides an operator with information about the system.

The symbol ⇔ in the predicate part can be read as 'if and only if'. The predicate therefore specifies that the light should be on if and only if reading is less than or equal to danger_level. That is, a 'low-contents' warning is signalled. At this stage, danger_level is not defined.

Given the specification of an indicator and a container, they can be combined (Figure 11.3) to define a storage tank with some capacity and an indicator light. The combined specification includes all the state variable declarations and predicates of the included specifications. Thus, Storage_tank combines the signatures of Container and Indicator and their predicates. These are combined with any new signatures and predicates introduced in the specification. Predicates are implicitly anded when schemas are composed so must all hold for the schema invariant to be true.

Storage_tank has three associated predicates which define constraints on the state variables introduced in the schemas Container and Indicator. In Z, writing

┌─ Indicator ───┐
│ light: {off, on}   │
│ reading: ℕ   │
│ danger_level: ℕ   │
├──┤
│ light = on ⟺ reading ≤ danger_level   │
└──┘

Figure 11.2
The specification of an
indicator.

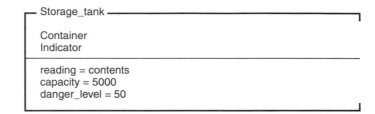

Figure 11.3
The specification of a
storage tank.

predicates on separate lines means that they are separated by an implicit 'and'. Thus the predicate can be read as 'reading equals contents and capacity equals 5000 and danger_level equals 50'. Predicates may also be written on the same line separated by an 'and' symbol ($\land$).

Including schemas in another schema as shown in Figure 11.3 is equivalent to merging these schemas (Figure 11.4). There is some redundancy here in that reading and contents represent the same thing; this results from the use of generalized schema building blocks. Z includes facilities for variable renaming which could remove this redundancy but I do not cover these constructs here.

The examples of schemas which we have seen so far show the specification of system state and the constraints or state invariants. Operations can be specified using schemas by defining their effect on the system state. That is, you define the state after the operation in terms of the state before the operation and the operation parameters.

Z uses various conventions to identify particular types of schema and state variable used in operation specification:

(1)   If any variable name, N, is followed by ', for example N', this means that it represents the value of the state variable N after the operation. In Z terminology, N is *decorated with* a dash.

(2)   If a schema name is decorated with ', this introduces the dashed values of all names defined in the specification together with the invariant applying to these values.

(3)   If a variable name is decorated with !, this means that it is an output, for example 'message!'.

```
┌─ Storage_tank ──────────────────────────────────────────┐
│                                                          │
│   contents: ℕ                                            │
│   capacity: ℕ                                            │
│   reading: ℕ                                             │
│   danger_level: ℕ                                        │
│   light: {off, on}                                       │
├──────────────────────────────────────────────────────────┤
│   contents ⩽ capacity                                    │
│   light = on  ⟺  reading ⩽ danger_level                  │
│   reading = contents                                     │
│   capacity = 5000                                        │
│   danger_level = 50                                      │
└──────────────────────────────────────────────────────────┘
```

Figure 11.4
Expanded specification
of a storage tank.

(4)   If a variable is decorated with ?, this means that it is an input, for example 'amount?'.

(5)   If a schema name is prefixed with the Greek character Xi (Ξ), this means that dashed versions of the variables defined in the named schema are introduced. For all variable names introduced in the schema, the values of corresponding dashed names are the same. That is, the values of state variables are not changed by the operation.

(6)   If a schema name is prefixed with the Greek character Delta (Δ), this implies that values of one or more state variables will be changed by the operation where that schema is introduced. For all variable names introduced in the named schema, corresponding dashed names are also introduced and may be referenced in operations.

Figure 11.5 shows part of the specification of the fill operation which adds an amount to a tank. The schema name is prefixed with Delta, indicating that the operation changes the state. The amount to be added to the tank is an input. The predicate associated with the operation specifies that the state is changed by the operation if there is enough capacity in the tank.

The predicate for Fill-OK specifies that the contents after completion of the operation (referenced as contents') is equal to the sum of the contents before the operation and the amount added to the tank. This is only true if adding the specified amount does not exceed the capacity of the tank. This is precluded because of the predicates defined in Container. If the addition of the specified amount would cause the tank to overflow, the operation is undefined.

A convention in writing Z specifications of operations is that they are specified in parts. The first schema defines the 'correct' operation. Following schemas define what should happen in exceptional situations. These schemas are then combined using a disjunction (or) operator to specify the operation completely.

Figure 11.6 is a specification of what should happen if adding the specified amount exceeds the capacity of the tank. In this situation, nothing is added to the tank and a warning message is output.

Note the use of the Xi schema here indicating that the values of state variables are not changed. The predicate associated with OverFill is true when the capacity of the tank is less than the current contents plus the amount to be added. Nothing is added to the tank if there is not enough room to add all the specified amount. A message 'Insufficient tank capacity – Fill cancelled' is output.

    ┌─ Fill-OK ───┐
    │ Δ Storage_tank
    │   amount?: $\mathbb{N}$
    ├──
    │   contents + amount? $\leq$ capacity
    │   contents' = contents + amount?
    └───┘

Figure 11.5
A partial specification of the fill operation.

Figure 11.6
Further specification of
the fill operation.

```
┌─ OverFill ──────────────────────────────────────────┐
│  Ξ Storage-tank                                      │
│  amount?: ℕ                                          │
│  r!: seq CHAR                                        │
├──────────────────────────────────────────────────────┤
│  capacity < contents + amount?                       │
│  r! = "Insufficient tank capacity – Fill cancelled"  │
└──────────────────────────────────────────────────────┘
```

Figure 11.7
The complete
specification of the
fill operation.

```
┌─ Fill ──────────────────────────────────────────────┐
│                                                      │
│  Fill-OK ∨ OverFill                                  │
└──────────────────────────────────────────────────────┘
```

To complete the specification of the fill operation, Fill-OK and OverFill must be combined using a disjunction (or) operator (Figure 11.7). The effect of this operator is to merge the signatures of Fill-OK and OverFill. These are identical in this case. The predicate parts are independent and are separated by an or operator (∨). Therefore either the predicate in Fill-OK or the predicate in OverFill must be true.

When schemas are very short, as in Figure 11.7, they may be written as text without the normal graphical highlighting. I use this form of schema where appropriate to save space. The complete specification of the fill operation could have been written:

Fill ≙ Fill-OK ∨ Overfill

11.2 The Z specification process

There are obviously many different processes which can be used to construct a formal model of a system. The formal specification of a non-trivial system or a sub-system interface is large and complex. An incremental approach must be used where individual system components are specified. These specification fragments are then composed to form the complete specification.

Figure 11.8 illustrates this process and shows the steps involved in constructing the specification for each component.

I illustrate this process by developing part of the specification for a data dictionary like that discussed in Chapter 6. In this example, data dictionaries are used to hold information about the components of semantic data models. Data dictionaries are information systems which maintain details of the names used in some design.

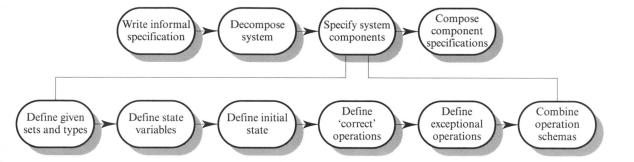

Figure 11.8
A process to develop a
Z specification.

The data dictionary described in Chapter 6 has four fields:

(1)   *Item name*   Holds the name of the entry.

(2)   *Description*   Holds a description of the entry.

(3)   *Type*   Holds the type of the entry. For this example, I assume that only types used in semantic data models will be allowed.

(4)   *Date*   Holds the date of creation of the entry.

The operations which I define are Add, which adds an entry to the dictionary, Delete, which removes an entry, Lookup, which returns the information associated with a given entry and Replace, which replaces one entry with another.

After constructing the informal specification, the next stage of the process is to define the types used. Types in Z are defined as sets. These sets may be defined explicitly or may be specified as *given sets*.

Given sets are incomplete type definitions where only the type name need be defined. Its details are not included in the specification. This facility is included in Z because it is sometimes appropriate to delay some details until system design or implementation.

Given sets are introduced by enclosing the type name in square brackets. In this case, the given sets are:

[NAME, DATE]

The type field in the data dictionary is restricted to types used in a semantic data model. These are defined by enumerating the values of the set members:

Sem_model_types = { relation, entity, attribute }

Schemas in Z may also be used as a basis for type definition. They are like a record type in Pascal or Ada or a structure in C. The state variables defined in the schema are referenced using dot notation in the same way as the fields of a record. Therefore, to access the name capacity defined in the schema Container, you write Container.capacity.

This type of schema is used to define a type representing an entry in the data dictionary (Figure 11.9). In this type definition, the description associated with a name is defined as a sequence of characters. A sequence is a collection of elements where each element is referenced by its position in the sequence. In this case, the predicate states that there is an arbitrary limit of 2000 characters on the length of the description. Sequences are described in Section 11.3.

The next stage of the specification process is to define the data dictionary and its initial state. In this case, functions are used to specify the data dictionary.

Functions or mappings are one of the most commonly used constructs in model-based specifications. In programming languages, a function is an abstraction over an expression. When provided with an input, it computes an output value based on the value of the input. Z functions are similar in effect. However, it is usually more convenient to think of them as a set of relationships between two sets called the *domain* and the *range* of the function. Figure 11.10 illustrates this for a simple function called SmallSquare. It relates the identifiers one to seven to members of a set of natural numbers. These are the squares of the numbers represented by the identifiers.

In Z, functions can be defined by listing the set of mappings from values in the domain to values in the range:

$$\text{SmallSquare} = \{\text{one} \mapsto 1, \text{two} \mapsto 4, \text{three} \mapsto 9, \text{four} \mapsto 16, \text{five} \mapsto 25,$$
$$\text{six} \mapsto 36, \ \text{seven} \mapsto 49\}$$

The domain of a function (written dom f in Z, where f is the function name) is the set of inputs over which the function has a defined result. The range of a function (written rng f in Z) is the set of results which the function can produce. If an input i is in the domain of some function f ($i \in$ dom f), the associated result may be specified as f (i), that is, f (i) $\in$ rng f. For example, in the function SmallSquare, SmallSquare (two) = 4, SmallSquare (five) = 25 and so on.

A function is a partial function if its input is a member of some set T but its domain (those inputs which produce a result) is a subset of T. For example, a partial function f may accept any number between 1 and 50 as an input but may only produce a result if the input is a multiple of 7. The domain of f is therefore (7, 14, 21, 28, 35, 42, 49).

Functions allow one value to be mapped onto another. They can therefore be used to define a data dictionary where a name is mapped onto a data dictionary entry. A schema defining the data dictionary is shown in Figure 11.11. A partial function

Figure 11.9
A schema defining a
data dictionary entry.

```
┌─ DataDictionaryEntry ─────────────────────────────────────┐
│                                                           │
│  entry: NAME                                              │
│  desc: seq char                                           │
│  type: Sem_model_types                                    │
│  creation_date: DATE                                      │
├───────────────────────────────────────────────────────────┤
│  #description ⩽ 2000                                      │
└───────────────────────────────────────────────────────────┘
```

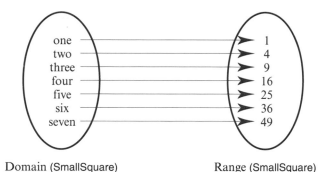

Domain (SmallSquare)   Range (SmallSquare)

Figure 11.10
The function
SmallSquare.

(indicated by the tagged arrow) is used in this example; not all sequences of characters have associated entries in the data dictionary. Enclosing the schema name DataDictionaryEntry in braces means that the range of DataDictionary is a set of values of type DataDictionaryEntry.

The schema DataDictionary defines ddict to be a partial function from NAME to DataDictionaryEntry. Given a name, the associated information such as desc, type and creation_date can be discovered. Sets may not have duplicate members so this definition ensures that names in the data dictionary are unique. However, it does not specify that the data dictionary must be ordered.

The next stage in the specification process is to define the initial state of the data dictionary. We do this by defining a schema that incorporates the schema DataDictionary'. This means that we are interested in the state of the data dictionary after some initialization has been applied. Its state before this is of no interest. Figure 11.12 shows that the initial value of the data dictionary is $\varnothing$ where this symbol represents the empty set. Initially, there are no entries in the data dictionary.

Now consider the informal definition of operations on the data dictionary:

(1)   **Add**   This operation takes a name and a data dictionary entry as parameters. If the name is not in the data dictionary, an entry is made in the dictionary.

(2)   **Delete**   Given a name, the entry associated with that name is deleted from the data dictionary.

(3)   **Lookup**   Given a name, this value of this operation is the data dictionary entry associated with that name.

(4)   **Replace**   Given a name and a data dictionary entry, the operation replaces the existing entry with the given name with the new entry.

For the **Add** operation, an error message is output if the name has already been entered in the data dictionary. For other operations, an error message is output if the name is not in the data dictionary and the data dictionary is unchanged.

```
┌─ DataDictionary ─────────────────────────────────────────┐
│                                                          │
│   DataDictionaryEntry                                    │
│   ddict: NAME ⇻ {DataDictionaryEntry}                    │
│                                                          │
└──────────────────────────────────────────────────────────┘
```

Figure 11.11
A schema defining a
data dictionary as a
partial function.

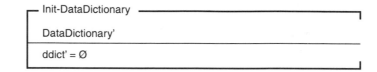

Figure 11.12
The initial state of the
data dictionary.

The specification of Add and Lookup uses Z constructs which have already
been discussed. Figure 11.13 shows the partial specification of the 'correct' operations. In the case of Add, the operation is defined when the name is not in the data
dictionary, that is, when the name is not a member of the domain of ddict. Lookup is
defined when the name is in the data dictionary.

Note the use of the Delta schema in Add_OK, indicating that the operation
causes a state change, and the Xi schema in Lookup_OK, indicating that no state
change occurs. For the Add_OK operation, the state of ddict after the operation is the
union of its state before the operation and a mapping from the input name to a data
dictionary entry. For the lookup operation, the result (entry!) is the data dictionary
entry associated with name? in ddict.

Once the normal mode of operation has been specified, the next stage is to
define operations where some exception occurs (Figure 11.14). In the Add operation,
an error state occurs when the name has already been added to the data dictionary.
In the Lookup operation, the error state occurs when the given name is not in the data
dictionary.

Finally the schemas are combined to complete the definition of the Add and
Lookup operations. To save space, I use the linear form of a schema definition here.

Add $\triangleq$ Add_OK $\lor$ Add_Error
Lookup $\triangleq$ Lookup_OK $\lor$ Lookup_Error

The specification of the Replace operation relies on the use of a Z operator called
the function overriding operator. The function overriding operator is, perhaps, best

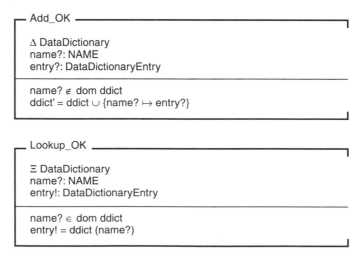

Figure 11.13
A partial specification
of Add and Lookup
operations.

```
┌─ Add_Error ──────────────────────────────────────────────┐
│                                                           │
│  Ξ DataDictionary                                         │
│  name?: NAME                                              │
│  error!: seq char                                         │
│ ─────────────────────────────────────────────────────────│
│  name? ∈ dom ddict                                        │
│  error! = "Name already in dictionary"                    │
│                                                           │
└───────────────────────────────────────────────────────────┘
```

```
┌─ Lookup_Error ───────────────────────────────────────────┐
│                                                           │
│  Ξ DataDictionary                                         │
│  name?: NAME                                              │
│  error!: seq char                                         │
│ ─────────────────────────────────────────────────────────│
│  name? ∉ dom ddict                                        │
│  error! = "Name not in dictionary"                        │
│                                                           │
└───────────────────────────────────────────────────────────┘
```

Figure 11.14
Add and Lookup specifications with input errors.

illustrated with a very simple example. Say we have a function which maps names to telephone numbers.

$$phone = \{ \text{Ian} \mapsto 3390, \text{Ray} \mapsto 3392, \text{Steve} \mapsto 3427 \}$$

Now assume we have another function newphone defined as follows.

$$newphone = \{ \text{Steve} \mapsto 3386, \text{Ron} \mapsto 3427 \}$$

The operation phone ⊕ newphone results in the following function:

$$phone \oplus newphone =$$
$$\{ \text{Ian} \mapsto 3390, \text{Ray} \mapsto 3392, \text{Steve} \mapsto 3386, \text{Ron} \mapsto 3427 \}$$

The function overriding operator acts like a set union operator if the name is not in the set. If the name is in the set, the name and its associated value are replaced. In the above example, an entry for Ron has been added and the number associated with Steve has been changed.

Figure 11.15 shows the schema defining the Replace operation when the name is in the dictionary.

```
┌─ Replace_OK ─────────────────────────────────────────────┐
│                                                           │
│  Δ DataDictionary                                         │
│  name?: NAME                                              │
│  entry?: DataDictionaryEntry                              │
│ ─────────────────────────────────────────────────────────│
│  name? ∈ dom ddict                                        │
│  ddict' ⊕ {name? ↦ entry?}                                │
│                                                           │
└───────────────────────────────────────────────────────────┘
```

Figure 11.15
Partial specification of the Replace operation.

The complete specification of the Replace operation can be constructed by combining the specification in Figure 11.15 with Lookup_Error. If the name is not in the data dictionary, the result is the same for this operation as it is for Lookup.

Replace $\triangleq$ Replace_OK $\vee$ Lookup_Error

The operation to delete an item from the data dictionary makes use of a special operator acting on functions. This is called the domain subtraction operator, which is written $\lhd$. Using the above example of telephone numbers, if Ian is to be removed from the domain of phone, this would be written

{Ian} $\lhd$ phone

The resulting function is:

{Ray $\mapsto$ 3392, Steve $\mapsto$ 3427}

The partial specification of the delete operation for the data dictionary is shown in Figure 11.16.

The domain subtraction operator removes a member from the domain of a function. In this case, the domain subtraction operation removes the data dictionary entry name from the domain of DataDictionary. Its related data dictionary entry in the range of the function is thus inaccessible. The effect of Delete is therefore to remove the mapping between name? and its associated data dictionary entry.

The partial specification Delete_OK can be combined with Lookup_error to construct the complete specification:

Delete $\triangleq$ Delete_OK $\vee$ Lookup_Error

This specification of the data dictionary is based on sets which are unordered entities. In practice, a data dictionary must be displayed and is usually stored in alphabetic order. In the next section, I discuss how Z sequences may be used to model ordered collections of items.

Figure 11.16
Partial specification of the delete operation.

```
┌─ Delete_OK ──────────────────────────────────────┐
│ Δ DataDictionary                                  │
│ name?: NAME                                       │
├───────────────────────────────────────────────────│
│ name? ∈ dom ddict                                 │
│ ddict' = {name?} ⋪ ddict                          │
└───────────────────────────────────────────────────┘
```

11.3 Specifying ordered collections

Ordered collections of items in Z may be specified using a built-in construct called a sequence. I have already used this when modelling a message as a sequence of characters.

Informally, a sequence is a collection where the elements are referenced by their position in the collection. Thus if a sequence is named S, S(1) references the first element in the sequence, S(5) references the fifth element and so on. A sequence can be thought of as a special kind of function where the domain of the function consists of consecutive natural numbers. This is illustrated in Figure 11.17 which illustrates a Z sequence called SqSeq. This is a sequence of the squares of the first seven natural numbers.

The domain of a sequence is naturally ordered. This means that it is straightforward to write a predicate which specifies that the range is also ordered. One way of doing this for a sequence s whose elements are of type T is:

$$\forall\ i, j: \text{dom } s \bullet (i < j) => s\ (i) <_T s\ (j)$$

The large dot in this predicate can be read as 'it is always the case that'. The entire predicate can therefore be read as 'for all values of i and j in the domain of s, it is always the case that if i is less than j then s(i) is less than s(j)'. The symbol '$<_T$' is the less than operation over entities of type T.

Assume now that a further operation (Extract) on the data dictionary is to be specified. The model of this Extract operation is shown in Figure 11.18. Informally, it may be defined as follows:

> The Extract operation extracts from the data dictionary all entries whose type is the same as the type input to the operation. The extracted list of entries is output in alphabetical order.

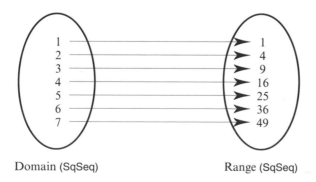

Domain (SqSeq)   Range (SqSeq)

Figure 11.17
A Z sequence.

```
┌─ Extract ──────────────────────────────────────────────┐
│                                                          │
│  DataDictionary                                          │
│  rep!: seq {DataDictionaryEntry}                         │
│  in_type?: Sem_model_types                               │
├──────────────────────────────────────────────────────── │
│  ∀n : dom ddict • ddict(n). type = in_type? ⇒ ddict (n) ∈ rng rep! │
│  ∀i : 1 ⩽ i ⩽ #rep! • rep! (i).type = in_type?          │
│  ∀i : 1 ⩽ i ⩽ #rep! • rep! (i) ∈ rng ddict              │
│  ∀i , j: dom rep! • (i < j) ⇒ rep. name(i) <_NAME rep.name (j) │
└──────────────────────────────────────────────────────── ┘
```

Figure 11.18
The specification of
the Extract operation.

The predicate in the Extract operation makes four assertions:

(1)   For all entries in the data dictionary whose type is in_type?, there is an entry in the output sequence.

(2)   The type of all members of the output sequence is in_type?. The notation #rep! means the number of members of the sequence called rep!.

(3)   All members of the output sequence are members of the range of ddict.

(4)   The output sequence is ordered.

The conjunction of 1 and 2 specifies that there are no members of the output sequence which are not in the data dictionary and that all members of the data dictionary with the given type also appear in the output sequence.

Finally, the complete specification of the data dictionary can be composed from all the above schemas (Figure 11.19).

This brief introduction to model-based specification has only scratched the surface of the technique. There are many other defined language operations. Examples of Z specifications of real systems are given by Earl *et al.* (1986) who specified part of a software engineering environment. Wordsworth (1990) specified a large part of IBM's CICS system and Spivey (1990) has specified a kernel for a real-time system.

Z has been fairly extensively used (mostly in the UK) for formally specifying moderately large systems. As Hall (1990b) describes, it can be used for specifying object-oriented systems by adopting various conventions of use. Alternatively, object-oriented variants of Z have been proposed. These, along with Hall's approach are summarized by Stepney *et al.* (1992). However, a problem with

```
┌─ The_Data_Dictionary ──────────────────────────────────┐
│                                                          │
│  DataDictionary                                          │
│  Init-DataDictionary                                     │
│  Add                                                     │
│  Lookup                                                  │
│  Delete                                                  │
│  Replace                                                 │
│  Extract                                                 │
└──────────────────────────────────────────────────────── ┘
```

Figure 11.19
The complete
specification of the
data dictionary.

Z is its lack of scoping and structuring facilities. Schemas are useful for defining specification fragments but they are concerned with low-level structuring rather than organizing the architecture of a specification.

Further reading

There are many books on Z which cover the notation and its use. Those below are good examples of Z texts.

Z: An Introduction to Formal Methods (2nd edn.). This is a good introduction to Z with many examples and a Z reference manual. It covers the required mathematical background, the use of Z in formal verification and presents a number of case studies. (A. Diller, 1994, John Wiley and Sons.)

Software Development with Z. As well as introducing Z, this book also describes a development process from formal specification to an implementation. (J.B. Wordsworth, 1992, Addison-Wesley.)

'Specifying a real-time kernel'. This is a good introductory paper on Z for readers who are familiar with real-time systems architecture. It includes a concise summary of Z notation. (J.M. Spivey, *IEEE Software*, **7** (5), September 1990.)

KEY POINTS

- Model-based specification relies on building a model of the system using mathematical entities such as sets which have a formal semantics. The Z specification language is based on typed sets.

- Z specifications consist of a mathematical model of the system state and a definition of operations on that state.

- A Z specification is presented as a number of schemas where a schema introduces some typed names and defines predicates over these names. Schemas in Z may be distinguished from surrounding text by graphical highlighting.

- Schemas are building blocks which may be combined and used in other schemas. The effect of including a schema A in schema B is that schema B inherits the names and predicates of schema A.

- Operations may be specified in Z by defining their effect on the system state. It is normal to specify operations incrementally and then combine the specification fragments to produce the complete specification.

- Z functions are sets of pairs where the domain of the function is the set of valid inputs. The range is the set of associated outputs. If ordering is important (sets are unordered), sequences can be used as a specification mechanism.

EXERCISES

11.1 Explain how Z's schema combination mechanism may be used to construct complex specifications.

11.2 Modify the specification of a storage tank (Figure 11.4) by adding a fill warning light which indicates when the tank is close to capacity. This should be switched on when the contents are some high percentage of the capacity.

11.3 Write a specification for an operation called **Dispense** which dispenses a given number of units from a tank.

11.4 Modify the specification of the **Fill** operation (Figure 11.7) so that it either adds the given amount or fills the tank completely.

11.5 What do you understand by the term *domain* and *range* of a function? Explain how functions may be used in defining keyed data structures such as tables.

11.6 Modify the specification of **DataDictionaryEntry** (Figure 11.9) so that the length of attribute descriptions is restricted to 500 characters, the description of relations to 1000 characters and the description of entities to 1500 characters.

11.7 Modify the specification of the **Extract** operation (Figure 11.18) so that it also takes a date as a parameter and only extracts entries from the data description which were entered after that date. You may assume that greater than and less than operators are defined for the type **DATE**.

11.8 Bank teller machines rely on using information on the user's card giving the bank identifier, the account number and the user's personal identifier. They also derive account information from a central database and update that database on completion of a transaction. Using your personal knowledge of the operation of such machines, write Z schemas defining the state of the system, card validation (where the user's identifier is checked) and cash withdrawal.

11.9 The Z schema shown in Figure 11.20 defines the state space of a lending library. Define an operation called **Borrow** which takes inputs called reader?

Figure 11.20
The state space of a library.

```
┌─ Library ─────────────────────────────────────────────────┐
│                                                            │
│   stock: ℙ Book                                            │
│   onLoan: Book ↦ Borrower                                  │
│ ──────────────────────────────────────────────────────────│
│   dom onLoan ⊆ Stock                                       │
│                                                            │
└────────────────────────────────────────────────────────────┘
```

and book? and which defines the effect on the state of a book being borrowed. The notation $\mathbb{P}$ **S** means Powerset **S**. That is, the type of stock is defined as the set of all sets of books. The notation $\subseteq$ can be read as 'is a subset of'.

11.10 Define two further operations on **Library**, namely **New** which adds a new book to the current stock and **Return** which returns a book which has been on loan to the library.

Part Three
Software Design

This part of the book is concerned with various aspects of software design. Chapter 12 introduces the process of design and Chapter 13 covers the important initial phase of architectural design. Chapters 14 and 15 describe the complementary design strategies of object-oriented and function-oriented design. Chapter 16 discusses the specialized problems of real-time system design. Finally, Chapter 17 introduces some principles of user interface design.

Contents

Software Design

Objectives

- To describe the process of software design where informal ideas are transformed to detailed implementation descriptions.

- To introduce the different stages in the design process including architectural design, interface design and data structure design.

- To explain why object-oriented and functional design strategies are complementary rather than opposing approaches to design.

- To describe design quality attributes such as cohesion, coupling, understandability and adaptability.

Contents

Good design is the key to effective engineering. However, it is not possible to formalize the design process in any engineering discipline. Design is a creative process requiring insight and flair on the part of the designer. It must be practised and learnt by experience and study of existing systems.

This chapter and the following five chapters are not, therefore, a design 'cook-book' but are an introduction to the design process, software design strategies and the specific problems of real-time systems and user interface design. The intention is to give you some understanding of design issues and guidance on ways to tackle design problems. Several illustrative examples are used to show how a design might evolve from initial conception through to detailed realization.

Any design problem must be tackled in three stages:

(1)   *Study and understand the problem*   Without this understanding, effective software design is impossible. The problem should be examined from a number of different angles or viewpoints as these provide different insights into the design requirements.

(2)   *Identify gross features of at least one possible solution*   It is often useful to identify a number of solutions and to evaluate them all. The choice of solution depends on the designer's experience, the availability of reusable components, and the simplicity of the derived solutions. Designers usually prefer familiar solutions even if these are not optimal, as they understand their advantages and disadvantages.

(3)   *Describe each abstraction used in the solution*   Before creating formal documentation, the designer may write an informal design description. This may be analysed by developing it in detail. Errors and omissions in the high-level design will probably be discovered during this analysis. These are corrected before the design is documented.

This problem-solving process is repeated for each abstraction identified in the initial design. The refinement process continues until a detailed design specification of each abstraction can be prepared. The problem is, of course, when to stop the process of design decomposition. A useful guideline is to stop when a component design can be described on a single sheet of paper.

12.1 The design process

A general model of a software design is a directed graph. The target of the design process is the creation of such a graph without inconsistencies. Nodes in this graph represent entities in the design such as processes, functions or types. Links represent relations between these design entities such as calls, uses and so on.

Software designers do not arrive at a finished design graph immediately but develop the design iteratively through a number of different versions. The design process involves adding formality and detail as the design is developed with constant backtracking to correct earlier, less formal, designs. The starting point is an informal design which is refined by adding information to make it consistent and complete (Figure 12.1).

The design process involves developing several models of the system at different levels of abstraction. As a design is decomposed, errors and omissions in earlier stages are discovered. These feed back to allow earlier design models to be improved. Figure 12.2 is a generic model of the design process and the design descriptions produced at different stages of design. There is not a rigid boundary between these stages but stage identification is useful to make the design process visible and thus allow it to be managed.

A specification of some kind is the output of each design activity. This specification may be an abstract, formal specification that is produced to clarify the requirements or it may be a specification of how part of the system is to be realized. As the design process continues, detail is added to the specification. The final results of the process are precise specifications of the algorithms and data structures to be implemented.

Figure 12.2 suggests that the stages of the design process are sequential. In fact, design process activities proceed in parallel. However, the activities shown are all part of the design process for large software systems. These design activities are:

(1)   *Architectural design*   The sub-systems making up the system and their relationships are identified and documented. This important topic is covered in Chapter 13.

(2)   *Abstract specification*   For each sub-system, an abstract specification of the services it provides and the constraints under which it must operate is produced.

(3)   *Interface design*   For each sub-system, its interface with other sub-systems is designed and documented. This interface specification must be unambiguous as it allows the sub-system to be used without knowledge of the sub-system operation. Formal specification methods as discussed in Chapters 9 to 11 may be used at this stage.

(4)   *Component design*   Services are allocated to different components and the interfaces of these components are designed.

(5)   *Data structure design*   The data structures used in the system implementation are designed in detail and specified.

(6)   *Algorithm design*   The algorithms used to provide services are designed in detail and specified.

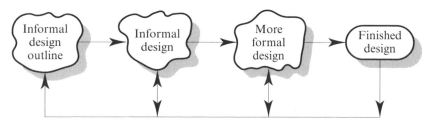

Figure 12.1
The progression from an informal to a detailed design.

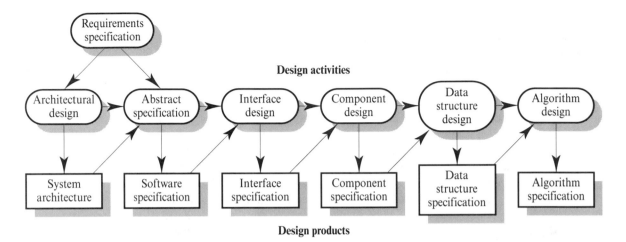

Figure 12.2
A general model of the design process.

This process is repeated for each sub-system until the components identified can be mapped directly into programming language components such as packages, procedures or functions.

Top-down design is one way of tackling a design problem. The problem is recursively partitioned into sub-problems until tractable sub-problems are identified. The general form of the design which usually emerges from such a design process is hierarchical (Figure 12.3). Cross-links in the graph emerge at lower levels of the design tree as designers identify possibilities for reuse.

However, large systems are never designed in a strictly top-down way. Designers always use their previous design knowledge in the design process. They may understand some parts of the design well so will delay decomposing them until other more problematical parts of the design have been considered. Furthermore, project planning may require poorly understood parts of the design to be tackled first. Managers can then make more informed estimates of the likely system development time.

Top-down design relies on the systematic decomposition of abstractions and clearly is a valid approach where design components are tightly coupled. However,

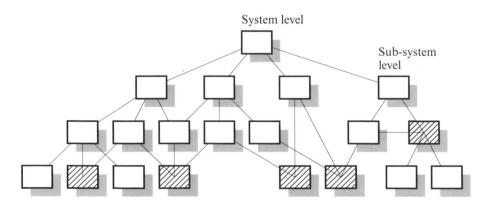

Figure 12.3
Top-down design.

when an object-oriented approach to design is adopted and many existing objects are available for reuse, the design process does not really start with a single encompassing abstraction. In an object-oriented approach, existing objects are used as a design framework and the design is built out from them. There is no concept of a single 'top' or of all objects existing in a single object hierarchy.

12.1.1 Design methods

In many software development projects, software design is still an ad hoc process. Starting from a set of requirements, usually in natural language, an informal design is prepared. Coding commences and the design is modified as the system is implemented. There is little or no formal change control or design management. When the implementation stage is complete, the design has usually changed so much from its initial specification that the original design document is an incorrect and incomplete description of the system.

A more methodical approach to software design is proposed by *structured methods* which are sets of notations and guidelines for software design. Budgen (1993) describes some of the most commonly used methods such as structured design (Constantine and Yourdon, 1979), structured systems analysis (Gane and Sarson, 1979), Jackson System Development (Jackson, 1983) and various approaches to object-oriented design (Robinson, 1992; Booch, 1994).

The use of structured methods normally involves producing large amounts of diagrammatic design documentation. CASE tools (see Part 4) have been developed to support particular methods. Structured methods have been applied successfully in many large projects. They can deliver significant cost reductions because they use standard notations and ensure that standard design documentation is produced.

A mathematical method (such as the method for long division) is a strategy that will always lead to the same result irrespective of who applies the method. The term 'structured methods' suggests, therefore, that designers should normally generate similar designs from the same specification.

In practice, the guidance given by the methods is informal so this situation is unlikely. These 'methods' are really standard notations and embodiments of good practice. By following these methods and applying the guidelines, a reasonable design should emerge. Designer creativity is still required to decide on the system decomposition and to ensure that the design adequately captures the system specification. Empirical studies of designers (Bansler and Bødker, 1993) have shown that they rarely follow methods slavishly. They pick and choose from the guidelines depending on local circumstances.

As discussed in Chapter 5, a structured method includes a set of activities, notations, report formats, rules and design guidelines. Although there are a large number of methods, they have much in common. Structured methods often support some or all of the following models of a system:

(1)   A data-flow model where the system is modelled using the data transformations which take place as it is processed. Data-flow diagrams are described in Chapter 15.

(2)   An entity-relation model which is used to describe the logical data structures being used. Entity-relation data modelling is covered in Chapter 6.

(3)   A structural model where the system components and their interactions are documented. One approach to providing a structural model is through 'structure charts', discussed in Chapter 15.

(4)   If the method is object-oriented it will include an inheritance model of the system, a model of how objects are composed of other objects and, usually, an object-use model which shows how objects are used by other objects. These object models are discussed in Chapters 6 and 14.

Particular methods supplement these with other system models such as state transition diagrams (Chapter 16), entity life histories that show how each entity is transformed as it is processed and so on. Most methods suggest a centralized repository for system information or a data dictionary should be used (Chapter 6). No one method is demonstrably better or worse than other methods; the success or otherwise of methods often depends on their suitability for an application domain. I have therefore made a deliberate decision not to cover any particular method in detail in this book.

12.1.2 Design description

A software design is a model of a real-world system that has many participating entities and relationships. This design is used in a number of different ways. It acts as a basis for detailed implementation; it serves as a communication medium between the designers of sub-systems; it provides information to system maintainers about the original intentions of the system designers, and so on.

Designs are documented in a set of design documents that describe the design for programmers and other designers. There are three main types of notation used in design documents:

(1)   *Graphical notations*   These are used to display the relationships between the components making up the design and to relate the design to the real-world system it is modelling. A graphical view of a design is an abstract view. It is most useful for giving an overall picture of the system.

(2)   *Program description languages*   These languages (PDLs) use control and structuring constructs based on programming language constructs but also allow explanatory text and (sometimes) additional types of statement to be used. These allow the intention of the designer to be expressed rather than the details of how the design is to be implemented.

(3)   *Informal text*   Much of the information that is associated with a design cannot be expressed formally. Information about design rationale or non-functional considerations may be expressed using natural language text.

Generally, all of these different notations may be used in describing a system design. The architecture and the logical data design should be described graphically, supplemented by design rationale and further informal or formal descriptive text. The interface design, the detailed data structure design and the algorithm design are best described using a PDL or, in some cases, using a formal notation as discussed in Chapters 9 to 11. Descriptive rationale may be included as embedded comments.

12.2 Design strategies

Until relatively recently, the most commonly used software design strategy involved decomposing the design into functional components with system state information held in a shared data area. Although Parnas (1972) suggested an alternative strategy in the early 1970s and versions of Smalltalk (Goldberg and Robson, 1983) were in existence in the 1970s, it is only since the late 1980s that this alternative, object-oriented design has been widely adopted.

These two design strategies may be summarized as follows:

(1)   *Functional design*   The system is designed from a functional viewpoint, starting with a high-level view and progressively refining this into a more detailed design. The system state is centralized and shared between the functions operating on that state. This strategy is exemplified by Structured Design (Constantine and Yourdon, 1979), SSADM (Cutts, 1988; Weaver, 1993) and step-wise refinement (Wirth, 1971, 1976). Methods such as Jackson Structured Programming (Jackson, 1975) and the Warnier–Orr method (Warnier, 1977) are techniques of functional decomposition where the structure of the data is used to determine the functional structure used to process that data.

(2)   *Object-oriented design*   The system is viewed as a collection of objects rather than as functions. Object-oriented design is based on the idea of information hiding (Parnas, 1972) and has been described by Meyer (1988), Booch (1994), Jacobsen *et al.* (1993) and many others. JSD (Jackson, 1983) is a design method that falls somewhere between function-oriented and object-oriented design.

In an object-oriented design, the system state is decentralized and each object manages its own state information. Objects have a set of attributes defining their state and operations which act on these attributes. Objects are usually members of an object class whose definition defines attributes and operations of class members. These may be inherited from one or more super-classes so that a class definition need only set out the differences between that class and its super-classes. Conceptually, objects communicate by exchanging messages; in practice, most object communication is achieved by an object calling a procedure associated with another object.

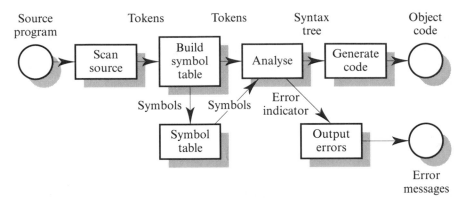

Figure 12.4
Functional view of a
compiler.

To illustrate the difference between functional and object-oriented approaches to software design, consider the structure of a compiler. It may be viewed as a set of functional transformations with information being passed from one processing unit to another (Figure 12.4).

The principal components in the functional view are identified as actions such as 'scan', 'build', 'analyse', 'generate', and so on. An alternative, object-oriented view of the same system is shown in Figure 12.5. The objects manipulated by the compiler are central with operations associated with each object. In this case, the main components are identified as entities such as 'Token stream', 'Symbol table', 'Syntax tree', and so on.

Enthusiasts for particular design techniques sometimes suggest that their favourite technique can be applied for all types of applications. Such assertions are dangerous because they over-simplify the problems of design. After experiment, disappointed users of a particular technique may reject it completely although it may well be applicable in some application domains.

There is no 'best' design strategy which is suitable for all projects and all types of application. Functional and object-oriented approaches are complementary rather than opposing techniques. Pragmatic software engineers select the most appropriate approach for each stage in the design process. In fact, large software systems are such complex entities that different approaches might be used in the design of different parts of the system.

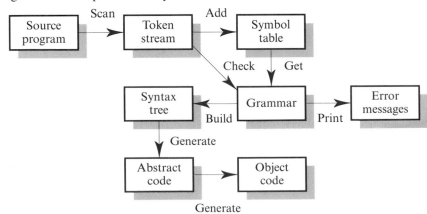

Figure 12.5
Object-oriented view
of a compiler.

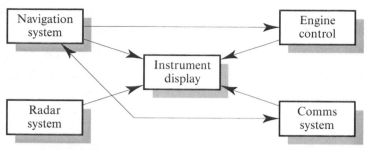

Figure 12.6
Aircraft sub-systems.

To illustrate this, consider the software systems (Figure 12.6) that might be part of a modern civil aircraft. Our natural high-level view of this software is as a set of sub-systems or objects. We use the definite article 'the' to refer to them so we talk of 'the navigation system', 'the engine control system', and so on. At this abstract design level, an object-oriented approach is completely natural.

When the system is examined in more detail, its natural description is as a set of interacting functions rather than objects. Some of these functions might be:

- Display_track (radar sub-system)
- Compensate_for_wind_speed (navigation sub-system)
- Reduce_power (engine control sub-system)
- Indicate_engine_failure (instrument sub-system)
- Lock_onto_frequency (communications sub-system)

This functional view may be taken by the requirements definition. This can be converted to an object-oriented design. However, system validation may be difficult because there is not a simple correspondence between design components and requirements definitions. A single logical function in the requirements definition may be implemented as a sequence of object interactions.

As the system design is further decomposed, an object-oriented view may again become the natural way to view the system. At the detailed design stage, the objects manipulated might be The_engine_status, The_aircraft_position, The_altimeter, The_radio_beacon, and so on. Thus an object-oriented approach to the lower levels of the system design is likely to be effective.

In summary, an object-oriented approach to software design seems to be natural at the highest and lowest levels of system design. In practice, of course, using different approaches to design may require the designer to convert his or her design from one model to another. Many designers are not trained in multiple approaches so prefer to use either object-oriented or functional design.

12.3 Design quality

There is no general agreement on the notion of a 'good' design. Apart from the obvious criterion that a design should correctly implement a specification, a good design might be a design that allows efficient code to be produced; it might be a minimal design where the implementation is as compact as possible; or it might be the most maintainable design.

A maintainable design can be adapted to modify existing functions and add new functionality. The design must therefore be understandable and changes should be local in effect. The design components should be cohesive which means that all parts of the component should have a close logical relationship. They should be loosely coupled which means that they should not be tightly integrated. Coupling is a measure of the independence of components. The looser the coupling, the easier it is to adapt the design as the effects of change are localized.

Design quality metrics may be used to assess if a design is a 'good' design. Proposed metrics have mostly been developed in conjunction with functional approaches such as Yourdon's structured design. I discuss some of these metrics here with a more general discussion of software measurement in Chapter 30.

Quality characteristics are equally applicable to object-oriented and function-oriented design. Because of the nature of object-oriented designs, which encourages the development of independent components, it is usually easier to achieve maintainable designs as information is concealed within objects.

12.3.1 Cohesion

The cohesion of a component is a measure of the closeness of the relationships between its components. A component should implement a single logical function or should implement a single logical entity. All parts of the component should contribute to this implementation. If the component includes parts that are not directly related to its logical function (for example, if it is a grouping of unrelated operations which are executed at the same time), it has low cohesion.

Cohesion is a desirable characteristic because it means that a unit represents a single part of the problem solution. If it becomes necessary to change the system, that part exists in a single place and everything to do with it is encapsulated in a single unit. There is no need to modify many components if a change has to be made.

Constantine and Yourdon (1979) identify seven levels of cohesion in order of increasing strength:

- *Coincidental cohesion*   The parts of a component are not related but simply bundled into a single component.
- *Logical association*   Components that perform similar functions such as input, error handling and so on are put together in a single component.
- *Temporal cohesion*   All of the components that are activated at a single time, such as start up or shut down, are brought together.
- *Procedural cohesion*   The elements in a component make up a single control sequence.
- *Communicational cohesion*   All of the elements of a component operate on the same input data or produce the same output data.

- *Sequential cohesion*   The output from one element in the component serves as input for some other element.

- *Functional cohesion*   Each part of the component is necessary for the execution of a single function.

These cohesion classes are not strictly defined. Constantine and Yourdon illustrate each by example. It is not always easy to decide under what cohesion category a unit should be classed.

Constantine and Yourdon's method is functional in nature so the most cohesive form of component is the function. However, a high degree of cohesion is also a feature of object-oriented systems. This approach to design leads naturally to components that are cohesive.

A cohesive object is one in which a single entity is represented and all the operations on that entity are included with the object. For example, an object representing a compiler symbol table is cohesive if all necessary functions such as 'Add a symbol', 'Search table' and so on are included with the symbol table object.

Thus, a further class of cohesion might be defined as follows:

- *Object cohesion*   Each operation provides functionality which allows the attributes of the object to be modified, inspected or used as a basis for service provision.

If a class in an object-oriented system inherits attributes and operations from a super-class, the cohesion of that class is reduced. It is no longer possible to consider that object class as a self-contained unit. All super-classes also have to be inspected if the object's functionality is to be completely understood. System browsers that display object classes and their super-classes assist with this process. However, understanding a component that inherits attributes from a number of super-classes can be particularly complex. This is especially true if multiple inheritance is used.

12.3.2 Coupling

Coupling is related to cohesion. It is an indication of the strength of interconnections between the components in a design. Highly coupled systems have strong interconnections, with program units dependent on each other. Loosely coupled systems are made up of components which are independent or almost independent.

As a rule, modules are tightly coupled if they make use of shared variables or if they interchange control information. Constantine and Yourdon call this *common coupling* and *control coupling*. Loose coupling is achieved by ensuring that details of the data representation are held within a component. Its interface with other components should be through a parameter list. If shared information is necessary, the sharing should be limited to those components which need access to the information. Globally accessible information should be avoided wherever possible.

Figures 12.7 and 12.8 illustrate tightly and loosely coupled modules.

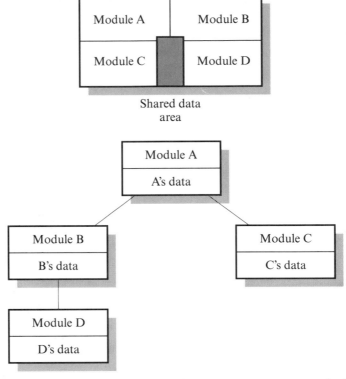

Figure 12.7
Tight coupling where components communicate through a shared data area.

Figure 12.8
Loosely coupled components.

Another form of coupling arises when names are prematurely bound to values. For example, if a program is concerned with tax computations and a tax rate of 30% is encoded as a number in the program, that program is tightly coupled with the tax rate. Changes to the tax rate require changes to the program. If the program reads in the tax rate at run-time, the coupling is looser. The tax rate may be changed without changing the program.

The nature of objects leads to the creation of loosely coupled systems. It is fundamental to object-oriented design that an object's representation is concealed within that object and is not visible to external components. The system does not have a shared state and any object can be replaced by another object with the same interface.

Inheritance in object-oriented systems, however, leads to a different form of coupling. Object classes which inherit attributes and operations are coupled to their super-classes. Changes to the super-class must be made carefully as the changes propagate to all classes which inherit their characteristics.

12.3.3 Understandability

The understandability of a design is important because anyone changing the design must first understand it. There are a number of component characteristics that affect understandability including:

(1) *Cohesion and coupling*   Can the component be understood without reference to other components?

(2) *Naming*   Are the names used in the component meaningful? Meaningful names are names which reflect the names of the real-world entities being modelled by the component.

(3) *Documentation*   Is the component documented so that the mapping between the real-world entities and the component is clear? Is the rationale for that mapping documented?

(4) *Complexity*   How complex are the algorithms used to implement the component?

The term 'complexity' is used here in an intuitive way. High complexity implies many relationships between different parts of the design component and deeply nested if-then-else statements. Complex components are hard to understand. Designers should always try to develop a component design that is as simple as possible.

Most work on design quality measurement (Chapter 30) has concentrated on trying to measure the complexity of a component. This assumes that complexity is directly related to understandability. Complexity affects understandability but there are other factors which influence understandability, such as data organization and the style used to describe the design. Complexity measures can only provide an indicator to the understandability of a component.

Inheritance in an object-oriented design affects its understandability in both positive and negative ways. Inheritance may be used to conceal design details; the design may therefore be presented in an abstract way that is easy to understand. On the other hand, the use of inheritance spreads information around the design. The reader has to look at many different object classes in the inheritance hierarchy, therefore more effort must be made to understand the design.

12.3.4 Adaptability

The adaptability of a design is a general estimate of how easy it is to change the design. Of course, this implies that its components should be loosely coupled. Adaptability also means that the design should be well documented, and that the component documentation should be easily understood. It should be consistent with the implementation. The program implementing the system should be written in a readable way.

An adaptable design should have a high level of traceability. This means that there should be a clear relationship between the different levels in the design. From one design model it should be easy to find related objects in another model. For example, Figure 12.9 shows two object models with an object interacting with other objects and the decomposition of that object into parts.

An adaptable design includes traceability links between different design representations in different documents. These traceability links are established

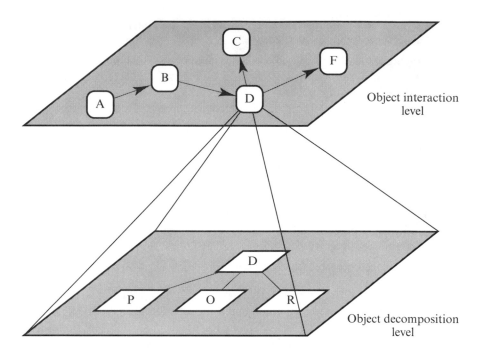

Figure 12.9
Design level
traceability.

between dependent information. When a change is made, all parts of the design and its documentation that are affected by the change can be found. If this is not the case, changes made to a design description may not be propagated to all related descriptions. The design documentation may become inconsistent. Later changes are more difficult to make (the component is less adaptable) because the modifier cannot rely on the design documentation.

For optimum adaptability, a component should be self-contained. Self-contained components are components which have no dependencies on other, external components. However, this is contrary to good practice which suggests that existing components should be reused. The designer must therefore strike a balance between the advantages of reusing components and the loss of component adaptability that this may entail.

Being self-contained is not the same as being loosely coupled. A component may be loosely coupled in that it only cooperates with other components by message passing. However, this loosely coupled component may rely on other components, such as system functions or error handling functions. Adaptations to the component may involve changing parts of the component that rely on external functions. The specification of these external functions must therefore also be understood by the person changing the design.

One of the principal advantages of inheritance in object-oriented systems is that components may be readily adapted. The adaptation mechanism does not rely on modifying existing components; rather, new components are created which inherit the attributes and operations of the original component. Only attributes and operations which need be changed have to be modified.

This simple adaptability is one reason why object-oriented languages are so effective for rapid prototyping. However, the problem with inheritance is that, as more and more changes are made, the inheritance network becomes increasingly complex. Functionality may be replicated at different points in the network and components are harder to understand. Experience of object-oriented programming has shown that the inheritance network must be periodically reviewed and restructured to reduce its complexity and functional duplication.

Further reading

Software Design. This is a general overview of software design covering a number of design methods and containing good general advice about design and the design process. (D. Budgen, 1993, Addison-Wesley.)

'Object-oriented and conventional analysis and design methodologies'. This is an excellent comparison of these approaches, which is written from the point of view of a practitioner rather than a zealot. It identifies the strengths and weaknesses of each approach and discusses the possible evolution of object-oriented methods. (R.G. Fichman and C.F. Kemerer, *IEEE Computer*, October 1992.)

KEY POINTS

■ Design is a creative process. Although methods and guidelines are helpful, judgement and flair are still required to design a software system.

■ The main design activities in the software process are architectural design, system specification, interface design, component design, data structure design and algorithm design.

■ Functional decomposition involves modelling a system as a set of interacting functional units. Object-oriented decomposition models the system as a set of objects where an object is an entity with state and functions to inspect and modify that state.

■ Function-oriented and object-oriented design are complementary rather than opposing design strategies. Different perspectives may be applied at different levels of design abstraction.

■ Cohesion is a measure of how closely the parts of a component relate to each other. Coupling is a measure of the strength of component interconnections. Designers should aim to produce strongly cohesive and weakly coupled designs.

■ Maintainability is an important design quality attribute. Maximizing cohesion and minimizing the coupling between components makes them easier to change. Understandability and adaptability are also important for maintainability.

EXERCISES

12.1   Describe the main activities in the software design process and the outputs of these activities. Using an entity-relation diagram, show possible relationships between the outputs of these activities.

12.2   What are the five components of a design method? Take any method which you know and describe its components. Assess the completeness of the method you have chosen.

12.3   Discuss the differences between object-oriented and function-oriented design strategies.

12.4   Explain why it is important to use different notations to describe software designs.

12.5   Suggest objects and functions that might be components in the design of the following systems:

(a) A cruise control system for a car which maintains a constant speed as set by the driver. The system should adjust the car controls depending on measured road speed.

(b) An automated library catalogue that is queried by users to find which books are available and which books are on loan.

(c) A self-service petrol (gas) pump where the driver sets the pump as required and fills his or her own tank. The amount used is recorded in a booth and the driver may pay by direct credit card debit.

12.6   What do you understand by the terms *cohesion, coupling,* and *adaptability*?

12.7   Explain why maximizing cohesion and minimizing coupling leads to more maintainable systems. What other attributes of a design might influence system maintainability?

12.8   Your company has been asked to design a software system with an estimated 20-year lifetime which will be regularly maintained. This design must be complete as the software is to be implemented in another country, this being a cheaper development option. Your company does not use any design measurements but uses a function-oriented structured method to develop the design and its documentation. Given that the company has limited control over the implementation, is it reasonable to claim that the software has been designed for maintainability?

Architectural Design

Objectives

- To introduce architectural design and to explain its role in the software process.
- To describe a number of different types of architectural model covering system structure, control and modular decomposition.
- To show how the architecture of a system may be modelled in different ways.
- To discuss how domain-specific reference models may be used to compare software architectures.

Contents

Large systems can be decomposed into sub-systems that provide some related set of services. The initial design process of identifying these sub-systems and establishing a framework for sub-system control and communication is called *architectural design*.

Architectural design usually comes before detailed system specification. Ideally, a specification should not include any design information. In practice, this is unrealistic except for very small systems. Architectural decomposition is necessary to structure and organize the specification. A good example of this was introduced in Figure 2.7 which shows the architecture of an air traffic control system. The architectural model is the starting point for the specification of the various parts of the system.

There are a number of parallels between the role of the software system architect and the role of the architect in a building project:

- He or she is the technical interface between the customer and the contractor responsible for building the system.

- A bad architectural design for a building cannot be rescued by good construction; a bad architectural design for a software system cannot be made good by effective implementation.

- There are specialist building architects and there are specialist system architects who concentrate on a small number of different types of system.

- There are schools or styles of building architecture and different models or styles of systems architecture.

However, this analogy should not be taken too far. Buildings are tangible while software is intangible. Building architecture cannot be changed except in detail after construction begins; software architectures can be modified. One of the roles of a building architect is to design a building with a pleasing external appearance. Although software architects may place constraints on the appearance of the software (the user interface), they are normally more concerned with the system structure. Architects usually try to avoid mixing different styles of building architecture. Heterogeneous software architectures, in which different architectural styles are used for different parts of the system, are the norm rather than the exception.

Furthermore, a building architect is usually employed by a customer to design the building and to oversee its construction. By contrast, a systems architect is usually an employee of the software contractor rather than the customer.

There is no generally accepted process model for architectural design. The process depends on application knowledge and on the skill and intuition of the system architect. As part of the process, the following activities are usually necessary:

(1) *System structuring* The system is structured into a number of principal sub-systems where a sub-system is an independent software unit. Communications between sub-systems are identified. This is covered in Section 13.1.

(2)   *Control modelling*   A general model of the control relationships between the parts of the system is established. This is covered in Section 13.2.

(3)   *Modular decomposition*   Each identified sub-system is decomposed into modules. The architect must decide on the types of module and their interconnections. This is covered in Section 13.3.

These activities are usually interleaved in some way. During any of these process stages, it may be necessary to develop the design in more detail to find out if architectural design decisions allow the system to meet its requirements.

The output of the architectural design process is an architectural design document. This consists of a number of graphical representations of the system models along with associated descriptive text. It should describe how the system is structured into sub-systems and how each sub-system is structured into modules.

There is no clear distinction between sub-systems and modules but I find it useful to think of them as follows:

- A *sub-system* is a system in its own right whose operation does not depend on the services provided by other sub-systems. Sub-systems are composed of modules and have defined interfaces which are used for communication with other sub-systems.

- A *module* is a system component that provides one or more services to other modules. It makes use of services provided by other modules. It is not normally considered to be an independent system. Modules are usually composed from a number of other simpler system components.

Architectural design may be based on a particular architectural model or style (Garlan and Shaw, 1993). An awareness of these models, their applications, strengths and weaknesses is important. I describe structural models, control models and modular decomposition models in this chapter.

It is convenient to discuss these models separately. However, most large systems do not follow a single model. Different parts of the system may be designed using different models. Furthermore, in some cases, the system architecture may follow a composite model. This is created by combining different architectural models. Design problems are rarely an exact fit to any one model. Designers must find the most appropriate model then modify it according to the problem requirements. An example of this is shown in Section 13.4 in the discussion of compiler architecture where a repository model is combined with a data-flow model.

The architectural model used affects the performance, robustness, distributability and maintainability of a system. The particular style chosen for an application may therefore depend on the non-functional system requirements. However, in some application domains, generic domain-specific architectures (covered in Section 13.4) have been established. These may be used as a starting point for the architectural design process.

13.1 System structuring

The first phase of the architectural design activity is usually concerned with decomposing a system into a set of interacting sub-systems. At its most abstract level, an architectural design may be depicted as a block diagram in which each box represents a sub-system. Boxes within boxes indicate that the sub-system has itself been decomposed to sub-systems. Arrows mean that data and/or control is passed from sub-system to sub-system in the direction of the arrows. This is illustrated in Figure 13.1.

Figure 13.1 is an architectural design for a packing robot system. This robotic system can pack different kinds of object. It uses a vision sub-system to pick out objects on a conveyor, identifies the type of object, and selects the right kind of packaging from a range of possibilities. It then moves objects from the delivery conveyor to be packaged. Packaged objects are placed on another conveyor.

An architectural block diagram presents an overview of the system structure. It is generally understandable to the various engineers who may be involved in the system development process. Other examples of architectural designs at this level are shown in Figures 2.7, 2.8, 14.9 and 26.4.

More specific models of the structure may be developed which show how sub-systems share data, how they are distributed and how they interface with each other. In this section I discuss three of these standard models, namely a repository model, a client–server model and an abstract machine model.

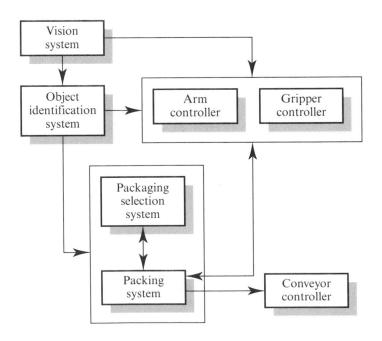

Figure 13.1
Block diagram of a packing robot control system.

13.1.1 The repository model

Sub-systems making up a system must exchange information so that they can work together effectively. There are two ways in which this can be done:

(1)   All shared data is held in a central database that can be accessed by all sub-systems. A system model based on a shared database is sometimes called a *repository model.*

(2)   Each sub-system maintains its own database. Data is interchanged with other sub-systems by passing messages to them.

The majority of systems which use large amounts of data are organized around a shared database or repository. This model is therefore suited to applications where data is generated by one sub-system and used by another. There are many examples of this type of system including command and control systems, management information systems and CAD systems.

Figure 13.2 is an example of a CASE toolset architecture based on a shared repository. The first shared repository for CASE tools was probably developed in the early 1970s by a UK company called ICL to support their operating system development (McGuffin *et al.,* 1979). This model became more widely known when Buxton (1980) made proposals for the Stoneman environment to support the development of systems written in Ada. Since then, many CASE toolsets have been developed around a shared repository. CASE toolsets are discussed in Chapters 26 and 27.

The advantages and disadvantages of a shared repository are as follows:

(1)   It is an efficient way to share large amounts of data. There is no need to transmit data explicitly from one sub-system to another.

(2)   However, sub-systems must agree on the repository data model. Inevitably, this is a compromise between the specific needs of each tool. Performance may be adversely affected by this compromise. It may be difficult or impossible to integrate new sub-systems if their data models do not fit the agreed schema.

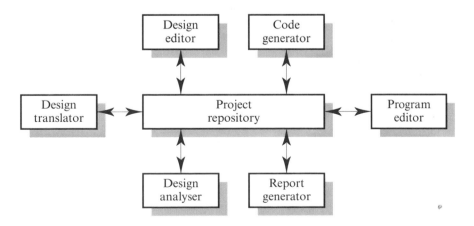

Figure 13.2
The architecture of an integrated CASE toolset.

(3)   Sub-systems which produce data need not be concerned with how that data is used by other sub-systems.

(4)   However, evolution may be difficult as a large volume of information is generated according to an agreed data model. Translating this to a new model will certainly be expensive and may be difficult or even impossible.

(5)   Activities such as backup, security, access control and recovery from error are centralized. They are the responsibility of the repository manager. Tools can focus on their principal function rather than be concerned with these issues.

(6)   However, different sub-systems may have different requirements for security, recovery and backup policies. The repository model forces the same policy on all sub-systems.

(7)   The model of sharing is visible through the repository schema. It is straightforward to integrate new tools given that they are compatible with the agreed data model.

(8)   However, it may be difficult to distribute the repository over a number of machines. Although it is possible to distribute a logically centralized repository, there may be problems with data redundancy and inconsistency.

In the above model, the repository is passive and control is the responsibility of the sub-systems using the repository. An alternative approach has been derived for AI systems that use a 'blackboard' model which triggers sub-systems when particular data becomes available. This is appropriate when the form of the repository data is less well structured. Decisions about which tool to activate can only be made when the data has been analysed. This model is discussed by Nii (1986).

13.1.2 The client–server model

The client–server architectural model is a distributed system model which shows how data and processing is distributed across a range of processors. The major components of this model are:

(1)   A set of stand-alone servers which offer services to other sub-systems. Examples of servers are print servers which offer printing services, file servers which offer file management services and a compile server which offers language translation services.

(2)   A set of clients that call on the services offered by servers. These are normally sub-systems in their own right. There may be several instances of a client program executing concurrently.

(3)   A network which allows the clients to access these services. In principle, this is not really necessary as both the clients and the servers could run on a single machine. In practice, however, this model would not be used in such a situation.

Clients must know the names of the available servers and the services that they provide. However, servers need not know either the identity of clients or how many clients there are. Clients access the services provided by a server through remote procedure calls.

An example of a system built around a client–server model is shown in Figure 13.3. This is a multi-user hypertext system to provide a film and photograph library. In this system, there are several servers which manage and display the different types of media. Video frames need to be transmitted quickly and in synchrony but at relatively low resolution. They may be compressed in a store. Still pictures, however, must be sent at a high resolution. The catalogue must be able to deal with a variety of queries and provide links into the hypertext information systems. The client program is simply an integrated user interface to these services.

The client–server approach can be used to implement a repository-based system where the repository is provided as a system server. Sub-systems accessing the repository are clients. Normally, however, each sub-system manages its own data. Servers and clients exchange data for processing. This can result in performance problems when large amounts of data are exchanged. However, as faster networks are developed, this problem is becoming less significant.

The most important advantage of the client–server model is that distribution is straightforward. Effective use can be made of networked systems with many distributed processors. It is easy to add a new server and integrate it gradually with the rest of the system or to upgrade servers transparently without affecting other parts of the system.

However, changes to existing clients and servers may be required to gain the full benefits of integrating a new server. There is no shared data model, and sub-systems usually organize their data in different ways. This means that specific data models may be established for each server which allow its performance to be optimized. The lack of a shared reference model for data may mean that it is difficult to anticipate problems in integrating data from a new server. Each server must take responsibility for data management activities such as backup, recovery and so on.

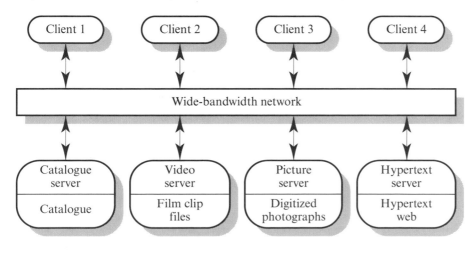

Figure 13.3
The architecture of a film and picture library system.

There is usually no central register of server names and services. Each client must know the services provided by each server. This is not usually a problem if the system is locally distributed. However, with fast, wide-area networking, systems are now being distributed over larger geographical areas. It is sometimes difficult for clients to find out exactly which servers they can use.

13.1.3 The abstract machine model

The abstract machine model of an architecture (sometimes called a layered model) models the interfacing of sub-systems. It organizes a system into a series of layers each of which provides a set of services. Each layer defines an *abstract machine* whose machine language (the services provided by the layer) is used to implement the next level of abstract machine. For example, a common way to implement a language is to define an ideal 'language machine' and compile the language into code for this machine. A further translation step then converts this abstract machine code to real machine code.

A well-known example of this approach is the OSI reference model of network protocols (Zimmermann, 1980) which is discussed in Section 13.4. Another influential example of this approach was proposed by Buxton (1980) who suggested a three-layer model for an Ada programming support environment (APSE). Figure 13.4 has something in common with this and shows how a version management system might be integrated using this abstract machine approach.

The version management system relies on managing versions of objects and provides general configuration management facilities as discussed in Chapter 33. To support these configuration management facilities, it uses an object management system which provides information storage and management services for objects. This system uses a database system to provide basic data storage and services such as transaction management, rollback and recovery, and access control. The database management uses the underlying operating system facilities and filestore in its implementation. This, of course, is layered on top of hardware although this is not shown in Figure 13.4.

The layered approach supports the incremental development of systems. As a layer is developed, some of the services provided by that layer may be made available to users. This architecture is also changeable and portable. If its interface

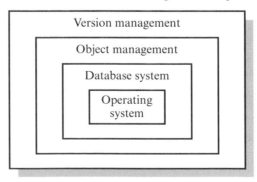

Figure 13.4
Abstract machine
model of a version
management system.

is preserved, a layer can be replaced by another layer. Even when layer interfaces change, only the adjacent layer is affected. As layered systems localize machine dependencies in inner layers, they can be ported to other computers relatively cheaply. Only the inner, machine-dependent layers need be reimplemented.

A disadvantage of the layered approach is that structuring systems in this way can be difficult. Basic facilities, such as file management, which are required by all abstract machines may be provided by inner layers. Services required by the user may therefore require access to an abstract machine that is several levels beneath the outermost layer. This subverts the model, as an outer layer is no longer simply dependent on its immediate predecessor.

Performance can also be a problem because of the multiple levels of command interpretation which are required. If there are many layers, some overhead is always associated with layer management. To avoid these problems, applications may have to communicate directly with inner layers rather than use facilities provided in the abstract machine.

13.2 Control models

The models for structuring a system are concerned with how a system is decomposed into sub-systems. To work as a system, sub-systems must be controlled so that their services are delivered to the right place at the right time. Structural models do not (and should not) include control information. Rather, the architect should organize the sub-systems according to some control model which supplements the structure model that is used. Control models at the architectural level are concerned with the control flow between sub-systems.

Two general approaches to control can be identified:

(1)   *Centralized control*   One sub-system has overall responsibility for control and starts and stops other sub-systems. It may also devolve control to another sub-system but will expect to have this control responsibility returned to it.

(2)   *Event-based control*   Rather than control information being embedded in a sub-system, each sub-system can respond to externally generated events. These events might come from other sub-systems or from the environment of the system.

Control models supplement structural models. All the above structural models may be implemented using either centralized or event-based control.

13.2.1 Centralized control

In a centralized control model, one sub-system is designated as the system controller and has responsibility for managing the execution of other sub-systems. Centralized control models fall into two classes depending on whether the controlled sub-systems execute sequentially or in parallel.

(1)   *The call-return model*   This is the familiar top-down subroutine model where control starts at the top of a subroutine hierarchy and, through sub-routine calls, passes to lower levels in the tree. The subroutine model is only applicable to sequential systems.

(2)   *The manager model*   This is applicable to concurrent systems. One system component is designated as a system manager and controls the starting, stopping and coordination of other system processes. A process is a sub-system or module which can execute in parallel with other processes. A form of this model may also be applied in sequential systems where a management routine calls particular sub-systems depending on the values of some state variables. This is usually implemented as a case statement.

The call-return model is illustrated in Figure 13.5. The main program can call Routines 1, 2 and 3, Routine 1 can call Routines 1.2 or 1.2, Routine 3 can call Routines 3.1 or 3.2, and so on. This is a model of the program dynamics. It is *not* a structural model; there is no need for Routine 1.1, for example, to be part of Routine 1.

This familiar model is embedded in programming languages such as Ada, Pascal and C. Control passes from a higher-level routine in the hierarchy to a lower-level routine. It then returns to the point where the routine was called. The currently executing subroutine has responsibility for control and can either call other routines or return control to its parent. It is poor programming style to return to some other point in the program.

This call-return model may be used at the module level to control functions or objects. Called subroutines in a programming language are naturally functional. However, in many object-oriented systems, operations on objects may be implemented as procedures or functions. When an object requests a service from another object, it does so by calling an associated procedure.

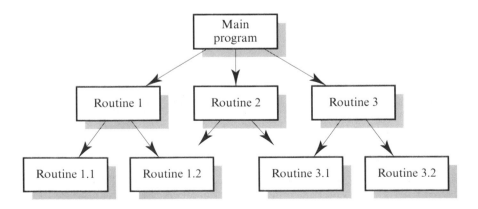

Figure 13.5
The call-return model
of control.

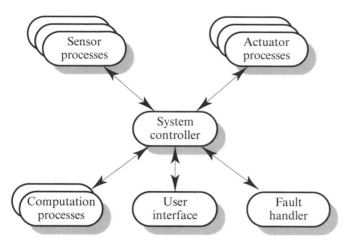

Figure 13.6
A centralized control
model for a real-time
system.

The rigid and restricted nature of this model is both a strength and a weakness. It is a strength because it is relatively simple to analyse control flows and work out how the system will respond to particular inputs. It is a weakness because exceptions to normal operation are awkward to handle. They either require the model to be corrupted or require a good deal of redundant checking code to be incorporated into the system. Exception management is discussed in Chapter 19.

Figure 13.6 is an illustration of a centralized management model of control for a concurrent system. This model is often used in 'soft' real-time systems which do not have very tight time constraints. The central controller manages the execution of a set of processes associated with sensors and actuators. The building monitoring system discussed in Chapter 16 follows this model of control.

The system controller process decides when processes should be started or stopped depending on system state variables. It checks if other processes have produced information to be processed or passes information to them for processing. The controller usually loops continuously, polling sensors and other processes for events or state changes. For this reason, this model is sometimes called an event-loop model.

13.2.2 Event-driven systems

In centralized control models, control decisions are usually determined by the values of some system state variables. By contrast, event-driven control models are driven by externally generated events. The term *event* in this context does not just mean a binary signal. It may be a signal which can take a range of values. The distinction between an event and a simple input is that the timing of the event is outside the control of the process which handles that event. A sub-system may need to access state information to handle these events but this state information does not usually determine the flow of control.

There are a variety of different types of event-driven systems which may be developed. These include spreadsheets where changing the value of a cell causes other cells to be modified, rule-based production systems as used in AI where a condition becoming true causes an action to be triggered, and active objects where changing a value of an object's attribute triggers some actions. Garlan *et al.* (1992) summarize these different approaches.

In this section, I discuss two event-driven control models:

(1)   *Broadcast models*   In these models, an event is, in principle, broadcast to all sub-systems. Any sub-system which is designed to handle that event responds to it.

(2)   *Interrupt-driven models*   These are exclusively used in real-time systems where external interrupts are detected by an interrupt handler. They are then passed to some other component for processing.

Broadcast models are effective in integrating sub-systems distributed across different computers on a network. Interrupt-driven models are used in real-time systems with stringent timing requirements.

In a broadcast model, sub-systems register an interest in specific events. When these events occur, control is transferred to the sub-system that can handle the event. This model is illustrated in Figure 13.7. The distinction between this model and the centralized model shown in Figure 13.6 is that the control policy is not embedded in the event and message handler. Sub-systems decide which events they require and the event and message handler ensures that these events are sent to them.

All events could be broadcast to all sub-systems but this imposes a great deal of processing overhead. More often, the event and message handler maintains a register of sub-systems and the events of interest to them. Sub-systems generate events indicating, perhaps, that some data is available for processing. The event handler detects the events, consults the event register and passes the event to those sub-systems that have declared an interest.

The event handler also usually supports point-to-point communication. A sub-system can explicitly send a message to another sub-system. There have been a number of variations of this model such as the Field environment (Reiss, 1990) and Hewlett-Packard's Softbench (Fromme and Walker, 1993). Both of these have been used to control tool interactions in software engineering environments.

The advantage of this broadcast approach is that evolution is relatively simple. A new sub-system to handle particular classes of events can be integrated by registering its events with the event handler. Any sub-system can activate any other

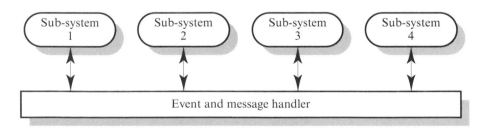

Figure 13.7
A control model based on selective broadcasting.

sub-system without knowing its name or location. The sub-systems can be implemented on distributed machines. This distribution is transparent to other sub-systems.

The disadvantage of this model is that sub-systems don't know if or when events will be handled. When a sub-system generates an event it does not know which other sub-systems have registered an interest in that event. It is quite possible for different sub-systems to register for the same events. This may cause conflicts when the results of handling the event are made available.

Real-time systems are usually event-driven. They sometimes require externally generated events to be handled very quickly. For example, if a real-time system is used to control the safety systems in a car, it must detect a possible crash and, perhaps, inflate an airbag before the driver's head hits the steering wheel. To provide this rapid response to events, an interrupt-driven control model may be used.

An interrupt-driven control model is illustrated in Figure 13.8. There are a known number of interrupt types with a handler defined for each type. Each type of interrupt is associated with the memory location where its handler's address is stored. When an interrupt of a particular type is received, a hardware switch causes control to be transferred immediately to its handler. This interrupt handler may then start or stop other processes in response to the event signalled by the interrupt.

This model should only be used in hard real-time systems where immediate response to some event is necessary. It may be combined with the centralized management model. The central manager handles the normal running of the system with interrupt-based control for emergencies.

The advantage of this approach to control is that it allows very fast responses to events to be implemented. Its disadvantages are that it is complex to program and difficult to validate. It may be impossible to replicate patterns of interrupt timing during the system testing process. It can be difficult to change systems developed using this model if the number of interrupts is limited by the hardware. Once this limit is reached, no other types of event can be handled. This limitation can be

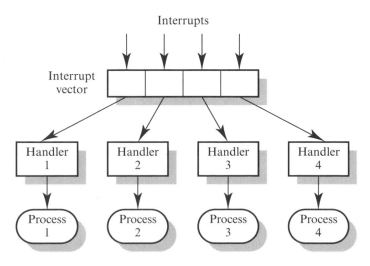

Figure 13.8
An interrupt-driven control model.

circumvented by mapping several types of event onto a single interrupt then leaving the handler to work out which event has occurred. However, timing requirements may limit the use of this option.

13.3 Modular decomposition

After a structural architecture has been designed, another level of decomposition may be part of the architectural design process. This is the decomposition of sub-systems into modules. There is not a rigid distinction between system decomposition and modular decomposition; the models discussed in Section 13.1 could be applied at this level. However, the components in modules are usually smaller than sub-systems and this allows alternative decomposition models to be used.

I consider two models which may be used when decomposing a sub-system into modules:

(1)   *An object-oriented model*   The system is decomposed into a set of communicating objects.

(2)   *A data-flow model*   The system is decomposed into functional modules which accept input data and transform it, in some way, to output data. This is also called a pipeline approach.

In the object-oriented model, modules are objects with private state and defined operations on that state. In the data-flow model, modules are functional transformations. In both cases, modules may be implemented as sequential components or as processes. Chapters 14 and 15 describe how objects and functions may be implemented sequentially and concurrently.

Designers should avoid, if possible, making premature decisions about concurrency. The advantage of avoiding a concurrent system design is that sequential programs are easier to design, implement, verify and test than parallel systems. Time dependencies between processes are hard to formalize, control and verify. It is best to decompose systems into modules then decide during implementation whether these need to execute in sequence or in parallel.

13.3.1 Object models

An object-oriented model of a system architecture structures the system into a set of loosely coupled objects with well-defined interfaces. Objects call on the services offered by other objects. I have already introduced object models in Chapters 6 and 12 and discuss them in more detail in Chapter 14.

Figure 13.9 is an example of an object-oriented architectural model of an invoice processing system. This system can issue invoices to customers, receive payments, issue receipts for these payments and reminders for unpaid invoices. I use

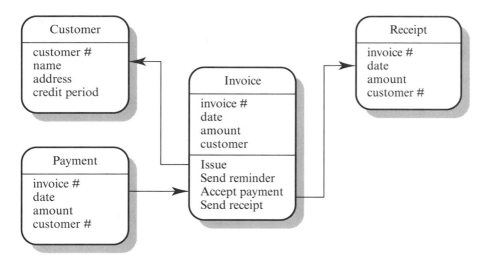

Figure 13.9
An object model of an
invoice processing
system.

the notation introduced in Chapter 6 where object classes have names and a set of associated attributes. Operations, if any, are defined in the lower part of the rounded rectangle representing the object. Arrows indicate that an object uses the attributes or services provided by another object.

An object-oriented decomposition is concerned with object classes, their attributes and operations. When implemented, objects are created from these classes and some control model is used to coordinate object operations. In this particular example, the 'Invoice' class has various associated operations which implement the system functionality. This class makes use of other classes representing customers, payments and receipts.

The advantages of the object-oriented approach are well known. Because objects are loosely coupled, the implementation of objects can be modified without affecting other objects. Objects are often representations of real-world entities so the structure of the system is readily understandable. Because these real-world entities are used in different systems, objects can be reused. Object-oriented programming languages have been developed which provide direct implementations of architectural components.

However, the object-oriented approach does have disadvantages. To use services, objects must explicitly reference the name and the interface of other objects. If an interface change is required to satisfy proposed system changes, the effect of that change on all users of the changed object must be evaluated. While objects may map cleanly to small-scale real-world entities, more complex entities are sometimes difficult to represent using an object model.

13.3.2 Data-flow models

In a data-flow model, functional transformations process their inputs and produce outputs. Data flows from one to another and is transformed as it moves through the sequence. Each processing step is implemented as a transform. Input data flows through these transforms until converted to output. The transformations may execute sequentially or in parallel. The data can be processed by each transform item by item or in a single batch.

When the transformations are represented as separate processes, this model is sometimes called the pipe and filter model after the terminology used in the Unix system. The Unix system provides pipes which act as data conduits and a set of commands which are functional transformations. Systems which conform to this model can be implemented by combining Unix commands using pipes and the control facilities of the Unix shell. The term 'filter' is used to signify that a transformation filters out the data of interest to it from its input for processing.

Variants of this data-flow model have been in use since automatic data processing began. When transformations are sequential with data processed in batches, this architectural model is a batch sequential model. This is a common architecture for some classes of data processing systems such as billing systems which generate large numbers of output reports derived from simple computations on a large number of input records.

An example of this type of system architecture is shown in Figure 13.10. An organization has issued invoices to customers. Once a week, payments which have been made are reconciled with the invoices. For those invoices which have been paid, a receipt is issued. For those invoices which have not been paid within the allowed payment time, a reminder is issued.

This is a model of only part of the invoice processing system; alternative transformations would be used for the issue of invoices. Notice the difference between this and its object-oriented equivalent discussed in the previous section. The object model is more abstract as it does not include information about the sequence of operations.

The advantages of this architecture are:

(1)   It supports the reuse of transformations.

(2)   It is intuitive in that many people think of their work in terms of input and output processing.

(3)   Evolving the system by adding new transformations is usually straightforward.

(4)   It is simple to implement either as a concurrent or a sequential system.

Figure 13.10
A data-flow model of an invoice processing system.

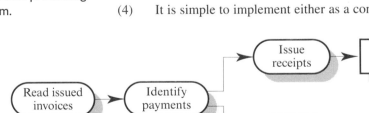

The principal disadvantage of the model stems from the need for a common format for data transfer which can be recognized by all transformations. Each transformation must either agree with its communicating transformations on the format of the data that will be processed or a standard format for all data communicated must be imposed. The latter approach is the only feasible approach when transformations are stand-alone and reusable. In Unix, the standard format is simply a character sequence. Each transformation must parse its input and unparse its output to the agreed form. This increases system overhead and may mean that it is impossible to integrate transformations which use incompatible data formats.

Interactive systems are difficult to write using the data-flow model because of the need for a stream of data to be processed. While simple textual input and output can be modelled in this way, graphical user interfaces have more complex I/O formats and control which is based on events such as mouse clicks or menu selections. It is difficult to translate this into a form compatible with the data-flow model.

13.4 Domain-specific architectures

The above architectural models are general models. They can be applied to many different classes of application. As well as these general models, architectural models which are specific to a particular application domain may also be used. Although instances of these systems differ in detail, the common architectural structure can be reused when developing new systems. These architectural models are called *domain-specific architectures*.

There are two types of domain-specific architectural model:

(1) *Generic models* which are abstractions from a number of real systems. They encapsulate the principal characteristics of these systems. The class of systems modelled using a generic model is usually quite restricted. For example, in real-time systems, there might be generic architectural models of different system types such as data collection systems, monitoring systems, and so on.

(2) *Reference models* which are more abstract and describe a larger class of systems. They provide a means of informing system architects about that class of system. For example, in Chapter 27, I describe a reference model for CASE environments.

There is not, of course, a rigid distinction between these different types of model. Generic models can also sometimes serve as reference models. I make a distinction between them here because generic models may be reused directly in a design. Reference models are normally used to communicate domain concepts and compare possible architectures.

This reflects the derivation of these models. Generic models are usually derived 'bottom-up' from existing systems whereas reference models are derived 'top-down'. They are abstract system representations. Reference models do not necessarily reflect the actual architecture of existing systems in the domain.

13.4.1 Generic models

Perhaps the best-known example of a generic architectural model is a compiler model. Thousands of compilers have been written. It is now generally agreed that compilers should include the following modules:

(1)   A lexical analyser which takes input language tokens and converts them to some internal form.

(2)   A symbol table that is built by the lexical analyser, which holds information about the names and types used in the program.

(3)   A syntax analyser which checks the syntax of the language being compiled using a defined grammar and builds a syntax tree.

(4)   A syntax tree which is an internal structure representing the program being compiled.

(5)   A semantic analyser which uses information from the syntax tree and the symbol table to check the semantic correctness of the input program.

(6)   A code generator which 'walks' the syntax tree and generates machine code.

Other components might also be included which transform the syntax tree to improve efficiency and remove redundancy from the generated machine code.

The components which make up a compiler can be organized according to different architectural models. As Garlan and Shaw (1993) point out, compilers can be implemented using a composite model. A data-flow architecture may be used with the symbol table acting as a repository for shared data. The phases of lexical, syntactic and semantic analysis are organized sequentially as shown in Figure 13.11.

This model is still widely used. It is effective in batch environments where programs are compiled and executed without user interaction. However, it is less effective when the compiler is to be integrated with other language processing tools such as a structured editing system, an interactive debugger, a program prettyprinter, and so on. The generic system components can then be organized in a repository-based model as shown in Figure 13.12.

In this model of a compiler, the symbol table and syntax tree act as a central information repository. Tools or tool fragments communicate through it. Other information such as the grammar definition and the definition of the output format for the program have been taken out of the tools and into the repository.

Figure 13.11
A data-flow model of a compiler.

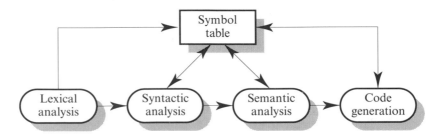

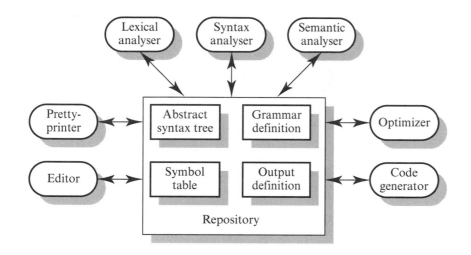

Figure 13.12
The repository model
of a language
processing system.

There are, in practice, a very large number of domain-specific architectural models. Some further examples of generic architectures for real-time systems are illustrated in Chapter 16. However, relatively few generic, domain-specific models have been published. Organizations that develop these models see them as valuable intellectual property which they need for future system development.

13.4.2 Reference architectures

Generic architectural models reflect the architecture of existing systems. In contrast, reference models are usually derived from a study of the application domain. They represent an idealized architecture which includes all the features that systems might incorporate.

Reference architectures may be used as a basis for system implementation. This was the intention behind the OSI reference model (Zimmermann, 1980) for open systems interconnection. The model was intended as a standard. If a system conformed to the model, it should be able to communicate with other conformant systems. Thus, a stock control system in a supermarket which followed the OSI model could exchange data directly with the supplier's ordering system.

However, reference models should not only or even primarily be considered as a route to implementation. Rather, their most important function is to serve as a means of comparing different systems in a domain. A reference model provides a vocabulary for comparison. It acts as a standard, against which systems can be evaluated.

The OSI model is a seven-layer model for open systems interconnection; it is illustrated in Figure 13.13. The exact functions of the different layers are not important here. In essence, the lower layers are concerned with physical interconnection, the middle layers with data transfer and the upper layers with the transfer of semantically meaningful application information such as standardized documents and so on.

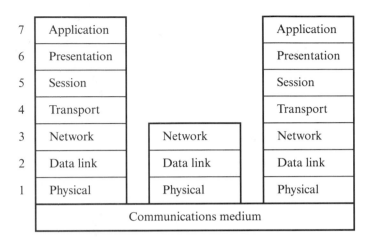

Figure 13.13
The OSI reference model architecture.

The designers of the OSI model had the very practical objective of defining a standard so that conformant systems could communicate with each other. Each layer should only depend on the layer beneath it. As technology developed, a layer could be transparently reimplemented without affecting the systems using other layers.

In practice, however, the problems of the layered approach to architectural modelling have compromised this objective. Because of the vast differences between networks, simple interconnection may be impossible. Although the functional characteristics of each layer are well defined, the non-functional characteristics are not defined. System developers have to implement their own higher-level facilities and skip layers in the model. Alternatively, they have to design non-standard features to improve system performance.

Consequently, the transparent replacement of a layer in the model is hardly ever possible. However, this does not negate the usefulness of the model as it provides a basis for the abstract structuring and systematic implementation of communications between systems.

Other reference models which have been proposed include a model for CASE environments (ECMA, 1991) and a model for software factories (Rockwell and Gera, 1993).

Further reading

'An introduction to software architecture'. This is an excellent paper which was derived from a course in software architectures. It discusses the development of architectural design and a number of architectural models (called styles, here). (D. Garlan and M. Shaw, *Advances in Software Engineering and Knowledge Engineering*, **1**, World Scientific Publishing, 1993.)

'Using tool abstraction to compose systems'. This paper discusses a number of different event models and proposes an approach to architectural design based on the composition of tool fragments. (D. Garlan, G. Kaiser and D. Notkin, *IEEE Computer*, **25** (6), June 1992.)

'Abstractions for Software Architectures and Tools to support them'. In my opinion, this is the best paper in a rather disappointing special issue of this journal on software architectures (M. Shaw, *et al.*, *IEEE Transactions on Software Engineering*, **21** (4), April 1995).

KEY POINTS

- The software architect is responsible for deriving an overall structural model of the system which identifies sub-systems and their relationships. Architects may also design a control model for the system and decompose sub-systems into modules.

- Large systems rarely conform to a single architectural model. They are heterogeneous and incorporate different models at different levels of abstraction.

- System decomposition models include repository models, client–server models and abstract machine models. Repository models share data through a common store. Client–server models usually distribute data. Abstract machine models are layered with each layer implemented using the facilities provided by its foundation layer.

- Examples of control models include centralized control and event models. In centralized models, control decisions are made depending on the system state; in event models external events control the system.

- Examples of modular decomposition models include data-flow and object models. Data-flow models are functional, whereas object models are based on loosely coupled entities which maintain their own state and operations.

- Domain-specific architectural models are abstractions over an application domain. Domain-specific models may be generic models which are constructed bottom-up from existing systems, or reference models which are idealized, abstract models of the domain.

EXERCISES

13.1 Explain why it may be necessary to design the system architecture before the specifications are written.

13.2 Construct a table showing the advantages and disadvantages of the different structural models discussed in this chapter.

13.3 Giving reasons for your answer, suggest an appropriate structural model for the following systems:

(a) an automated ticket issuing system used by passengers at a railway station;

(b) a computer-controlled video conferencing system which allows video, audio and computer data to be visible to several participants at the same time;

(c) a robot floor cleaner which is intended to clean relatively clear spaces such as corridors. The cleaner must be able to sense walls and other obstructions.

13.4 Design an architecture for the above systems based on your choice of model. Make reasonable assumptions about the system requirements.

13.5 Explain why a call-return model of control is not usually suitable for real-time systems which control some process.

13.6 Giving reasons for your answer, suggest an appropriate control model for the following systems:

(a) a batch processing system which takes information about hours worked and pay rates and prints salary slips and bank credit transfer information;

(b) a set of software tools which are produced by different vendors but which must work together;

(c) a television controller which responds to signals from a remote control unit.

13.7 Distributed applications which execute on a number of processors connected by a high-speed network are now common. Application designers must take distributability into account when proposing a system architecture. Discuss their advantages and disadvantages as far as distributability is concerned of the data-flow model and the object model. Assume that both single machine and distributed versions of an application are required.

13.8 You are given two integrated CASE toolsets and are asked to compare them. Explain how you could use a reference model to make this comparison. You will find it helpful to read Chapter 27, which describes a software engineering environment reference model, before tackling this question.

13.9 Should there be a separate profession of 'software architect' whose role is to work independently with a customer to design a software architecture? This would then be implemented by some software company. What might be the difficulties of establishing such a profession?

Object-oriented Design

Objectives

- To explain how a software design may be represented as a set of interacting objects which manage their own state and which encapsulate state operations.
- To develop an example which illustrates the process of object-oriented design.
- To introduce various models which may be used to describe an object-oriented design.
- To explain how objects can be implemented as concurrent processes.

Contents

Object-oriented design is a design strategy based on information hiding. It differs from the functional approach to design in that it views a software system as a set of interacting objects, with their own private state, rather than as a set of functions that share a global state (Figure 14.1). Since the late 1980s, object-oriented design has been widely publicized and adopted. Outside the business systems domain, it is perhaps the predominant design strategy for new software systems.

The characteristics of an object-oriented design (OOD) are:

(1)   Objects are abstractions of real-world or system entities which are responsible for managing their own private state and offering services to other objects.

(2)   Objects are independent entities that may readily be changed because state and representation information is held within the object. Changes to the representation may be made without reference to other system objects.

(3)   System functionality is expressed in terms of operations or services associated with each object.

(4)   Shared data areas are eliminated. Objects communicate by calling on services offered by other objects rather than sharing variables. This reduces overall system coupling. There is no possibility of unexpected modifications to shared information.

(5)   Objects may be distributed and may execute either sequentially or in parallel. Decisions on parallelism need not be taken at an early stage of the design process.

Object-oriented systems are easier to maintain as the objects are independent. They may be understood and modified as stand-alone entities. Changing the implementation of an object or adding services should not affect other system objects. Furthermore, there is often a clear mapping between real-world entities (such as hardware components) and their controlling objects in the system. This improves the understandability and hence the maintainability of the design.

As I discuss in Chapter 20, objects are appropriate reusable components because they are independent encapsulations of state and operations. Designs can be developed using objects that have been created in previous designs. This reduces

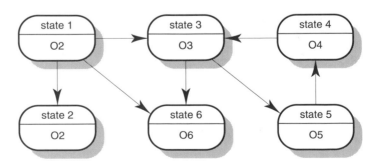

Figure 14.1
The structure of an object-oriented design.

design, programming and validation costs. It may also lead to the use of standard objects (hence improving design understandability) and reduces the risks involved in software development.

Object-oriented analysis, design and programming are all part of *object-oriented development* whereby an object-oriented strategy is used throughout the development process. However, they are not the same thing:

- *Object-oriented analysis* is concerned with developing an object-oriented model of the application domain. The identified objects may or may not map directly into system objects.

- *Object-oriented design* is concerned with developing an object-oriented model of a software system to implement the identified requirements. These requirements may or may not be structured around objects in the problem domain.

- *Object-oriented programming* is concerned with realizing a software design using an object-oriented programming language. An object-oriented programming language supports the direct implementation of objects and provides object classes and inheritance.

Object-oriented programming languages such as C++ or languages with data encapsulation capabilities (Ada or Modula-2) make an object-oriented design easier to implement. However, an object-oriented design can also be implemented in languages such as C or Pascal which do not have such features. A standard programming style can be used in these languages to represent objects.

Many object-oriented design methods have been proposed (Coad and Yourdon, 1990; Robinson, 1992; Jacobson *et al.,* 1993; Booch, 1994; Graham, 1994). I don't describe any particular design method here but cover object-oriented concepts and design activities that are common to the object-oriented design process which is proposed by all methods. These include:

- the identification of the objects in the system along with their attributes and operations;

- the organization of objects into an aggregation hierarchy which shows how objects are 'part-of' other objects;

- the construction of dynamic 'object-use' diagrams that show which object services are used by other objects;

- the specification of object interfaces.

The nature of the design process is such that all of the above activities are intermingled rather than carried out in sequence, so I do not suggest any process model for object-oriented design. The services or operations associated with the objects must also be designed in detail. However, this implementation should not affect other parts of the design so this is usually seen as an implementation rather than a design task. The detailed design of operations may use a program description language as discussed in Chapter 15 to show the control structure of the system. I do not cover the detailed design of objects and object operations here.

The details of objects are shown here in two programming languages, namely Ada and C++. Ada is a more secure and less error-prone language than C++, so is often chosen as the implementation language for very large-scale software projects. C++ was originally designed as an object-oriented language whereas Ada was developed with abstract data types rather than object classes. The most recent revision of Ada (Ada 95) has modified the language to include object-oriented concepts such as inheritance.

14.1 Objects, object classes and inheritance

The terms *object* and *object-oriented* are now widely used buzzwords. They are applied to different types of entity, design methods, systems and programming languages. Anything that is not purely functional has been termed 'object-oriented'.

My definition of an object and an object class is:

> An object is an entity that has a state and a defined set of operations which operate on that state. The state is represented as a set of object attributes. The operations associated with the object provide services to other objects (clients) which request these services when some computation is required. Objects are created according to some object class definition. An object class definition serves as a template for objects. It includes declarations of all the attributes and services which should be associated with an object of that class.

An object-oriented design process is normally concerned with designing object classes. When the design is implemented, the required objects are created using these class definitions.

Objects communicate by requesting services from other objects and, if necessary, exchange information required for service provision. In some distributed systems, object communications are implemented directly as text messages which are exchanged by objects. The receiving object parses the message, identifies the service and the associated data and carries out the requested service.

More commonly, however, object communication is implemented as procedure or function calls. The name of service required corresponds to the name of the object operation providing the service. The copies of information needed to execute the service and the results of service execution are passed as parameters. Some examples of this form of communication are:

```
- - Call the printing service associated with lists to print the list L1
List.Print (L1)
- - Call the service associated with integer arrays which finds the
- - maximum value of array XX. Return the result in Max_value
IntArray.Max ( XX, Max_value]
```

When service requests are implemented as procedure calls, communication between objects is synchronous. However, requests may also be implemented as calls to entries associated with a concurrent process, so communication may be asynchronous. An object-oriented design may therefore be realized as a parallel or as a sequential program.

Objects that are implemented as instances of abstract data types are passive objects. All state changes are implemented by operations defined in the object interface. Active objects are objects which can change their own state without an explicit call to an interface operation.

The notation used here to denote objects was introduced in Chapter 6. An object class is represented as a named round-edged rectangle with two sections. The object attributes are listed in the top section. The services provided by the object are set out in the bottom section. Figure 14.2 illustrates this notation using an object class which models an electronic mail message.

The attributes of Mail message are the identifiers of the sender and receiver, the addresses of the sender and receiver, the date the message was sent, the date it was received, its route from sender to receiver, a message title and the text of the message itself. Operations are Send, Present (display the message on a user's terminal), File and Print.

It is good design practice to hide information so the representation of the object should not be accessible from outside the object. When the object design is developed, the attributes should be accessed and modified through appropriate access and update functions. This allows the representation to be changed at a later stage in the design or implementation process without affecting other objects.

Figures 14.3 and 14.4 show how this object class may be defined as an Ada abstract data type and as a C++ class. I do not have space to go into the differences between Ada and C++. However, it is important to understand that the Ada design here is not truly object-oriented. Rather, it defines an abstract data type. The C++

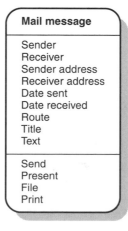

Figure 14.2
A mail message object class.

```
package Mail is
    type MESSAGE is private ;
    -- Object operations
    procedure Send (M: MESSAGE; Dest: DESTINATION) ;
    procedure Present (M: MESSAGE; D: DEVICE) ;
    procedure File (M: MESSAGE; File: FILENAME) ;
    procedure Print (M: MESSAGE; D: DEVICE) ;
    -- Sender attribute
    function Sender (M: MESSAGE) return MAIL_USER ;
    procedure Put_sender (M: in out MESSAGE; Sender: MAIL_USER) ;
    -- Receiver attribute
    function Receiver (M: MESSAGE) return MAIL_USER ;
    procedure Put_receiver (M: in out MESSAGE; Receiver: MAIL_USER) ;
    -- Access functions and Put operations for other attributes here
    ...
private
    -- The representation of the attributes is concealed by
    -- representing it as an access type. Details are inside the package body
    type MAIL_MESSAGE_RECORD ;
    type MESSAGE is access MAIL_MESSAGE_RECORD ;
end Mail ;
```

Figure 14.3
The interface design, in Ada, of an object class representing a mail message.

```
class Mail_message {
public:
    Mail_message () ;
    ~Mail_message () ;
    void Send () ;
    void File (char* filename) ;
    void Print (char* printer_name) ;
    void Present (char* device_name) ;
    char* Sender () ;
    void Put_sender (char* S) ;
    char* Receiver () ;
    void Put_receiver (char* R) ;
    // Other access and inspection functions here
private:
    char* sender, receiver, senderaddr, receiveraddr ;
    char* title, text ;
    date datesent, datereceived ;
} ;
```

Figure 14.4
The interface design, in C++, of an object class representing a mail message.

example, by contrast defines an object class. In Ada, entities are defined to be of some abstract type but the objects themselves do not have associated operations. These are associated with the type. In C++, the operations are associated with the declared object.

```
                              Ada

with Mail ;
—— define an object of type mail message by declaring a
—— variable of the specified abstract data type
Office_memo: Mail.MESSAGE ;
—— Call an operation on mail message
Mail.Print (Office_memo, Laser_printer) ;


                              C++

// define an object of type Mail_message
Mail_message Office_memo ;
// Call an operation on mail message
Office_memo.Print ("Laser_printer") ;
```

Figure 14.5
Object definition in
Ada and C++.

This leads to a different style of operation declaration. In Ada, the entity on which the operation acts is usually passed as a parameter to the operation. In C++, the entity is not passed as a parameter since its value can be accessed directly in the object.

In both Ada and C++, object names and associated operation or attribute names are separated by a dot. Objects are defined using the standard language declaration features. Figure 14.5 shows how objects are created using the above object class definitions and how operations associated with objects are activated. Notice how in Ada, the operation is associated with the package and the object is passed as a parameter. In C++, the operation is associated with the object so the name of the object rather than the name of the type is used.

14.1.1 Inheritance

When objects are created they inherit the attributes and operations of their class. Object classes are themselves objects so inherit their attributes from some other class (their 'super-class'). Inheritance trees (class hierarchies) show how objects inherit attributes and services from their super-classes.

In the class hierarchy shown in Figure 14.6, programmers are employees and inherit attributes from class Employee. The class Programmer then adds particular attributes specific to programmers such as the current project and known programming languages. Project managers are both managers and employees. They inherit their attributes from the class Manager which has already inherited attributes from Employee.

An inheritance hierarchy or tree is created when a class inherits its attributes and services from a single super-class. Multiple inheritance means that attributes are inherited from more than one immediate super-class. An inheritance network rather than an inheritance tree is created (Figure 14.7). When a class has multiple parents,

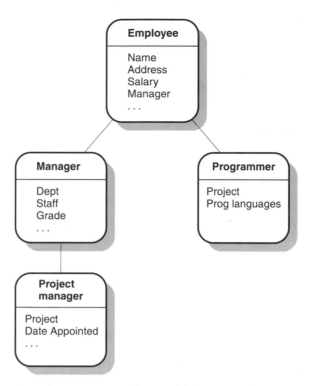

Figure 14.6
A class hierarchy
showing attribute
inheritance.

its attributes and services are created by combining the attributes and services from all of its super-classes.

Figure 14.7 shows that a programmer has been appointed as a project manager. The arrows show the direction of inheritance. The class Software project manager inherits its attributes from two super-classes Manager and Programmer. This diagram also illustrates one of the problems of multiple inheritance where the same name (Project) is inherited from different super-classes. The usual solution to name clashes is to rename attributes and operations as shown in Figure 14.7.

Constructing a consistent inheritance hierarchy is not simple. Good object-oriented programmers regularly review and rewrite their inheritance hierarchy. They remove duplicate attributes that have been introduced on different branches of the hierarchy. They check that attributes and operations are provided at the right level of abstraction.

Inheritance has two clear roles in an object-oriented development process:

(1)   It is an abstraction mechanism which can be used to classify entities in system models as discussed in Chapter 6.

(2)   It is a reuse mechanism for program code and allows rapid changes to be made to an object without side-effects that corrupt other parts of the system. This is discussed in Chapter 20.

Inheritance is clearly valuable for object-oriented modelling and object-oriented programming. However, if inheritance hierarchies are developed during the design

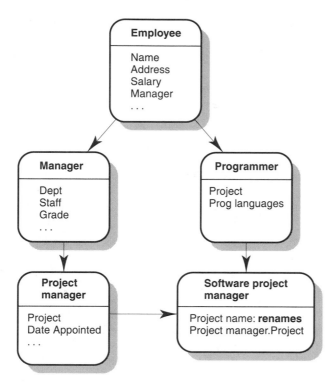

Figure 14.7
A class network showing multiple inheritance.

process, these may confuse rather than clarify the design. There are three reasons for this:

(1)   Object classes are not self-contained. They cannot be understood on their own without reference to any super-classes.

(2)   Designers have a tendency to reuse the inheritance graph created during analysis. This may lead to inefficient designs as this graph reflects the application domain rather than the system to be developed.

(3)   The needs of analysis, design and implementation are all different. While the inheritance graphs may be similar, they are rarely identical. This is likely to confuse future maintainers of the system.

There is not a consensus among designers on this issue. My opinion is that there is not a strong case for developing inheritance graphs during design so I have not included them in the examples in this chapter.

14.2 Object identification

The main problem in object-oriented design is identifying the objects that make up the system, their attributes and associated operations. There is no simple formula which allows objects to be identified. Designers must use their skill and experience in this task.

There have been various proposals made about how to identify objects:

- Use a grammatical analysis of a natural language description of a system. Objects and attributes are nouns, operations or services are verbs (Abbott, 1983).

- Use tangible entities (things) in the application domain such as aircraft, roles such as manager, events such as request, interactions such as meetings, locations such as offices, organizational units such as companies, and so on (Shlaer and Mellor, 1988; Coad and Yourdon, 1990; Wirfs-Brock *et al.,* 1990).

- Use a behavioural approach in which the designer first understands the overall behaviour of the system. The various behaviours are assigned to different parts of the system and an understanding derived of who initiates and participates in these behaviours. Participants who play significant roles are recognized as objects (Rubin and Goldberg, 1992).

- Use a scenario-based analysis where various scenarios of system use are identified and analysed in turn. As each scenario is analysed, the team responsible for the analysis must identify the required objects, attributes and operations (Jacobsen *et al.,* 1993). A method of analysis called CRC cards whereby analysts and designers take on the role of objects is effective in supporting this scenario-based approach (Beck and Cunningham, 1989).

These approaches are not exclusive. Good designers may use all of them when trying to identify objects. The methods are informal and different designers will discover different objects when applying them. Nevertheless, they are a useful way to start identifying objects.

Very few object-oriented methods make specific recommendations on object identification. One method which uses grammatical analysis to identify objects is the HOOD method (Robinson, 1992). The basis of this approach is that the nouns in a system description identify objects and the verbs (actions) identify operations or object services.

To illustrate this process, consider the following short description of a system which acts as an office information retrieval system. This system is used as a design example in the next chapter where an object-oriented design is compared to a functional design.

> The Office Information **Retrieval System** (OIRS) can *file* **documents** under some name in one or more **indexes**, *retrieve* **documents**, *display* and *maintain* **document** indexes, *archive* **documents** and *destroy* **documents**. The **system** is activated by a *request* from the **user** and always *returns* a message to the **user** indicating the success or failure of the request.

The language analysis approach starts by identifying key nouns (emboldened) and verbs (italicized) in the system description. This suggests that the objects and associated operations should be as shown in Figure 14.8. Of course, the above description is incomplete. More attributes and services should be added as further information about the system becomes available.

The Retrieval system object does not have identified services which can be called by other objects. The reason for this is that it acts as a controller whose main function is the coordination of other objects. It identifies user inputs and calls for services from other objects depending on that input. It does not provide services to other objects.

The problem with a natural language description is that there may be different ways to reference the same object. Designers cannot simply assume that nouns are always objects and verbs are their associated operations.

For example, in the last sentence of the above description, the objects are the retrieval system (simply referenced as the system) and the user. The operations on the system object are retrieval system operations Get user request and Return status message. However, the word 'request' is used as a noun in that sentence. This might imply that it is an object rather than an operation. In fact, because the sentence is written in the passive voice, request is actually an action associated with the User object.

Natural language descriptions are usually written on the assumption that the reader has a 'common sense' understanding of the application domain. The description leaves out 'obvious' knowledge that the index itself must have a name, that documents have owners, and so forth. Therefore, not all objects, attributes and services are explicitly mentioned in the description. If designers do not have sufficient domain knowledge, it is likely that they will make design errors and leave out important system services.

In practice, many different sources of knowledge have to be used to discover objects and object classes. Objects and operations which are initially identified from the informal system description can be a starting point for the design. Further information from application domain knowledge or scenario analysis may then be used to refine and extend the initial objects. This information may be collected from requirements documents, from discussions with users and from an analysis of existing systems.

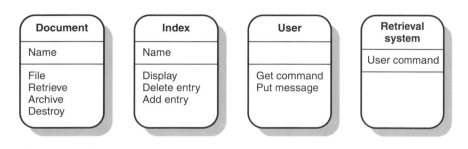

Figure 14.8
Preliminary object identification from a natural language description.

14.3 An object-oriented design example

Examples of software design are inevitably artificial. Designs for large software systems involve creating hundreds of pages of documentation. However, in a book, only a few pages are available to convey the essence of the design. Readers must take on trust assertions about the advantages of object-oriented design. It is only when you practise this approach in a real, evolving system design that the advantages become clear.

The example I use to illustrate object-oriented design is a system for creating weather maps using automatically collected meteorological data. I cannot show the complete design. However, I have tried to convey the essence of OOD by focusing on a self-contained part of this system (automated data collection).

The requirements for such a weather mapping system would take up many pages. However, an outline design can be developed from a relatively brief system description:

> A weather data collection system is required to generate weather maps on a regular basis using data collected from remote, unattended weather stations. Each weather station collects meteorological data over a period and produces summaries of that data. On request, it sends the collected, processed information to an area computer for further processing. Data on the air temperature, the ground temperature, the wind speed and direction, the barometric pressure and the amount of rainfall is collected by each weather station.
>
> Weather stations transmit their data to the area computer in response to a request from that machine. The area computer collates the collected data and integrates it with reports from other sources such as satellites and ships. Using a digitized map database it then generates a set of local weather maps.

Figure 14.9 is a block diagram of the system architecture. For simplicity, I ignore satellite and manually collected data and consider only the weather station information in the rest of this example.

From the outline description of the system and the architectural diagram, four main abstract objects can be identified:

(1)   A Weather station which collects information and communicates it for processing.

(2)   A Map database which provides templates of maps for weather data to be added. Assume this is a database of survey information that allows maps of the area to be generated at various scales.

(3)   A Map which is displayed and printed. Assume that a weather map is an outline of an area with superimposed weather information.

(4)   Weather data which is used to produce the map and which is archived.

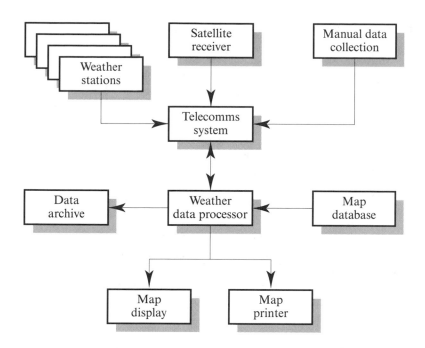

Figure 14.9
The architecture of
the weather mapping
system.

A description of the automatic weather station may be used to identify its objects:

> A weather station is a package of software-controlled instruments which collects data, performs some data processing and transmits this data for further processing. The instruments include air and ground thermometers, an anemometer, a wind vane, a barometer and a rain gauge. Data is collected every five minutes. When a command is issued to transmit the weather data, the weather station processes and summarizes the collected data. The summarized data is transmitted to the mapping computer when a request is received.

From this description, it is possible to identify some objects, attributes and operations of a weather station:

(1)   Objects are air and ground thermometers, anemometer, wind vane, barometer and rain gauge. The instrument package may also be an object in its own right but this is not clear at this stage.

(2)   Operations are collect data, perform data processing, transmit data.

(3)   Attributes are 'summarized data'.

At this stage in the design process, knowledge of the application domain may be used to identify further objects and services. In this case, we know that weather stations are often located in remote places. They include various instruments which sometimes go wrong. Instrument failures should be reported automatically. This implies that attributes and operations to check the correct functioning of the instruments are necessary.

We also know that there are many remote weather stations. The description does not explicitly state that weather stations need a unique identifier. However, this is the normal way to distinguish one station from another. Each weather station should therefore have its own identifying attribute.

This leads to the object class description for Weather station shown in Figure 14.10. The state includes a unique station identifier, a weather data record (which will be described in more detail later), and an instrument status record. The weather station includes operations to initialize the state, to transmit weather data, to run a self-checking program, to transmit status information and to shut itself down. There is no explicit operation to collect weather information. Data collection starts automatically when the system is switched on.

The weather station object includes hardware control objects which manage and control its instruments. The term 'hardware control object' means an object which interacts directly with a hardware unit. It is a good design principle to associate a hardware control object with each piece of hardware in the system.

Hardware control objects are used to hide details of the system hardware. Say a hardware unit provides information by writing into a known memory location. The address of that location should be concealed in the hardware control object. If the hardware is redesigned and a different address used, there is no need to change the software which interfaces to the hardware control object.

When each instrument is considered as an object that conceals hardware details, the instrument design and the software design can go on in parallel. During system validation, the hardware can be implemented as a simulator. There is no need to connect the control object to a real instrument.

Figure 14.11 shows a possible design for the hardware control objects in the weather station. The object attributes represent the data collected by the instrument. All objects have a Test operation which runs a self-test program on the instrument. As the rain gauge measures cumulative rainfall, it must have a Reset operation. The barometer object must have a Height attribute as the barometric pressure reading must be adjusted to compensate for the height of the instrument.

Figure 14.10
A model of a class description for a weather station.

Weather station
Identifier
Weather data
Instrument status
Initialize
Transmit data
Transmit status
Self test
Shut down

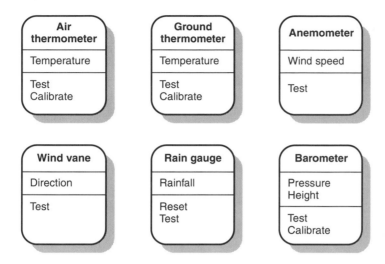

Figure 14.11
Hardware control
objects in the weather
station.

For implementation, these objects could be arranged in an inheritance hierarchy with an object class such as Instrument with a Test operation at the top of the hierarchy. Developing a hierarchy at this stage, however, does not help our understanding of the design.

The lowest-level system objects and high-level objects have now been identified. Object-oriented design is rarely a top-down process. Other objects must now be defined to bridge the gap between the hardware control objects and the weather station object itself. For this stage of the design more information about the data to be collected is required. Assume that the requirements are as follows:

In the course of a collection period (typically one hour, four hours maximum), the following data should be collected by the weather station:

- Air temperature: Maximum, minimum and average temperature
- Ground temperature: Maximum, minimum and average temperature
- Wind speed: Average speed, maximum gust speed
- Pressure: Average barometric pressure
- Rainfall: Cumulative rainfall
- Wind direction: Direction every five minutes

Measurements should be made every five minutes and the above data computed from these measurements.

With this information, the object Weather data, which gathers and stores this information, can be defined. Weather data accumulates the data to be transmitted to the mapping system. The attributes of Weather data are objects which have an associated vector of readings that holds collected data. When a Read operation is called, a reading is made and added to this vector. Figure 14.12 shows Weather data and its associated objects. Air temperature data and Ground temperature data are both instances of the class Temperature data.

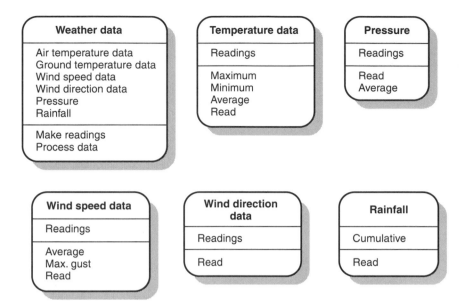

Figure 14.12
Weather data and
associated objects.

Weather data acts as a focus for the data collection. When a set of data is to be collected, Weather station requests Weather data to Make readings. Weather data then calls all lower-level objects to evaluate the hardware control objects. The results are saved in the local Readings attribute.

The operation Process data in Weather data is initiated when a transmission of weather data is required. Process data calls the appropriate operations on lower-level objects (Maximum, Minimum, and so on). Using the raw weather data that is stored in Readings, these lower-level objects compute the information (such as the maximum and minimum temperatures) required by Process data.

So far, the identified objects in the weather station system have been directly related to the collection of data. Other objects are required to handle communications and instrument status checking. The operations concerned with the transmission of weather data and instrument status suggest that there should be an object which handles data communications (Comms). The attribute recording instrument status information suggests that the weather station instruments should be packaged in some way under a single object (Instruments). Data is collected at regular intervals so there is a need for a hardware clock and an associated hardware control object (Clock).

These objects with their attributes and operations are shown in Figure 14.13. Comms is an *active object* as discussed in the following section. It should be implemented as a continuously running process. It monitors the communications hardware for an incoming signal. When a signal is detected, the input command is entered into the input buffer. An internal operation parses this input and calls the appropriate operation in Weather station. When the weather station is switched on, Clock and Comms are started and initialized. The clock is synchronized when data is transmitted to the weather mapping computer.

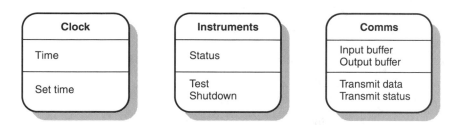

Figure 14.13
Further objects in the
weather station.

14.3.1 Object aggregation

So far, various objects have been identified without considering the static structure of the system. In practice, of course, objects are organized into an aggregation structure that shows how one object is composed of a number of other objects. The aggregation relationship between objects is a static relationship. When implemented, objects which are part of another object may be implemented as sub-objects. Their definition may be included in the definition of the object of which they are a part.

We have already seen an example of an aggregation hierarchy in Chapter 6 (Figure 6.10). Aggregation is shown by using links annotated with a circular blob. Figure 14.14 shows part of a comparable aggregation hierarchy for the weather mapping system. To simplify the diagram, object attribute and operation details have been hidden.

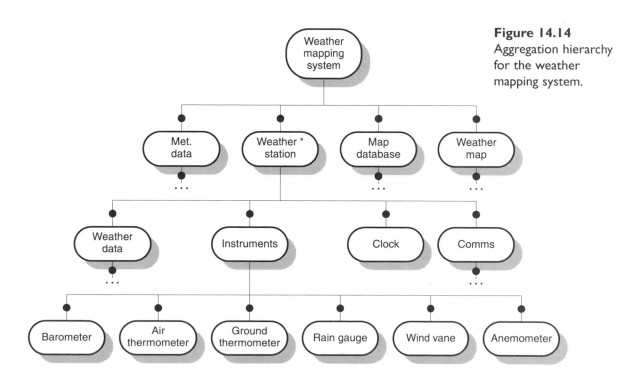

Figure 14.14
Aggregation hierarchy
for the weather
mapping system.

There are too many objects to show the complete hierarchy in a single diagram. The existence of hidden objects is indicated by ellipses (...). The star (*) in Weather station indicates that there are many instances of this object in the system.

14.3.2 Service usage

Figure 14.14 describes the static structure of the system but does not show how objects interact when the system is executing. It is useful to complement an aggregation hierarchy with a dynamic structure diagram. This describes which services are used by objects. We have already seen an example of this type of model in Chapter 6 (Figure 6.11).

For each operation in the weather station, an interaction diagram can be produced showing how a call to that operation triggers requests for service from other objects in the system. Figure 14.15 shows how the Transmit data operation in Weather station results in calls to other objects to compute the required information. The arrowed lines indicate that an object calls on a service provided by another object (at the head of the arrow) with the service names indicated in a box on the line. The service name may be either an operation name or an attribute name. If it is an operation, the object receiving the request should execute that operation. If it is an attribute name, the value of that attribute should be delivered.

The Comms object calls Weather station with a Transmit data command. This causes Weather station to request processed weather data which is collected from other objects. Weather station then calls Comms to transmit the collected data.

Figure 14.15
Object interactions for the Transmit data operation.

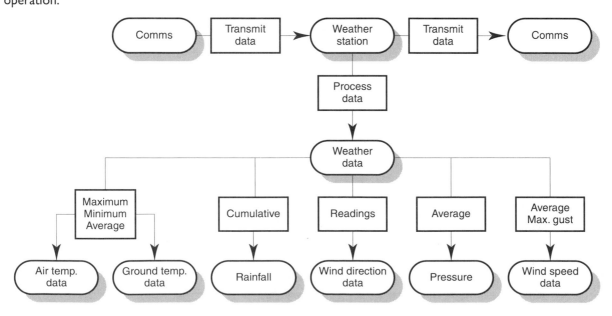

When object interaction charts have been prepared for all operations which are part of Weather station, a composite object interaction chart may be drawn (Figure 14.16). This summarizes all object–object communications. Obviously, in some systems, there are so many interactions that it is impractical to produce a composite chart. In such cases, designers must make their own judgement about which object interactions need be documented.

After identifying the object hierarchy and the object interactions, the next step is to develop the design of the object interfaces. Once the interface design has been established and agreed, it is then possible to implement each object, without reference to other object designs.

Figure 14.16
Object interaction summary for Weather Station.

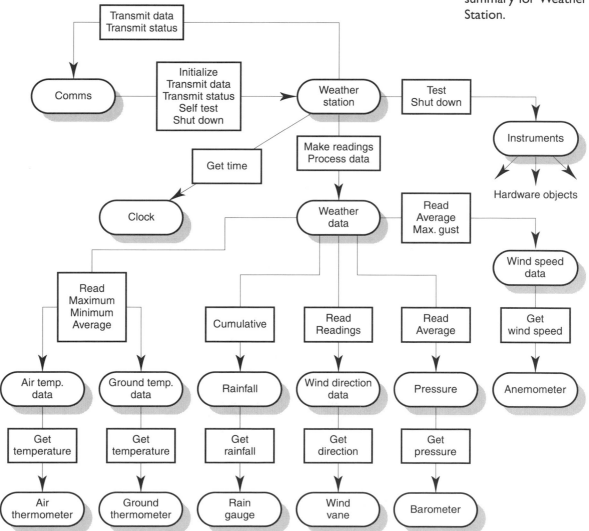

14.3.3 Object interface design

Object interface design is concerned with specifying the detail of the object interfaces. This means defining the types of the object attributes and the signatures and the semantics of the object operations. If an object-oriented programming language is being used for implementation, it is natural to use it to express the interface design.

Designers should avoid interface representation information in their interface design. Rather, the representation should be hidden and object operations provided to access and update the data. If the representation is hidden, it can be changed without affecting the objects that use these attributes. This leads to a design which is inherently more maintainable. For example, an array representation of a stack may be changed to a list representation without affecting other objects which use the stack.

Figure 14.17 shows an interface design, in Ada, for the weather station. The weather station has been represented as an abstract data type (Weather_station.T)

```
with Weather_data, Instrument_status, Mapping_computer ;
package Weather_station is
    type T is  private ;
    type STATION_IDENTIFIER is STRING (1..6) ;
    procedure Initialize (WS: T) ;
    procedure Transmit_data (   Id: STATION_IDENTIFIER ;
                                WR: Weather_data.REC ;
                                Dest: Mapping_computer.ID ) ;
    procedure Transmit_status ( Id: STATION_IDENTIFIER ;
                                IS: Instrument_status.REC ;
                                Dest: Mapping_computer.ID ) ;
    procedure Self_test (WS: T) ;
    procedure Shut_down (WS: T) ;

    -- Access and constructor procedures for object attributes
    -- Attribute: Station identifier
    function Station_identifier (WS: T) return STATION_IDENTIFIER ;
    procedure Put_identifier (WS: in out T ; Id: STATION_IDENTIFIER) ;
    -- Attribute: Weather data record
    function Weather_data (WS: T ) return Weather_data.REC ;
    procedure Put_weather_data (WS: in out T ; WR: Weather_data.REC ) ;
    -- Attribute: Instrument status
    procedure Put_instrument_status ( WS: in out T; IS:
                                            Instrument_status.REC ) ;
    function Instrument_status (WS: T) return Instrument_status.REC ;
private
    type T is record
        Id: STATION_IDENTIFIER ;
        Weather_data: Weather_data.REC ;
        Instrument_status: Instrument_status.REC ;
    end record ;
end Weather_station ;
```

Figure 14.17
The interface design of the weather station object in Ada.

```
class Weather_station {
public:
    Weather_station () ;
    ~Weather_station () ;
    void Transmit_data (computer_id dest) ;
    void Transmit_status (computer_id dest) ;
    void Self_test () ;
    void Shut_down () ;

    // Access and constructor functions
    char* Identifier () ;
    void Put_identifier (char* Id) ;
    instrument_status Inst_status () ;
    void Put_instrument_status (Instrument_status ISD) ;
    weather_data_rec Weather_data () ;
    void Put_weather_data (weather_data_rec WDR) ;
private:
    char* station_identifier ;
    weather_data_rec Weather_data ;
    instrument_status inst_status ;
} ;
```

Figure 14.18
The interface design of
the weather station
object class in C++.

which is like an object class. Any number of instances of that type may be created by declaring them as Weather_station.T.

In Ada, object interfaces are represented using a package specification. The representation is hidden in the 'private' part of the package. Functions are provided in the interface to access this representation. Functions which should always be provided for each attribute include functions to store and retrieve information in that attribute. Other functions, such as comparison functions, may also be required.

Figure 14.18 shows the corresponding design in C++. The services associated with Weather_station are declared in the public part of a C++ class declaration. The private part of the C++ class declaration is similar to the private part of the Ada package. Entities declared within this part may not be accessed from outside the object.

14.3.4 Design evolution

An important advantage of an object-oriented approach to design is that it simplifies the problem of making changes to the design. The reason for this is that object state representation does not influence the design. Changing the internal details of an object is unlikely to affect any other system objects. Furthermore, because objects are loosely coupled, it is usually straightforward to introduce new objects without significant effects on the rest of the system.

To illustrate the robustness of the object-oriented approach, assume that pollution monitoring capabilities are to be added to each weather station. This involves adding an air quality meter to compute the amount of various pollutants in the atmosphere. The pollution readings are transmitted at the same time as the weather data. To modify the design, the following changes must be made:

(1)   An object Air quality should be introduced as part of Weather station at the same level as Weather data.

(2)   An operation Transmit pollution data should be added to Weather station to send the pollution information to the central computer. The weather station control software must be modified so that pollution readings are automatically collected when the system is switched on.

(3)   Objects representing the types of pollution which can be monitored should be added. Levels of nitrous oxide, smoke and benzene can be measured.

(4)   A hardware control object Air quality meter should be added as a sub-object to Air quality. This has attributes representing each of the types of measurement which can be made.

Apart from at the highest level of the system (Weather station) no software changes are required. The addition of pollution data collection does not affect weather data collection in any way. Data representations are encapsulated in objects so they are not affected by the additions to the design.

Figure 14.19 shows Weather station and the new objects added to the system. The abbreviation NO in Air quality stands for nitrous oxide.

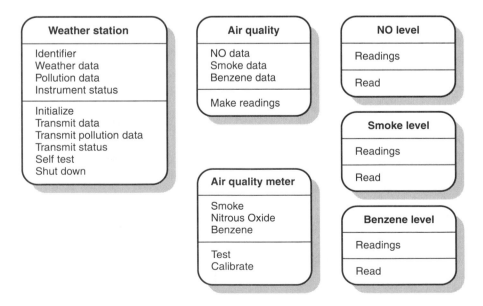

Figure 14.19
New objects to support pollution monitoring.

14.4 Concurrent objects

Conceptually, an object requests a service from another object by sending a 'service request' message to that object. In practice, this is usually implemented as a procedure or function call. However, the message-passing model allows objects to be implemented as concurrent processes. Agha (1990) discusses concurrent object-oriented design.

There are two kinds of concurrent object implementation:

(1)   *Passive objects* where the object is realized as a parallel process with entry points corresponding to the defined object operations. If no calls to the process are available for processing, the object process suspends itself.

(2)   *Active objects* where the state of the object may be changed by internal operations executing within the object itself. The process representing the object continually executes these operations so never suspends itself.

Objects may be implemented as processes in any system which supports some form of concurrency. In Ada, sequential objects are implemented as packages; concurrent objects are implemented as Ada tasks (Burns and Wellings, 1990; Barnes, 1994). C++ does not have any built-in support for concurrency. The implementation of concurrent objects depends on operating system support. I have not, therefore, included C++ versions of the examples in this section.

Consider a very simple object such a counter associated with sensors in a real-time system. It has a value and two associated operations. These are Add, which increments the current value, and Initialize, which sets the value to some given value. Figure 14.20 shows the specification and the detailed design of this simple counter as a concurrent object. It is implemented as an Ada task with entries associated with the counter operations. An entry is also provided to allow the counter value to be inspected.

Task types are equivalent to object classes. Concurrent objects may therefore be created by declaring them to be of the appropriate task type:

    Geiger1, Geiger2: Concurrent_counter ;

The operations associated with tasks are accessed in the same way as object operations, that is, by using the object name. Unlike Ada packages, the package name is not used.

When Geiger1 is specified as a task type, there are task entries corresponding to the defined operations Add, Initialize and Get. Each **accept** statement handles an entry and has an associated queue of 'calls'. When an entry is 'called', that call joins the queue associated with the accept statement. It is processed (ultimately) by the task according to the code specified between **accept** and **end**. While an **accept** clause is in execution, mutual exclusion is guaranteed. An object wishing to evaluate a counter enters into what is called a *rendezvous* with the Geiger1 task. The appropriate entry in Geiger1 as defined in the task type is called:

    Geiger1.Get (The_value)

```
task type Concurrent_counter is
    entry Add (N: NATURAL) ;
    entry Initialize (N: NATURAL) ;
    entry Get (N: out NATURAL) ;
end Concurrent_counter ;
task body Concurrent_counter is
    Value: NATURAL := 0 ;
begin
    loop
        select
            accept Add (N: NATURAL) do
                Value := Value + N ;
            end Add ;
        or
            accept Initialize (N: NATURAL) do
                Value := N ;
            end Initialize ;
        or
            accept Get (N: out NATURAL) do
                N := Value ;
            end Get ;
        end select ;
    end loop ;
end Counter ;
```

Figure 14.20
Specification and task
implementation of a
counter object in Ada.

This request for service joins the queue of Get entries. The Ada **select** construct is used to specify that one outstanding entry should be accepted each time the loop is executed. If there are no pending entries to be processed, Geiger1 suspends itself till further processing is required.

Active objects are used when an object updates its own state at specified intervals. We have already seen an example of this in the weather station example. The Comms object in that system updated its own state by monitoring the communications hardware and changing its state in response to an incoming signal.

Figure 14.21 shows how a task representing an active object may be specified and implemented in Ada. This object represents a transponder on an aircraft. The transponder keeps track of the aircraft's position using a satellite navigation system. It provides the current aircraft position in response to a request to the Give_position service.

This object is implemented as a task with a continuous loop updating the aircraft's position. When a Give_position entry is accepted, the position (as computed by the previous loop iteration) is returned to the calling task. In this case a conditional **select** statement is used. If there are no entries to be accepted, the task carries out the position computation as specified in the else part of the **select** statement.

Active objects such as Transponder or the Comms object in the weather station are commonly used in real-time systems where hardware devices must be continually monitored.

```
task Transponder is
   entry Give_position (Pos: POSITION ) ;
end Transponder ;
task body Transponder is
   Current_position: POSITION ;
   C1, C2: Satellite.COORDS ;
   loop
      select
         accept Give_position (Pos: out POSITION) do
            Pos:= Current_position ;
         end Give_position ;
      else
         C1 := Satellite1.Position ;
         C2 := Satellite2.Position ;
         Current_position := Navigator.Compute (C1, C2) ;
      end select ;
   end loop ;
end Transponder ;
```

Figure 14.21
An active transponder object.

Further reading

Object-oriented Design with Applications, 2nd edition. This book describes a general approach to object-oriented design in which C++ is used as the object-oriented programming language. (G. Booch, 1993, Benjamin-Cummings.)

Software Engineering with Ada, 3rd edition. This book is an excellent introduction to Ada and object-oriented design. The authors make it look easy but that is a criticism that can be made of many textbooks, including, perhaps, this one. (G. Booch and D. Bryan, 1994, Benjamin-Cummings.)

Object-oriented Software Engineering. A book which covers object-oriented development in general from analysis through design to programming. (I. Jacobson, M. Christerson, P. Jonsson and G. Overgaard, 1992, Addison-Wesley.)

KEY POINTS

- Object-oriented design is a means of designing with information hiding. Information hiding allows the information representation to be changed without other extensive system modifications.

- An object is an entity which has a private state. It should have constructor and inspection functions allowing its state to be inspected and modified. The object provides services (operations using state information) to other objects.

- Object identification is a major problem in object-oriented design. One way to identify objects is to consider the nouns (objects) and verbs (operations) in a short system description. Other approaches are based on identifying tangible entities in the application domain, on behavioural analysis and on scenario analysis.

- Object interfaces must be defined precisely so that they can be used by other objects. Graphical descriptions are usually too imprecise for interface definition. A programming language such as Ada or C++ should be used.

- When documenting an object-oriented design, it is useful to draw a hierarchy chart showing objects and their sub-objects. It is also useful to draw an object interaction network showing which objects call on the services of which other objects.

- Objects may be implemented sequentially or concurrently. A concurrent object may be a passive object whose state is only changed through its interface or an active object that can change its own state without outside intervention.

EXERCISES

14.1   Explain why adopting a design approach based on information hiding should lead to a design which may be readily modified.

14.2   Using examples, explain the difference between an object and an object class.

14.3   Using the graphical notation introduced here, design the following objects. Use your own experience to decide on the attributes and operations associated with these objects.

(a) a telephone

(b) a printer for a personal computer

(c) a personal stereo system

(d) a bank account

(e) a library catalogue

14.4   Develop the design of the weather station design in detail by writing interface descriptions of the identified objects. This may be expressed in Ada or in any object-oriented programming language.

14.5   Modify the design of the weather station so that it makes readings every minute and transmits the raw data immediately to the weather data processing system.

14.6   Identify possible objects in the following systems and develop an object-oriented design for them. You may make any reasonable assumptions about the systems when deriving the design.

(a) A group diary and time management system is intended to support the timetabling of meetings and appointments across a group of co-workers. When an appointment is to be made which involves a number of people, the system finds a common slot in each of their diaries and arranges the appointment for that time. If no common slots are available, it interacts with the user to rearrange their personal diary to make room for the appointment.

(b) A petrol (gas) station is to be set up for fully automated operation. Drivers swipe their credit card through a reader connected to the pump, the card is verified by communication with a credit company computer and a fuel limit established. The driver may then take the fuel required. When fuel delivery is complete and the pump hose is returned to its holster, the driver's credit card account is debited with the cost of the fuel taken. The credit card is returned after debiting. If the card is invalid, it is returned by the pump before fuel is dispensed.

14.7   Write precise interface definitions in Ada, C++ or in some other object-oriented programming language for the objects you defined in Exercise 14.3.

14.8   Under what circumstances might it be appropriate to develop a design where objects execute concurrently?

Function-oriented Design

Objectives

- To explain how a software design may be represented as a set of functions which share system state information.

- To introduce notations which may be used to represent a function-oriented design.

- To develop an example which illustrates the process of function-oriented design.

- To compare, using a common example, sequential and concurrent function-oriented design and object-oriented design.

Contents

A function-oriented design strategy relies on decomposing the system into a set of interacting functions with a centralized system state shared by these functions (Figure 15.1). Functions may also maintain local state information but only for the duration of their execution.

Function-oriented design has been practised informally since programming began. Programs were decomposed into subroutines which were functional in nature. In the late 1960s and early 1970s several books were published which described 'top-down' functional design. They specifically proposed this as a 'structured' design strategy (Myers, 1975; Wirth, 1976; Constantine and Yourdon, 1979). These led to the development of many design methods based on functional decomposition.

Function-oriented design conceals the details of an algorithm in a function but system state information is not hidden. This can cause problems because a function can change the state in a way which other functions do not expect. Changes to a function and the way in which it uses the system state may cause unanticipated changes in the behaviour of other functions.

A functional approach to design is therefore most likely to be successful when the amount of system state information is minimized and information sharing is explicit. Systems whose responses depend on a single stimulus or input and which are not affected by input histories are naturally function-oriented. Many transaction-processing systems and business data-processing systems fall into this class. In essence, they are concerned with record processing where the processing of one record is not dependent on any previous processing.

An example of such a transaction processing system is the software that controls automatic teller machines (ATMs) which are now installed outside many banks. The service provided to a user is independent of previous services provided so can be thought of as a single transaction. Figure 15.2 illustrates a simplified functional design of such a system. Notice that this design follows the centralized management control model introduced in Chapter 13.

In this design, the system is implemented as a continuous loop and actions are triggered when a card is input. Functions such as Dispense_cash,

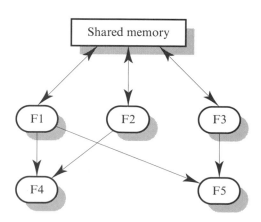

Figure 15.1
A function-oriented
view of design.

```
loop
   loop
   Print_input_message (" Welcome – Please enter your card") ;
      exit when Card_input ;
   end loop ;
   Account_number := Read_card ;
   Get_account_details (PIN, Account_balance, Cash_available) ;
   if Validate_card (PIN) then
   loop
      Print_operation_select_message ;
      case Get_button is
         when Cash_only =>
            Dispense_cash (Cash_available, Amount_dispensed) ;
         when Print_balance =>
            Print_customer_balance (Account_balance) ;
         when Statement =>
            Order_statement (Account_number) ;
         when Check_book =>
            Order_checkbook (Account_number) ;
      end case ;
      Eject_card ;
      Print ("Please take your card or press CONTINUE") ;
      exit when Card_removed ;
   end loop ;
   Update_account_information (Account_number, Amount_dispensed) ;
   else
      Retain_card ;
   end if ;
end loop ;
```

Figure 15.2
The functional design
of software for an
ATM.

Get_account_number, Order_statement, Order_checkbook and so on which implement system actions can be identified. The system state maintained by the program is minimal. The user services operate independently and do not interact with each other. An object-oriented design would be similar and would probably not be significantly more maintainable.

As object-oriented design has become more widely used, some people have suggested that function-oriented design is obsolete, and should be superseded by an object-oriented approach. There are several good reasons why this should not and will not happen:

(1)   As discussed above, there are classes of system, particularly business systems, where object-oriented design does not offer significant advantages in terms of system maintainability or reliability. In these cases, an object-oriented approach may result in a less efficient system implementation.

(2)   Many organizations have developed standards and methods based on functional decomposition. They are understandably reluctant to discard these in

favour of object-oriented design. Many design methods and associated CASE tools are function-oriented. A large capital and training investment in these systems has been made.

(3)   An enormous number of systems have been developed using a functional approach. These legacy systems will have to be maintained for the foreseeable future. Unless they are radically re-engineered, their design structure will remain functional.

It is not sensible to view the function-oriented and object-oriented approaches as competing design strategies. Rather, they are applicable in different circumstances and for different types of application. Good designers choose the most appropriate strategy for the application that is being developed rather than use a single approach.

In this chapter, I illustrate a function-oriented design process using a number of examples. The activities in that process are:

(1)   *Data-flow design*   Model the system design using data-flow diagrams. This should show how data passes through the system and is transformed by each system function. This model may be derived from data-flow models developed during the analysis process.

(2)   *Structural decomposition*   Model how functions are decomposed into sub-functions using graphical structure charts.

(3)   *Detailed design description*   Describe the entities in the design and their interfaces. These descriptions may be recorded in a data dictionary. Also describe the control structure of the design using a program description language (PDL) which includes conditional statements and looping constructs.

As with all design processes, these activities are not carried out in sequence but are interleaved during the design process.

15.1 Data-flow design

Data-flow design is concerned with designing a sequence of functional transformations that convert system inputs into the required outputs. The design is represented as data-flow diagrams. These diagrams illustrate how data flows through a system and how the output is derived from the input through a sequence of functional transformations.

Data-flow diagrams are a useful and intuitive way of describing a system. They are normally understandable without special training, especially if control information is excluded. They show end-to-end processing: that is, the flow of processing from when data enters the system to where it leaves the system can be traced.

Data-flow design is an integral part of a number of design methods and most CASE tools support data-flow diagram creation. Different methods may use different icons to represent data-flow diagram entities but their meanings are similar. The notation which I use is based on the following symbols:

- *Rounded rectangles* represent functions which transform inputs to outputs. The transformation name indicates its function.

- *Rectangles* represent data stores. Again, they should be given a descriptive name.

- *Circles* represent user interactions with the system which provide input or receive output.

- *Arrows* show the direction of data flow. Their name describes the data flowing along that path.

- *The keywords* 'and' *and* 'or'. These have their usual meanings as in boolean expressions. They are used to link data flows when more than one data flow may be input or output from a transformation.

This notation is illustrated in Figure 15.3 which shows a data-flow design of a design report generator. The report generator produces a report which describes all of the named entities in a data-flow diagram. The user inputs the name of the design

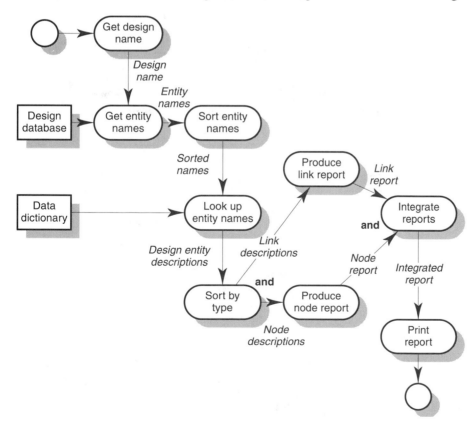

Figure 15.3
Data-flow diagram of a design report generator.

represented by the diagram. The report generator then finds all the names used in the data-flow diagram. It looks up a data dictionary and retrieves information about each name. This is then collated into a report which is output by the system.

Data-flow diagrams show functional transformations but do not suggest how these might be implemented. A system described in this way might be implemented as a single program using functions or procedures to implement each transformation. Alternatively, it could be implemented as a number of communicating tasks.

15.2 Structural decomposition

As well as a data-flow model of a system, it is also useful to develop a structural system model. This structural model shows how a function is realized by a number of other functions which it calls. Structure charts are a graphical way to represent this decomposition hierarchy. Like data-flow diagrams, they are dynamic rather than static system models. They show how one function calls others. They do not show the static block structure of a function or procedure.

A function is represented on a structure chart as a rectangle. The hierarchy is displayed by linking rectangles with lines. Inputs and outputs (which may be implemented either as parameters or shared variables) are indicated with annotated arrows. An arrow entering a box implies input, leaving a box implies output. Data stores are shown as rounded rectangles and user inputs as circles.

Converting a data-flow diagram to a structure chart is not a mechanical process. It requires designer insight and creativity. However, there are several 'rules of thumb' which may be applied to help designers assess if their decomposition is likely to be a reasonable one:

(1)   Many systems, particularly business systems for which functional design is most appropriate, can be considered as three-stage systems. These stages are: input some data, perhaps with validation and checking, process the data then output the data, perhaps in the form of a report or perhaps to some other file. A master file may also be updated. The first-level structure chart may therefore have three or four functions corresponding to input, process, master-file update and output. Figure 15.4 illustrates this structure although, in this case, there is no master file processing.

(2)   If data validation is required, functions to implement these should be subordinate to an input function. Output formatting, printing and writing to disk or tape should be subordinate to an output function.

(3)   The role of functions near the top of the structural hierarchy may be to control and coordinate a set of lower-level functions.

(4)   The objective of the design process is to have loosely coupled, highly cohesive components (cohesion and coupling were discussed in Chapter 12). Functions should therefore do one thing and one thing only.

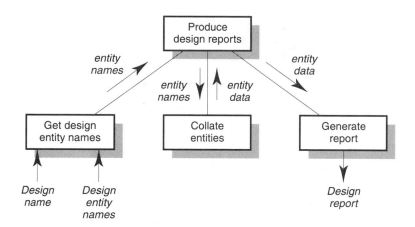

Figure 15.4
Initial structure chart
for the design report
generator.

(5)   Each node in the structure chart should have between two and seven sub-
        ordinates. If there is only a single subordinate, this implies that the unit
        represented by that node may have a low degree of cohesion. The component
        may not be single function. A single subordinate means that another function
        has been factored out. If a node has too many subordinates, this may mean
        that the design has been developed to too low a level at that stage.

Three process steps, which follow these guidelines, can be identified for the transformation process from data-flow diagram to structure chart:

(1)   *Identify system processing transformations*   These are the transformations in
        the diagram which are responsible for central processing functions. They are
        not concerned with any input or output functions such as reading or writing
        data, data validation or filtering or output formatting. These transformations
        should be grouped under a single function at the first level in the structure
        chart.

(2)   *Identify input transformations*   These are concerned with reading data,
        checking it, removing duplicates, and so on. These should also be grouped
        under a single function at the first level in the structure chart.

(3)   *Identify output transformations*   These are transformations which prepare
        and format output or write it to the user's screen or other device.

In the design report generator data-flow diagram (Figure 15.3), the processing
functions are those that sort the input, look up the data dictionary and sort the
information retrieved from the data dictionary. In the structure chart (Figure 15.4)
these are collected together into a single function called Collate entities. This initial
structure chart can be decomposed to show subordinate functions which also reflect
transformations in the data-flow diagram (Figure 15.5).

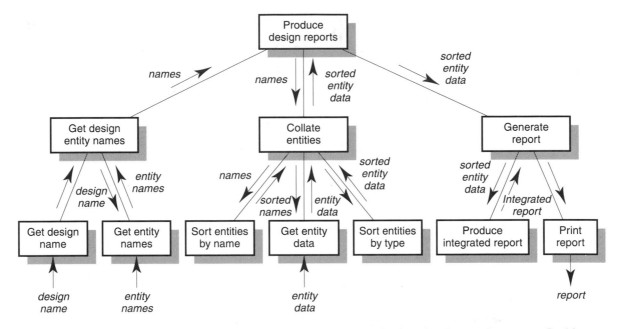

Figure 15.5
Second-level structure chart for the design report generator.

The input transformations stop at the function Sort entity names. In this case they are simply concerned with reading information. No data checking is required. They are represented as a function called Get design entity names.

The output transformations are concerned with producing reports for link and node type, report integration and printing. These are all concerned with the formatting and organization of design entity descriptions. They are grouped under the function Generate report.

All the principal routines in the design report generator have now been identified. It only remains to add a final level of more detailed routines and to show how the system data stores are accessed. The final structure chart is shown in Figure 15.6. This chart does not show the access functions to the data dictionary and the design database. I assume that these data stores are like abstract data types and have their own access functions.

Other components may be included in a structure chart which are not directly concerned with data transformation. Because they do not transform data, they do not appear on the data-flow diagram. For example, components which are concerned with logging-in and logging-out a user, system initialization and any other components concerned with system control rather than data processing may be included at the structural decomposition level.

15.3 Detailed design

At this stage in the design process, the designer should know the organization of the design and what each function should do. Design entity description is concerned

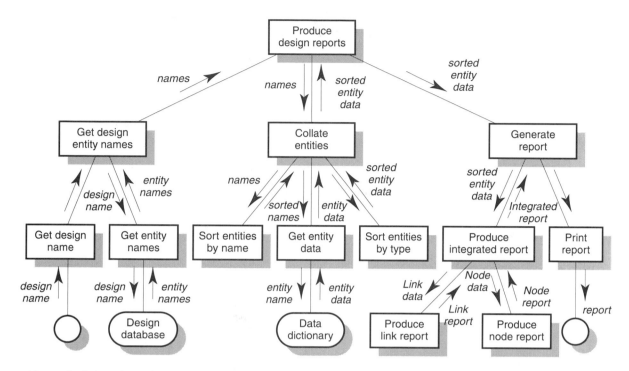

Figure 15.6
Final structure chart for the design report generator.

with producing a short design specification (sometimes called a *minispec*) of each function. This describes the function, its inputs and its outputs.

Making this information explicit usually reveals flaws in the initial decomposition or functions which have been omitted. The data-flow diagrams and structure charts must be revisited and modified to incorporate the improved understanding of the design.

The best way to manage these functional descriptions is to maintain them in a data dictionary. Data dictionaries were introduced in Chapter 6 as a way of recording information in system models developed as part of the requirements analysis process. They can also be used to record information about design entities. Maintaining names and descriptions in a data dictionary reduces the chances of mistakenly reusing names and provides design readers with insights into the designer's thinking.

Data dictionary entries can vary in detail from a short informal description to a specification of the function in a design description language. Figure 15.7 shows some of the data dictionary entries that might be made for the design report generator. As you can see, it includes information about data as well as the functions in the system.

Some CASE tools may include facilities which allow data dictionaries to be accessed at the same time as a design diagram. This allows information about individual entities to be viewed at the same time as the diagram showing all entities and their relationships. The tool may allow a design entity to be selected then display the corresponding information from the data dictionary. Figure 15.8 is

Entity name	Type	Description
Design name	STRING	The name of the design assigned by the design engineer
Get design name	FUNCTION	*Input:* Design name *Function:* This function communicates with the user to get the name of a design that has been entered in the design database *Output:* Design name
Get entity names	FUNCTION	*Input:* Design name *Function:* Given a design name, this function accesses the design database to find the names of the entities (nodes and links) in that design *Output:* Entity names
Sorted names	ARRAY of STRING	A list of the names of the entities in a design held in ascending alphabetical order

Figure 15.7
Data dictionary entries for the design report generator.

an example of this facility. It shows a pop-up window which includes a form describing the selected transform in the data-flow diagram.

The next stage of the functional design process is to produce detailed designs for each part of the design. These detailed designs should include control information and more precise information about the data structures manipulated. The detailed designs may be expressed using some program description language, in

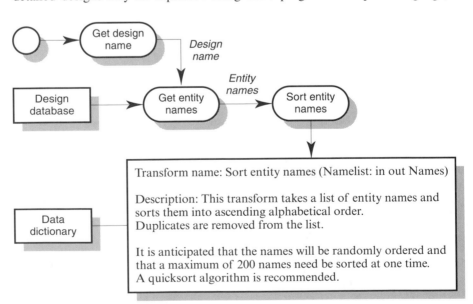

Figure 15.8
Information about design entities from a data dictionary.

some more detailed graphical notation or directly in a programming language. I have already shown examples of how a PDL may be used to describe a design in Figure 15.2. Further examples are shown in Figures 15.11, 15.14 and 15.16.

15.4 A comparison of design strategies

In Chapter 14, I introduced an example of an office information system. This was used to illustrate object identification using a grammatical analysis of a system description. In this section, this example will be expanded and used to compare functional and object-oriented approaches to design. I will also show how a design can be developed for the same system using concurrent processes.

The Office Information Retrieval System (OIRS) is an office system which can file documents in one or more indexes, retrieve documents, display and maintain document indexes, archive documents and delete documents. Users request operations from a menu-based interface and the system always returns a message to the user indicating the success or failure of the request.

The interface to this system is a form which has a number of fields (Figure 15.9). Some of these fields are menu fields where the user can choose a particular option. Other fields allow user textual input. Menu items may be selected by pointing with a mouse or by moving a cursor using keyboard commands.

The fields displayed in the form are as follows:

(1)   *The operation field*   Selecting this field causes a menu of allowed operations to be displayed as shown in Figure 15.9.

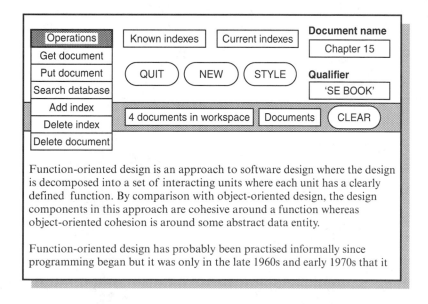

Figure 15.9
The OIRS user interface.

(2)   *The known indexes field*   Selecting this field causes a menu of existing index names to be displayed. Selecting an item from this list adds it to the current index list.

(3)   *The current indexes field*   Selecting this field displays a list of the indexes where the current document is to be indexed.

(4)   *The document name field*   This specifies the name of the document to be filed or the name of the document to be retrieved. If this name is not filled in, the user is prompted for a value.

(5)   *The qualifier field*   This is a pattern which is used in searching. For example, the pattern 'A–K' may be specified with a command to look up the names of documents in the current index lists. The qualifier causes only those names which begin with a letter from A to K to be listed. Alternatively, the qualifier field might contain a keyword such as 'Software Engineering'. An index search retrieves all documents which contain this keyword.

(6)   *The current workspace*   Documents are retrieved to the current workspace which may contain several documents. The user may choose a document in the workspace by selecting its name from the workspace menu. Clicking on the Clear button in the workspace control bar removes the selection from the workspace. Moving the cursor into the workspace causes the system to enter document edit mode.

When developing a functional design, the initial stage should treat the system as a black box. It should simply show the inputs and outputs of the system with the system itself represented as a single transformation (Figure 15.10). The arc annotated with 'or' joining the output data flows means that one or the other but not both of these data flows occur. Notice that the document database and the current workspace are both inputs and outputs.

Functional designs of interactive systems often follow a common detailed architectural model. This is a command 'fetch and execute' loop. Figure 15.11 describes the general form of a fetch-execute loop. The ATM design, described in Figure 15.2, is an example of this model.

In this design, the Get command function has been separated from the Execute command function to allow for different types of user interface and user

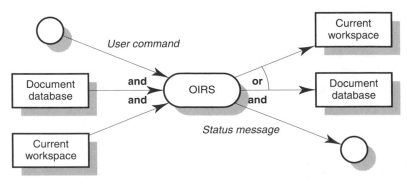

Figure 15.10
Inputs and outputs of
the OIRS.

```
procedure Interactive_system is
begin
   loop
      Command := Get_command;
      if Command = "quit" then
         -- Make sure files etc. are closed properly
         Close_down_system ;
         exit ;
      else
         Input_data := Get_input_data ;
         Execute_command (Command, Input_data, Output_data) ;
      end if ;
   end loop ;
end Interactive_system ;
```

Figure 15.11
Fetch-execute model
of an interactive
system.

interface evolution. If the system is moved from a computer without a mouse to a computer with a mouse (say), only the Get command function need be changed. It is generally good design practice to separate, as far as possible, the user interface of a system from the data processing functions. This is discussed in Chapter 17.

A data-flow diagram for the OIRS based on this model is shown in Figure 15.12. The central transform is concerned with command execution and further functions are incorporated to manage the database and the workspace.

The Execute command transformation can now be considered in isolation and can be decomposed into simpler transformations (Figure 15.13).

Figure 15.13 shows that there are three different classes of command in the OIRS. These are commands to update the workspace (Get document, Search database, Clear workspace and the implicit Edit command), commands to update the database (Put document, Delete document) and index commands (Add index, Delete index, Display index lists).

For brevity, I have skipped the structural decomposition and entity description stages in the functional design process and have gone straight to detailed design description. Figure 15.14 is a design, expressed in a PDL, for the top level of the

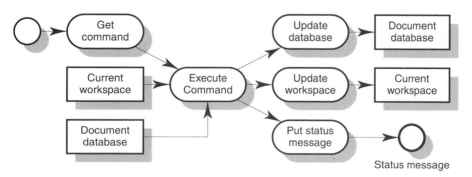

Figure 15.12
Top-level data-flow
design for the OIRS.

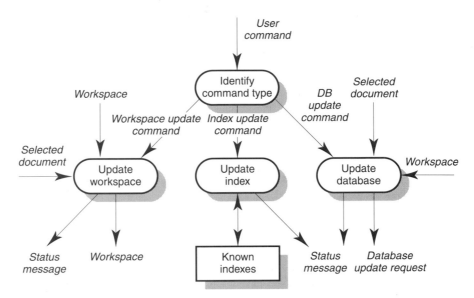

Figure 15.13
Data-flow diagram for
Execute command.

OIRS. As discussed in the previous section, additional functions have been included for login and initialization which are not shown in the data-flow diagram.

Note that the control structure design shown in Figure 15.14 is not a syntactically correct program. It does not include declarations of the entities which are

```
procedure OIRS is
begin
    User := Login_user ;
    Workspace := Create_user_workspace (User) ;
    -- Get the user's own document database using the user id
    DB_id := Open_document_database (User) ;
    -- get the user's personal index list;
    Known_indexes := Get_document_indexes (User) ;
    Current_indexes := NULL ;
    -- command fetch and execute loop
    loop
        Command := Get_command ;
        exit when Command = Quit ;
        Execute_command ( DB_id, Workspace, Command, Status) ;
        if Status = Successful then
            Write_success_message ;
        else
            Write_error_message (Command, Status) ;
        end if ;
    end loop ;
    Close_database (DB_id) ;
    Logout (User) ;
end OIRS ;
```

Figure 15.14
High-level design
description of the
OIRS.

used. As discussed above, these names should be entered in a data dictionary along with a description of the entities which they identify.

The design process continues by decomposing each of the design components in more detail. This decomposition should stop when the design has been described at a sufficiently detailed level that a program can be developed in the chosen implementation language. This level of detail will obviously vary depending on the language used. The lower level the implementation language, the more detail is required in the design.

15.4.1 Concurrent systems design

The above functional design models the OIRS as a sequential system with a single control loop which fetches and executes commands in sequence. An alternative approach to the detailed design is to implement the system as a number of concurrent processes. As data-flow diagrams explicitly exclude control information, they can also be the starting point for a concurrent design. A standard implementation technique for real-time systems (see Chapter 16) is to take a data-flow diagram and to implement each of its transformations as a separate process.

In this case, implementing each data-flow transformation as a separate process would not be an efficient way of designing the system. There is a scheduling overhead involved in starting and stopping processes and managing process communications. Unless it is absolutely necessary because of real-time requirements, it is best to avoid decomposing a system into many small processes.

However, to improve real-time response in window-based systems, it is often necessary to identify those parts of the system which must respond to user events and implement these as separate processes. This allows the system to be responsive to time-critical user events such as mouse movements. The strict sequence which is forced by a fetch-execute cycle can be avoided. In the OIRS, there are two situations in which user actions cause an event to be generated:

(1)   When a command is selected. The user moves the cursor into a menu and makes a choice. An event is generated informing the system that a command has been chosen.

(2)   When the cursor is moved into the workspace and the user starts to type.

The user can move the cursor between these areas at any time so the system must be able to cope with the change. This can be handled in a fetch-execute system by making sure that the workspace editor keeps track of the cursor, but some code duplication in such a situation is inevitable.

Given that the input processing (commands and text) is to be implemented using separate processes, it then makes sense to identify corresponding processes to handle command execution and output processing. This leads to a set of four processes as shown in Figure 15.15. Control passes from process to process in response to events such as a cursor being positioned in a workspace, a command menu being selected, and so on.

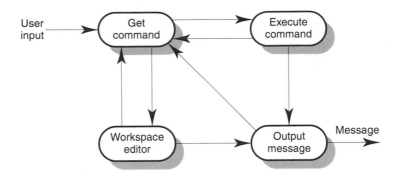

Figure 15.15
Process decomposition
of the OIRS.

The Get command task tracks the mouse and responds to low-level mouse events. When a command area is selected, it initiates the command execution process. Similarly, the command execution process produces status messages which are processed by the output task. Workspace editing is also implemented as a parallel task. The editor is initiated and suspended as the cursor is moved in and out of the workspace window.

The detailed design of the overall system and the Get command process is shown, in Ada, in Figure 15.16. This uses Ada's facilities (tasks) for implementing parallel systems. Ada task entries correspond to procedure calls. Therefore, calling an entry Display indexes in Execute command is like calling a function of that name. Details of Ada tasking can be found in Ada textbooks (Burns and Wellings, 1990; Barnes, 1994).

15.4.2 Object-oriented design

Both the sequential and concurrent designs of the OIRS are functional because the principal decomposition strategy identifies functions such as Execute command, Update index, and so on. By contrast, an object-oriented design focuses on the entities in the system with the functions part of these entities. There is not enough space here to develop a complete object-oriented design but I show the entity decomposition in this section. Notice that this is quite different from the functional system decomposition.

We have already seen an initial object identification for the OIRS in Chapter 14. The objects identified from that description are shown in Figure 15.17.

This object decomposition leaves out entities such as the database, the workspace and so on, the reason being that this decomposition was based on a simple description. This description did not describe all system facilities. Nor did it describe how these facilities are presented to users. We therefore need to define further system objects as shown in Figure 15.18.

Documents which are being used are held in a workspace and referenced in indexes. We therefore need objects which correspond to the workspace and each index. Index list is an object class used to create different lists of indexes. The document database is also represented as an object.

```
procedure Office_system is
    task Get_command ;
    task Process_command is
        entry Command_menu ;
        entry Display_indexes ;
        entry Edit_qualifier ;
        -- Additional entries here. One for each command
    end Process_commands ;
    task Output_message is
        entry Message_available ;
    end Output_message ;
    task Workspace_editor is
        entry Enter ;
        entry Leave ;
    end Workspace_editor ;

    task body Get_command is
    begin
    -- Fetch/execute loop
    loop
        loop
            Cursor_position := Get_cursor_position ;
        exit when cursor positioned in workspace or
        (cursor positioned over menu and button pressed)
        Display_cursor_position ;
        end loop ;
        if In_workspace (Cursor_position) then
            Workspace_editor.Enter ;
        elsif In_command_menu (Cursor_position) then
            Process_command.Command_menu ;
        elsif In_Known_indexes (Cursor_position) then
            Process_command.Display_indexes ;
        elsif In_Current_indexes (Cursor_position) then
                ...
                Other commands here
            ...
    end loop ; -- Fetch/execute
    end Get_command ;
-- other task implementations here
end Office_system ;
```

Figure 15.16
Detailed process
design in Ada.

The initial object decomposition was based on a simple system description. With further information we now have to revisit this decomposition and see if it is still appropriate. We know that the user interface is a graphical interface with various fields and buttons so this should be represented as an object. It can serve as a replacement for the User object, so this can now be discarded and its operations incorporated into Display. As a general design guideline, displays map onto objects.

Figure 15.17
Initial decomposition of
the OIRS into classes
and objects.

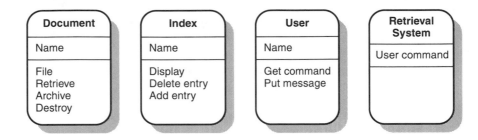

Object attributes represent fields on the display. We can see an example of this in Figure 15.19 which should be compared with Figure 15.9 showing the OIRS display.

The Retrieval system object is also modified to add attributes representing the workspace and the indexes used. This object does not have any associated operations. The object is an active object which controls other objects but does not provide services to them. All its functionality is therefore concealed.

The principal objects in the OIRS have now been identified. The next stage of the design process is to set out object aggregation hierarchies and how these objects interact as discussed in Section 14.3. In essence, the fetch-execute loop as discussed above is still part of the design. Commands are fetched from the display object. Services provided by the workspace, document and index objects are called on to execute these commands.

Given the limited information here, it is impossible to say which design strategy is the best one for this system. The functional approach to design using data-flow diagrams is probably the most intuitive way to describe the overall design. However, the focus on function means that the reader of the design finds it more difficult to understand the entities which are manipulated by the system.

The object-oriented approach solves this difficulty as it is very good for entity description. Because of information encapsulation, object-oriented design generally leads to more robust systems where system data is less likely to be corrupted in the event of a program error. It may also be easier to change although this depends on the nature of the change. However, as Fichman and Kemerer (1992) point out, decomposing a system into loosely coupled objects often means that there is no overall picture of end-to-end processing in the design.

Designers must use the most appropriate approach to design. They should not be forced into the straitjacket of any particular design method or strategy. My own

Figure 15.18
Additional OIRS
system objects.

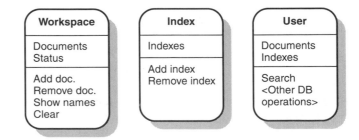

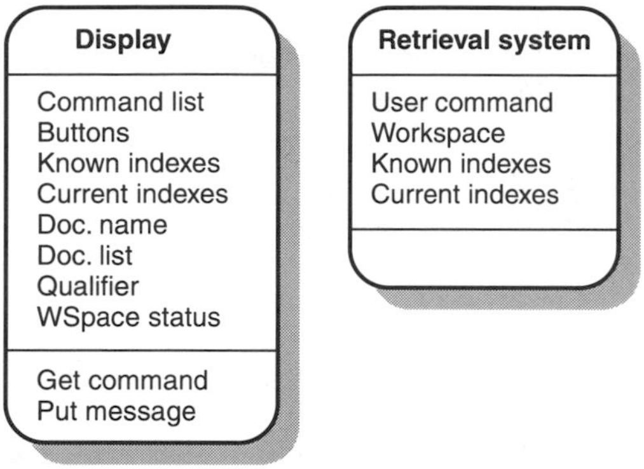

Display

Command list
Buttons
Known indexes
Current indexes
Doc. name
Doc. list
Qualifier
WSpace status

Get command
Put message

Retrieval system

User command
Workspace
Known indexes
Current indexes

Figure 15.19
Modified OIRS objects.

preference in this instance is to take a heterogeneous approach to the design. The basic functional fetch-execute loop should be retained and data-flow diagrams used to illustrate and understand the system's processing. The display management should be implemented as a separate process. The objects identified in this section should be used and referenced from the fetch-execute loop.

Further reading

Software Design. This book is a good general survey of software design techniques. Its orientation is towards functional approaches to design for the valid reason that these are more mature than object-oriented approaches. (D. Budgen, 1993, Addison-Wesley.)

'Object-oriented and conventional analysis and design methodologies'. This is an excellent comparison of object-oriented and functional approaches to design. Its conclusion is that the claimed advantages of object-oriented design have not been conclusively demonstrated. (*IEEE Computer*, **25** (10), October 1992.)

KEY POINTS

■ Function-oriented design relies on identifying functions which transform their inputs to create outputs. In most systems, functions share some global system state.

■ Many business systems which process transactions are naturally functional. Furthermore, there is a huge amount of legacy code which has been designed using this approach. For these reasons, function-oriented design will continue alongside object-oriented design as an important design strategy.

■ The functional design process involves identifying data transformations in the system, decomposing functions into a hierarchy of sub-functions, describing the operation and interface of each system entity and documenting the flow of control in the system.

- Data-flow diagrams are a means of documenting end-to-end data flow through a system. They do not include control information. Structure charts are a way of representing the hierarchical organization of a system. Control may be documented using a program description language (PDL).

- Data-flow diagrams can be implemented directly as a set of cooperating sequential processes. Each transform in the data-flow diagram is implemented as a separate process. Alternatively, they can be realized as a number of procedures in a sequential program.

- Functional design and object-oriented design usually result in totally different system decompositions. However, the most appropriate design strategy is often a heterogeneous one in which both functional and object-oriented approaches are used.

EXERCISES

15.1 Using examples, describe how data-flow diagrams may be used to document a system design. What are the advantages of using this type of design model?

15.2 Draw possible data-flow diagrams of system designs for the following applications. You may make any reasonable assumptions about these applications.

(a) Part of an electronic mail system which presents a mail form to a user, accepts the completed form and sends it to the identified destination.

(b) A salary system which computes employee salaries and deductions. The input is a list of employee numbers who are to be paid that month. The system maintains tables holding tax rates and the annual salary for each employee. The output is a salary slip for each employee plus a list of automated payments to be made by the company's bank.

15.3 Modify the design of the report generator shown in Figure 15.3 so that it becomes an interactive system. The user may give a design entity name and the report generator provides information about that entity. Alternatively, the user may provide a type name and the report generator produces a report about each entity of that type in a design. Document your modified design using data-flow diagrams and structure charts.

15.4 Convert the data-flow diagram of the report generator system described in Figure 15.3 into a design consisting of concurrent processes.

15.5 Using a design description language, describe a possible design for the design report generator whose data-flow diagram is given in Figure 15.3 and structure chart in Figure 15.7.

15.6   Explain how data dictionaries may be used to supplement design information in data-flow diagrams and structure charts.

15.7   Develop the data-flow diagrams shown in Figure 15.12 so that all transforms are documented with more detailed data-flow diagrams.

15.8   Develop the design of **Execute Command** in the office information retrieval system and describe its detailed design in a design description language.

15.9   Develop function-oriented designs for the systems described in Exercise 14.6. What are the principal differences between these and object-oriented designs?

16

Real-time Systems Design

Objectives

- To introduce real-time systems design and to explain why real-time systems are usually implemented as a set of concurrent processes.

- To show how state machine models may be used to describe real-time systems.

- To describe real-time executives which are used to control the processes in real-time systems.

- To describe, using simple examples, generic architectures for some types of real-time system.

Contents

Computers are now used to control an increasing number of systems ranging from simple domestic machines to entire manufacturing plants. These computers interact directly with hardware devices. The system software must be sufficiently responsive to react to events generated by the hardware and issue control signals in response to these events. This software is called an embedded real-time system. It is *embedded* in some larger hardware system and must respond in *real-time* to events from the system's environment.

Real-time systems are different from other types of software system. Their correct functioning is dependent on the system responding to events within a given (usually short) time interval. I define a real-time system as follows:

> A real-time system is a software system whose correct functioning depends on the results produced and the time at which these results are produced. A 'soft' real-time system is a system whose operation is *degraded* if results are not produced according to the specified timing requirements. A 'hard' real-time system is a system whose operation is *incorrect* if results are not produced according to the timing specification.

One way of looking at a real-time system is as a stimulus/response system. Given a particular input stimulus, the system must produce a corresponding response. The behaviour of a real-time system can therefore be defined by listing stimuli, associated responses and the time at which the response must be produced.

Stimuli fall into two classes:

(1) *Periodic stimuli*   These occur at predictable time intervals. For example, the system may examine a sensor every 50 milliseconds and take action (respond) depending on that sensor value (the stimulus).

(2) *Aperiodic stimuli*   These occur irregularly. They are usually signalled using the computer's interrupt mechanism. An example of such a stimulus would be an interrupt indicating that an I/O transfer was complete and that data was available in a buffer.

Periodic stimuli in a real-time system are usually generated by sensors associated with the system. These provide information about the state of the system's environment. The responses are directed to a set of actuators that control some hardware unit which influences the system's environment. Aperiodic stimuli may be generated either by the actuators or by sensors. They often indicate some exceptional condition, such as a hardware failure, which must be handled by the system.

This sensor–system–actuator model of an embedded real-time system is illustrated in Figure 16.1. A real-time system must respond to stimuli which occur at different times. Its architecture must therefore be organized so that control is transferred to the appropriate handler for that stimulus as soon as it is received. This is normally achieved by designing the system as a set of concurrent, cooperating processes. Part of the real-time system (the real-time executive) is dedicated to managing these processes.

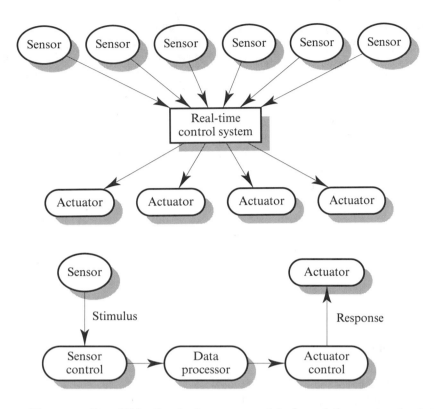

Figure 16.1
General model of a
real-time system.

Figure 16.2
Sensor/actuator
control processes.

The generality of this stimulus/response model of a real-time system leads to the generic architectural model illustrated in Figure 16.2 in which three processes execute concurrently. In general, each class of sensor has an associated process. A process also manages each class of actuator and further processes may be responsible for computational tasks within the system. This model allows data to be collected quickly from the sensor (before the next input becomes available) but allows for processing and the associated response to be carried out later.

16.1 System design

As discussed in Chapter 2, part of the system design process involves deciding which system capabilities are to be implemented in software and which in hardware. Most hardware components now include embedded software. Timing constraints or other requirements may mean that some system functions (for example, signal processing) have to be implemented using specially designed hardware. The system design process therefore involves parallel hardware and software design as shown in Figure 16.3.

Until relatively recently, it was only economic to develop special-purpose hardware for very large systems or specialized military systems. However, special-purpose integrated circuits are now much cheaper and faster to produce. For simple circuits, it is now possible to go from an idea to a delivered microchip in a few weeks. It is becoming increasingly cost-effective to delay decisions about which functions should be implemented in hardware and which functions should be software components.

Hardware components deliver much better performance than the equivalent software. System processing bottlenecks (for example, signal processing) can be identified and replaced by hardware thus avoiding expensive software optimization. Providing performance in hardware means that the software design can be structured for adaptability and that performance considerations can take second place.

Decisions on hardware/software partitioning should be left until as late as possible in the design process. This implies that the system architecture should be made up of stand-alone components which can be implemented in either hardware or software. Fortunately, building a design in this way is exactly the aim of the designer trying to design a maintainable system. A good system design process should therefore result in a system which can be implemented in either hardware or software.

There are several stages in the design process for real-time embedded software:

(1)   Identify the stimuli that the system must process and the associated responses.

(2)   For each stimulus and associated response, identify the timing constraints which apply to both stimulus and response processing.

(3)   Aggregate the stimulus and response processing into a number of concurrent processes. A good general model for the system architecture is to associate a process with each class of stimulus and response as shown in Figure 16.2.

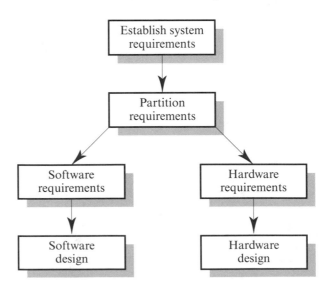

Figure 16.3
Parallel hardware and software design.

(4)   For each stimulus and response, design algorithms to carry out the required computations. Algorithm designs often have to be developed relatively early in the design process to give an indication of the amount of processing required and the time required to complete that processing.

(5)   Design a scheduling system which will ensure that processes are started in time to meet their deadlines.

(6)   Integrate the system under the control of a real-time executive.

Naturally, this is an iterative process. Once a process architecture has been established and a scheduling policy decided, extensive assessments and simulations are needed to check that the system will meet its timing constraints. These may reveal that the system will not perform adequately. The process architecture, the scheduling policy, the executive or all of these may then have to be redesigned.

Carrying out a timing assessment of a real-time system is difficult. Because of the unpredictable nature of aperiodic stimuli, the designers must make some assumptions as to the probability of these stimuli occurring (and therefore requiring service) at any particular time. These assumptions may be incorrect and system performance after delivery may not be adequate. Dasarthy (1985) and Burns (1991) discuss general issues of timing validation. Gomaa (1993) includes a good discussion of methods for performance analysis.

Processes in a real-time system must be coordinated. Process coordination mechanisms ensure mutual exclusion to shared resources. When one process is modifying a shared resource, other processes should not be able to change that resource. Mechanisms for ensuring mutual exclusion include semaphores (Dijkstra, 1968a), monitors (Hoare, 1974) and critical regions (Brinch-Hansen, 1973). I do not cover these mechanisms here as they are well documented in operating system texts (Silberschaltz *et al.,* 1991; Tanenbaum, 1992).

Because real-time systems must meet their timing constraints, it may not be practical to use design strategies which involve additional implementation overhead. For example, object-oriented design involves hiding data representations and accessing attribute values through operations defined with the object. This involves an inevitable overhead and consequent loss of performance. I know of an aerospace project where object-oriented design was abandoned midway through the project. The system could not meet its timing requirements because of the overhead associated with object communications.

The programming language used for implementing a real-time system may also influence the design. Hard real-time systems are still often programmed in assembly language so that tight deadlines can be met. Other languages used include systems-level languages such as C which requires extra run-time support for parallelism.

Ada was originally designed for embedded systems implementation and has features such as tasking, exceptions and representation clauses. Its *rendezvous* capability is a good general-purpose mechanism for task synchronization (Burns and Wellings, 1990; Barnes, 1994). Unfortunately, the designers of the original version of Ada (Ada 83) made a number of design errors which mean that the language is unsuitable for hard real-time systems implementation. It is impossible to specify task deadlines, there is no inbuilt exception if a deadline is not met and a strict first-in, first-out policy for servicing a queue of task entries is imposed.

Ada 95, the revised version of the 1983 Ada standard (Barnes, 1993) has gone some way towards addressing these limitations. However, the designers of Ada 95 were limited as they had to maintain compatibility, as far as possible, with the earlier version of the language. It remains to be seen whether these changes provide all the facilities required for hard real-time system engineers. At the time of writing, implementations of Ada 95 are not generally available and the language is untested.

16.2 State machine modelling

As discussed in the introduction to this chapter, real-time systems have to respond to events occurring at irregular intervals. These events (or stimuli) often cause the system to move to a different state. For this reason, state machine modelling may be used as a way of describing a real-time system.

A state model of a system assumes that, at any time, the system is in one of a number of possible states. When a stimulus is received, this may cause a transition to a different state. For example, a system controlling a valve may move from a state 'Valve open' to a state 'Valve closed' when an operator command (the stimulus) is received. This approach to system modelling is illustrated in Figure 16.4. This shows

Figure 16.4
State machine model of a simple microwave oven.

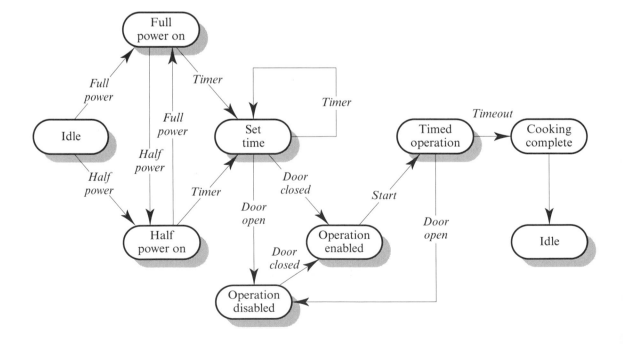

State	Description
Half power on	The oven power is set to 300 watts
Full power on	The oven power is set to 600 watts
Set time	The cooking time is set to the user's input value
Operation disabled	Oven operation is disabled for safety. Interior oven light is on
Operation enabled	Oven operation is enabled. Interior oven light is off
Timed operation	Oven in operation. Interior oven light is on. Timer is counting down
Cooking complete	Timer has counted down to zero. Audible alarm signal is on. Oven light is off

Stimulus	Description
Half power	The user has pressed the half power button
Full power	The user has pressed the full power button
Timer	The user has pressed one of the timer buttons
Door open	The oven door switch is not closed
Door closed	The oven door switch is closed
Start	The user has pressed the start button
Timeout	Timer signal indicating that set cooking time is finished

Figure 16.5
Microwave oven state
and stimulus
description.

a state machine model of a simple microwave oven equipped with buttons to set the power and the timer and to start the system.

The rounded rectangles in Figure 16.4 represent system states and the arrowed labels represent stimuli which force a transition from one state to another. The names chosen in the state machine diagram are descriptive and give an indication of operation. However, in a more complete design it is necessary to provide more detail about both the stimuli and the system states (Figure 16.5). Data dictionaries, as discussed in Chapters 6 and 15, could be used in real-time systems development to maintain such information.

The problem with the state machine approach is that the number of possible states increases rapidly. The simplified microwave oven state model (a very small system) is a relatively complex diagram. For large system models, therefore, some structuring of these state models is necessary. One way to do this is by drawing individual thread diagrams that show how a sequence of actions 'thread' their way through the system. A thread diagram should be produced for every identified combination of messages.

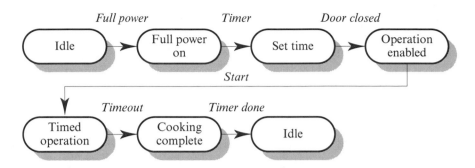

Figure 16.6
A thread diagram for a microwave oven.

Figure 16.6 shows a single message thread from the microwave oven system model.

State machine models are a good, language-independent way of representing the design of a real-time system. For this reason, they are an integral part of real-time design methods such as that proposed by Ward and Mellor (1985) and Harel (1987, 1988). Harel's method, which is based on a notation called *Statecharts,* has addressed the problem of the inherent complexity of state machine models. Statecharts structure state models so that groups of states can be considered as a single entity. The notation also allows concurrent systems to be represented as state models.

16.3 Real-time executives

A real-time executive is analogous to an operating system in a general-purpose computer. It manages processes and resource allocation in a real-time system. It starts and stops appropriate processes so that stimuli can be handled, and allocates memory and processor resources. It does not, however, usually include more complex operating system facilities such as file management.

The components of an executive depend on the size and complexity of the real-time system being developed. Normally, for all except the simplest systems, they will include the following:

- *A real-time clock*   This provides information to schedule processes periodically.
- *An interrupt handler*   This manages aperiodic requests for service.
- *A scheduler*   This component is responsible for examining the processes which can be executed and choosing one of these for execution.
- *A resource manager*   Given a process which is scheduled for execution, the resource manager allocates appropriate memory and processor resources.
- *A despatcher* This component is responsible for starting the execution of a process.

These components and their interactions are illustrated in Figure 16.7.

Systems that must provide a continuous service, such as telecommunication and monitoring systems with high reliability requirements, may also include further executive capabilities:

- *A configuration manager* This is responsible for the dynamic reconfiguration (Kramer and Magee, 1985) of the system's hardware. Hardware modules may be taken out of service and the system upgraded by adding new hardware without shutting down the system.

- *A fault manager* This component is responsible for detecting hardware and software faults and taking appropriate action to recover from these faults. Principles of fault tolerance and recovery are discussed in Chapter 19.

Stimuli processed by a real-time system usually have different levels of priority. For some stimuli, such as those associated with certain exceptional events, it is essential that their processing should be completed within the specified time limits. Other processes may be safely delayed if a more critical process requires service. Consequently, real-time systems usually need at least two priority levels:

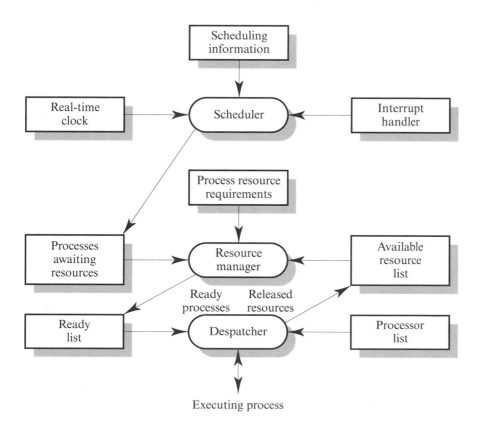

Figure 16.7
Components of a real-time executive.

(1)   *Interrupt level*   This is the highest priority level. It is allocated to processes which need a very fast response. One of these processes will be the real-time clock process.

(2)   *Clock level*   This level of priority is allocated to periodic processes.

Within both of these priority levels, different classes of process may be allocated different priorities. For example, there may be several interrupt lines. An interrupt from a very fast device may have to pre-empt processing of an interrupt from a slower device to avoid information loss. The allocation of process priorities so that all processes are serviced in time usually requires extensive analysis and simulation. There may be a further priority level allocated to background processes (such as a self-checking process) that do not need to meet real-time deadlines. These processes are scheduled for execution when processor capacity is available.

16.3.1 Process management

When an interrupt is detected by the executive, this indicates that some service is required. The computer's interrupt mechanism causes control to transfer to a predetermined memory location that contains an instruction to jump to an interrupt service routine. Interrupt service routines must be simple, short and have fast execution times. While the interrupt is being serviced, other interrupts are disabled and will be ignored by the system. To make the probability of information loss as low as possible, the time spent in this state must be minimized.

The service routine should disable further interrupts to avoid being interrupted itself. It should discover the cause of the interrupt and initiate, with a high priority, a process to handle the stimulus causing the interrupt. In some cases of high-speed data acquisition, the interrupt handler will buffer the data that the interrupt signalled was available. After this initial processing, interrupts are again enabled and control is returned to the executive.

Periodic processes are processes which must be executed at pre-specified time intervals for data acquisition and actuator control. The executive uses its real-time clock to determine when a process is to be executed. In most real-time systems, there will be several classes of periodic process. These will have different periods (the time between process executions), execution times and deadlines (the time by which processing must be complete). The executive must choose the appropriate process for execution at any one time.

The real-time clock is configured to 'tick' periodically where a 'tick' period might typically be a few milliseconds. The clock 'tick' initiates an interrupt level process which then schedules the process manager for periodic processes. The interrupt level process is not normally responsible for managing periodic processes because interrupt processing must be completed as quickly as possible.

The actions taken by the executive for periodic process management are shown in Figure 16.8. The list of periodic processes is examined by the scheduler

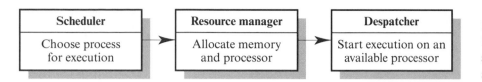

Figure 16.8
Real-time executive
actions required to
start a process.

which selects a process to be executed. The choice depends on the process priority, the process periods, the expected execution times and the deadlines of the ready processes. Sometimes, two processes with different deadlines should be executed at the same clock tick. In such a situation, one must be delayed so long as its deadline can still be met.

At any one time, there may be several processes, with different priorities, which should be executed. If *pre-emptive scheduling* is used, the currently executing process may be pre-empted and its execution halted to allow an alternative, higher-priority process to execute.

Information about the process to be executed is passed to the resource manager. The resource manager allocates memory and, in a multi-processor system, a processor to this process. The process is then placed on the 'ready list', a list of processes which are ready for execution. When a processor finishes executing a process and becomes available, the despatcher is invoked. It scans the ready list to find a process which can be executed on the available processor and starts its execution.

Baker and Scallon (1986) present a good discussion of the facilities required in real-time executives. Cooling (1991) also covers this topic and briefly discusses real-time system products. Although there are several real-time executive products available, the specialized requirements of many real-time systems often require that the executive be designed as part of the system.

16.4 Monitoring and control systems

Real-time systems are usually designed according to some generic architecture. There are a number of fairly standard system types such as monitoring systems, data acquisition systems, command and control systems, and so on. When a system is developed, its architecture is usually based on one of these standard types. Therefore, rather than discuss general design issues, I illustrate real-time systems design using some of these generic architectural models.

Presenting realistic examples of a real-time system design is difficult because these systems are usually very specialized. Application domain knowledge is essential if the examples are to be understood. This is particularly true of 'hard' real-time systems which interact with system hardware. The examples presented here are therefore simplified but I hope they give some indications of how to tackle a real-time system design.

Monitoring and control systems are an important class of real-time system. They check sensors providing information about the system's environment and take actions depending on the sensor reading. Monitoring systems take action when some exceptional sensor value is detected. Control systems continuously control hardware actuators depending on the value of associated sensors.

Consider the following example:

A burglar alarm system is to be implemented for a building. This makes use of several different types of sensor. These include movement detectors in individual rooms, window sensors on ground floor windows which detect if a window has been broken, and door sensors which detect door opening on corridor doors. There are 50 window sensors, 30 door sensors and 200 movement detectors in the system.

When a sensor detects the presence of an intruder, the system automatically calls the local police and, using a voice synthesizer, reports the location of the alarm. It also switches on lights in the rooms around the active sensor and sets off an audible alarm. Multiple sensor alerts may be received by the system and the building lights must be switched on around each sensor. Calls to the police and the audible alarm initiation are not repeated in the event of multiple sensor alerts.

The sensor system is normally powered by mains power but is equipped with a battery backup which can allow operation for 24 hours after mains power has been lost. Power loss is detected using a separate power circuit monitor that monitors the mains voltage. It interrupts the alarm system when a voltage drop is detected. The system must be manually switched back to mains power. A separate alarm system (not described here) is used to notify a power loss.

This system is a 'soft' real-time system which does not have stringent timing requirements. The sensors do not need to detect high-speed events so they need only be polled twice per second.

The design process starts by identifying the aperiodic stimuli which the system receives and the associated responses. I have simplified the design by ignoring stimuli generated by system self-checking procedures and external stimuli generated to test the system or to switch it off in the event of a false alarm. This means, there are only two classes of stimulus which must be processed:

(1)   *Power failure* This is generated by the circuit monitor. The required response is to switch the circuit to backup power by signalling an electronic power switching device.

(2)   *Intruder alarm* This is a stimulus generated by one of the system sensors. The response to this stimulus is to compute the room number of the active sensor, set up a call to the police, initiate the voice synthesizer to manage the call, and switch on the audible intruder alarm and the building lights in the area.

The next step in the design process is to consider the timing constraints associated with each stimulus and associated response. These timing constraints are shown in

Figure 16.9. In this diagram, the different classes of sensor which can generate an alarm stimulus have been listed separately as these have different timing requirements.

Allocation of the system functions to concurrent processes is the next design stage. There are three different types of sensor which must be polled periodically so each of these sensor types has an associated process. There is an interrupt-driven system to handle power failure and switching, a communications system, a voice synthesizer, an audible alarm system and a light switching system to switch on lights around the sensor. Each of these systems is controlled by an independent process. This suggests the system architecture shown in Figure 16.10.

Annotated arrows joining processes indicate data flows between processes with the annotation indicating the type of data flow. The arrow associated with each process on the top right indicates control. The arrows on a periodic process use solid lines with the minimum number of times a process should be executed per second as an annotation. The rate of period scheduling is determined by the number of sensors and the timing requirements of the system. For example, there are 30 door sensors which must be interrogated twice per second. This means that the associated door sensor process must run 60 times (60 Hz) per second. Similarly, the movement detector process must run 400 times per second.

Aperiodic processes have dashed lines on the control arrows. The lines are annotated with the event which causes the process to be scheduled. The control information on the actuator processes (that is, the audible alarm controller, the lighting controller and so on) indicates that they are started by an explicit command from the Alarm system process.

All processes need not receive data from other processes. For example, the process responsible for managing a power failure has no need for data from elsewhere in the system.

Stimulus/response	Timing requirements
Power fail interrupt	The switch to backup power must be completed within a deadline of 50 ms
Door alarm	Each door alarm should be polled twice per second
Window alarm	Each window alarm should be polled twice per second
Movement detector	Each movement detector should be polled twice per second
Audible alarm	The audible alarm should be switched on within $1/2$ second of an alarm being raised by a sensor
Lights switch	The lights should be switched on within $1/2$ second of an alarm being raised by a sensor
Communications	The call to the police should be started within 2 seconds of an alarm being raised by a sensor
Voice synthesizer	A synthesized message should be available within 4 seconds of an alarm being raised by a sensor

Figure 16.9
Stimulus/response timing requirements.

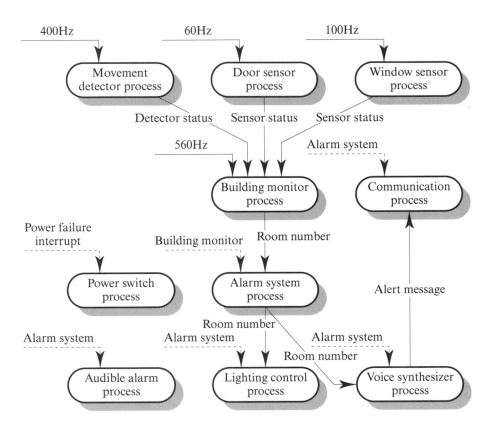

.Figure 16.10
Process architecture of
the intruder alarm
system.

The designs of each of these processes may be expressed in more detail using some design description language. Figure 16.11 shows the Ada specification of the Building_monitor process which polls the system sensors. If these signal an intruder, the software activates the associated alarm system. It is assumed in this design that the timing requirements (included as comments) can be met.

C and C++ can be used for implementing real-time systems but these languages do not have built-in support for concurrency. The facilities provided by the operating system or real-time executive must be used for process creation, initialization and so on. Because of the lack of language support for concurrency, I have not included C++ equivalents of the Ada examples in this chapter.

Once the system process architecture has been established, algorithms for stimulus processing and response generation should be designed. As discussed in Section 16.2, this detailed design stage is necessary early in the design process to ensure that the system can meet its specified timing constraints. If the associated algorithms are complex, changes to the timing constraints may be required. Unless signal processing is required, real-time system algorithms are often very simple. They only require a memory location to be checked, some simple computations to be carried out or a signal to be despatched. This is the case with the burglar alarm system so I leave algorithm design as an exercise for the reader.

```
task Building_monitor is
    entry Initialize ;
    entry Test ;
    entry Monitor ;
end Building_monitor ;

task body Building_monitor is
    type ROOMS is array (NATURAL range <>) of ROOM_NUMBER ;
    Move_sensor, Window_sensor, Door_sensor : SENSOR ;
    Move_sensor_locations: ROOMS (0..Number_of_move_sensors–1) ;
    Window_sensor_locations: ROOMS (0.. Number_of_window_sensors–1) ;
    Corridor_sensor_locations : ROOMS (0..Number_of_corridor_sensors–1) ;
    Next_movement_sensor, Next_window_sensor,
    Next_door_sensor: NATURAL := 0;
begin
    select
        accept Initialize do
            –– code here to read sensor locations from a file and
            –– initialize all location arrays
        end Initialize ;
    or
        accept Test do
            –– code here to activate a sensor test routine
            end Test ;
    or
        accept Monitor do
            –– the main processing loop
        loop
         –– TIMING: Each movement sensor twice/second
        Next_move_sensor :=
            Next_move_sensor + 1 rem Number_of_move_sensors ;
        –– rendezvous with Movement detector process
        Movement_detector.Interrogate (Move_sensor) ;
        if Move_sensor /= OK then
            Alarm_system.Initiate
                    (Move_sensor_locations (Next_move_sensor)) ;
        end if ;
        –– TIMING: Each window sensor twice/second
        –– rendezvous with Window sensor process
        Next_window_sensor :=
            Next_window_sensor + 1 rem Number_of_window_sensors ;
        Window_sensor.Interrogate (Window_sensor) ;
        if Window_sensor /= OK then
            Alarm_system.Initiate (Window_sensor_locations
                                    (Next_move_sensor)) ;
        end if ;
        –– TIMING: Each door sensor twice/second
        –– rendezvous with Door sensor process
        –– Comparable code to the above here
        end loop ;
    end select ;
end Building_monitor ;
```

Figure 16.11
Design specification of the Building_monitor process.

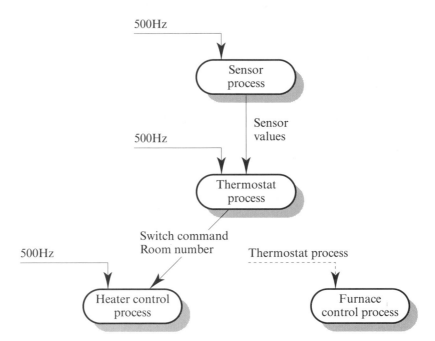

Figure 16.12
Process architecture of
a temperature control
system.

The final step in the design process is to design a scheduling system which ensures that a process will always be scheduled to meet its deadlines. In this example, deadlines are not tight. Process priorities should be organized so that all sensor polling processes have the same priority. The process for handling a power failure should be a higher-priority interrupt level process. The priorities of the processes managing the alarm system should be the same as the sensor processes.

The burglar alarm system is a monitoring system rather than a control system as it does not include actuators that are directly affected by sensor values. An example of a control system is a building heating control system. This system monitors temperature sensors in different rooms in the building and switches a heater unit off and on depending on the actual temperature and the temperature set on the room thermostat. The thermostat also controls the switching of the furnace in the system.

The process architecture of this system is shown in Figure 16.12. It is clear that its general form is similar to the burglar alarm system. Further development of this example is left as an exercise for the reader.

16.5 Data acquisition systems

Data acquisition systems are another class of real-time system which are usually based on a generic architectural model. These systems collect data from sensors for subsequent processing and analysis.

To illustrate this class of system, consider the system model shown in Figure 16.13. This represents a system which collects data from six sensors monitoring the

Sensors (each data flow is a sensor value)

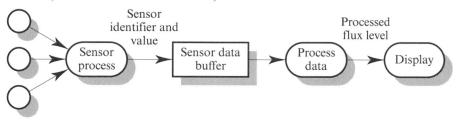

Figure 16.13
Architecture of a flux
monitoring system.

neutron flux in a nuclear reactor. The sensor data is placed in a buffer from which it is extracted and processed, and the average flux level is displayed on an operator's display.

Each sensor has an associated process which converts the analogue input flux level into a digital signal. It passes this flux level, with the sensor identifier, to the sensor data buffer. The process responsible for data processing takes the data from this buffer, processes it and passes it to a display process for output on an operator console.

In real-time systems which involve data acquisition and processing, the execution speeds and periods of the acquisition process and the processing process may be out of step. Sometimes, when significant processing is required, the data acquisition will go faster than the data processing. At other times where only simple computations need be carried out, the processing will be faster than the data acquisition.

To smooth out these speed differences, most data acquisition systems buffer input data using a circular buffer. The process producing the data (the producer) adds information to this buffer and the process using the data (the consumer) takes information from the buffer (Figure 16.14).

Obviously, mutual exclusion must be implemented to prevent the producer and consumer processes accessing the same element in the buffer at the same time. The system must also ensure that the producer does not try to add information to a full buffer and the consumer does not take information from an empty buffer. This means that the buffer itself should be implemented as an abstract data type with the buffer operations implemented as parallel processes.

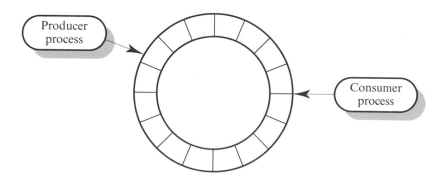

Figure 16.14
A ring buffer for data
acquisition.

Figure 16.15
Task specification of
Sensor_data_buffer.

```
task Sensor_data_buffer is
    -- Get and Put are like procedures which may
    -- execute in parallel. They are the only interface to the buffer.
    entry Put ( Val: SENSOR_RECORD ) ;
    entry Get ( Val: in out SENSOR_RECORD) ;
end Sensor_data_buffer ;
```

```
task body Sensor_data_buffer is
    Size: constant NATURAL := 50000 ;
    type BUFSIZE is range 0..Size ;
    Store: array (BUFSIZE) of SENSOR_RECORD ;
    Entries: NATURAL := 0 ;
    Front, Back: BUFSIZE := 1 ;
begin
loop
    -- A call to the Get and Put operations will only be accepted when
    -- one of the expressions associated with when is true.
    -- Thus, Put can only execute when there is space in the buffer,
    -- Get can only take items from the buffer when it is not empty.
    select
        when Entries < Size =>
            accept Put (Val: SENSOR_RECORD) do
                Store (Back) := Val ;
            end Put ;
        Back := Back rem BUFSIZE'LAST + 1 ;
        Entries := Entries + 1 ;
    or
        when Entries > 0 =>
            accept Get (Val: in out SENSOR_RECORD) do
                Val := Store (Front) ;
            end Get ;
        Front := Front rem BUFSIZE'LAST + 1 ;
        Entries := Entries − 1 ;
    end select ;
end loop ;
end Sensor_data_buffer ;
```

Figure 16.16
Detailed design of
Sensor_data_buffer.

The design of the sensor data buffer process shown in Figure 16.13 may be described as an abstract data type with concurrent operations. Assume that the information passed to the buffer is of type SENSOR_RECORD. Figure 16.15 shows the specification of the task describing the abstract data type.

The task specification shown in Figure 16.16 describes the buffer interface and shows that Get and Put are the only operations defined on the buffer. The detailed design description shows that the buffer is implemented as a ring buffer with a maximum of 50000 entries. If the number of entries exceeds 50000, the processes calling Sensor_data_buffer must wait until there is buffer space available before making a buffer entry.

Further reading

Real-time Systems and their Programming Languages. This is an excellent book on comparative real-time programming languages. Its coverage of real-time systems design is limited. It has good chapters on exception handling and reliability that are useful background for Chapters 18 and 19. (A. Burns and A. Wellings, 1990, Addison-Wesley.)

Software Design Methods for Concurrent and Real-time Systems. This book has a good survey of real-time systems design methods plus several very informative case studies of real-time systems design. (H. Gomaa, 1993, Addison-Wesley.)

Advances in Real-time Systems. This is an excellent IEEE tutorial volume that covers various aspects of real-time systems design and implementation. Some of the chapters assume that the reader has some familiarity with the subject area but others are good introductions. (J.A. Stankovic and K. Ramamritham, 1993, IEEE Press.)

KEY POINTS

- A real-time system is a software system which must respond to events in real-time. Its correctness does not just depend on the results it produces but also on the time when these results are produced.

- Systems design includes hardware and software design. It is good design practice to delay partitioning of a design into hardware and software elements until as late as possible in the design process.

- The architectural design of a real-time system usually involves organizing the system as a set of interacting, concurrent processes.

- A general model for real-time systems architecture involves associating a process with each class of sensor and actuator device. Other coordination processes may also be required.

- A real-time executive is responsible for process and resource management. It always includes a scheduler which is the component responsible for deciding which process should be scheduled for executing. Scheduling decisions are made using process priorities.

- Monitoring and control systems periodically poll a set of sensors which capture information from the system's environment. They take actions, depending on the sensor readings, by issuing commands to actuators.

- Data acquisition systems are usually organized according to a producer–consumer model. The producer process inputs the data into a circular buffer where it is consumed by the consumer process. The buffer is also implemented as a process so that conflicts between the producer and consumer are eliminated.

EXERCISES

16.1 Using examples, explain why real-time systems usually have to be implemented using concurrent processes.

16.2 Explain why an object-oriented approach to software development may not be suitable for real-time systems.

16.3 Draw state machine models of the control software for the following systems:

(a) An automatic washing machine which has different programs for different types of clothes.

(b) The software which controls a compact disc player.

(c) A telephone answering machine which records incoming messages and displays the number of accepted messages on an LED display. The system should allow the telephone owner to dial in, type a sequence of numbers (identified as tones) and have the recorded messages replayed over the phone.

(d) A drinks vending machine which can dispense coffee with or without milk and sugar. The user deposits a coin and makes his or her selection by pressing a button on the machine. This causes a cup with powdered coffee to be output. The user places this cup under a tap, presses another button and hot water is dispensed.

16.4 Draw a thread diagram for the action 'dispense coffee with milk' in the above drinks vending machine system.

16.5 Using the real-time system design techniques discussed in this chapter, redesign the weather station data collection system covered in Chapter 14.

16.6 Design a process architecture for an environmental monitoring system which collects data from a set of air quality sensors situated around a city. There are 5000 sensors organized into 100 neighbourhoods. Each sensor must be interrogated four times per second. When more than 30% of the sensors in a particular neighbourhood indicate that the air quality is below an acceptable level, local warning lights are activated. All sensors return the readings to a central computer which generates reports every 15 minutes on the air quality in the city.

16.7 Write a detailed algorithm design for the processes identified in Figure 16.12. Your design may be expressed in Ada or in some other appropriate language.

16.8 Develop the producer/consumer example discussed in Section 16.5 by designing the details of the producer and consumer processes. They should be implemented as concurrent processes.

16.9 You are asked to work on a real-time development project for a military application but have no previous experience of projects in that domain. Discuss what you, as a professional software engineer, should do before starting work on the project.

User Interface Design

Objectives

- To propose some general design principles which should be followed by engineers responsible for user interface design.

- To describe direct manipulation interfaces as a means of system interaction.

- To discuss factors which should be taken into account when designing information presentation.

- To describe the user support which should be built into user interfaces and the associated user documentation.

- To introduce the notion of usability attributes and simple approaches to system evaluation.

Contents

Computer system design encompasses a spectrum of activities from hardware design to user interface design. Electronic engineers have always been responsible for hardware design. However, few organizations employ specialist interface designers. Software engineers must often take responsibility for user interface design as well as the design of the software to implement that interface. Human factors specialists may assist with this process in large organizations; however, in smaller companies such specialists are rarely used.

The user interface of a system is often the yardstick by which that system is judged. An interface which is difficult to use will, at best, result in a high level of user errors. At worst, it will cause the software system to be discarded, irrespective of its functionality. If information is presented in a confusing or misleading way, the user may misunderstand the meaning of an item of information. They may initiate a sequence of actions which corrupt data or even cause catastrophic system failure.

When the first edition of this book was published in 1982, the standard interaction device was a 'dumb' alphanumeric terminal with green or blue characters displayed on a black background. User interfaces had to be textual or form-based. Most computer users now have a personal computer with a very powerful processor and a high-resolution colour display. These include graphical user interfaces (GUIs) which support high-resolution colour screens and interaction using a mouse as well as a keyboard.

Although text-based interfaces will remain in use for many years, users increasingly expect application systems to have some form of graphical interface. I therefore concentrate on this style of interface here. I do not discuss interfaces which require special (perhaps very simple) displays such as those incorporated in consumer and business products such as video recorders, televisions, copiers and fax machines.

Graphical user interfaces will be familiar to most readers of this book. They are available on all PCs, Apple computers and Unix workstations. Figure 17.1 shows the principal characteristics of this type of interface.

The advantages of GUIs are:

- They are relatively easy to learn and use. Users with no computing experience can learn to use the interface after a brief training session.

- The user has multiple screens (windows) for system interaction. Switching from one task to another is possible without losing sight of information generated during the first task.

- Fast, full-screen interaction is possible with immediate access to anywhere on the screen.

User interface design cannot be covered in any depth in a single chapter. My intention is to introduce important issues in this complex subject and, perhaps, help engineers to avoid dangerous design errors. There are many textbooks on user interface design such as those by Shneiderman (1992), Dix *et al.* (1993) and Preece *et al.* (1994).

Characteristic	Description
Windows	Multiple windows allow different information to be displayed simultaneously on the user's screen.
Icons	Icons represent different types of information. On some systems, icons represent files; on others, icons represent processes.
Menus	Commands are selected from a menu rather than typed in a command language.
Pointing	A pointing device such as a mouse is used for selecting choices from a menu or indicating items of interest in a window.
Graphics	Graphical elements can be mixed with text on the same display.

Figure 17.1
The characteristics of graphical user interfaces.

This chapter does not discuss user interface implementation. Graphical interfaces are much more complex than simple textual interfaces. A significant fraction of the resources devoted to application development must be spent on implementing the user interface. Bass and Coutaz (1991) have written an excellent book on this topic, and Young's book (1990) is a good introduction to X-windows programming. There are innumerable books on user interface programming for PCs and Apple computers.

17.1 Design principles

User interface design must take into account the needs, experience and capabilities of the system user. Potential users should be involved in the design process. It is impossible to judge user interfaces from an abstract description. Prototyping (discussed in Chapter 8) is essential for user interface development. The prototype should be made available to users and the resulting feedback used to improve the user interface design.

Designers must take into account the physical and mental limitations of the humans who use computer systems. The most important, perhaps, is the need to recognize the limitations on the size of short-term memory and to avoid overloading the user with information. This is discussed in Chapter 28. People do many regular tasks without thinking explicitly about them. User interface consistency reduces the probability of error in these tasks.

Human capabilities are the basis for the design guidelines discussed in this chapter (Figure 17.2). These are general principles which are applicable to all user interface designs. A longer list of user interface design guidelines is given by Shneiderman (1992) and Maguire (1985). Organizations may also develop their own guidelines to implement a 'house-style' in their software.

Users should not be forced to adapt to an interface because it is convenient to implement. The interface should use terms familiar to the user and the objects

Principle	Description
User familiarity	The interface should use terms and concepts which are drawn from the experience of the anticipated class of user.
Consistency	The interface should be consistent in that comparable operations should be activated in the same way.
Minimal surprise	Users should never be surprised by the behaviour of a system.
Recoverability	The interface should include mechanisms to allow users to recover from their errors.
User guidance	The interface should incorporate some form of context-sensitive user guidance and assistance.

Figure 17.2
User interface design principles.

manipulated by the system should have direct analogues in the user's environment. For example, if a system is designed for use by secretarial staff, the objects manipulated should be letters, documents, diaries, folders, and so on. Operations might be 'file', 'retrieve', 'index', 'discard', and so on. Secretaries should not be forced to cope with computing concepts such as directories, file identifiers, file suffixes, and so forth.

Interface consistency means that system commands and menus should have the same format, parameters should be passed to all commands in the same way, and command punctuation should be similar. Consistent interfaces reduce user learning time. Knowledge learnt in one command or application is applicable in other parts of the system.

Interface consistency across sub-systems is also important. As far as possible, commands with similar meanings in different sub-systems should be expressed in the same way. It is dangerous for a keyboard command, such as 'Control-k', to mean 'keep this file' in a word processor and the same command to mean 'kill this transaction' in an information retrieval system.

This level of consistency is low-level consistency. Interface designers should always try to achieve this in a user interface. Consistency at a higher level is also sometimes desirable. For example, it may be appropriate to support the same operations (such as print, copy, and so on) on all types of system entities. However, Grudin (1989) points out that complete consistency is neither possible or desirable. It may be sensible to implement deletion from a desktop by dragging entities into a trashcan. Implementing deletion in the same way in a word processor would be unnatural.

Users become particularly irritated when a computer system behaves in a way which is unexpected. As a system is used, users build a mental model of how the system works. If an action in one context causes a particular type of change, it is reasonable to expect that the same action in a different context will cause a comparable change. If something completely different happens, the user is both surprised and confused. Interface designers must therefore ensure that comparable actions have comparable effects.

Users inevitably make mistakes when using a system. The interface design can minimize these mistakes (for instance, using menus means that typing mistakes are avoided) but mistakes can never be completely eliminated. The interface should contain facilities allowing users to recover from their mistakes. These can be of two kinds:

(1) *Confirmation of destructive actions* If a user specifies an action which is potentially destructive, he or she should be asked to confirm that this is really what is intended before any information is destroyed.

(2) *The provision of an undo facility* Undo restores the system to a state before the action occurred. Many levels of undo are useful as users don't always recognize immediately that a mistake has been made. In practice, this is expensive to implement. Most systems therefore only allow the last command issued to be 'undone'.

Finally, interfaces should have built-in user assistance or help facilities. These should be integrated with the system and should provide different levels of help and advice. Levels should range from basic information on getting started with the system to a full description of system facilities. These help facilities should be structured; users should not be overwhelmed with information when they ask for help. Help facilities and other forms of user guidance are discussed in Section 17.4.

These principles emphasize that the interface design process should be *user-centred* (Norman and Draper, 1986). Computer users are trying to solve some problem using the computer yet many existing systems do not take user needs and limitations into account. The designer should always bear in mind that system users have a task to accomplish and the interface should be oriented towards that task. Users may participate directly in the design process as team members. This approach has been used with some success in Scandinavia in what is called *participatory design* (Kyng, 1988; Greenbaum and Kyng, 1991).

17.2 User–system interaction

The designer of a user interface to a computer is faced with two key issues. How can information from the user be provided to the computer system and how can information from the computer system be presented to the user? A coherent user interface must integrate user interaction and information presentation through some common framework such as an interface metaphor.

Most of this section is concerned with direct manipulation interfaces where users interact by modifying information as it is presented on their screen, and issue commands using menus. I also briefly discuss command-line interfaces. Issues concerning the presentation of information are covered in Section 17.3.

17.2.1 Direct manipulation

A direct manipulation interface presents users with a model of their information space. They interact with this information through direct actions such as replacing information, moving information, and so on. Explicit commands to modify information are not necessary. Modifications to the presented model immediately change the underlying information.

A familiar example of a direct manipulation interface is the interface provided by most word processors or screen editors. In this case, the information space is composed of a sequence of paragraphs which are presented to the user as a document. To insert text the cursor is positioned at the appropriate place in the display and text is typed. It appears immediately, showing users the effects of their action. Another example is the graphical user interface, where the user is presented with a list of filenames. To change the name of a file, the user selects the text on the display then types the replacement name.

The advantages of direct manipulation interfaces are:

● Users feel in control of the computer and are not intimidated by it.

● User learning time is relatively short.

● Users get immediate feedback on their actions. Mistakes can often be detected and corrected quickly.

Problems of designing a direct manipulation interface are:

● How can an appropriate information model and metaphors be derived? In some cases, this is straightforward. For example, in the Apple Macintosh, deletion of an entity involves dragging its icon into a trashcan which is an obvious metaphor for throwing something away. However, it is not always easy to find an appropriate model if there is no obvious real-world analogy which can be used.

● Given that users have a large information space (normally the case in large systems), how can they navigate around that space and always be aware of their current position? This is comparable to the problems of dealing with multi-level menus, covered in Section 17.2.3.

Direct manipulation interfaces are complex to program and make heavy demands on the underlying processor and memory. However, performance problems due to inadequate hardware are lessening because of the availability of fast, relatively cheap, processors.

One of the simplest and easiest to understand direct manipulation interfaces is a form-based interface. The user is presented with a form to fill in. The fields in the form are labelled with the field names indicating the information to be provided. Figure 17.3 shows an example of a form-based interface which might be used to collect information for a library cataloguing system.

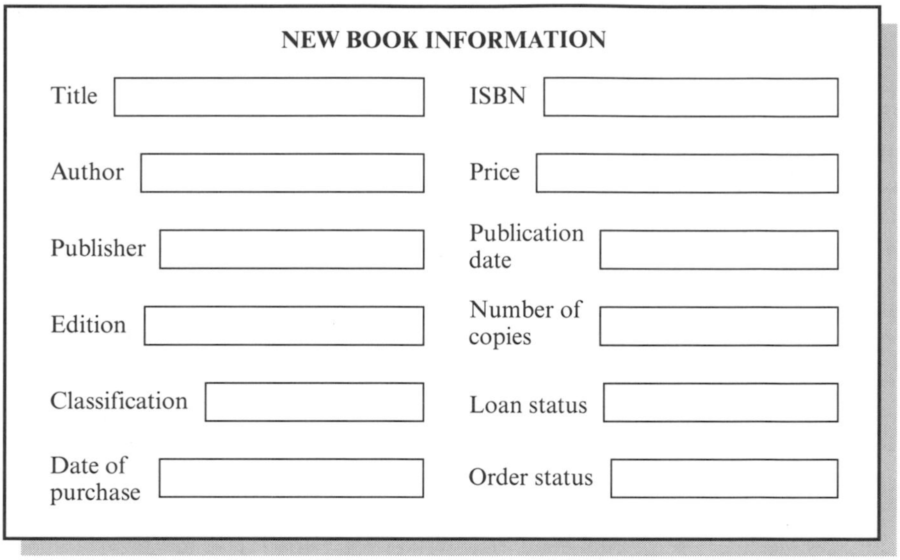

Figure 17.3
Form-based interface for a library cataloguing system.

The user inputs the information requested and moves to the next input field using the tab key or by selecting the field using a mouse. Checks can be associated with each field to ensure that the data input is of the correct form. Where there are relatively few possible inputs for a particular field, a menu of possibilities may be offered to the user.

Form-based interfaces are suitable for applications where users can be given some training. They are not really suitable for casual use. Untrained users will not know exactly what form the data in each field should take.

17.2.2 Interface models

The need for user interface consistency was identified as a basic principle of user interface design in the first part of this chapter. One way of helping achieve consistency is to define a consistent model or metaphor for user–computer interaction. The user interface model should be analogous to some real-world model which the user understands.

The best-known metaphor is the desktop metaphor (Ellis and Nutt, 1980) where the user's screen represents a desktop. System entities are represented by icons on that desktop. Deleting an entity involves dragging it to a trashcan, reading electronic mail is accomplished by 'opening' a mailbox. Documents may be stored by dragging them into a filing cabinet. This metaphor was first implemented on Xerox computers. In slightly different forms, it is the basis of the graphical interfaces designed by Apple, Microsoft and IBM.

The desktop metaphor is not suitable for supporting complex system interactions such as that offered by applications such as editors, database systems and so on. These systems maintain the desktop metaphor to some extent but supplement this by adding a control panel which is a graphical representation of system commands. This control panel can be a simple ribbon of icons where each icon represents a particular command. Clicking on the command icon is equivalent to selecting the command from a menu or typing its name. More complex control panels which replicate the control panels on complex hardware systems may include additional user interface objects such as display fields, sliders, indicators and so on.

Figure 17.4 shows an example of a control panel which is part of a CASE tool editing system. This control panel shows the style of interfaces which can be produced using the X-windows/Motif toolkit.

Control panels may include several kinds of entity to support user interaction:

(1) *Buttons* Picking (pressing) a button causes a single action to be initiated. Two buttons are shown, 'Print' and 'Quit', in Figure 17.4.

(2) *Switches* These may be set at a number of positions to configure a system or to move a system from one state to another. In Figure 17.4, the switches are named 'Units' (which turns a screen grid on and off) and 'Reduce' (which scales the display).

(3) *Menus* These are collections of buttons or switches which may be made visible and selected. They are represented by the dark grey rectangles along the base of the control panel labelled 'Nodes', 'Links' and so on. Picking a menu title causes a pull-down menu to appear.

(4) *Indicators* These are activated to show some action is taking place. The black rectangle marked 'Busy' in Figure 17.4 is an indicator.

(5) *Displays* Areas of the panel where graphical or textual information may be displayed. They have a name and a value. In Figure 17.4, displays named 'Title', 'Method', 'Type' and 'Selection' are shown. The interface designer may control whether or not a display may be edited.

(6) *Sliders* Input devices used to set a specific input value from a scale. They are like slider controls on hardware such as the volume control on a stereo system. The user drags the slider along the scale to set the required value. Sliders are not used in the example in Figure 17.4.

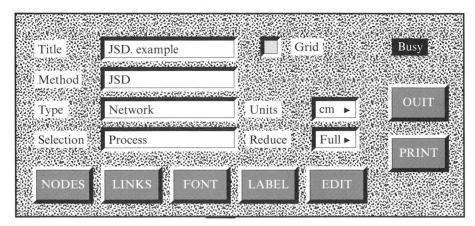

Figure 17.4
Design editor control panel – Motif style.

This control panel metaphor may be used to provide a consistent interface to many interactive systems ranging from information retrieval systems to CASE tools.

17.2.3 Menu systems

In a menu interface, users select one of a number of possibilities to issue a command to the machine. Users may type the name or the identifier of the selection; they may point at it with a mouse or some other pointing device; they may use cursor-moving keys to position the cursor over it. On some types of touch-sensitive terminals, they can point at the selection with a finger or a pen.

Menu-based systems have several advantages:

(1)   Users do not need to know command names. They are always presented with a valid command list. Meaningful command names such as 'Save' imply the command function.

(2)   Typing effort is minimal. This is important for occasional system users who cannot type quickly.

(3)   Some kinds of user error are avoided. Invalid menu options can be disabled by the system. Command syntax errors are never made.

(4)   Context-dependent help can be provided. With a menu system, it is easy to keep track of the user's context and to link this with a help system.

Menus can either be pull-down or pop-up. Pull-down menus display the menu title. Selecting this 'pulls down' the menu for command selection. Pop-up menus are associated with entities (such as a field on a form). Selecting the entity then clicking a mouse button (say) causes the menu to appear.

Pull-down menus have the advantage that the user always knows that they are there. They can predict the result of clicking on them. However, they take up screen space which is a problem if some commands are rarely used. Pop-up menus are more tailorable. The options can change to suit the entity with which they are associated. However, popping-up a menu may contradict the principle that the interface should not surprise users. They may be confused by it and may have to spend time understanding the menu before making a command selection.

The major problem with menu interfaces is the need to structure large menus. In some cases there may be tens, hundreds or thousands of possible menu choices. These have to be organized so that they are displayed in reasonably sized chunks.

There are several ways to tackle this problem:

(1)   *Scrolling menus*   When a choice is not displayed on a menu, the menu scrolls to display the next set of choices. This is impractical if there are thousands of menu choices.

(2)   *Hierarchical menus*   The menus are organized in a hierarchy. Selecting a menu item causes the current menu to be replaced by another menu

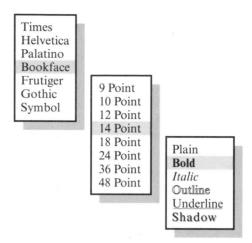

Figure 17.5
Walking menus.

representing its subtree. Hierarchical menus can manage very large numbers of choices but they are difficult to navigate around. Users get lost in the menu hierarchy.

(3) *Walking menus* Walking menus are a form of hierarchical menus which are possible when the tree is shallow. When a menu item is selected, this causes a further menu to be displayed adjacent to it (Figure 17.5). This is feasible if there are tens rather than hundreds of choices presented.

(4) *Associated control panels* These are a different form of hierarchical menu where the sub-menu is represented as a control panel. Clicking on a menu command causes a control panel to be popped up offering further options. This approach is used in many word processing systems. Selecting a 'Paragraph format' option may pop-up a control panel which shows all possibilities.

Menu navigation can be simplified by displaying a *menu map* which is a compressed picture of the menu hierarchy. This shows the user's current position in the hierarchy, the path followed to reach that position and other reachable parts of the hierarchy. The menu map may include facilities for user navigation. They may select a menu by pointing at it on the map. This allows large jumps from one part of the hierarchy to another to be made with ease. I discuss this approach, in the context of help systems, in Section 17.4.

17.2.4 Command-line interfaces

Command interfaces require the user to type a text command to the system. The command may be a query, a request for some service or it may call up a sequence of other commands. These were the first type of interface offered by interactive systems as they can be implemented using relatively cheap, alphanumeric displays and limited processing power. A very large number of systems have been developed with command-line interfaces and these continue in use. Users of some operating systems prefer command-line interfaces because they allow faster interaction than GUIs.

The advantages and disadvantages of a command-line interface are:

- Language processing techniques are well developed because of the work done on compiler techniques. Creating a command language processor is usually much easier than implementing a graphical user interface.

- However, users have to learn a command language which is sometimes very complex. In some cases (such as the Unix shell language) few users ever learn the complete language.

- Commands of almost arbitrary complexity can be created by combining individual commands. A powerful feature of the Unix system is its facility to write command language programs.

- However, users inevitably make errors in expressing commands. This requires error handling and message generation facilities to be included in the command language processor.

- The interface can be made concise with little typing effort on the part of the user.

- However, system interaction is through a keyboard. The interface cannot make full use of pointing devices, like a mouse.

Command-line interfaces are not suitable for casual and inexperienced users. The time taken to learn the command language is disproportionate to the time spent interacting with the computer. For such users a menu-based interface (or, perhaps, a natural language interface) is the only acceptable interface style.

Experienced, regular computer users sometimes prefer a command-based interface as the overhead involved in menu selection irritates them and slows down their work. Command interfaces allow faster interaction with the computer and simplify the input of complex requests. Experienced users may also wish to combine commands into procedures and programs.

Of course, command language interfaces and menu-based interfaces are not mutually exclusive. Many large software systems must accommodate a wide variety of users from experienced computer professionals to casual users with no computing background. Some systems which have a standard menu interface also provide a simple command language (sometimes called keyboard shortcuts) which allows commands to be input without choosing them from a menu.

This can be generalized so that a number of different user interface processors can be associated with a system. Different interface styles may be provided for different classes of user (Figure 17.6). The full functionality of the command language can be offered to regular experienced users with a simpler menu interface offered to less experienced or occasional users.

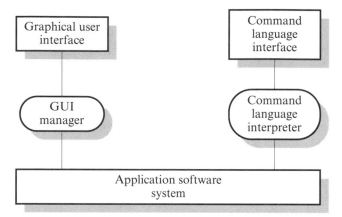

Figure 17.6
Multiple user
interfaces.

17.3 Information presentation

All interactive systems have to provide some way of presenting information to users. The information presentation may simply be a direct representation of the input information (for example, text in a word processor) or it may present the information in some other, more meaningful way. There are many systems such as command and control systems, geographical information systems and so on whose principal function is to present large amounts of information to users. They must understand the information and the relationships between information items. Finding the best presentation of information needs knowledge of the background of the users of that information and the ways in which they use the system.

It is good system design practice to keep the software required for information presentation separate from the information itself. To some extent, this contradicts object-oriented philosophy which suggests that operations on data should be defined with the data itself. However, this presupposes that the designer of the objects always knows the best way to present information; this is definitely not always true. It is often difficult to know the best way to present data when it is being defined and object structures should not 'hard-wire' presentation operations.

By separating the presentation system from the data, the representation on the user's screen can be changed without having to change the underlying computational system. This is illustrated in Figure 17.7.

In deciding how to present information, the designer must take a number of factors into account:

(1) Is the user interested in precise information or in the relationships between different data values?

(2) How quickly do the information values change? Should the change in a value be indicated immediately to the user?

(3) Must the user take some action in response to a change in information?

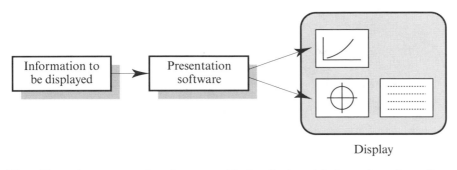

Display

Figure 17.7
Information
presentation.

(4)   Does the user need to interact with the displayed information via a direct manipulation interface?

(5)   Is the information to be displayed textual or numeric? Are relative values of information items important?

Information which does not change during a session may be presented either graphically or as text depending on the application. Textual presentation is usually better as it takes up less screen space. Static information (which does not change) should be distinguished from dynamic information by using a different presentation style. For example, all static information may be presented in a particular font, may be highlighted using a particular colour or may always have an associated icon.

Information should be represented as text when precise numeric information is required and the information changes relatively slowly. If the data changes quickly or if the relationships between data are significant, graphical presentation should usually be used.

For example, consider a system which records and summarizes the sales figures for a company on a monthly basis. Figure 17.8 illustrates how the same information can be presented as text or in a graphical form.

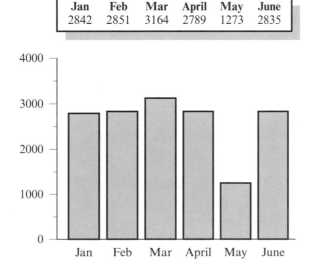

Jan	Feb	Mar	April	May	June
2842	2851	3164	2789	1273	2835

Figure 17.8
Textual and graphical
information
presentation.

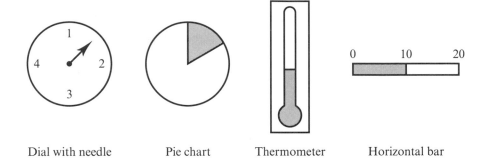

Figure 17.9
Methods of presenting
dynamically varying
numeric information.

Dial with needle   Pie chart   Thermometer   Horizontal bar

Managers studying sales figures are usually more interested in trends or anomalous figures rather than precise values. Graphical presentation of this information, as a histogram, makes the anomalous figures in March and May stand out from the others. Figure 17.8 also illustrates how textual presentation takes less space than a graphical representation of the same information.

Dynamically varying numeric information is usually best presented graphically using an analogue representation. Constantly changing digital displays are confusing as precise information is difficult to assimilate quickly. The graphical display can be supplemented if necessary with a precise digital display. Some different ways of presenting dynamic numeric information are shown in Figure 17.9.

Continuous analogue displays give the viewer some sense of relative value. In Figure 17.10, the values of temperature and pressure are approximately the same. However, the graphical display shows that temperature is close to its maximum value whereas pressure has not reached 25% of its maximum. With only a digital value, the viewer needs to know the maximum values. They must mentally compute the relative state of the reading. The extra thinking time required can lead to human errors in a stressful situation. Such situations are common when problems occur and many operator displays are showing abnormal readings.

When precise alphanumeric information is presented, graphics can be used to pick out the information from its background. Rather than presenting a line of information, it can be displayed in a box or indicated using an icon (Figure 17.11). The box displaying the message overlays the current screen display. The user's attention is immediately drawn to it.

Graphical highlighting may also be used in the display of text which is dynamically updated. The user's attention may be drawn to the change by temporarily applied highlighting or colour change. However, if changes occur rapidly, graphical highlighting should not be used. Rapid changes cause the display to flash which distracts and irritates users.

Figure 17.10
Graphical information
display showing relative
values.

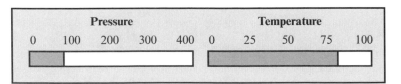

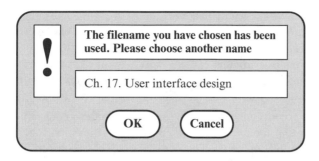

Figure 17.11
Textual highlighting of
alphanumeric
information.

17.3.1 Data visualization

The above advice on information presentation is concerned with relatively small amounts of information. Very large amounts of information must usually be visualized graphically if they are to be meaningful. This presentation may be used to navigate through the information or may be a way of exposing relationships which are not obvious from the raw data. Examples of possible data visualizations are:

- Weather information, gathered from a number of sources, is shown as a weather map with isobars, weather fronts and so on.

- The state of a telephone network is displayed graphically in a network management centre.

- A model of a molecule is displayed and manipulated in three dimensions using a virtual reality system.

Information visualization usually requires a vast amount of information processing to compute the relationships between data. It is only relatively recently that it has become practical to use it outside specialized laboratories.

Systems for information visualization rely on high-performance computers, colour graphics and, sometimes, specialized equipment such as a virtual reality helmet display, data glove and so on. As the cost of this equipment falls, information visualization will move from specialized domains into mainstream user interfaces. The details of the topic are, however, too complex to cover here. Watson and Earnshaw (1993) cover this topic in an introduction to visualization.

17.3.2 The use of colour

Colour gives the user interface designer an extra dimension which can be exploited in the display of complex information structures. In some cases, such as VLSI layout systems, system complexity is so high that, without colour, the display is incomprehensible. In other cases, colour may be used to draw the operator's attention to important events which have been detected by the software.

Unfortunately, it is easy to misuse colour to produce displays that are error-prone and disturbing to many users. The most common errors made by designers when incorporating colour in a user interface are:

(1)   Colour is used to communicate meaning. A significant number of men are colour-blind and may misinterpret the meaning. Human colour perceptions are different and there are different conventions in different professions about the meaning of particular colours. Users with different backgrounds may unconsciously interpret the same colour in different ways. For example, to a driver red usually means *danger*. However, to a chemist, red means *hot*.

(2)   Too many colours are used in the display and/or the colours are used in inconsistent ways. If too many colours are used or if the colours are too bright, the display may be confusing. The mass of colour may disturb the user (in the same way that some abstract paintings cannot be viewed comfortably for a long time) and cause visual fatigue. User confusion is also possible if colours are used inconsistently.

Shneiderman (1992) has expanded on his original colour usage guidelines presented in Shneiderman (1986) and gives 14 key guidelines for the effective use of colour in user interfaces. I think that the most important of these are:

(1)   Limit the number of colours used and be conservative how these are used. No more than four or five separate colours should be used in a window and no more than seven in a system interface. Colour should be used selectively and consistently. It should not simply be used to brighten up an interface.

(2)   Use colour change to show a change in system status. If a display changes colour, this should mean that a significant event has occurred. Thus, in a fuel gauge, a change of colour may indicate that fuel is running low. Colour highlighting is particularly important in complex displays where hundreds of distinct entities may be displayed.

(3)   Use colour coding to support the task which users are trying to perform. If they have to identify anomalous instances, highlight these instances; if similarities are also to be discovered, highlight these using a different colour.

(4)   Use colour coding in a thoughtful and consistent way. If one part of a system displays error messages in red (say), all other parts should do likewise. Red should not be used for anything else. If it is, the user may interpret the red display as an error message. Be aware of the assumptions which the users may have about the meaning of particular colours.

(5)   Be careful about colour pairings. Because of the physiology of the eye, people cannot focus on red and blue simultaneously. Eyestrain is a likely consequence of a red on blue display. Other colour combinations may also be visually disturbing or difficult to read.

Colour can improve user interfaces by helping users understand and manage complexity. However, there is still much to be learned about the effective use of colour. Given our current knowledge, user interface designers should therefore be conservative in their use of colour in user displays.

17.4 User guidance

A design principle suggested in the first section of this chapter was that user interfaces should always provide some form of on-line help system. Help systems are one facet of a general part of user interface design, namely the provision of user guidance which covers three areas:

(1)   the messages produced by the system in response to user actions;
(2)   the on-line help system;
(3)   the documentation provided with the system.

There is usually a distinction made between the provision of help (asked for by the user) and the output of messages (asynchronously produced by the system). However, they are really different aspects of a single user guidance system (Figure 17.12).

The design of useful and informative information for users should be taken seriously and should be subject to the same quality process as designs or programs. Managers must allow sufficient time and effort for message design and it may be appropriate to involve professional writers and graphic artists in the process. When designing error messages or help text, the factors shown in Figure 17.13 should be taken into account.

17.4.1 Error messages

The first impression which users may have of a software system is the system error messages. Inexperienced users may start work, make an initial error and

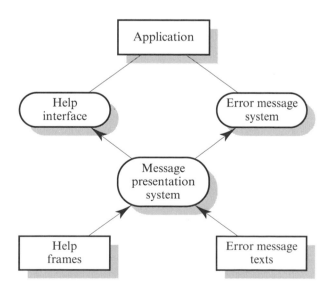

Figure 17.12
An integrated help and message system.

Factor	Description
Context	The user guidance system should be aware of what the user is doing and should adjust the output message to the current context.
Experience	As users become familiar with a system they become irritated by long, 'meaningful' messages. However, beginners find it difficult to understand short terse statements of the problem. The user guidance system should provide both types of message and allow the user to control message conciseness.
Skill level	Messages should be tailored to the user's skills as well as their experience. Messages for the different classes of user may be expressed in different ways depending on the terminology which is familiar to the reader.
Style	Messages should be positive rather than negative. They should use the active rather than the passive mode of address. They should never be insulting or try to be funny.
Culture	Wherever possible, the designer of messages should be familiar with the culture of the country where the system is sold. There are distinct cultural differences between Europe, Asia and America. A suitable message for one culture might be unacceptable in another.

Figure 17.13
Design factors in
message wording.

immediately have to understand the resulting error message. This can be difficult enough for skilled software engineers; it is often impossible for inexperienced or casual system users.

Error messages should always be polite, concise, consistent and constructive. They must not be abusive and should not have associated beeps or other noises which might embarrass the user. Wherever possible, the message should suggest how the error might be corrected. The error message should be linked to a context-sensitive on-line help system.

The background and experience of users should be anticipated when designing error messages. For example, say a system user is a nurse in an intensive-care ward in a hospital. Patient monitoring is carried out by a computer system. To view a patient's current state (heart rate, temperature, and so on), the system user selects 'display' from a menu and inputs the patient's name (Figure 17.14).

In this case, say the patient's name was Pates rather than Bates so that the name input by the nurse could not be recognized. A badly designed (but all too typical) system error message is shown in Figure 17.15.

This message is negative (it accuses the user of making an error), it is not tailored to the user's skill and experience level and it does not take context information into account. It does not suggest how the situation might be rectified. As well as the negative connotation of user error, this message uses system-specific terms (patient-id) rather than user-oriented language.

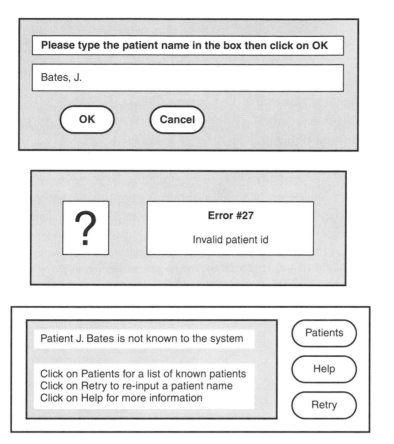

Figure 17.14
Nurse input of a patient's name.

Figure 17.15
A badly designed error message.

Figure 17.16
A user-oriented error message.

Figure 17.16 shows a better error message which might be issued when an incorrect patient name is input. This message is positive implying that the problem is a system rather than a user problem. The message identifies the problem in the nurse's terms, and offers an easy way to correct the mistake by pressing a single button. The help system is available if required.

17.4.2 Help system design

When users are presented with an error message they do not understand, they turn to the help system for information. This is an example of *help!* meaning 'help, I'm in trouble'. Another form of help request is *help?* which means 'help, I want information'. Different system facilities and message structures may be needed to provide these different types of help.

Help systems should provide a number of different user entry points (Figure 17.17). These should allow the user to enter the help system at the top of the message hierarchy and browse for information. Alternatively, they may enter the help system to get an explanation of an error message or may request an explanation of a particular application command.

All comprehensive help systems have a complex network structure in which each frame of help information may refer to several other information frames. The structure of this network is usually hierarchical with cross-links as shown in Figure 17.17. General information is held at the top of the hierarchy, detailed information at the bottom.

Problems can arise with help systems when users enter the network after making a mistake and then navigate around the network. Within a short time, they can become hopelessly lost. They must abandon the session and start again at some known point in the network.

Displaying help information in multiple windows can help alleviate this situation. Figure 17.18 shows a screen display in which there are three help windows. However, screen space is always limited and the designer must be aware that displaying extra windows may obscure other information which is important.

The actual text which is included in a help system should be prepared with the help of application specialists. The help frame should not simply be a reproduction of the user manual as people read paper and screens in different ways. The text itself, its layout and style have to be carefully designed to ensure that it is readable in a relatively small window.

In Figure 17.18, the help frame ('Mail redirection') is relatively short. It is best not to overwhelm the user with information in any one frame. Three buttons are provided in the help frame to request more information, to move onto the next help frame and to call up a list of topics on which help is available.

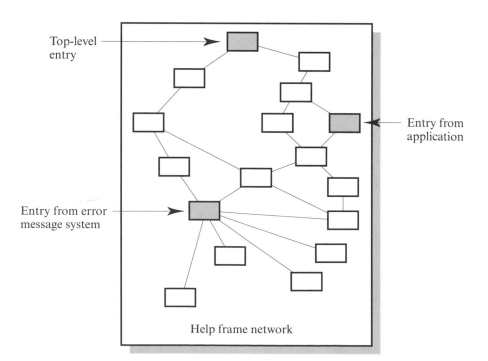

Figure 17.17
Entry points to a help system.

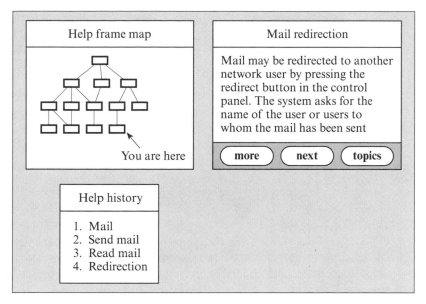

Figure 17.18
Help system windows.

The 'history' window shows the frames which have already been visited. It should be possible to return to these frames by picking an item from this list. The navigation window is a graphical 'map' of the help system network. The current position in this map should be highlighted by using colour, shading or, in this case, by annotation.

Users should be able to move to another frame by selecting it from the frame being read, by selecting a frame in the 'history window' to reread or to retrace their steps or by selecting a node in the network 'map' to move to that node.

Hypertext and hypermedia systems (Conklin, 1987; Neilson, 1990) may be used to implement a message system. Hypermedia systems are systems where information in the form of text, graphics, sound and video is structured hierarchically rather than linearly. The hierarchy may be easily traversed by selecting parts of a message or display. These systems have the advantage that help information can be provided in different ways. However, it is sometimes difficult to integrate them with applications so that they are context-sensitive as this requires the hypertext system to be controlled by context information from the application.

17.4.3 User documentation

Help and message systems are usually geared towards the end-user of the software system. The paper documentation which accompanies the system must also provide information for technical staff and engineers responsible for administering the system and diagnosing and repairing system faults.

To cater for these different classes of user and different levels of user expertise, there are at least five documents (or perhaps chapters in a single document) which should be delivered with a software system (Figure 17.19).

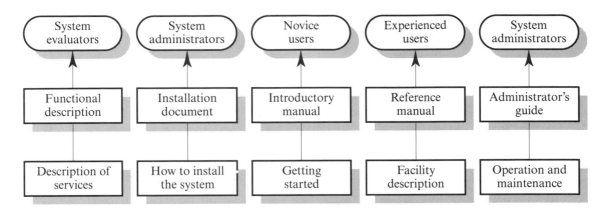

Figure 17.19
Types of document
produced to support
users.

These documents are:

(1)   *A functional description* which should describe, very briefly, the services that the system provides. Users should be able to read this document with an introductory manual and decide if the system is what they need.

(2)   *An introductory manual* which should present an informal introduction to the system, describing its 'normal' usage. It should describe how to get started and how end-users might make use of the common system facilities. It should be liberally illustrated with examples. It should include information on how to recover from mistakes and restart useful work. Carroll (1992) suggests that focusing on error recovery and minimizing the information that users have to read by eliminating redundancy is an effective way to organize introductory manuals.

(3)   *A system reference manual* which should describe the system facilities and their usage, provide a complete listing of error messages and describe how to recover from detected errors.

(4)   *A system installation manual* which should provide details of how to install the system. It should describe the disks or tape on which the system is supplied, the files on these disks and the minimal hardware configuration required. It should include installation instructions and details of how to set up configuration-dependent files.

(5)   *A system administrator's manual* may be provided for some types of system. This should describe the messages generated when the system interacts with other systems and how to react to these messages. If system hardware is involved, it might explain how to maintain that hardware. For example, it might describe how to clear faults in the system console, how to connect new peripherals and so on.

As well as manuals, other, easy-to-use documentation might be provided. A quick reference card listing available system facilities and how to use them is particularly convenient for experienced system users.

17.5 Interface evaluation

It is easy to be seduced by the attractiveness of the displays provided by modern personal computers and to assume that any interface which uses these displays must be better than a simple command interface. However, this is not necessarily so. Part of the system quality assurance process should therefore be concerned with an evaluation of the user interface. This evaluation should be concerned with assessing the usability of the interface and checking that it meets user requirements.

Unfortunately, it is rare for quantitative usability requirements to be included in the system requirements specification. Indeed, it is unusual for any user interface requirements to be specified apart from very general requirements such as the windowing system to be used or the particular type of display. This makes objective evaluation of user interfaces difficult.

Ideally, an evaluation should be conducted against a usability specification. Possible usability attributes are shown in Figure 17.20. Metrics for these usability attributes can be devised. For example, a learnability metric might state that an operator who is familiar with the work supported by the system should be able to use 80% of the system functionality after a three-hour training session.

Systematic evaluation of a user interface design can be an expensive process. It may involve cognitive scientists and graphics designers. It may involve designing and carrying out a statistically significant number of experiments with typical users in specially constructed laboratories fitted with monitoring equipment. A user interface evaluation of this kind is economically unrealistic for systems developed by small organizations with limited resources.

There are a number of simpler, less expensive techniques of user interface evaluation which can identify particular user interface design deficiencies:

- questionnaires which collect information about what users thought of the interface;

Attribute	Description
Learnability	How long does it take a new user to become productive with the system?
Speed of operation	How well does the system response match the user's work practice?
Robustness	How tolerant is the system of user error?
Recoverability	How good is the system at recovering from user errors?
Adaptability	How closely is the system tied to a single model of work?

Figure 17.20
Usability attributes.

- observation of users at work with the system and 'thinking aloud' about how they are trying to use the system to accomplish some task;
- video 'snapshots' of typical system use;
- the inclusion in the software of code which collects information about the most-used facilities and the most common errors.

Surveying users by using a questionnaire is a relatively cheap way of evaluating an interface. The questions should be precise rather than general. It is no use asking questions like 'Please comment on the usability of the interface' as the responses will probably vary so much that no common trend will emerge. Rather, specific questions such as 'Please rate the understandability of the error messages on a scale from 1 to 5. A rating of 1 means very clear and 5 means incomprehensible' are better. They are both easier to answer and more likely to provide useful information to improve the interface.

Users should be asked to rate their own experience and background when filling in the questionnaire. This allows the designer to find out if users from any particular background have problems with the interface. Questionnaires can even be used before any executable system is available if a paper mock-up of the interface is constructed and evaluated.

Observation-based evaluation simply involves watching users as they use a system, looking at the facilities used, the errors made, and so on. This can be supplemented by 'think aloud' sessions where users talk about what they are trying to achieve, how they understand the system and how they are trying to use the system to accomplish their objectives.

Relatively low-cost video equipment means that direct observation can be supported by recording user sessions for later analysis. Complete video analysis is expensive and requires a specially equipped evaluation suite with several cameras focused on the user and on the screen. However, video recording of selected user operations can be helpful to detect problems. Other evaluation methods must be used to find out which are the operations that cause user difficulties.

Analysis of recordings allows the designer to find out if the interface requires too much hand movement (a problem with some systems is that users must regularly move their hand from keyboard to mouse) and to see if unnatural eye movements are necessary. An interface which requires many shifts of focus may mean that the user makes more errors and misses parts of the display.

Instrumenting code to collect usage statistics allows interfaces to be improved in a number of ways. The most common operations can be detected. The interface can be reorganized so that these are the fastest to select. For example, if pop-up or pull-down menus are used, the most frequent operations should be at the top of the menu and destructive operations towards the bottom. Code instrumentation also allows error-prone commands to be detected and modified.

Finally, a means of easy user response can be provided by equipping each program with a 'gripe' command which the user can use to pass messages to the tool maintainer. This makes users feel that their views are being considered. The interface designer and other engineers can gain rapid feedback about individual problems.

None of these relatively simple approaches to user interface evaluation is foolproof and they are unlikely to detect all user interface problems. However, the techniques can be used with a group of volunteers before a system is released without a large outlay of resources. Many of the worst problems of the user interface design can then be discovered and corrected.

Further reading

Human–Computer Interaction. A good general text whose strengths are a focus on design issues and cooperative work. (A. Dix, J. Finlay, G. Abowd and R. Beale, 1993, Prentice-Hall.)

Designing the User Interface. This is a revision of what was probably the first textbook in this area. It is a great improvement on the first edition and provides a wide-ranging survey of the field. Contrary to its title, however, its discussion of design is implicit rather than explicit. (B. Shneiderman, 1992, Addison-Wesley.)

Developing Software for the User Interface. This is a good book on user interface engineering. It concentrates on graphical interfaces and, unlike some books on this subject, covers the engineering problems of building a user interface. (L. Bass and J. Coutaz, 1991, Addison-Wesley.)

KEY POINTS

- The interface design process should be user-centred. An interface should interact with users in their terms, should be logical and consistent and should include facilities to help users with the system and to recover from their mistakes.

- Menu systems are good for casual users because they have a low learning overhead. They can be awkward to use when the number of options is very large.

- Graphical information display should be used when it is intended to present trends and approximate values. Digital display should only be used when precision is required.

- Colour must be used sparingly and consistently in user interfaces. Designers should take account of the fact that a significant number of people are colour-blind.

- User help systems should provide two kinds of help. Help! which is 'help, I'm in trouble' and Help? which is 'help, I need information'.

- Error messages should not suggest that the user is to blame. They should offer suggestions how to repair the error and provide a link to a help system.

- User documentation should include beginners' and reference manuals. Separate documents for system administrators should be provided.

■ The system specification should include, wherever possible, quantitative values for usability attributes and the evaluation process should check the system against these requirements.

EXERCISES

17.1 I suggested in Section 17.1 that the objects manipulated by users should be drawn from their domain rather than a computer domain. Suggest appropriate objects for the following types of user and system.

  (a) a warehouse assistant using an automated parts catalogue;

  (b) an airline pilot using an aircraft safety monitoring system;

  (c) a manager manipulating a financial database;

  (d) a policeman using a patrol car control system.

17.2 Suggest situations in which it is unwise or impossible to provide a consistent user interface.

17.3 What factors have to be taken into account when designing a menu-based interface for 'walk-up' systems such as bank ATM machines? Write a critical commentary on the interface of an ATM that you use.

17.4 Discuss the advantages of graphical information display and suggest four applications where it would be more appropriate to use graphical rather than digital displays of numeric information.

17.5 What are the guidelines which should be followed when using colour in a user interface? Suggest how colour might be used to improve the interface of an application system which you use.

17.6 Write a short set of guidelines for designers of user guidance systems.

17.7 Consider the error messages produced by MS-Windows, Unix, MacOS or some other operating system. Suggest how these might be improved.

17.8 Design a questionnaire to gather information about the user interface of some tool (such as a word processor) with which you are familiar. If possible, distribute this questionnaire to a number of users and try and evaluate the results. What do these tell you about the user interface design?

17.9 Discuss if it is ethical to instrument software without telling end-users that their work is being monitored.

17.10 What ethical issues might user interface designers face when trying to reconcile the needs of end-users of a system with the needs of the organization that is paying for the system to be developed?

Part Four
Dependable Systems

This part of the book addresses the development of systems that must be dependable. Dependable systems are systems which have critical non-functional requirements for reliability, safety or security. Chapter 18 introduces the topic of software reliability and discusses reliability assessment. Chapter 19 covers some techniques for implementing highly reliable systems. Chapter 20 is concerned with software reuse. This is included in this section because reuse is an effective way to achieve dependability. Finally, Chapter 21 discusses the development of software that is safety-critical.

Contents

Software Reliability

Objectives

- To introduce the notion of software reliability and to discuss the problems of reliability specification and measurement.

- To describe a number of metrics which may be used to quantify reliability.

- To explain why it may be necessary to express the reliability of different parts of large software systems in different ways.

- To describe the process of statistical testing for reliability assessment.

- To show how reliability growth models may be used to help managers decide when system testing and debugging may stop.

Contents

Reliability is the most important dynamic characteristic of almost all software systems. As general expectations of quality in all types of system have increased, it is no longer acceptable to deliver software which fails on a regular basis. Unreliable software results in high costs for end-users. Developers of unreliable systems may acquire a bad reputation for quality and lose future business opportunities.

Informally, the reliability of a software system is a measure of how well users think it provides the services that they require. More formally, reliability is usually defined as the probability of failure-free operation for a specified time in a specified environment for a specific purpose. Say it is claimed that software installed on an aircraft will be 99.99% reliable during an average flight of five hours. This means that a software failure of some kind will probably occur in one flight out of 10 000.

General assertions about software reliability are of little value. Expressing the reliability of a software system as a probability is only valid in a particular context of use. Different sets of input data may cause the software to fail in different ways. Quantitative measures of reliability are therefore only valid when the software is used in comparable environments. It may be possible to quantify the reliability of an embedded system which always controls the same hardware; it is meaningless to specify the reliability of an interactive system which is used in many different ways.

However, a formal definition of reliability may not equate to users' experience of the software. The difficulty in relating such a figure to user experience arises because it does not take the nature of the failure into account. Users do not consider all services to be of equal importance. A system might be thought of as unreliable if it ever failed to provide some critical service. For example, say a system was used to control braking on an aircraft but failed to work under a single set of very rare conditions. If the aircraft crashed because these failure conditions occurred, pilots of similar aircraft would (reasonably) regard the software as unreliable.

On the other hand, say the same software provided some visual indication of its actions to the pilot. Assume this failed fairly regularly in predictable circumstances without the main system function being affected. Pilots might not consider the software as unreliable as the system which caused the catastrophic failure because the failure was not safety-critical.

Software reliability is a function of the number of failures experienced by a particular user of that software. A software *failure* occurs when the software is executing. It is a situation in which the software does not deliver the service expected by the user. Software failures are not the same as software *faults* although these terms are often used interchangeably.

Software faults may be programming or design errors whereby the delivered program does not conform to the system specification. Alternatively, they can be specification or documentation errors. The software behaves in a way that users did not expect. Software faults are static. They are characteristics of the program code. They are discovered either through program inspections or by inferring their existence from software failures.

Software faults cause software failures when the faulty code is executed with a set of inputs which expose the software fault. The code works properly for most inputs. Figure 18.1, derived from Littlewood (1990) shows a software system as a

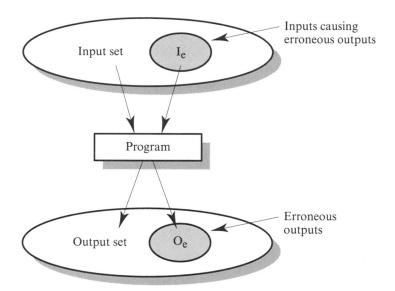

Figure 18.1
A system as an
input/output mapping.

mapping of an input to an output set. A program has many possible inputs (for simplicity, combinations and sequences of inputs are considered as a single input). The program responds to these inputs by producing an output or a set of outputs.

Some of these inputs (shown in the shaded ellipse in Figure 18.1) cause system failures where erroneous outputs are generated by the program. The software reliability is related to the probability that, in a particular execution of the program, the system input will be a member of the set of inputs which cause an erroneous output.

There is a complex relationship between observed system reliability and the number of latent software faults. Mills *et al.* (1987) point out that not all software faults are equally likely to cause software failure. Usually, there are a number of members of I_e which are more likely to be selected than others. If these inputs do not cause the faulty parts of the software to be executed, there will be no failures. The reliability of the program, therefore, mostly depends on the number of inputs causing erroneous outputs which arise during normal, rather than exceptional, use of the system.

Reliability is related to the probability of an error occurring in operational use. Removing software faults from parts of the system that are rarely used makes little real difference to the perceived reliability. Mills *et al.* found that, in their software, removing 60% of product defects would only have led to a 3% reliability improvement. This was confirmed in a separate study of errors in IBM software products. Adams (1984) noted that many defects in the products were only likely to cause failures after hundreds or thousands of months of product usage.

Therefore, a program may contain known faults but may still be seen as reliable by its users. They may never select an erroneous input so program failures never arise. Furthermore, experienced users often 'work around' software faults which are known to cause failures. They deliberately avoid using system features which they know can cause problems for them. Repairing the faults in these features may make no practical difference to the reliability as perceived by these users.

For example, the word processor used to write this book has an automatic hyphenation capability. This is used when text columns are short and any faults might manifest themselves when users produce multi-column documents. I never use hyphenation. Faults in the hyphenation code do not affect the reliability of the word processor as far as I am concerned.

Each user of a system uses it in different ways. Faults which affect the reliability of the system for one user may never be revealed under a different mode of working (Figure 18.2). In Figure 18.2, the set of erroneous inputs corresponding to the shaded ellipse in Figure 18.1 is shaded. The set of inputs produced by User 2 intersects with this erroneous input set. User 2 will therefore experience some system failures. User 1 and User 3, however, never use inputs from the erroneous set. For them, the software will always be reliable.

It is sometimes claimed that the use of formal methods for system development leads to more reliable systems. There is no doubt that a formal system specification is less likely to contain anomalies which must be resolved by the system designer. As I discussed in Chapter 9, developing a specification forces a detailed analysis which is useful for error discovery. It may also be possible to prove that an implementation is consistent with its specification so does not contain programming faults.

However, formal specification and proof do not guarantee that the software will be reliable in practical use. The reasons for this are:

(1) *The specification may not reflect the real requirements of system users*   Lutz (1993) discovered that many failures experienced by users were a consequence of specification errors and omissions which could not be detected by formal system specification. It may even be the case that the opaqueness of formal notations makes it more difficult for users to establish whether or not a system meets their real requirements.

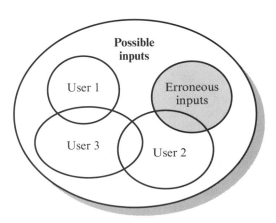

Figure 18.2
Software usage patterns.

(2)   *The proof may contain errors*   Program proofs are large and complex so, like large and complex programs, they usually contain errors.

(3)   *The proof may assume a usage pattern which is incorrect*   If the system is not used as anticipated, the proof may be invalid.

Because of additional design, implementation and validation overheads, increasing reliability can dramatically increase development costs. Figure 18.3 shows the relationship between costs and incremental improvements in reliability.

It is not possible to measure if a system is 100% reliable as this would require an amount of time equal to the lifetime of the system. However, as reliability requirements increase, system costs usually rise exponentially. This is mostly due to the need for redundant hardware as discussed in the next chapter and to vastly increased testing costs to check that the required reliability has been achieved. As I discuss in Section 18.2, some specifications which call for ultra-reliable systems are unrealistic. The number of tests required to validate these specifications cannot be carried out in a reasonable time.

There is, of course, an efficiency penalty which must be paid for increasing reliability. Reliable software must include extra, often redundant, code to perform the necessary checking for exceptional conditions as discussed in the next chapter. This reduces program execution speed and increases the amount of store required by the program. However, reliability should always take precedence over efficiency for the following reasons:

(1)   *Computers are now cheap and fast*   There is little need to maximize equipment usage. Paradoxically, however, faster equipment leads to increasing expectations on the part of the user so efficiency considerations cannot be completely ignored.

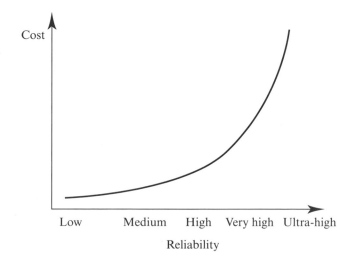

Figure 18.3
Costs versus reliability.

(2)   *Unreliable software is liable to be discarded by users*   If a company attains a reputation for unreliability because of a single unreliable product, this is likely to affect future sales of all of that company's products.

(3)   *System failure costs may be enormous*   For some applications, such as a reactor control system or an aircraft navigation system, the cost of system failure is orders of magnitude greater than the cost of the control system.

(4)   *Unreliable systems are difficult to improve*   It is usually possible to tune an inefficient system because most execution time is spent in small program sections. An unreliable system is more difficult to improve as unreliability tends to be distributed throughout the system.

(5)   *Inefficiency is predictable*   Programs take a long time to execute and users can adjust their work to take this into account. Unreliability, by contrast, usually surprises the user. Software that is unreliable can have hidden errors which can violate system and user data without warning and whose consequences are not immediately obvious. For example, a fault in a CAD program used to design aircraft might not be discovered until there have been several plane crashes.

(6)   *Unreliable systems may cause information loss*   Information is very expensive to collect and maintain; it may sometimes be worth more than the computer system on which it is processed. A great deal of effort and money is spent duplicating valuable data to guard against data corruption caused by unreliable software.

The reliability of the software product is influenced by the software process used to develop that product. A repeatable process which is oriented towards defect avoidance is likely to develop a reliable system. However, there is not a simple relationship between product and process reliability. Conforming to a particular process does not allow any quantitative product reliability assessment to be made. The relationships between process and product quality are discussed in Chapters 30 and 31 which cover quality management and process improvement.

Users often complain that systems are unreliable. This may be due to poor software engineering. However, a common cause of perceived unreliability is incomplete specifications. The system performs as specified but the specifications do not set out how the software should behave in exceptional situations. As professionals, software engineers must do their best to produce reliable systems which take meaningful and useful actions in such situations.

18.1 Software reliability metrics

Software reliability metrics have, by and large, evolved from hardware reliability metrics. However, hardware metrics are not always applicable for software reliability specification because of the differing nature of software and hardware failures. A hardware component failure tends to be permanent: the component stops working. The system is unavailable until it is repaired. The repair time is usually a factor in hardware reliability quantification. By contrast, software component failures are transient: they only manifest themselves with some inputs. The system can often continue in operation after a failure has occurred.

This distinction has meant that commonly used hardware reliability metrics such as *mean time to failure* (MTTF) are not really useful if we are interested in whether or not a software system will be available to meet a demand. It is not simple to relate system availability to software system failure because it depends on factors such as the time needed to re-initialize the system, the degree (if any) of data corruption caused by the software failure and so on.

Metrics which have been used for software reliability specification are shown in Figure 18.4. The choice of which metric should be used depends on the type of system to which it applies and the requirements of the application domain. For some systems, it may be appropriate to use different reliability metrics for different sub-systems.

In some cases, system users are most concerned about how often the system will fail, perhaps because there is a significant cost in restarting the system. In those

Metric	Explanation	Example systems
POFOD Probability of failure on demand	This is a measure of the likelihood that the system will fail when a service request is made. For example, a POFOD of 0.001 means that 1 out of 1000 service requests may result in failure.	Safety-critical and non-stop systems, such as hardware control systems.
ROCOF Rate of failure occurrence	This is a measure of the frequency of occurrence with which unexpected behaviour is likely to occur. For example, a ROCOF of 2/100 means that 2 failures are likely to occur in each 100 operational time units. This metric is sometimes called the failure intensity.	Operating systems, transaction processing systems.
MTTF Mean time to failure	This is a measure of the time between observed system failures. For example, an MTTF of 500 means that 1 failure can be expected every 500 time units. If the system is not being changed, it is the reciprocal of the ROCOF.	Systems with long transactions such as CAD systems. The MTTF must be greater than the transaction time.
AVAIL Availability	This is a measure of how likely the system is to be available for use. For example, an availability of 0.998 means that in every 1000 time units, the system is likely to be available for 998 of these.	Continuously running systems such as telephone switching systems.

Figure 18.4
Reliability metrics.

cases, a metric based on a *rate of failure occurrence* (ROCOF) or the mean time to failure should be used.

In other cases, it is essential that a system should always meet a request for service because there is some cost in failing to deliver the service. The number of failures in some time period is less important. In those cases, a metric based on the *probability of failure on demand* (POFOD) should be used. Finally, users or system operators may be mostly concerned that the system is available when a request for service is made. They will incur some loss if the system is unavailable. *Availability* (AVAIL), which takes into account repair or restart time, is then the most appropriate metric.

There are three kinds of measurement which can be made when assessing the reliability of a system:

(1)   The number of system failures given a number of system inputs. This is used to measure the POFOD.

(2)   The time (or number of transactions) between system failures. This is used to measure ROCOF and MTTF.

(3)   The elapsed repair or restart time when a system failure occurs. Given that the system must be continuously available, this is used to measure AVAIL.

Time is a factor in all of these reliability metrics. It is essential that the appropriate time units should be chosen if measurements are to be meaningful. Time units which may be used are calendar time, processor time or may be some discrete unit such as number of transactions. Calendar time may not be appropriate as some systems, such as telephone switching systems, spend much of their time waiting to respond to a service request. Basing reliability on calendar time would give an optimistic figure. Processor time is therefore probably the most appropriate unit for these systems.

Calendar time is an appropriate time unit to use for systems which are in continuous operation. For example, monitoring systems, such as alarm systems, and other types of process control systems fall into this category. Systems which process transactions such as bank ATMs or airline reservation systems have very variable loads placed on them depending on the time of day. In these cases, the unit of 'time' used should be the number of transactions; that is, the ROCOF would be number of failed transactions per N thousand transactions.

Reliability metrics are all based around the probability of a system failure. They cannot take account of the consequences of such a failure. Some faults, particularly those which are transient and whose consequences are not serious, are of little practical importance in the operational use of the software. For example, say a software system averaged several temperature readings taken at one minute intervals. The loss of some of this data is unlikely to have any significant effect on the average value computed.

Other types of failure may be catastrophic and might cause complete system failure with loss of life, property or valuable data. These are not equivalent to transient, inconsequential failures yet we do not have any metrics which can distinguish between them. When specifying reliability, therefore, different metrics for different failure classes may be necessary. I discuss failure classes in the following section.

18.2 Software reliability specification

In most system requirements documents, reliability requirements are expressed in an informal, qualitative, untestable way. Ideally, the required level of reliability should be expressed quantitatively in the software requirements specification. Depending on the type of system, one or more of the metrics discussed in the previous section may be used for reliability specification. Statistical testing techniques (discussed later) should be used to measure the system reliability. The software test plan should include an operational profile of the software to assess its reliability.

Unfortunately, reliability specifications are sometimes expressed in a form which is subjective, irrelevant or unmeasurable. For example, statements such as 'The software shall be as reliable as possible' are meaningless. Quasi-quantitative statements such as 'The software shall exhibit no more than N faults/1000 lines' are equally irrelevant. It is impossible to measure the number of faults per 1000 lines of code as you can't tell when all faults have been discovered. Furthermore, the statement means nothing in terms of the dynamic behaviour of the system. It is software failures not software faults which affect the reliability of a system.

The types of failure which can occur are system specific and, as previously discussed, the consequences of a system failure depend on the nature of that failure. When writing a reliability specification, the specifier should identify different types of failure and consider whether these should be treated differently in the specification. Examples of different types of failure are shown in Figure 18.5. Obviously combinations of these, such as a failure which is transient, recoverable and corrupting, can occur.

Most large systems are composed of several sub-systems which often have different reliability requirements. Because very highly reliable software is expensive, it is usually sensible to assess the reliability requirements of each sub-system separately rather than impose the maximum reliability requirement on all sub-systems.

Failure class	Description
Transient	Occurs only with certain inputs
Permanent	Occurs with all inputs
Recoverable	System can recover without operator intervention
Unrecoverable	Operator intervention needed to recover from failure
Non-corrupting	Failure does not corrupt system state or data
Corrupting	Failure corrupts system state or data

Figure 18.5
Failure classification.

The steps involved in establishing a reliability specification are as follows:

(1) For each identified sub-system, identify the different types of system failure which may occur and analyse the consequences of these failures.

(2) From the system failure analysis, partition failures into appropriate classes. A reasonable starting point is to use the failure types shown in Figure 18.5.

(3) For each failure class identified, define the reliability requirement using the appropriate reliability metric. It is not necessary to use the same metric for different classes of failure. For example, where a failure requires some intervention to recover from it, the probability of that failure occurring on demand might be the most appropriate metric. When automatic recovery is possible and the effect of the failure is some user inconvenience, ROCOF might be more appropriate.

As an example of a reliability specification, consider the bank auto-teller system which has been described elsewhere in the book. Assume that each machine in the network is used about 300 times per day. The lifetime of the system hardware is eight years and the software is normally upgraded every two years. Therefore, during the lifetime of a software release, each machine will handle about 200 000 transactions. A bank has 1000 machines in its network. This means that there are 300 000 transactions on the central database per day (say 100 million per year).

Failures fall into two broad classes: those that affect a single machine in the network and those that affect the database and therefore all ATMs in the network. Clearly, the latter type of failure is less acceptable than those failures which are local to the ATM.

Figure 18.6 shows possible failure classes and possible reliability specifications for different types of system failure. The reliability requirements state that it is acceptable for a permanent failure to occur in a machine roughly once per three years. This means that, on average, one machine in the banking network might be affected each day. By contrast, faults which simply mean that a transaction has to be

Failure class	Example	Reliability metric
Permanent, non-corrupting	The system fails to operate with any card which is input. Software must be restarted to correct failure	ROCOF 1 occurrence/1000 days
Transient, non-corrupting	The magnetic stripe data cannot be read on an undamaged card which is input	POFOD 1 in 1000 transactions
Transient, corrupting	A pattern of transactions across the network causes database corruption	Unquantifiable! Should never happen in the lifetime of the system

Figure 18.6
Examples of reliability specification.

aborted and the user must start again can occur relatively frequently. Their only effect is to cause minor user inconvenience.

Ideally, faults which corrupt the database should never occur in the lifetime of the software. Therefore, the reliability requirement which might be placed on this is that the probability of a corrupting failure occurring when a demand is made is less than one in 200 million transactions. That is, in the lifetime of an ATM software release, there should never be an error which causes database corruption.

However, a reliability requirement like this cannot actually be tested. Say each transaction takes one second of machine time and a simulator can be built for the ATM network. Simulating the transactions which take place in a single day across the network will take 300000 seconds. This is approximately 3.5 days. Clearly this period could be reduced by reducing the transaction time and using multiple simulators but it is still very difficult to test the system to validate the reliability specification.

In general, it is impossible to validate qualitative requirements which demand a very high level of reliability. For example, say a system was intended for use in a safety-critical application so it should never fail over the total lifetime of the system. Assume that 1000 copies of the system are to be installed and the system is 'executed' 1000 times per second. The projected lifetime of the system is 10 years.

This means that the total estimated number of system executions is approximately $3*10^{14}$. There is no point whatsoever in specifying that the probability of a failure in demand should be $1/10^{15}$ (allowing some safety factor, say). There is no way in which this reliability can be validated in the developed software system.

The cost of developing and validating a reliability specification for a software system is very high. As discussed in the following section, an operational profile to validate the reliability specification must be derived. A statistical testing and reliability measurement programme is necessary. Organizations must be realistic about whether these costs are worthwhile. They are clearly justified in systems where reliable operation is critical such as telephone switching systems or where system failure may result in large economic losses. They are probably not justified for many types of business or scientific system. These usually have relatively modest reliability requirements as the costs of failure are not high.

18.3 Statistical testing

Statistical testing is a software testing process in which the objective is to measure the reliability of the software rather than to discover software faults. It uses different test data from defect testing (Chapter 23), which is intended to find faults in the software. Statistical testing can be combined with reliability growth modelling which is discussed in the following section. Predictions of the final system reliability and when that will be achieved can be made. As failures are discovered, the underlying faults causing these failures are repaired so that the reliability of the system should improve in the course of the testing process.

The steps involved in statistical testing are:

(1)   Determine the operational profile of the software. The operational profile is the probable pattern of usage of the software. This can be determined by analysing historical data to discover the different classes of input to the program and the probability of their occurrence.

(2)   Select or generate a set of test data corresponding to the operational profile.

(3)   Apply these test cases to the program, recording the amount of execution time between each observed system failure. It may not be appropriate to use raw execution time. As discussed in the previous section, the time units chosen should be appropriate for the reliability metric used.

(4)   After a statistically significant number of failures have been observed, the software reliability can then be computed. This involves using the number of failures detected and the time between these failures to compute the required reliability metric.

This conceptually attractive approach to reliability estimation is not easy to apply in practice. The principal difficulties which arise are due to:

(1)   operational profile uncertainty;
(2)   high costs of operational profile generation;
(3)   statistical uncertainty when high reliability is specified.

The operational profile of the software reflects how it will be used in practice. It consists of a specification of classes of input and the probability of their occurrence. When a new software system replaces an existing manual or automated system, it is reasonably easy to assess the probable pattern of usage of the new software. It should roughly correspond to the existing usage with some allowance made for the new functionality which is (presumably) included in the new software. For example, an operational profile can be specified for telecommunication switching systems because telecommunication companies know the call patterns which these systems have to handle.

Typically, the operational profile is such that the inputs which have the highest probability of being generated fall into a small number of classes as shown on the left of Figure 18.7. There is an extremely large number of classes where inputs are highly improbable but not impossible. These are shown on the right of Figure 18.7. The ellipsis (…) means that there are many more of these unusual inputs which are not shown.

Musa (1993) provides guidelines and advice on the development of operational profiles. In the application domain in which he works (telecommunication systems), there is a long history of collecting usage data so the process of operational profile development is relatively straightforward. For a system taking about 15 person-years of development, an operational profile was developed in

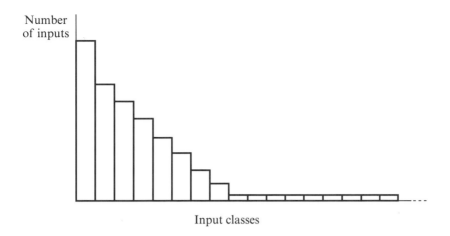

Number
of inputs

Input classes

Figure 18.7
An operational profile.

about one person-month. In other cases, the time needed was much longer (two to three person-years) but the cost, of course, is written off over a number of system releases. Musa reckons that his company (a telecommunications company) had at least a 10-fold return on the investment required to develop an operational profile.

However, when a software system is new and innovative it is more difficult to anticipate how it will be used. Systems are used by a range of users with different expectations, backgrounds and experience. There is no historical usage database. Computer users often make use of systems in ways which are not anticipated by their developers. The problem is further compounded by the fact that the operational profile may change as the system is used. When the abilities and confidence of users change as they gain experience with the system, they may use it in more sophisticated ways. Because of these difficulties, Hamlet (1992) suggests that it is often impossible to develop a trustworthy operational profile. Reliability measurements, therefore, are unreliable.

Statistical testing, as the name implies, relies on using a large test data set to exercise the software. It is based on the assumption that only a small percentage of the test inputs is likely to cause a system failure. By far the best way to create a large data set is to use some form of test data generator which can be set up to automatically generate random inputs. However, it is difficult to automate the production of test data for some classes of system, particularly interactive systems. Data sets for these systems have to be generated manually with correspondingly higher costs.

It is often straightforward to generate tests taken from the most common inputs. However, it is important that a statistically significant percentage of the unlikely inputs are also included in the test set. Creating these may be difficult. This is particularly true if a test data generator is used as it may have to be specially modified to create these rare but valid inputs. This is a particular problem for safety-related systems (see Chapter 21) where very unlikely combinations of inputs may have to be generated to exercise the system.

18.4 Reliability growth modelling

During software validation, software managers must decide how much effort should be devoted to system testing. They must try to predict when the required level of system reliability will be achieved. The goal of a project manager should be to test and debug the system until this required level of reliability is reached. As testing is very expensive, it is important to stop testing as soon as possible and not to 'over-test' the system. Sometimes, of course, reliability predictions may reveal that the required level of reliability will never be achieved. In this case, the manager must make difficult decisions about rewriting parts of the software or renegotiating the system contract.

A reliability growth model is a mathematical model of software reliability which predicts how software reliability should improve over time as faults are discovered and repaired. There are various models which have been derived from reliability experiments in a number of different application domains. The simplest of these models is a step function model (Jelinski and Moranda, 1972) where the reliability increases by a constant increment each time a fault is discovered and repaired (Figure 18.8).

There are two problems with this model. It assumes that software repairs are always correct and never increase the number of faults present in the software. As these repairs are made, the reliability of the software should (but may not) increase. Reliability will not necessarily increase after a fault has been repaired. The repair may introduce new faults whose probability of occurrence might be higher than the occurrence probability of the fault which has been repaired.

The simple equal-step model also assumes that all faults contribute equally to reliability and that each fault repair contributes the same amount of reliability growth. However, not all faults are equally probable. Repairing faults which are

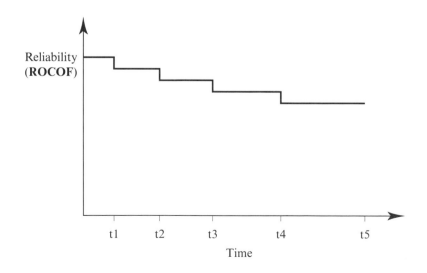

Figure 18.8
Equal-step function model of reliability growth.

more likely to occur contributes more to reliability growth than repairing faults which only manifest themselves occasionally.

Later models, such as that suggested by Littlewood and Verrall (1973), take these problems into account by introducing a random element into the reliability growth improvement effected by a software repair. Thus, each repair does not result in an equal amount of reliability improvement but varies depending on the random perturbation (Figure 18.9).

Littlewood and Verrall's model allows for negative reliability growth when a software repair introduces further errors. It also models the fact that as faults are repaired, the average improvement in reliability per repair decreases. The reason for this is that the most probable faults are likely to be discovered early in the testing process. Repairing these contributes most to reliability growth.

Note that in Figures 18.8 and 18.9, the reliability is measured in terms of the rate of occurrence of failures. Therefore, over time, this figure decreases indicating reliability improvements.

The above models are discrete, logical models. They match real reliability growth which is incremental. When a new version of the software with repaired faults is delivered for testing it should have a lower ROCOF than the previous version. However, to predict reliability, continuous mathematical models are needed and many different models, derived from different application domains, have been proposed. Musa *et al.* (1987) discuss a number of these models and Abdel-Ghaly *et al.* (1986) describe and compare several reliability growth models.

Reliability growth models can be used to predict when (or if) a particular level of reliability is likely to be attained. The model provides a way of assessing how fast the software quality is improving with time. The software is tested using a statistical approach and the reliability is measured. Discovered faults are repaired and the software re-tested until a number of reliability measurements have been made. The reliability measurements are compared with the growth model and reliability predications made.

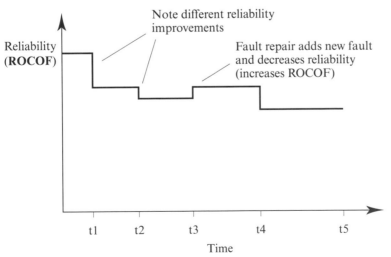

Figure 18.9
Random-step function model of reliability growth.

The different levels of reliability are plotted against the time between releases of the system which are statistically tested. The target system reliability is indicated on the graph. Given that the target reliability has not been reached when the model is being used, the next step is to fit the observed reliability data to one of the known reliability models (Figure 18.10).

Once the best curve-fit has been achieved, the model formula can then be used to suggest when the required reliability will be reached. The system testers can then estimate when system testing can finish. Alternatively, the reliability growth model may show that the required level of reliability is never likely to be reached. The reliability growth of the software may be so small that it will not reach the required value in the projected lifetime of the system. Either the reliability requirements have to be modified or the software has to be rewritten to eliminate large numbers of inherent faults.

Littlewood (1990), in a comparison of eight different reliability models, points out that there is no universally applicable reliability growth model. This is to be expected as the pattern of reliability growth is not independent of the application domain. He recommends that reliability growth predictions should be based on fitting observed data to several growth models. Whichever model exhibits the best fit should then be used to predict the reliability for that system. Brocklehurst and Littlewood (1992) reiterate this and discuss ways of calibrating different models to give more accurate predictions.

A complete discussion on reliability growth models and their use requires an understanding of statistical theory and is outside the scope of this book. Readers who

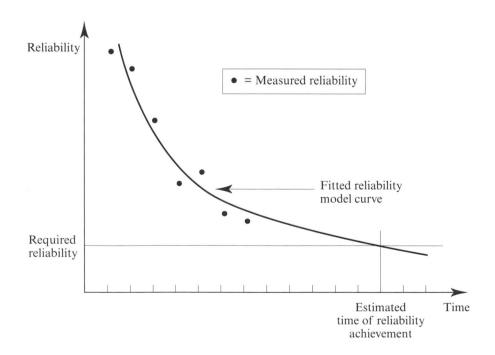

Figure 18.10
Reliability prediction.

are interested in this topic should refer to Musa's book and the articles by Littlewood referenced here. Practical experience of the use of reliability growth models is described by Sheldon *et al.* (1992), Schneidewind and Keller (1992) and Ehrlich *et al.* (1993).

Further reading

IEEE Software, July 1992. This special issue is concerned with reliability measurement. It includes a number of articles which discuss reliability growth models and their practical application.

Software Reliability Handbook. In spite of its title this book has a much broader scope than simply reliability issues. It also has excellent sections on metrics and quality assurance. (P. Rook (ed.), 1990, Elsevier.)

'Quantifying software validation: When to stop testing'. This is an excellent article by Musa and Ackerman which introduces the notions of statistical testing and reliability growth and shows how these can be used in test planning. They provide details of actual experiences with statistical testing. (J.D. Musa and A. Frank Ackerman, *IEEE Software,* **6** (3), May 1989.)

Software Reliability: Measurement, Prediction, Application. This book is a detailed description of reliability modelling from both a practical and a theoretical standpoint. It explores in depth the ideas introduced in the above paper (J.D. Musa, A. Iannino and K. Okumoto, 1987, McGraw-Hill.)

KEY POINTS

- The most important dynamic characteristic of most software systems is their reliability. The reason for this is that the costs of system failure often exceed the costs of developing the software system.

- Reliability specifications are often imperfect but software engineers are still responsible for producing reliable systems. Programs should not produce incorrect output, should not corrupt themselves or other programs and should take meaningful actions in unexpected situations.

- The reliability of a software system is not a simple measure which can be associated with the system. It depends on the pattern of usage of that system. It is quite possible for a system to contain faults yet be seen as reliable by users of the system.

- Reliability requirements should be defined quantitatively in the system requirements specification.

- There are several different reliability metrics. The most appropriate metric for a specific system depends on the type of system and application domain. Different metrics may be used for different sub-systems.

■ Statistical testing is used to estimate software reliability. It relies on testing the system with a test data set which reflects the operational profile of the software. Test data may be generated automatically.

■ Reliability growth models model the change in reliability as faults are removed from software. They can be used to predict when the required reliability will be achieved. Various models have been developed and the most appropriate model should be chosen by fitting observed reliability measurements to one of these models.

EXERCISES

18.1 Suggest six reasons why software reliability is important. Using an example, explain the difficulties of describing what software reliability means.

18.2 Why is it inappropriate to use reliability metrics which were developed for hardware systems in estimating software system reliability? Illustrate your answer with an example.

18.3 Assess the reliability of some software system which you use regularly by keeping a log of system failures and observed faults. Write a user's handbook which describes how to make effective use of the system in the presence of these faults.

18.4 Suggest appropriate reliability metrics for the following classes of software system. Give reasons for your choice of metric. Make some predictions about the usage of these systems and suggest appropriate values for the reliability metric.

(a) a system which monitors patients in a hospital intensive care unit,

(b) a word processor,

(c) an automated vending machine control system,

(d) a system to control braking in a car,

(e) a system to control a refrigeration unit,

(f) a management report generator.

18.5 You are responsible for writing the specification for a software system which controls a network of EPOS (electronic point of sale) terminals in a supermarket. The system accepts bar code information from a terminal, queries a product database and returns the item name and its price to the terminal for display. The system must be continually available during the supermarket's opening hours.

Giving reasons for your choice, choose appropriate reliability metrics for specifying the reliability of such a system and write a plausible reliability specification taking into account the fact that some faults are more serious than others. You should consider three classes of fault, namely faults which result in data corruption, faults which result in a system being unavailable for service and faults which cause incorrect information to be transmitted to the EPOS terminal. It may be necessary to use different metrics for different fault classes.

18.6 Describe how you would go about validating the reliability specification you defined in Exercise 18.5. Your answer should include a description of any validation tools which might be used. You may find it useful to read Section 26.3 in Chapter 26 before attempting this exercise.

18.7 Using the literature as background information, write a report for management (who have no previous experience in this area) on the use of reliability growth models.

18.8 Is it ethical for an engineer to agree to deliver a software system with known faults to a customer? Does it make any different if the customer is told of the existence of these faults in advance? Would it be reasonable to make claims about the reliability of the software in such circumstances?

19

Programming for Reliability

Objectives

- To describe a number of programming techniques for reliable systems development.

- To explain how faults in programs can be avoided by minimizing the use of error-prone constructs and by effective use of the programming language type system.

- To introduce the notion of fault-tolerant systems and to describe methods of achieving fault tolerance.

- To show how exception handling facilities in a programming language may be used to create robust programs.

- To describe defensive programming which is intended to detect faults and ensure that they do not result in system failure.

Contents

There is a general requirement for more reliable systems in all application domains. Customers expect their software to operate without failures and to be available when it is required. Improved programming techniques, better programming languages and better quality management have led to very significant improvements in reliability for most software. However, for some systems, such as those which control unattended machinery, these 'normal' techniques may not be enough to achieve the level of reliability required. In these cases, special programming techniques may be necessary to achieve the required reliability. Some of these techniques are discussed in this chapter.

Reliability in a software system can be achieved using three complementary strategies:

(1) *Fault avoidance*   This is the most important strategy which is applicable to all types of system. The design and implementation process should be organized with the objective of producing fault-free systems.

(2) *Fault tolerance*   This strategy assumes that residual faults remain in the system. Facilities are provided in the software to allow operation to continue when these faults cause system failures.

(3) *Fault detection*   Faults are detected before the software is put into operation. The software validation process uses static and dynamic methods to discover any faults which remain in a system after implementation.

Fault avoidance and fault detection strategies are often sufficient to achieve the required level of reliability. Although there may be a small number of residual faults in the software, the costs of failures due to these faults may be acceptable. However, when software is safety-critical or has very high reliability requirements, the program must be designed so that residual faults do not cause catastrophic failure. When a fault occurs, the software must be fault-tolerant. It must continue to operate (perhaps in a degraded way) so that the system in which the software is embedded does not completely fail.

Fault avoidance and fault tolerance are covered in this chapter. Fault detection techniques are discussed in Chapters 22 to 24 which cover program testing.

19.1 Fault avoidance

A good software process should be oriented towards fault avoidance rather than fault detection and removal. It should have the objective of developing fault-free software. *Fault-free software* means software which conforms to its specification. Of course, there may be errors in the specification or it may not reflect the real needs of the user so fault-free software does not necessarily mean that the software will always behave as the user wants.

Fault avoidance and the development of fault-free software relies on:

(1)   The availability of a precise (preferably formal) system specification which is an unambiguous description of what must be implemented.

(2)   The adoption of an organizational quality philosophy in which quality is the driver of the software process. Programmers should expect to write bug-free programs.

(3)   The adoption of an approach to software design and implementation which is based on information hiding and encapsulation and which encourages the production of readable programs.

(4)   The use of a strongly typed programming language so that possible errors are detected by the language compiler.

(5)   Restrictions on the use of programming constructs, such as pointers, which are inherently error-prone.

Achieving fault-free software is virtually impossible if low-level programming languages with limited type checking are used for program development. In strongly typed languages, such as Ada, the compiler can find many faults before the program is executed. Ada is, in my opinion, the best language for developing reliable systems because of its strong typing, its emphasis on compile-time error detection and its constructs for writing readable programs.

However, C++ is becoming increasingly used for this type of system development because it allows the development of very efficient systems. C++ has much better type checking than C. However, it is practically impossible to write efficient C++ programs without using some of the error-prone constructs discussed in the next section. Furthermore, many C++ programmers use a rather terse style which does not make for particularly readable programs.

Although perfection should be the aim, we must be realistic and accept that human errors will always occur. Faults may remain in the software after development. Therefore, the development process must include a validation phase which checks the developed software for the presence of faults. This validation phase is usually very expensive. As faults are removed from a program, the cost of finding and removing remaining faults tends to rise exponentially (Figure 19.1). As the software becomes more reliable, more and more testing is required to find fewer and fewer faults.

Consequently, a software development organization may decide that some residual faults are acceptable. If and when the system fails, it may be cheaper to pay for the consequences of failure rather than discover and remove the faults before system delivery. This is a fairly common practice among vendors of software products for personal computers. However, as I discuss in Chapter 21, the decision to release faulty software is not simply an economic decision. The social and political acceptability of system failure must also be taken into account.

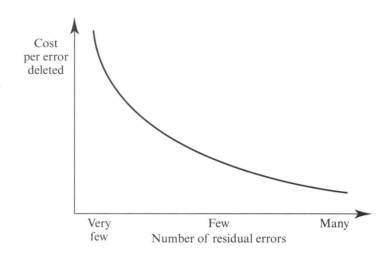

Figure 19.1
The increasing costs of
residual fault removal.

19.1.1 Structured programming and error avoidance

Structured programming is a term which was coined in the late 1960s to mean programming without using goto statements, programming using only while loops and if statements as control constructs and designing using a top-down approach. The adoption of structured programming was an important milestone in the development of software engineering because it was the first step away from an undisciplined approach to software development.

Dijkstra (1968) recognized that the goto statement was an inherently error-prone programming construct. The disciplined use of control structures forces programmers to think carefully about their program. Hence they are less likely to make mistakes during development. Structured programming means programs can be read sequentially and are therefore easier to understand and inspect. However, avoiding unsafe control statements is only the first step in programming for reliability.

Apart from gotos, there are also several other constructs in programming languages which are inherently error-prone. Faults are less likely to be introduced into programs if the use of these constructs is minimized. These constructs include:

(1)   *Floating-point numbers*   Floating-point numbers are inherently imprecise. They present a particular problem when they are compared because representation imprecision may lead to invalid comparisons. Fixed-point numbers, where a number is represented to a given number of decimal places, are safer as exact comparisons are possible.

(2)   *Pointers*   Pointers are low-level constructs which refer directly to areas of the machine memory. They are dangerous because errors in their use can be devastating and because they allow 'aliasing'. This means the same entity may be referenced using different names. Aliasing makes programs harder to understand so that errors are more difficult to find. However, efficiency requirements mean that it is often impractical to avoid the use of pointers.

(3) *Dynamic memory allocation*   Program memory is allocated at run-time rather than compile-time. The danger with this is that the memory may not be de-allocated so that the system eventually runs out of available memory. This can be a very subtle type of error to detect as the system may run successfully for a long time before the problem occurs.

(4) *Parallelism*   Parallelism is dangerous because of the difficulties of predicting the subtle effects of timing interactions between parallel processes. Timing problems cannot usually be detected by program inspection and the peculiar combination of circumstances which cause a timing problem may not result during system testing. Parallelism may be unavoidable but its use should be carefully controlled to minimize inter-process dependencies. Programming language facilities, such as Ada tasks, help avoid some of the problems of parallelism as the compiler can detect some kinds of programming errors.

(5) *Recursion*   Recursion is the situation in which a subroutine calls itself or calls another subroutine which then calls the calling subroutine. Its use can result in very concise programs but it can be difficult to follow the logic of recursive programs. Errors in using recursion may result in the allocation of all the system's memory as temporary stack variables are created.

(6) *Interrupts*   Interrupts are a means of forcing control to transfer to a section of code irrespective of the code currently executing. The dangers of this are obvious as the interrupt may cause a critical operation to be terminated.

Some standards for safety-critical systems development completely prohibit the use of these constructs. However, this extreme position is not normally practical. All of these constructs and techniques are useful but they must be used with great care. Wherever possible, their potentially dangerous effects should be controlled by using them within abstract data types or objects. These act as natural 'firewalls' limiting the damage caused if errors occur.

19.1.2 Data typing

A security principle which is adopted by military organizations is the 'need to know' principle. Only those individuals who need to know a particular piece of information to carry out their duties are given that information. Information which is not directly relevant to their work is withheld.

When programming, an analogous principle should be adopted to control access to system data. Program components should only be allowed access to data which they need to implement their function. Access to other data should be denied by using the scope rules of the programming language to conceal its existence.

The advantage of using 'information hiding' is that hidden information cannot be corrupted by program components which are not supposed to use it. If the interface remains the same, the data representation may be changed without affecting other components in the system.

The key to effective information hiding is to use the programming language type system to its fullest extent. It is possible to implement information hiding in languages like C or Pascal which have limited data typing facilities. However, it is much easier and more secure to use a language such as Ada, Modula-2 or C++, which offers direct support for information hiding.

Many errors arise because programmers accidentally assign incorrect values to program variables. If a language with strong typing is used, many of these errors can be detected by the language compiler before the program is executed. The effective use of type names makes programs more readable and reduces the chances of accidental misuse of names. Program entities should be assigned types which reflect their function in the real world. For example, if a traffic light system is being implemented in C++, the following declarations might be made:

```
typedef enum { red, redamber, amber, green} TrafficLightColour ;
TrafficLightColour ColourShowing, NextColour ;
```

The possible values of the traffic light colour are named as an enumerated type. The objects ColourShowing and NextColour, which are modelling the traffic light display, may only be assigned the values red, redamber, amber, and green. Similar type definition facilities are available in Ada.

The above example declares a *scalar type,* which is the name given to a type where the set of all possible values is known. Ada also includes an alternative means of declaring a scalar type, the range declaration:

```
type POSITIVE is INTEGER range 1..MAXINT ;
```

The type POSITIVE consists of the set of integers between 1 and the maximum integer which may be represented on a particular computer. Declaring the type as a range is a shorthand way of defining the set of values associated with the type. Any attempt to assign a negative value to variables of that type is trapped by the compiler. C++ does not include explicit type definition using ranges. However, it is possible to implement a class which includes range checking on assignment.

Ada allows types to be renamed so that they inherit the operations of the existing type but are distinct from it. For example, if several entities are logical variables but should not be assigned to each other, the following type declarations can be made:

```
type OIL_STATUS is new BOOLEAN ;
type DOOR_STATUS is new INTEGER ;
type FUEL_STATUS is new BOOLEAN ;
```

When variables are declared of these types, the compiler ensures that the oil pressure (for example) cannot be assigned to the fuel status indicator. This type renaming improves program readability and reduces the chances of incorrect assignment.

Ada has a very strict type regime so that variables of type BOOLEAN cannot be assigned to OIL_STATUS and vice versa. This is not the case in all object-oriented languages where inheritance is used to create a sub-type from a parent type. Most object-oriented languages have a less strict notion of derived types. If a type B inherits its attributes from type A, it is usually possible to assign variables of type B to variables of type A. This is a logical consequence of the semantics of inheritance but it is inherently less safe than the Ada approach.

As well as using meaningful names, the operations which are associated with a type should be packaged with the type declaration to create an abstract data type or object class. The representation of the type in terms of lower-level program entities should be concealed from the rest of the program. Operation implementation and the type representation may be changed without changing those parts of the program which use the abstract type.

Abstract data types and object classes are similar but not identical constructs. The most significant practical distinction is that an object class is like a template. It is used to create objects which have operations and attributes as defined in the object class. In an abstract data type, the operations are associated with the type rather than the variable assigned that type. In practice, if we have an Ada variable S of type STACK with an associated operation Push, this might be referenced as follows:

    STACK.Push (S, somevalue) ;

The stack is passed as a parameter to the type operation. In C++, by contrast, the push operation is associated with the object S. There is no need to pass this object as a parameter. It would be referenced as follows:

    S.Push (somevalue) ;

I use the terms 'abstract data type' and 'object class' interchangeably in the remainder of this chapter. I only distinguish between them if it makes a difference to the meaning of the description.

Both abstract data types and object classes include an interface specification and an implementation. The interface specification defines the type or object class name and the operations which act on that type or object class.

The implementation of the abstract type defines the representation and the implementation of operations on the type. If the specification part remains unchanged, the implementation part may be modified without requiring changes to other parts of the program which use the abstract data type.

Figure 19.2 shows the specification of a simple abstract data type (a 100-element integer queue) in Ada. Figure 19.3 shows the comparable class definition in C++.

The name of the Ada type shown in Figure 19.2 is Queue.T. The defined operations are Queue.Put, Queue.Remove and Queue.Size. The type T (the name is meaningful when prefixed by the type name to give Queue.T) is specified as a private type. In Ada, this means that the only operations allowed on that type are assignment, test for equality and the operations defined in the Queue package.

In Figure 19.3, the C++ object class is named Queue and has comparable associated operations. It has additional operations Queue () and ~Queue (). Queue ()

```
package Queue is
    type T is private ;
    procedure Put (IQ : in out T; X: INTEGER);
    procedure Remove (IQ : in out T; X : out INTEGER);
    function Size (IQ : T ) return NATURAL;
private
    type Q_RANGE is range 0..99 ;
    type Q_VEC is array ( Q_RANGE ) of INTEGER ;
    type T is record
        The_queue: Q_VEC ;
        front, back : Q_RANGE ;
    end record;
end Queue;
```

Figure 19.2
An integer queue declaration as an Ada package specification.

is a constructor operation which is automatically called when a variable is declared of type Queue. ~Queue () is used when that variable is no longer required. Typically, it is used to de-allocate any memory which has been allocated to the queue.

Figures 19.2 and 19.3 define a fixed-size queue where the elements are integers. However, queues are general data structures and queue operations are usually independent of the type of queue element and the size of the queue. Both Ada and C++ support generics which can be used to specify this abstract type independently of the element type and size (Figures 19.4 and 19.5).

Generics are a way of creating parameterized, reusable general-purpose templates for packages and subroutines. The use of generics means that programmers are less likely to make mistakes in type or class implementation. Faults are therefore avoided and program reliability improved.

In Figures 19.4 and 19.5, the type of the queue element and the size of the queue are generic parameters. They are assigned values when the package is instantiated. Figure 19.6 shows how generics are instantiated in Ada and C++. It defines an integer queue with a maximum of 50 elements and a queue whose elements are lists (defined in another package, we assume) with 200 elements.

Creating a new version of a generic package is a compile-time operation. A generic declares a template for a package and the compile-time instantiation of this

```
class Queue {
public:
    Queue () ;
    ~Queue () ;
    void Put ( int x ) ; // adds an item to the queue
    int Remove () ; // this has side effect of changing the queue
    int Size( ) ; // returns number of elements in the queue
private:
    int front, back ;
    int qvec [100] ;
} ;
```

Figure 19.3
An integer queue declaration as a C++ class declaration.

```
generic
   type ELEM is private ;
   type Q_SIZE is range <> ;
package Queue is
   type T is private ;
   procedure Put (IQ : in out T; X: ELEM );
   procedure Remove (IQ : in out T; X : out ELEM );
   function Size (IQ : in T ) return NATURAL ;
private
   type Q_VEC is array (Q_SIZE) of ELEM ;
   type T is record
        The_queue: Q_VEC ;
        Front : Q_SIZE := Q_SIZE'FIRST ;
        Back: Q_SIZE := Q_SIZE'FIRST ;
   end record;
end Queue;
```

Figure 19.4
A generic queue
specification (Ada).

```
template
   <class elem>
class Queue {
public:
   Queue ( int size = 100 ) ; // default to queue of size 100 elements
   ~Queue () ;
   void Put ( elem x ) ;
   elem Remove ( ) ; // this has side effect of changing queue
   int Size ( ) ;
private:
   int front, back ;
   elem* qvec ;
} ;
```

Figure 19.5
A generic queue
specification
(C++).

```
                           Ada

type IQ_SIZE is range 0..49 ; type LQ_SIZE is range 0..199 ;
package Integer_queue is new Queue (ELEM => INTEGER,
                                    Q_SIZE => IQ_SIZE ) ;
package List_queue is new Queue (ELEM => List.T,
                                  Q_SIZE => LQ_SIZE ) ;

                           C++

//Assume List has been defined elsewhere as a type
Queue <int> Int_queue (50) ;
Queue <List> List_queue (200) ;
```

Figure 19.6
Generic instantiation in
Ada and C++.

generic adds detail to the template. The effect is as if a new package or object class had been declared. C++'s generic facilities are used to provide type parameters to classes and functions. Ada generics can be used for this purpose but may also have parameters which define the size of data structures and generic function parameters.

19.2 Fault tolerance

A fault-tolerant system can continue in operation after some system failures have occurred. Fault tolerance is needed in situations where system failure would cause some catastrophic accident or where a loss of system operation would cause large economic losses. For example, the computers in an aircraft must continue in operation until the aircraft has landed; the computers in an air traffic control system must be continuously available.

Given a fault-free system, you might think that fault-tolerance facilities do not have to be included in a reliable system. If there are no errors in the system, there would not seem to be any chance of system failure. However, 'fault-free' does not mean 'failure-free'. It can only mean that the program corresponds to its specification. The specification may contain errors or omissions and may be based on incorrect assumptions about the system's environment. And, of course, we can never conclusively demonstrate that a system is completely fault-free.

Fault-tolerance facilities are required if the system is to be resilient to failure. There are four aspects to fault tolerance:

(1)   *Failure detection*   The system must detect that a particular state combination has resulted or will result in a system failure.

(2)   *Damage assessment*   The parts of the system state which have been affected by the failure must be detected.

(3)   *Fault recovery*   The system must restore its state to a known 'safe' state. This may be achieved by correcting the damaged state (forward error recovery) or by restoring the system to a known 'safe' state (backward error recovery). Forward error recovery is more complex as it involves diagnosing system faults and knowing what the system state should have been had the fault not caused a system failure.

(4)   *Fault repair*   This involves modifying the system so that the fault does not recur. In many cases, software failures are transient and due to a peculiar combination of system inputs. No repair is necessary as normal processing can resume immediately after fault recovery. This is an important distinction between hardware and software faults.

When a fault is not a transient fault, a new version of the faulty software component must be installed. It may be necessary to stop the system then install a new version of the system. However, for systems which must be continuously available, the system must be dynamically reconfigured (Kramer and Magee, 1985). The replacement must be substituted for the faulty component without stopping the system.

There has been a need for many years to build fault-tolerant hardware. The most commonly used hardware fault-tolerant technique is based around the notion of triple-modular redundancy (TMR). The hardware unit is replicated three (or sometimes more) times. The output from each unit is compared. If one of the units fails and does not produce the same output as the other units, its output is ignored. The system functions with two working units (Figure 19.7).

This approach to fault tolerance relies on most hardware failures being the result of component failures rather than design faults. It assumes that, when fully operational, all hardware units perform to specification. There is a low probability of simultaneous component failure in all hardware units.

Of course, they could all have a common design fault and thus all produce the same (wrong) answer. The chances of this can be reduced by using hardware units which have a common specification but which are designed and built by different manufacturers. It is assumed that the probability of different teams making the same design or manufacturing error is small.

There have been two comparable approaches to the provision of software fault tolerance (Figures 19.8 and 19.9). Both have been derived from the hardware model where a component (or the whole system) is replicated.

(1)   *N-version programming*   Using a common specification, the software system is implemented in a number of different versions by different teams. These versions are executed in parallel. Their outputs are compared using a voting system and inconsistent outputs are rejected. At least three versions of the system should be available. The assumption is that it is unlikely that different teams will make the same design or programming errors. Avizienis (1985, 1995) describes this approach to fault tolerance.

(2)   *Recovery blocks*   This is a finer grain approach to fault tolerance. Each program component includes a test to check if the component has executed successfully. It also includes alternative code which allows the system to back-up and repeat the computation if the test detects a failure. Unlike N-version programming, the implementations are different rather than independent implementations of the same specification. They are executed in sequence rather than in parallel. Randell (1975) and Randell and Xu (1995) describe this method.

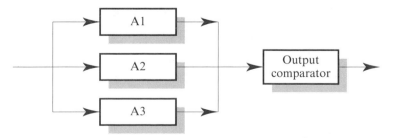

Figure 19.7
Triple-modular redundancy to cope with hardware failure.

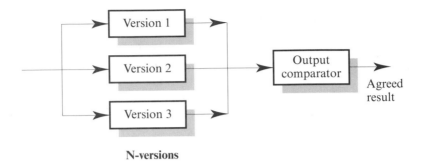

Figure 19.8
N-version
programming.

N-version programming is the most used approach to software fault tolerance. However, a number of experiments have suggested that the assumption that different design teams are unlikely to make the same mistakes may not be valid (Knight and Leveson, 1986; Brilliant *et al.*, 1990). Different development teams may make the same mistakes because of common misinterpretations of the specification or because they independently arrive at the same algorithms to solve the problem. Recovery blocks reduce the probability of common errors because different algorithms must be used for each recovery block.

The weakness of both these approaches to fault tolerance is that they are based on the assumption that the specification is correct. They do not tolerate specification errors. In many cases, however, the specification is incorrect or incomplete so that the system behaves in an unexpected way. Defensive programming, as discussed in Section 19.4, is an approach which may be used to reduce the consequences of some types of specification error.

The provision of software fault tolerance requires the software to be executed under the control of a fault-tolerant controller which will ensure that the steps involved in tolerating a fault are executed. Laprie *et al.* (1995) describe fault-tolerant systems architectures. Interested readers should follow up the further reading for more information on this topic.

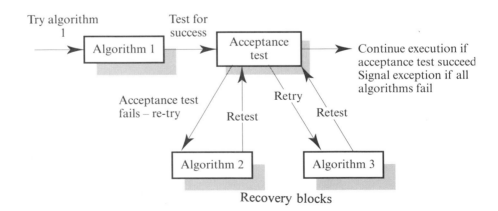

Figure 19.9
Recovery blocks.

19.3 Exception handling

When an error of some kind or an unexpected event occurs during the execution of a program, this is called an *exception*. Exceptions may be caused by hardware or software errors. When an exception has not been anticipated, control is transferred to a system exception handling mechanism. If an exception has been anticipated, code must be included in the program to detect and handle that exception.

Most programming languages do not include facilities to detect and handle exceptions. The normal decision constructs (if statements) of the language must be used to detect the exception and control constructs used to transfer control to exception handling code. This is possible in a monolithic program but, when an exception occurs in a sequence of nested procedure calls, there is no easy way to transmit it from one procedure to another. Control is passed down through a sequence of procedures. When an exception occurs, this control structure has to be unwound.

Consider a number of nested procedure calls where procedure A calls procedure B which calls procedure C (Figure 19.10). If an exception occurs during the execution of C this may be so serious that execution of B cannot continue. Procedure B has to return immediately to Procedure A which must also be informed that B has terminated abnormally and that an exception has occurred.

In a nested structure, exceptions may be signalled by associating a shared boolean variable with each exception. The conditions which could cause an exception are tested before the exception arises and the normal processing is stopped if the effect of a statement is to cause an exception. In a sequence of nested procedure calls, the same test must be repeated several times. If there is no test for the exception, program execution continues incorrectly or a system exception handler forces the program to terminate.

An alternative approach to unwinding a sequence of nested calls is to signal an exception when a problem is detected. When an exception is detected, control is immediately transferred to an exception handler. This is a segment of code which should deal with the exceptional situation.

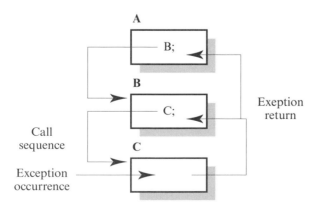

Figure 19.10
Exception return in embedded procedure calls.

An exception handler is something like a case statement. It states exception names and appropriate actions for each exception. Not every exception raised in a component need necessarily be handled by that unit. The exception may be propagated to the exception handler associated with the calling routine.

Both Ada and C++ have recognized that exception handling is a normal part of system development. They include constructs to support exception signalling and exception handling. In Ada, signalling an exception is achieved using a **raise** statement. In C++, the comparable statement is a **throw** statement. The handler of an exception is indicated by the keyword **exception** in Ada; in C++, the keyword **catch** is used.

Figures 19.11 and 19.12 illustrate the use of exceptions and exception handling. These program fragments show the design of a temperature controller on a food freezer. The required temperature may be set between –18 and –40 degrees Celsius. Food may start to defrost and bacteria become active at temperatures over –18 degrees. The control system maintains this temperature by switching a refrigerant pump on and off depending on the value of a temperature sensor. If the required temperature cannot be maintained, the controller sets off an alarm.

```
with Pump, Temperature_dial, Sensor, Globals, Alarm;
use Globals ;

procedure Control_freezer is
    Ambient_temperature: FREEZER_TEMP ;
begin
    loop
        Ambient_temperature := Sensor.Get_Temperature ;
        if Ambient_temperature > Temperature_dial.Setting then
            if Pump.Status = Off then
                Pump.Switch (State => On) ;
                -- Wait for the freezer to cool
                Wait (Cooling_time ) ;
            elsif Pump.Status = On then
                -- Switch pump off because temperature is low
                Pump.Switch (State => Off) ;
            end if ;
        end if ;
        -- Problem - can't lower temperature
        if Ambient_temperature > Danger_temperature then
            raise Freezer_too_hot ;
        end if ;
    end loop ;
exception
    when Freezer_too_hot => Alarm.Activate ;
        raise ;
    when others => Alarm_activate ;
        raise Control_problem ;
end Control_freezer;
```

Figure 19.11
Exceptions in a freezer temperature controller (Ada).

```
void Control_freezer ( const float Danger_temp)
{
    float Ambient_temp ;
    // try means exceptions will be handled in this block
    // Assume that Sensor, Temperature_dial and Pump are
    //objects which have been declared elsewhere
    try {
        while (true) {
            Ambient_temp = Sensor.Get_temperature () ;
            if (Ambient_temp > Temperature_dial.Setting () )
                if (Pump.Status () == off)
                {
                    Pump.Switch (on) ;
                    Wait (Cooling_time) ;
                }
                else
                    if (Pump.Status () == on)
                            Pump.Switch (off) ;
            if ( Ambient_temp > Danger_temp )
                    throw Freezer_too_hot ( ) ;
        } // end of while loop
    } // end of exception handling try block
    // catch indicates the exception handling code.
    catch ( Freezer_too_hot )
        Alarm.Activate () ;
}
```

Figure 19.12
Exceptions in a freezer
temperature controller
(C++).

The temperature of the freezer is discovered by interrogating an object called Sensor and the required temperature by inspecting an object called Temperature_dial. A pump object responds to signals to switch its state. Assume that the exceptions Freezer_too_hot and Control_problem and the type FREEZER_TEMP are declared, in Ada, in a package called Globals. There are no built-in exceptions in C++ but other information is declared in a separate header file.

The temperature controller tests the temperature and switches the pump as required. If the temperature is too hot, it transfers control to the exception handler which activates an alarm. In Ada, the fact that an exception has occurred can be signalled to the calling procedure by re-raising the exception within the exception handler. This is shown in the first part of the exception handler where the Freezer_too_hot exception causes an alarm to be signalled then that particular exception is re-raised. In C++, it is not normal to adopt this approach. Once an exception has been handled, it is not re-thrown.

The definition of Ada includes five built-in exceptions as shown in Figure 19.13. The Ada run-time system includes a handler for these exceptions and, of course, they may be handled by the application program.

Writing a fault-tolerant Ada program requires the developer to include handlers for all of these exceptions if, of course, the requisite facility is used. If

Exception	Description
CONSTRAINT_ERROR	Raised when an attempt is made to assign an out-of-range value to a state variable. Such an error would result, for example, when an attempt is made to access an array element using an index outside the bounds of the array.
NUMERIC_ERROR	Raised when some arithmetic operation goes wrong (division by zero, for example).
PROGRAM_ERROR	Raised when a control structure is violated e.g. calling a sub-program whose specification exists but whose body has not been defined.
STORAGE_ERROR	Raised when storage space for dynamically allocated values is exhausted.
TASKING_ERROR	Raised when there is some failure of inter-task communication.

Figure 19.13
Built-in exceptions in Ada.

dynamic storage allocation and tasking are avoided, the exceptions STORAGE_ERROR and TASKING_ERROR obviously cannot occur.

In Ada 83, the exception management system does not provide a facility to discover the cause of an exception after it has occurred. For instance, a CONSTRAINT_ERROR can arise from a number of different causes. The exception handler may have to check a large number of possibilities to detect the error and repair the affected state variables. This has been addressed, to some extent, in Ada 95 which provides built-in functions to discover further information about exceptions. At the time of writing, there has been little practical experience of Ada 95. It is therefore impossible to say if these completely solve Ada 83's exception management problems.

C++ does not include the notion of built-in exceptions. Exceptions are defined as classes in C++ so they may inherit facilities from other exceptions and may have associated operations. This offers more flexibility than Ada's exception mechanism. However, its lack of built-in exceptions means that programmers must remember to declare exceptions and write exception handlers wherever it is necessary to do so.

19.4 Defensive programming

Defensive programming is an approach to program development whereby programmers assume that there may be undetected faults or inconsistencies in their programs. Redundant code is incorporated to check the system state after modifications and to ensure that the state change is consistent. If inconsistencies are detected, the state change is retracted or the state is restored to a known correct state.

Defensive programming is an approach to fault tolerance which can be carried out without a fault-tolerant controller. The techniques used, however, are fundamental to the activities in the fault tolerance process, namely detecting a failure, damage assessment, and recovering from that failure. In practical implementations, failure detection and damage assessment are often combined as they rely on common checks of the system state variables.

19.4.1 Failure prevention

Programming languages such as Ada and C++ allow many errors which cause state corruption and system failure to be detected at compile-time. The compiler can detect those problems which breach the strict type rules of the language. Compiler checking is obviously limited to static values but the compiler can also automatically add code to a program to perform run-time checks.

For example, when programming in Ada, the exception handling mechanism can be used with a range specification to detect some run-time errors. An assignment which results in a variable's value going out of range results in a CONSTRAINT_ERROR exception being raised which can then be handled locally. This works for some classes of check but has two principal limitations:

(1)   Checks which involve relationships between variables (such as if A is zero then B must be 1) cannot be expressed.

(2)   The exception handler is informed that a CONSTRAINT_ERROR exception has been raised but not where that exception occurred. Further processing may be needed to discover the source of the problem.

An alternative approach is to use state assertions. These are logical predicates (see Chapter 9) over the state variables which assert conditions on that state. This predicate is checked immediately before an assignment is made to a referenced state variable and, if an anomalous value for the variable would result from the assignment, an error has occurred. Examples of assertions might be:

> A = 1 **and** B = 0 **or** A = 0 **and** B = 1
> **forall** i **in** (1..20) : A (i) > 0

A few programming languages allow assertions to be written as part of the program and the compiler generates code to check the assertion. In most languages, however, it is up to the programmer to include explicit assertion checks along with state variables. Stroustrup (1991) explains how to do this in a standard way in C++.

Assertion checking is simplified if all assignments to state variables are always implemented as operations on abstract data types or objects. The assertion checking code need only be included in the abstract type implementation.

```
                            Ada

package Positive_even is
   type NUMB is limited private ;
   procedure Assign (A: in out NUMB; B: NATURAL;
           State_error: in out BOOLEAN) ;
   function Eval (A: NUMB) return NATURAL ;
   -- overload operator =
   function "=" (A, B: NUMB) return BOOLEAN ;
private
   type NUMB is new NATURAL ;
end Positive_even ;
```

```
                            C++

class Positive_even {
public:
   // New assignment function to assign integer to
   // positive even number object
   void Assign ( int b, Error_type &State_error) ;
   int Eval ( ) ;
   // Equals can be re-defined because it is always true or false
   int operator == (Positive_even b) ;
private:
   int numb ;
} ; //Positive_even
```

Figure 19.14
An even number
abstract data type.

```
                            Ada

procedure Assign (A: in out NUMB; B: NATURAL;
           State_error: in out BOOLEAN) is
begin
   if B rem 2 /= 0 then
        State_error := TRUE ;
   else
        State_error := FALSE ;
        A := NUMB (B ) ;
   end if ;
end Assign ;
```

```
                            C++

void Positive_even:: Assign ( int b, Error_type &State_error)
{
   if (b%2 != 0)
        State_error = failure ;
   else {
        State_error = OK ;
        numb = b ;
   }
}
```

Figure 19.15
The assignment
operation for even
numbers.

Figures 19.14 and 19.15 illustrate an abstract type specification and the implementation of the associated assignment procedure. This procedure includes a check that the value assigned is always a positive even number. If not, the return variable State_error is set. Notice that exception handling is not included in the abstract type as the abstract type cannot know how the calling procedure or function wishes state errors of this type to be handled.

Generalized assertion checking on all assignments takes up space and slows down the system. An alternative to this is to run a procedure that checks the system state explicitly before critical operations. If the state is corrupt or invalid, the operation is delayed while damage assessment and fault recovery procedures are initiated.

19.4.2 Damage assessment

Damage assessment involves analysing the system state to gauge the extent of the state corruption. In many cases, corruption can be avoided by checking for fault occurrence before finally committing a change of state. If a fault is detected, the state change is not accepted so that no damage is caused. However, damage assessment may be needed when a fault arises because a sequence of state changes (all of which are individually correct) causes the system to enter an incorrect state.

The role of the damage assessment procedures is not to recover from the fault but to assess what parts of the state space have been affected by the fault. Damage can only be assessed if it is possible to apply some 'validity function' which checks if the state is consistent. If inconsistencies are found, these are highlighted or signalled in some way.

Figures 19.16 and 19.17 illustrate how it is possible to define data structures which can be checked for damage. In these examples, the system state is represented as an array of values of type ELEM. There is a corresponding array of type BOOLEAN that is used to signal problems with the state space.

The routine Assess_damage takes a 'validity function' as a parameter and applies this to each element in the state space. If its value is incorrect or inconsistent, the corresponding value in the array Checks is set to false. I have written the Ada version of this example (Figure 19.16) in Ada 95 rather than Ada 83. I have used Ada 95 here because it offers a much simpler and clearer solution. Ada 83 does not allow functions to be parameters to other procedures.

Other techniques which can be used for fault detection and damage assessment are dependent on the system state representation and on the application. Possible methods are:

- the use of checksums in data exchange and check digits in numeric data;
- the use of redundant links in data structures which contain pointers;
- the use of watchdog timers in concurrent systems.

```
generic
    type ELEM is private ;
    type INDEX is range <> ;
package Robust_array is
    type T is private ;
    -- This is Ada 95. Access types to functions are not defined in Ada 83
    type CHECK_FUNCTION is access function (E: ELEM) return
            BOOLEAN ;
    function Eval (A: T; I: INDEX) return ELEM ;
    procedure Assign (A: in out T; I: INDEX;
                            E: ELEM ) ;
    -- This is Ada 95 NOT Ada 93
    -- Test is a pointer to a function which checks elements against
    -- some condition and returns a boolean value. If they are damaged
    -- it sets the corresponding element in the array Checks
    procedure Assess_damage (A: T ; Test: CHECK_FUNCTION) ;
    -- Returns TRUE if any array element is damaged
    function Is_damaged (A: T ) return BOOLEAN ;
    -- Access the state associated with element I
    function Eval_state (A: T; I: INDEX) return BOOLEAN ;
private
    type T is record
        Vals: array (INDEX) of ELEM ;
        Checks: array (INDEX) of BOOLEAN ;
    end record ;
end Robust_array ;
```

Figure 19.16
An array type with
damage assessment
operations (Ada).

```
template <class elem> class Robust_array {
public:
    Robust_array (int size = 20) ;
    ~Robust_array () ;
    void Assign ( int Index, elem Val) ;
    elem Eval (int Index) ;
    // Damage assessment functions
    // Assess_damage takes a pointer to a function as a parameter
    // It sets the corresponding element of Checks if a problem is
    // detected by the function Test
    void Assess_damage ( void (*Test ) (boolean*)) ;
    boolean Eval_state (int Index) ;
    boolean Is_damaged () ;
private:
    elem* Vals ;
    boolean* Checks ;
} ;
```

Figure 19.17
An array type with
damage assessment
operations (C++).

Coding checks can be used when data is exchanged where a checksum is associated with numeric data. Fujiwara and Pradhan (1990) discuss coding checks and their application. A checksum is a value that is computed by applying some mathematical function to the data. The function used should give a unique value for the packet of data which is exchanged. This checksum is computed by the sender which applies the checksum function to the data and appends that function value to the data. The receiver applies the same function to the data and compares the checksum values. If these differ, some data corruption has occurred.

When linked data structures are used, the representation can be made redundant by including backward pointers. That is, for every reference from A to B, there exists a comparable reference from B to A. It is also possible to keep count of the number of elements in the structure. Checking can determine whether or not all pointers have an inverse value and whether or not the stored size and the computed structure size are the same.

When processes must react within a specific time period, a watch-dog timer may be installed. A watch-dog timer is a timer which must be reset by the executing process after its action is complete. It is started at the same time as a process and times the process execution. It may be interrogated by a controller at regular intervals. If, for some reason, the process fails to terminate, the watch-dog timer is not reset. The controller can therefore detect that a problem has arisen and take action to force process termination.

19.4.3 Fault recovery

Fault recovery is the process of modifying the state space of the system so that the effects of the fault are minimized. The system can continue in operation, perhaps in some degraded form. Forward recovery involves trying to correct the damaged system state. Backward recovery restores the system state to a known 'correct' state.

Forward error recovery is sometimes application-specific with domain knowledge used to compute possible state corrections. However, where the state information includes built-in redundancy, forward error recovery strategies may sometimes be used. There are two general situations where forward error recovery can be applied:

(1)   *When coded data is corrupted*   The use of coding techniques which add redundancy to the data allows errors to be corrected as well as detected.

(2)   *When linked structures are corrupted*   If forward and backward pointers are included in the data structure, the structure can be recreated if enough pointers remain uncorrupted. This technique is frequently used for file system and database repair.

Backward error recovery is a simpler technique which restores the state to a known safe state after an error has been detected. Most database systems include backward error recovery. When a user initiates a database computation a *transaction* is initiated. Changes made during that transaction are not immediately incorporated in the database. The database is only updated after the transaction is finished and no problems are detected. If the transaction fails, the database is not updated.

Transactions allow error recovery because they do not commit changes to the database until they have completed. However, they do not permit recovery from state changes that are valid but incorrect. Checkpointing is a technique which can be used to recover from this situation. The system state is duplicated periodically. When a problem is discovered, a correct state may be restored from one of these copies.

As an example of how backward recovery can be implemented using exceptions, consider the sort procedures shown in Figures 19.18 and 19.19 which include code for error detection and backward recovery. It is assumed that the type ELEM_ARRAY and the exception Sort_error are declared outside Sort. For brevity, I do not show here the code which sorts the array. Any sorting algorithm could be used.

```
procedure Safe_Sort (X: in out INT_ARRAY ) is
    Copy: INT_ARRAY ;
begin
    -- Take a copy of the array to be sorted.
    for i in INT_ARRAY'RANGE loop
        Copy (i) := X (i) ;
    end loop ;
    -- Code here to sort the array X in ascending order
    -- Now test that the array is actually sorted
    for i in INT_ARRAY'FIRST..INT_ARRAY'LAST-1 loop
        if X (i) > X (i + 1) then
            -- a problem has been detected - raise exception
            raise Sort_error ;
        end if ;
    end loop ;
exception
-- restore state and indicate to calling procedure
-- that a problem has arisen
    when Sort_error =>
        for i in INT_ARRAY'RANGE loop
            X (i) := Copy (i) ;
        end loop ;
        raise ;
        -- unexpected exception. Restore state and indicate
        -- that the sort has failed
    when Others =>
        for i in INT_ARRAY'RANGE loop
            X (i) := Copy (i) ;
        end loop ;
        raise Sort_error;
end Safe_Sort ;
```

Figure 19.18
Safe sort procedure with backward error recovery (Ada).

```
void Safe_Sort (int* X, int N, err_status &Err )
{
    // Allocate memory for array copy
    int* Copy = new int [N] ;

    // Take a copy of the array to be sorted.
    for ( int i=0; i < N ; i++ )
        Copy [i]= X [i] ;
    try
    {
        // Code here to sort the array X in ascending order
        //...
        Err = OK ;
        // Now test that the array is actually sorted
        for ( i=0; i<N-1 ; i++)
            if (X [i] > X [i + 1] )
                throw Sort_error ;
    } // try block
    // restore state and indicate to calling procedure
    // that a problem has arisen
    catch (Sort_error )
    {
        for ( i=0; i < N ; i++)
            X [i] = Copy [i] ;
        Err = failure ;
    }
    // No pre-defined exceptions in C++ to be caught
    // return memory used by array copy
    delete [ ] Copy ;
} // Safe_sort
```

Figure 19.19
Safe sort procedure
with backward error
recovery (C++).

The procedure copies the array before the sort operation. After the sort code has been executed, the procedure checks that the elements have been sorted. If not, the copy of the array is used to restore its state before the procedure was called. A Sort_error exception is raised to indicate that the call to the sort routine has been unsuccessful and that the array is unsorted.

Note the different style of exception management in Ada and C++. The C++ code can cope with the defined exception where a state error has been detected. However, the Ada code is more robust. It can also cope with other standard exceptions and restore the array to a safe state if these exceptions occur.

When a system includes cooperating processes, the sequence of process communications can be such that the checkpoints of the processes are out of synchronization. To recover from a fault, each process has to be rolled back to its starting state. This makes fault recovery very complex. A discussion of this is too long for this chapter and interested readers are referred to Randell (1975) who proposes a solution to this problem.

Further reading

Software Fault Tolerance. This collection includes several articles discussing recovery blocks and N-version programming. It also includes a good article on fault-tolerant system architectures. (M.R. Lyu (ed.), 1995, John Wiley & Sons.)

'Software fault tolerance'. This is a good overview of the subject with an excellent comparison of N-version programming and recovery blocks as approaches to software fault tolerance. (M. Moulding, in *Software Reliability Handbook*, P. Rook (ed.), 1990, Elsevier.)

High-Integrity Software. This is a book of chapters by different authors all on the topic of high-integrity systems development. Moulding's chapter above appears in a revised form and a chapter by Carré discusses unsafe features in Ada and Pascal. (C. Sennett, 1989, Pitman.)

KEY POINTS

- Reliability in a program can be achieved by avoiding the introduction of faults and by including fault-tolerance facilities which allow the system to remain operational after a fault has caused a system failure.

- Some programming language constructs such as goto statements, pointers, recursion and floating-point numbers are inherently error-prone. They should be avoided wherever possible.

- The use of data typing facilities for real-world modelling helps to avoid the introduction of software faults. The reason for this is that programs are easier to understand and information is protected. Programming errors are therefore less likely.

- Software that is fault-tolerant can continue execution in spite of faults which cause system failures.

- There are four aspects of program fault tolerance, namely failure detection, damage assessment, fault recovery and fault repair.

- N-version programming and recovery blocks are approaches to providing software fault tolerance which rely on redundant code for function execution. A fault-tolerant controller coordinates the execution of the different program units.

- The exception handling facilities provided in languages such as Ada and C++ are designed to help with the development of programs which can detect and recover from run-time failures.

- Defensive programming is a programming technique which involves incorporating checks for faults and fault recovery code in the program. Faults are detected before they cause a system failure.

EXERCISES

19.1 Given that pointers are an inherently error-prone construct, design an abstract type that implements binary trees which does not make use of pointers or recursion in its implementation.

19.2 Design an abstract data type called **List** to implement the list specifications set out in Chapter 10. Produce alternative implementations of this abstract type with and without using pointers.

19.3 Give two reasons why all the different system versions in an N-version system may all fail in a similar way.

19.4 Using a table, compare the exception handling facilities provided in Ada and C++. Exceptions in Ada are described in Chapter 10 of Barnes's book (Barnes, 1994) on Ada and in Chapter 9 of Stroustrup's book on C++ (Stroustrup, 1991).

19.5 Design an abstract data type in Ada or an object class in C++ which implements a binary tree without duplicate entries. If a duplicate entry is entered, it should be rejected and a status variable set indicating that the entry was unacceptable.

19.6 Discuss the problems of developing and maintaining 'non-stop' systems such as telephone exchange software. How might exceptions be used in the development of such systems?

19.7 What pre-conditions must hold before forward error recovery can be implemented in a fault-tolerant system? Is forward error recovery possible in interactive systems?

19.8 Design an abstract data type or object class called **Robust_list** which implements forward error recovery in a linked list. You should include operations to check the list for pointer corruption and to rebuild the list if corruption has occurred. Assume that you can check corruption by maintaining redundant pointers.

20

Software Reuse

Objectives

To explain the advantages and disadvantages of reusing software components.

To describe the processes involved in software development with reuse and software development for reuse.

To discuss the characteristics of reusable software components and to provide an example of a generic reusable component.

To describe methods of developing application systems so that they can be reused across a range of different computers and operating systems.

Contents

The design process in most engineering disciplines is based on component reuse. Mechanical or electrical engineers do not specify a design in which every component has to be manufactured specially. They base their design on components that have been tried and tested in other systems. These components obviously include small components such as nuts and bolts. However, they may also be major sub-systems such as engines, condensers or turbines.

By contrast, software system design usually assumes that all components are to be implemented specially for the system being developed. Apart from libraries such as window system libraries, there is no common base of reusable software components which is known by all software engineers. However, this situation is slowly changing. We need to reuse our software assets rather than redevelop the same software again and again. Demands for lower software production and maintenance costs along with increased quality can only be met by widespread and systematic software reuse.

This chapter on software reuse has been included in this section because improved reliability is one of the benefits of reuse. Software components are not just used in one system but are tried and tested in a variety of different environments. Design and implementation faults are discovered and eliminated so that the reusable component contains few errors. Although absolute reliability specification is impossible, reusable components may have an associated quality certification. This allows reusers to incorporate them with confidence in their systems.

Component reuse, of course, does not just mean the reuse of code. It is possible to reuse specifications and designs. The potential gains from reusing abstract products of the development process, such as specifications, may be greater than those from reusing code components. Code contains low-level detail which may specialize it to such an extent that it cannot be reused. Designs or specifications are more abstract and hence more widely applicable.

Over the past few years, software reuse has been widely publicized (Tracz, 1988; Biggerstaff and Perlis, 1989). A number of companies have instigated programs to investigate how the systematic reuse of software can be incorporated in their development process. In Japan, the leverage which can be gained from reuse has been recognized for a long time (Matsumoto, 1984). Reuse is an integral part of the Japanese 'factory' approach to software development (Cusamano, 1989). There is now a much greater awareness of the benefits of reuse in both Europe and North America (Joos, 1994; Lim, 1994). However, putting reuse into practice and integrating it into software development processes remains a major challenge for most organizations.

The reuse of software can be considered at a number of different levels:

(1) *Application system reuse* The whole of an application system may be reused. The key problem here is ensuring that the software is portable; it should execute on several different platforms. I cover portability in Section 20.4.

(2) *Sub-system reuse* Major sub-systems of an application may be reused. For example, a pattern-matching system developed as part of a text processing system may be reused in a database management system.

(3)   *Module or object reuse*   Components of a system representing a collection
        of functions may be reused. For example, an Ada package or a C++ object
        implementing a binary tree may be reused in different applications.

(4)   *Function reuse*   Software components which implement a single function,
        such as a mathematical function, may be reused.

Currently, application system reuse is widely practised as software companies
implement their systems across a range of machines. Function reuse is also widely
practised as use is made of standard libraries of reusable functions such as graphics
and mathematical libraries. However, sub-system and module reuse are less common. The problems which inhibit software reuse apply particularly to these types of
component.
        In this chapter, I focus on four aspects of software reuse:

(1)   *Software development with reuse*   What are the advantages and problems of
        developing software with reusable components? How must software
        processes evolve to incorporate reuse?

(2)   *Software development for reuse*   How can software components be gener-
        alized so that they are usable across a range of systems?

(3)   *Generator-based reuse*   How do application generators support the reuse of
        domain concepts?

(4)   *Application system reuse*   How can entire application systems be reused
        by making them available on a range of machines? What implementation
        strategies should be used to develop portable software?

20.1   Software development with reuse

Software development with reuse is an approach to development which tries to
maximize the reuse of existing software components. An obvious advantage of this
approach is that overall development costs should be reduced. Fewer software
components need be specified, designed, implemented and validated. However, cost
reduction is only one potential advantage of reuse. Systematic reuse in the development process offers further advantages:

(1)   *System reliability is increased*   Reused components, which have been
        exercised in working systems, should be more reliable than new components.
        These components have been tested in operational systems and have there-
        fore been exposed to realistic operating conditions.

(2)   *Overall process risk is reduced*   If a component exists, there is less
        uncertainty in the costs of reusing that component than in the costs of devel-
        opment. This is an important factor for project management as it reduces the

uncertainties in project cost estimation. This is particularly true when relatively large components such as sub-systems are reused.

(3)   *Effective use can be made of specialists*   Instead of application specialists doing the same work on different projects, these specialists can develop reusable components which encapsulate their knowledge.

(4)   *Organizational standards can be embodied in reusable components*   Some standards, such as user interface standards, can be implemented as a set of standard components. For example, reusable components may be developed to implement menus in a user interface. All applications present the same menu formats to users. The use of standard user interfaces improves reliability as users are less likely to make mistakes when presented with a familiar interface.

(5)   *Software development time can be reduced*   Bringing a system to market as early as possible is often more important than overall development costs. Reusing components speeds up system production because both development and validation time should be reduced.

Reuse can be incorporated into the systems development process by incorporating a specific reuse activity as shown in Figure 20.1. The system designer completes a high-level design and specifications of the components of that design. These specifications are used to find components to reuse. These may be incorporated at the architectural level or at more detailed design levels.

Although this model can result in significant reuse, it contrasts with the approach adopted in other engineering disciplines where reusability drives the design process. Rather than design then search for reusable components, engineers first search for reusable components. They base their design on these components (Figure 20.2).

In reuse-driven development, the system requirements are modified according to the reusable components available. The design is also based around existing components. Of course, this means that there may have to be requirements compromises. The design may be less efficient than a special-purpose design. However, the lower costs of development and increased system reliability will often compensate for this.

There are three conditions for software development with reuse:

(1)   It must be possible to find appropriate reusable components. Organizations need a base of properly catalogued and documented reusable components. The cost of finding an appropriate component in this catalogue must be relatively low.

Figure 20.1
Reuse in a standard
development process.

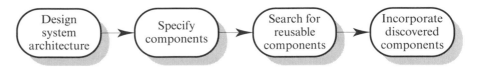

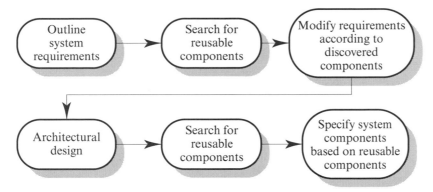

Figure 20.2
A reuse-driven
development process.

(2)   The reuser of the components must have confidence that the components will
behave as specified and will be reliable. Ideally, all components in an organization's catalogue should be certified to confirm that they have reached some
quality standards.

(3)   The components must have associated documentation to help the reuser
understand them and adapt them to a new application. The documentation
should include information about where components have been reused and
any reuse problems which have been found.

The introduction of a development process with reuse is difficult because, like so
many other technological advances, we have a 'chicken and egg' problem. Before
managers can be convinced of the merits of reuse, these must be demonstrated in real
projects. However, before they can be demonstrated, some initial investment is
needed to achieve the above conditions. Organizations have seen reuse as inherently
risky and have been reluctant to make this initial investment.

Apart from the problems of funding a reuse program, other difficulties in
introducing development with reuse are:

(1)   It is difficult to quantify what the cost reductions might be as there are
usually costs associated with reuse. Software components have to be discovered in a library, understood and sometimes adapted to work in a new
environment. These reuse costs may sometimes be greater than the cost of
re-implementing the component.

(2)   CASE toolsets do not support development with reuse. It may be difficult or
impossible to integrate these tools with a component library system.

(3)   Some software engineers sometimes prefer to rewrite components as they
believe that they can improve on the reusable component. This is a natural
consequence of an educational process which concentrates on original software development rather than reuse.

(4)   Our current techniques for classifying, cataloguing and retrieving software
components are immature. Engineers must be reasonably confident of finding
a component in the library before they will routinely include a component
search as part of their normal development process.

These difficulties have meant that development with reuse has been the exception rather than the norm in Europe and the Americas. Furthermore, there are organizational problems in introducing a reuse program which can cause difficulties (Farchamps, 1994). Nevertheless, systematic development with reuse (Frakes and Isoda, 1994) will become an increasingly important software engineering strategy.

20.2 Software development for reuse

Systematic reuse requires a properly catalogued and documented base of reusable components. A common misconception is that these components are available in existing systems. A component library might therefore be created cheaply by extracting and documenting them.

In fact, components that are created as part of an application system development are unlikely to be immediately reusable. These components are geared towards the requirements of the system in which they are originally included. To be reusable, they have to be generalized to satisfy a wider range of requirements.

Ideally, once a component has been developed and used in a system, it can be reused without change. More commonly, however, it will be necessary to adapt the component in some way to take account of the particular requirements for the system being developed. Figure 20.3 shows the process of improving the reusability of a component.

Adapting a component to make it reusable may involve making different types of changes:

(1)   *Name generalization*   The names used in the component may be modified so that they are neutral rather than a direct reflection of some specific application entity.

(2)   *Operation generalization*   This may involve adding operations to a component or removing operations which are very specific to some application domain.

(3)   *Exception generalization*   This may involve checking each component to see which exceptions it might generate and including these exceptions in the component interface.

Figure 20.3
The process of reusability enhancement.

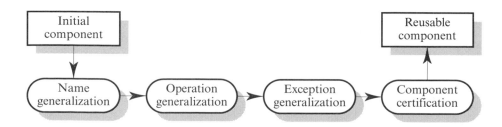

After generalization, the quality of the generalized component should be checked. This may require program inspections or testing. Ideally, the test data for a component should be made available to reusers so that it also may be reused. The component may be certified as having reached the required quality standards.

In general, component reuse is likely to be domain-specific. If a component is written for some domain such as library systems, it is unlikely to be reusable cost-effectively in other domains. Of course, some domains (such as the user interface domain) are used in many different types of application so reuse across applications is possible.

Domain analysis is concerned with understanding the domain so that domain abstractions can be modelled as reusable components. A good summary of domain analysis is given by Prieto-Díaz and Arango (1991). One domain which is both very general and widely studied is the domain of abstract data structures (ADS) (Booch, 1987). Booch has developed an extensive classification structure for such components and discusses how generalized components can be implemented.

To show what is involved in generalizing a component, let us now look at how to produce a reusable component implementing a linked list abstract data structure. Abstract data structures may be implemented as Ada packages or as objects in C++. Figure 20.4 shows a model of an abstract data structure illustrating the different types of operation which might be included in a generalized reusable component.

- *Exported type names* are the names of types declared within the ADS which are available for use.

- *Access operations* are used to inspect the value of the elements of the component.

- *Constructor operations* are used to add or subtract elements from the component.

- *I/O operations* are used to read and write the component to and from disk and to print the component.

- *Iterator operations* allow each component of the ADS to be inspected without removing it from the structure.

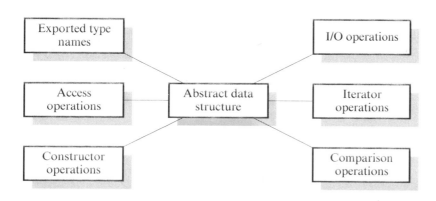

Figure 20.4
A model of a reusable abstract data structure.

● *Comparison operations* are used to compare one instance of the ADS with another.

Few applications will require all the functionality which is implied by the operation classes shown in Figure 20.4. However, the needs of applications can't be predicted in advance. To make the component truly general, all these operation classes are required. Let us now look at what this means in practice.

Figure 20.5 shows part of the specification, in Ada, of a reusable list abstract data structure. The exported type names and comparison operations are shown in this figure and the remaining operations shown in separate figures; I include a C++ version of the complete specification in Figure 20.10.

The linked list ADS is based on design guidelines for reusable abstract data structures:

(1) If data structures are composed of many elements, implement them using generics. This avoids the need to develop a separate implementation of the abstract data structure for each type of element (for example, integer, string and so on).

(2) Provide operations to create instances of the abstract type and an assignment procedure.

(3) Provide a mechanism for operations on the abstract structure to return an indication of whether or not they have been successful. In the examples here, operations return a variable of type STATUS. STATUS is an enumerated type whose members reflect the possible errors which can arise. STATUS is set in

```
generic
    type ELEMENT is private ;
package Linked is
    -- Exported type declarations
    type LIST is limited private ;
    type STATUS is range 1..10 ;
    type ITERATOR is private ;

    -- Comparison operations
    function Equals (L1, L2: LIST) return BOOLEAN ;
    function Equivalent (L1, L2: LIST) return BOOLEAN ;

    -- Access operations (Fig 20.6)
    -- Constructor operations (Fig. 20.7)
    -- I/O operations (Fig. 20.8)
    -- Iterator operations (Fig. 20.9)
private
    type LIST_ELEM;
    type LIST is access LIST_ELEM ;
    type ITERATOR is access LIST_ELEM ;
end Linked ;
```

Figure 20.5
Ada package specification for a linked list component.

each procedure or function to indicate whether or not it has finished execution successfully.

(4) Minimize the amount of representation information defined in the component specification. Here, a list is simply represented as a pointer.

(5) Implement operations which can result in an error as procedures and return the error status as well as the operation result. Implement operations which cannot fail as functions.

(6) Provide an equality operation. In this case, two operations are provided. The Equals operation tests whether two lists are the same size and all corresponding members have the same values. The operation named Equivalent tests whether different list references point to the same list.

(7) Provide an iterator which allows each element in the structure to be visited without affecting the structure itself. This is discussed later.

Some operations on an abstract data structure can be implemented by combinations of other operations. However, this is often inefficient. If the component exhibits poor performance, it may not be reused. On the other hand, if the component is too complex, it is hard to understand and therefore again may not be reused. It is always a difficult decision for the reusable component designer to find an acceptable balance between providing a minimal and an efficient set of operations.

The operations on an abstract structure should always include access operations to discover characteristics of the structure and to access structure components (Figure 20.6). If the abstract type is a composite type (that is, a collection of elements), access operations to provide information about attributes of the composition (such as its size) may also be included. Access operations simply return values. They do not change the abstract data structure.

Constructor operations are intended to update the ADS in some way (Figure 20.7). Operations to add objects to and to delete objects from the collection should

```
-- true if the list has no elements
function Is_empty (L: LIST) return BOOLEAN ;
-- returns the number of elements in the list
function Size_of (L: LIST ) return NATURAL ;
-- true if a list element is the same as E
function Contains (E: ELEMENT; L: LIST )
        return BOOLEAN ;
-- returns the first list element
procedure Head (L: LIST; E: in out ELEMENT ;
        Error_level: out STATUS ) ;
-- removes the first list element and returns the remaining list
procedure Tail (L: LIST; Outlist: in out LIST ;
        Error_level: out STATUS ) ;
```

Figure 20.6
Access operations for linked list component.

```
-- Append adds an element to the end of the list
procedure Append ( E: ELEMENT; Outlist: in out LIST ;
                              Error_level: out STATUS ) ;
-- Add adds an element to the front of the list
procedure Add ( E: ELEMENT; Outlist: in out LIST ;
                              Error_level: out STATUS ) ;
-- Add_before adds an element before element value E
procedure Add_before ( E: ELEMENT ; Outlist: in out LIST ;
                              Error_level: out STATUS ) ;
-- Add_after adds an element after element E
procedure Add_after ( E: ELEMENT; Outlist: in out LIST ;
                              Error_level: out STATUS ) ;
-- Replace replaces the element matching E1 with E2
procedure Replace ( E1, E2: ELEMENT; Outlist: in out LIST ;
                              Error_level: out STATUS ) ;
-- Clear deletes all members of a list
procedure Clear ( Outlist: in out LIST ;
                              Error_level: out STATUS ) ;
-- Prune removes the last element from the list
procedure Prune ( Outlist: in out LIST ;
                              Error_level: out STATUS ) ;
-- Prune_to deletes the list up to and including
-- the element matching E
procedure Prune_to ( E: ELEMENT; Outlist: in out LIST ;
                              Error_level: out STATUS ) ;
-- Prune_from deletes list after element matching E
procedure Prune_from( E: ELEMENT; Outlist: in out LIST ;
                              Error_level: out STATUS ) ;
-- Remove deletes the element which matches E
procedure Remove ( E: ELEMENT; Outlist: in out LIST ;
                              Error_level: out STATUS ) ;
-- Remove_before and Remove_after delete the element before
-- and after E respectively
procedure Remove_before ( E: ELEMENT; Outlist: in out LIST;
                              Error_level: out STATUS ) ;
procedure Remove_after ( E: ELEMENT; Outlist: in out LIST ;.
                              Error_level: out STATUS ) ;
```

Figure 20.7
Constructor
operations for linked
list component.

be provided. If the collection is ordered, add and delete functions should be provided which maintain the order of the collection. For a list type, operations should be available to add and delete an element to and from the front and the end of the list.

For lists, a particularly rich set of constructor operations is required to make the component practically reusable. It is possible to implement most of these constructor operations using the simple operations Create, Append, Head, Tail and Equals but the implementation is inefficient.

It is particularly important that I/O operations should be incorporated as part of a reusable component. These are usually inefficient and sometimes impossible to

```
-- print onto standard output
procedure Print_list (L: LIST; Error_level: out STATUS ) ;
procedure Write_list (F: TEXT_IO.FILE_TYPE ; L: LIST;
                               Error_level: out STATUS ) ;
procedure Read_list (F: TEXT_IO.FILE_TYPE ;
                  Outlist: out LIST ; Error_level: out STATUS ) ;
```

Figure 20.8
I/O procedures for
linked list component.

implement without access to the data representation. Operations to print the structure, to write it to permanent store and to read it from permanent store should be provided (Figure 20.8) for all types of component where this may be necessary.

For every possible exception condition which might occur, a test function should be available to check that condition before initiating the operation. For example, if an operation might fail when presented with an empty list, a function should be provided which allows the user to check if the list has any members. In this example, the Is_empty operation can be used but other types may need special exception checking procedures.

If the abstract type is a composite type, an iterator should be provided to allow simple access to all elements of the structure (Figure 20.9). Iterators allow each component of a composite to be visited and evaluated without destroying the structure of the composite. This is useful if every element must be examined to check whether it meets some criterion. Again, such operations can be implemented using simpler operations but are inefficient.

Iterator operations which should be provided are: an operation to initialize it (set it to reference the first structure element), an operation to evaluate the currently referenced element, an operation to check if all elements have been visited and an operation to advance the reference to the next element.

The complete C++ implementation of the linked list ADS is shown in Figure 20.10. Note that the iterator in C++ is implemented as a separate class (a 'friend' class) which has access to the representation of the list. The type error_indic corresponds to the Ada type STATUS.

The above guidelines are language independent but the language used does influence the reusability of a component. To give a trivial example of this, a reusable C function which processes arrays should have the array size passed as a parameter to it. The same component, implemented in Ada, should not. Rather, the array size should be discovered in the component using the FIRST and LAST language attributes.

```
procedure Iterator_initialize (L: LIST; Iter: in out ITERATOR;
        Error_status: in out STATUS) ;
procedure Go_next (L: LIST; Iter: in out ITERATOR;
        Error_status: in out STATUS) ;
procedure Eval (L: List; Iter: in out ITERATOR;
        Val: out ELEMENT; Error_status: in out STATUS) ;
function At_end (L: LIST; Iter: ITERATOR) return BOOLEAN ;
```

Figure 20.9
Iterator operations for
linked list component.

```
template <class elem> class List
{
public:
    List();        // Automatic constructor
    ~List();       // Automatic destructor

    // Basic list operations
    elem Head (error_indic &Err) ;
    int Length ( ) ;
    List <elem> Tail (error_indic &Err) ;

    // Equality operations
    friend List <elem> operator == (List <elem> L1, List <elem> L2) ;
    friend List <elem> Equivalent (List <elem> L1, List <elem> L2) ;

    // Constructor operations for linked list
    void Append (elem E, error_indic &Err) ;
    void Add (elem E, error_indic &Err) ;
    void Add_before (elem E, error_indic &Err) ;
    void Add_after (elem E, error_indic &Err) ;
    void Replace (elem E, error_indic &Err) ;
    void Clear (error_indic &Err ) ;
    void Prune (error_indic &Err ) ;
    void Prune_to (elem E, error_indic &Err ) ;
    void Prune_from (elem E, error_indic &Err ) ;
    void Remove (elem E, error_indic &Err ) ;
    void Remove_before (elem E, error_indic &Err ) ;
    void Remove_after (elem E, error_indic &Err ) ;

    // I/O functions
    void Print(error_indic &Err) ;
    void Write_list(char* filename, error_indic &Err) ;
    void Read_list(char* filename, error_indic &Err) ;
private:
    typedef struct Linkedlist {
    elem        val;
    Linkedlist* next;
    } Linkedlist;

    Linkedlist* Listhead ; // (Internal) Pointer to start of list
};
template <class elem> class Iterator {
    friend class List <elem> ;
public:
    Iterator () ;
    ~Iterator () ;
    void Create (List <elem> L, error_indic &Err) ;
    void Go_next (error_indic &Err) ;
    elem Eval (error_indic &Err) ;
    boolean At_end () ;
private:
    Linkedlist* iter ;
} ;
```

Figure 20.10
C++ implementation
of reusable list
abstract data
structure.

If the array size is not passed as a C function parameter, the function must be modified to work with arrays of different sizes. Ada, however, has a built-in attribute which can be used to find the size of arrays. This should be used rather than a parameter as there is then no possibility of the array size being incorrect. Reusability guidelines may therefore be produced for each programming language used although most work on this area has focused on Ada (Braun and Goodenough, 1985; Gautier and Wallis, 1990) and on object-oriented languages (Gamma *et al.*, 1995).

The conversion of existing components to generic reusable components obviously incurs considerable costs. If these costs have to be met from a single project budget, the project manager is unlikely to support reusable component development. As the principal responsibility of project managers is to minimize costs, they are understandably reluctant to invest any extra effort in creating components which will not bring them any direct return.

To develop reusable components therefore requires an organizational policy decision to increase short-term costs for potential long-term gain. It is difficult to quantify this potential gain so few organizations have been willing to make this investment in a component library. However, more and more organizations are now considering software components as assets to be exploited and are developing components for reuse.

20.2.1 Reuse and inheritance

When an object-oriented programming language is used for systems development, the inheritance mechanism in that language can be used to adapt components for reuse. Furthermore, the encapsulation provided by the language object/object class mechanism makes components self-contained which improves their reusability. It is often claimed, with some justification, that reuse is one of the principal benefits of an object-oriented approach to software development (Gamma *et al.*, 1995).

When an implementation language supports inheritance, a base object class with minimal functionality can be provided. When additional or different functionality is required, a new version is created taking the base class as a starting point. The functions provided in the base object need not be re-implemented; they are reused in the new implementation.

Multiple inheritance allows several objects to act as base objects. It is supported in object-oriented languages such as C++ and Eiffel (Meyer, 1988). The characteristics of several different object classes can be combined to make up a new object. For example, in Figure 20.11, the component named 'Laser' represents a laser printer. However, as these printers may incorporate a disk drive, it also inherits the attributes and operations of 'Disk'.

When inheritance is supported in a programming language, a class lattice is created as shown in Figure 20.11. This lattice shows the super-classes for each class in the system. As more and more classes are reused, the lattice becomes increasingly complex.

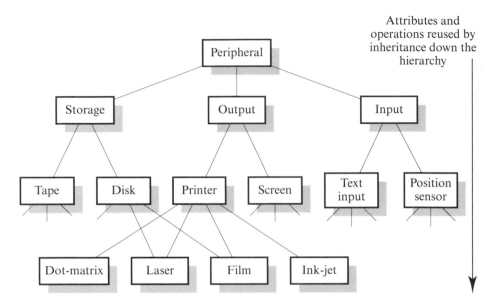

Figure 20.11
A class lattice.

Reuse through inheritance is common in object-oriented programming languages. However, the reusability of classes has proved to be less effective than is sometimes suggested by enthusiasts for object-oriented programming. The reasons for this are:

(1) With inheritance, the code of a component is not collected together in one place. Rather, it is spread through the class lattice and the reuser must examine a number of classes before a component can be understood.

(2) Adaptation through inheritance tends to lead to extra unwanted functionality which can make components inefficient and bulky.

(3) As more and more classes are added to the class lattice, it becomes increasingly difficult to manage. Functionality tends to be duplicated and periodic reorganizations are necessary. Even in a mature and widely used object-oriented language like Smalltalk, the hierarchy of basic classes is still being reorganized after more than 20 years of use.

Inheritance is not, therefore, a simple answer to reusability but does make some kinds of reuse easier to implement. As object-oriented programming languages become increasingly widely used, there is no doubt that standard object libraries will be more effectively exploited.

20.3 Generator-based reuse

An alternative to the component-oriented view of reuse is the generator view. In this approach to reuse, reusable knowledge is captured in a program generator system which can be programmed in a domain-oriented language. The application description specifies, in an abstract way, which reusable components are to be used, how they are to be combined and their parameterization. Using this information, an operational software system can be generated. Figure 20.12 illustrates this approach to reuse.

The most widely used 'program generators' are high-level language compilers where the reusable components are fragments of object code corresponding to high-level language constructs. The reused elements are abstractions corresponding to programming language statements. When a domain-specific notation is used to describe the application, larger domain abstractions can be reused. Examples of this more abstract approach are:

(1) *Application generators for business data processing* The input to these may be a 4GL or may be completely interactive where the user defines screens and processing actions. The output is a program in a language such as COBOL or SQL (Guerrieri, 1994).

(2) *Parser generators for language processing* The generator input is a grammar describing the language to be parsed and the output is a language parser.

(3) *Code generators in CASE tools* The input to these generators is a software design and the output is a program implementing the designed system.

Application generators for business systems are successful because many data processing applications involve abstracting information from a database, performing some relatively simple information processing and producing reports from that information. This stereotypical structure was recognized and components to carry out these operations devised. The generator includes a control language which allows these components to be composed into programs. A complete application can then be generated.

Generator-based reuse is cost-effective but depends on identifying stereotypical domain abstractions. This has been possible for business data processing. O'Connor *et al.* (1994) also report on a successful application of this approach in the domain of command and control systems. Some systems have been produced to describe domain abstractions and generate 'generators' (Neighbours, 1984) but these have not been widely used. We do not have a deep enough understanding of many application domains for such generators to be produced.

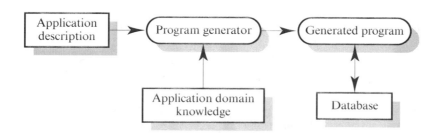

Figure 20.12
Reuse of domain knowledge through application generation.

20.4 Application system portability

A special case of software reuse is application system reuse where a whole application system is reused by implementing it across a range of different computers and operating systems. The problem here is not to discover components for reuse but to develop the system so that it is portable across different platforms.

The rate of change of computer hardware technology is so fast that computers become obsolete long before the programs which execute on them. Techniques for achieving software portability have been widely documented although there are few recent publications in this area (Tanenbaum *et al.*, 1978; Wallis, 1982; Nissen and Wallis, 1985; Mooney, 1990). These techniques include:

- emulating one machine on another using microcode;

- compiling a program into some abstract machine language then implementing that abstract machine on a variety of computers;

- using pre-processors to translate from one dialect of a programming language to another.

The portability of an application is proportional to the amount of work needed to make it work in a new environment. If significantly less work is required than the original development effort, the application is portable.

Mooney (1990) points out that there are two major aspects of program portability:

(1) *Transportation* This is the movement of the program's code and associated data from one environment to another.

(2) *Adaptation* This is the changes required to the program to make it work in a new environment.

Transportation problems have become less significant as commercial pressures have forced manufacturers to produce systems which read the disks and tapes written by other manufacturer's machines. Widespread networking means that electronic interchange of programs and data can replace physical transportation. The problems of physical device incompatibility which were significant in the 1970s and 1980s have now almost disappeared.

The environment in which a program operates is made up of the system hardware, operating system, libraries and language run-time support system. An application system communicates with this environment through a set of interfaces as shown in Figure 20.13.

When this environment is changed, those dependent parts of the program must be identified and may have to be modified to adapt the program to its new environment. Communication with the operating system, libraries and the run-time system is usually through procedure or function calls. However, communications with the memory and CPU (machine architecture) are more subtle. They involve the information representation scheme used by whatever programming language has been used to develop the application.

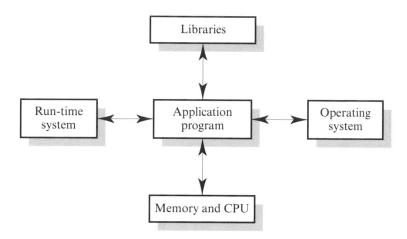

Figure 20.13
Application program
interfaces.

20.4.1 Portability problems

As standardized high-level languages have become almost universally used for large
system development, problems of portability due to compiler unavailability are now
less serious than in the past. However, simply because a program is written in a
standard high-level language does not mean that it can be moved without change
from one machine to another. Indeed, for non-trivial programs, there will almost
always be some adaptation required.

We can classify the different portability problems which arise according to
the interfaces shown in Figure 20.13.

(1) *Machine architecture problems* The program makes some assumptions
     about information representation on the underlying machine and these
     assumptions are not true for all machines.

(2) *Operating system problems* The program calls on operating system
     facilities which are not available on all potential host machines.

(3) *Run-time system problems* The program makes use of particular run-time
     system features which are not universal. Alternatively, it may rely on some
     behavioural characteristic of the run-time system (such as some dynamic
     checking) which is not shared by all implementations.

(4) *Library problems* The program uses libraries which are not available on all
     potential host machines. A particularly subtle and common manifestation of
     this problem is when a program relies on a particular version of a library
     which is not universally available.

Run-time system problems and library problems are particularly difficult to solve.
Run-time systems and libraries are usually large, complex and unavailable as source
code. While standards should be used as far as possible, these standards are often not
completely defined. There is still scope for differences between different implementations.

It is also often the case that the implementation of new versions of different standard libraries (such as X-windows) will not all be available at the same time on different machines. Therefore, a program which is based on the latest version (say) may not be portable because the target machine only has an older version of the standard libraries.

Machine architecture and operating system dependencies can be isolated by developing a *portability interface* as shown in Figure 20.14. Rather than call operating system and I/O procedures directly, abstract versions of these procedures are called by the application program. These abstract procedures are, of course, implemented using the operating system facilities.

Similarly, rather than access built-in language data types directly, these should all be represented as abstract data types which are called by the program. These abstract data types are then implemented using built-in types such as integer and string. When the program is moved to another operating system or machine architecture, it is only necessary to re-implement the portability interface. All platform dependent references are routed through this portability interface.

The problem with using this approach is that there is a significant overhead in routing all references though the portability interface. Typically, the overhead of calling an operating system or I/O function is doubled, as two procedure calls rather than a single call must be made. The overhead of data access to primitive types is even greater as all access requires at least one procedure call through the abstract data type interface.

In practice, therefore, system designers do not usually isolate all operating system and machine architecture dependencies behind a portability interface. Rather, they use their knowledge of the application and target platform to identify which parts of the program are likely to cause portability problems when moved to another machine. These are then hidden behind the portability interface.

Portability problems are likely to arise when:

(1)   The program relies on some specific feature of the data representation. For example, it may include assumptions about the order of bits in a data word or

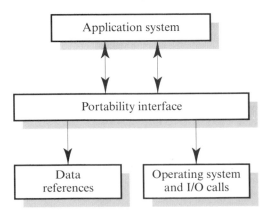

Figure 20.14
A portability interface hiding platform details.

may generate data values at the extremes of the ranges supported by the machine.

(2)   The program uses operating system calls which provide facilities which are not available on all target platforms. Examples of such calls are calls which provide a particular method of process management (for instance, Unix's fork) or file system calls.

As an example of the first of these situations, consider a control program which is intended to be built into a range of different laboratory instruments. These incorporate different kinds of counter. The company developing these instruments hope to sell into different markets. These vary from school laboratories who need low-cost instruments to research laboratories who need high-performance (and therefore expensive) instruments.

The cheaper instruments use very low-cost 8-bit and 16-bit microprocessors whereas the more expensive instruments use 32-bit machines. The length of a computer word directly affects the range of integers available on that machine, the precision of real numbers and the number of characters which may be packed into a single word.

The counters in these instruments must be able to cope with a wide range of values. Because of the different machine architectures which may be used, these counters should not simply be implemented as integers. The maximum integer which may be represented depends on the underlying machine word length. Rather, the counter should be implemented as an abstract data type or object (Figure 20.15) which may be implemented on different machine architectures. On 32-bit machines, the built-in integers may be used for implementation. On 8-bit and 16-bit machines, however, character strings may be used to implement the counter.

Only the type name and related operations need be visible outside the package with representation details confined to the package. When the program is ported to a different system which uses a different counter representation, only the counter package need be changed. None of the uses of the counter should be affected.

Where a program needs to make use of operating system calls for file and process management, these can also be isolated in one or more packages or objects. For example, Figure 20.16 shows a package specification for process management. This provides operations to start and stop processes, wait for processes to finish execution, and so on. These are normally implemented using operating system calls.

Portability interfaces can also be used when a system has to be implemented across a range of database management system or filing systems. A portability interface was used in the implementation of the design editing system discussed in earlier chapters. The intention in building this system was to make it possible to store the design representation in either a Unix file system or in a database. Thus, we had to avoid building representation dependencies into the system.

A logical design representation was specified and implemented as an abstract data interface (ADI). All operations on the design representation took place through this ADI (Figure 20.17). Porting the program to a different underlying database or filestore was accomplished by rewriting the ADI code.

```
                              Ada

package Counter is
    type T is limited private;
    procedure Inc (Cnt : in out T ) ;
    procedure Dec (Cnt : in out T ) ;
    procedure Copy (Cnt1: T ; Cnt2: out T ) ;
    function Cequals (Cnt1, Cnt2: T ) return BOOLEAN ;
private
    type T is range 0..500_000 ;
end Counter;


                              C++

class Counter {
public:
    Counter () ;
    void Inc () ;
    void Dec () ;
    friend Counter Copy ( Counter c1, Counter c2 ) ;
    // Overload the operator == to compare two counters
    friend Counter operator == ( Counter c1, Counter c2 ) ;
private:
    int value ;
};
```

Figure 20.15
A portable counter
component.

As an illustration of the relative amount of work involved, the ADI was implemented in about 1000 lines of C code which was about 7% of the total system code. Porting the program to another data storage system takes about 1/20th of the effort required to write a complete system.

20.4.2 Standards

The emergence of workable standards and their acceptance by large segments of the software development community means that it is now easier to produce portable application systems than it was in the 1970s and 1980s. If a standard is adopted by the implementors of an application system, that system should be portable, without change, to any other system which follows that standard. Standards which have been developed include:

(1) *Programming language standards* Standards for Ada, COBOL, Pascal, C, C++ and FORTRAN have been agreed. Programs which follow these standards are readily portable to any compiler following the standards. However, differences between language translators can still introduce portability problems.

Ada

```
package Process_manager is
   type PROCESS is private ;
   type STATUS is (READY, RUNNING, WAITING, KILLED)
   function Create return PROCESS ;
   function Kill (P: PROCESS ) return STATUS ;
   function Get_status (P: PROCESS ) return STATUS ;
   function Wake_up (P: PROCESS ) return STATUS ;
   function Sleep (P: PROCESS ) return STATUS ;
   procedure Wait (P: PROCESS ; S: STATUS) ;
private
   type PROCESS is record
       PID: NATURAL ;
       State: STATUS ;
   end record ;
end Process_manager ;
```

C++

```
class Process {
public:
   Process () ;
   P_state Kill () ;
   P_state Get_status () ;
   P_state Wake_up () ;
   P_state Sleep ();
   void Wait (P_state &status) ;
private:
   int PID ;
   P_state status ;
} ;
```

Figure 20.16
Portable process
management.

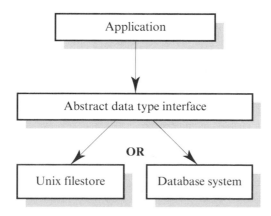

Figure 20.17
Implementation of a
portability interface.

(2)   *Operating system standards*   Microsoft Windows has become a de facto standard for the current generation of personal computers with MacOS favoured by a relatively small number of users. Unix is the standard operating system for workstations. However, there are subtle differences between different implementations of Unix. These arise because different manufacturers implement non-standard system extensions. Large mainframe computers used for transaction processing do not have a standard operating system.

(3)   *Networking standards*   There is a great deal of international standardization effort going on concerned with networking standards and the OSI layer model has been adopted although not widely implemented. TCP/IP protocols and Sun's Network File System (NFS) have become standards for local area networks running Unix. They are also supported by most personal computers.

(4)   *Window system standards*   The X-window system (Scheifler and Gettys, 1986) has become accepted as the standard for graphical user interfaces for workstations. The Motif toolkit has been widely adopted on top of X-windows as a standard toolkit (OSF, 1993). Microsoft Windows is the standard on the majority of PCs. Although these systems have a similar 'look and feel', they are implemented in quite different ways. The cost of moving from one window system to another is fairly high.

These standards significantly reduce the problems of moving an application system from one environment to another. However, there is still a need to think carefully about application system portability and to design the portability interface to minimize portability problems.

Further reading

'Software reuse'. This survey article takes a rather unusual view of reuse and seems to leave out what I would consider to be key reuse references. However, it is still worth reading for the rather different perspective which it offers. (*ACM Computing Surveys*, **24** (2), June 1992.)

IEEE Software, **11** (5), September 1994. This special issue on systematic reuse includes several good papers. The overview by Frakes and Isoda and the article by Farchamps which discusses reuse experience at Hewlett-Packard are particularly recommended.

Design Patterns: Elements of Reusable Object-oriented Software. This is one of the few books I have seen on object-oriented reuse which provides a set of useful generic components for reuse. (E. Gamma, R. Helm, R. Johnson and J. Vlissides, 1995, Addison-Wesley.)

'Strategies for supporting application portability'. There are few recent articles on portability apart from specific case studies. Although several years old, this is an excellent article. It focuses on operating system portability but is also of general interest. (J.D. Mooney, *IEEE Computer*, **23** (11), November 1990.)

KEY POINTS

- Software reuse involves reusing existing components rather than developing them specially for an application. Systematic reuse can improve reliability, reduce management risk and reduce development costs.

- Software development with reuse needs a library of reusable components that can be understood by the reuser. Information on how to reuse the components should also be provided.

- Reusable software components do not simply emerge as a by-product of software development. Extra effort must be added to generalize system components to make them reusable.

- Abstract data types and objects are effective encapsulations of reusable components.

- Generator-based reuse depends on the identification of domain abstractions that are known to the application generator.

- Application system portability is a specialized form of reuse in which an entire application system is adapted for reuse on a different computer.

- Portable systems should be implemented so that environment dependent sections are isolated in a portability interface.

- Development according to standards for languages, operating systems, networking and graphical user interfaces minimizes the costs of implementing a system on different types of computer.

EXERCISES

20.1 What are the major technical and non-technical factors which militate against widespread software reuse? From your own experience, do you reuse much software? If not, why not?

20.2 Write a set of guidelines for Ada or C++ programmers which give advice on how to make functions or procedures reusable.

20.3 Using the suggestions set out in the chapter, design reusable packages for the following abstract data structures:

(a) a stack

(b) a table with keyed access to table elements

(c) a binary tree

(d) a priority queue

(e) an array

(f) a character string

20.4 Suggest a set of software tools which might be provided to support software development with and for reuse.

20.5 Design an experiment which might demonstrate the advantages of software development with reuse. You may assume that you have a component catalogue which is populated with abstract data structure components.

20.6 The manipulation of individual bits within a machine word can cause portability problems because of different information representations in different machines. Design and specify (in Ada or C++) a reusable, bit manipulation package which can be used to conceal these differences.

20.7 Explain why the use of a standard high-level language does not guarantee that software will be portable across a range of machines.

20.8 You have been given the task of implementing a calendar and clock which gives time and data information. This has to operate on a range of computers from 8-bit micros to 64-bit special processors. Design and implement an abstract data type to represent the calendar and clock which can be readily ported from machine to machine.

20.9 Using your knowledge of a compiler or some other application, suggest which parts of the system are most likely to lead to portability problems. Suggest an architectural design of the application which can minimize the cost of developing a portable system.

20.10 The reuse of software raises a number of copyright and intellectual property issues. If a customer pays a software contractor to develop some system, who has the right to reuse the developed code? Does the software contractor have the right to use that code as a basis for a generic component? What payment mechanisms might be used to reimburse providers of reusable components? Discuss these issues and other ethical issues associated with the reuse of software.

21

Safety-critical Software

Objectives

- To introduce the notion of safety-critical software, the malfunction of which can threaten human life or the environment.

- To describe the process of safety-critical systems development and some methods of safety analysis.

- To discuss methods of safety assurance which are intended to increase confidence in the safety of the software.

- To use a simple example (software for an embedded drug delivery system) to illustrate some aspects of safety-critical systems programming.

Contents

There are now many systems where failure or malfunctioning of the system software can pose a threat to human life. Examples of such *safety-critical systems* are control and monitoring systems in aircraft, process control systems in chemical and pharmaceutical plants and automobile control systems.

Until relatively recently, most safety-critical systems avoided the use of software and relied on hardware safety devices. Safety validation and assurance techniques that had been developed for hardware systems could not be transferred, without change, to software. Because the software could not be certified as safe, its use was avoided. Methods for hardware safety assurance often relied on physical characteristics of the system to make it safe. For example, a bimetallic strip which bent when heated might have been used as a switch. Obviously, comparable techniques cannot work with software.

However, we are now building systems of such complexity that they cannot be controlled by hardware systems. Some software control is essential because of the need to manage large numbers of sensors and actuators. An example of such complexity is found in advanced military aircraft which are aerodynamically unstable. They require continual software-controlled adjustment of their flight surfaces to ensure that they do not crash.

It is a useful shorthand to use the term 'safety-critical software' to refer to software in systems whose malfunction can be dangerous. Obviously, however, software on its own does not pose a threat to anyone. Hardware failure of some kind is the ultimate result of software malfunction. Thus, when considering safety-critical issues, you have to take a systems viewpoint. You must consider the interactions of the hardware, software and people who make up the complete system. Safety considerations are therefore part of the systems engineering process as discussed in Chapter 2.

Safety-critical software falls into two classes:

(1)   *Primary, safety-critical software*   This is software which is embedded as a controller in a system. Malfunctioning of such software can cause a hardware malfunction which results in human injury or environmental damage.

(2)   *Secondary safety-critical software*   This is software which can indirectly result in injury. Examples of such systems are computer-aided engineering design systems whose malfunctioning might result in a design fault in the object being designed. This fault may pose a threat to humans if the designed system malfunctions. Another example of a secondary safety-critical system is a medical database holding details of drugs administered to patients. Errors in this system might result in an incorrect drug dosage being administered.

It is sometimes difficult to decide if a system is a secondary safety-critical system. For example, say an automobile manufacturer maintains a database holding details of car owners. They use this database to recall cars for repair if a design fault has to be rectified. Say this system malfunctions and, when recalled, some owners are not notified. In some of these cases, the design fault occurs and causes an accident.

Should this database be considered as safety-critical or is the problem in the process which relies on the database? The answer to such questions depends on the organization and the systems used. It can't be discussed in general so, in this chapter, I only cover primary, safety-critical software.

A specialized vocabulary has evolved to discuss safety-critical systems and it is important to understand the specific terms used. As defined by Leveson (1985), one of the most authoritative safety-critical systems researchers, these are:

(1) *Mishap (or accident)* An unplanned event or sequence of events which results in human death or injury, damage to property or to the environment. A computer-controlled machine injuring its operator is an example of an accident.

(2) *Hazard* A condition with the potential for causing or contributing to a mishap. A failure of the sensor which detects an obstacle in front of a machine is an example of a hazard.

(3) *Damage* A measure of the loss resulting from a mishap. Damage can range from many people killed as a result of an accident to minor injury or property damage.

(4) *Hazard severity* An assessment of the worst possible damage which could result from a particular hazard. Hazard severity can range from catastrophic where many people are killed to minor where only minor damage results.

(5) *Hazard probability* The probability of the events occurring which create a hazard. Probability values tend to be arbitrary but range from *probable* (say, 1/100 chance of a hazard occurring) to *implausible* (no conceivable situations are likely in which the hazard could occur).

(6) *Risk* This is a measure of the probability that the system will cause an accident. The risk is assessed by considering the hazard probability, the hazard severity and the probability that a hazard will result in an accident.

Software reliability and software safety are not the same thing. Of course, a safety-critical system should be reliable in that it should conform to its specification and should operate without failures. It may incorporate fault-tolerant characteristics. However, fault-tolerant systems are not necessarily safe. The software may still malfunction and cause system behaviour that results in an accident.

Apart from the fact that we can never be 100% certain that a software system is fault-free and fault-tolerant, there are several other reasons why software systems which are reliable are not necessarily safe:

(1) The specification may be incomplete in that it does not describe the required behaviour of the system in some critical situations. A high percentage of system malfunctions (Boehm *et al.*, 1975; Endres, 1975; Nakajo and Kume, 1991; Lutz, 1993) are the result of specification rather than design errors. In a study of errors in embedded systems, Lutz concludes:

'... difficulties with requirements are the key root cause of the safety-related software errors which have persisted until integration and system testing'

(2)   Hardware malfunctions may cause the system to behave in an unpredictable way and may present the software with an unanticipated environment. For example, when components are close to failure they may behave erratically and generate signals outside the ranges which can be handled by the software.

(3)   The operator of the system may generate inputs which are not individually incorrect but which, in particular situations, can lead to a system malfunction. An anecdotal example of this is that of a mechanic instructing the utility management software on an aircraft to raise the undercarriage. The software carried out the mechanic's instruction in spite of the fact that the plane was on the ground!

Accidents generally occur when several things go wrong at the same time. An analysis of serious accidents (Perrow, 1984) suggested that they were almost all due to a combination of malfunctions rather than single failures. The unanticipated combination led to interactions which resulted in system failure. Perrow also suggests that it is impossible to anticipate all possible combinations of system malfunction and that accidents are an inevitable part of using complex systems. Software tends to increase system complexity so using software control *may* increase the probability of system accidents.

This does not mean that software control invariably increases the risk associated with a system. Software-controlled systems can monitor a wider range of conditions than electromechanical systems. They can be adapted relatively easily. They involve the use of computer hardware which has very high inherent reliability and which is physically small and lightweight. Software-controlled systems can provide sophisticated safety interlocks. They can support control strategies which reduce the amount of time people need to spend in hazardous environments.

Software control and monitoring can therefore increase the safety of systems. Even when there are doubts over the 'safeness' of the software, overall system safety may be improved even when potentially hazardous software failures can occasionally occur. Additional hazards may be introduced with software control. However, these may be compensated by a reduction in other forms of system hazard which are detected or avoided by the software.

21.1 An insulin delivery system

Understanding safety-critical control and monitoring systems obviously requires an understanding of the underlying system being controlled. It is difficult to find an example for discussion which does not require specialized application-domain knowledge. The example used in this chapter is an insulin delivery system for the control of diabetes. I hope that most readers will have general knowledge of this condition and its treatment.

Diabetes is a relatively common condition (affecting about one per cent of the population) in which the human body is unable to produce sufficient quantities of a hormone called insulin. Insulin metabolizes glucose in the blood. The conventional treatment of diabetes involves regular injections of genetically engineered insulin.

The problem with this treatment is that the level of insulin in the blood does not depend on the blood glucose level but is a function of the time when the insulin injection was taken. This can lead to very low levels of blood glucose (if there is too much insulin) or very high levels of blood sugar (if there is too little insulin). Low blood sugar is, in the short term, a more serious condition as it can result in temporary brain malfunctioning and, ultimately, unconsciousness and death. In the long term, continually high levels of blood sugar can lead to eye damage, kidney damage and heart problems.

Current advances in developing miniaturized sensors have meant that it is now possible to develop automated insulin delivery systems. These monitor blood sugar levels and deliver an appropriate dose of insulin when required. Insulin delivery systems already exist for the treatment of hospital patients. In future, it may be possible for many diabetics to use such systems which will be permanently attached to their bodies.

An insulin delivery system might work by using a micro-sensor embedded in the patient to measure some blood parameter which is proportional to the sugar level. This is then sent to the pump controller. This controller computes the sugar level, judges how much insulin is required and sends signals to a miniaturized pump to deliver the insulin via a permanently attached needle. Insulin delivery systems are likely to be software-controlled. A data-flow model of such a system is shown in Figure 21.1. Note that the design of this system follows the architectural model discussed in Section 13.3.2.

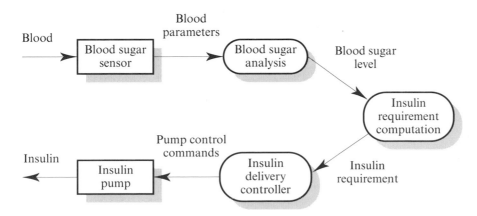

Figure 21.1
An insulin delivery system.

21.2 Safety specification

Safe operation is the required characteristic of a safety-related software system. This requires that particular attention should be paid during the specification of a system to potential hazards which might arise. Each hazard should be assessed for the risk it poses and the specification may either describe how the software should behave to minimize the risk or might require that the hazard should never arise. It then becomes the responsibility of the safety assurance process to demonstrate that the safety specification has been met. The process of safety specification and assurance is sometimes called the 'safety life cycle' (IEE, 1989) and is illustrated in Figure 21.2.

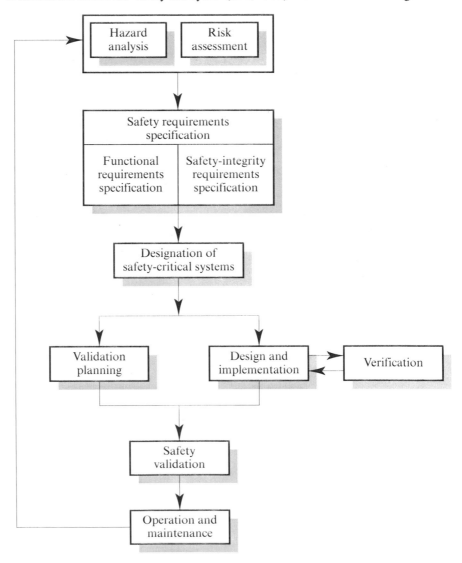

Figure 21.2
The safety life cycle.

The first stages of the life cycle involve assessing the potential system hazards and estimating the risk they pose. This is followed by safety requirements specification. This activity is concerned with identifying safety-critical functions (functional requirements specification) and the safety integrity level for each of these functions. The safety integrity level is a statement of the acceptability of safety-related failures. It can range from intolerable (that is, there should be no such failures) to acceptable.

The designation of safety-critical systems involves assigning explicit responsibility for safety to individual engineers. A 'normal' process model is then followed with particular attention paid to the validation of the system. Part of that validation should be an explicit safety validation activity.

Of course, it is possible that potential hazards might not be foreseen by the specifier. Part of the specification should be concerned with how the software should behave should an unforeseen condition arise. Exception handling mechanisms, as discussed in Chapter 19, can be used to handle unforeseen errors.

21.2.1 Hazard analysis

Hazard analysis involves analysing the system and the environment in which it is to be installed. Its objective is to discover potential hazards which might arise in that environment and the root causes of these hazards. This is a complex and difficult process which requires lateral thinking and input from many different sources of expertise. It should be undertaken by systems engineers in conjunction with domain experts and professional safety advisers. Group working techniques such as brainstorming may be used.

Hazard analysis is difficult and needs input from a group because many hazards are extremely rare. They are caused by very unusual combinations of circumstances. Hazards are often identified because one of the analysts involved has direct experience of some previous incident which resulted in a hazard.

Hazard analysis is carried out in several iterative steps:

(1) *Hazard identification*   Potential hazards which might arise are identified. These will always be dependent on the environment in which the system is to be used.

(2) *Hazard classification*   The hazards are considered separately. Those which are potentially serious and not implausible are selected for further analysis. At this stage, some hazards may be eliminated simply because they are very unlikely ever to arise (for example, simultaneous lightning strike and earthquake).

(3) *Hazard decomposition*   Each hazard is considered individually and its root cause discovered.

(4) *Safety specification*   The system safety specification is written, setting out how each hazard must be taken into account when the system is designed.

For large systems, hazard analysis is usually structured into a number of phases (Leveson, 1986):

(1)   *Preliminary hazard analysis*   This activity is undertaken early in the specification phase. The principal hazards which can arise are identified and the risk of each hazard is assessed.

(2)   *Sub-system hazard analysis*   This is a more detailed hazard analysis which is carried out for each safety-critical sub-system. This process may involve *zonal analysis* whereby the effects of a sub-system failure on other sub-systems that are located close to it are analysed.

(3)   *System hazard analysis*   This analysis is concerned with hazards which arise through sub-system interaction involving interface errors and incompatibilities, simultaneous failure of several sub-systems, and so on.

(4)   *Software hazard analysis*   This analysis is explicitly concerned with discovering software-related hazards in the system or sub-system. It may be undertaken as part of sub-system or system hazard analysis.

(5)   *Operational hazard analysis*   This is a study of the hazards which might arise as a result of the use of the system. In safety-critical software systems, it is concerned with user interface analysis and possible related operator errors.

These analyses identify hazards and associate a risk with each hazard. This involves estimating the probability that the hazard will arise, estimating the probability that the hazard will cause a mishap and estimating the likely severity of that mishap. Engineering judgement is the only way of making such risk assessments.

The process of hazard analysis generally involves considering different classes of hazard such as physical hazards, electrical hazards, biological hazards, radiation hazards (where appropriate), hazards due to service failure and so on. Each of these classes is then analysed in detail to discover associated hazards.

For the insulin delivery system, introduced above, the hazards and their associated classes are:

- insulin overdose (service failure),
- insulin underdose (service failure),
- power failure due to exhausted battery (electrical),
- machine interferes electrically with other medical equipment such as a heart pacemaker (electrical),
- poor sensor and actuator contact caused by incorrect fitting of machine (physical),
- parts of machine break off in patient's body (physical),
- infection caused by introduction of machine (biological),
- allergic reaction to the materials or insulin used in the machine (biological).

Because this is a small system, multiple phases of hazard analysis are not necessary. Many safety-critical systems (such as a chemical plant), however, are very large and hazard analysis is a long, complex and expensive process.

21.2.2 Fault-tree analysis

For each identified hazard, a detailed analysis should be carried out to discover the conditions which might cause that hazard. Hazard analysis techniques can either be deductive or inductive. Deductive techniques, which tend to be easier to use, start with the hazard and work from that to the possible system failure; inductive techniques start with a proposed system failure and identify which hazards might arise. Wherever possible, both inductive and deductive techniques should be used for hazard analysis.

There are various techniques which have been proposed as possible approaches to such analyses. These include reviews and checklists, and more formal techniques such as Petri net analysis (Peterson, 1981), formal logic (Jahanian and Mok, 1986) and fault-tree analysis (Leveson and Harvey, 1983).

I cover fault-tree analysis here. This is a widely used hazard analysis technique which is relatively easy to understand without specialist domain knowledge. Fault-tree analysis involves identifying the undesired event and working backwards from that event to discover the possible causes of the hazard. The hazard is at the root of the tree and the leaves of the tree represent potential causes of the hazard.

Software-related hazards are normally concerned with service failure or with the failure of monitoring systems. These monitoring systems detect potentially hazardous conditions such as power failures. Figure 21.3 is the fault tree which can be identified for the possible software-related hazards in the insulin delivery system. Insulin underdose and insulin overdose really represent a single hazard namely 'incorrect insulin dose administered' and a single fault tree can be drawn. Of course, when specifying how the software should react to hazards, the distinction between an insulin underdose and overdose must be taken into account.

The fault tree in Figure 21.3 is incomplete. Only potential software faults have been fully decomposed. Hardware faults such as low battery power causing a sensor failure are not shown. At this level, further analysis is not possible. However, as a design and implementation is developed more detailed fault tree analysis should be carried out. Leveson and Harvey (1983) and Leveson (1985) show how fault trees can be developed throughout the software design down to the individual programming language statement level.

21.2.3 Risk assessment

The process of risk assessment begins after all hazards have been identified. Risk assessment considers the severity of each hazard, the probability that it will arise and the probability that an accident will result from the hazard. For each hazard, the outcome of the risk assessment process is a statement of acceptability. This classifies the acceptability of the hazard as follows:

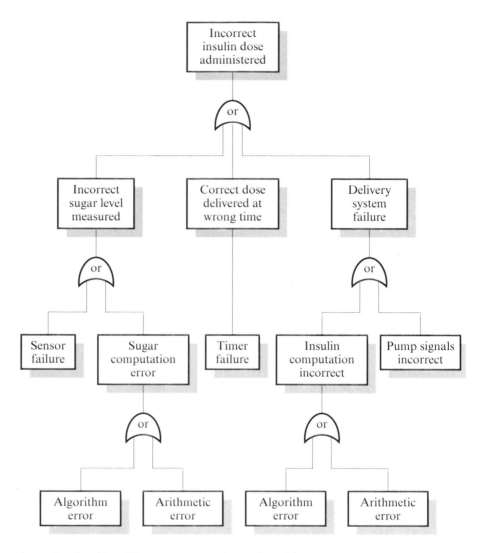

Figure 21.3
Fault tree for insulin
delivery system.

(1) *Intolerable* The system must be designed in such a way so that either the hazard cannot arise or, if it does arise, it will not result in an accident.

(2) *As low as reasonably practical (ALARP)* The system must be designed so that the probability of an accident arising because of the hazard is minimized subject to other considerations such as cost, delivery and so on.

(3) *Acceptable* While the system designers should take all possible steps to reduce the probability of this hazard arising, these should not increase costs, delivery time or other non-functional system attributes.

Figure 21.4 (Brazendale and Bell, 1994) shows these three regions. The shape of the diagram reflects the costs of ensuring that hazards do not result in accidents. The cost of system design to cope with the hazard is a function of the width of the

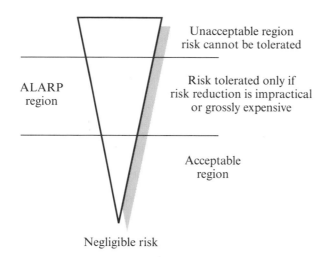

Unacceptable region
risk cannot be tolerated

Risk tolerated only if
risk reduction is impractical
or grossly expensive

ALARP
region

Acceptable
region

Negligible risk

Figure 21.4
Levels of risk.

triangle so the highest costs are incurred by hazards at the top of the diagram, the lowest costs by hazards at the apex.

The boundaries between the regions in Figure 21.4 are not fixed for any particular class of system. Rather, they are pushed downwards with time, due to public expectations of safety and political considerations. Although the financial costs of accepting hazards and paying for any resulting accidents may be less than the costs of accident prevention, public opinion may mean that the additional costs must be accepted. For example, it may be cheaper for a company to clean up pollution on the rare occasion it occurs rather than install systems for pollution prevention. This may have been acceptable in the 1960s and 1970s but it is not likely to be publicly or politically acceptable now. The boundary between the intolerable region and the ALARP region has moved downwards so that hazards which may have been accepted in the past are now intolerable.

The risk assessment process involves estimating the hazard probability and the hazard severity. This is usually very difficult to do in an exact way and generally depends on making engineering judgements. Probabilities and severities are assigned using relative terms such as 'probable', 'unlikely' and 'rare', and 'high', 'medium' and 'low'. Previous system experience may allow some numeric value to be associated with these terms. However, because accidents are relatively uncommon, it is usually very difficult to validate the accuracy of this value.

Figure 21.5 shows a risk classification for the hazards identified in the previous section for the insulin delivery system. As I am not a physician, the estimates in that table are for illustration only. Notice that an insulin overdose is potentially more serious than an insulin underdose in the short term.

Hazards 3–8 are not software-related so I don't discuss them further here. To counter these hazards, the machine should have built-in self-checking software which should monitor the system state and warn of some of these hazards. The warning will often allow the hazard to be detected before it causes an accident. Examples of hazards which might be detected are power failure and incorrect placement of the

Identified hazard	Hazard probability	Hazard severity	Estimated risk	Acceptability
Insulin overdose	Medium	High	High	Intolerable
Insulin underdose	Medium	Low	Low	Acceptable
Power failure	High	Low	Low	Acceptable
Machine incorrectly fitted	High	High	High	Intolerable
Machine breaks in patient	Low	High	Medium	ALARP
Machine causes infection	Medium	Medium	Medium	ALARP
Electrical interference	Low	High	Medium	ALARP
Allergic reaction	Low	Low	Low	Acceptable

Figure 21.5
Risk analysis of
identified hazards.

machine. The monitoring software is, of course, safety-related as failure to detect a hazard could result in an accident.

21.2.4 Risk reduction

Once potential hazards and their causes have been identified, the system specification should be formulated in such a way that these hazards are unlikely to result in an accident. There are several approaches which may be used:

(1)   *Hazard avoidance*   The system is designed in such a way that the hazard cannot arise. For example, say a potential hazard in some machine is that the operator's hand might be trapped in the machine. The user interface might be redesigned so that both hands are needed for machine operation. It is therefore impossible for the operator's hand to be in a potentially dangerous position.

(2)   *Hazard probability reduction*   The system is designed in such a way that the probability of a hazard arising is reduced. This is usually achieved by ensuring that hazards cannot arise as a result of any single failure or operating error.

(3)   *Accident prevention*   The system is designed in such a way that hazards can be detected. Other systems may be activated to remove the hazard before an accident is caused. This approach is widely used in control systems. The process which is being controlled is monitored by a separate system. If a hazard or the cause of a hazard is detected, the monitoring system takes action to avoid an accident. This usually involves putting the system into some safe state.

These approaches are not independent. Normally, the designers of a system would use a combination of these approaches. For example, intolerable hazards may be handled by reducing their probability as far as possible and adding an accident prevention system should the hazard arise.

In an insulin delivery system, a 'safe state' is a shut-down state in which no insulin is injected. Over a short period this will not pose a threat to the diabetic's health. If the potential software problems identified in Figure 21.3 are considered, the following 'solutions' might be developed:

(1)   *Arithmetic error*   This arises when some arithmetic computation causes a representation failure. The specification must identify all possible arithmetic errors which may occur. These depend on the algorithm used. The specification should set out the action to be taken for each of these errors if they arise. A safe action is to shut down the delivery system and activate a warning alarm.

The specification might set out that software development must be in Ada with an appropriate exception handler to handle NUMERIC_ERROR exceptions which arise. However, the physical size of a delivery system is restricted and all software must fit into ROM. Using Ada means that a substantial run-time system must be present. This may not be acceptable because of the need to keep the device size as small as possible. If another language is used, each possible exception must be individually handled.

(2)   *Algorithmic error*   This is a more difficult situation as no definite anomalous situation can be detected. It might be detected by comparing the required insulin dose computed with the previously delivered dose. If it is much higher, this may mean that the amount has been computed wrongly. At the same time, the system may keep track of the dose sequence. After a number of above-average doses have been delivered, a warning may be issued and further dosage limited. If the diabetic's condition genuinely requires unusually large doses of insulin, it probably means that medical intervention is necessary. A warning is appropriate even if no error has occurred.

The fault tree is also used to identify potential hardware problems. It may provide insights into requirements for software to detect and, perhaps, correct these problems. For example, insulin doses are not administered at a very high frequency, typically two or three times per hour. There is, therefore, available processor capacity in the system to run diagnostic and self-checking programs. Hardware errors such as sensor, pump or timer errors can be discovered and warnings issued before they have a serious effect on the patient.

21.3   Safety assurance

General design principles for safety-critical software revolve around information hiding and software simplicity. Those parts of the system which are safety-critical should be isolated from other parts of the system. This may be achieved through the use of data and control abstraction or may be achieved using physical separation. The safety-critical software may execute on a separate computer with minimal communication links to other parts of the system.

Safety-critical software should be as simple as possible. Potentially error-prone language features, such as those discussed in Chapter 19, should be avoided. They may even be disallowed by standards for safety-critical systems development. I recommend against the use of C and C++ for safety-critical systems development and have therefore deliberately excluded C++ examples in this chapter. These languages are particularly unsafe because of their low-level features such as pointers. Their terse style can be hard to understand so systems are more difficult to validate.

Subsets of languages such as Pascal and Ada have been devised for safety-critical applications. These subsets have excluded language features which are not properly defined and features which are inherently unsafe such as real numbers, pointers and so on.

It is arguable whether or not fault-tolerant techniques should be adopted. One view is that they increase complexity so making the software harder to validate. Furthermore, Knight and Leveson (1986) and Brilliant *et al.* (1990) have demonstrated that the arguments for reliability through diversity (N-version programming) are not always valid. When developing software from the same specification, different teams made the same mistakes; software redundancy did not give the theoretically predicted increase in system reliability. Furthermore, if the specification is incorrect, all versions will include the common specification error.

This does not mean that N-version programming is useless, as it may well reduce the absolute number of failures in the system. While admitting that common faults were present in the different system versions, Bishop *et al.* (1986) found that the number of system failures were reduced with this approach. N-version programming gives increased confidence but not absolute confidence in the system reliability.

Rather than use N-version programming which increases system complexity, an alternative approach is to keep the system as simple as possible and devote a lot of resources to system validation. Keeping software simple not only reduces the probability that errors will be introduced, it also means that the very high costs of safety validation are reduced. Only a relatively small amount of software is safety-related.

Parnas *et al.* (1990) support this approach. They suggest that safety can best be assured by minimizing and isolating safety-critical code components and by using the simplest possible techniques for writing safety-critical code sections. They suggest that validation should be based on a combination of thorough testing, reviews based on mathematical specifications and a certified development process.

21.3.1 Formal methods and safety-critical software

There is a continuing debate in the safety-critical systems community about the role of formal methods in the safety-critical software development process. The use of formal mathematical specification and associated verification is mandated in UK defence standards for safety-critical software (MOD, 1995). However, many safety-critical systems developers are unconvinced that formal methods are cost-effective and argue that they may even reduce rather than increase system safety.

The argument for the use of formal specification and associated program verification is that formal specification forces a detailed analysis of the specification. It may reveal potential inconsistencies or omissions which might not otherwise be discovered until the system is operational. Formal validation demonstrates that the developed program meets its specification so that implementation errors do not compromise safety.

The argument against the use of formal specification is that it requires specialized notations. These can only be used by specially trained staff and cannot be understood by domain experts. Hence, problems with the system requirements can be concealed by formality. Potential difficulties with the requirements are not recognized by the software engineers developing the specification. The specification may be consistent but it does not specify the system properties that are really required.

It is also argued that formal verification is not cost-effective. The same level of safety can be achieved at lower cost by using other validation techniques such as inspections and system testing. It is currently impossible to either confirm or refute this assertion as so few systems have been developed using formal methods.

My view is that formal methods should be used to support the development of software which has safety implications. It is certain that the use of formal approaches will increase as procurers demand it and as more and more engineers become familiar with these techniques. However, many people are unconvinced by formal methods. It will, therefore, be many years before their use is universal for safety-critical systems development.

21.3.2 Process assurance

The life-cycle model for safety-critical systems development makes clear that explicit attention should be paid to safety during all stages of the software process. This means that specific safety assurance activities must be included in the process. These include:

- the creation of a hazard logging and monitoring system which traces hazards from preliminary hazard analysis through to testing and system validation;

- the appointment of project safety engineers who have explicit responsibility for the safety aspects of the system;

- the extensive use of safety reviews throughout the development process;

- the creation of a safety certification system whereby safety-critical components are formally certified for their assessed safety;

- the use of a very detailed configuration management system (see Chapter 33) which is used to track all safety-related documentation and keep it in step with the associated technical documentation. There is little point in having stringent validation procedures if a failure of configuration management means that an unchecked system is delivered to the customer.

The central safety document is the hazard log in which hazards identified during the specification process are documented. This hazard log is then used at each stage of the software development process to assess how that development stage has taken the hazards into account. A simplified example of a hazard log entry for the insulin delivery system is shown in Figure 21.6.

As shown in Figure 21.6, individuals who have some safety responsibilities should be explicitly identified. It is important to appoint a project safety engineer who should not be involved in the system development. The responsibility of this engineer is to ensure that appropriate safety checks have been made and documented. The system procurer may also require an independent safety assessor to be appointed from an outside organization who reports directly to the client on safety matters.

Extensive reviews are essential during a safety-oriented development process. Parnas *et al.* (1990) suggest five classes of review which should be mandatory for safety-critical systems:

Hazard Log. Page 4: Printed 21.12.94

System: Insulin Delivery System   *File: Insulin System/Safety/HLog*
Safety Engineer: James Brown   *Log version 1.3*

Identified Hazard: Insulin overdose delivered to patient

Identified by: Jane Williams

Criticality Class: 1

Identified Risk: High

Fault tree identified: YES   *Date:* 10.11.94   *Location:* Hazard Log, Page 5

Fault tree creator: Jane Williams and Bill Smith

Fault tree checked: YES   *Date:* 20.11.94   *Checker:* James Brown

System design safety requirements:

1.   Incorporate self-testing software for sensor system, clock and delivery system. This should be executed at least once per minute and should cause an audible warning to be emitted if a fault is discovered. If a fault is discovered, no further insulin deliveries should be made until the system has been reset.

2.   Incorporate a patient override facility so that the patient may modify the dose to be delivered by manual intervention. However, a limit should be set on the dose administered by the patient. This limit should be set by medical staff when the system is installed.

3.   …

Figure 21.6
A simplified hazard log page.

(1)   review for correct intended function,

(2)   review for maintainable, understandable structure,

(3)   review to verify that the algorithm and data structure design are consistent with the specified behaviour,

(4)   review the code for consistency with the algorithm and data structure design, and

(5)   review the adequacy of the system test cases.

Currently an international standard for safety-critical systems development (IEC, 1995) has been proposed. It is likely that this standard will be the basis for process standards required by particular system procurers such as government and defence departments.

In many types of application, system engineers who have safety responsibilities must be certified engineers. In the UK, this means that they have to have been accepted as a member of one of the engineering institutes (civil, electrical, mechanical and so on) and have to be chartered engineers. Inexperienced, poorly qualified engineers may not take responsibility for safety. This does not currently apply to software engineers. However, future process standards for safety-critical software development may require that project safety engineers should be formally certified as having undergone appropriate training.

21.3.3 Product safety assurance

Product safety assurance is part of an effective safety process. As discussed in the previous section, it is generally based on testing and reviews. The testing of safety-critical systems has much in common with the testing of any other systems with high reliability requirements. Thus, the techniques discussed in Chapters 18 and 22–24 should be applied. However, because of the ultra-low failure rates required in many safety-critical systems, it is unlikely that statistical testing can provide a quantitative estimate of the system reliability because of the unrealistically large number of tests required. Engineering judgement must be used to assess the safety of the product.

An assumption which underlies work in system safety is that the number of system faults which can lead to hazards is significantly less than the total number of faults which may exist in the system. Safety assurance can concentrate on these faults with hazard potential. If it can be demonstrated that these faults cannot occur or, if they occur, the associated hazard will not result in an accident, then the system is safe.

Static analysis techniques based on the use of automatic static analysers are useful in detecting potential faults in a system. Their use is mandated by some safety process standards. These techniques and some currently available tools are discussed in Chapter 24.

21.3.4 Safety proofs

Proofs of program correctness have been proposed as a key validation technique for over 20 years. However, these have been little used except in research laboratories. The practical problems of constructing a correctness proof (discussed in Chapter 24) are so great that few organizations have considered them to be cost-effective in normal system development. However, for some critical applications, it may be economic to develop correctness proofs in order to increase confidence that the system meets its safety or security requirements.

Although it may not be cost-effective to develop correctness proofs for most systems, it is sometimes possible to develop a weaker proof, namely a safety proof which demonstrates that the program meets its safety obligations. It is not necessary to prove that the program meets its specification. It is only necessary to prove that program execution cannot result in an unsafe state.

A useful technique in developing safety proofs is to use proof by contradiction. This means assuming that the unsafe state (identified by the hazard analysis) can be reached then demonstrating that the pre-conditions for this state are contradicted by the post-conditions of all program paths leading to that state. If this is the case, the initial assumption of an unsafe state is incorrect so the software is safe.

As an example, consider the (hypothetical) code in Figure 21.7 which might be part of the implementation of the insulin delivery system. Some comments have been added to this code to relate it to the safety proof shown in Figure 21.8.

```
-- The insulin dose to be delivered is a function of
-- blood sugar level, the previous dose delivered and
-- the time of delivery of the previous dose
Insulin_dose := Compute_insulin ( Blood_sugar_level,
            Previous_dose, Previous_time) ;
-- if statement 1
if Insulin_dose > Previous_dose + Previous_dose then
    Insulin_dose := Previous_dose + Previous_dose ;
end if ;
-- Don't administer very small doses
-- if statement 2
if Insulin_dose < Minimum_dose then
    Insulin_dose := 0 ;
-- Don't deliver more than maximum dose
elsif Insulin_dose > Maximum_dose then
    Insulin_dose := Maximum_dose ;
end if ;
-- root of fault tree
-- if statement 3
if Insulin_dose > 0 then
    Administer_insulin (Insulin_dose) ;
end if ;
```

Figure 21.7
Insulin delivery code.

Developing a safety proof of this code involves demonstrating that the dose of insulin administered is never greater than some maximum level which is established for each individual diabetic. Therefore, it is not necessary to prove that the system delivers the 'correct' dose, merely that it never delivers an overdose to the patient.

The method used here is to identify the pre-condition for the unsafe state which, in this case, is that Insulin_dose > Maximum dose. The system is shown to be safe by demonstrating that all program paths lead to a contradiction of this unsafe assertion. If this is the case, the unsafe condition cannot be true. Therefore, the system is safe.

Safety arguments, such as that shown in Figure 21.8, are much shorter than formal system verifications. The argument need only consider the last assignment to each state variable on the path leading to the potentially unsafe state. Previous computations (such as if statement 1 in Figure 21.7) do not appear in the safety argument as the variable Insulin_dose is modified by later statements.

In the safety proof shown in Figure 21.8, there are three possible program paths which lead to the Administer_insulin procedure call:

(1)   Neither branch of if statement 2 is executed. This can only happen if Insulin_dose is either greater than or equal to Minimum_dose and less than or equal to Maximum_dose.

(2)   The then branch of if statement 2 is executed. In this case, the assignment setting Insulin_dose to zero is executed. Therefore, its post-condition is Insulin_dose = 0.

(3)   The elsif branch of if statement 2 is executed. In this case, the assignment setting Insulin_dose to Maximum_dose is executed. Therefore, its post-condition is Insulin_dose = Maximum_dose.

(4)   If Insulin_dose is less than or equal to zero, the Administer_insulin function is not called so this is a safe condition.

In all three cases, the post-conditions contradict the unsafe pre-condition so the system is safe.

21.3.5 Safety assertions

The use of assertions in defensive programming was discussed in Chapter 19 and a similar technique can be used in safety-critical systems. Assertions are predicates which describe conditions that must hold before the following statement can be executed. In safety-critical systems, the assertions should be generated from the safety specification rather than the system specification. They are intended to assure safe behaviour rather than behaviour which conforms to the specification.

Assertions can be particularly valuable to assure the safety of communications between components of the system. For example, in the insulin delivery system, the dose of insulin administered involves generating signals to the insulin pump to deliver a specified number of insulin increments (Figure 21.9). The number

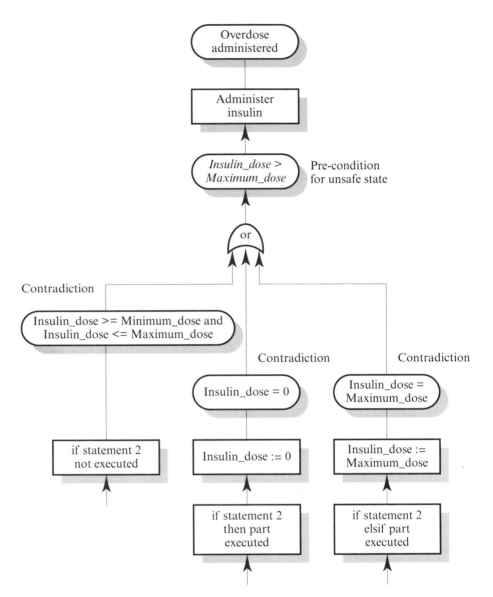

Figure 21.8
Informal safety proof
based on demonstrating
contradictions.

of insulin increments associated with the allowed maximum insulin dose can be
pre-computed and included as an assertion in the system.

Assertions may be included as formal comments in the program. They may
be used as reminders during program inspections. Alternatively, it may be possible
to use a language pre-processor to generate assertion checking code. This is inserted
into the program as conditional statements. Function execution is terminated if the
assertion does not hold. A general exception handler takes over. However, it may be
impossible to write a general exception handler. In this case, automatically generated
assertion checking can only log violations of these assertions.

```
procedure Administer_insulin (Insulin_dose: DOSE) is
    Insulin_increments: NATURAL ;
begin
    --* assert Insulin_dose <= Maximum_dose
    Insulin_increments := Compute_requirement (Insulin_dose) ;
    --* assert Insulin_increments <= Maximum_increments
    for i in range 1..Insulin_increments loop
        Generate_pump_signal ;
        --* assert i <= Maximum_increments ;
    end loop ;
end Administer_insulin ;
```

Figure 21.9
Insulin administration.

Further reading

'Software safety in embedded control systems'. This is a good introduction to the problems of developing safe software-controlled systems. The article updates Leveson's original survey article (*ACM Computer Surveys*, 1986) but leaves out issues such as human factors. For readers with no background in this area, the article is an excellent starting point. (*Comm. ACM*, **34** (2), 1991.)

Safety-critical Systems: Current Issues, Techniques and Standards. This collection of papers illustrates the breadth of this field. It includes papers on current problems, formal methods, requirements, training of safety engineers, case studies and standards. (Chapman and Hall, 1993.)

Computer-related Risks. This is a collection drawn from the Internet Risks Forum of incidents which have occurred in automated systems. It shows how much can actually go wrong in safety-related systems. (P.G. Neumann, 1995, Addison-Wesley.)

KEY POINTS

- Software is increasingly used in safety-critical control and monitoring systems. Existing hardware safety assurance techniques have to be modified to cope with software systems.

- The use of software control can increase system safety by improving the number of control variables which can be monitored and by increasing the sophistication of safety interlocks.

- It is important to have a well-defined, certified process for safety-critical systems development. The process must include the identification and monitoring of potential hazards.

- Hazard analysis is a key activity in the safety specification process. It involves identifying hazardous conditions which can compromise system safety. Fault-tree analysis is a technique which can be used in the hazard analysis process.

- Risk analysis is the process of assessing the likelihood that a hazard will result in an accident. Risk analysis identifies critical hazards which must be avoided in the system and classifies risks according to their seriousness.

- Risk can be reduced by applying design strategies which eliminate the hazard, which reduce the probability of the hazard occurring or which prevent the hazard causing an accident. Usually, more than one of these strategies is used.

- Safety assurance should be the responsibility of named individuals who are external to the software development team.

- Safety proofs are an effective product safety assurance technique. They show that an identified hazardous condition can never occur. They are usually simpler than proving that a program meets its specification.

EXERCISES

21.1   Identify six consumer products which may contain, or which may contain in future, safety-critical software systems.

21.2   Explain why ensuring system reliability is not a guarantee of system safety.

21.3   Suggest two constructs in Ada or some other programming language which should be avoided when developing safety-critical systems. Explain, in a single sentence, why these constructs are potentially unsafe.

21.4   For the insulin delivery system example, write a possible safe implementation of a procedure called **Compute_sugar** which computes the **Blood_sugar_level**. The function takes a parameter **BP** which is some blood characteristic. Your function should take into account the previously measured blood sugar levels and likely blood sugar levels which can occur.

21.5   Develop a safety proof of your function which demonstrates that it cannot compute an artificially low level (and thus cause excessive insulin to be administered).

21.6   The door lock control mechanism in a nuclear waste storage facility is designed for safe operation. It ensures that entry to the storeroom is only permitted when radiation shields are in place or when the radiation level in the room falls below some given value (danger level). That is,

(a) If remotely controlled radiation shields are in place within a room, the door may be opened by an authorized operator.

(b) If the radiation level in a room is below a specified value, the door may be opened by an authorized operator.

```
1        Entry_code := Get_entry_code
2        if Entry_code = Authorized_code then
3            Shield_status := Get_shield_status;
4            Radiation_level := Get_sensor_readings;
5            if radiation_level < danger_level then
6                State := safe;
7            else
8                State := unsafe;
9            end if;
10               if shield_status = in_place then
11                   State := safe;
12           end if;
13           if State = safe then
14               Door_locked := false ;
15               Unlock_door;
16           end if ;
17       else
18           Lock_door;
19           Door_locked := true ;
20       end if ;
```

Figure 21.10
Door lock controller.

(c) An authorized operator is identified by the input of an authorized door entry code.

The Ada code shown in Figure 21.10 is used to control the door locking mechanism. Note that the safe state is that entry should not be permitted.

Develop a safety argument which shows that this code is potentially unsafe. Modify the code to make it safe.

21.7 A software-controlled radiation therapy machine is used for treating hospital patients. On each visit to the hospital, medical staff assess the machine setting (expressed in units of radiation/minute) and the number of minutes for which the patient is to be treated. These figures are input to the system. A system parameter called **Max_permitted_dose** holds the maximum allowed radiation dose in a single session. Furthermore, each patient has a specified monthly maximum dose which is input at the beginning of each month. The system checks that the dose to be delivered does not cause the cumulative dose to be exceeded. The Ada routine which computes the radiation dose is shown in Figure 21.11.

Identify the unsafe states for the radiation therapy machine and develop an informal safety proof which shows that the above code will always ensure that the dose computed for a patient is not unsafe. You may assume that the I/O operations and the **Lookup** operation do not compromise the safety of the procedure.

```
procedure Compute_radiation (Patient_id: PATIENT;
    Machine_setting: in out NATURAL ;
    Exposure_time: in out NATURAL ) is
begin
    Console_IO.Read (Machine_setting) ;
    Console_IO.Read (Exposure_time) ;
    Radiation_dose := 0 ;
    for i in (1..Exposure_time) loop
        Radiation_dose := Radiation_dose + Machine_setting
    end loop ;
    Cumulative_dose := Lookup (Patient_id) ;
    if Radiation_dose + Cumulative_dose > Monthly_maximum then
        TEXT_IO.Put ("Dose exceeds monthly maximum
                            – check inputs") ;
        TEXT_IO.Put ("Radiation dose reset to zero") ;
        Radiation_dose := 0 ;
    end if ;
    if Radiation_dose > Max_permitted_dose then
        Exposure := 0;
        TEXT_IO.Put ("Exposure overdose – check inputs") ;
    end if ;
    if Radiation_dose = 0 then
        Exposure_time := 0 ; Machine_setting := 0;
    end if ;
end Compute_radiation ;
```

Figure 21.11
Radiation dose
computation.

21.8 Explain the function of the for loop in the code shown in Figure 21.11. Explain why this operation is implemented using iteration rather than the built-in multiplication operator.

21.9 Assume you were part of a team that developed software for a chemical plant which went wrong and caused a serious pollution incident. Your boss is interviewed on television and states that there are no faults in the software and that the problems must be due to poor operational procedures. You are approached by a newspaper for your opinion. Discuss how you should handle such an interview.

21.10 Should software engineers working on the development of safety-related systems be professionally certified in some way?

Part Five

Verification and Validation

This part of the book is concerned with the checking processes which are required to ensure that software meets its specification and the user's requirements. Chapter 22 introduces verification and validation and covers the overall testing process. Chapter 23 looks specifically at techniques for discovering defects in a program. Chapter 24 introduces static verification techniques which rely on analysis of the source code rather than program execution.

Contents

22

Verification and Validation

Objectives

- To introduce software verification and validation.
- To describe the various stages of the testing process.
- To explain why test planning is important and to show how test plans are used in the context of software life cycle models.
- To describe a number of complementary testing strategies which may be used during system validation.

Contents

Verification and validation (V & V) is the generic name given to checking processes which ensure that software conforms to its specification and meets the needs of the software customer. The system should be verified and validated at each stage of the software process using documents produced during the previous stage. Verification and validation therefore starts with requirements reviews and continues through design and code reviews to product testing.

Verification and validation are sometimes confused. They are, in fact, different activities. The difference between them is succinctly summarized by Boehm (1979):

- 'Validation: Are we building the right product?'
- 'Verification: Are we building the product right?'

Verification involves checking that the program conforms to its specification. Validation involves checking that the program as implemented meets the expectations of the software customer. Requirements validation techniques, such as prototyping, help in this respect. However, flaws and deficiencies in the requirements can sometimes only be discovered when the system implementation is complete.

To satisfy the objectives of the V & V process, both static and dynamic techniques of system checking and analysis should be used. Static techniques are concerned with the analysis and checking of system representations such as the requirements document, design diagrams and the program source code. They may be applied at all stages of the process through structured reviews. Dynamic techniques or tests involve exercising an implementation. Dynamic techniques are discussed in this chapter and in Chapter 23. Static verification techniques are covered in Chapter 24.

Figure 22.1 shows the place of static and dynamic techniques in the software process. Static techniques can be used at all stages of the software process. Dynamic techniques, however, can only be used when a prototype or an executable program is available.

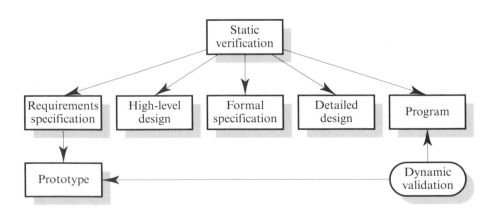

Figure 22.1
Static and dynamic verification and validation.

Static techniques include program inspections, analysis and formal verification. Some purists have suggested that these techniques should completely replace dynamic techniques in the verification and validation process and that testing is unnecessary. This is nonsense. Static techniques can only check the correspondence between a program and its specification (verification); they cannot demonstrate that the software is operationally useful.

Although static verification techniques are becoming more widely used, program testing is still the predominant verification and validation technique. Testing involves exercising the program using data like the real data processed by the program. The existence of program defects or inadequacies is inferred from unexpected system outputs. Testing may be carried out during the implementation phase to verify that the software behaves as intended by its designer and after the implementation is complete. This later testing phase checks conformance with requirements and assesses the reliability of the system.

Different kinds of testing use different types of test data:

(1)   *Statistical testing* may be used to test the program's performance and reliability. This has already been discussed in Chapter 18. Tests are designed to reflect the frequency of actual user inputs. After running the tests, an estimate of the operational reliability of the system can be made. Program performance may be judged by measuring the execution of the statistical tests.

(2)   *Defect testing* is intended to find areas where the program does not conform to its specification. Tests are designed to reveal the presence of defects in the system. This form of testing is covered in Chapter 23.

When defects have been found in a program, these must be discovered and removed. This is called *debugging*. Defect testing and debugging are sometimes considered to be parts of the same process. In fact, they are quite different. Testing establishes the existence of defects. Debugging is concerned with locating and correcting these defects.

Figure 22.2 illustrates a possible debugging process. Defects in the code must be located and the program modified to meet its requirements. Testing must then be repeated to ensure that the change has been made correctly.

The debugger must generate hypotheses about the observable behaviour of the program then test these hypotheses in the hope of finding the fault which caused the output anomaly. Testing the hypotheses may involve tracing the program code manually. It may require new test cases to localize the problem. Interactive debugging tools which show the intermediate values of program variables and a trace of the statements executed may be used to help the debugging process.

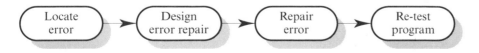

Figure 22.2
The debugging process.

It is impossible to present a set of instructions for program debugging. The skilled debugger looks for patterns in the test output where the defect is exhibited and uses knowledge of the defect, the pattern and the programming process to locate the defect. Process knowledge is important. Debuggers know of common programmer errors (such as failing to increment a counter) and match these against the observed patterns.

After a defect in the program has been discovered, it must be corrected and the system should then be re-tested. This form of testing is called *regression testing*. Regression testing is used to check that the changes made to a program have not introduced new faults into the system.

In principle, all tests should be repeated after every defect repair; in practice this is too expensive. As part of the test plan, dependencies between parts of the system and the tests associated with each part should be identified. When a change is made, it may only be necessary to run a subset of the entire test data set to check the modified component and its dependants.

22.1 The testing process

Except for small programs, systems should not be tested as a single, monolithic unit. Large systems are built out of sub-systems which are built out of modules which are composed of procedures and functions. The testing process should therefore proceed in stages where testing is carried out incrementally in conjunction with system implementation.

The most widely used testing process consists of five stages as shown in Figure 22.3. In general, the sequence of testing activities is component testing, integration testing then user testing. However, as defects are discovered at any one stage, they require program modifications to correct them and this may require other stages

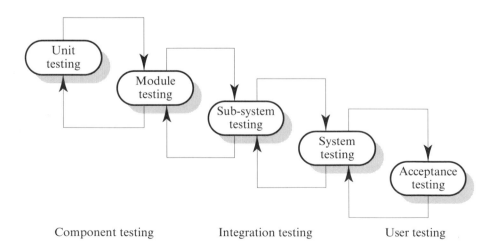

Figure 22.3
The testing process.

Component testing   Integration testing   User testing in the testing process to be repeated. Errors in program components, say, may come to light at a later stage of the testing process. The process is therefore an iterative one with information being fed back from later stages to earlier parts of the process.

In Figure 22.3, the arrows from the top of the boxes indicate the normal sequence of testing. The arrows returning to the previous box indicate that previous testing stages may have to be repeated. The stages in the testing process are:

(1)   *Unit testing*   Individual components are tested to ensure that they operate correctly. Each component is tested independently, without other system components.

(2)   *Module testing*   A module is a collection of dependent components such as an object class, an abstract data type or some looser collection of procedures and functions. A module encapsulates related components so can be tested without other system modules.

(3)   *Sub-system testing*   This phase involves testing collections of modules which have been integrated into sub-systems. Sub-systems may be independently designed and implemented. The most common problems which arise in large software systems are sub-system interface mismatches. The sub-system test process should therefore concentrate on the detection of interface errors by rigorously exercising these interfaces.

(4)   *System testing*   The sub-systems are integrated to make up the entire system. The testing process is concerned with finding errors which result from un-anticipated interactions between sub-systems and system components. It is also concerned with validating that the system meets its functional and non-functional requirements.

(5)   *Acceptance testing*   This is the final stage in the testing process before the system is accepted for operational use. The system is tested with data supplied by the system procurer rather than simulated test data. Acceptance testing may reveal errors and omissions in the system requirements definition because the real data exercises the system in different ways from the test data. Acceptance testing may also reveal requirements problems where the system's facilities do not really meet the user's needs or the system performance is unacceptable.

Acceptance testing is sometimes called *alpha testing*. Bespoke systems are developed for a single client. The alpha testing process continues until the system developer and the client agree that the delivered system is an acceptable implementation of the system requirements.

When a system is to be marketed as a software product, a testing process called *beta testing* is often used. Beta testing involves delivering a system to a number of potential customers who agree to use that system. They report problems to the system developers. This exposes the product to real use and detects errors which may not have been anticipated by the system builders. After this feedback, the system is modified and either released for further beta testing or for general sale.

22.1.1 Object-oriented system testing

The model of system testing shown in Figure 22.3 is based on the notion of incremental system integration where simple components are integrated to form modules. These modules are integrated into sub-systems and finally the sub-systems are integrated into a complete system. In essence, we should finish testing at one integration level before moving on to the next level.

When object-oriented systems are developed, the levels of integration are less distinct. Clearly, operations and data are integrated to form objects and object classes. Testing these object classes corresponds to unit testing. There is no direct equivalent to module testing in object-oriented systems. However, Murphy *et al.* (1994) suggest that groups of classes which act in combination to provide a set of services should be tested together. They call this *cluster testing*.

At higher levels of integration, namely sub-system and system levels, thread testing may be used (Section 22.3.3). Thread testing is based on testing the system's response to a particular input or set of input events. Object-oriented systems are often event-driven so this is a particularly appropriate form of testing to use.

A related approach to testing groups of interacting objects is proposed by Jorgensen and Erickson (1994). They suggest that an intermediate level of integration testing can be based on identifying 'method-message' (MM) paths. These are traces through a sequence of object interactions which stop when an object operation does not call on the services of any other object. They also identify a related construct which they call an 'Atomic System Function' (ASF). An ASF consists of some input event followed by a sequence of MM-paths which is terminated by an output event. This is similar to a thread in a real-time system, discussed in Section 22.3.3.

22.2 Test planning

System testing is expensive. For some large systems, such as real-time systems with complex non-functional constraints, half the system development budget may be spent on testing. Careful planning is needed to get the most out of testing and to control testing costs.

Test planning is concerned with setting out standards for the testing process rather than describing product tests. Test plans are not just management documents. They are also intended for software engineers involved in designing and carrying out system tests. They allow technical staff to get an overall picture of the system tests and to place their own work in this context. Test plans also provide information to staff who are responsible for ensuring that appropriate hardware and software resources are available to the testing team.

The major components of a test plan are shown in Figure 22.4. This plan should include significant amounts of contingency so that slippages in design and implementation can be accommodated and staff allocated to testing can be deployed in other activities. A good description of test plans and their relation to more general quality plans is given in Frewin and Hatton (1986).

The testing process
A description of the major phases of the testing process. These might be as described earlier in this chapter.

Requirements traceability
Users are most interested in the system meeting its requirements and testing should be planned so that all requirements are individually tested.

Tested items
The products of the software process which are to be tested should be specified.

Testing schedule
An overall testing schedule and resource allocation for this schedule. This, obviously, is linked to the more general project development schedule.

Test recording procedures
It is not enough simply to run tests. The results of the tests must be systematically recorded. It must be possible to audit the testing process to check that it has been carried out correctly.

Hardware and software requirements
This section should set out software tools required and estimated hardware utilization.

Constraints
Constraints affecting the testing process such as staff shortages should be anticipated in this section.

Figure 22.4
Test plan contents.

Like other plans, the test plan is not a static document. It should be revised regularly as testing is an activity which is dependent on implementation being complete. If part of a system is incomplete, the system testing process cannot begin.

The preparation of the test plan should begin when the system requirements are formulated and it should be developed in detail as the software is designed. Figure 22.5 shows the relationships between test plans and software process activities.

Figure 22.5
Testing phases in the software process.

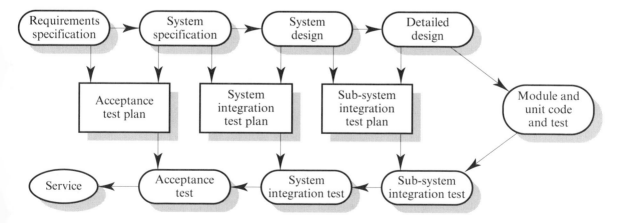

Figure 22.5 is a horizontal version of what is sometimes called the V-model of the software process. This V-model is an extension of the simple waterfall model where each process phase concerned with development has an associated verification and validation phase. The individual test plans are the links between these activities.

Unit testing and module testing may be the responsibility of the programmers developing the component. Programmers make up their own test data and incrementally test the code as it is developed. This is an economically sensible approach as the programmer knows the component best and is most able to generate test data. Unit testing is part of the implementation process and it is expected that a component conforming to its specification will be delivered as part of that process.

As it is a natural human trait for individuals to feel an affinity with objects they have constructed, programmers responsible for system implementation may feel that testing threatens their creations. Psychologically, programmers do not usually want to 'destroy' their work. Consciously or subconsciously, tests may be selected which will not demonstrate the presence of system defects.

If unit testing is left to the component developer, it should be subject to some monitoring procedure to ensure that the components have been properly tested. Some of the components should be re-tested by an independent tester using a different set of test cases. If independent testing and programmer testing come to the same conclusions, it may be assumed that the programmer's testing methods are adequate.

Later stages of testing involve integrating work from a number of programmers and must be planned in advance. They should be undertaken by an independent team of testers. Module and sub-system testing should be planned as the design of the sub-system is formulated. Integration tests should be developed in conjunction with the system design. Acceptance tests should be designed with the program specification. They may be written into the contract for the system development.

22.3 Testing strategies

A testing strategy is a general approach to the testing process rather than a method of devising particular system or component tests. Different testing strategies may be adopted depending on the type of system to be tested and the development process used.

The testing strategies which I discuss in this section are:

(1) *Top-down testing* where testing starts with the most abstract component and works downwards.

(2) *Bottom-up testing* where testing starts with the fundamental components and works upwards.

(3) *Thread testing* which is used for systems with multiple processes where the processing of a transaction threads its way through these processes.

(4)   *Stress testing* which relies on stressing the system by going beyond its specified limits and hence testing how well the system can cope with overload situations.

(5)   *Back-to-back testing* which is used when versions of a system are available. The systems are tested together and their outputs are compared.

Large systems are usually tested using a mixture of these testing strategies rather than any single approach. Different strategies may be needed for different parts of the system and at different stages in the testing process.

Whatever testing strategy is adopted, it is always sensible to adopt an incremental approach to sub-system and system testing (Figure 22.6). Rather than integrate all components into a system and then start testing, the system should be tested incrementally. Each increment should be tested before the next increment is added to the system.

In the example shown in Figure 22.6, tests T1, T2 and T3 are first run on a system composed of module A and module B. Module C is integrated and tests T1 and T2 are repeated to ensure that there have not been unexpected interactions with A and B. Test T4 is also run on the system. Finally, module D is integrated and tested using existing and new tests.

The process should continue until all modules have been incorporated into the system. When a module is introduced at some stage in this process, tests, which were previously unsuccessful, may now detect defects. These defects are probably due to interactions with the new module. The source of the problem is localized to some extent, thus simplifying defect location and repair.

22.3.1 Top-down testing

Top-down testing tests the high levels of a system before testing its detailed components. The program is represented as a single abstract component with sub-components represented by stubs. Stubs have the same interface as the component

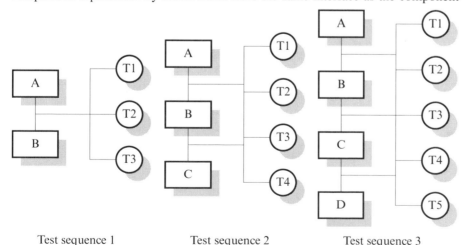

Test sequence 1   Test sequence 2   Test sequence 3

Figure 22.6
Incremental testing.

but very limited functionality. After the top-level component has been tested, its sub-components are implemented and tested in the same way. This process continues recursively until the bottom-level components are implemented. The whole system may then be completely tested. Figure 22.7 illustrates this sequence.

Top-down testing should be used with top-down program development so that a system component is tested as soon as it is coded. Coding and testing are a single activity with no separate component or module testing phase.

If top-down testing is used, unnoticed design errors may be detected at an early stage in the testing process. As these errors are usually structural errors, early detection means that they can be corrected without undue costs. Early error detection means that extensive re-design and re-implementation may be avoided.

Top-down testing has the further advantage that a limited, working system is available at an early stage in the development. This is an important psychological boost to those involved in the system development. It demonstrates the feasibility of the system to management. Validation, as distinct from verification, can begin early in the testing process as a demonstrable system can be made available to users.

Strict top-down testing is difficult to implement because of the requirement that program stubs, simulating lower levels of the system, must be produced. These program stubs may either be implemented as a simplified version of the component required which returns some random value of the correct type or by manual simulation. The stub simply requests the tester to input an appropriate value or to simulate the action of the component.

If the component is a complex one, it may be impractical to produce a program stub which simulates it accurately. Consider a function which relies on the conversion of an array of objects into a linked list. Computing its result involves internal program objects, the pointers linking elements in the list. It is unrealistic to generate a random list and return that object. The list components must correspond to the array elements. It is equally unrealistic for the programmer to input the created list. This requires knowledge of the internal pointer representation. Therefore, the routine to perform the conversion from array to list must exist before top-down testing is possible.

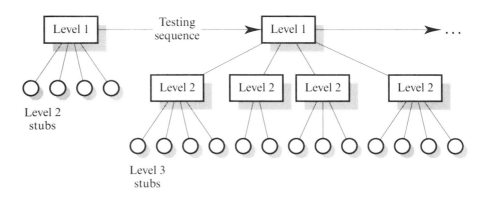

Figure 22.7
Top-down testing.

Another disadvantage of top-down testing is that test output may be difficult to observe. In many systems, the higher levels of that system do not generate output but, to test these levels, they must be forced to do so. The tester must create an artificial environment to generate the test results.

Collections of objects are not usually integrated in a strictly hierarchical way so a strict top-down testing strategy is not appropriate for object-oriented systems. However, individual objects may be tested using this approach where operations are replaced by stubs.

22.3.2 Bottom-up testing

Bottom-up testing is the converse of top-down testing. It involves testing the modules at the lower levels in the hierarchy, and then working up the hierarchy of modules until the final module is tested (Figure 22.8). The advantages of bottom-up testing are the disadvantages of top-down testing and vice versa.

When using bottom-up testing, test drivers must be written to exercise the lower-level components. These test drivers simulate the components' environment and are valuable components in their own right. If the components being tested are reusable components, the test drivers and test data should be distributed with the component. Potential reusers can then run these tests to satisfy themselves that the component behaves as expected in their environment.

If top-down development is combined with bottom-up testing, all parts of the system must be implemented before testing can begin. Architectural faults are unlikely to be discovered until much of the system has been tested. Correction of these faults might involve the rewriting and consequent re-testing of lower-level modules in the system.

Because of this problem, bottom-up testing was criticized by the proponents of top-down functional development in the 1970s. However, a strict top-down development process including testing is an impractical approach, particularly if existing software components are to be reused. Bottom-up testing of critical, low-level system components is almost always necessary.

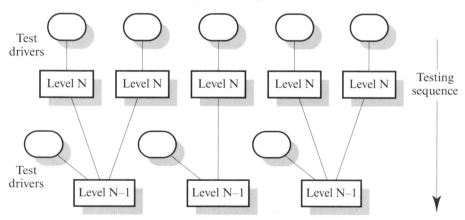

Figure 22.8
Bottom-up testing.

Bottom-up testing is appropriate for object-oriented systems in that individual objects may be tested using their own test drivers. They are then integrated and the object collection is tested. The testing of these collections should focus on object interactions. An approach such as the 'method-message' path strategy, discussed in Section 22.1.1, may be used.

22.3.3 Thread testing

Thread testing is a testing strategy which was devised for testing real-time systems. It is an event-based approach where tests are based on the events which trigger system actions. A comparable approach may be used to test object-oriented systems as they may be modelled as event-driven systems. Bezier (1990) discusses this approach in detail but he calls it 'transaction-flow testing' rather than thread testing.

Thread testing is a testing strategy which may be used after processes or objects have been individually tested and integrated into sub-systems. The processing of each external event 'threads' its way through the system processes or objects with some processing carried out at each stage. Thread testing involves identifying and executing each possible processing 'thread'. Of course, complete thread testing may be impossible because of the number of possible input and output combinations. In such cases, the most commonly exercised threads should be identified and selected for testing.

Consider the real-time system made up of five interacting processes shown in Figure 22.9. Some processes accept inputs from their environment and generate outputs to that environment. These inputs may be from sensors, keyboards or from some other computer system. Similarly, outputs may be to control lines, other computers or user terminals. Inputs from the environment are labelled with an I, outputs with an O. The arrows connecting processes mean that an event of some kind (with associated data) is generated by the source of the arrow and processed by the process at the head of the arrow.

As part of the testing process, the system should be analysed to identify as many threads as possible. Threads are not just associated with individual events but also with combinations of inputs which can arise. These threads should be identified

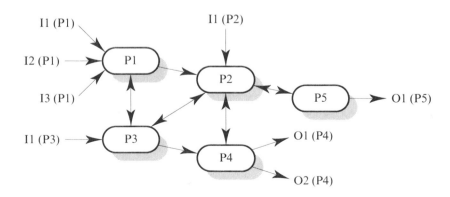

Figure 22.9
Real-time process
interactions.

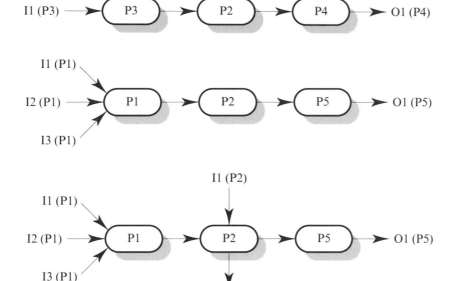

Figure 22.10
Single thread testing.

Figure 22.11
Multiple-input thread testing.

Figure 22.12
Multiple thread testing.

from an architectural model of the system which shows process interactions and from descriptions of system input and output.

A possible thread is shown in Figure 22.10 where an input is transformed by a number of processes in turn to produce an output. In Figure 22.10, the thread of control passes through a sequence of processes from P3 to P2 to P4. Threads can be recursive so that processes or objects appear more than once in the thread. This is normal in object-oriented systems where control returns to the calling object from the called object. The same object therefore appears at different places in the thread.

After each thread has been tested with a single event, the processing of multiple events of the same type should be tested without events of any other type. For example, a multi-user system might first be tested using a single terminal then multiple terminal testing gradually introduced. In the above model, this type of testing might involve processing all inputs in multiple-input processes. Figure 22.11 illustrates an example of this process where three inputs to the same process are used as test data.

After the system's reaction to each class of event has been tested, it can then be tested for its reactions to more than one class of simultaneous event. At this stage, new event tests should be introduced gradually so that system errors can be localized. This might be tested as shown in Figure 22.12.

22.3.4 Stress testing

Some classes of system are designed to handle a specified load. For example, a transaction processing system may be designed to process up to 100 transactions per second; an operating system may be designed to handle up to 200 separate terminals. Tests have to be designed to ensure that the system can process its intended load. This usually involves planning a series of tests where the load is steadily increased.

Stress testing continues these tests beyond the maximum design load of the system until the system fails. This type of testing has two functions:

(1) It tests the failure behaviour of the system. Circumstances may arise through an unexpected combination of events where the load placed on the system exceeds the maximum anticipated load. In these circumstances, it is important that system failure should not cause data corruption or unexpected loss of user services. Stress testing checks that overloading the system causes it to 'fail-soft' rather than collapse under its load.

(2) It stresses the system and may cause defects to come to light which would not normally manifest themselves. Although it can be argued that these defects are unlikely to cause system failures in normal usage, there may be unusual combinations of normal circumstances which the stress testing replicates.

Stress testing is particularly relevant to distributed systems based on a network of processors. These systems often exhibit severe degradation when they are heavily loaded as the network becomes swamped with data which the different processes must exchange.

22.3.5 Back-to-back testing

Back-to-back testing may be used when more than one version of a system is available for testing. The same tests are presented to both versions of the system and the test results compared. Differences between these test results highlight potential system problems (Figure 22.13).

Of course, it is not usually realistic to generate a completely new system just for testing so back-to-back testing is usually only possible in the following situations:

(1) When a system prototype is available.
(2) When reliable systems are developed using N-version programming.
(3) When different versions of a system have been developed for different types of computer.

Alternatively, where a new version of a system has been produced with some functionality in common with previous versions, the tests on this new version can be compared with previous test runs using the older version.

The steps involved in back-to-back testing are:

(1) Prepare a general-purpose set of test cases.
(2) Run one version of the program with these test cases and save the results in one or more files.

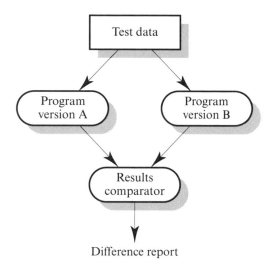

Figure 22.13
Back-to-back testing.

Difference report

(3) Run another version of the program with the same test cases, saving the results to a different file.

(4) Automatically compare the files produced by the modified and unmodified program versions.

If the programs behave in the same way, the file comparison should show the output files to be identical. Although this does not guarantee that they are valid (the implementors of both versions may have made the same mistake), it is probable that the programs are behaving correctly. Differences between the outputs suggest problems which should be investigated in more detail.

Further reading

Comm. ACM, **34** (9), September 1994. This special issue includes a number of articles on the testing of object-oriented systems. The best articles are those concerned with integration testing and with the distinction between an object-oriented and a functional approach to testing.

IEEE Software, **6** (3), May 1989. This special issue has several articles concerned with verification and validation. These present a good overview of the topic and its relevance in the software process. Testing and static verification techniques are covered in separate articles.

Comm. ACM, **31** (6), June 1988. This issue of the journal includes several papers on testing. The introduction by Hamlet and the paper by Gelperin and Hetzel are good background reading for the material in this chapter.

KEY POINTS

- Verification and validation are not the same thing. Verification is intended to show that a program meets its specification. Validation is intended to show that the program does what the user requires.

- Testing has a dual function; it is used to establish the presence of defects in a program and it is used to help judge whether or not the program is usable in practice.

- Testing can only demonstrate the presence of errors. It cannot show that there are no errors in a program.

- The testing process may involve unit testing, module testing, sub-system testing, integration testing and acceptance testing.

- Object classes are the fundamental units which should be tested in object-oriented systems. Clusters of objects may be tested as loose collections of objects providing related services.

- Testing should be scheduled as part of the project planning process. Adequate resources must be made available for testing.

- Test plans should include a description of the items to be tested, the testing schedule, the procedures for managing the testing process, the hardware and software requirements and any testing problems which are likely to arise.

- Testing strategies which may be adopted include top-down testing, bottom-up testing, stress testing, thread testing of real-time and object-oriented systems and back-to-back testing of different program versions.

EXERCISES

22.1 Discuss the differences between verification and validation and explain why validation is a particularly difficult process.

22.2 What is the distinction between alpha and beta testing? Explain why these forms of testing are particularly valuable.

22.3 Explain why top-down testing is not an effective strategy for testing object-oriented systems.

22.4 Design a process model for running system tests and recording their results.

22.5 Describe four classes of system which can be encountered in everyday life which might be subjected to stress testing.

22.6 Write a report for non-technical management explaining the problems of verifying and validating real-time systems.

22.7 Explain why regression testing is necessary and how automated testing tools can assist with this type of testing.

22.8 Explain how back-to-back testing may be used to test critical systems with replicated software.

22.9 Discuss whether it is possible for engineers to test their own programs in an objective way.

22.10 One approach which is commonly adopted to system testing is to test the system until the testing budget is exhausted and then deliver the system to customers. Discuss the ethics of this approach.

23

Defect Testing

Objectives

- To describe approaches to program testing which are geared to discovering program defects.

- To show, using a simple example, how test case design guidelines may be used to design defect tests.

- To explain how program structure analysis can be used in the defect testing process.

- To explain why finding defects in module or object interfaces is particularly difficult.

- To suggest design guidelines for module or object interface tests.

Contents

Defect testing is intended to exercise a system so that latent defects are exposed before the system is delivered. This contrasts with validation testing which is intended to demonstrate that a system meets its specification. Validation testing requires the system to perform correctly using given acceptance test cases. A successful defect test is a test which causes the system to perform *incorrectly* and hence exposes a defect. This emphasizes an important fact about testing. It demonstrates the presence, *not the absence*, of program faults.

Following Myers (1979), I define a good defect test as one that reveals the presence of defects in the software being tested. Defect testing is not intended to show that a program meets its specification. If the test suite for a program does not detect defects, this means that the tests chosen have not exercised the system so that defects are revealed. It does not mean that program defects do not exist.

A generic model of the defect testing process is shown in Figure 23.1. In this diagram, I distinguish between test cases and test data. Test data are the inputs which have been devised to test the system; test cases are input and output specifications plus a statement of the function under test. Test data can sometimes be generated automatically. Automatic test case generation is impossible as it needs the output of the test to be predicted.

It is practically impossible for defect testing to be exhaustive. Exhaustive testing requires every statement in the program and every possible path combination through the program to be executed. In practice, this is impossible in a program that contains loops which can be executed a variable number of times. There is an infinite number of path combinations as each sequence of loop executions represents a separate path.

Testing, therefore, must be based on a sub-set of possible test cases. Organizations should develop policies for choosing this sub-set rather than leave this to arbitrary judgements of the development team. These policies might be based on some testing methods. For example, they may require all program statements to be executed at least once. Alternatively, the policies may be more general and based on guidelines such as those suggested by Petschenik (1985):

- 'Testing a system's capabilities is more important than testing its components.' Users are interested in getting a job done and test cases should be chosen to identify aspects of the system that will stop them doing their job. Although errors, such as screen corruption, are irritating, they are less disruptive than errors which cause loss of data or program termination.

Figure 23.1
The defect testing process.

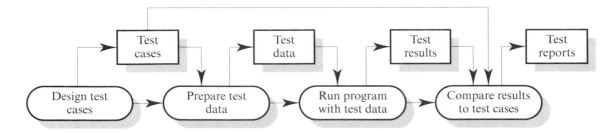

- 'Testing old capabilities is more important than testing new capabilities.' If a program is a revision of an existing system, users expect existing features to keep working. They are usually less affected by failure of new capabilities which they may not need.

- 'Testing typical situations is more important than testing boundary value cases.' It is more important that a system works under normal usage conditions than under occasional conditions that only arise with extreme data values. This does not mean that boundary value testing (discussed below) is unimportant. It simply means that if it is necessary to restrict the number of test cases, it may be advisable to concentrate on typical input values.

In this chapter, I consider three approaches to defect testing:

(1)   Functional or black-box testing where the tests are derived from the program specification.

(2)   Structural or white-box testing where the tests are derived from knowledge of the program's structure and implementation.

(3)   Interface testing where the tests are derived from the program specification plus knowledge of its internal interfaces. This type of testing is particularly important for object-oriented systems.

Any of these approaches may be applied, in principle, at any stage of the testing process. However, as shown in Figure 23.2, each of these approaches to testing is most applicable to different types of component. Figure 23.2 also shows who might be responsible for running defect tests. Functional system testing is usually the job of a separate testing team. Unit and module testing are the responsibility of the development team. Interface testing may sometimes be carried out by the development team and sometimes by a testing team depending on the nature of the sub-system being tested.

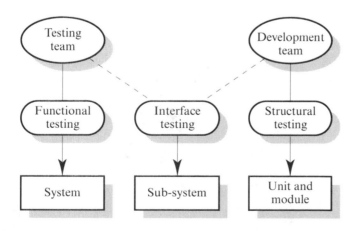

Figure 23.2
Application of defect testing approaches to system components.

Basili and Selby (1987) conducted an experiment to compare the effectiveness of black-box and structural testing. They found that black-box testing was more effective in discovering faults than structural testing. However, the rate of fault detection (the number of faults discovered per unit time) was similar for each approach.

This experiment also found that static code reviewing was more effective and less expensive than defect testing in discovering program faults. This is confirmed by Gilb and Graham (1993). Although program defect testing is still widely used, I predict that it will gradually be replaced by program inspections and code reviews. These static defect detection methods are covered in Chapter 24.

23.1 Black-box testing

Black-box testing relies on the specification of the system or component which is being tested to derive test cases. The system is a 'black box' whose behaviour can only be determined by studying its inputs and the related outputs. Another name for this is *functional testing* because mathematical functions can be specified using only their inputs and outputs.

Figure 23.3 illustrates the model of a system which is assumed in black-box testing. This model is the same as that used for reliability testing, discussed in Chapter 18.

The key problem for the defect tester is to select inputs that have a high probability of being members of the set I_e. In many cases, the selection of these test cases is based on the previous experience of test engineers. They use domain knowledge

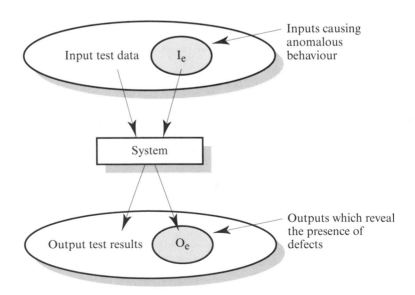

Figure 23.3
Black-box testing.

to identify test cases which are likely to reveal defects. However, the systematic approach to test data selection discussed in the next section may also be used to supplement this heuristic knowledge.

23.1.1 Equivalence partitioning

The input data to a program usually fall into a number of different classes. These classes have common characteristics, for example positive numbers, negative numbers, strings without blanks, and so on. Programs normally behave in a comparable way for all members of a class. Because of this equivalent behaviour, these classes are sometimes called equivalence partitions or domains (Bezier, 1990). A systematic approach to defect testing is based on identifying a set of equivalence partitions which must be handled by a program. Test cases are designed so that the inputs or outputs lie within these partitions.

Input equivalence partitions are sets of data where the set members should all be processed in an equivalent way by the program. Output equivalence partitions are program outputs which have common characteristics so can be considered as a distinct class. Partitions may be discrete or they may overlap. In situations where partitions do not overlap, further partitions might be identified where the inputs are deliberately selected to lie outside the partitions. These test if the program handles invalid input correctly.

In Figure 23.4, each equivalence partition is shown as an ellipse. Both input and output equivalence partitions are shown. Valid and invalid inputs also form partitions.

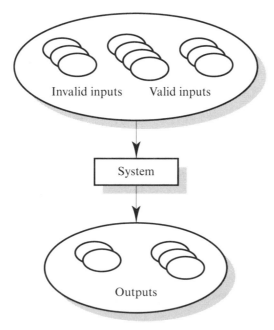

Figure 23.4
Equivalence partitioning.

Once a set of partitions has been identified, particular test cases from each of these partitions should be chosen. A good guideline to follow for test case selection is to choose test cases on the boundaries of the partitions plus cases close to the mid-point of the partition. The rationale for this guideline is that designers and programmers tend to consider typical values of inputs when developing a system. These are tested by choosing the mid-point of the partition. Boundary values are often atypical (for example, zero may behave differently from other non-negative numbers) so are overlooked by developers. Program errors often occur when processing these atypical values.

The equivalence partitions may be identified by using the program specification or user documentation and by the tester using experience to predict which classes of input value are likely to detect errors. For example, say a program specification states that the program accepts four to eight inputs which are 5 digit integers greater than 10 000. Figure 23.5 shows the identified equivalence partitions and possible test input data values. For complete testing, test data should be selected so that each partition in each class is tested with all instances of partitions in other classes.

Input values which generate outputs in each output partition should also be chosen as tests. Say a program is designed to produce between three and six outputs, with each output lying in the range 1000–2500. Test input should be selected to produce:

- three values at 1000,
- three values at 2500,
- six values at 1000,
- six values at 2500.

To illustrate the derivation of test cases, I use the specification of a small example (a search routine). This is unavoidably artificial but a practical testing example would be unmanageably large. The specification of this routine, using pre- and

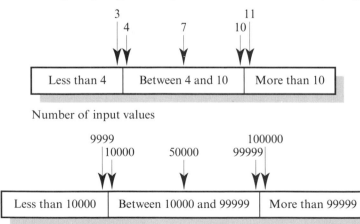

Figure 23.5
Equivalence partitions.

post-conditions, is shown in Figure 23.6. Assume that this is a generic routine where the key and array elements are of type ELEM.

The pre-condition states that the search routine has not been designed to work with empty arrays. The post-condition states that the variable Found is set if the key element is in the array. The position of the key element is indicated by the index L. The index is undefined if the element is not in the array.

From this specification, two obvious equivalence partitions can be identified:

(1)   Inputs where the key element is a member of the array (Found = true).

(2)   Inputs where the key element is not a member of the array (Found = false).

An equivalence partition may be necessary if the programming language used allows arrays of zero length. In Ada, this is not permitted and errors of this type are trapped by the compiler. It is possible in C++ because arrays are implemented as pointers.

As well as deriving equivalence partitions from the system specification, there are various testing guidelines that can also be used. Some examples of these general testing guidelines which apply when arrays are used are:

(1)   Test software with arrays which have only a single value. Programmers naturally think of arrays as a sequence of values and sometimes they embed this assumption in their programs. Consequently, the program may not work properly when presented with an exceptional array.

(2)   Use different arrays of different sizes in different tests. This decreases the chances that a program with defects will accidentally produce a correct output because of some accidental characteristics of the input.

(3)   Derive tests so that the first, middle and last elements of the array are accessed. This means that any problems due to boundary effects are more likely to be revealed.

```
procedure Search (Key : ELEM ; T: ELEM_ARRAY;
        Found : in out BOOLEAN; L: in out ELEM_INDEX) ;

Pre-condition
        -- the array has at least one element
        T'FIRST <= T'LAST
Post-condition
        -- the element is found and is referenced by L
        ( Found and T (L) = Key)
    or
        -- the element is not in the array
        ( not Found and
            not (exists i, T'FIRST >= i <= T'LAST, T (i) = Key ))
```

Figure 23.6
The specification of a search routine.

Figure 23.7
Identified input
partitions for search
routine.

Array	Element
Single value	In array
Single value	Not in array
More than 1 value	First element in array
More than 1 value	Last element in array
More than 1 value	Middle element in array
More than 1 value	Not in array

Figure 23.8
Test cases for search
routine.

Input array (T)	Key (Key)	Output (Found, L)
17	17	true, 1
17	0	false, ??
17, 29, 21, 23	17	true, 1
41, 18, 9, 31, 30, 16, 45	45	true, 6
17, 18, 21, 23, 29, 41, 38	23	true, 4
21, 23, 29, 33, 38	25	false, ??

Using these guidelines, two further equivalence partitions of the input array can be identified:

(1)   The input array has a single value.

(2)   The number of elements in the input array is greater than 1.

These partitions must be combined with the previously identified equivalence partitions giving the set of equivalence partitions summarized in Figure 23.7.

A set of possible test cases based on these partitions is shown in Figure 23.8. If the key element is not in the array, the value of L is undefined ('??'). The guideline that different arrays of different sizes should be used has been applied in these test cases. These are tests for arrays where the lower bound is 1 rather than 0.

The set of input values used to test the search routine is not exhaustive. The routine may fail if the input array happens to be 1, 2, 3, 4 but the tester cannot be expected to guess this from the specification. It is reasonable to surmise that if the test fails to detect defects when one member of a class is processed, no other members of that class will identify defects. Of course, defects may still exist. Some equivalence partitions may not have been identified, errors may have been made in equivalence partition identification or the test data may have been incorrectly prepared.

I have deliberately left out tests that are designed to present the system with parameters in the wrong order, of the wrong type, and so on. This type of error is best detected using program inspection or automated static analysis. Similarly, the tests do not check for unexpected corruption of data outside the component. It does not make sense for black-box tests to check such corruption. Code inspection can reveal whether this kind of problem is likely to arise. It is most likely in weakly typed languages where pointers are used.

23.2 Structural testing

A complementary approach to black-box testing is sometimes called structural, 'white-box' or 'glass-box' testing (Figure 23.9). As the name implies, the tester can analyse the code and use knowledge about the structure of a component to derive test data. The advantage of structural testing is that an analysis of the code can be used to find how many test cases are needed to guarantee a given level of test coverage. A dynamic analyser can then be used to measure the extent of this coverage and help with test case design.

Knowledge of the algorithm used to implement some function can be used to identify further equivalence partitions. To illustrate this, I have instantiated the search routine specification (Figure 23.6) as a binary search routine (Figures 23.10 and 23.11). Of course, this has stricter pre-conditions. The input array must be ordered and the value of the lower bound must be less than the value of the upper bound. This latter condition is usually checked by the compiler. Few languages allow arrays where the indexes are in descending rather than ascending order.

By examining the code of the search routine, we can see that binary searching involves splitting the search space into three parts. Each of these parts makes up an equivalence partition (Figure 23.12). Test cases where the key lies at the boundaries of each of these partitions should be chosen to exercise the code.

The test cases shown in Figure 23.8 must be modified so that the input array is arranged in ascending order. Further cases based on knowledge of the algorithm used should also be added to the test set. These are elements which are adjacent to the mid-point of the array. Figure 23.13 shows a set of test cases for the binary search routine.

23.2.1 Path testing

Path testing is a white-box testing strategy whose objective is to exercise every independent execution path through the component. If every independent path is executed then all statements in the program must have been executed at least once. Furthermore, all conditional statements are tested for both true and false cases.

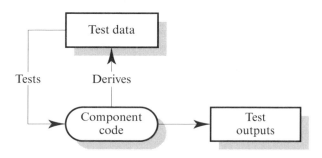

Figure 23.9
White-box testing.

```
procedure Binary_search (Key: ELEM ; T: ELEM_ARRAY ;
    Found: in out BOOLEAN ; L: in out ELEM_INDEX ) is
    -- Preconditions
    -- T'FIRST < =T'LAST and
    -- forall i: T'FIRST..T'LAST-1, T (i) <= T(i+1)
    Bott : ELEM_INDEX := T'FIRST ;
    Top : ELEM_INDEX := T'LAST ;
    Mid : ELEM_INDEX;
begin
    L := (T'FIRST + T'LAST ) / 2;
    Found := T( L ) = Key;
    while Bott <= Top and not Found loop
        Mid := (Top + Bott) mod 2;
        if T( Mid ) = Key then
            Found := true;
            L := Mid;
        elsif T( Mid ) < Key then
            Bott := Mid + 1;
        else
            Top := Mid - 1;
        end if;
    end loop;
end Binary_search;
```

Figure 23.10
Ada implementation of
a binary search
routine.

```
void Binary_search (elem key, elem* T, int size,
                    boolean &found, int &L)
{
    int bott, top, mid ;
    bott = 0 ;
    top = size - 1 ;
    L = ( top + bott ) / 2 ;
    if (T[L] == key)
        found = true ;
    else
            found = false ;
    while (bott <=top && !found)
    {
        mid = top + bott / 2 ;
        if ( T [mid] == key )
        {
                found = true;
                L = mid ;
        }
        else if (T [mid] < key )
            bott = mid + 1 ;
        else
            top = mid - 1 ;
    } // while
} //binary_search
```

Figure 23.11
C++ implementation of
a binary search
routine.

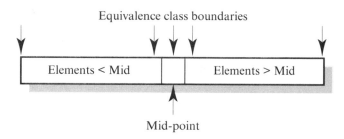

Figure 23.12
Binary search
equivalence classes.

Input array (T)	Key (Key)	Output (Found, L)
17	17	true, 1
17	0	false, ??
17, 21, 23, 29	17	true, 1
9, 16, 18, 30, 31, 41, 45	45	true, 7
17, 18, 21, 23, 29, 38, 41	23	true, 4
17, 18, 21, 23, 29, 33, 38	21	true, 3
12, 18, 21, 23, 32	23	true, 4
21, 23, 29, 33, 38	25	false, ??

Figure 23.13
Test cases for search
routine.

The starting point for path testing is a program flow graph. This is a skeletal model of all paths through the program. A flow graph consists of nodes representing decisions and edges showing flow of control. The flow graph is constructed by replacing program control statements by equivalent diagrams. The flow graph representation for if-then-else, while-do and case statements is shown in Figure 23.14.

If there are no goto statements in a program, it is a straightforward manual or automatic process to derive its flow graph. The representations shown in Figure 23.14 are simply substituted for program statements. Sequential statements (assignments, procedure calls and I/O statements) can be ignored in the flow graph construction.

The flow graph for the binary search procedure is shown in Figure 23.15.

In Figure 23.15, the compound condition in the while statement has been simplified into a simple while and an if statement.

```
while Bott <= Top loop
    if Found then
            exit
    else
        ...
```

Complete path testing means that both the true and false branches of all conditions must be executed. By simplifying compound expressions into two simpler conditions, it is easier to construct the flow graph and to see what test cases are needed.

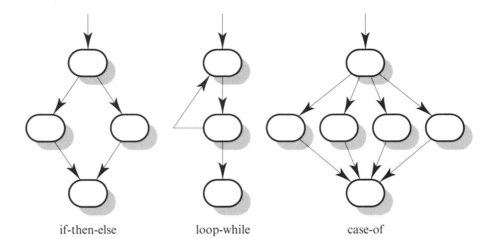

Figure 23.14
Flow graph
representations.

if-then-else   loop-while   case-of

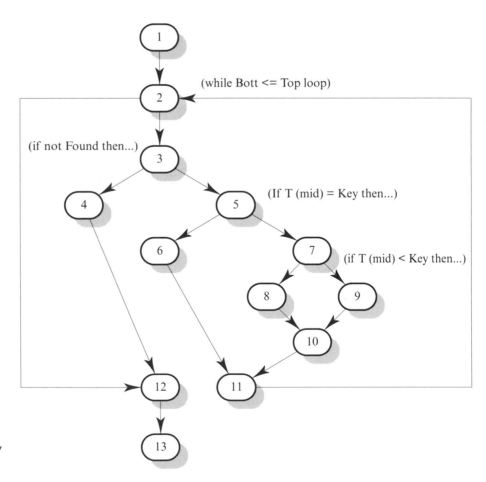

Figure 23.15
Flow graph for a binary
search routine.

An independent program path is one which traverses at least one new edge in the flow graph. In program terms, this means exercising one or more new conditions. By tracing the flow, therefore, we see that the independent paths through the binary search flow graph are:

1, 2, 3, 4, 12, 13
1, 2, 3, 5, 6, 11, 2, 12, 13
1, 2, 3, 5, 7, 8, 10, 11, 2, 12, 13
1, 2, 3, 5, 7, 9, 10, 11, 2, 12, 13

If all of these paths are executed we can be sure that:

- every statement in the routine has been executed at least once and
- every branch has been exercised for true and false conditions.

The number of independent paths in a program can be discovered by computing the cyclomatic complexity (McCabe, 1976) of the program flow graph. The cyclomatic complexity, CC, of any graph G may be computed according to the following formula:

CC (G) = Number (edges) – Number (nodes) + 1

For programs without goto statements, the cyclomatic complexity is simply equal to the number of conditions in the program. Compound conditions with N simple predicates are counted as N conditions. Thus, if there are 6 if-statements and a while loop, with all conditional expressions simple, the cyclomatic complexity is 7. If a conditional expression is a compound expression with two logical operators ('and' or 'or') the cyclomatic complexity is 9. The cyclomatic complexity of the binary search routine shown in Figures 23.10 and 23.11 is 4.

After discovering the number of independent paths through the code by computing the cyclomatic complexity, the next step is to design test cases to execute each of these paths. The minimum number of test cases required to test all program paths is equal to the cyclomatic complexity.

Test case design is quite easy in the case of the binary search routine. However, when programs have a complex branching structure, it may be difficult to predict how any particular test case will be processed. In these cases, a dynamic program analyser can be used to discover the program's execution profile.

Dynamic program analysers are testing tools which instrument the program with additional code. This code counts the number of times each program statement has been executed. After the program has been run, an execution profile can be printed which shows which parts of the program have and have not been executed using particular test cases. This execution profile therefore reveals untested program sections.

This level of analysis is not necessary for the binary search routine. By studying the logic of the code, it is clear that the test cases that have been derived are sufficient to exercise all independent program paths.

Figure 23.16
Control and data-
driven programs.

```
case A is
    when "One" => i := 1 ;
    when "Two" => i := 2 ;
    when "Three" => i := 3 ;
    when "Four" => i := 4 ;
    when "Five" => i := 5 ;
end case ;
```

```
Strings: array (1..4) of STRING :=
    ("One", "Two", "Three", "Four", "Five");
i := 1 ;
loop
    exit when Strings (i) = A ;
    i := i + 1 ;
end loop ;
```

A problem with cyclomatic complexity as a measure of the minimum number of test cases required for path coverage is that the data complexity is not taken into account. The program fragments in Figure 23.16 are equivalent in function but have different cyclomatic complexities.

These examples use different ways of representing a table. Complete path testing requires that A should take all of the values "One", "Two", "Three", "Four", "Five". However, code fragment (a) has a cyclomatic complexity of 5 and fragment (b) a cyclomatic complexity of 1. This implies that the exhaustive testing of fragment (b) requires only a single test case. Of course, both fragments should be tested in exactly the same way.

This illustrates a general problem with testing metrics. They may give a misleading impression that the program has been thoroughly tested. In fact, all that can be said is that some percentage (perhaps 100%) of the independent control paths in a program have been executed. There is no simple relationship between this assertion and the adequacy of the test coverage.

Path testing does not test all possible combinations of all paths through the program. For any components apart from very trivial ones without loops, this is an impossible objective. There are an infinite number of possible path combinations in programs with loops. Defects may manifest themselves when particular path combinations arise even although all program statements have been executed at least once.

The number of paths through a program is usually proportional to its size. As modules are integrated into systems, it becomes unfeasible to use structural testing techniques. Path testing techniques are therefore only really usable at the unit testing and module testing stages of the testing process.

23.3 Interface testing

Interface testing takes place when modules or sub-systems are integrated to create larger systems. Each module or sub-system has a defined interface which is called by other program components. The objective of interface testing is to detect faults which may have been introduced into the system because of interface errors or invalid assumptions about interfaces.

Figure 23.17 illustrates interface testing. The arrows to the box boundary mean that the test cases are not applied to the individual components but to the sub-system created by combining these components.

This form of testing is particularly important for object-oriented development, particularly when objects and object classes are reused. Objects are essentially defined by their interfaces and may be reused in combination with different objects in different systems. Unit testing cannot detect most interface errors as the errors are a result of the interaction between components rather than the isolated behaviour of a single component.

There are different types of interface between program components and, consequently, different types of interface error that can occur:

(1)   *Parameter interfaces*   These are interfaces where data or sometimes function references are passed from one component to another.

(2)   *Shared memory interfaces*   These are interfaces where a block of memory is shared between sub-systems. Data is placed in the memory by one sub-system and retrieved from there by other sub-systems.

(3)   *Procedural interfaces*   These are interfaces where one sub-system encapsulates a set of procedures which can be called by other sub-systems. Objects and abstract data types have this form of interface.

(4)   *Message passing interfaces*   These are interfaces where one sub-system requests a service from another sub-system by passing a message to it. A return message includes the results of executing the service. Some object oriented systems have this form of interface as do client-server systems.

Interface errors are one of the most common forms of error in complex systems (Lutz, 1993). These errors fall into three classes:

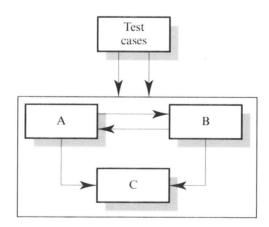

Figure 23.17
Interface testing.

(1) *Interface misuse*   A calling component calls some other component and makes an error in the use of its interface. This type of error is particularly common with parameter interfaces where parameters may be of the wrong type, may be passed in the wrong order or where the wrong number of parameters may be passed.

(2) *Interface misunderstanding*   A calling component misunderstands the specification of the interface of the called component and embeds assumptions about the behaviour of the called component. The called component does not behave as expected and this causes unexpected behaviour in the calling component. For example, a binary search routine may be called with an unordered array to be searched.

(3) *Timing errors*   These occur in real-time systems which use a shared memory or a message passing interface. The producer of data and the consumer of data may operate at different speeds. Unless particular care is taken in the interface design, the consumer can access out-of-date information because the producer of the information has not updated the shared interface information.

Testing for interface defects is particularly difficult because interface faults may only manifest themselves under unusual conditions. For example, say an object implements a queue as a fixed length data structure. A calling object may assume that the queue is implemented as an infinite data structure and may not check for queue overflow when an item is entered. This condition can only be detected during testing by designing test cases which force the queue to overflow and cause that overflow to corrupt the object behaviour in some detectable way.

A further problem may arise because of interactions between faults in different modules or objects. Faults in one object may only be detected when some other object behaves in an unexpected way. For example, an object may call some other object to receive some service and may assume that the response is correct. If there has been a misunderstanding about the value computed, the returned value may be valid but incorrect. This will only manifest itself when some later computation goes wrong.

Some general guidelines for interface testing are:

(1) Examine the code to be tested and explicitly list each call to an external component. Design a set of tests where the values of the parameters to the external components are at the extreme ends of their ranges. These extreme values are most likely to reveal interface inconsistencies.

(2) Where pointers (Ada access values) are passed across an interface, always test the interface with null pointer parameters.

(3) Where a component is called through a procedural interface, design tests which should cause the component to fail. Differing failure models are one of the most common specification misunderstandings.

(4)   Use a stress testing strategy in message passing systems. Design tests which generate many more messages than are likely to occur in practice. Timing problems may be revealed in this way.

(5)   Where several components interact through shared memory, design tests that vary the order in which these components are activated. These tests may reveal implicit assumptions made by the programmer about the order in which the shared data is produced and consumed.

Static techniques are often more cost-effective than testing for discovering interface errors. A strongly typed language such as Ada allows many interface errors to be trapped by the compiler. Where a weaker language, such as C, is used, a static analyser such as LINT can detect interface errors. Program inspections can concentrate on component interfaces and questions about the assumed interface behaviour can be asked during the inspection process.

Further reading

There is very little recent introductory material on testing. Although the suggestions below are several years old, they are still relevant.

Software Testing Techniques. This is the definitive book on defect testing for programs which are developed using a function-oriented approach. It is incredibly detailed and thorough. Bezier's approach is practical rather than theoretical which makes the book useful for test engineers. (B. Bezier, 1990, Van Nostrand Rheinhold.)

IEEE Software, **8** (2), March 1991. This special issue is devoted to testing. It includes papers covering user interface testing, automated test case generation and program analysis for interface testing.

Comm. ACM, **31** (6), June 1988. Another special issue which contains a number of papers on software testing concerned with functional testing, the testing process and test coverage.

KEY POINTS

- It is more important to test the parts of the system which are commonly used rather than parts which are only rarely exercised.

- Equivalence partitioning is a way of deriving test cases. It depends on finding partitions in the input and output data sets and exercising the program with values from these partitions. Often, the value which is most likely to lead to a successful test is a value at the boundary of a partition.

- Black-box testing does not need access to source code. Test cases are derived from the program specification.

- Structural testing relies on analysing a program to determine paths through it and using this analysis to assist with the selection of test cases.

- Test coverage measurements can ensure that the test cases exercise all statements in the program and cause all branches to be selected at least once. However, it is not possible to exercise all possible path combinations in programs which contain loops.

- Interface defects may arise because of errors made in reading the specification, specification misunderstandings or errors or invalid timing assumptions. Interface testing is intended to discover defects in the interfaces of objects or modules.

EXERCISES

23.1 Discuss the differences between black-box and structural testing and suggest how they can be used together in the defect testing process.

23.2 Identify equivalence partitions for the **New_list**, **Queue** and **Binary_tree** components whose specifications are given in Chapter 10.

23.3 What testing problems might arise in numerical routines designed to handle very large and very small numbers?

23.4 Derive a set of test cases for the following components:

(a) a keyed table in which entries are made and retrieved using some alphabetic key;

(b) a sort routine which sorts arrays of integers;

(c) a routine which takes a line of text as input and counts the number of non-blank characters in that line;

(d) a routine which examines a line of text and replaces sequences of blank characters with a single blank character;

(e) an abstract data type which provides operations on character strings. These include concatenation, length (to give the length of a string) and substring selection.

23.5 Program the above routines using a language of your choice and, for each routine, derive its cyclomatic complexity.

23.6 Show, using a small example, why it is practically impossible to exhaustively test a program.

23.7 By examining the code of the routines which you have written, derive further test cases in addition to those you have already considered. Has the code analysis revealed omissions in your initial set of test cases?

23.8 Explain why interface testing is necessary given that individual units have been extensively validated through unit testing and program inspections.

24

Static Verification

Objectives

- To explain why static verification techniques are cost-effective in discovering program defects.

- To describe the program inspection process in terms of activities, participants and process results.

- To introduce the notion of rigorous mathematical arguments as a means of verifying that a program meets its specification.

- To show how static analysis tools can discover program anomalies that may indicate program faults.

- To describe the 'Cleanroom' development process where static verification rather than defect testing is used.

Contents

Systematic program testing is expensive because a large number of tests must be developed and executed. The main problem with defect testing, particularly in its early stages, is that each test run tends to discover one fault or, at best, only a few faults. A fault can cause system data corruption so it is sometimes difficult to tell if output anomalies are a result of a new fault or a side-effect of an existing fault.

Static verification does not require the program to be executed. Rather, it involves examining the source code of a program (or a design) and detecting faults before execution. Each error can be considered in isolation. Error interactions are not significant and an entire component can be validated in a single session. This means that less time is required to find each error. Static verification is therefore more cost-effective than defect testing.

Fagan (1986) reported that more than 60% of the errors in a program can be detected using informal program inspections. Mills *et al.* (1987) suggest that a more formal approach, using mathematical verification, can detect more than 90% of the errors in a program. Furthermore, the program inspection process can also consider other quality attributes (see Chapter 30) such as compliance with standards, portability and maintainability.

This does not mean that static verification can completely replace testing. Rather, it should be used as an initial verification process to find most program defects. Static verification can check conformance with a specification but it cannot predict dynamic behaviour. Testing is necessary for reliability assessment, performance analysis, user interface validation and to check that the software requirements are what the user really wants.

I discuss program inspections in this chapter but the techniques used may be applied to any of the outputs of the software process. Comparable inspection techniques can also be applied to requirements specifications, detailed design definitions, data structure designs, test plans and user documentation.

24.1 Program inspections

Program inspections are reviews whose objective is program defect detection. The notion of a formalized inspection process was first developed at IBM in the 1970s and is described by Fagan (1976, 1986). It is now a widely used method of program verification. Other types of quality assurance reviews are discussed in Chapter 30.

The key difference between program inspections and other types of review is that the principal objective of inspections is defect detection rather than broader design issues. Defects may either be logical errors, anomalies in the code that might indicate an erroneous condition or non-compliance with organizational or project standards.

When an organization decides to introduce inspection into its software process it must:

(1)   Prepare a checklist of likely errors to drive the inspection process. This
        should be established initially by discussion with experienced staff and
        regularly updated as more experience is gained of the inspection process.

(2)   Accept that static verification will 'front-load' project costs so that more
        money is spent in earlier stages of a software project. This should lead to a
        consequent reduction in testing costs.

(3)   Define a policy which states that inspections are part of the verification
        process and not personnel appraisals. Inspection results should never be used
        in an individual's career reviews.

(4)   Be prepared to invest in the training of inspection team leaders. Each team
        leader will require three to five days' training before participating in an
        inspection process.

The process of inspection is a formal one carried out by a small team of at least four
people. Team members systematically analyse the code and point out possible
defects. In Fagan's original proposals, he suggested roles such as author, reader,
tester and moderator. The reader reads the code aloud to the inspection team, the
tester inspects the code from a testing perspective and the moderator organizes the
process.

As organizations have gained experience with inspection, other proposals
for team roles have emerged. In a discussion of how inspection was successfully
introduced in Hewlett-Packard's development process, Grady and Van Slack (1994)
suggest six roles as shown in Figure 24.1. Different roles may be adopted by the
same person so the team size may vary from one inspection to another.

Grady and Van Slack report that there is not always a need for a reader role.
In this respect, they have modified the process from that originally proposed by
Fagan, where an integral part of the process involved reading the program aloud.

Role	Description
Author or owner	The programmer or designer responsible for producing the program or document. Responsible for fixing defects discovered during the inspection process.
Inspector	Finds errors, omissions and inconsistencies in programs and documents. May also identify broader issues which are outwith the scope of the inspection team.
Reader	Paraphrases the code or document at an inspection meeting.
Scribe	Records the results of the inspection meeting.
Chairman or moderator	Manages the process and facilitates the inspection. Reports process results to the chief moderator.
Chief moderator	Responsible for inspection process improvements, checklist updating, standards development and so on.

Figure 24.1
Roles in the inspection
process.

Before a program inspection is started, it is essential that:

(1)   There is a precise specification of the code to be inspected. It is impossible to inspect a component at the level of detail required to detect defects without a complete specification.

(2)   The members of the inspection team are familiar with the organizational standards.

(3)   There is an up-to-date, syntactically correct version of the code available. There is no point in inspecting code which is 'almost complete' even if a delay causes schedule disruption.

A generic inspection process is shown in Figure 24.2. This is adapted as required by organizations using program inspections.

The moderator is responsible for inspection planning. This involves selecting an inspection team, organizing a meeting room and ensuring that the material to be inspected and its specifications are complete. The material to be inspected is presented to the inspection team during the overview stage. This is followed by a period of individual preparation. Each inspection team member studies the specification and the program and looks for defects in the code.

The inspection itself should be relatively short (no more than two hours) and should be exclusively concerned with identifying defects, anomalies and non-compliance with standards. The inspection team should not suggest how these defects should be corrected nor recommend changes to other components.

Following inspection, the program is modified by its author to correct the identified problems. In the follow-up stage, the moderator must decide whether a re-inspection of the code is required. Alternatively, he or she may decide that a complete re-inspection is not required and that the defects have been successfully fixed. The document is then approved by the moderator for release.

The inspection process should be driven by a checklist of common programmer mistakes. This checklist will vary, depending on the checking provided by the language compiler. For example, an Ada compiler checks that functions have the correct number of parameters, a C compiler does not. Possible checks which might be made during the inspection process are shown in Figure 24.3.

Figure 24.2
The inspection process.

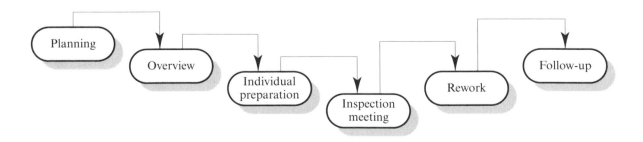

Fault class	Inspection check
Data faults	Are all program variables initialized before their values are used? Have all constants been named? Should the lower bound of arrays be 0, 1, or something else? Should the upper bound of arrays be equal to the size of the array or Size – 1? If character strings are used, is a delimiter explicitly assigned?
Control faults	For each conditional statement, is the condition correct? Is each loop certain to terminate? Are compound statements correctly bracketed? In case statements, are all possible cases accounted for?
Input/output faults	Are all input variables used? Are all output variables assigned a value before they are output?
Interface faults	Do all function and procedure calls have the correct number of parameters? Do formal and actual parameter types match? Are the parameters in the right order? If components access shared memory, do they have the same model of the shared memory structure?
Storage management faults	If a linked structure is modified, have all links been correctly reassigned? If dynamic storage is used, has space been allocated correctly? Is space explicitly de-allocated after it is no longer required?
Exception management faults	Have all possible error conditions been taken into account?

Figure 24.3
Inspection checks.

Gilb and Graham (1993) emphasize that each organization should develop its own inspection checklist. This should be based on local standards and practices and it should be regularly updated as new types of defects are discovered.

As an organization gains experience of the inspection process, it can use the results of that process as a means of process improvement. An analysis of defects found during the inspection process can be made. The inspection team and the authors of the code or documents which were being inspected can suggest reasons why these defects occurred. Wherever possible, the process should then be modified to eliminate the reasons for defects so they will not recur in future systems.

Gilb and Graham report that a number of organizations are abandoning unit testing in favour of program inspections. They have found that program inspections are so effective at finding errors that the costs of unit testing are not justifiable. As I discuss later in the chapter, this is an inherent part of the Cleanroom software development process.

The amount of code which can be inspected in a given time depends on the experience of the inspection team, the programming language and the application domain. When the inspection process was measured in IBM, Fagan made the following observations:

(1)   About 500 source code statements per hour can be considered during the overview stage.

(2)   During individual preparation, about 125 source code statements per hour can be examined.

(3)   From 90 to 125 statements per hour can be inspected.

These figures are confirmed by data collected by AT & T (Barnard and Price, 1994) where measurements of the inspection process showed comparable values.

Fagan suggests that the maximum time spent on an inspection should be about two hours, as the efficiency of the defect detection process falls off after that time. Inspection should therefore be a frequent process, carried out on relatively small software components, during program development.

With four people involved in an inspection team, the cost of inspecting 100 lines of code is roughly equivalent to one person-day of effort. This assumes that the inspection itself takes about an hour and that each team member spends one to two hours in preparing for the inspection. Although testing costs are very variable, this is probably less than half the effort that would be required for equivalent defect testing.

24.2 Mathematically based verification

The deficiencies of defect testing have been recognized for a long time. Rather than detect defects after programs have been written, some software engineering researchers have suggested that proving that a program meets its specification should be a more effective approach to software verification.

Formal program verification involves proving, using mathematical arguments, that a program is consistent with its specification. Research on program verification has been going on for more than 30 years. This is built on the work of McCarthy (1962), and a number of other authors such as Floyd (1967), Hoare (1969) and Dijkstra (1976).

Mathematically formal verification is only possible under the following conditions:

- The semantics of the programming language must be formally defined.
- The program must be formally specified in a notation which is consistent with the mathematical verification techniques used.

Although there has been some work done in formal language definition, the semantics of most programming languages are not formally defined. This means that, for most programs, it is not possible to prove them in the strict mathematical sense.

The lack of complete formal semantics for most languages mean that program verification is usually only possible if a language sub-set, excluding features such as pointers, is used for development. Even in this situation, developing mathematical proofs is a very expensive and time-consuming exercise. Complex theorem prover programs (Lindsay, 1988) are needed to support the process. For large systems, this is so expensive that it is impractical to prove them mathematically.

This does not mean that formal mathematical verification cannot ever be used. For safety-critical systems, secure systems and very reliable systems the high cost of developing a proof may be justified. The critical parts of these systems are sometimes relatively small so it may be possible to verify these parts formally. However, for the majority of systems, program inspection is probably a more cost-effective defect detection technique.

Program inspection relies on the experience and judgement of the inspectors to discover program defects. A more rigorous approach to inspection can be developed where mathematically based arguments are used to verify the program. A formal specification of the program must be available. A rigorous, although not mathematically formal, argument can then be developed to show that it meets its specification. This is much less expensive than complete mathematical verification.

These correctness arguments must demonstrate two things:

(1)   that the program code is logically consistent with the program specification;
(2)   that the program will always terminate.

To demonstrate the use of mathematically based arguments, I use an approach to verification called the axiomatic approach. The basis of this approach is as follows.

(1)   There are a number of points in a program component where assertions can be made about program variables and their relationships.
(2)   Assertions A_1, A_2,....., A_n are associated with points P_1, P_2,...P_n in the component. A_1 (the pre-condition) must be an assertion about the input of the component and A_n (the post-condition) an assertion about the component output. As discussed in Chapter 9, the pre-condition and the post-condition, along with the signature of the component being verified, make up its formal specification.
(3)   To show that the code between points P_i and P_{i+1} is correct, the verifier must show that the statements separating these points causes assertion A_i to be transformed to assertion A_{i+1}.
(4)   If it can be argued that A_1 always leads to A_2, A_2 to A_3 and so on until all statements have been considered, the combination of these arguments shows that assertion A_1 leads to A_n. The component is therefore partially correct. To demonstrate complete correctness, it must also be argued that the program will always terminate.

The example which I use is, again, the binary search routine. Its specification is shown in Figure 24.4.

The function specification includes the function signature (its parameters and their types) and pre- and post-conditions. The pre-condition is a predicate which must be true for the function to execute correctly. The post-condition is a predicate which holds after function execution. The value returned by the function is referenced in the post-condition by using the function name.

In the notation which I use, the mathematical symbol ($\exists$) is represented by a mnemonic **exists**. The symbol ($\forall$) is replaced by the mnemonic **for_all.** The membership operator ($\in$) is replaced by the keyword **in** which may be applied to arrays as well as to sets.

Slices of an array may be specified, as in Ada, by writing their upper and lower bounds. For example, A (3..6) specifies the part of the array which includes elements indexed from 3 to 6 inclusive.

The binary search routine code, annotated with assertions, is shown in Figure 24.5. The C++ version of this code was shown in Figure 23.11 so I do not show it again here.

The correctness of this routine is demonstrated in two stages:

(1)   A logical argument is produced showing how the pre-condition plus the program statements leads to the post-condition. This can be expressed in various ways but I find the tabular form, shown in Figure 24.6, to be a particularly readable way to present this type of argument.

(2)   A logical argument that the program will terminate is made.

To demonstrate that the routine will terminate, it must be demonstrated that the exit condition for all loops in the program will be satisfied. This involves making an argument that variables are changed in such a way by the computation that the loop termination condition will always be satisfied at some stage. In this case, the program contains a single while loop. This terminates when Found becomes true or when Bott becomes greater than Top. The argument for loop termination is set out below:

Figure 24.4
The specification of a binary search procedure.

```
procedure Binary_search (Key : ELEM ; T: ELEM_ARRAY;
            Found : in out BOOLEAN; L: in out ELEM_INDEX) ;

Pre-condition
    T'LAST – T'FIRST >= 0 and
        for_all i, T'FIRST >= i <= T'LAST–1, T (i) <= T (i + 1)

Post-condition
    ( Found and T (L) = Key) or
        ( not Found and not (exists i, T'FIRST >= i <= T'LAST, T (i) = Key ))
```

```
procedure Binary_search (Key: ELEM ; T: ELEM_ARRAY ;
        Found: in out BOOLEAN ; L: in out ELEM_INDEX ) is
    -- Pre: T'LAST – T'FIRST > 0 and
    -- for_all i, T'FIRST >= i <= T'LAST–1, T (i) <= T (i + 1)
    Bott : ELEM_INDEX := T'FIRST;
    Top : ELEM_INDEX := T'LAST ;
    Mid : ELEM_INDEX;
begin
    L := ( T'FIRST + T'LAST ) mod 2;
    Found := T( L ) = Key;
    -- loop invariant
    -- 1. Found and T(L) = Key or
    -- not Found and not Key in T(T'FIRST..Bott–1, Top+1..T'LAST)
    while Bott <= Top and not Found loop
        Mid := (Top + Bott) / 2;
        if T( Mid ) = Key then
            Found := true;
            L := Mid;
        -- 2. Key = T(Mid) and Found
        elsif T( Mid ) < Key then
            -- 3. not Key in T(T'FIRST..Mid)
            Bott := Mid + 1;
        -- 4. not Key in T(T'FIRST..Bott–1)
        else
            -- 5. not Key in T( Mid..T'LAST )
            Top := Mid – 1;
        -- 6. not Key in T(Top+1..T'LAST)
        end if;
    end loop;
    -- Post: Found and T (L) = Key or
    --    ( not Found and not (exists i, T'FIRST >= i <= T'LAST, T (i) = Key ))
end Binary_search;
```

Figure 24.5
The binary search
routine annotated with
assertions.

(1) If an element equal to the key is found during loop execution then Found is explicitly set to true. The loop will terminate.

(2) The condition Bott <= Top means that (Top – Bott) $\geqslant 0$ for the loop to execute. If it can be shown that (Top–Bott) < 0, loop termination is guaranteed.

(3) If an element matching Key is not found during an execution of the loop, either the statement Bott := Mid + 1 or the statement Top := Mid – 1 must be executed. As Mid is computed by dividing the sum of Top and Bott by 2, it is always true that Top < Mid ≤ Bott and is therefore not negative. Therefore, the assignments within the program either reduce Top or increase Bott. Consequently, (Top – Bott) must ultimately become negative. Therefore the loop will terminate.

Assertion	Statement	Argument
Pre-condition	The array is arranged in ascending order and has at least one member.	We assume that the parameters to the array satisfy this pre-condition. No checking code is included.
(1) (loop invariant)	Either a value matching Key does not lie in the portion of the array which has been examined or the value at the mid-point of the array matches Key.	True on the first entry to the loop. None of the array has been examined so a value matching Key cannot lie in the examined portion of the array.
(2)	The key matches the middle element of the array and Found is true.	Follows because of successful test, Key = Mid.
(3)	The key does not lie in that part of the array 'below' the mid-point.	Follows from the fact that T is ordered and T(Mid) < Key. If T(Mid) is less than Key, all values with an index less than Mid must also be less than Key.
(4)	The key is not in the range T (T'FIRST).. T (Bott–1).	Follows by substituting Bott–1 for Mid.
(5)	The key does not lie in that part of the array 'above' the mid-point.	Follows using a similar argument to 3 for values greater than Key. All array elements whose index is between Mid and T'LAST must be greater than Key.
(6)	The key is not in the range T (Top+1).. T (T'LAST).	Follows from 5 by substituting Top–1 for Mid.
(1) (loop re-entry)	The loop is re-entered at 1 because neither Found is true nor is Bott ≤Top.	There is no value in the part of the table searched so far that equals key so the loop invariant holds.
Post (loop termination)	The loop terminates because the key has been found in the array or the whole array has been checked.	Found is explicitly set true because the key has been found at T (L) or T(T'FIRST..Bott–1, Top+1..T'LAST) includes the entire array. There is no value in T which is equal to Key.
	Therefore, the binary search program is correct.	

Figure 24.6
Correctness argument based on program assertions.

The axiomatic approach to demonstrating program correctness can be applied when the system is modelled as functions but it is difficult to apply it to object-based systems. An alternative approach is used in the Cleanroom process, discussed later in this chapter. This is more suited to object-oriented systems. It uses a stimulus-response model to specify the actions of a program component which is represented as a black box (Mills, 1988).

In the stimulus-response approach to specification, a component is specified by listing the responses it produces when presented with different stimuli and different stimulus histories. Given that components can respond to a number of different stimuli and that their associated responses vary depending on the previous stimuli, there are usually a large number of stimulus-response combinations. Specifications tend to be large and are often presented as a table.

Once the specification has been produced, the black box is developed in a step-wise fashion. Rigorous arguments are produced at each stage to demonstrate that the development step is correct with respect to the specification. In general, the verification is based on informal correctness arguments but a more detailed, formal verification can be produced for critical systems. I don't have space to describe this approach to verification in any detail here. Interested readers should consult the original text by Linger *et al.* (1979) or the article by Mills (1988) for more details.

24.3 Static analysis tools

Static program analysers are software tools which scan the source text of a program and detect possible faults and anomalies. They do not require the program to be executed. They may be used as part of the verification process to complement the error detection facilities provided by the language compiler.

The intention of automatic static analysis is to draw the verifier's intention to anomalies in the program such as variables which are used without initialization, variables which are unused, and so on. While these are not necessarily erroneous conditions, it is probable that many of these anomalies are a result of errors or omissions. Some of the checks which can be detected by static analysis are shown in Figure 24.7.

The stages involved in static analysis include:

(1)   *Control flow analysis*   This stage identifies and highlights loops with multiple exit or entry points and unreachable code. Unreachable code is code which is surrounded by unconditional goto statements and which is not referenced elsewhere in the program. If goto statements are avoided, unreachable code cannot be written.

(2)   *Data use analysis*   This stage is concerned with examining how variables in the program are used. It detects variables which are used without previous initialization, variables which are written twice without an intervening assignment and variables which are declared but never used. Data use analysis can also detect ineffective tests where the test condition always has the same value.

Fault class	Static analysis check
Data faults	Variables used before initialization
	Variables declared but never used
	Variables assigned twice but never used between assignments
	Possible array bound violations
	Undeclared variables
Control faults	Unreachable code
	Unconditional branches into loops
Input/output faults	Variables output twice with no intervening assignment
Interface faults	Parameter type mismatches
	Parameter number mismatches
	Non-usage of the results of functions
	Uncalled functions and procedures
Storage management faults	Unassigned pointers
	Pointer arithmetic

Figure 24.7
Automated static
analysis checks.

(3)   *Interface analysis*   This analysis checks the consistency of routine and procedure declarations and their use. It is unnecessary if a strongly typed language like Ada is used for implementation as the compiler carries out these checks. Interface analysis can detect type errors in weakly typed languages like FORTRAN and C. Interface analysis can also detect functions and procedures which are declared and never called or function results which are never used.

(4)   *Information flow analysis*   This phase of the analysis identifies all input variables on which output variables depend. While it does not detect anomalies, the derivation of the values used in the program are explicitly listed. Erroneous derivations should therefore be easier to detect during a code inspection or review. Information flow analysis can also show the conditions on which a variable's value depends.

(5)   *Path analysis*   This phase of semantic analysis identifies all possible paths through the program and sets out the statements executed as part of that path. It essentially unravels the program's control and allows each possible predicate to be analysed individually.

Information flow analysis and path analysis generate an immense amount of information. This information is really another way of viewing the program and does not highlight anomalous conditions. Because of the large amount of information generated, these phases of static analysis are sometimes left out of the process. Only the early phases, which detect anomalous conditions directly, are used.

To illustrate static analysis tools, I use an example of a static analyser for C programs called LINT. LINT provides static checking which is equivalent to that provided by the compiler in a strongly typed language such as Ada. An example of the output produced by LINT is shown in Figure 24.8. In this transcript of a Unix terminal session, commands are shown in italics. The first command lists the (non-sensical) program. It defines a function with one parameter called printarray then causes this function to be called with three parameters. Variables i and c are declared but never assigned values. The value returned by the function is never used.

The line numbered 139 shows the C compilation of this program with no errors reported by the C compiler. This is followed by a call of the LINT static analyser which detects and reports program errors.

The static analyser shows that the scalar variables c and i have been used but not initialized and that printarray has been called with a different number of arguments than are declared. It also identifies the inconsistent use of the first argument in printarray and the fact that the function value is never used.

Static analysers may be used by programmers before the inspection process to discover potential problems in their code. These tools are particularly valuable when a programming language like C is used. C does not have strict type rules and the checking which the C compiler can do is limited. Therefore, there is a great deal of scope for programmer errors which can be automatically discovered by the analysis tool.

```
138% more lint_ex.c

#include <stdio.h>
printarray (Anarray)
  int Anarray;
{
  printf("%d",Anarray);
}
main ()
{
  int Anarray[5]; int i; char c;
  printarray (Anarray, i, c);
  printarray (Anarray) ;
}

139% cc lint_ex.c
140% lint lint_ex.c

lint_ex.c(10): warning: c may be used before set
lint_ex.c(10): warning: i may be used before set
printarray: variable # of args. lint_ex.c(4) :: lint_ex.c(10)
printarray, arg. 1 used inconsistently lint_ex.c(4) :: lint_ex.c(10)
printarray, arg. 1 used inconsistently lint_ex.c(4) :: lint_ex.c(11)
printf returns value which is always ignored
```

Figure 24.8
LINT static analysis.

However, tool-based analysis cannot replace inspections as there are a significant number of error types which static analysers cannot detect. For example, they can detect uninitialized variables but they cannot detect initializations which are incorrect. They can detect (in a language like C) functions which have the wrong numbers and types of arguments. They cannot detect situations in which an incorrect argument of the correct type has been passed to a function.

24.4 Cleanroom software development

Cleanroom software development (Mills *et al.*, 1987; Cobb and Mills, 1990; Linger, 1994) is a software development philosophy which is based on static verification techniques. The objective of this approach to software development is zero-defect software. The name 'Cleanroom' was derived by analogy with semiconductor fabrication units. In these units (cleanrooms) defects are avoided by manufacturing in an ultra-clean atmosphere.

A model of the process, adapted from the description given by Linger (1994), is shown in Figure 24.9.

The Cleanroom approach to software development is based on the notion that defects in software should be avoided rather than detected and repaired. It relies on a strict, formalized inspection process to discover faults before the software is tested.

There are five key characteristics of the Cleanroom development process.

(1) *Formal specification* The software to be developed is formally specified. A stimulus-response model is used to express the specification.

(2) *Incremental development* The software is partitioned into increments which are developed separately using the Cleanroom process. These are defined, with customer input, at an early stage in the process.

Figure 24.9
The Cleanroom development process.

(3) *Structured programming* Only a limited number of control and data abstraction constructs are used. The program development process is a process of stepwise refinement of the specification.

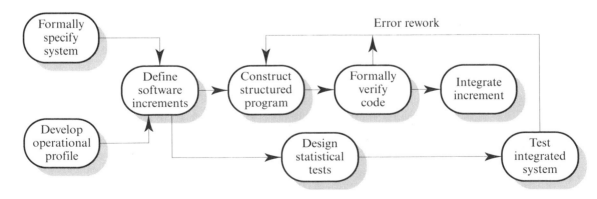

(4)   *Static verification*   The developed software is statically verified using mathematically based correctness arguments. Code components are not executed
or tested in any way.

(5)   *Statistical testing*   The integrated software increment is tested statistically,
as discussed in Chapter 18, to determine its reliability. These statistical tests
are based on an operational profile which is developed in parallel with the
system specification as shown in Figure 24.9.

Incremental development (Figure 24.10) involves producing and delivering the software in parts which are made available for user assessment. An increment can
be executed by user commands and is a useful, albeit limited, system in its own
right. Users can then feed back reports of the system and propose changes that
are required. Incremental development is important because it minimizes the
disruption caused to the development process by customer-requested requirements
changes.

When a specification is specified as a single unit, changes in customer
requirements (which are inevitable) disrupt the specification and development
process. The specification and design must be continually reworked. With incremental development, the specification for the increment is frozen although change
requests for the rest of the system are accepted. The software increment is delivered
on completion.

The most effective approach to incremental development is to deliver critical
customer functionality in early increments. Less important system functions are
included in later increments. The customer therefore has the opportunity of trying
these critical increments before the whole system has been delivered. If requirements problems are discovered, the customer may then feed back this information to
the development team and request a new release of the increment.

Given the emphasis on static verification, it is perhaps paradoxical that this
approach means that the most important customer functions receive the most testing.
As new increments are developed, they are integrated with the existing increments
and the complete system is tested. Therefore, increments are re-tested with new test
cases as more increments are added to the system.

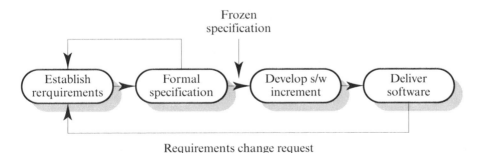

Figure 24.10
An incremental
development process.

There are three teams involved when the Cleanroom process is used for large system development:

(1) *The specification team* This group is responsible for developing and maintaining the system specification. Customer-oriented specifications (requirements definition) and mathematical specifications for verification are produced by this team. In some cases, when the specification is complete, the specification team will also take responsibility for development.

(2) *The development team* This team has the responsibility of developing and verifying the software. The software is not executed or even compiled during the development process. A structured, formal approach to verification based on inspection of code supplemented with correctness arguments is used.

(3) *The certification team* This team is responsible for developing a set of statistical tests to exercise the software after it has been developed. These tests are based on the formal specification. Test case development is carried out in parallel with software development. The test cases are used to certify the software reliability. Reliability growth models, discussed in Chapter 18, are used to decide when to stop testing.

The Cleanroom approach results in software with very few errors and does not seem to be any more expensive than conventional development. Cobb and Mills (1990) discuss several successful Cleanroom development projects which have a uniformly low failure rate in delivered systems. The costs of these projects were comparable with other projects which used conventional development techniques.

Selby *et al.* (1987), using students as developers, compared Cleanroom development with conventional techniques. They found that most teams could successfully use the Cleanroom method. More of the Cleanroom teams met the development schedule. The developed source code had more comments and a simpler structure. Use of the Cleanroom method resulted in products of higher quality than those developed using traditional techniques.

Static verification is cost-effective in the Cleanroom process. The vast majority of defects are discovered before execution and are not introduced into the developed software. Linger (1994) reports that, on average, only 2.3 defects per thousand lines of source code were discovered during testing for Cleanroom projects. Overall development costs are not increased because less effort is required to test and repair the developed software.

Cleanroom development works well when practised by skilled and committed engineers. However, use of the method has been confined to a few, technologically advanced, organizations. Reports of the success of this approach in industry have mostly come from its developers. We don't know if this process can be transferred effectively to other types of software development organization. These organizations usually have fewer, less committed and less skilled engineers. Transferring the Cleanroom approach to such organizations remains a challenge for the future.

Further reading

Software Inspection. A very thorough book which covers program inspections as a defect detection technique in detail. It tends to be rather wordy at times but the case studies are particularly useful for illustrating the practice of inspection. (T. Gilb and D. Graham, Addison-Wesley, 1993.)

'Using inspections to investigate program correctness'. This article discusses how a mathematically based but not completely formal inspection process is effective in discovering program errors. (R. N. Britcher, *IEEE Computer,* **21** (11), November 1988.)

'Cleanroom software engineering'. This article describes the development technique used in IBM's Federal Systems Division which is based on program correctness arguments and statistical quality checks. (H. D. Mills, M. Dyer, and R. Linger, *IEEE Software*, **4** (5), September 1987.)

'Cleanroom process model'. This article updates the earlier presentation of the Cleanroom approach with more description of the development process that is used. (R. C. Linger, *IEEE Software*, **11** (2), March 1994.)

KEY POINTS

- Static verification techniques involve examination and analysis of the program source code to detect errors. They should be used with program testing as part of the V & V process.

- Program inspections are effective in finding program errors. The aim of an inspection is to locate faults and the inspection process is often driven by a fault checklist.

- Program code is systematically checked by a small team. Team members include a team leader or moderator, the author of the code, a reader who presents the code during the inspection and a tester who considers the code from a testing perspective.

- Mathematical program verification involves producing a mathematically rigorous argument that a program conforms to its specification.

- The axiomatic approach to verification relies on programs being specified as a pair of predicates defining pre- and post-conditions. The program is shown to be correct by arguing that the application of the program statements lead from the pre-condition to the post-condition. It also involves demonstrating that the program terminates.

- Static analysers are software tools which process a program source code and draw attention to anomalies such as unused code sections and uninitialized variables. These anomalies may be the result of faults in the code.

■ Cleanroom software development is an approach to software development which relies on static techniques for program verification and statistical testing for system reliability certification. It has been successful in producing systems which have a high level of reliability.

EXERCISES

24.1 The technique of program inspections was derived in a large organization which had a plentiful supply of potential inspectors. Suggest how the method might be revised for use in a small programming group with no outside assistance.

24.2 Using your knowledge of Ada, C++, C or some other programming language, derive a checklist of common errors (not syntax errors) which could not be detected by a compiler but which might be detected in a program inspection.

24.3 Write a set of routines to implement an abstract data type called **SYMBOL_TABLE** which could be used as part of a compilation system. Organize a program inspection of your routines and keep a careful account of the errors discovered. Test the routines using a black-box approach and compare errors which are revealed by testing with those discovered by inspection.

24.4 The specification of a routine called **Max_value** which finds the largest element in an array is shown in Figure 24.11. Code this routine and demonstrate the correctness of your implementation using logical correctness arguments. The specification function **Initialized** verifies that all elements of the array have been assigned an initial value.

24.5 Modify the routine in Figure 24.11 (**Max_value**) so that it sums the elements of the array and returns the value of that sum. Modify the correctness arguments accordingly.

Figure 24.11
The specification of Max_value.

```
function Max_value (X: ELEM_ARRAY) return ELEM ;
-- FIRST and LAST are predefined attributes giving the lower and
-- the upper bounds of the array respectively
--|   Pre: X'LAST - X'FIRST >= 0 and
--|      for_all i in {X'FIRST..X'LAST}, Initialized (X(i))
--|   Post: for_all i in {X'FIRST..X'LAST}, Max_value (X) >= X (i) and
--|      exists j in {X'FIRST..X'LAST}, Max_value (X) = X (j)
```

24.6 Formally specify, implement and produce correctness arguments for the following routines:

(a) a linear search routine;

(b) a routine which sorts an array of integers using bubblesort;

(c) a routine which finds the greatest common divisor of two integers;

(d) a routine which inserts an element into an ordered list.

24.7 Produce a list of conditions which could be detected by a static analyser for Ada or C++.

24.8 Read the published papers on Cleanroom development and write a management report highlighting the advantages, costs and risks of adopting this approach to software development.

24.9 A manager decides to use the reports of program inspections as an input to the staff appraisal process. These reports show who made and who discovered program errors. Is this ethical managerial behaviour? Would it be ethical if the staff were informed in advance that this would happen? What difference might it make to the inspection process?

Part Six
CASE

The chapters in this part of the book introduce CASE (computer-aided software engineering) and the part it plays in the software process. Chapter 25 classifies various CASE systems, discusses CASE integration and the CASE life cycle. Chapter 26 describes CASE workbenches for design, programming and testing. Chapter 27 introduces large-scale CASE in the form of software engineering environments. These provide support for all software process activities.

Contents

25

Computer-aided Software Engineering

Objectives

- To introduce computer-aided software engineering (CASE) and to cover some general issues relating to CASE and CASE technology.

- To propose a classification for CASE systems based on the functions provided, the activities supported and the breadth of coverage offered by the system.

- To discuss a number of types of CASE integration.

- To describe the CASE life cycle from initial procurement through to obsolescence.

Contents

Historically, the most significant productivity increases in manufacturing or building processes have come about when human skills are augmented by powerful tools. One man and a bulldozer can probably shift more earth in a day than 50 men working with hand tools. Similarly, the productivity of engineering designers is improved when they are supported by CAD systems which take over tedious drawing chores and which check the design for errors and omissions.

Automated tool support for software engineers should therefore lead to improvements in software productivity. Since the early 1980s, a wide range of tools to support software development have been developed. The term *computer-aided software engineering* (CASE) is now generally accepted as the name for this automated support for the software engineering process.

Three different levels of CASE technology can be identified:

(1)   *Production-process support technology*   This includes support for process activities such as specification, design, implementation, testing, and so on. These were among the earliest and consequently are the most mature CASE products. Different types of production-support products are covered in Chapter 26.

(2)   *Process management technology*   This includes tools to support process modelling and process management. These tools will call on production-process support tools to support specific process activities. A few products in this area are available but it is still the subject of considerable research.

(3)   *Meta-CASE technology*   Meta-CASE tools are generators which are used to create production-process and process management support tools. This topic is covered in Chapter 26. Some meta-CASE tools are available but they are not easy to use and have not been widely adopted.

At the time of writing (1995), there are many different CASE suppliers who offer hundreds of different products. The market for these products expanded very rapidly in the late 1980s and early 1990s but now seems to have entered a period of slower growth. This is partly due to general economic circumstances. However, the first generations of CASE products have not led to the high level of productivity improvements which were predicted by their vendors.

There are various reasons for this:

●   For large system development, the fundamental problems were accurately identified by Brooks (1987). They are the problems of managing complexity both in the product being developed and in the development process. Brooks suggested that CASE technology can provide some support but cannot address this essential problem of complexity to any significant extent.

●   Current CASE products represent 'islands of automation' where various process activities are supported to a greater or lesser extent. Integration between these different products is limited. This limits the applicability of the technology.

- Adopters of CASE technology sometimes underestimated the training and process adaptation costs which are essential for the effective introduction of CASE. They often skimped on these costs with the consequence that the CASE technology was under-utilized.

We now have a more realistic view of the costs and benefits of CASE technology. It has not revolutionized software development nor has it produced orders of magnitude productivity improvements. Software engineering has not yet benefited from automation to the same extent as other engineering disciplines.

Nevertheless, CASE technology can be applied in a cost-effective way to reduce software costs and development time significantly and to increase software quality. The availability of CASE support makes it possible to re-engineer some software processes so that they are more effective. Thus, CASE has contributed and will continue to contribute to the development of software engineering.

25.1 CASE classification

The area of CASE has developed very rapidly and, as a consequence, different terminology is used by different people to describe CASE systems. Terms such as tools, toolkits, workbenches and environments are used inconsistently. A classification scheme for CASE technology allows different types of tool to be assessed and compared. It also provides a conceptual basis for understanding and explaining the field.

Figure 25.1 lists a number of different types of CASE tool and gives specific examples of each tool. There are other, more specialized, tool classes, such as tools to support software reuse, tools for software re-structuring and so on, which might be included in some systems.

Functionality is one possible classification dimension where the tools are classified according to the functions they support. Other possible classification dimensions are:

- *Process support* What process phases are supported by the CASE technology? Tools can be classified as design tools, programming tools, maintenance tools and so on.
- *Breadth of support* What is the extent of process activity supported by the technology? Narrow support means support for very specific tasks in the process such as creating an entity-relation diagram, compiling a program, etc. Broader support includes broader support for process phases such as design with the most general support covering all or most phases of the software process.

Figure 25.2 is an activity-based classification which shows the process phases supported by a number of different types of CASE tool. Tools for planning and

Tool type	Examples
Management tools	PERT tools, estimation tools
Editing tools	Text editors, diagram editors, word processors
Configuration management tools	Version management systems, change management systems
Prototyping tools	Very high-level languages, user interface generators
Method support tools	Design editors, data dictionaries, code generators
Language processing tools	Compilers, interpreters
Program analysis tools	Cross-reference generators, static analysers, dynamic analysers
Testing tools	Test data generators, file comparators
Debugging tools	Interactive debugging systems
Documentation tools	Page layout programs, image editors
Re-engineering tools	Cross-reference systems, program restructuring systems

Figure 25.1
Functional classification
of CASE tools.

estimating, text editing, document preparation and configuration management may be used throughout the software process.

Figure 25.2 shows that tool support is available for all process activities from specification through to verification and validation. Obviously, these tools are also used in system maintenance. This would appear to suggest that computer-aided software engineering has now matured with good coverage of all process activities. However, the quality of the available support is uneven. Very good support for design and implementation activities is available but significantly weaker support for requirements and maintenance. These differences are illustrated in Figure 25.3. Obviously, this picture may change over the lifetime of the book as new tools become available.

The excellent quality of the support for system modelling, design and programming reflects the fact that these activities are relatively well understood. The more difficult activities of requirements definition, formal specification and maintenance are not well supported by CASE. CASE support is most successful when it is based on some method. We currently do not have effective methods for these activities.

The breadth of support for the software process offered by CASE technology is another possible classification dimension. Fuggetta (1993) proposes that CASE systems should be classified in three categories:

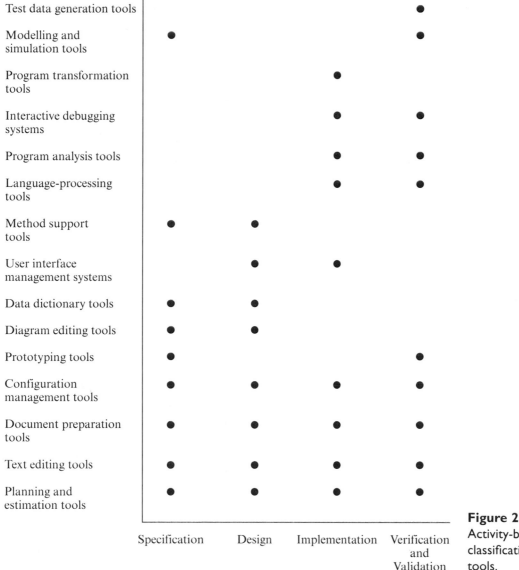

Figure 25.2
Activity-based
classification of CASE
tools.

(1)   *Tools* support individual process tasks such as checking the consistency of a design, compiling a program, comparing test results and so on. Tools may be general-purpose, stand-alone tools (for example, a word processor) or may be grouped into workbenches.

(2)   *Workbenches* support process phases or activities such as specification, design and so on. They normally consist of a set of tools with some greater or lesser degree of integration. Workbenches are discussed in more detail in Chapter 26.

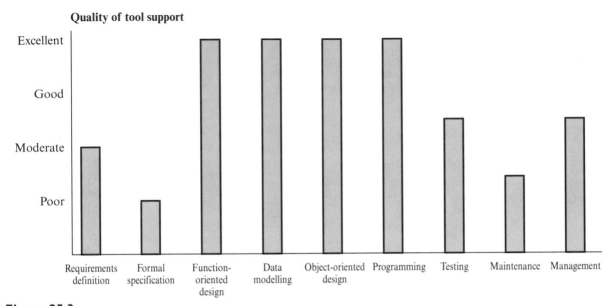

Figure 25.3
Quality of CASE
support for software
process activities.

(3)   *Environments* support all or at least a substantial part of the software process. They will normally include several different workbenches which are integrated in some way. Environments are the topic of Chapter 27.

When I need to make general statements about any of these types, I use the generic term *CASE system* to mean either tool, workbench or environment.

Figure 25.4 illustrates this classification and shows some examples of these different classes of CASE support. Of course, Figure 25.4 is simply an illustrative example; many types of tool and workbench have been left out of this diagram.

Figure 25.4 shows only general-purpose tools rather than tools which are built into workbenches. General-purpose tools are used at the discretion of the software engineer who makes decisions about when to apply them for process support. Workbenches, however, usually support some method which includes a process model and a set of rules/guidelines which apply to the software being developed. The workbench should therefore provide some guidance on how to apply the method and when tools in the workbench should be used.

I have classified environments as integrated environments or process-centred environments. Integrated environments provide infrastructure support for data, control and presentation integration as discussed in the next section. Process-centred environments are more general. They also include software process knowledge and a process engine which uses this process model to advise engineers on what tools or workbenches to apply and when they should be used.

In practice, the boundaries between these different classes are not clear-cut. Tools may be sold as a single product but may embed support for different activities. For example, many word processors now provide a built-in diagram editor. As

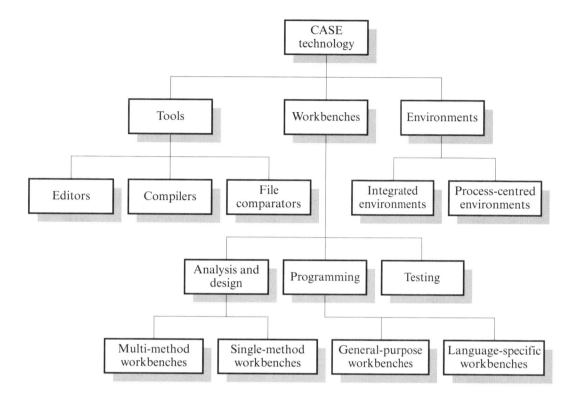

CASE workbenches mature and are made available on more powerful hardware, they offer increasing support for programming and testing so they resemble software engineering environments. It may therefore not always be easy to position a product using a classification. Nevertheless, it provides a useful first step to help understand the degree of process support which a tool is likely to provide.

Figure 25.4
Tools, workbenches
and environments.

25.2 Integrated CASE

Individual CASE tools are useful and cost-effective. However, more leverage is obtained when CASE tools work together in an integrated way. The principal benefit of integration is that specialized tools can be combined to provide wider support for process activities. An effective integration framework makes evolution possible as new systems are added without perturbing existing systems. With an integrated system, training costs are potentially reduced as existing software is reused when new systems are added. If CASE system user interfaces are integrated, the learning time and the user error rate are likely to be reduced.

Examples of situations where benefits are gained from integration include:

(1)   The integration of a design workbench with a documentation workbench. The documentation automatically generated by the design tools can be formatted

neatly and included in system documentation produced using the documentation workbench.

(2)   The integration of specification, design and programming tools with a configuration management workbench. The outputs from the tools can be managed using the CM system. The organization can keep track of different changes, versions, releases and so on.

Wasserman (1990) proposed a five-level model for discussing integration in software engineering environments. These apply to tools within a workbench or environment.

(1)   *Platform integration*   Tools run on the same hardware/operating system platform.

(2)   *Data integration*   Tools operate using a shared data model.

(3)   *Presentation integration*   Tools offer a common user interface.

(4)   *Control integration*   Tools may activate and control the operation of other tools.

(5)   *Process integration*   Tool usage is guided by an explicit process model and associated process engine.

From the user's perspective, integration means that CASE tools exhibit some measure of uniformity. The degree of uniformity supported varies considerably. Loosely coupled systems may only provide limited data interchange. By contrast, in tightly integrated systems, tools operate on a single, shared representation of the software using a consistent user interface. There is a seamless transition from one tool to another.

25.2.1 Platform integration

Platform integration means that the tools or workbenches to be implemented run on the same platform where 'platform' can mean either a single computer/operating system combination or a network of systems. Most CASE tools are either available for Unix systems or PCs running Microsoft Windows. Platform integration on a single system does not constitute a major problem unless, of course, there is a need to integrate PC and Unix tools.

The major problems which arise with platform integration occur when an organization runs a heterogeneous network with different computers running different operating systems. Even when machines are all bought from the same supplier, this can be a problem. New machines may be delivered with new operating system versions and installed in a network with machines running older versions of the operating system. In some circumstances, existing CASE systems will not immediately run under the new operating system. Newly purchased CASE systems may not work with older versions of the operating system.

These problems of platform integration can only be solved in the long term. They require either a universally used operating system or operating system standards which are widely adopted. This does not seem to be imminent so problems of network heterogeneity will continue for the foreseeable future.

25.2.2 Data integration

Data integration means that different CASE tools can exchange data. Thus, results from one tool can be passed as inputs to another tool. Support can therefore be provided by multi-purpose 'tool fragments' rather than monolithic tools or workbenches.

There are a number of different levels of data integration:

(1)   *Shared files*   All tools recognize a single file format. The most general-purpose shareable file format is where files are made up of lines of characters.

(2)   *Shared data structures*   The tools make use of shared data structures which usually include programming or design language information. The details of the data structure are agreed in advance by all tools and are 'hard-wired' into the tools.

(3)   *Shared repository*   The tools are integrated around an object management system which includes a public, shared data model describing the data entities and relationships which can be manipulated by the tools. This model is accessible to all tools but not an inherent part of them.

The simplest form of data integration is integration around a shared set of files, as supported by the Unix system. Unix has a simple model of files which are unstructured sequences of characters. Any tool can write character files and can read the files produced by other tools. The simple file format allows I/O devices to be treated as files. It makes it easy to provide pipes for direct process communication. When processes are connected by a pipe, streams of characters are passed directly from one process to another without the need for intermediate file creation.

Files are a physically simple approach to information exchange. However, applications must know the logical structure of a file if they are to use the information produced by another tool. This logical structure is embedded in the program which wrote the file. Either all tools follow that format, which then becomes a standard, or a tool which uses information must know which tool created that information.

A file-based integration strategy leads to a point-to-point approach to integration. Each pair of tools to be integrated must either agree on file interchange formats or must be provided with a filter to convert the shared file from one representation to another. This is illustrated in Figure 25.5.

Shared file integration requires, in principle, a conversion filter program to be written for every pair of tools which are to be integrated. As the formats used by different tools may be radically different, the cost of writing these filters may be

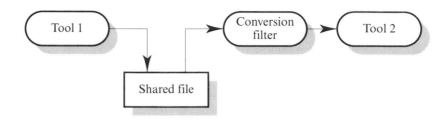

Figure 25.5
Point-to-point tool integration through shared files.

high. Rader *et al.* (1993), in a study of CASE tool integration, report that, in some cases, one to two years of effort were required to implement the conversion filter for point-to-point integration.

Alternatively, file format conventions can be agreed and tools programmed to work to these conventions. This was the approach used in the early versions of the Unix system which was one of the first effective programming environments. However, new tools may find that these agreed conventions are unduly restrictive. They may therefore ignore them and use their own formats. It becomes progressively more difficult to make these compatible with existing tools in the system.

A number of CASE tool vendors have proposed a CASE data exchange format (Imber, 1991) which is intended as a standard data exchange format for CASE systems. At the time of writing, standards proposals have been made but they do not yet seem to have had a significant impact on available CASE systems. The future of this standard and its level of support by CASE system vendors is not clear.

An alternative approach to data integration which incorporates shared syntactic and semantic information is based on shared data structures. These data structures may be representations of notations such as data-flow diagrams, entity-relation diagrams or programming languages.

Perhaps the best examples of this form of integration can be found in many programming language translation and support tools. These tools rely on a syntactic and semantic analysis of the program and are often bundled with the compilation system. The tools share the syntax tree and symbol table which are generated by the compiler. The generated code is linked to this symbol table and syntax tree so that program execution information can be presented in high-level language terms. Figure 25.6 illustrates this form of data integration in a programming language workbench.

Integration around the shared data structures hides the differences between individual tools and the user is presented with what appears to be a coherent program development system. However, it is difficult to import tools into this environment because of the complex data integration representation. Any new tools must know the details of the shared structures. These are usually proprietary to the compiler vendor. Hence, workbenches based on this form of integration are usually stand-alone systems. The only possible form of integration with other CASE tools is through shared programming language source code.

Integration around a repository or object management system is the most flexible form of data integration. An object management system is a database system which includes facilities for typing entities in the system, associating

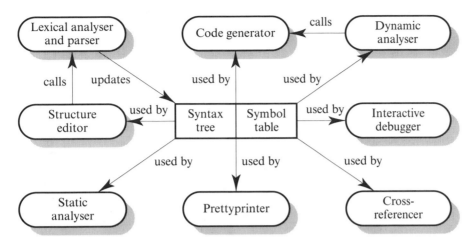

Figure 25.6
Integration through shared data structures.

attributes with these entities and establishing typed relationships between them. Object management systems are discussed in more detail in Chapter 27.

The essence of this form of integration is a public database schema in which are defined the entity types and relationships that are used. Tools read and write data according to this schema. If a tool wishes to use data produced by another tool, the schema is used to discover the data structure generated by that tool (Figure 25.7).

There are two principal disadvantages of this approach to data integration:

(1)   Tools have to be specially written to make use of the object management system. Existing tools cannot usually be adapted without considerable effort.

(2)   As well as the tool or workbench, the CASE user must also buy the object management system. This is additional expense and risk which many companies are unwilling to incur.

Research in this area has been under way since the early 1980s and environment frameworks such as PCTE (Thomas, 1989; Wakeman and Jowett, 1993) have been defined and implemented. However, CASE tool vendors have shown a reluctance to adopt any framework standards. They have mostly preferred their own proprietary

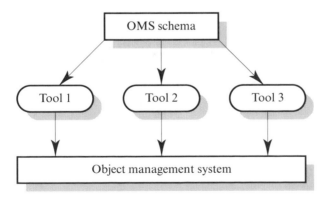

Figure 25.7
Integration through an OMS.

approaches. This has meant that, at the time of writing, the market for CASE systems based on this form of integration is limited and reliant on a few specialized organizations.

25.2.3 Presentation integration

Presentation or user interface integration means that the tools in a system use a common metaphor or style and a set of common standards for user interaction. Tools have a similar appearance. Users have a reduced learning overhead when a new tool is introduced as some of the interface is already familiar.

There are three different levels of presentation integration:

(1) *Window system integration*   Tools which are integrated at this level use the same underlying window system and present a common interface for window manipulation commands. Windows have the same appearance and the same commands for window movement, re-sizing, iconification and so on.

(2) *Command integration*   Tools which are integrated at this level use the same form of commands for comparable functions. If a textual interface is used, the syntax of command lines and parameters is the same for all commands. If a graphical interface using menus and buttons is used, comparable commands have the same name. The menu items are positioned in the same place in each application. The same representation (icons) is used in all sub-systems for buttons, menus and so on.

(3) *Interaction integration*   This applies in systems with a direct manipulation interface where the user interacts directly with a graphical or textual view of an entity. Interaction integration means that the same direct manipulation operations, such as selection, deletion and so on, are provided in all sub-systems. Therefore, if text is selected by double-clicking, it should be possible to select entities in a diagram in the same way. Examples of systems where interaction integration is supported include word-processing systems and graphical editing systems.

Command integration means that application and environment control functions are supported in a uniform way. As an example, all applications require some mechanism which allows the user to stop their execution. For instance, all applications might have the same kind of 'quit' button. If the tools are driven by textual commands, the commands should have similar or identical formats and parameter names.

Command integration can be achieved if implementors follow a set of guidelines defining the representations of abstract user interface actions. These representations may include selection of a choice from a set of alternatives, toggling a switch, numerical and character information display and so on. An early example of such guidelines was defined for the ECLIPSE environment. The user interface was defined in terms of menus, buttons, display panels, toggles and 'lights' (Sommerville *et al.*, 1989).

Most software tools depict the objects which they manipulate as either diagrams or text. Interaction integration means that the mechanisms used to interact with these graphical or textual objects are, wherever possible, consistent and uniform. For example, if text is normally selected by traversing it using cursor control keys, all tools which require text selection should use the same approach.

Providing guidelines for interaction integration is particularly difficult. This is because of the number of interaction possibilities and the range of potential textual and graphical object representations. It is relatively straightforward to define possible interactions with unstructured text and untyped graphical objects; it is more difficult when the text or diagram represents a structured entity with operations initiated through the screen representation.

In open systems, user interface integration above the windowing system level is more difficult to achieve. In these environments or workbenches, tools are developed at different times by different developers. As the system evolves and new tools are introduced, it becomes progressively harder to maintain user interface uniformity. Although comprehensive guidelines for user interface integration may be provided, the guideline designers cannot anticipate every possible use of the environment. New facilities, such as the use of sound, may not be covered by the guidelines so *ad hoc* user interface conventions are invented to support them. Inevitably, uniformity is lost in this process.

The *de facto* standard for window system integration for Unix workstations is X-windows with the Motif toolkit (Berlage, 1991; OSF, 1993). Virtually all Unix-based CASE tools conform to this standard. However, it only addresses the window level of integration. Unix tools and workbenches from different vendors are rarely well integrated at the command and interaction level. These CASE systems may provide command tailoring facilities to improve presentation integration. However, user control over detailed interaction integration is not usually supported.

On the PC platform, the *de facto* standard is Microsoft Windows. This is rather better than X/Motif as it supports all three levels of presentation integration. As well as a common windowing system, Windows includes toolbox support for menu construction guidelines and specific forms of interaction. The easiest way to implement a tool interface is to follow these guidelines with the result that most CASE tools running under Windows have a consistent appearance.

CASE workbenches which are closed systems usually have good user interface integration. As new tools cannot be introduced by other suppliers it is possible to achieve user interface commonality across the tools in the workbench. Conventions and standards for the different tools in the workbench can be developed. Users can seamlessly move from one tool to another.

25.2.4 Control integration

Control integration is concerned with providing mechanisms for one tool in a workbench or environment to control the activation of other tools in the CASE system. As well as being able to start and stop other tools, a tool can call on services provided by another tool in the system. These services are accessed through a program interface where facilities in a tool which are made available to other tools are published. For example, a structured editing system within a language toolkit may call a parser to check the syntax of a program fragment which has been input.

Some workbenches have developed special-purpose mechanisms for control integration. However, a more general approach based on message passing has been adopted by several vendors. This is implemented in systems such as Hewlett-Packard's SoftBench, DEC's FUSE and Sun's ToolTalk. Brown (1993) describes this approach to tool integration and compares several implementations of message passing systems.

In the message passing approach, CASE systems interchange information by passing messages to each other. These messages may provide status information, informing other tools about what is going on or requests for specific services provided by a CASE system. A generic *message server* manages communications between the CASE systems.

Figure 25.8 illustrates this general model. Each tool to be integrated provides a control interface which allows access to the tool's facilities. The message server includes information about the interfaces of all of the accessible tools and the location of these tools. It takes care of information encoding and decoding for network transmission.

When a tool needs to communicate with another tool, it constructs a message using a known format, addresses it and sends this to the message server. The tool does not need to know where the called tool is situated; it simply calls the message server which then passes the message to the called tool. Therefore, the model supports a distributed CASE system where different components of the system execute on different computers.

Logically, tools broadcast messages to be picked up by other tools with an interest in them. In practice, this is an inefficient approach. The message server knows the messages which can be processed by each CASE system so only passes on appropriate messages.

As an illustration of this approach, assume that the CASE system includes a design editor, a code generator and a compiler. These are implemented as separate components. On the conclusion of an editing session, the following actions might take place:

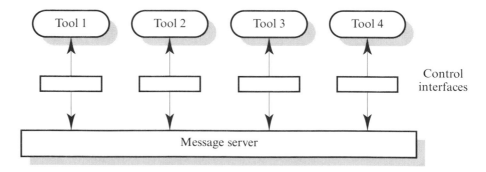

Figure 25.8
Control integration through message passing.

(1)   The design editor sends a message to the code generator requesting the design to be processed and code generated.

(2)   After generating the code, the code generator sends a message which is intercepted by both the design editor and the compiler. The design editor links the generated code file to the design; the compiler compiles the generated code.

(3)   After the code has been generated, the compiler sends a message which is intercepted by the design editor. It indicates to the user that the compilation is complete.

Control integration also requires some level of data integration so that the parameters of tool operations can be exchanged. The format of the data to be exchanged during an operation is normally encoded in an interface definition language (IDL). This IDL incorporates a set of standard types which every tool must use. Each tool must convert the data to be exchanged into these types so that it may be processed by the receiving tool.

However, this does not solve the data integration problems which arise when large amounts of data have to be shared. It is only suitable for the interchange of relatively short messages. Bulk data exchange must still be organized through files or objects. Therefore, the messages passed between systems normally include references to files whose data must be shared.

25.2.5 Process integration

Process integration means that the CASE system has embedded knowledge about the process activities, their phasing, their constraints and the tools needed to support these activities. The CASE system participates actively in the scheduling of these activities and in checking that the required activity sequence is maintained (Figure 25.9).

Process integration requires that the CASE system maintains a model of the software process and uses this model to drive the process activities. In essence, activities and deliverables are identified, a coordination strategy defined and the tools required to support activities are specified. All of this is embedded in the model and a process interpreter or 'engine' then enacts this model to drive the software process.

Current thinking is that this process enactment should not be prescriptive but should provide guidance to the engineers working on process activities. It is also recognized that not all activities can be modelled or supported. Process support systems have 'opt-outs' which allow parts of the process to be left to the discretion of the engineer.

Many activities are concurrent activities and this must be reflected in the process model. As activities and their coordination are interdependent, the process model should be dynamic and should change as more information regarding process activities is obtained.

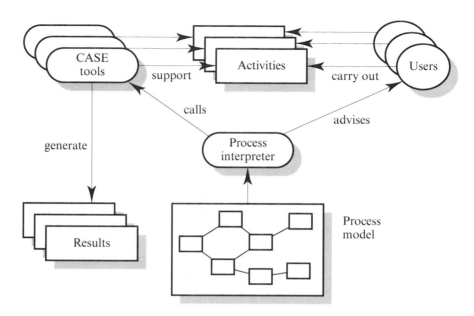

Figure 25.9
Process integration.

Supporting process integration with CASE technology relies on designing process models. There are some problems in creating realistic models:

(1)   Models of the software process as discussed in Chapter 1 are generic models. They rely on human interpretation to instantiate them in any particular set of circumstances. The activities and their implementation are not defined in detail in these process models. Breaking down the process into finer-grain activities is a project specific task. If a model is to be used to integrate activities, there is a significant cost in process programming and validation which adds to the project management costs.

(2)   There is never a single right way to organize a software development and both the project manager and the development engineers change the process 'on the fly' as the system is being developed. Humans can switch between activities relatively quickly if unforeseen circumstances (for example, a printer failure) arise. Embedding this flexibility in a model is difficult.

(3)   Process models specify the products of the software process and the communications between developers. Communication specification is possible for well-structured tasks such as invoice processing. However, the coordination patterns in loosely structured, problem-solving tasks which are normal in software development are difficult to specify.

A further difficulty with process integration is that engineers and managers may view this as a form of de-skilling. They may feel a loss of autonomy and that the CASE system challenges their professional judgement. These engineers may have evolved their own, informal, undocumented ways to tackle development and might be reluctant to conform to the more rigid strategies imposed by an environment.

Consequently, they may resist the introduction of CASE systems with activity integration.

At the time of writing there are a number of process modelling workbenches available such as Process Weaver (Fernström, 1993) where process models can be specified and enacted. These can be linked to other CASE tools using a control integration framework as discussed above. A number of examples of experimental process-centred environments have been built (Taylor *et al.*, 1988; Fernström *et al.*, 1992). These have not yet been developed into commercial products. In their study, Rader *et al.* (1993) did not find a significant commercial demand for this type of integration. It is therefore unlikely that CASE systems integrated through process models will be widely used before the end of the 20th century.

25.3 The CASE life cycle

The introduction and use of CASE technology requires careful planning. CASE tools are expensive and they must be maintained until all of the software produced using these tools becomes obsolete. Unless adequate resources are devoted to CASE procurement and support, it is unlikely that the benefits of using that technology will be achieved. If wrong decisions are made, software costs may increase rather than decrease when CASE systems are put into use.

CASE systems in an organization follow a life cycle from initial procurement through to ultimate obsolescence (Figure 25.10). The stages of this CASE life cycle are:

(1)   *Procurement*   This involves choosing an appropriate CASE system for the type of software being developed.

(2)   *Tailoring*   This phase adapts a CASE system to a particular set of organizational or project requirements.

(3)   *Introduction*   This phase introduces the CASE system into a working context. During this phase, engineers are trained in the use of the system.

(4)   *Operation*   This is the phase where the CASE system is in everyday use for software development.

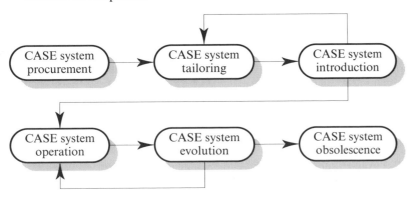

Figure 25.10
The CASE system life cycle.

(5)   *Evolution*   Evolution is not really a separate phase but is a continuing activity throughout the life of the CASE system. It involves modifying the hardware or software to adapt the system to new requirements.

(6)   *Obsolescence*   During this phase the CASE system is taken out of use. It must be ensured that software developed using the system can still be supported by the organization.

There is obviously feedback from the introduction phase to the tailoring phase as tailoring problems are discovered. There is also a feedback loop between evolution and usage.

Management must adopt a sensitive approach when introducing CASE technology so that engineers are convinced of its usefulness. The cost advantages of CASE systems are long-term rather than short-term, and immediate cost savings are unlikely. As discussed in the introduction, orders of magnitude reductions in cost from the use of CASE should not be expected.

25.3.1 CASE procurement

Hundreds of different CASE systems are now available. The majority of these are analysis and design workbenches, most of which seem, superficially at least, to be similar. However, there are also many other types of CASE system ranging from specialized tools through workbenches to complete environments.

The factors which must be taken into account when procuring a company-wide CASE system are:

(1)   *Existing company standards and methods*   The system should support existing practices rather than introduce new standards and methods which are likely to be resisted by users.

(2)   *Existing computers and future computer procurement*   It may be sensible to buy a system which runs on existing computers. However, if the current hardware is heavily used, there may not be spare capacity for CASE systems so significant capital expenditure on new machines may be required. Environments have a long lifetime so it is unwise to procure a system which does not run on industry-standard computers.

(3)   *The class of applications to be developed*   Clearly, a CASE system should be chosen which provides facilities for developing the type of applications required by an organization. There is no point in investing in a CASE system for commercial systems development if the organization is mostly involved in developing scientific FORTRAN programs.

(4)   *Security*   Some classes of system development require that the software and its associated documentation are classified. The system must provide appropriate security features so that the security manager can specify access permissions in the environment. Most CASE workbenches are not particularly secure.

Another factor is, obviously, the cost of the CASE system. Huff (1992) estimates that the acquisition cost of a reasonable CASE system is about $18,000 per person with support cost over five years of $40,000 per person. These figures obviously vary considerably from one organization to another. They also depend on the type of CASE system and associated support platform. However, they illustrate that CASE technology is a major capital expenditure for an organization and the decision on procurement is an important one.

25.3.2 CASE system tailoring

CASE systems are general-purpose software systems which must be adapted when installed in an organization to conform to the specific standards and working practices of that organization. The activities required to customize a CASE system for a particular organization and application domain include:

(1) *Installation*   The system must be installed and tested on the organization's hardware configuration. This may involve changing system dependent parameters. Scripts may have to be written to support installation and usage of the system.

(2) *Process model definition*   Even when the CASE system is not process driven, some kind of process model is needed to work out what system tailoring is required. The process model allows the CASE manager to see where the tool can be applied and what interfaces to other tools may need to be constructed.

(3) *Tool integration*   New CASE systems may have to be integrated with other installed CASE systems. If the system is integrated through a shared object management system, the schema must be defined and validated. This involves identifying all of the entities and relationships which are important in an organization's software development process. Getting the schema right is essential for successful integration so this stage is likely to take several months of development. If the system is integrated through files, shared file formats must be agreed and, where necessary, conversion filter programs must be written.

(4) *Documentation*   As part of the tailoring process, the particular instantiation of the CASE system must be documented.

The time required for tailoring and the costs involved should not be underestimated. Tailoring a CASE system, unless it is a very simple system, will always take several months; it may take more than a year before an effective system is available.

25.3.3 CASE system introduction and operation

Introducing a CASE system into an organization inevitably means changing working practices. The full benefit from using the system will not be gained until it has been in use for some time. There are predictable difficulties which are likely to arise but there will probably also be unanticipated problems. Resources must be available for tackling these problems.

Some of the problems which may arise when a CASE system is introduced are:

* *User resistance*   With few exceptions, humans are innately conservative and tend to resist new developments unless they have obvious advantages. CASE has advantages for management as it usually provides more control over the software process. The advantages for the individual software developer are less obvious. It may be argued that CASE systems are prescriptive and constrain the creativity of individual engineers.

* *Lack of training*   Some engineers may feel that new developments are inherently difficult and that they cannot understand some of the system facilities. This is most likely to be a problem with staff who have little formal training in software engineering. The pace of change in software development has been very fast. They may just have adapted to working with some other system and they may be reluctant to spend time learning a new system.

* *Management resistance*   Some managers may be resistant to introducing CASE technology into a known development process. Managers are responsible for cost control but the cost advantages of introducing CASE are difficult to quantify in advance. Using an unknown support system increases the risk associated with a project.

These objections to CASE systems may be valid in some cases. However, a properly designed system should provide tools to assist with the tedious chores which are part of software development (such as redrawing design diagrams, finding associated code and documentation, and so on). Individual engineers should therefore have more time for the creative and fulfilling parts of their job. CASE need not de-skill the software engineering process.

The second objection can only be addressed by ensuring that proper training is given to all engineers who are to use the CASE systems. This is expensive and managers must ensure that resources to cover these training costs are available. The CASE systems should be introduced in conjunction with existing support systems and the benefits demonstrated to staff working on other projects.

The final objection, that of management resistance, is more difficult to overcome especially as we now know that CASE systems have not lived up to their initial heady expectations. Adopting new software process technology is a leap into the unknown and there must be clear evidence of the benefits of the approach before management will be convinced by it.

Imposition of technology is rarely successful. Project managers should be closely involved in organizational decisions concerned with CASE system procurement and the technology should be introduced incrementally. As new projects are started using CASE support, costs should be carefully measured and the experiences of the project engineers and managers noted. This information may then be used to convince other managers of the effectiveness of the CASE system.

25.3.4 CASE system evolution

Like all software systems, CASE systems cannot remain static if they are to remain useful. They must evolve as new requirements become apparent and as new hardware and software platforms become available. New CASE tools may be added, inputs and output formats changed and new methods of tool use developed.

One of the problems of CASE system evolution is that new and old versions of the CASE system may be incompatible. It may be impossible to maintain all software using the new version of the system so several versions of the CASE system may be in use at any one time. If the incompatibilities are due to hardware changes, this may mean that old hardware also has to be maintained to support the software systems. If the incompatibilities are due to operating system dependencies, a heterogeneous network must be supported with different machines running different versions of the operating system.

25.3.5 CASE system obsolescence

At some stage in a CASE system's lifetime, a decision may be made to replace it. This may be forced on the organization because of the lack of support provided by the CASE system vendor or because of other decisions to change hardware and software platforms. Alternatively, it may be decided that other CASE systems offer a more suitable framework for that particular organization and that these should replace the system which is in use.

CASE systems cannot simply be scrapped and subsequently replaced by some other system. Rather, a transition period, which may be several years, should be planned where the new and the old systems are both in use. During this transition period, software which was developed using the old system and whose maintenance must continue must be moved to the new CASE system.

The scale of this problem depends on the amount of software to be moved and the compatibility of the old and new systems. A decision to make a CASE system obsolete may depend on a related decision to scrap the software systems it supports. The CASE support is therefore redundant and there are no significant costs involved in discontinuing the system.

Further reading

'Tools that bind: Creating integrated environments'. This article discusses CASE integration and describes a number of individual CASE products which may be part of an integrated framework. (D. Sharon and R. Bell, *IEEE Software*, **12** (2), March 1995.)

'A classification of CASE technology'. The classification scheme proposed in this article has been used here but Fuggetta goes into more detail and illustrates how a number of commercial products fit into this scheme. (A. Fuggetta, *IEEE Computer,* **26** (12), December 1993.)

IEEE Software, **9** (2), March 1992. This special issue is devoted to integrated CASE. The articles by Thomas and Nejmeh and by Brown and McDermid are particularly recommended to complement the discussion on integration in this chapter.

'Elements of a realistic CASE tool adoption budget'. This is an excellent article which discusses the real costs of CASE technology and cuts through the hype of CASE tool vendors. (C.C. Huff, *Comm. ACM*, **35** (4), April 1992.)

KEY POINTS

- Computer-aided software engineering (CASE) is the term for software tool support for the software engineering process.

- CASE technology may be classified according to the functions it provides, according to the software process activities which are supported and according to the size of the tasks supported.

- CASE tools support individual process activities; CASE workbenches support a set of related activities; CASE environments support all or most software process activities.

- Integrated CASE involves five levels of integration, namely platform integration, data integration, presentation integration, control integration and process integration.

- Data integration can be implemented via shared files, shared data structures or through an object management system described by a published schema.

- Process integration means that the CASE system has knowledge of the software process used and can advise on process activities. This has been the topic of a good deal of research but few products in this area are available.

- The CASE system life cycle has six stages, namely procurement, tailoring, introduction, usage, evolution and obsolescence.

- The true costs of adopting CASE technology are relatively high; over a five-year period, they are likely to exceed $50,000 per person.

EXERCISES

25.1 Suggest how a CASE technology classification scheme may be helpful to managers responsible for CASE system procurement.

25.2 Survey the tool availability in your local development environment and classify the tools according to the parameters (function, activity, breadth of support) suggested here.

25.3 Suggest potential benefits and practical problems of integrating CASE workbenches from different suppliers.

25.4 Different Unix commands may be integrated using pipes and shared files. Explain why this simple approach to tool integration is reasonably successful. Suggest where it might break down.

25.5 Write user interface guidelines for menus in a user interface so that applications offer an integrated presentation interface. These guidelines should cater for the situation where the number of menu items is more than can reasonably be displayed on a single menu. You should not simply follow those used in Windows or Apple Macintosh systems.

25.6 Survey the available literature and write a report summarizing the current state of the art in process modelling. A good starting point is the article by Fuggetta suggested as further reading.

25.7 Using a diagram which is different from Figure 25.10, briefly describe the different stages in the CASE system life cycle.

25.8 Using examples from your own experience, explain why CASE systems must be adapted for use in a given environment.

25.9 Using illustrative examples, explain why CASE technology in an organization must evolve if it is to remain useful.

25.10 Historically, the introduction of technology has caused profound changes in the labour market and, temporarily at least, displaced people from jobs. Discuss if the introduction of CASE technology is likely to have the same consequences for software engineers. If you don't think it will, explain why not. If you think that it will reduce job opportunities, is it ethical for the engineers affected to resist, passively and actively, the introduction of this technology?

26

CASE Workbenches

Objectives

- To describe different types of CASE workbench which are now available.
- To explain the difference between open and closed CASE workbenches.
- To describe the structure and components of design, programming and testing workbenches.
- To introduce meta-CASE tools which may be used to create CASE workbenches.

Contents

As discussed in the previous chapter, a CASE workbench is a set of tools which supports a particular phase of the software process such as design, implementation or testing. The advantage of grouping CASE tools into a workbench is that tools can work together to provide more comprehensive support than is possible with a single tool. Common services can be implemented and called by all other tools. Workbench tools may be integrated either through shared files, a shared repository or shared data structures.

CASE workbenches are available to support most software process activities. However, some activities (notably analysis and design, programming and program testing) are much better supported than others. Workbenches to support these activities are widely used in industry. Because of this, their relative maturity and their generality across application domains, I concentrate on these three types of workbench here.

This does not imply that these are the only workbenches which are required to support software development. Depending on the type of software developed and the application domain, other types of CASE workbench may also be used. These include:

- *Cross-development workbenches* These are workbenches which support host–target working (see Chapter 27) where software is developed on one machine for execution on some other system. The tools which might be included in a cross-development workbench include cross-compilers, target machine simulators, communication packages to download software from host to target, and remote execution monitoring tools.

- *Configuration management (CM) workbenches* These are workbenches to support configuration management. They may include version management tools, change tracking systems, system building tools and so on. These tools are discussed in Chapter 33.

- *Documentation workbenches* These are workbenches to support the production of high-quality documents. They may include word processors, desktop publishing systems, diagram and image editors, document viewing systems and so on.

- *Project management workbenches* These support project management activities. They may include tools for project planning and scheduling, cost estimation and budget tracking. Some of these tools are described in Chapters 3 and 29.

CASE workbenches are intended to support a software process phase such as system design or a set of interrelated software process activities such as configuration management. Clearly, these activities vary significantly from one application domain to another and from one organization to another. It is therefore desirable that CASE workbenches should be *open systems*.

An open workbench is a system where control integration mechanisms are either provided or can be programmed and where the data integration protocols are public rather than proprietary. Because standards for data integration have not been generally accepted, the majority of open systems have therefore relied on a file-based integration strategy.

The advantages of open workbenches are:

(1) New specialist tools which meet an organization's particular needs can be added to the workbench or existing tools may be replaced by more suitable alternatives.

(2) The outputs from tools are files which may be managed by a configuration management system.

(3) Incremental workbench introduction and evolution are possible. An organization can introduce CASE technology using a workbench with a few, easy-to-use tools. As its engineers gain experience, new tools can be added to the system. The initial tools may be replaced by more powerful systems as demands increase.

(4) Organizations need not depend on a single workbench supplier but can buy tools from a range of different vendors. This diversity of supply is important. If tool support is withdrawn by a tool vendor, this only affects part of the workbench. The remainder of the tools may continue in use.

Although open workbenches are preferable, many CASE workbench vendors have made a decision to provide *closed* systems. Closed systems are systems where the integration protocols are proprietary to the workbench vendor. Many workbenches are closed systems because this allows much tighter data, presentation and control integration. The workbench can appear to the user as a unified whole rather than as a toolbox of different tools. However, the addition of third-party or specially written tools to the workbench is usually impossible.

Since the mid-1980s there have been strenuous efforts made to define, implement and introduce standards for open repositories. Such standards allow open workbenches to be created but with tighter integration between the workbench components. These standards have included work on CAIS for Ada environments (Oberndorf, 1988), ATIS (Black, 1991) an object-oriented approach based on work by Atherton Technology and Digital, and PCTE (Wakeman and Jowett, 1993). At the time of writing, PCTE (described in Chapter 27) seems to be the most widely accepted of these. However, none of them are widely used and most CASE products still use proprietary approaches to integration.

26.1 Programming workbenches

A programming workbench is made up of a set of tools to support the process of program development. Programming workbenches were the first CASE systems when a set of software tools such as compilers, editors and debuggers were put together on a host machine which was dedicated to program development (Ivie, 1977). Language-oriented programming systems such as InterLisp (Teitleman and Masinter, 1984) were also developed around the same time.

Assemblers and compilers which translate higher-level programming languages to machine code are the central components of a programming workbench. The syntactic and semantic information generated from the source program during compilation may also be used by other tools. These include program analysers which show where variables are defined and used, program viewers which display the program structure and dynamic analysers which create a dynamic program execution profile. Debugging systems which help programmers discover faults also use the information in the syntax tree and symbol table.

Figure 26.1 illustrates a programming workbench. CASE tools are represented as round-edged boxes and tool inputs and outputs are shown as rectangles. In this workbench, tools are integrated through an abstract syntax tree and symbol table which is a shareable representation of the source language program.

Some of the tools which might be part of a programming workbench are:

(1)   *Language compiler*   Translates source programs to object code. As part of this translation process, an abstract syntax tree (AST) and a symbol table is created.

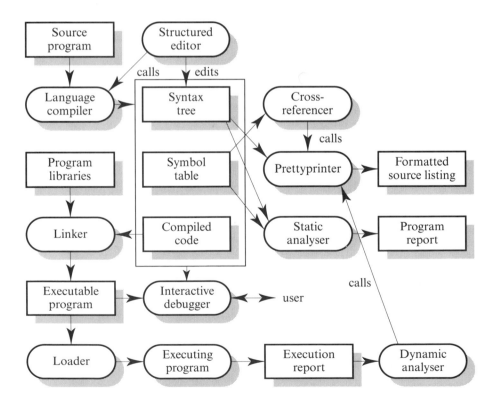

Figure 26.1
A programming
workbench.

(2) *Structured editor*   Incorporates embedded programming language knowledge and edits the syntactic representation of the program in the AST rather than its source code text.

(3) *Linker*   Links the object code program with components which have already been compiled.

(4) *Loader*   Loads the executable program into the computer memory prior to execution.

(5) *Cross-referencer*   Produces a cross-reference listing showing where all program names are declared and used.

(6) *Prettyprinter*   Scans the AST and prints the source program according to embedded formatting rules.

(7) *Static analyser*   Analyses the source code to discover anomalies such as uninitialized variables, unreachable code, uncalled functions and procedures, etc.

(8) *Dynamic analyser*   Produces a source code listing annotated with the number of times each statement was executed when the program was run. It may also generate information on program branches and loops and statistics of processor usage.

(9) *Interactive debugger*   Allows the user to control the execution sequence and view the program state as execution progresses.

Figure 26.1 shows the syntax tree and symbol table as shared structures which integrate the tools in the programming workbench. Logically, this is the approach adopted in all programming workbenches which offer a range of programming tools. However, in open systems, it may be difficult to share data structures in this way. Sharing in open systems requires data interchange through files. Creating file representations of complex linked structures is difficult. It is often easier and more efficient to re-create the syntactic and semantic information as required. Data shared by tools is usually interchanged as program source code which is generated by unparsing the program syntax tree.

Programming workbenches may be implemented as collections of tools running under a general-purpose operating system like Unix or may be bundled with the programming language compiler. Unix-based systems are invariably open systems. These have evolved from early experiments in providing programming support through the Unix Programmers Workbench (Ivie, 1977; Dolotta *et al.*, 1978). Some of the tools developed in these experiments (such as Make) are now sold along with the Unix system.

There are many programming workbenches available for personal computers. For marketing reasons, these are not usually sold as workbenches but as language compilers that include additional tool support. These workbenches are usually closed systems. There is very tight integration, using shared data structures, between the compiler and other tools. Languages which are sold in this way include Basic, C, C++, Pascal, Lisp and Smalltalk.

These language workbenches usually include a language-oriented editor, compiler and debugging system. When a program fails during execution, the editor is initiated and the editing cursor is positioned at the source language statement which caused the failure. A debugging window is opened showing the program state when it failed.

These workbenches may also include program viewing systems which allow users to decide how they wish to view the program and how much detail is to be presented (Figure 26.2). Multiple program views are very useful for program understanding as they give a picture of the overall structure of the program. The program viewing system may fold structures so that, for example, procedures are represented by their header. The user of the system can request information (for example, the procedure body) to be displayed or concealed.

Imperative languages such as C, Ada or C++ are usually integrated through the AST and symbol table as illustrated in Figure 26.1. Fourth-generation languages (4GLs) are an alternative approach which are now widely used for the implementation of commercial systems. Although termed 'languages', these 4GLs are really programming workbenches as they always include facilities apart from a programming language. Figure 26.3 shows the components which are normally part of a 4GL workbench.

4GL workbenches are geared towards producing interactive applications which rely on abstracting information from an organizational database, presenting it to end-users on their terminal or workstation and then updating the database with changes made by users. The user interface usually consists of a set of standard forms or a spreadsheet.

The tools which may be included in a 4GL workbench are:

(1) A database query language such as SQL (Date and Darwen, 1993) which may either be input directly or generated automatically from forms filled in by an end-user.

(2) A form design tool which is used to create forms for data input and display.

(3) A spreadsheet which is used for the analysis and manipulation of numeric information.

(4) A report generator which is used to define and create reports from information in the database.

Figure 26.2
Multiple program
views.

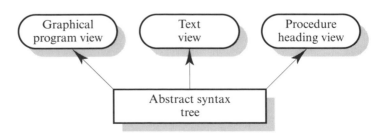

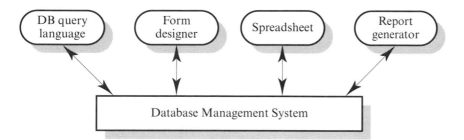

Figure 26.3
A 4GL programming workbench.

Instead of the program being central as is the case with imperative programming languages, the database is the central component of a 4GL workbench. Therefore, the database rather than the abstract syntax tree and symbol table is the integrating 'glue' which binds the workbench components.

4GLs have radically changed the development of business systems by reducing the time required to create working systems. The extent of this saving varies depending on the type of system and how much automatic generation is possible. In general, it seems that a system can be produced using a 4GL workbench in 10–25% of the time required for a system developed with a conventional programming language. However, such systems are usually much less efficient than those produced using imperative languages. The use of a 4GL may therefore be impractical for large system development.

26.2 Analysis and design workbenches

Analysis and design workbenches are designed to support the analysis and design stages of the software process where models of the system (for example, a data-flow model, an entity-relation model and so on) are created. These workbenches are usually oriented towards the support of the graphical notations used in structured design methods. Workbenches designed to support analysis and design are sometimes called upper-CASE tools. They support the early (upper) parts of the software process. By contrast, programming workbenches may be referred to as lower-CASE tools.

These workbenches may support a specific design or analysis method, such as JSD or Booch's object-oriented analysis (Cameron, 1986; Booch, 1994). Alternatively, they may be more general diagram editing systems with knowledge of the diagram types in the most common methods. Method-oriented workbenches incorporate method rules and guidelines. Some automatic checking of the diagrams is therefore possible.

Figure 26.4 shows the tools which may be included in an analysis and design workbench. These tools are normally integrated through a shared repository whose structure is proprietary to the workbench vendor. Analysis and design workbenches are therefore usually closed environments. It is difficult for users to add their own tools to them or to modify the tools which are provided.

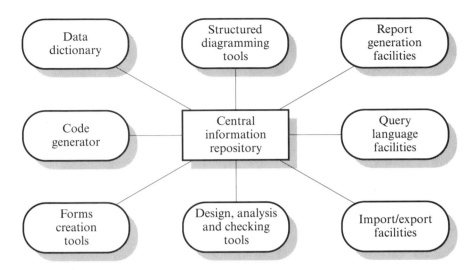

Figure 26.4
An analysis and design
workbench.

The components of the analysis and design workbench shown in Figure 26.4 are:

- *Diagram editors* to create data-flow diagrams, structure charts, entity-relationship diagrams and so on. These editors are not just drawing tools but are aware of the types of entities in the diagram. They capture information about these entities and save this information in the central repository (called an encyclopaedia in some workbenches).

- *Design analysis and checking tools* which process the design and report on errors and anomalies. These may be integrated with the editing system so that user errors are trapped at an early stage in the process.

- *Repository query languages* which allow the designer to find designs and associated design information in the repository.

- A *data dictionary* which maintains information about the entities used in a system design.

- *Report definition and generation tools* which take information from the central store and automatically generate system documentation.

- *Forms definition tools* which allow screen and document formats to be specified.

- *Import/export facilities* which allow the interchange of information from the central repository with other development tools.

- *Code generators* which generate code or code skeletons automatically from the design captured in the central store.

Analysis and design workbenches are now available for most widely used structured methods. Chikofsky and Rubenstein (1988) suggest that productivity improvements of up to 40% may be achieved with these CASE systems. They also found that the quality of the developed systems was improved with fewer errors and inconsistencies. The developed systems were better suited to the user's real needs.

Practical difficulties which arise with analysis and design workbenches are mostly a consequence of the fact that they are usually closed environments. They incorporate their own storage management system. Some of these difficulties are:

(1) Import/export facilities are limited. Although all workbenches provide for the import and export of ASCII text representations of the design and most will provide Postscript output of diagrams, other import/export formats may not be supported. This can cause problems where data must be exchanged with other workbenches.

(2) Facilities for tailoring and adapting a design method to a particular application or class of application are limited. For example, it is not usually possible for users to override a built-in rule and replace it with their own.

(3) Workbenches may provide their own configuration management system which is incompatible with the system used in an organization. If no configuration management support is provided in the workbench, it may be difficult to export the system designs in a form which may be managed by the organization's configuration management system.

The code generators which are included in analysis and design workbenches may generate code in a language such as Ada, C or C++. As designs deliberately exclude low-level details, the code generator in a design workbench may not be able to generate the complete system. As much as possible of the code is generated automatically but some hand-coding is usually necessary to complete the generated program. Many analysis and design workbenches, such as HoodNice which supports the HOOD method (Robinson, 1992), adopt this approach.

The code generation approach means that code maintenance must be carried out by changing the design then regenerating the code. If the code is directly maintained, it is impossible to prevent the design and the code becoming inconsistent.

Some analysis and design workbenches are intended to support methods which are geared to the development of business system applications. The development platform and the application platform are the same so a database system such as Ingres or Oracle is used to implement the shared tool repository. These workbenches include most of the facilities of a 4GL programming environment so, instead of generating a conventional programming language from a design, they may generate a 4GL database language.

This programming language may be concealed behind standard forms and scripts so that no explicit programming is required. There is a seamless interface between analysis, design and implementation with no separate implementation phase in the software development process. This leads to the rapid production of applications and avoids some of the maintainability problems of 4GLs. However, the applications which are created using this approach often include redundant information. They are therefore bulky and may execute slowly. These inefficiences usually mean that this approach is unsuitable for the production of large commercial systems or transaction processing systems.

26.3 Testing workbenches

Testing is an expensive and laborious phase of the software process. As a result, testing and debugging tools were among the first software tools to be developed. These tools now offer a range of facilities and their use may significantly reduce the cost of the testing and debugging process.

Testing tends to be application and organization specific. Consequently, there is not a large market for closed testing workbenches. Rather, companies prefer to create their own testing workbenches using a combination of bought-in and locally implemented testing tools. Testing workbenches are therefore invariably open systems which evolve to suit the needs of the system being tested.

Figure 26.5 shows some tools which may be included in a testing workbench and the interactions between these tools.

The tools which might be included in a testing workbench are:

● *Test manager*   Manages the running and reporting of program tests. This involves keeping track of test data, expected results, program facilities tested and so on.

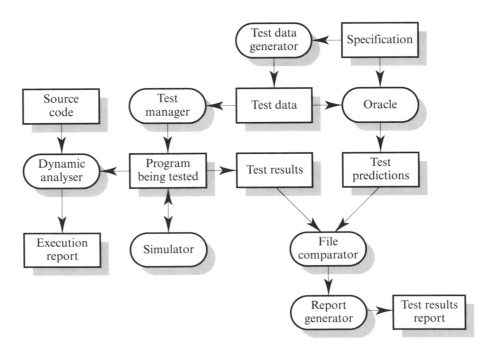

Figure 26.5
A testing workbench.

- *Test data generator*   Generates test data for the program to be tested. This may be accomplished by selecting data from a database or by using patterns to generate random data of the correct form.

- *Oracle*   Generates predictions of expected test results. Oracles may either be previous program versions or prototype systems. Back-to-back testing involves running the oracle and the program to be tested in parallel. Differences in their outputs are highlighted.

- *File comparator*   Compares the results of program tests with previous test results and reports differences between them. Comparators are particularly useful in regression testing where the results of executing old and new versions are compared. Differences in these results indicate potential problems with the new version of the system.

- *Report generator*   Provides report definition and generation facilities for test results.

- *Dynamic analyser*   Adds code to a program to count the number of times each statement has been executed. After the tests have been run, an execution profile is generated showing how often each program statement has been executed. Test cases should be designed so that all statements in the program are executed at least once. This is discussed in Chapter 23.

- *Simulator*   Different kinds of simulator may be provided. Target simulators simulate the machine on which the program is to execute. User interface simulators are script-driven programs which simulate multiple simultaneous user interactions. Using simulators for I/O means that the timing of transaction sequences is repeatable. This is particularly useful when testing real-time systems which may contain subtle timing faults.

The testing requirements for large systems depend on the application which is being developed. Consequently, testing workbenches invariably have to be adapted to suit the test plan of each system. Examples of adaptations which may be required are:

- Scripts may have to be written for user interface simulators and patterns defined for test data generators. Report formats may also have to be defined.

- Sets of expected test results may have to be prepared manually if no previous program versions are available to serve as an oracle.

- Special-purpose file comparators may have to be written which include knowledge of the structure of the test results on file.

A significant amount of effort and time is usually needed to create a comprehensive testing workbench. Complete test workbenches as shown in Figure 26.5 are therefore only used when relatively expensive systems are being developed. In this case, the overall testing costs may be up to 50% of the total development costs so testing workbench adaptation costs are usually justified.

26.4 Meta-CASE workbenches

Programming workbenches for different languages have much in common. Although they may differ in detail, they are all based on the manipulation and display of an abstract syntax tree representing the program and the program symbol table. Similar operations (for example, add and remove a node from the tree, display a node in a particular representation) must be provided for all languages.

Because of this similarity, it is possible to write a program which can generate programming workbenches for specific languages. This is similar to the notion of a 'compiler-compiler' which can generate a programming language compiler given information about the syntax and semantics of the language. The workbench generator takes information about language syntax and semantics and creates a standard workbench tailored for that language.

This possibility was recognized in the early 1980s and the first generation of these workbench generators is typified by systems such as Mentor (Donzeau-Gouge *et al.,* 1984), the Synthesizer Generator (Reps and Teitlebaum, 1984) and the Gandalf system (Habermann and Notkin, 1986). These systems include a generic environment which is driven by a set of tables representing specific programming language information. These tables are generated from a language syntax definition attributed with semantic information (Figure 26.6).

These environment generators were the first examples of what are now called meta-CASE tools. Meta-CASE tools are incorporated into workbenches which are used to create other CASE tools and workbenches.

The development of language-oriented (or, more accurately, syntax-oriented) programming workbenches is relatively straightforward as the programming language has a well-defined syntax and an 'accepted' semantics. This is not true for most diagrammatic notations used as part of design methods. Their syntax is usually defined informally. The semantics are embedded in rules and guidelines associated with the design and analysis method.

Research in the mid-1980s tackled this problem by producing a language which could be used for the description of design methods (Beer *et al.,* 1987). This language incorporated facilities for defining method types, the icons associated with

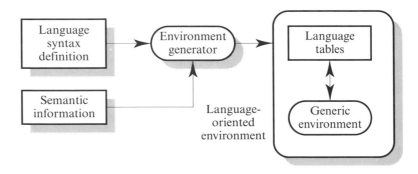

Figure 26.6
Environment
generation.

these types and the rules of the design method. In the same way as a language description can be used to generate a programming workbench, this method description language was used to generate CASE tools for design editing.

The general principle used was similar to the model illustrated in Figure 26.6. The method description was compiled to create a set of tables for a generic editing system. As methods usually incorporate a number of different graphical notations such as data-flow diagrams and structure charts, separate tables were generated for each of these notations. A single editor was used for all designs so that users were always presented with a consistent user interface. The method description tables were linked dynamically with the editor as editing operations on a particular type of diagram were required (Figure 26.7).

Figure 26.7 shows descriptions of entity-relation diagrams, data-flow diagrams and finite state machines being processed to create an editing system which can handle all of these diagram types. This approach leads to very good presentation integration since a common interface for all graphical editing operations is provided.

This model of a generic system which is tailored by defining the characteristics of a particular tool and then linking these with the generic tool is the basis of meta-CASE. As well as a diagram editing system, other tools in a meta-CASE workbench might include:

- A general-purpose repository (such as PCTE) plus schema description and editing tools.
- Tools to create structure editors for textual notations and programming languages.
- A code generator plus pattern definition tools defining how code is to be generated from particular design structures.
- A forms editor and report generator linked to the repository.

Alderson (1991) describes a meta-CASE workbench called Toolbuilder which is geared towards producing CASE tools for method support. This system is based on the fact that all design methods represent designs as attributed, directed graphs so

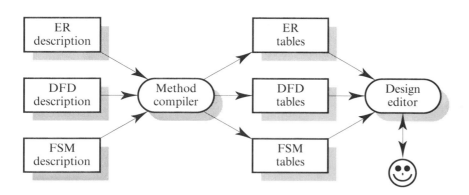

Figure 26.7
A multi-notation design editor.

generic systems for manipulating these graphs can be developed. Five different aspects of the method are specified in this approach:

(1)   A data model for data capture and output generation.

(2)   A frame model which defines the views of the data model to be generated. Each possible view of the data model is termed a frame. Links between frames which allow navigation from one representation to another are defined in this model.

(3)   Diagrammatic notions for each diagram frame.

(4)   Textual presentations for each text frame.

(5)   Report structures.

The Toolbuilder system has been used to implement a variety of different workbenches including itself. Alderson reports that prototype workbenches can be produced in a few weeks. New methods and associated CASE support can therefore be developed quickly in response to particular application needs.

Meta-CASE tools reduce the costs of generating CASE workbenches but perhaps a more significant advantage is that they address the problem of method inflexibility. Organizations may wish to tailor design methods to their own requirements but modifying supporting tools is usually impossible. However, if these tools have been produced using a meta-CASE system, then the costs of method adaptation are relatively low. The method definition is simply modified and a new workbench generated.

Further reading

'A classification of CASE technology'. As well as CASE classification, Fuggetta describes a number of different types of CASE workbench and commercial products which were available in 1993. (A. Fuggetta, *IEEE Computer*, **26** (12), December 1993.)

IEEE Software, **9** (3), May 1992. This special issue is devoted to CASE and includes a number of articles which are worth reading. The article by Forte describes a number of commercially available workbenches. Although the market has changed since this article was published, the general description of the product functionality is still relevant.

A comprehensive list of CASE tools and workbenches is accessible through the WWW at URL: http://www.qucis.queensu.ca/Software-Engineering/tools.html

KEY POINTS

■ CASE workbenches are sets of tools that are integrated in some way and which are intended to support a coherent software process activity such as design or management.

- Workbenches may be open or closed systems. Open systems are loosely integrated but it is usually possible to add new tools to them. Closed systems have tighter integration but it is difficult or impossible to extend them.

- The most widely used CASE workbenches are programming workbenches, analysis and design workbenches and testing workbenches.

- Programming workbenches may include compilers, debugging systems, static and dynamic program analysers and structured program editors.

- Analysis and design workbenches may include design editors, forms editors, code generators, report generators and a data dictionary.

- Testing workbenches may include test managers, dynamic analysers, test data generators, file comparators and different types of simulator.

- Meta-CASE workbenches are CASE tools which are used to generate other CASE tools. They are usually based on a description of the rules and notations of design or analysis methods.

EXERCISES

26.1   Using the integration classification described in Chapter 25, explain why tight tool integration in open workbenches is difficult to achieve.

26.2   Describe two types of workbench, apart from those discussed here, which might be used to support the software engineering process. Your description should include a description of the workbench tools and how these might be integrated.

26.3   Suggest how a programming workbench should be integrated with a configuration management workbench to provide control over the program development process. Describe any tools which might be required to link these systems. Using your knowledge of existing compilers, discuss integration problems which may arise.

26.4   What are the advantages and disadvantages of using workbenches which support multiple program views for system maintenance?

26.5   Using an example, explain how the design checking tools in an analysis and design workbench might use information stored in the central repository to check design consistency.

26.6   Many organizations have experienced problems in integrating analysis and design workbenches with their organizational software process. Suggest two reasons why problems might arise and write associated advice for CASE adopters discussing how these problems might be anticipated.

26.7 Giving reasons for your answer, explain why it is not necessary for programming and testing workbenches to be tightly integrated.

26.8 Explain how meta-CASE workbenches may contribute to the development of new analysis and design methods. Suggest limitations which they might have in this respect.

26.9 A friend wishes to invest money in a small company specializing in meta-CASE tools. Assuming the company is well managed, what investment advice would you give? You should take into account the risks and benefits of this technology.

27

Software Engineering Environments

Objectives

- To define software engineering environments and the basic support infrastructure which these environments provide.

- To discuss the advantages and disadvantages of software engineering environments.

- To describe an architectural reference model for software engineering environments and the services associated with the reference model.

- To introduce PCTE, a proposed framework standard for software engineering environments.

Contents

545

CASE workbenches, as described in Chapter 26, are 'islands of automation' in which different phases of the software process are supported in different ways. Each workbench manages its own data so it may be difficult to provide consistent configuration management across all software process outputs. Reusing information generated in one workbench in a different workbench may be difficult or impossible.

A software engineering environment (SEE) is intended to address these difficulties and provide support for all or most software process activities. The notion of such an environment was first given wide publicity by Buxton (1980) who, with US Defense Department support, proposed a set of requirements for an Ada Programming Support Environment (APSE). Buxton proposed a model of the APSE as shown in Figure 27.1.

Buxton realized that it was unlikely that a complete APSE could be built in 1980 and suggested an incremental approach to environment development based on three levels of functionality:

(1) A kernel APSE which extended an operating system with infrastructure support for the environment. Infrastructure support for environments is discussed in Section 27.3. It was suggested that this kernel APSE should be standardized and should have a public tool interface. Different environment products could therefore be built on top of the same kernel.

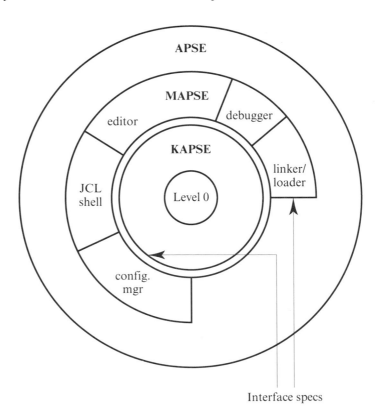

Figure 27.1
The organization of an APSE.

(2)   A minimal APSE which was basically a programming workbench. Given the available hardware platforms in 1980 (timesharing systems with text-only terminals), this was probably all that could realistically be provided when the APSE proposals were made.

(3)   A complete software engineering environment which could be developed incrementally. As tools to support other process activities became available, they could be added to the minimal APSE to extend its capabilities.

These proposals were very far-sighted and have been tremendously influential in the software engineering community. The notion of a standardized kernel led to various activities such as CAIS (Oberndorf, 1988) and PCTE, as discussed later in this chapter. Many government organizations and large companies started research programmes in the mid-1980s to develop APSEs or more general software engineering environments (Boehm *et al.*, 1984; Taylor *et al.*, 1988; Bott, 1989). The general view in the software engineering community was that software engineering environments would provide very significant improvements in software productivity and quality.

Unfortunately, these hopes have not been realized and expectations have now been scaled down. Most of these research prototype environments were not developed into commercial CASE products. There are both technical and non-technical reasons for this:

- It was much more difficult to define and implement a standard environment kernel than was originally anticipated. Without a standardized and efficiently implemented kernel, tool vendors were unwilling to devote effort to tool production for software engineering environments.

- The graphical facilities offered by low-cost personal computers encouraged the development of analysis and design workbenches for specific methods such as structured analysis. The vendors of these systems wanted to bring their products to market quickly rather than wait for standards to be developed. They therefore did not create a demand for a standard environment kernel.

- Data integration requirements were not well understood so defining the database requirements for an environment was difficult.

- The proposals for environments were made at the same time as a remarkable increase in the rate of evolution of hardware technology. Personal computers and graphical workstations started to supplant time-sharing systems and text-only terminals. Because of the fast rate of technological change, it was impossible to develop standards for user interface technology and human–computer interaction. This meant that tools from different vendors could not be integrated at the presentation level.

- Experience with CASE tools for PCs showed that the potential productivity improvements were less than originally anticipated by both vendors and users. The prediction of orders of magnitude productivity improvement from

SEEs were clearly over-estimates. Potential environment buyers postponed plans to introduce an SEE until their CASE requirements were better understood.

● The geopolitical changes in the late 1980s which culminated in the collapse of the communist bloc and the dissolution of the Soviet Union led to large-scale defence cuts in the US and in Europe. As defence contractors were probably the principal market for SEEs and defence agencies the principal funders of research, this resulted in a significant decline in community interest in software engineering environments.

Nevertheless, there remains a need for integrated support for the development of large, long-lifetime systems. Efforts to develop integrated environments are continuing but it is now accepted that these will mostly be used for large systems engineering projects. They are unlikely to be cost-effective for small or medium-sized systems development.

These environments will be based around a standard framework. Depending on the use made of the environment, different tools will be integrated with this framework as required. I therefore focus on the framework for software engineering environments in the rest of this chapter.

27.1 Integrated environments

The term 'environment' is used to describe a vast range of support systems ranging from simple systems that support program development in a single language to very large systems offering support for multiple projects using many different languages and design methods. As discussed in Chapter 25, I use the term to describe CASE systems which support all (or a large number of) software process activities.

More specifically, a software engineering environment can be defined as follows:

> A software engineering environment (SEE) is a set of hardware and software tools which can act in combination in an integrated way to provide support for the whole of the software process from initial specification through to testing and system delivery.

The key characteristics of an SEE which distinguish it from CASE workbenches are:

(1)   The environment facilities are integrated. Ideally, the environment should support all five levels of integration identified in Chapter 25. These are platform integration, data integration, presentation integration, control integration and process integration.

(2)   The environment assumes team-based rather than individual development and provides configuration management support for all activities. The management of multiple versions of system documents and code and their dependencies is a particularly expensive activity for large long-lifetime systems.

(3)   Facilities are available to support a wide range of software development activities. Thus, the SEE might include workbenches which support specification, design, documentation, programming, testing, debugging and so on.

The general definition of a software engineering environment is relatively simple but, of course, this simple definition hides an immense amount of complexity. Software processes are extremely complex so an environment to support the whole software process is a large and complex software system.

SEEs usually support integration by providing a shared repository of project information. All tools are interfaced to this repository and exchange information through it. Outputs of one tool can become the inputs to another. Although most tool interactions are predictable, there are many cases of serendipitous tool combinations. The repository allows these combinations to occur when required. This addresses a major problem with CASE workbenches, namely the problem of exchanging information with other tools. Project management can access project information and management tools can use product data collected during the course of a project.

Configuration management costs are reduced in SEEs because all project documents are stored in one place and links between these documents may be automatically managed. Configuration management may be extended to entities such as individual variable declarations if the environment repository supports fine-grain objects. This simplifies the development of traceability tools which help discover dependencies when changes have to be made.

To provide the support required for different projects, software engineering environments must accommodate a range of CASE tools and workbenches. It must be possible to add new facilities as required. This means that an SEE may be considered as a set of services which are used by facilities which provide end-user support. Services may be provided by the platform on which the SEE is executing or by an environment framework. This three-layer model is illustrated in Figure 27.2.

In this model, an SEE consists of a set of CASE workbenches which are integrated using environment services. These services may be provided either by the platform on which the environment is running or by an environment framework. Framework services are analogous to the environment kernel introduced above in the discussion of the APSE.

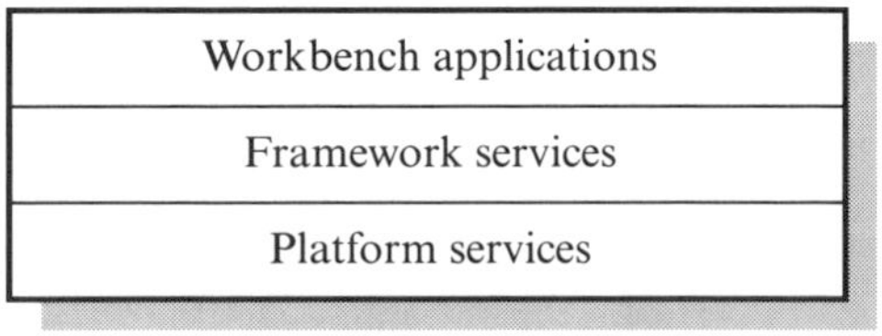

Figure 27.2
Layered model of a software engineering environment.

Brown *et al.* (1992) point out that there are many different perspectives on this software engineering environment model, depending on the role of the environment user. Some of the most important of these perspectives are:

(1)   Developers of application software see the environment as a set of workbenches supporting the software process. Their principal focus is on the upper layer in Figure 27.2. The workbenches available may include those discussed in Chapter 26 but the particular environment configuration depends on the organization using the environment and the type of software which is being developed.

(2)   SEE integrators see the environment as a set of common services and tools which must be integrated in a particular context to create an effective support environment. Their principal focus is on the boundary between the workbench and the framework layer in Figure 27.2.

(3)   Tool or workbench developers see the environment as a set of common services which may be used to integrate their tool with other tools in the environment. Their principal focus is on the middle layer in Figure 27.2. As they do not know which other tools will be part of the environment, they are not concerned with the workbench application layer in Figure 27.2.

(4)   Framework developers see the environment as a set of services which must be implemented on some host computer system. They are concerned with using the facilities of that machine to provide an efficient service implementation. Their focus is on the interface between the middle and the lowest layer in Figure 27.2.

Clearly, the services provided by an environment to support tool implementation and integration are critical. I therefore concentrate here on describing the service layers in Figure 27.2. The top layer in Figure 27.2, namely workbench applications, has already been covered in Chapter 26.

27.2 Platform services

The platform on which an SEE runs is called its host system. In some cases, the software developed using the SEE will run on the same platform but, in many cases, the developed software will be delivered for some target system which may have a completely different architecture and operating system. Figure 27.3 illustrates this host–target development where the developed software is to be delivered on different target machines.

Host–target development is necessary for the following reasons:

(1)   In some cases, the application software under development may be for a machine with no software development facilities. This is most likely in the

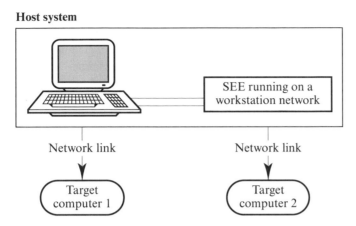

Host system

SEE running on a
workstation network

Network link   Network link

Target
computer 1

Target
computer 2

Figure 27.3
Host–target
development.

case of real-time systems for special-purpose computers. These computers
may not even have an operating system but only a simple real-time executive.

(2)   The target machine may be application-oriented (a vector processor, say) and
not well suited to supporting software engineering environments.

(3)   The target machine may be in use and dedicated to running a particular
application (such as a transaction processing system) and this must be given
priority over software development.

It is generally assumed that the platform which hosts software engineering
environments will consist of a number of workstations connected by a high-speed
local or wide area network. This platform will offer a range of services such as:

● *File services* which provide facilities for files to be named, created, stored,
deleted and organized into a directory structure. Files will normally be stored
on one or more file servers which are accessible to all machines on the
network.

● *Process management services* which are used to create, start, stop and
suspend processes running on computers in the network.

● *Network services* which are used to move processes and their associated data
from one computer to another on the network.

● *Communication services* which are used to communicate with other computers in the organization and elsewhere. If target machines are connected to the
network, this service must support program downloading to these machines.

● *Window management services* which allow windows on the user's display to
be created, moved, deleted, re-sized and so on.

● *Print services* which allow information from the environment to be printed on
paper or on some other permanent medium such as CD-ROM or microfiche.

In general, the environment platform will consist of a heterogeneous range of
distributed computers. This may include workstations of different types (for

example, Unix workstations and PCs), Unix workstations from the same manufacturer running different operating system versions (for example, Solaris 2.1 and Solaris 2.4) and Unix workstations from different manufacturers.

This heterogeneity is inevitable in large organizations with many different computers. New workstations often only run the most recent version of the operating system. These have to run alongside existing systems which run older versions of the operating system. Therefore, different versions of the same operating system must run concurrently on the same network. Furthermore, different parts of an organization may have different computing needs so buy different types of machine (for example, graphics workstations). They obviously wish to use these to run the SEE rather than buy other computers specifically for software development.

27.3 Framework services

Framework services in an SEE extend the set of services provided by the environment host and are usually implemented using these platform services. They are specifically designed to support the operation of CASE tools or workbenches which are integrated in some way.

The best way to understand these framework services is in the context of a reference model of a software engineering environment architecture. Recall that architectural reference models (introduced in Chapter 13) are abstractions which provide a basis for comparing different architectures. The reference model for software engineering environments was originally developed by the European Computer Manufacturers Association (ECMA). It has now also been adopted by the US National Institute of Standards and Technology (NIST). The 'official' model is described in a NIST/ECMA report (ECMA, 1991) but a more accessible description of the model is given by Brown *et al.* (1992), who also compare various environment framework proposals using this model.

The structure of the model (which has become known as the 'toaster' model) is shown in Figure 27.4. In essence, the reference model identifies five sets of services which an environment should provide. It should also provide 'plug-in' facilities for tools and workbenches which use these services. Thus, environments can be configured with different tools and workbenches depending on the software process used and the type of software which is to be developed.

The services which might be provided by an SEE support the different forms of integration introduced in Chapter 25. They can be discussed under five headings:

(1) *Data repository services* These provide facilities for the storage and management of data items and their relationships.

(2) *Data integration services* These provide facilities for managing groups or configurations of data items. They support the naming of configurations and the establishment of relationships between them. These services and data repository services are the basis of data integration in the environment.

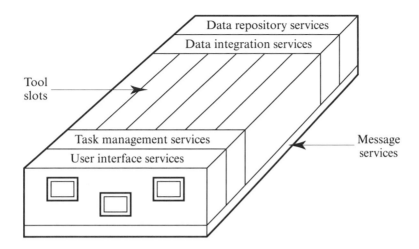

Figure 27.4
A reference model for
an SEE.

(3) *Task management services* These provide facilities for the definition and enactment of process models. They support process integration.

(4) *Message services* These provide facilities for tool–tool, environment–tool and environment–environment communications. They support control integration.

(5) *User interface services* These provide facilities for user interface development. They support presentation integration.

27.3.1 Data repository services

The data repository services provide a basic set of facilities for naming and managing entities and establishing relationships between these entities. The data repository services identified in the reference model are described in Figure 27.5.

These data repository services are often provided by a system known as an object management system (OMS). Most object management systems which have been implemented are based on an entity-relation model with built-in entity and relationship types reflecting the needs of the software process.

Figure 27.6 illustrates how entities representing procedures or functions may be linked in an OMS. This diagram assumes that the environment uses an entity-relation model of data. Entities, attributes and relationships are typed and this type information is used by SEE tools.

This example models a situation where there are four routines A, B, C and D written in different programming languages. Each of these has various attributes such as the development language used, the creator, its status and the library where it is stored. For the purposes of the diagram, I have not shown all attributes for all objects.

The model shows that Procedure A calls Function B. Both are written in Pascal and B is optimized in some way. Procedure C, which is written in Ada,

Service	Description
Data storage	Provides support for creating, reading, updating and deleting entities where entities are named, have a set of attributes and may participate in relationships.
Relationship	Provides support for defining and managing relationships between environment entities.
Name	Provides support for entity naming. Entities also have a unique identifier which is assigned by the repository services.
Location	Provides support for the distribution of entities over a network of workstations so has associated operations such as move, copy, replicate and so on.
Data transaction	Provides support for atomic transactions which allow database recovery in the event of a failure.
Concurrency	Provides support for multiple simultaneous transactions.
Process support	Provides process operations such as start, stop, suspend and so on.
Archive	Provides support for the off-line storage and recovery of entities.
Backup	Provides support for recovery of data in the event of system failure.

Figure 27.5
Data repository
services.

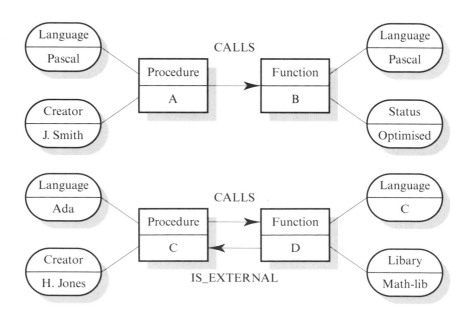

Figure 27.6
Typed entities,
attributes and
relationships in an
OMS.

calls Function D. This is an external function, written in C, which is held in a library called Math-lib. Tools can be provided which navigate this structure and allow engineers to view the information about the system. The attributes can be used to ensure that the correct versions of tools such as compilers are used for processing.

The granularity of an object management system or database is the minimum size of entity which may be efficiently stored and manipulated. If the smallest size of entity which can be efficiently manipulated is a file, the types of relation which can be managed allow documents to be linked. However, relationships between entities within these documents cannot be established. By contrast, if fine-grain entities only a few bytes long can be managed then a richer set of relationships can be used. For example, the OMS can record links between the variable declarations in a program and their use.

Fine-grain systems require many more database accesses than coarse-grain systems when data is to be retrieved. This means that the performance of these systems is often significantly worse than coarse-grain systems. Consequently, most proposals for data repositories have recommended that they should be used for coarse-grain rather than fine-grain data management.

27.3.2 Data integration services

The set of data integration services provided in a framework extends the basic data repository services. While the data repository operations are general-purpose, the operations associated with the data integration services are explicitly intended to support software development. The data integration services proposed in the SEE reference model are described in Figure 27.7.

Service	Description
Version	Provides support for the management of multiple versions of entities.
Configuration	Provides support for entity grouping into named configurations and managed as a composite entity.
Query	Provides access and update services to versions.
Meta-data	Provides facilities for schema definition and management.
State monitoring	Provides triggering facilities which allow particular operations to be initiated when a particular database state is reached.
Sub-environment	Provides support for the definition and management of subsets of the data and operations in the environment and to consider them as a separate, named environment.
Data interchange	Provides mechanisms to import and export data from the environment.

Figure 27.7
Data integration
services.

I suggested in the definition of an SEE at the beginning of this chapter that the provision of integrated configuration management is an essential feature. While file-based configuration management workbenches are widely used, they suffer from the disadvantage that the entities managed can only be loosely linked through data incorporated in the workbench. By providing configuration support as a service, all repository items can be linked. Versions and version sets can be created and managed, changes tracked and traceability relationships established between environment entities.

The meta-data services and the sub-environment services allow local environments with their own data and relationship types to be created. Meta-data means data about data so meta-data services provide a mechanism to define new entity and relationship types and to query the types which have been defined. The sub-environment services allow the environment data to be partitioned. Sub-projects can have their own environment. They may therefore be isolated from other projects going on at the same time.

The state monitoring services are provided so that changes in database state can initiate particular actions. For example, when a new version of an entity is created, this might trigger an operation which automatically informs all users of that entity that the new version is available. Finally, the data interchange services address the problems discussed in Chapter 26. They recognize that some tools will maintain their own repositories and they allow information to be transferred into and out of these local stores.

27.3.3 Task management services

Task management services are those services which provide support for process integration in the environment. The defined reference model services are shown in Figure 27.8. In this context, the term 'task' means an atomic unit of activity in some process. In the discussion of process modelling in Chapter 31, I use the term 'activity' rather than 'task'.

In essence, the task management services provide operations to define and enact (execute) process models. These models include entities such as activities, roles, deliverables and so on. These process models must be enacted to provide active support for the development process. It must be possible to assign activities to roles and to trigger activities when some event (such as the commencement of a task) occurs. They should allow activity history to be recorded and for records to be maintained of resource usage and so on.

The task management services in the reference model are perhaps the least well-defined services. We have little practical experience of process integration and it is therefore very difficult to specify, in any detail, what these services should do. In their comparison of several framework proposals against the reference model, Brown *et al.* (1992) noted that this area was not well supported by any of these systems.

Service	Description
Task definition	Provides facilities for task definition including pre- and post-conditions, inputs and outputs, resources required and the roles involved in the task.
Task execution	Provides facilities for supporting the execution of tasks. This may involve specifying task interactions in a process programming language.
Task transaction	Provides support for transactions which involve one or more task executions over a considerable period of time. Recovery from failure should be possible without rolling back the system to its state before the task started.
Task history	Provides facilities to record task executions and to query previous executions.
Event monitoring	Supports the definition of events or triggers which cause some task to be executed.
Audit and accounting	Provides a record of what has been done and what resources have been used in the environment.
Role management	Provides facilities to define and manage roles in the environment.

Figure 27.8
Task management
services.

27.3.4 Message services

Message services allow tools and framework services to communicate. There are only two message services defined in the SEE reference model:

(1) *Message delivery*   This service provides support for tool–tool, service–service, tool–service and framework–framework message passing. It may allow for point-to-point (that is, direct) message exchange, broadcast messages where the message is sent to all tools and services and multicast messages where some agent identifies which tools or services should receive the message. Associated operations include send, receive, acknowledge and so on. This corresponds to the message server discussed in Chapter 25.

(2) *Tool registration*   This service allows a tool or service to register with the message services as the recipient of certain types of message.

This relatively simple model has been implemented in a number of commercial products such as Hewlett-Packard's SoftBench. As discussed in Chapter 25, it provides control integration over a distributed network. A tool or service can register an interest in certain types of message with some central agent. When another tool or service wishes to communicate, it sends the message to the message delivery service. This locates potential receivers of the message on the network and passes the message to them.

27.3.5 User interface services

The user interface services in the SEE reference model are intended to support presentation integration. The developers of the SEE reference model have not proposed a new set of user interface services but propose that the user interface services should be based on the OSF's layered user interface model (Figure 27.9) which was developed from early work on X-windows (Scheifler and Gettys, 1986).

The first two levels of this reference model provide basic physical support including screen and input device handlers and a set of basic graphical primitives (X-lib). The next two levels build on these primitives to provide a set of interface objects which may be used at the presentation level to create user interfaces. The Motif toolkit has emerged as a *de facto* standard for this level. These lower-level services are, in my view, platform rather than framework services.

Above this level, the definition of the support which might be provided is vague. The presentation level provides support for arranging the toolkit elements into application interfaces. It might include tools such as form design tools, user interface layout tools (Colebourne *et al.,* 1993) and so on. The dialogue level provides support for synchronizing interface operations so might include user interface management systems (UIMS) and dialogue specification languages (Myers, 1988). Finally, the application level is concerned with the communications between the application and the user interface.

Unlike the other levels in the reference model, the description of the user interface services do not really provide a basis for comparing and assessing framework proposals. It is assumed in the reference model that all frameworks will support X/Motif (OSF, 1993) and some supporting tools. However, this assumption may not be true.

The designers of the SEE reference model appear to have assumed that most SEEs will run on workstations running Unix or some comparable operating system. Personal computers, running different operating systems, are now powerful enough to act as nodes in a networked environment. These may run some alternative window management system, such as MS Windows. They do not, therefore, conform to the SEE reference model.

Figure 27.9
The user interface
reference model.

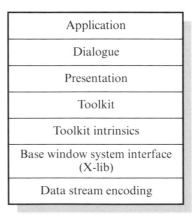

| Application |
| Dialogue |
| Presentation |
| Toolkit |
| Toolkit intrinsics |
| Base window system interface (X-lib) |
| Data stream encoding |

27.3.6 Tools

The environment framework exists to provide a set of common services for tool implementation. However, these services will not necessarily be used by all tools. Some tools will provide comparable services themselves and it should be possible to integrate them into the environment. The environment should therefore provide facilities for integrating tools at the platform as well as at the framework level.

There are three levels of tool integration with the services provided by software engineering environments as shown in Figure 27.10.

(1) *Integrated tools*   These are tools which manage all of their data using framework services and implement their data structures in the object management system.

(2) *Semi-detached tools*   These are less tightly integrated with the framework services. They manage their own data structures but the files containing the data structures are managed using the framework services. Therefore, OMS links can be established between files but not between the contents of these files.

(3) *Foreign tools*   These are tools that run on the same machine as the SEE but which use only the platform services. They manage their own data but may transfer data to and from the SEE using the data interchange services.

It is relatively easy to migrate existing tools to software engineering environments as foreign tools and semi-detached tools if they run on the same platform as the environment. However, the problem of tightly integrating tools with framework services is a 'chicken and egg' problem.

The full power of an environment can only be realized when a significant proportion of tools have been implemented as integrated tools. Once this has happened, the market for SEEs will expand significantly. However, tool vendors are reluctant to develop SEE-integrated tools until there is a significant market (which currently does not exist). To have a good integrated toolset, there needs to be a market for SEEs; for such a market to develop, there needs to be an integrated toolset! It remains to be seen how this problem will be solved.

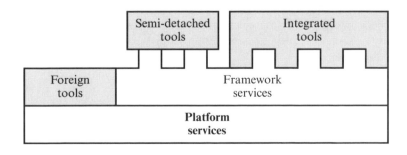

Figure 27.10
Tool integration with a software engineering environment.

27.4 PCTE

The development of a common set of framework services derived from the Stoneman proposals for an APSE. In both the US and Europe, a number of research projects were established to define a common tool interface. In the US, these efforts were driven by the DoD and the focus was on the development of a kernel-APSE for an Ada environment. This led to the development of the Common APSE Interface Set or CAIS (Munck *et al.*, 1988; Oberndorf, 1988). This was originally intended as a standard but there was little commercial interest in this.

At the same time as the US CAIS work, the European Commission funded a multi-national project under the ESPRIT research programme to define a comparable public tool interface. This was called PCTE (portable common tool environment) and the first version of the PCTE was published in 1984 (Campbell, 1986). By contrast with the CAIS standard which was Ada-oriented, the PCTE standard was Unix and C-oriented. It was intended for general-purpose rather than language-oriented environment support.

PCTE had a number of technical deficiencies (for instance, it lacked support for security and access control) and was very closely tied to Unix as a platform. To resolve these, further projects were set up including a defence-funded project to develop PCTE+ (Boudier *et al.*, 1988; Tedd, 1989) and a project funded by the European Computer Manufacturers Association (ECMA). This ECMA PCTE has now superseded these earlier versions and has been accepted as a standard (Dawes and Davis, 1991; Wakeman and Jowett, 1993).

There is a significant overlap between the PCTE and the CAIS proposals and a project was established to integrate these to develop what was called PCIS (Portable Common Interface Standard). The first version of the PCIS framework definition was published in early 1994. At the time of writing, it is currently being prototyped.

However, ECMA PCTE has been widely accepted in both Europe and the US. A number of manufacturers such as Digital and IBM have developed implementations of this standard. PCTE has been accepted as part of a very large integrated-CASE project, sponsored by the US Department of Defense. The existence of PCTE and the development of implementations and tools may mean that PCIS never really gets off the ground. PCTE will probably become the *de facto* standard for SEE frameworks.

Object management in PCTE is based on an entity-relationship-attribute (ERA) model where objects may participate in relationships with other objects and may have associated attributes. PCTE provides support for objects and links between these objects.

Objects are typed and user-defined sub-typing is supported. For example, from a basic type TEXT, it is possible to derive subtypes such as C-SOURCE-TEXT. This typing allows tools to check that the objects which they manipulate are the correct type and thus reduces the scope for error. Typed links are used to establish relationships between objects. Types are defined in a *schema definition set*

(SDS) and any program running in PCTE has an associated working schema which is made up of one or more SDSs.

To provide data recovery and resilience, transactions are supported. A transaction is an atomic set of actions whose effect on data is to apply either all or none of these actions. If a failure occurs during the transaction, it is possible to restore the database to a consistent state. Facilities for execution management and inter-process communication are provided. These allow processes to be started, terminated and controlled. Processes may be stored in the OMS so the OMS query facilities can be used to discover process information. The framework is intended to run on a network of workstations so process and data distribution is supported.

Brown *et al.* (1992) describe ECMA PCTE and evaluate it using the framework reference model introduced in Section 27.3. Figure 27.11 summarizes the results of their evaluation.

PCTE incorporates a sophisticated security model (not covered in the reference model) controlling access to objects in the OMS. Various security levels, such as confidential, secret and so on, are provided thus making the framework potentially suitable for military applications.

The comparison in Figure 27.11 shows that ECMA PCTE provides a reasonably complete set of low-level framework services but must be extended considerably to address all of the areas covered by the SEE reference model. This can be achieved by implementing other services alongside or on top of PCTE. For example, in the US DoD proposal for environment framework services, PCTE will be used to provide data repository and data integration services. Control services will be provided by some separate system such as Hewlett-Packard's SoftBench, user interface services by X/Motif and task management services by Process Weaver (Fernström, 1993).

Services	Description
Data repository	All data repository services are provided by ECMA PCTE with the exception of a backup service.
Data integration	Provides all data integration services apart from a general query service. Some services such as state monitoring and data interchange services are more limited than those proposed in the reference model.
Task management	No task management services are provided apart from auditing and accounting services.
Message	Provides a service for message delivery but no tool registration service.
User interface	It is assumed that PCTE-based environments will use X-windows for implementing their user interface. No specific library is mandated.

Figure 27.11
A comparison of PCTE and the SEE framework reference model.

Further reading

Software Engineering Environments. This book includes an excellent description of the SEE reference model and comparisons of various frameworks, including ECMA PCTE, against this reference model. The authors present a realistic picture of the problems of developing and introducing SEEs. (A. W. Brown, A. N. Earl and J. McDermid, McGraw-Hill, 1992.)

'PCTE interfaces: Supporting tools in software engineering environments'. Although this article discusses an early version of the system, the basic concepts of PCTE have not changed. The article is a good introduction to PCTE and its use as a basis for an SEE called PACT. (*IEEE Software*, **6** (6), December 1989.)

IEEE Software, **9** (2), March 1992. This special issue covers integrated CASE. It includes several articles on software engineering environments.

'Tools that bind: Creating integrated environments'. A brief but well-described introduction to integrated environments. This paper also includes a description of a number of commercial CASE products. (D. Sharon and R. Bell, *IEEE Software*, **12** (2), March 1995.)

KEY POINTS

- A software engineering environment provides support for a wide range of software process activities. This distinguishes it from other CASE systems which provide less comprehensive support.

- SEEs should support the five levels of tool and workbench integration (platform, data, presentation, control and process) described in Chapter 25.

- Software engineering environments are generally designed to operate on a network of host workstations and to deliver software for some target platform.

- The services which may be provided by an SEE platform (host computer and operating system) include file services, process management services, network services, communication services, window management services and printing services.

- The SEE reference model includes a description of environment framework services. These include data repository services, data integration services, task management services, message services and user interface services.

- Tools which are provided as part of an SEE may be foreign tools (integrated through platform services), semi-detached tools (integrated through coarse-grain environment objects) or integrated tools (integrated though fine-grain environment objects).

- ECMA PCTE has been widely accepted as a potential framework for software engineering environments. It supports many of the framework services defined in the SEE reference model.

EXERCISES

27.1 What are the principal advantages and disadvantages of introducing a software engineering environment to support the development of large systems?

27.2 Suggest three software tools which should be included in an SEE to support host–target development.

27.3 Explain how the platform services discussed in Section 27.2 are provided on Unix workstations.

27.4 Suggest entity and relation types which might be defined in a data repository to support object-oriented or function-oriented design.

27.5 What entity types, attributes and relations are required for configuration management support in an SEE (see Chapter 33)?

27.6 Explain why it is difficult to define the task management services in an environment framework.

27.7 Survey the tool availability in your local development environment and produce a table showing what software process activities are supported.

27.8 How could existing CASE workbenches be integrated with a software engineering environment? What problems are likely to arise?

27.9 What are the barriers to the acceptance of PCTE as a standard framework for software engineering environments?

27.10 Some governments favour the use of software from national suppliers for publicly funded contracts. This has, perhaps, affected the acceptance of PCTE which is perceived as a European product. Discuss the rights and wrongs of this position.

Part Seven
Management

This part of the book extends the introduction of management given in Chapter 3. Chapter 28 is concerned with the management of the people involved in the software process. Chapter 29 describes software cost and schedule estimation. Chapters 30 and 31 are concerned with quality management and quality improvement. Chapter 30 includes an extensive discussion of software metrics and Chapter 31 discusses process maturity and improvement models.

Contents

28

Managing People

Objectives

- To emphasize the importance of people in the software engineering process.

- To describe basic cognitive factors such as the structure of human memory which influence the performance of software engineers.

- To discuss factors which managers might consider when choosing staff for a software project.

- To describe factors which affect group working and group organization for software development.

- To explain why the working environment of software engineers affects their productivity.

Contents

The people working in a software organization are its greatest assets. They represent intellectual capital and it is up to software managers to ensure that the organization gets the best possible return on its investment in people. In successful companies and economies, this is achieved when people are respected by the organization. They should have a level of responsibility and reward that is commensurate with their skills.

Effective management is therefore about managing the people in an organization. Project managers have to solve technical and non-technical problems by using the people in their team in the most effective way possible. They have to motivate people, plan and organize their work and ensure that the work is being done properly. Some of these responsibilities have been covered in Chapter 3. Others will be covered in this chapter and other chapters in this section of the book.

The chapter does not present any particular management theory or approach. Rather, I base my discussion of management on cognitive and social factors. Software engineering is a cognitive and social activity so these factors are important in developing an understanding of how people write software. If managers have some understanding of these fundamentals, they can do a better job of getting the best from the people who work for them.

28.1 Cognitive fundamentals

There is great diversity in individual abilities reflecting differences in intelligence, education and experience but all of us seem to be subject to some basic constraints on our thinking. These are a consequence of the way in which information is stored and modelled in our brains. An awareness of this model can help you understand some fundamental cognitive limitations which affect software engineering.

28.1.1 Memory organization

Software systems are abstract entities and engineers must remember their characteristics during the development process. For example, programmers must understand and remember the relationship between a source code listing and the dynamic behaviour of the program. They apply this stored knowledge in further program development.

The retention of information in the memory depends on the memory structure. This seems to be hierarchical with three distinct, connected areas (Figure 28.1):

(1)   *A limited capacity, fast-access, short-term memory*   Input from the senses is received here for initial processing. This memory is comparable with registers in a computer; it is used for information processing and not information storage.

(2)   *A larger capacity, working memory area*   This memory area has a longer access time than short-term memory. It is used for information processing but can retain information for longer periods than short-term memory. It is not

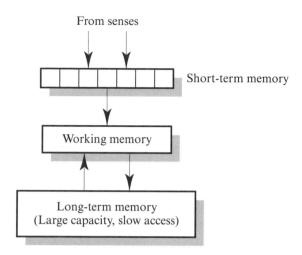

Figure 28.1
Human memory
organization.

used for long-term information retention. By analogy with the computer, this is like RAM where information is maintained for the duration of a computation.

(3)   *Long-term memory*   This has a large capacity, relatively slow access time and unreliable retrieval mechanisms (we forget things). Long-term memory is used for the 'permanent' storage of information. To continue the analogy, long-term memory is like disk memory on a computer.

Problem information is input to the short-term memory from reading documents and talking to people. It is integrated with existing, relevant information from long-term memory in working memory. The result of this integration forms the basis for problem solutions. These are stored in long-term memory for future use. Of course, the solution may be incorrect so, in future, the long-term memory must be modified. However, incorrect information is not completely discarded but is retained in some form. We know this because we learn from our mistakes.

The limited size of short-term memory constrains our cognitive processes. In a classic experiment, Miller (1957) found that the short-term memory can store about seven quanta of information. A quantum of information is not a fixed size but is rather a coherent information entity. It may be a telephone number, the function of a procedure or a street name. Miller also describes the process of 'chunking' where information quanta are collected together into chunks.

If a problem involves the input of more information than the short-term memory can handle, there has to be information processing and transfer during the input process. This can result in information being lost. Errors arise because this information processing cannot keep up with the memory input.

This is a particular problem when new information is being processed. For example, if people are shown pictures of common animals, they can usually process them quickly. Most people learn to recognize these animals when they are children. On the other hand, it takes people much longer to recognize unfamiliar things. This is particularly difficult when these are abstract concepts, related to an unfamiliar application, and encoded in a programming language.

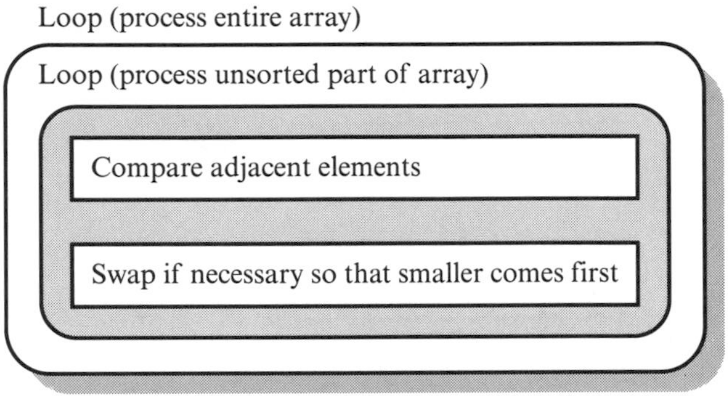

Loop (process entire array)

Loop (process unsorted part of array)

Compare adjacent elements

Swap if necessary so that smaller comes first

Figure 28.2
Cognitive 'chunks' in a
bubblesort program.

Shneiderman (1980) conjectures that an information chunking process is used in understanding programs. Program readers abstract the information in the program into chunks which are built into an internal semantic structure. Programs are not understood on a statement by statement basis unless a statement represents a logical chunk. Figure 28.2 shows how a simple bubblesort program might be 'chunked' by a reader.

Once the internal semantic structure representing the program has been established, this knowledge is transferred to long-term memory. If it is regularly used, it is not usually forgotten. It can be reproduced in different notations without much difficulty.

For example, consider the binary search algorithm where an ordered collection is searched for a particular item. This involves examining the mid-point of the collection and using knowledge of the ordering relationship to check if the key item is in the upper or the lower part of the collection. A programmer who understands this algorithm can easily produce a version in C, Ada or other programming language. The information is retained in some abstract form that can be translated into any appropriate concrete syntax.

28.1.2 Knowledge modelling

Information enters short-term memory and is processed before being stored in long-term memory. We don't store raw information but store information abstractions which we call *knowledge*. Neural information processing involves the integration of new and existing information to create knowledge.

The knowledge acquired during software development and stored in long-term memory falls into two classes:

(1) *Semantic knowledge* This is the knowledge of concepts such as the operation of an assignment statement, the notion of a linked list, how a hash search technique operates and how organizations are structured. This knowledge is acquired through experience and learning and is retained in a representation independent fashion.

(2)   *Syntactic knowledge*   This is detailed representation knowledge such as how
       to write a function declaration in C, what standard functions are available in
       a programming language, whether an assignment is written using an '=' or a
       ':=' sign, and so on. This knowledge seems to be retained in an unprocessed
       form.

This knowledge organization is illustrated in Figure 28.3, adapted from
Shneiderman's book on user interface design (Shneiderman, 1992).
       Semantic knowledge is acquired by experience and through active learning.
New information is consciously integrated with existing semantic structures.
Syntactic knowledge, on the other hand, seems to be acquired by memorization.
New syntactic knowledge is not immediately integrated with existing knowledge but
may interfere with it. It is more easily forgotten than deeper semantic knowledge.
       The different acquisition modes for syntactic and semantic knowledge help
explain how experienced programmers learn a new programming language.
Normally, they have no difficulty understanding language concepts such as assignments, loops, conditional statements and so on. The language syntax, however, tends
to get mixed up with the syntax of familiar languages. An Ada programmer learning
C++ might write the assignment operator as ':=' rather than '='; a Pascal programmer learning Ada might write 'type x =...' rather than 'type x is ...' , and so on.
       As an understanding of a concept develops, it is stored in memory as seman-
tic knowledge. Semantic knowledge appears to be stored in an abstract conceptual
form. The concept details can be regenerated in a number of different concrete
representations (Soloway *et al.,* 1982; Card *et al.,* 1983).
       Problem solving requires task and computer concepts to be integrated.
Organizational factors such as the need to complete a solution within budget also
need to be considered. Thus, a user may be expert in the task concepts, a software
designer an expert in the computer concepts and a manager an expert in the organization factors. During the software engineering process, all of this expertise may
have to be used and integrated.

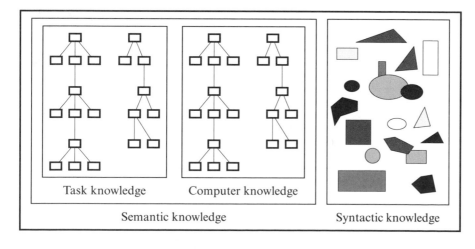

Task knowledge   Computer knowledge

Semantic knowledge   Syntactic knowledge

Figure 28.3
Syntactic and semantic
knowledge.

The model explains why, for many people, learning to program is a skill which seems to arrive all at once, after a period of difficulties. Programming skills require an understanding of the semantic concepts and a separation of semantic and syntactic concepts. Instructors sometimes have difficulties understanding student problems. They have successfully understood and processed the semantic information so only have to consider syntactic information. They may therefore find it hard to explain the semantic concepts in ways that novice programmers can understand.

28.1.3 Motivation

One of the roles of project managers is to motivate the people who work for them. Maslow (1954) suggested that people are motivated by satisfying their needs and that needs can be arranged in a series of levels as shown in Figure 28.4. Human priorities are to satisfy lower-level needs (like hunger) before the more abstract, higher-level needs.

The lower levels of this hierarchy represent fundamental needs for food, sleep and so on, as well as the need to feel secure in an environment. Social needs are concerned with the need to feel part of a social grouping. Esteem needs are the need to feel respected by others, while self-realization needs are needs concerned with personal development.

For people working in software development organizations, it can usually be assumed that low-level physiological and safety needs are satisfied. People are not hungry or thirsty and generally do not feel physically threatened by their environment. Therefore, ensuring the satisfaction of social, esteem and self-realization needs is most significant from a management point of view. I discuss this in the following section.

There is some value in Maslow's model of motivation. However, it is simplistic in that it has a personal focus. It does not take adequate account of the fact that people feel themselves to be part of an organization, a professional group and, usually, some culture. People are not just motivated by personal needs but may also be motivated by the goals of these broader groups.

People with fulfilling jobs are not solely motivated by material rewards. They often like to go to work because they are motivated by the people they work with

Figure 28.4
Human needs
hierarchy.

and by the work that they do. In a psychological study, Bass and Dunteman (1963) classified professionals into three types:

(1) *Task-oriented* who are motivated by the work they do. In software engineering, they are technicians who are motivated by the intellectual challenge of software development.

(2) *Self-oriented* who are principally motivated by personal success and recognition. They are interested in software development as a means of achieving their own goals.

(3) *Interaction-oriented* who are motivated by the presence and actions of co-workers. As software development becomes more user-centred, interaction-oriented individuals are becoming more and more involved in software engineering.

Each individual's motivation is made up of elements of each class but one type of motivation is usually dominant. However, personalities are not static and individuals can change. For example, technical people who feel they are not being properly rewarded can become self-oriented and put personal interests before technical concerns.

Typically, interaction-oriented personalities prefer to work in a group whereas task-oriented and self-oriented people often prefer to work alone. Women are more likely to be interaction-oriented than men. Whether this is a result of natural tendencies or of role stereotyping is not clear.

28.2 Management implications

Software engineers and project managers should be aware of how cognitive processes affect software management, design and development. Devising and writing a program is a problem-solving process. The software engineer must understand the problem, work out a solution strategy then translate it into a program. The first stage involves the problem statement entering working memory from short-term memory. It is integrated with existing knowledge from long-term memory and analysed to work out an overall solution. Finally, the general solution is refined into an executable program (Figure 28.5).

The development of the solution (the program) involves building an internal semantic model of the problem and a corresponding model of the solution. When this model has been built, it may be represented in any appropriate syntactic notation. The process of program design is therefore an iterative process involving several steps:

(1) Integrate existing computer and task knowledge to create new knowledge and hence understand the problem. Curtis *et al.* (1988) suggest that application experience is particularly important at this stage.

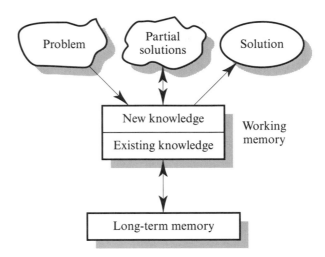

Figure 28.5
Problem solving.

(2)   Construct a semantic model of the solution. Test this against the problem and refine it until it is satisfactory.

(3)   Represent the model in some programming language or design notation.

Once a problem has been understood, experienced programmers will have roughly the same degree of difficulty in writing a program, irrespective of the programming language used. Language skills are necessary and take time to develop (particularly for complex languages like C++ or Ada) but managers should be wary of hiring staff simply on the basis of previous language experience.

The translation from semantic model to program is more likely to be error-free if the syntactic facilities of the notation match the lowest-level semantic structures used. These vary from individual to individual but probably correspond with concepts such as assignments, loops, conditional statements, information hiding, inheritance and so on. The closer the fit between the programming language and these concepts, the easier it is to write the program.

Programs written in Ada should therefore contain fewer errors than those written in assembly code because low-level semantic concepts can be encoded directly as language statements. However, problems may arise if functional and object-oriented concepts are mixed up. These can be a problem if a company has standardized on one type of method for analysis (for example, SADT) but uses an object-oriented design and programming process.

Structured programming, discussed in Chapter 19, is the best strategy for program control structure design. Because it is based on semantic concepts such as loops and conditional statements, it does not overload short-term memory. Errors are therefore less likely and people find structured programs easier to understand.

Short-term memory capacity is limited, information is encoded in chunks and semantic and syntactic knowledge is stored in our brains. Structured programs can be read from top to bottom so the abstractions involved in forming chunks can be made sequentially. There is no need to look at other parts of the program. Short-term memory can be devoted to a single section of code. It is not necessary to maintain information about several sections connected by arbitrary goto statements. Information from working memory about other parts of the program which interfere with that section need not be retrieved.

28.2.1 Training

People are motivated by opportunities to develop their skills. Training, therefore, is not simply a way of ensuring that engineers have the necessary skills to work on a particular project. It is also a way of demonstrating that an organization is interested in the personal development of its staff. However, if training is not designed for the trainees, it can have the opposite effect. People are demotivated and do not benefit from the organizational investment in developing their skills.

As discussed above, programming ability is not closely related to knowledge of any particular programming language. It is usually easy for programmers who know one programming language to learn a new language of the same type. If the semantic concepts underlying the languages are the same, they only need to learn a new syntax. The concepts are already understood. For example, FORTRAN programmers have few real difficulties learning C. Both languages reflect an underlying Von Neumann architectural model. However, the same programmers might have difficulty learning C++ as this requires them to understand new object-oriented concepts.

When organizing programmer training, experienced and inexperienced programmers have different requirements. Experienced programmers need to know the syntax of a language. By contrast, novice programmers need to be taught concepts such as how an assignment statement works, the notion of a procedure and so on.

Language-directed editing systems are useful for novices as they handle syntactic detail leaving the beginner to concentrate on the semantic concepts. Experienced programmers may have evolved a programming style where syntactic program correctness is not always maintained and may thus find language-directed editors obtrusive.

Languages like C++ and Ada present particular training problems. They are based on a Von Neumann model but introduce concepts such as information hiding (objects and packages), exceptions and, in Ada, tasking. These ideas may be unfamiliar to C or FORTRAN programmers. They may learn to write simple C++ or Ada programs fairly quickly but they need to spend much more time learning the new features of the language.

28.2.2 Motivating people

To motivate their staff, managers have to recognize that there are three factors to be considered. These are the satisfaction of needs as discussed in Section 28.1.3, the development of a cohesive group and the organization of work so that people are assigned tasks according to their skills and abilities.

In terms of the needs hierarchy (Figure 28.4), social, esteem and self-realization needs must be satisfied. Satisfying social needs means allowing people time to meet their co-workers and providing places for them to meet. Informal communication channels such as electronic mail should be available. Satisfying esteem needs means showing people that they are valued by the organization. Public recognition of achievements is a simple yet effective way of doing this. Obviously, people must also feel that they are paid at a level that reflects their skills and experience. Finally, satisfying self-realization needs involves giving people responsibility for their own work, assigning people demanding (but not impossible) tasks and providing a training programme where people can develop their skills.

Being a member of a cohesive group is highly motivating to most people. Therefore, managers should promote 'team building' so that all members of a team feel that they are respected and have a role to play. This is discussed later in Section 28.4.2.

28.3 Project staffing

One of the roles of a project manager is to choose staff to work on the project. In exceptional cases, project managers can appoint the people who are best suited to the job irrespective of their other responsibilities or budget considerations. More normally, however, project managers do not have a free choice of staff. They may have to use whoever is available in an organization, they may have to find people very quickly and they may have a limited budget. This limited budget may constrain the number of (expensive) experienced engineers who may work on the project.

If a manager has some choice of staff who can work on the project, there are a number of factors which may be used to influence the decision who to appoint. Some of these factors are shown in Figure 28.6.

There is no way of rating these factors in terms of importance as this varies depending on the application domain, the type of project and the skills of other members of the project team.

The decision on who to appoint to a project is usually made using three types of information:

(1)   Information provided by candidates about their background and experience (their resumé or CV).

(2)   Information gained by interviewing candidates.

(3)   Recommendations from other people who have worked with the candidates.

Some companies make use of various types of test to assess candidates. These include programming aptitude tests and psychometric tests. Psychometric tests are intended to produce a psychological profile of the candidate indicating attitude and suitability for certain types of task. Managers have radically different views about these tests. Some consider them nonsense; others think they provide useful informa-

Factor	Explanation
Application domain experience	For a project to develop a successful system, the developers must understand the application domain.
Platform experience	May be significant if low-level programming is involved. Otherwise, not usually a critical attribute.
Programming language experience	Normally only significant for short-duration projects where there is insufficient time to learn a new language.
Educational background	May provide an indicator of the basic fundamentals which the candidate should know and of their ability to learn. This factor becomes increasingly irrelevant as engineers gain experience across a range of projects.
Communication ability	Very important because of the need for project staff to communicate orally and in writing with other engineers, managers and customers.
Adaptability	Adaptability may be judged by looking at the different types of experience which candidates have had. This is an important attribute as it indicates an ability to learn.
Attitude	Project staff should have a positive attitude to their work and should be willing to learn new skills. This is an important attribute but often very difficult to assess.
Personality	Again, an important attribute but difficult to assess. Candidates must be reasonably compatible with other team members. No particular type of personality is more or less suited to software engineering.

Figure 28.6
Factors governing staff selection.

tion for staff selection. As discussed above, problem-solving ability seems to be related to the building of semantic models which is a long-term process. Aptitude and psychometric tests usually rely on the rapid completion of questions. The relationships between this and problem-solving ability are unclear.

Project managers are sometimes faced with difficulties in finding people with appropriate skills and experience. Teams have to be built using relatively inexperienced engineers. This may lead to problems because of a lack of understanding of the application domain or the technology used in the project.

One reason for this situation is that, in some organizations, technically skilled staff quickly reach a career plateau. To progress further, they must take on managerial responsibilities. These require different abilities from their technical skills. Promotion of these people to managerial status often means that useful technical skills are lost. To avoid a loss of technical skills to a project, some companies have developed parallel technical and managerial career structures of equal worth. Experienced technical people are rewarded at the same level as managers. As an engineer's career develops, they may specialize in either technical or managerial activities. They may move between them without loss of status or salary.

28.4 Group working

The image of programmers presented in the media is an individualistic one. They are often shown as technology-mad teenagers, who are inherently anti-social and who are most interested in hacking into other computers. While this is obviously exaggerated, there is some evidence that many programmers do not feel the need to work closely with other people (Cougar and Zawacki, 1978; Cougar, 1988).

In reality, most software engineers work in teams which vary in size from two to several hundred people. In a study undertaken by IBM (McCue, 1978), the proportion of time spent in various activities is as shown in Figure 28.7. I don't know of any more recent figures on work distribution but I would be surprised if there was any significant change from McCue's study.

About half of a typical programmer's time is spent interacting with other team members, 30% working alone and 20% in non-productive activities, such as travel and training. While the public and the self-image may be an individual one, the truth is that most software engineering is a team activity.

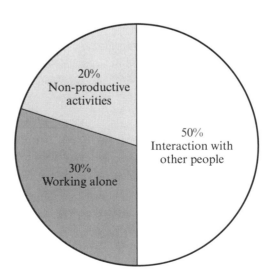

Figure 28.7
Distribution of a software engineer's time.

Managers are faced with a difficult task when forming groups. The group should have the right balance of technical skills and experience and personalities. This requires an understanding of the factors which affect successful group working. These include group composition, cohesion, leadership, communications and organization.

28.4.1 Group composition

Most software engineers are motivated primarily by their work. Software development groups, therefore, are likely to be composed of individuals who have their own idea on how technical problems should be solved. This is borne out by regularly reported problems of interface standards being ignored, systems being redesigned as they are coded, unnecessary system embellishments and so on.

A group which has complementary personalities may work better as a team than a group which has been selected on technical ability. People who are motivated by the work are likely to be the strongest technically. People who are self-oriented will probably be best at pushing the work forward to finish the job. It is particularly important to have interaction-oriented people in a team. They may act as a focus for communications within the group as they like to talk to people. They can detect tensions at an early stage and resolve personality problems before these can have a serious impact on the group.

It is sometimes impossible to choose a group with complementary personalities. In this case, the tendency of group members to go their own way implies that strict managerial control is needed to stop individual goals transcending organizational and group objectives. This control is easier to achieve if all group members participate in each stage of the project. Individual initiative is most likely when group members are given instructions without being aware of the part that their task plays in the overall project.

For example, say an engineer is given a program design for coding and notices possible design improvements. If these improvements are implemented without understanding the rationale for the original design, they might have adverse implications on other parts of the system. If the whole team are involved in the design from the start, they will understand why design decisions have been made. They will identify with these decisions rather than oppose them.

Within a group, the group leader has an important role. He or she may be responsible for providing technical direction and project administration. Group leaders must keep track of the day-to-day work of their team, ensure that people are working effectively and work closely with project managers on project planning.

Leaders are normally appointed and report to the overall project manager. However, the appointed leader may not be the real leader of the group as far as technical matters are concerned. The group members may look to another group member for leadership. He or she may be the most technically competent engineer or may be a better motivator than the appointed group leader.

Sometimes, it is effective to separate technical leadership and project administration. People who are technically competent are not always the best administrators. When they are given an administrative role, this reduces their overall value to the group. It is best to support them with an administrator who relieves them of day-to-day administrative tasks. This is the basis of a model of team organization known as 'chief programmer teams' as discussed in Section 28.4.4.

If an unwanted leader is imposed on a group, this is likely to introduce tensions. The members will not respect the leader and may reject group loyalty in favour of individual goals. This is a particular problem in a fast-changing field such as software engineering where new members may be more up-to-date and better educated than experienced group leaders. Some people with experience may resent the imposition of a young leader with new ideas.

28.4.2 Group cohesiveness

In a cohesive group, members think of the group as more important than the individuals in it. Members of a well-led, cohesive group are loyal to the group. They identify with group goals and with other group members. They attempt to protect the group, as an entity, from outside interference. This makes the group robust and able to cope with problems and unexpected situations. The group can cope with change by providing mutual support and help.

Specific advantages of a cohesive group are:

(1)   *A group quality standard can be developed*   Because this standard is established by consensus, it is more likely to be observed than external standards imposed on the team.

(2)   *Team members work closely together*   The team can learn from each other. Inhibitions caused by ignorance are minimized as mutual learning is encouraged.

(3)   *Team members can get to know each other's work*   Continuity can be maintained should a team member leave.

(4)   *Egoless programming can be practised*   Programs are regarded as team property rather than personal property.

Egoless programming (Weinberg, 1971) is a style of group working in which designs, programs and other documents are considered to be the common property of the group rather than the individual who developed them. If engineers think of their work in this way, they are more likely to offer it for inspection by other group members, to accept criticism, and to work with the group to improve the program. Group cohesiveness is improved because all members feel that they have a shared responsibility for the software.

As well as improving the quality of designs, programs and documents, egoless programming also improves communications within the group. It encourages uninhibited discussion without regard to status, experience or gender. Individual members actively cooperate with other group members throughout the course of the project. This all serves to draw the members of the group together and make them feel part of a team.

Group cohesiveness depends on many factors including the overall organizational culture and the personalities in the group. Managers can encourage cohesiveness in a number of ways. They may organize social events for group members and their families. They may try to establish a sense of group identity by naming the group and establishing a group identity and territory. They may get involved in explicit team building activities such as sports and games.

However, in my experience, one of the most effective ways of promoting cohesion is to ensure that group members are treated as responsible and trustworthy and given access to information. Often, managers feel that they cannot reveal certain information to all of the group. This invariably creates a climate of mistrust. Simple information exchange is a cheap and efficient way of making people feel that they are part of a group.

Cohesive groups, however, can sometimes suffer from two problems:

(1) *Irrational resistance to a leadership change* If the leader of a cohesive group has to be replaced by someone outside the group, the group members may band together against the new leader. Group members may spend time resisting changes proposed by the group leader with a consequent loss of productivity. Whenever possible, new leaders are best appointed from within groups.

(2) *Groupthink* This is the name given to a situation where the critical abilities of group members are eroded by group loyalties (Janis, 1972). Consideration of alternatives is replaced by loyalty to group norms and decisions. Any proposal favoured by the majority of the group may be adopted without proper consideration of alternatives. Groupthink is most likely when a team is stressed by imminent deadlines. In this situation, it is particularly important to make reasoned decisions.

To avoid groupthink, formal sessions may be organized where group members are encouraged to criticize decisions. Outside experts may be introduced to review the group's decisions. People who are naturally argumentative, questioning and disrespectful of the *status quo* may be appointed as group members. They act as a devil's advocate, constantly questioning group decisions thus forcing other group members to think about and evaluate their activities.

28.4.3 Group communications

Effective communication among the members of a software development group is essential if the group is to work efficiently. Factors which affect the effectiveness of intra-group communications include:

- the size of the group,
- the structure of the group,
- the status and personalities of group members,
- the physical work environment of the group.

The number of potential communication links between individual members increases as the square of the group size. If there are two members A and B, there are two links AB and BA. If there are three members A, B, and C, there are six links. For an n-member group, the number of potential communication links is $n * (n-1)$. Even in relatively small groups there are, therefore, many potential communication channels. Figure 28.8 describes some other factors that also affect communications within a group. Work environments are discussed in Section 28.5.

28.4.4 Group organization

Software engineering team sizes should normally have no more than eight members. When small teams are used, communication problems are reduced. The whole team can get round a table for a meeting and can meet in each other's offices. Complex communication structures are not required.

Factor	Description
Status of group members	Higher-status members tend to dominate communications with lower-status members who may be reluctant to start a conversation. Higher-status members should always encourage uninhibited communication in the group.
Personalities in the group	If there are too many people in the group who are task-oriented, this may inhibit effective communications. All of them may have their own ideas on technical issues and wish to discuss these in detail before making a decision. Sometimes people do not like each other because they have clashing personalities.
Sexual composition of group	Marshall and Heslin (1975) found that men and women prefer to work in mixed-sex groups. Within these groups, communications were better than in single-sex groups. As women tend to be more inter-action-oriented than men, the female group members may act as interaction controllers within the group.
Communication channels	Communications are more effective if anyone in a group can easily contact anyone else. Communications that are channelled through a central coordinator are less effective.

Figure 28.8
Factors affecting communications in a group.

For big projects which cannot be tackled by a single team in the time available, multiple teams must be used. They should work independently with each team tackling a significant part of the project in an autonomous way. The system architecture should be designed so that the interface between the sub-systems developed by the independent teams is simple and well defined.

Small programming teams are usually organized in an informal way. The team leader gets involved in the software development with the other team members. A technical leader may emerge who effectively controls software production. In an informal team, the work to be carried out is discussed by the team as a whole and tasks allocated according to ability and experience. High-level system design is carried out by senior team members but low-level design is the responsibility of the member allocated a particular task.

Informal teams can be very successful particularly where the majority of team members are experienced and competent. The team functions as a democratic unit, making decisions by consensus. Psychologically, this improves team spirit with a resultant increase in cohesiveness and performance. If a team is composed mostly of inexperienced or incompetent members, informality can be a hindrance. No definite authority exists to direct the work, causing a lack of coordination between team members and, possibly, eventual project failure.

An alternative programming team organization (chief programmer teams) was suggested by Baker (1972) and is also described, in a slightly different form, by Brooks (1975) and Aron (1974). Productivity measurements (Walston and Felix, 1977) suggested that this method of team organization resulted in a doubling of team productivity.

The underlying principle of the chief programmer team is that skilled and experienced staff should be responsible for all software development. They should not be concerned with routine matters and should have good technical and administrative support for their work. Their communications with people outside the group should be limited (Figure 28.9).

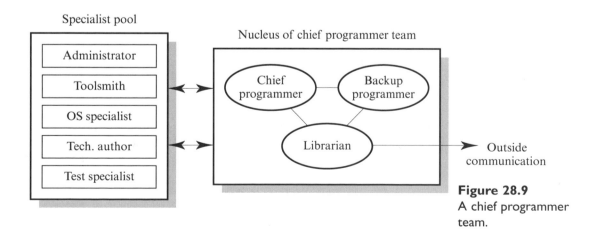

Figure 28.9
A chief programmer team.

The nucleus of a chief programmer team consists of three members:

(1)   A chief programmer who takes full responsibility for the design, programming, testing and installation of the system.

(2)   An experienced backup programmer whose job is to support the chief programmer and take responsibility for software validation.

(3)   A librarian whose role is to assume all the clerical functions associated with a project. The librarian is assisted by an automated library system.

Depending on the size and type of the application, other experts might be drawn from a specialist pool to work temporarily or permanently with a team. These might be administrators, operating system or language specialists, test engineers and so on.

Apart from the difficulty of finding talented chief programmers and deputy programmers, this team structure can cause personnel and organizational difficulties. Team members may be resentful if the chief programmer takes credit for a successful project. Projects might collapse if both the chief programmer and his or her deputy are ill or leave the organization.

Organizational structures may not be able to accommodate the introduction of this type of team. Large companies may have a well-developed grading structure. Appointing chief programmers outside this structure may be very difficult. In small companies, the number of technical staff may be limited. It may simply be impossible for one of them to be completely devoted to one task.

Chief programmer teams, although sometimes effective, may be a risky strategy for organizations to adopt. However, we can learn from the experiences of this type of team. It makes sense to support technically talented people with project librarians, administrators and so on. Their abilities can therefore be used in the best way. Making specialists available for short times can be more productive than using programmers with general experience for a longer period.

28.5 Working environments

The workplace has important effects on the performance of people. Psychological experiments have shown that behaviour is affected by room size, furniture, equipment, temperature, humidity, brightness and quality of light, noise and the degree of privacy available. Group behaviour is affected by architectural organization and telecommunication facilities.

DeMarco and Lister (1985) compared the productivity of programmers in different types of workplace. They found that factors such as a private workspace and the ability to cut off interruptions had a significant effect. Programmers who had good working conditions were more than twice as productive as equally skilled programmers who had to work in poorer conditions.

There is a real and significant cost in failing to provide good working conditions. When people are unhappy about their working conditions, staff turnover increases. More costs must therefore be expended on recruitment and training. Software projects may be delayed because of lack of qualified staff.

Most software engineering still takes place in environments designed for other functions, principally business offices. Software development staff often work in large open-plan office areas and only senior management have individual offices. McCue (1978) carried out a study that showed that the open-plan architecture favoured by many organizations was neither popular nor productive. The most important environmental factors identified in that design study were:

(1)   *Privacy*   Programmers require an area where they can concentrate and work without interruption.

(2)   *Outside awareness*   People prefer to work in natural light and with a view of the outside environment.

(3)   *Personalization*   Individuals adopt different working practices and have different opinions on decor. The ability to rearrange the workplace to suit working practices and to personalize that environment is important.

Providing individual offices for software engineering staff makes a significant difference to productivity. There is much less disruption than in open-plan organizations. In open-plan offices, people are denied privacy and a quiet working environment. They are limited in the ways that they can personalize their workspace.

Development groups require areas where all members of the group can get together as a group and discuss their project, both formally and informally. Meeting rooms must be able to accommodate the whole group in privacy. It is unreasonable to expect group meetings to take place in the corner of some larger office.

Individual privacy requirements and group communication requirements seem to be exclusive objectives. The way round this problem, described by McCue, is to group individual offices round larger central rooms which are used for group meetings and discussions (Figure 28.10).

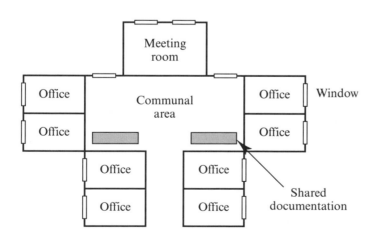

Figure 28.10
Office and meeting room grouping.

Each office should have adequate computing and communication facilities. The normal development environment used by software engineers is a powerful networked workstation with installed software such as CASE tools, documentation tools and so on. Electronic mail can facilitate rapid information exchange and can reduce the number of face-to-face meetings and unanswered telephone calls. Groupware systems, such as Lotus Notes, may be provided to assist with group working. Such systems provide repositories for group information and are becoming increasingly widely used.

Although individual offices make for better productivity, it is more difficult for informal communications between members of the same or different programming groups to take place. Individuals tend to 'disappear' into their offices and may not communicate much with their co-workers. This is a particular problem for those people who are not gregarious by nature and who are shy about seeking out other people to talk to.

This type of communication helps people solve their problems and exchange information in an informal but effective way. Weinberg cites an anecdotal example of how an organization wanted to stop programmers 'wasting time' talking to each other around a coffee machine. They removed the machine then immediately had a dramatic increase in requests for formal programming assistance. An organization should therefore provide informal meeting places as well as formal conference rooms.

Further reading

Software Management, 4th edition. This is an IEEE tutorial text which has several articles about managing and motivating people. (D. J. Reifer, IEEE Press, 1993.)

Working with Computers: Theory versus Outcome. This book is a collection of papers on human factors. They are mostly written by cognitive scientists with an interest in software development. (G. van der Veer, T. R. Green, J-M Hoc and D. M. Murray (eds), 1988, Academic Press.)

KEY POINTS

- Software management is principally concerned with managing people. Managers should therefore have some understanding of human factors so that they do not make unrealistic demands on themselves or their staff.

- Humans have a fast, short-term memory, a working memory and a long-term memory. Knowledge may be arbitrary syntactic knowledge and deeper semantic knowledge. Semantic knowledge is held in some internal way rather than in a language-oriented way.

- An understanding of memory organization helps explain why structured programming and information hiding is effective.

- Factors which might be used to select staff include application domain experience, adaptability and personality.

- Software development groups should be small and cohesive. They should be led by a technically competent person who is given administrative and technical support.

- Communications within a group are influenced by factors such as the status of group members, the size of the group, the sexual composition of the group, personalities and available communication channels.

- Providing a private working environment with appropriate computing and communication facilities can improve the productivity and satisfaction of programmers.

EXERCISES

28.1 Briefly describe the human memory hierarchy and explain why the organization of this hierarchy suggests that object-oriented systems are easier to understand than systems based on functional decomposition.

28.2 What is the difference between syntactic and semantic knowledge? From your own experience, write down a number of instances of each of these types of knowledge.

28.3 As a training manager, you are responsible for the initial programming language training of a new graduate intake to your company whose business is the development of communication systems. The principal programming language used is CHILL, which is a language for communications systems programming. The trainees may be computer science graduates, engineers or physical scientists. Some but not all of the trainees have previous programming experience; none have previous experience in CHILL. Explain how you would structure the programming training for this group of graduates.

28.4 What factors should be taken into account when selecting staff to work on a software development project?

28.5 Explain why keeping all members of a group informed about progress and technical decisions in a project can improve group cohesiveness.

28.6 Explain what you understand by 'groupthink'. Describe the dangers of this phenomenon and explain how it might be avoided.

28.7 You are a programming manager who has been given the task of rescuing a project that is critical to the success of the company. Senior management has given you an open-ended budget and you may choose a project team of up to five people from any other projects going on in the company. However, a rival company, working in the same area, is actively recruiting staff and several staff working for your company have left to join them.

Describe two models of programming team organization which might be used in this situation and make a choice of one of these models. Give reasons for your choice and explain why you have rejected the alternative model.

28.8 Why are open-plan and communal offices less suitable for software development than individual offices?

28.9 Should managers become friendly and mix socially with more junior members of their group?

28.10 Is it ethical to provide the answers which you think the tester wants rather than saying what you really feel when taking psychological tests?

29

Software Cost Estimation

Objectives

- To introduce software cost and schedule estimation.

- To describe the problems of objectively assessing the productivity of software developers and factors which affect productivity.

- To explain a number of different techniques which may be used for software cost estimation.

- To describe algorithmic cost modelling and to illustrate this approach with examples.

Contents

In Chapter 3, I introduced the project planning process. During that process, a project is split into a number of activities which may be enacted in parallel or in sequence. The discussion of project planning in Chapter 3 concentrated on ways to represent these activities, their dependencies and the allocation of people to carry out these tasks.

In this chapter, I turn to the problem of associating estimates of effort and time with the identified project activities. Project managers must estimate the answers to the following questions:

- How much effort is required to complete an activity?

- How much calendar time is needed to complete an activity?

- What is the total cost of an activity?

Project estimation and project scheduling are carried out together. However, some cost estimation may be required at an early stage of the project before detailed schedules are drawn up. These estimates may be needed to establish a budget for the project or to set a price for the software for a customer.

Once a project is underway, estimates should be updated regularly. This assists with the planning process and allows the effective use of resources. If actual expenditure is significantly greater than the estimates then the project manager must take some action. This may involve applying for additional resources for the project or modifying the work to be done.

There are three parameters involved in computing the total cost of a software development project:

- hardware and software costs including maintenance,
- travel and training costs,
- effort costs (the costs of paying software engineers).

For most projects, the dominant cost is the effort cost. Computers that are powerful enough for software development are relatively cheap. Although travel costs can be significant where a project is developed at different sites, they are relatively low for most projects. Furthermore, the use of electronic mail, fax and teleconferencing can reduce the travel required.

Effort costs are not simply the costs of the salaries of the software engineers involved in the project. Organizations compute effort costs in terms of overhead costs where they take the total cost of running the organization and divide this by the number of productive staff. Therefore, the following costs are all part of the total effort cost:

- costs of providing, heating and lighting office space;
- costs of support staff such as accountants, secretaries, cleaners, and so on;
- costs of networking and communications;

- costs of central facilities such as a library, recreational facilities and so on;
- costs of pensions, health insurance and so on.

Typically, this overhead factor is somewhere around twice the software engineer's salary. Therefore, if a software engineer is paid $50,000 per year, the total cost to the organization is $150,000 per year or $12,500 per month.

If the project cost has been computed as part of a project bid to a customer, a decision then has to be made about the price quoted to the customer. Classically, price is simply cost plus profit. However, the relationship between the project cost and the price to the customer is not usually so simple.

Software costing should be carried out objectively with the aim of accurately predicting the cost to the contractor of developing the software. Software pricing must take into account broader organizational, economic, political and business considerations. Factors which may be taken into account are shown in Figure 29.1.

Because of the organizational considerations involved, project pricing usually involves senior management in the organization as well as software project managers.

Factor	Description
Market opportunity	A development organization may quote a low price because it wishes to move into a new segment of the software market. Accepting a low profit on one project may give the opportunity of more profit later. The experience gained may allow new products to be developed.
Cost estimate uncertainty	If an organization is unsure of its cost estimate, it may increase its price by some contingency over and above its normal profit.
Contractual terms	A customer may be willing to allow the developer to retain ownership of the source code and reuse it in other projects. The price charged may then be less than if the software source code is handed over to the customer.
Requirements volatility	If the requirements are likely to change, an organization may lower its price to win a contract. After the contract is awarded, high prices may be charged for changes to the requirements.
Financial health	Developers in financial difficulty may lower their price to gain a contract. It is better to make a small profit or break even than to go out of business.

Figure 29.1
Factors affecting software pricing.

29.1 Productivity

Productivity in a manufacturing system can be measured by counting the number of units output and dividing this by the number of hours input to the work. However, for any software problem, there are many different solutions which have different attributes. One solution may execute more efficiently while another may be more readable. When solutions with different attributes are produced, comparing their production rates is not really meaningful.

Nevertheless, the productivity of engineers in the software development process may have to be estimated by managers. These estimates may be needed for project estimation and to assess whether process or technology improvements are effective. These productivity estimates are usually based on measuring some attributes of the software and dividing this by the total effort required for development. There are two types of measure which may be used:

(1) *Size-related measures*   These are related to the size of some output from an activity. The most common size-related measure is lines of delivered source code. Other measures which may be used are the number of delivered object code instructions or the number of pages of system documentation.

(2) *Function-related measures*   These are related to the overall functionality of the delivered software. Productivity is expressed in terms of the amount of useful functionality produced in some given time. There have been various proposals made for measuring functionality. Function points (see below) are the best known measure of this type.

The most commonly used measure of productivity is lines of source code per programmer-month. This is computed by counting the total number of lines of source code which are delivered. This count is divided by the total time in programmer-months required to complete the project. This time includes analysis and design time, coding time, testing time and documentation time.

This approach was first developed when most programming was in FORTRAN, assembly language or COBOL. Then, programs were typed on cards, with one statement on each card. The number of lines of code was easy to compute. It corresponded to the number of cards in the program deck.

However, programs in languages like Ada or C++ consist of declarations, executable statements and commentary. They may include macro instructions that expand to several lines of code. There may be more than one statement per line. There is not, therefore, a simple relationship between program statements and lines on a listing.

Some line counting techniques consider executable statements only; others count executable statements and data declarations; some count each non-blank line in the program, irrespective of what is on that line. So long as an organizational standard is established and used consistently, it doesn't matter which model of a line of code is used. However, because different organizations may count lines of code in different ways, programmer productivity across organizations cannot be reliably compared.

Low-level language

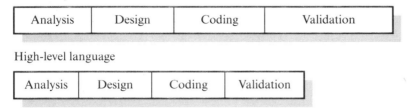

High-level language

Figure 29.2
Development times
with high-level and
low-level languages.

It is also meaningless to compare productivity across different programming languages. The more expressive the programming language, the lower the apparent productivity. This is a consequence of using a measurement of only part of the software process.

The time required for programming normally represents much less than half the time needed to complete a project (Figure 29.2). Analysis, design and documentation time are language-independent activities. They take roughly the same time irrespective of the programming language used. Low-level language programs have more lines of code than high-level language programs. These programs take longer to develop. However, the large number of lines of code produced make it look as though low-level language programming is more productive than programming in a higher-level language.

For example, consider a system which might be coded in 5000 lines of assembly code or 1500 lines of high-level language code. The development time for the various phases is shown in Figure 29.3. The assembler programmer has a productivity of 714 lines/month and the high-level language programmer less than half of this, 300 lines/month. Yet the development costs for the high-level language system are lower and it is produced in less time.

An alternative to using code size as the estimated product attribute is to use some measure of the functionality of the code. MacDonell (1994) briefly describes and compares several different function-based measures. The best-krown of these measures is the function-point count. This was proposed by Albr_cht (1979) and refined by Albrecht and Gaffney (1983). Function points are language-independent so productivity in different programming languages can be compared. Productivity is expressed as function points produced per person-month.

	Analysis	Design	Coding	Testing	Documentation
Assembly code	3 weeks	5 weeks	8 weeks	10 weeks	2 weeks
High-level language	3 weeks	5 weeks	8 weeks	6 weeks	2 weeks
	Size	**Effort**	**Productivity**		
Assembly code	5000 lines	28 weeks	714 lines/month		
High-level language	1500 lines	20 weeks	300 lines/month		

Figure 29.3
System development
times

Function points are biased towards data-processing systems which are dominated by input and output operations. A function point is not a single characteristic but is a combination of program characteristics. The total number of function points in a program is computed by measuring or estimating the following program features:

- external inputs and outputs
- user interactions
- external interfaces
- files used by the system

Each of these is individually assessed for complexity and given a weighting value that varies from 3 (for simple external inputs) to 15 for complex internal files. Either the weighting values proposed by Albrecht may be used or values based on local experience.

The unadjusted function-point count (UFC) is computed by multiplying each raw count by the estimated weight and summing all values.

$$\text{UFC} = \sum(\text{number of elements of given type}) \times (\text{weight})$$

This initial function-point count is then further modified by factors whose value is based on the overall complexity of the project. This takes into account the degree of distributed processing, the amount of reuse, the performance and so on. The unadjusted function-point count is multiplied by the project complexity factors to produce a final function-point count.

Symons (1988) notes that the subjective nature of complexity estimates means that the function-point count in a program depends on the estimator. Different people have different notions of complexity. There are wide variations in function-point count depending on the estimator's judgement.

Function-point counts can be used in conjunction with lines of code estimation techniques. The number of function points is used to estimate the final code size. Using historical data analysis, the average number of lines of code, AVC, in a particular language required to implement a function point can be estimated. The estimated code size for a new application is computed as follows:

$$\text{Code size} = \text{AVC} \times \text{Number of function points}$$

Values of AVC vary from 2–300 LOC/FP in assembly language to 2–40 LOC/FP for a fourth-generation language. The advantage of this function-based approach is that the number of function points may be estimated once the external interactions of the system have been designed. This is usually at a relatively early stage of the design process. A program size estimate can be produced without the need for detailed design.

The productivity of individual engineers working in an organization is affected by a number of factors. Some of the most important of these are summarized in Figure 29.4. However, individual differences in ability are more significant than any of these factors. In an early assessment of productivity, Sackman *et al.* (1968) found that some programmers were more than 10 times more productive than

Factor	Description
Application domain experience	Knowledge of the application domain is essential for effective software development. Engineers who already understand a domain are likely to be the most productive.
Process quality	The development process used can have a significant effect on productivity. This is covered in Chapter 31.
Project size	The larger a project, the more time required for team communications. Less time is available for development so individual productivity is reduced.
Technology support	Good support technology such as CASE tools, supportive configuration management systems and so on, can improve productivity.
Working environment	As discussed in Chapter 28, a quiet working environment with private work areas contributes to improved productivity.

Figure 29.4
Factors affecting software engineering productivity.

others. My experience is that this is almost certainly still true. Large teams are likely to have a mix of abilities so will have 'average' productivity. In small teams, however, overall productivity is mostly dependent on individual aptitudes and abilities.

For large, complex embedded systems, productivity may be as low as 30 lines/programmer-month. For straightforward, well-understood application systems it may be as high as 900 lines/month. There is no such thing as an 'average' value for productivity that applies across application domains and organizations.

The problem with measures expressed as volume/time is that they take no account of non-functional software characteristics. They imply that more always means better. What we really want to estimate is the cost of deriving a particular system with given functionality, quality, performance, maintainability and so on. This is only indirectly related to tangible measures such as the system size.

This becomes a particular problem if managers use productivity measurements to judge the abilities of staff. In such situations, engineers may compromise on quality in order to become more 'productive'. It may be the case that the 'less productive' programmer produces more reliable code which is easier to understand and cheaper to maintain. Productivity measures must therefore only be used as a guide. They should not be used without careful analysis.

29.2 Estimation techniques

There is no simple way to make an accurate estimate of the effort required to develop a software system. Initial estimates may have to be made on the basis of a requirements definition which may have very little detail. The software may have to run on unfamiliar computers or use new development technology. The people involved in the project and their skills will probably not be known. All of these factors mean that it is practically impossible to produce an accurate estimate of system development costs at an early stage in the project.

Nevertheless, organizations need to make software effort and cost estimates. To do so, one or more of the techniques described in Figure 29.5 may be used (Boehm, 1981).

Hihn and Habib-agahi (1991) describe an experiment in which they asked managers to estimate the size of a software system to be developed and the effort required. The managers used expert judgement and estimation by analogy. It was found that they were reasonably accurate in estimating required effort but their estimates of code size were much less accurate. This means that cost estimates which are computed using a code size estimate will also be inaccurate.

These approaches to cost estimation can be tackled using either a top-down or a bottom-up approach. A top-down approach starts at the system level. The estimator starts by examining the overall functionality of the product and how that functionality is provided by interacting sub-functions. The costs of system-level

Technique	Description
Algorithmic cost modelling	A model is developed using historical cost information that relates some software metric (usually its size) to the project cost. An estimate is made of that metric and the model predicts the effort required.
Expert judgement	Several experts on the proposed software development techniques and the application domain are consulted. They each estimate the project cost. These estimates are compared and discussed. The estimation process iterates until an agreed estimate is reached.
Estimation by analogy	This technique is applicable when other projects in the same application domain have been completed. The cost of a new project is estimated by analogy with these completed projects. Myers (1989) gives a very clear description of this approach.
Parkinson's Law	Parkinson's Law states that work expands to fill the time available. The cost is determined by available resources rather than by objective assessment. If the software has to be delivered in 12 months and 5 people are available, the effort required is estimated to be 60 person-months.
Pricing to win	The software cost is estimated to be whatever the customer has available to spend on the project. The estimated effort depends on the customer's budget and not on the software functionality.

Figure 29.5
Cost estimation techniques.

activities such as integration, configuration management and documentation are taken into account.

The bottom-up approach, by contrast, starts at the component level. The system is decomposed into components and the effort required to develop each of these is computed. These costs are then added to give the effort required for the whole system development.

The disadvantages of the top-down approach are the advantages of the bottom-up approach and vice versa. Top-down estimation can underestimate the costs of solving difficult technical problems associated with specific components such as interfaces to non-standard hardware. There is no detailed justification of the estimate that is produced. By contrast, bottom-up estimation produces such a justification and considers each component. However, this approach is more likely to underestimate the costs of system activities such as integration. Bottom-up estimation is also more expensive. There must be an initial system design to identify the components to be costed.

Each estimation technique has its own advantages and disadvantages. Boehm makes the point there is no best or worst technique. For large projects, several cost estimation techniques may be used in parallel and their results compared. If these predict radically different costs, this implies that not enough costing information is available. More information should be sought and the costing process repeated. The process should then iterate until the estimates converge.

An assumption which seems to underlie all of the published cost models is that a firm set of requirements has been drawn up and costing is carried out using these requirements as a basis. Although this is an appropriate model of some projects (particularly military projects which have funded a separate requirements phase), the costs of many projects must be estimated using only an outline of the work which is to be done. This means that the estimators have very little information to work with. Their estimates are probably even less accurate than those developed from a requirements definition.

This can be justifiably criticized as an unscientific approach but it may be cost-effective from a business point of view. Requirements capture and definition is expensive and the cost may not be justified if the project does not gain funding approval.

The notion of 'pricing to win' may seem unethical and unbusinesslike. However, this is a common approach to costing which has some advantages. A project cost is agreed on the basis of an outline proposal. Negotiations then take place between client and customer to establish the detailed project specification. This specification is constrained by the agreed cost. The buyer and seller must agree on what is acceptable system functionality. The fixed factor in many projects is not the project requirements but the cost. The requirements may be changed so that the cost is not exceeded.

The estimation techniques introduced above rely on experience or political judgement and these skills can't be explained in a book of this nature. Managers need to understand both the application domain and the organization to make reasonably accurate estimates. Hihn and Habib-agahi (1991) found that managers with more than six years of estimating experience usually produced the most accurate estimates.

29.3 Algorithmic cost modelling

The most systematic, although not necessarily the most accurate, approach to software estimation is algorithmic cost estimation. An algorithmic cost model can be built by analysing the costs and attributes of completed projects. A mathematical formula is used to predict costs based on estimates of project size, number of programmers and so on. Kitchenham (1990a) describes 13 different models which have been developed from empirical observations.

Most algorithmic estimation models have an exponential component. This reflects the fact that costs do not increase linearly with project size. As the size increases, extra costs are incurred because of the need for larger teams, more complex configuration management and so on. Models usually also have a component which reflects product attributes such as complexity and components reflecting the attributes of the process and the software developers. They can therefore be expressed as follows:

$$\text{Effort} = C \times PM^s \times M$$

C is a complexity factor and PM is some product metric that may either be a size metric or a functionality metric. M is a multiplier made up by combining different process, product and development attributes. The exponent s is usually close to 1 but reflects the increasing effort required for large projects. Depending on product complexity, different values of s may be proposed. In some models, some of the attributes contributing to the value of M may also have an associated exponent.

All models suffer from the same basic difficulties:

(1)   It is very difficult to estimate PM at an early stage in a project where only a specification is available.

(2)   The estimates of C and the factors contributing to M are subjective. Estimates of their value vary from one person to another depending on their background and experience. Models typically classify factors and assign values to each class. However, this classification is inherently imprecise and only an approximate reflection of reality.

The most commonly used metric for cost estimation is the number of lines of source code in the finished system. Size estimation may involve estimation by analogy with other projects, estimation by ranking the sizes of system components and using a known reference component to estimate the component size, or it may simply be a question of engineering judgement. Application domain knowledge may be used to provide a reasonable size estimate. However, many projects break new ground and estimating their size is difficult.

Design decisions, which may not be known when the initial estimates are made, influence the size of the final system. For example, an application which requires complex data management may either use a commercial database or implement its own data manager. If a commercial database is used, the code size will be smaller. The programming language used is also significant. A language like Ada might mean that more lines of code are necessary than if C++ (say) were used. However, this extra code allows more compile-time checking so validation costs are likely to be reduced. How should this be taken into account?

Kemerer (1987) compared four different cost models using business data-processing applications. One of these was the COCOMO model discussed here. He compared this with Putnam's model (Putnam, 1978) and with other models which were not based on lines of source code as an input parameter. Very wide variations in the predicted costs were found from 230 person-months to 3857 person-months for the same project. Kemerer used a historical database for cost estimation. He found that the costs predicted by uncalibrated models could vary by several hundred per cent from the actual project costs. However, after calibration of the model using local data, the model prediction errors were reduced.

If algorithmic models are used for project costing, their outputs must be carefully interpreted. The estimator should develop a range of estimates (worst, expected and best) rather than a single estimate. The costing formula should be applied to all of these. Errors in initial estimates are likely to be significant. Estimates are most likely to be accurate when the product is well understood, the model has been calibrated for the organization using it, and language and hardware choices are predefined.

There is no doubt that algorithmic cost models have been successfully used. However, project cost estimates are often self-fulfilling. The estimate is used to define the project budget and the product is adjusted so that the budget figure is realized. I do not know of reports of controlled experiments with cost modelling where the model outputs were not used to bias the experiment. A controlled experiment would not reveal the cost estimate to the project manager and then would compare actual with estimated costs.

29.3.1 The COCOMO model

A well-documented software costing model, whose parameters can be tailored to particular modes of working, is the COCOMO model described by Boehm (1981). This model and that of Putnam (1978) are probably the most widely used algorithmic costing models. Software products are available to support both of these models.

I concentrate on the COCOMO model to give the reader an overview of algorithmic cost estimation. The COCOMO model exists in basic (simple), intermediate and detailed forms. I introduce the basic and intermediate COCOMO models here. The detailed form is comparable but breaks the project down into different parts and estimates these separately.

The form of the COCOMO model follows the formula introduced above. However, as well as different values of the complexity multiplier, different exponents are suggested, depending on the complexity of the project. This leads to three formulae as shown in Figure 29.6.

In the basic COCOMO model, the multiplier M is 1. This gives an order of magnitude estimation of software costs. It only uses the estimated size of the software project and the type of software being developed. KDSI is the number of thousands of delivered source instructions. Figure 29.7 is a graph of effort against project size for the basic COCOMO model.

Boehm's interpretation of a delivered source instruction is any line of source text irrespective of the actual number of instructions on that line. If there are two or more statements on a line this counts as a single delivered source instruction. If a statement is spread over five lines this counts as five DSIs. Comments are excluded. Undelivered support software, whose development may take up a significant fraction of the project's resources, is not included when counting lines of code.

The basic COCOMO model is a starting point for project estimation. However, there are many factors apart from project size and type which affect the effort involved in a project. The intermediate COCOMO model takes some of these factors into account.

The intermediate model is based on the basic COCOMO effort and schedule computations. A series of multipliers is then applied to the basic COCOMO estimates. These multipliers take into account factors such as required product

Project complexity	Formula	Description
Simple	$PM = 2.4 \, (KDSI)^{1.05} \times M$	Well-understood applications developed by small teams. Boehm refers to these as organic mode projects.
Moderate	$PM = 3.0 \, (KDSI)^{1.12} \times M$	More complex projects where team members may have limited experience of related systems. Boehm refers to these as semi-detached mode projects.
Embedded	$PM = 3.6 \, (KDSI)^{1.20} \times M$	Complex projects where the software is part of a strongly coupled complex of hardware, software, regulations and operational procedures.

Figure 29.6
Different forms of the COCOMO model.

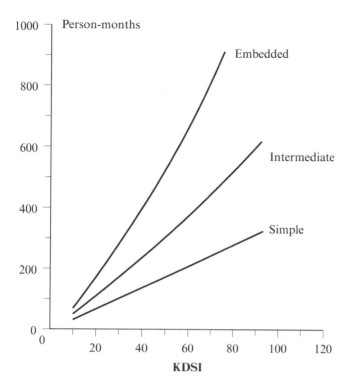

Figure 29.7
COCOMO effort
estimates.

reliability, data base size, execution and storage constraints, personnel attributes and the use of software tools. Multipliers are assigned values from 0.7 to 1.66. A value less than one means that this multiplier reduces the required effort, a value greater than one increases the required effort.

The attributes that were suggested in the original COCOMO model fall into four classes, namely product attributes, computer attributes, personnel attributes and project attributes.

(1)   *Product attributes* are concerned with required characteristics of the software product being developed. They include reliability, database size, and product complexity.

(2)   *Computer attributes* are constraints imposed on the software by the hardware platform. These affect software productivity because effort must be expended to overcome the hardware limitations. Computer attributes include execution time constraints, storage constraints, and the stability of the hardware/software platform on which the software must execute.

(3)   *Personnel attributes* are multipliers which take into account the experience of the people working on the project. These attributes are analyst capability, application experience, virtual machine experience, programmer capability and programming language experience.

(4)   *Project attributes* are concerned with the use of software tools, the project development schedule and the use of modern programming practices. When originally proposed, modern programming practice corresponded to structured programming; now it would probably mean object-oriented development.

The schedule attribute is a measure of how well the required development schedule fits the nominal schedule estimated using the COCOMO model. Either an accelerated or an extended schedule requirement will give positive values to this multiplier.

Figure 29.8 shows an example of how these multipliers influence effort estimates. The figures are rather contrived but they show how significantly the multipliers can affect the total effort required.

The basic and intermediate COCOMO models suffer from the disadvantage that they consider the software product as a single entity and apply multipliers to it as a whole. In fact, most large systems are made up of sub-systems which are not homogeneous and which have different non-functional requirements. The complete COCOMO model takes this into account and estimates the costs of each sub-system separately.

29.3.2 Model calibration

To use any estimation model effectively, it must be tuned to reflect local circumstances. The tuning or calibration process must be based on a database of schedule and effort measurements made for completed projects. It should take into account local definitions of complexity and local attribute multipliers which may be significant.

It is sometimes possible to eliminate or combine intermediate COCOMO attributes or to add new, locally significant attributes. For example, the personnel

Figure 29.8
The effect of multipliers on effort estimates.

System type	Embedded
System size	128 000 DSI
Basic COCOMO estimate	**1216 person-months**
Reliability	Very high, multiplier = 1.4
Complexity	Very high, multiplier = 1.3
Memory constraint	High, multiplier = 1.2
Tool use	Low, multiplier = 1.1
Schedule	Accelerated, multiplier = 1.23
Intermediate COCOMO estimate	**3593 person-months**
Reliability	Very low, multiplier = 0.75
Complexity	Very low, multiplier = 0.7
Memory constraint	None, multiplier = 1
Tool use	High, multiplier = 0.9
Schedule	Normal, multiplier = 1
Intermediate COCOMO estimate	**575 person-months**

attributes might be combined into a single attribute. Interactive working may be the only development mode and the use of a standard development system, such as Unix, may mean that a standard toolset is always available. New attributes might be added. For example, an attribute might take into account the additional costs of working with classified data and its associated security requirements.

Boehm discusses how the COCOMO model may be re-calibrated by comparing actual costs to predicted costs. This allows the constant factor and the scale factor in the basic COCOMO model to be re-computed to take local factors into account. The costs are predicted using published values of the model parameters and the actual costs are then measured (Figure 29.9).

A least squares approximation is used to fit estimated to measured costs. The least squares technique is a statistical technique which allows the best-fit line to the measured values to be discovered. Graphical software usually includes curve-fitting capabilities and can be used in model calibration. The constant value in the COCOMO equation is the constant value in the curve fitted to the measured effort. The predicted cost curve therefore matches the measured costs.

The exponent value can be calculated in a similar way but requires more data, particularly for large projects, for a valid calibration to be made. However, as this

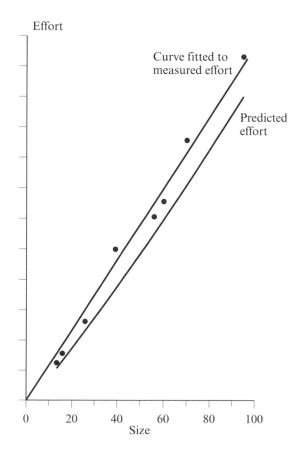

Figure 29.9
Predicted and measured costs.

exponent value is close to one, it is unlikely that small changes in its value are significant. The value suggested by Boehm is probably accurate enough.

Values for multipliers may be computed by estimating the product costs without using a particular multiplier, measuring the actual costs then finding the best multiplier value that fits the measured data. However, multipliers are not independent variables. Say an organization decides to invest in a CASE system, thus affecting the tools attribute, the virtual machine volatility attribute and the experience attribute; calibrating the model accurately would require each attribute to be considered in isolation which is practically impossible.

29.3.3 Algorithmic cost models in project planning

Project managers can use an algorithmic cost model to compare different ways of investing money to reduce project costs. This is particularly important where there must be hardware/software cost trade-offs and where there may be a need to recruit new staff with specific project skills.

Consider an embedded system to control an experiment that is to be launched into space. Spaceborne experiments have to be very reliable and are subject to stringent weight limits. The number of chips on a circuit board may have to be minimized. In terms of the COCOMO model, the multipliers based on computer constraints and reliability are greater than one.

There are three components to be taken into account in costing this project:

(1)   The cost of the target hardware to execute the system.

(2)   The cost of the platform (computer plus software) to develop the system.

(3)   The cost of the effort required to develop the software.

Figure 29.10 shows some possible options which may be considered. These include spending more on target hardware to reduce software costs or investing in better development tools.

Additional hardware costs may be acceptable in this case because the system is a specialized system that does not have to be mass-produced. If hardware is embedded in consumer products, however, investing in target hardware to reduce software costs is rarely acceptable because it increases the unit cost of the product.

Assume that the basic COCOMO model predicts an effort of 45 p.m. to develop an embedded software system for this application. The average cost for one person-month of effort is $12,500. To allow for estimation error, assume that the 'best-case' estimate is 30 p.m. and the 'worst-case' is 60 p.m.

Figure 29.11 shows the hardware, software and total costs for the options shown in Figure 29.10. The relevant multipliers are based on storage and execution time constraints (TIME and STOR), the availability of tool support (cross-compilers and so on) for the development system (TOOL) and development team's experience (EXP). In all options, the reliability multiplier (RELY) is 1.2, indicating that extra effort is needed to develop a reliable system.

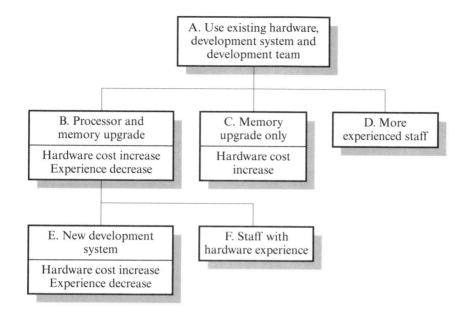

Figure 29.10
Management options.

The software cost (SC) is computed as follows:

$$SC = \text{Basic cost} \times RELY \times TIME \times STOR \times TOOL \times EXP \times \$12,\!500$$

Option A represents the cost of building the system with existing support and staff. It represents a baseline for comparison. All other options involve either more hardware expenditure or the recruitment (with associated costs and risks) of new staff. Option B shows that upgrading hardware does not necessarily reduce costs because the experience multiplier is more significant. It is actually more cost-effective to upgrade memory rather than the whole computer configuration.

Option F appears to offer the lowest costs for all basic estimates. However, this option has additional risk in that the staff with appropriate hardware experience have to be recruited and integrated into the organization. This takes time and the project schedule requirements may be such that this is an unacceptable risk. Option D, which is only marginally more expensive, also involves extra staff recruitment.

The comparisons show the importance of staff experience as a multiplier. If good quality people with the right experience are recruited, this can significantly reduce project costs. This is consistent with the discussion of productivity factors in Section 29.1.

29.4 Project duration and staffing

As well as estimating the effort required to develop a software system and the overall cost of that effort, project managers must also estimate how long the software will

Option	Multipliers	Basic COCOMO	Hardware cost	Software cost	Total cost
A	STOR = 1.1	30 p.m. (best)	$100,000	$435,600	$535,600
	TIME = 1.1	45 p.m. (expected)	$100,000	$653,400	$753,400
	TOOLS = 0.8	60 p.m. (worst)	$100,000	$871,200	$971,200
	EXP = 1				
B	STOR = 0.8	30 p.m.	$135,000	$427,680	$562,680
	TIME = 0.9	45 p.m.	$135,000	$641,520	$776,520
	TOOLS = 1.1	60 p.m.	$135,000	$855,360	$990,360
	EXP = 1.2				
C	STOR = 0.9	30 p.m.	$110,000	$356,400	$466,400
	TIME = 1.1	45 p.m.	$110,000	$534,600	$644,600
	TOOLS = 0.8	60 p.m.	$110,000	$712,800	$822,800
	EXP = 1				
D	STOR = 1.1	30 p.m.	$100,000	$326,700	$426,700
	TIME = 1.1	45 p.m.	$100,000	$490,050	$590,050
	TOOLS = 0.8	60 p.m.	$100,000	$653,400	$753,400
	EXP = 0.75				
E	STOR = 0.8	30 p.m.	$235,000	$315,900	$550,900
	TIME = 0.9	45 p.m.	$235,000	$473,850	$708,850
	TOOLS = 0.75	60 p.m.	$235,000	$631,800	$866,800
	EXP = 1.3				
F	STOR = 0.8	30 p.m.	$135,000	$285,120	$420,120
	TIME = 0.9	45 p.m.	$135,000	$427,680	$562,680
	TOOLS = 1.1	60 p.m.	$135,000	$570,240	$705,240
	EXP = 0.8				

Figure 29.11
Management options.

take to develop and when staff will be needed to work on the project. The relationship between the number of staff working on a project, the total effort required and the development time is not linear. As the number of staff increases, more effort may be needed. People must spend more time communicating. More time is required to define interfaces between the parts of the system. Doubling the number of staff (for example) does not mean that the duration of the project will be halved.

The COCOMO model includes a formula to estimate the calendar time (TDEV) required to complete a project. This depends on the type of project and the initial effort estimate. The time computation formulae are:

Simple projects $TDEV = 2.5 \, (PM)^{0.38}$
Intermediate projects $TDEV = 2.5 \, (PM)^{0.35}$
Embedded projects $TDEV = 2.5 \, (PM)^{0.32}$

To illustrate the basic COCOMO model, assume that an organic mode software project has an estimated size of 32 000 delivered source instructions. From the effort equation, the number of person-months required for this project is:

PM = 2.4 $(32)^{1.05}$ = 91 p.m.

From the schedule equation, the time required to complete the project is:

TDEV = 2.5 $(91)^{0.38}$ = 14 months

The basic COCOMO model is intended to give an order of magnitude estimate of the effort required to complete a software project. The model uses an implicit productivity estimate which was presumably derived from existing project data. In the case of organic mode projects, the productivity is 352 DSI/p.m. which is about 16 instructions per person-day. The effort required for the embedded system implies a productivity of 105 DSI/p.m. which is about four instructions per person-day. These figures roughly correspond to productivity estimates from other sources.

An interesting implication of the COCOMO model is that the time required to complete the project is a function of the total effort required for the project. It does not depend on the number of software engineers working on the project. This confirms the notion that adding more people to a project that is behind schedule is unlikely to help that schedule to be regained. Myers (1989) discusses the problems of schedule acceleration. He suggests that projects are likely to run into significant problems if they try to develop software without allowing sufficient calendar time.

Dividing the effort required on a project by the development schedule does not give a useful indication of the number of people required for the project team. Generally, the number of people employed on a software project builds up from a relatively small number to a peak then declines. Studies of this build-up showed that plotting staff levels against time resulted in a curve whose shape was like a Rayleigh curve.

A Rayleigh curve is a probability curve whose equation is:

dy/dt = 2 Kat exp $(-at^2)$

where dy/dt is the staff build-up rate, K is the area under the curve, t is time and a is a constant that determines the shape of the curve. Various curves for different values of the constant a are shown in Figure 29.12.

Only a small number of people are needed at the beginning of a project to carry out planning and specification. As the project progresses and more detailed work is required, the number of staff builds up to a peak. After implementation and unit testing is complete, the number of staff required starts to fall until it reaches one or two when the product is delivered.

Putnam's estimation model (Putnam, 1978) is based on this model of project staffing. Londeix (1987) discusses Rayleigh curves and project staffing in some detail. Putnam's model also includes development time as a key factor. As development time is reduced, the effort required to develop the system grows exponentially.

Experience has shown that a very rapid build-up of project staff often correlates with project schedule slippage. Project managers should therefore avoid adding too many staff to a project early in a project's lifetime.

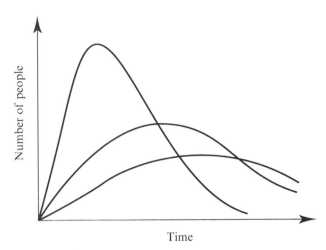

Figure 29.12
Rayleigh manpower
curves.

Further reading

'Nine management guidelines for better cost estimating'. Sound practical advice on cost estimation. (*Comm. ACM*, **35** (2), February 1992.)

'Allow plenty of time for large-scale software'. A good introduction to cost estimation. Myers makes the point that compressing the project schedule invariably leads to significant extra costs. (W. Myers, *IEEE Software*, **6** (4), July 1989.)

Software Reliability Handbook. Includes a chapter on algorithmic cost modelling written by users rather than model developers and a comparison of 13 different cost models. (P. Rook (ed.), 1990, Elsevier.)

KEY POINTS

- Factors which affect productivity include individual aptitude (the dominant factor), domain experience, the development process, the size of the project, tool support and the working environment.

- Measurements of programmer productivity do not usually take the quality of the developed system into account.

- There are various techniques of software cost estimation. In preparing an estimate, several of these should be used. If the estimates diverge widely, this means that inadequate estimating information is available.

- Software is often priced to gain a contract and the functionality of the system is then adjusted to meet the price.

- Algorithmic cost modelling suffers from the fundamental difficulty that it relies on attributes of the finished product to make the cost estimate. At early stages of the project, these attributes are impossible to estimate accurately.

- The COCOMO costing model is a well-developed model that takes project, product, hardware and personnel attributes into account when formulating a cost estimate. It also includes a means of estimating development schedules.

- Algorithmic cost models are valuable to management as they support quantitative option analysis. They allow the cost of various options to be computed and, even with errors, the options can be compared on an objective basis.

- The time required to complete a project is not simply proportional to the number of people working on the project. Adding more people to a late project can make it later.

EXERCISES

29.1 Describe two metrics which have been used to measure programmer productivity. Comment briefly on the advantages and disadvantages of these metrics.

29.2 In the development of large, embedded real-time systems, suggest five factors which are likely to have a significant effect on the productivity of the software development team.

29.3 Cost estimates are inherently risky irrespective of the estimation technique used. Suggest four ways in which the risk in a cost estimate can be reduced.

29.4 A software manager is in charge of the development of a safety-critical software system which is designed to control a radiotherapy machine to treat patients suffering from cancer. This system is embedded in the machine and must run on a special-purpose processor with a fixed amount of memory (one Mbyte). The machine communicates with a patient database system to obtain the details of the patient and, after treatment, automatically records the radiation dose delivered and other treatment details in the database.

 The basic COCOMO method is used to estimate the effort required to develop this system and an estimate of 26 person-months is computed.

 Explain why this estimate is adjusted in the intermediate COCOMO method.

 Suggest four factors that might be used in this case to adjust the basic COCOMO estimate and propose realistic values for each of these factors. Justify why you have included each factor.

29.5 Give three reasons why algorithmic cost estimates prepared in different organizations are not directly comparable.

29.6 Explain how the algorithmic approach to cost estimation may be used by project managers for option analysis. Give an example of a situation where managers may choose an approach that is not based on the lowest project cost.

29.7 Implement the COCOMO model using a spreadsheet such as Microsoft Excel or Lotus 1-2-3.

29.8 Some very large software projects involve the writing of millions of lines of code. Suggest how useful the cost estimation models are likely to be for such systems. Why might the assumptions on which they are based be invalid for very large software systems?

29.9 Is it ethical for a company to quote a low price for a software contract knowing that the requirements are ambiguous and that they can charge a high price for subsequent changes requested by the customer?

29.10 Should measured productivity be used by managers during the staff appraisal process? What safeguards are necessary to ensure that quality is not affected by this?

30

Quality Management

Objectives

- To introduce the essentials of quality management and the ISO 9000 quality assurance standard.

- To discuss the quality management process and to explain why process quality influences the quality of the developed software.

- To explain how standards may be used in the quality management process.

- To explain how software metrics may be used for quality assessment and to describe a number of product quality metrics which may be used.

Contents

Achieving a high level of product or service quality is now the objective of most organizations. It is no longer acceptable to deliver poor quality products and then repair problems and deficiencies after they have been delivered to the customer. In this respect, software is the same as any other manufactured product such as cars, televisions or computers.

The responsibility of quality managers is to ensure that the required level of quality is achieved. Quality management involves defining appropriate procedures and standards and checking that these are followed by all engineers. It depends on developing a 'quality culture' where everyone responsible for product development is committed to quality.

Software quality is a multi-dimensional concept that is not easy to define in a simple way. Classically, the notion of quality has been that the developed product should meet its specification (Crosby, 1979). In an ideal world, this definition should apply to all products but, for software systems, there are difficulties with it:

- The specification should be oriented towards the characteristics of the product which the customer wants. However, the development organization may also have requirements (such as maintainability requirements) which are not included in the specification.

- We do not know how to specify certain quality characteristics (for example, maintainability) in an unambiguous way.

- Software specifications are usually incomplete.

Obviously, efforts should be made to improve specifications but we cannot wait for ideal specifications to emerge before trying to improve quality. Rather, we should recognize the problems with existing specifications and put procedures in place to improve quality within the constraints imposed by an imperfect specification.

Quality management is not therefore just concerned with ensuring that software is developed without faults and conforms to its specification. It is also concerned with broader aspects of software quality such as those shown in Figure 30.1. A critical part of quality planning is selecting critical quality attributes and planning how these can be achieved.

Software quality managers are responsible for three kinds of activity:

(1) *Quality assurance* They must establish organizational procedures and standards which lead to high-quality software.

Figure 30.1
Software quality attributes.

Safety	Understandability	Portability
Security	Testability	Usability
Reliability	Adaptability	Reusability
Resilience	Modularity	Efficiency
Robustness	Complexity	Learnability

(2) *Quality planning*   They must select appropriate procedures and standards and tailor them for a specific software project.

(3) *Quality control*   They must ensure that procedures and standards are followed by the software development team.

Quality assurance is concerned with defining how an organization aims to achieve quality. It involves defining or selecting standards that should be applied to the software development process or software product. These standards must be embedded in procedures or processes which are applied during development. These processes may be supported by tools that may have to be bought or specially developed during the quality assurance process.

Quality control involves overseeing the software development process to ensure that quality assurance procedures and standards are being followed. The quality control process has its own set of procedures and reports that must be defined and applied during the development process. As far as possible, these procedures should be straightforward and easily understood by the engineers developing the software.

An international standard which can be used in the development of a quality management system in all industries is called ISO 9000. IS0 9000 is a set of standards that can be applied to a range of organizations from manufacturing through to service industries. ISO 9001 is the most general of these standards and applies to organizations concerned with the quality process in organizations which design, develop and maintain products. A supporting document (ISO 9000-3) interprets ISO 9000 for software development.

Each country has its own national standards which instantiate the ISO 9000 standards for that country. In the UK, the appropriate standard is BS 5750. The standards themselves are expressed in a rather formal and stilted way and a better understanding of them can be gained from books such as that by Johnson (1993).

ISO 9001 is a generic model of a quality process. It describes various aspects of that process and defines which standards and procedures should exist within an organization. As it is not industry-specific, these are not defined in detail. Within any specific organization, a set of appropriate quality processes should be defined and documented in an organizational quality manual.

Figure 30.2 shows the areas which are covered in ISO 9001. I do not have space here to discuss this standard (or any other standard) in any depth. Ince (1994) gives a more detailed account of how the standard can be used to develop software quality management processes.

The quality assurance procedures in an organization should be documented in a quality manual which defines the quality process. In some countries, bodies exist which will certify that the quality process as expressed in the quality manual conforms to ISO 9001. Increasingly, customers look for ISO 9000 certification in a supplier as an indicator of how seriously that supplier takes quality.

The relationship between ISO 9000, the quality manual and individual project quality plans is shown in Figure 30.3. This is derived from a model given in Ince's book (1994).

Management responsibility	Quality system
Control of non-conforming products	Design control
Handling, storage, packaging and delivery	Purchasing
Purchaser-supplied products	Product identification and traceability
Process control	Inspection and testing
Inspection and test equipment	Inspection and test status
Contract review	Corrective action
Document control	Quality records
Internal quality audits	Training
Servicing	Statistical techniques

Figure 30.2
Areas covered by ISO 9001 model for quality assurance.

Quality planning should begin at an early stage in the software process. A quality plan should set out the desired product qualities. It should define how these are to be assessed. It therefore sets out what 'high quality' software actually means. Without such a definition, different engineers may work in an opposing way so that different product attributes are optimized.

The quality plan should clearly set out which quality attributes are most significant for the product being developed. It may be that efficiency is paramount and other factors have to be sacrificed to achieve this. If this is set out in the plan, the engineers working on the development can cooperate to achieve this. The plan should also define the quality assessment process. This process should be a standard way of assessing whether some quality, such as maintainability, is present in the product.

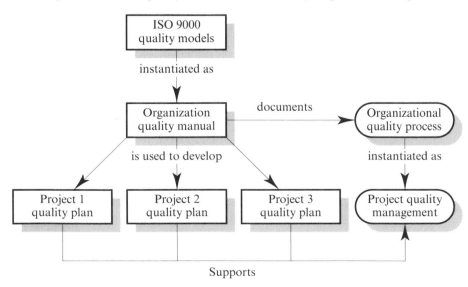

Figure 30.3
ISO 9000 and quality management.

The quality plan should select those organizational standards that are appropriate to a particular product and development process. New standards may have to be defined if the project uses new methods and tools. The plan need not include details of particular standards. It may simply reference these in the quality manual. Quality management should ensure that the standards documents are generally available. Humphrey (1989) and Frewin (1990) discuss structures for quality plans.

Within an organization, quality management should be separate from project management. This ensures that quality considerations are not compromised by management responsibilities for project budget and schedule. This can be achieved by devolving quality management responsibilities to an independent team which reports directly to management above the project manager level. The quality management team should not be associated with any particular development group but should be responsible for quality management across the organization. Alternatively, the project manager for some project can take on the role of quality manager for a different project.

30.1 Process quality assurance

An underlying assumption of quality management is that the quality of the development process directly affects the quality of delivered products. This assumption is derived from manufacturing systems where product quality is intimately related to the production process. Indeed, in automated mass production systems once an acceptable level of process quality has been attained, product quality naturally follows. This approach to quality assurance is illustrated in Figure 30.4.

Process quality is particularly important in software development. The reason for this is that it is difficult to measure software attributes, such as maintainability, without using the software for a long period. Quality improvement focuses on identifying good quality products, examining the processes used to develop these products then generalizing these processes so that they may be applied across a range of projects. However, the relationship between software process and software product quality is complex. Changing the process does not necessarily lead to improved product quality.

Figure 30.4
Process-based quality.

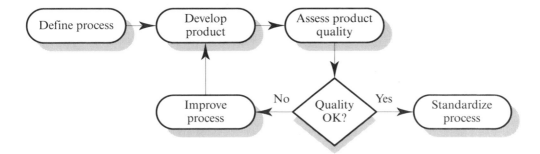

There is a clear link between process and product quality in manufacturing because the process is relatively easy to standardize and monitor. Once manufacturing systems are calibrated, they can be run again and again to output high-quality products. Software is not manufactured but is designed. As software development is a creative rather than a mechanical process, the influence of individual skills and experience is significant. Furthermore, external factors, such as the novelty of an application or commercial pressure for an early product release, might mean that product quality is impaired irrespective of the process used.

Nevertheless, software process quality is important. Quality managers must ensure the quality of the software process that is used. This involves:

(1)   defining process standards such as how reviews should be conducted, when reviews should be held and so on;

(2)   monitoring the development process to ensure that the standards are being followed;

(3)   reporting the software process to project management and to the buyer of the software.

A danger of process-based quality assurance is that the prescribed process may be inappropriate for the type of software which is being developed. For example, process quality standards may specify that specification must be complete and approved before implementation can begin. However, some systems may require prototyping which involves program implementation. The quality team may suggest that this prototyping should not be carried out because its quality cannot be monitored. In such situations, senior management must intervene to ensure that the quality process supports rather than hinders product development.

I return to the relationships between process and product quality in the next chapter which is concerned with process improvement.

30.2 Quality reviews

Reviews are the principal method of validating the quality of a process or product. They involve a group of people examining part or all of a software process, system or its associated documentation to discover potential problems. The conclusions of the review are formally recorded and passed to the author or whoever is responsible for correcting the discovered problems.

Figure 30.5 shows that there are several different types of review. Program inspections have already been covered in Chapter 24. Progress reviews are part of the management process as discussed in Chapter 3. In this chapter, I concentrate on reviews as part of the quality management process.

Quality reviews have three functions:

(1)   A quality function in that they are part of the general quality assurance procedures used in the organization.

Review type	Principal purpose
Design or program inspections	To detect detailed errors in the design or code and to check whether standards have been followed. The review should be driven by a checklist of possible errors.
Progress reviews	To provide information for management about the overall progress of the project. This is both a process and a product review and is concerned with costs, plans and schedules.
Quality reviews	To carry out a technical analysis of product components or documentation to find faults or mismatches between the specification and the design, code or documentation. It may also be concerned with broader quality issues such as adherence to standards and other quality attributes.

Figure 30.5
Types of review.

(2)   A project management function whereby they provide information to management about progress. Documents may be 'signed off' at a review indicating that further development can proceed. Signing off a document does not necessarily mean that it is fault-free. Rather, the manager may decide that problems identified during the review are relatively simple to solve. Further development in the project does not depend on their detailed solutions.

(3)   A training function in that engineers explain their design and justify their design decisions. Newcomers to the project or designers who must interface with the system being designed may attend the review as observers. It offers an excellent opportunity to learn about the system design.

The process of setting up and holding a review is illustrated in Figure 30.6. A quality review is distinct from a design or code inspection in that the system may not be described (or even developed) in detail. The review need not examine individual system components but may be more concerned with the validation of component interactions and with conformance to user's requirements.

Figure 30.6
The review process.

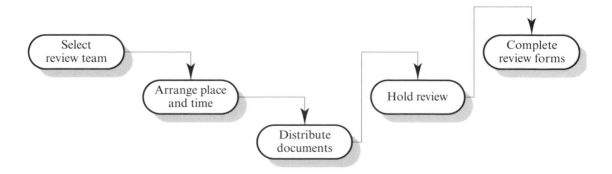

The remit of the review team is to detect errors and inconsistencies and point them out to the designer or document author. Reviews are document-based but are not limited to specifications, designs or code. Documents such as process models, test plans, configuration management procedures, process standards and user manuals may all be reviewed.

The review team should include those project members who can make an effective contribution. For example, if a sub-system design is being reviewed, designers of related sub-systems should be included in the review team. They may bring important insights into sub-system interfaces which could be missed if the sub-system is considered in isolation.

The review team should not be too large. It may have a core of three or four people who are selected as principal reviewers. At least one member should be a senior designer who can take the responsibility for making significant technical decisions. The principal reviewers may invite other project members to contribute to the review. They may not be involved in reviewing the whole document. Rather, they concentrate on those parts which affect their work. Alternatively, the review team may circulate the document being reviewed and ask for written comments from other project members.

Documents to be reviewed must be distributed well in advance of the review to allow reviewers time to read and understand them. Although this delay can disrupt the development process, reviewing is ineffective if the review team is not given time to understand the documents to be reviewed.

The review itself should be relatively short (two hours at most). If possible, the author of the document being reviewed should 'walk through' the document with the review team. One member of the team should chair the review and another should formally record all review decisions. During the review, the chairman is responsible for ensuring that all written comments are considered.

On completion of the review, the actions are noted and forms recording the comments and actions are signed by the designer and the review chairman. These are then filed as part of the formal project documentation. If only minor problems are discovered, a further review may be unnecessary. The chairman is responsible for ensuring that the required changes are made. If major changes are necessary, it is normal practice to schedule a further review.

All comments should be considered along with other written submissions to the review team. Comments should be classed under one of three categories:

(1)   *No action*   Either the comment was factually incorrect or the review decided that the cost of rectifying the problem was unjustified.

(2)   *Refer for repair*   The review detected a problem and asked the document originator or designer to fix that problem.

(3)   *Reconsider overall design*   The best way to solve an identified problem is to change the overall design of the system or process. The review chairman will normally set up a meeting between the engineers involved to reconsider the problem.

Some of the errors discovered in a review may be errors in the software specification and requirements definition. Requirements errors must be reported to the software contractor and the impact of changing the requirements assessed. Sometimes the requirements must change. However, if the change involves large-scale modification of the system architecture or hardware changes, it may be more cost-effective to design around the fault. The software may be redesigned to compensate for the fault and to correct adverse consequences which result from it.

30.3 Software standards

One of the most important roles of the quality assurance team is the development of product and process standards. Product standards define characteristics that all product components should exhibit; process standards define how the software process should be conducted. An example of a product standard is a review form which defines the information to be collected during a review. An example of a process standard is a procedural definition of how design reviews should be organized.

Standards are important for a number of reasons:

(1)   They provide an encapsulation of best, or at least most appropriate, practice. This knowledge is often only acquired after a great deal of trial and error. Building it into a standard avoids the repetition of past mistakes. The standard should capture some wisdom which is of value to the organization.

(2)   They provide a framework around which the quality assurance process may be implemented. Given that standards encapsulate best practice, quality assurance becomes the activity of ensuring that standards have been properly followed.

(3)   They assist in continuity where work carried out by one person is taken up and continued by another. Standards ensure that all engineers within an organization adopt the same practices. Consequently, learning effort when starting new work is reduced.

The development of software engineering project standards is a difficult and time-consuming process. National and international bodies such as the US DoD, ANSI, BSI, NATO and the IEEE have been active in the production of standards. These are usually of a general rather than a specific nature. Bodies such as NATO and other defence organizations may require that their own standards are followed in software contracts.

National and international standards have been developed covering software engineering terminology, programming languages such as Pascal and Ada, notations such as charting symbols, procedures for deriving and writing software requirements, quality assurance procedures and software verification and validation processes (IEEE, 1994).

Quality assurance teams who are developing standards should normally base organizational standards on national and international standards. Using these standards as a starting point, the quality assurance team should draw up a standards 'handbook' which should define those standards which are appropriate for their organization. Examples of standards that might be included in such a handbook are shown in Figure 30.7.

Software engineers sometimes consider standards to be bureaucratic and irrelevant to the technical activity of software development. This is particularly likely when the standards require tedious form-filling and work recording. Although they usually agree about the general need for standards, engineers often find good reasons why standards are not necessarily appropriate to their particular project.

Product standards such as standards setting out program formats, design documentation and document structures are often tedious to follow and to check. Unfortunately, these standards are sometimes written by staff who are remote from the software development process and who are not aware of modern practices. Thus, the standards may appear to be out of date and unworkable.

To avoid these problems, the quality assurance organization that set the standards must be adequately resourced and must take the following steps:

(1) Involve software engineers in the development of product standards. They should understand the motivation behind the development of the standards and be committed to these standards. The standards document should not simply state a standard to be followed but should include a rationale of why particular standardization decisions have been made.

(2) Review and modify standards regularly to reflect changing technologies. Once standards are developed they tend to be enshrined in a company standards handbook and there is often a reluctance to change them. A standards handbook is essential but it should evolve with changing circumstances and technology.

(3) Where standards set out clerical procedures such as document formatting, software tools should be provided to support these standards. Clerical standards are the cause of many complaints because of the tedious work involved in implementing them. If tool support is available, there is not a great deal of additional effort involved in development to the standards.

Figure 30.7
Product and process
standards.

Product standards	Process standards
Design review form	Design review conduct
Document naming standards	Submission of documents to CM
Procedure header format	Version release process
Ada programming style standard	Project plan approval process
Project plan format	Change control process
Change request form	Test recording process

The project manager and the quality manager can avoid the difficulties and resentment that inappropriate standards cause by planning which standards should be used. They should decide, at the beginning of a project, which of the standards in the handbook should be used without change, which should be modified and which should be ignored. New standards may have to be created in response to a particular project requirement. For example, standards for formal specifications may be required if these have not been used in previous projects. These new standards must be allowed to evolve in the course of the project.

Process standards may cause difficulties if an impractical process is imposed on the development team. Such standards are often simply guidelines which must be sympathetically interpreted by individual project managers. There is no point in prescribing a particular way of working if it is inappropriate for a project or project team. Each project manager should therefore have the authority to modify process standards according to individual circumstances. However, standards that relate to product quality and the post-delivery process should only be changed after careful consideration.

30.4 Documentation standards

Documentation standards in a software project are particularly important as documents are the only tangible way of representing the software and the software process. Documents produced according to appropriate standards have a consistent appearance, structure and quality. Documents make the software process visible so must be consistent and readable.

There are three types of documentation standards:

(1) *Documentation process standards* These standards define the process which should be followed for document production.

(2) *Document standards* These are standards which govern the documents themselves.

(3) *Document interchange standards* It is increasingly important to exchange copies of documents via electronic mail and to store documents in databases. Interchange standards ensure that all electronic copies of documents are compatible.

30.4.1 Documentation process standards

Process standards define the process used to produce documents. This means defining the procedures involved in document development and the software tools used for document production. The checking and refinement procedures which ensure that documents are of a high quality should also be defined.

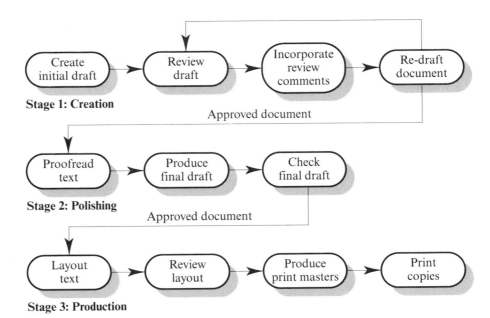

Stage 1: Creation

Approved document

Stage 2: Polishing

Approved document

Figure 30.8
A document
production process
including quality
checks.

Stage 3: Production

Document process quality assurance standards must be flexible and must be able to cope with all types of document. For working papers or memos, there is no need for explicit quality checking. However, where documents are formal documents used for further development or are released to customers, a formal quality process should be adopted. Figure 30.8 is a model of one possible process.

Drafting, checking, revising and re-drafting is an iterative process. It should be continued until a document of acceptable quality is produced. The acceptable quality level will depend on the document type and the potential readers of the document.

30.4.2 Document standards

Document standards apply to all documents produced in the course of the software development. Documents should have a consistent appearance and documents of the same class should have a consistent structure. Although document standards should be adapted to the needs of a specific project, it is good practice for the same 'house style' to be used in all of the documents produced by an organization.

Examples of document standards which may be developed are:

(1) *Document identification standards* As large projects typically produce thousands of documents, each document must be uniquely identified. For formal documents, this identifier may be the formal identifier defined by the configuration manager. For informal documents, the style of the document identifier should be defined by the project manager.

(2)   *Document structure standards*   Each class of document produced during a
       software project should follow some standard structure. Structure standards
       should define the sections to be included and should specify the conventions
       used for page numbering, page header and footer information, and section
       and sub-section numbering.

(3)   *Document presentation standards*   Document presentation standards define
       a 'house style' for documents and they contribute significantly to document
       consistency. They include the definition of fonts and styles used in the docu-
       ment, the use of logos and company names, the use of colour to highlight doc-
       ument structure and so on.

(4)   *Document update standards*   As a document is changed to reflect changes in
       the system, a consistent way of indicating these changes should be used. These
       might include the use of different colours of cover to indicate a new document
       version and the use of change bars to indicate modified or added paragraphs.

Document standards should apply to all project documents and to the initial drafts of
user documentation. In many cases, however, user documentation (see Chapter 17)
has to be presented in a form appropriate to the user rather than the project. It should
be recast into that form during the production process.

30.4.3 Document interchange standards

Document interchange standards are increasingly important as electronic rather than
paper copies of documents are passed from one engineer to another during the development process. Assuming that the use of standard tools is mandated in the process
standards, interchange standards define the conventions for using these tools. The
use of interchange standards allows documents to be transferred electronically and
re-created in their original form.

       Examples of interchange standards include the use of an agreed standard
macro set if a text formatting system is used for document production or the use of
a standard style sheet if a word processor is used. Interchange standards may also
limit the fonts and text styles used because of differing printer and display capabilities.

       The use of standard style sheets is applicable if all documents are produced
using the same word processing system. However, sometimes different word processors are used in which case documents should be stored in a standard format that can
be read by all systems. The most general standard is SGML (Standard Generalized
Mark-up Language) but this is not recognized by all word processors. A widely used
de facto standard is the RTF format, developed by Microsoft. Programs such as
Adobe Acrobat are becoming increasingly used for viewing formatted text.

30.5 Software metrics

A software metric is any type of measurement which relates to a software system,
process or related documentation. Examples are measures of the size of a product in

lines of code, the Fog index (Gunning, 1962) which is a measure of the readability of a product manual, the number of reported faults in a delivered software product and the number of person-days required to develop a system component.

Metrics fall into two classes namely control metrics and predictor metrics (Figure 30.9). Control metrics are those used by management to control the software process. Examples of these metrics are effort expended, elapsed time and disk usage. Estimates and measurements of these metrics can be used in the refinement of the project planning process. Control metrics can provide information about process quality and are therefore related, in some way, to product quality. This is discussed in Section 34.3 which covers the role of metrics in process improvement.

Predictor metrics are measurements of a product attribute that can be used to predict an associated product quality. For example, it has been suggested that the readability of a product manual may be predicted by estimating its Fog index, or the ease of maintenance of a software component may be predicted by measuring its cyclomatic complexity (McCabe, 1976).

Whether or not valid quality predictions can be made from such measurements is open to question. Ideally, a predictor metric would allow us to predict the value of some external attribute of the software (such as maintainability, say), by measuring an internal attribute (cyclomatic complexity, say). An external attribute is something which we can only discover after the software has been put into use. An internal attribute is an attribute of the software we can measure directly from the software itself. External attributes cannot usually be measured directly so we have to assume that a relationship exists between what we can measure and what we want to know.

Figure 30.10 shows some external quality attributes which might be of interest and internal attributes which can be measured and which might be related to the external attribute. The figure suggests that there may be a relationship between external and internal attributes but it does not say what that relationship is. If the measure of the internal attribute is to be a useful predictor of the external software characteristic, three conditions must hold (Kitchenham, 1990b):

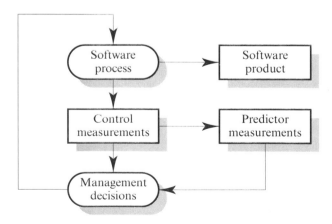

Figure 30.9
Predictor and control metrics.

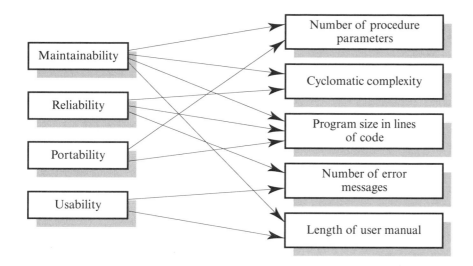

Figure 30.10
Possible relationships between internal and external software attributes.

(1)   The internal attribute must be measured accurately.

(2)   A relationship must exist between what we can measure and the external behavioural attribute.

(3)   This relationship is understood, has been validated and can be expressed in terms of a formula or model.

Kitchenham points out that this critical third assumption is often ignored. For example, McCabe's cyclomatic complexity measure is claimed to be useful in predicting the maintainability of a component. It is a reasonable assumption that maintainability is related to the overall component complexity but this is much more than the cyclomatic complexity. Because cyclomatic complexity is not necessarily the dominant factor influencing component complexity, the relationship between this metric and the software maintainability is difficult to formulate and validate.

Model formulation involves identifying the functional form of the model (linear, exponential and so on) by analysis of collected data, identifying the parameters which are to be included in the model and calibrating these using existing data. Such model development, if it is to be trusted, requires significant experience in statistical techniques. A professional statistician should be involved in the process.

Up till now metrics have been relatively little used in the software industry. However, there is an increasing awareness that they have an important role in quality improvement. A number of large companies such as Hewlett-Packard (Grady, 1993) and AT&T (Barnard and Price, 1994) are collecting metrics and using them for process improvements. Most of the focus has been on collecting metrics on program defects and the verification and validation processes. As awareness of the value of quantitative information develops, the industrial use of metrics will increase.

30.5.1 Data collection

Software metrics must be calibrated so that they reflect the characteristics of individual organizations. Locally relevant metrics may also be defined. This means that the organization must build and maintain a database of quantitative software information. The database of measurements must be reasonably large. Small and perhaps atypical data sets lead to unreliable metrics which will not be trusted by project managers.

Because of the overheads of manual data collection and the tedious nature of the task, Kitchenham (1990b) suggests that data collection should be automated and integrated into the development process. Three types of automated data collection can be identified:

(1)   *Static product analysis*   This involves developing or buying software tools that statically analyse the software product and measure various product parameters. These tools may analyse source code, design documents, user manuals and so on. Examples of metrics which can be collected include program size (from source code), module cohesion (from design documents) and Fog index (from user documentation).

(2)   *Dynamic product analysis*   This involves instrumenting the software system so that it collects information about its own usage and about faults of various kinds which occur (Figure 30.11). With this information, it is possible to measure some external software attributes.

(3)   *Process data collation*   Given that project management tools are used, it is sometimes possible to modify or extend these tools to process management data (such as time spent on a task) input to the tools so that it is collated in a useful form for further analysis.

Some data cannot be collected automatically from the product source or during program execution. Examples include the number of modules reused in a system or the number of lines of code changed in response to a modification request. Process data which is not normally collected for project management must also be collected manually. Examples include the time taken to modify user documentation and the time spent in meetings with customers.

Data collection is expensive. Humphrey (1989) quotes experience in NASA where data collection costs were about 15% of development costs and Rombach

Figure 30.11
Automated data collection.

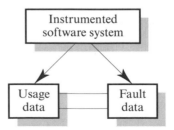

(1990) found that data collection and analysis costs are between 7% and 10% of development costs. The actual cost will vary from organization to organization and from project to project depending on the data required. However, it is usually a significant fraction of project costs.

To get the best return on investment, a metrics programme must ensure that it is collecting useful and accurate data. This means that:

(1) The questions that the measurement is intended to answer should be decided before the data is collected or analysed. Measurements which are not directly relevant to these questions need not be collected. Basili's GQM (Goal-Question-Metric) paradigm (Basili and Rombach, 1988), discussed in the following chapter, is a good approach to use when deciding what data is to be collected.

(2) Development staff should be informed why the data is being collected. It must be made clear that the data collection is not part of the personnel evaluation process. If this is not clear, engineers are likely to alter their normal working practices to ensure that collected data shows them, as individuals, in the best light.

(3) Data which cannot be automatically collected should be collected during development and should not be based on recollections of past events. Data which might be collected includes the time required to fix individual faults, the time spent in meetings, and so on. This adds some overhead as engineers must complete data collection forms as part of the development process.

Collected data should be maintained as an organizational resource and historical records of all projects should be maintained even when data has not been used during a particular project. Once a sufficiently large database has been established, comparisons across projects may be made.

30.5.2 Analysis of measurements

One of the problems with collecting quantitative data about software and software projects is understanding what that data really means. While there may be 'obvious' inferences to be drawn from measurements, the fact that these inferences are obvious does not necessarily mean that they are correct. Measurements therefore have to be carefully analysed to understand what they really imply.

To illustrate how collected data can be interpreted in different ways consider the following scenario:

A manager decides to monitor the number of change requests submitted by a customer and makes the reasonable assumption that there is a relationship between these change requests and product usability and suitability. The higher the number of change requests, the less the software meets the needs of the customer.

Processing change requests and changing the software is expensive. The organization therefore decides to modify its process to increase customer satisfaction and, at the same time, reduce the costs of change. It is intended that the process changes will result in better products and fewer change requests.

Process changes are initiated which involve more customer involvement in the software design process. Beta-testing of all products is introduced and customer-requested modifications are incorporated in the delivered product. New versions of products, developed with this modified process are delivered. In some cases, the number of change requests is reduced; in others, it is increased. The manager is baffled and cannot judge the effects of the process changes on the product quality.

To understand why this kind of thing can happen, we must understand why change requests are made. One reason is that the delivered software does not do what customers want it to do. Another possibility is that the software is very good and is widely and heavily used, sometimes for purposes for which it was not originally designed. Because there are so many people using it, it is natural that more change requests are generated.

A third possibility is that the company producing the software is very responsive to customers' change requests. Customers are therefore satisfied with the service they receive. They generate a lot of change requests because they know that these requests will be taken seriously. Their suggestions will probably be incorporated in later versions of the software.

The number of change requests might decrease because the process changes have been effective and have made the software more usable and suitable. Alternatively, the number might have decreased because the product has lost market share to a rival product. There are consequently fewer product users. The number of change requests might increase because there are more users, because the beta-testing process has convinced users that the company is willing to make changes or because the beta-test sites were not typical of most usage of the program.

In order to analyse the change request data, we do not simply need to know the number of change requests. We need to know who made the request, how they use the software and why the request was made. We need to know if there are external factors such as modifications to the change request procedure or market changes which might have an effect. With this information, it is then possible to find out if the process changes have been effective in increasing product quality.

This illustrates that collecting quantitative data about a product or a process does not necessarily mean that the data can be simply interpreted. Processes of any kind are not insulated from their environment and changes to that environment may make comparisons of data invalid. Quantitative data about human activities cannot always be taken at face value. The underlying reasons for the measured value should be investigated. There are no general guidelines which may be used here as data analysis is only possible when local circumstances are understood.

30.6 Product quality metrics

An organization that is committed to software measurement must experiment with and evaluate metrics using locally collected data rather than rely on external experience. To discover if a particular metric is a useful predictor of product quality, the quality assurance team must assess that metric in a systematic way using local data. They must take local procedures and standards into account.

The process of using metrics for quality prediction is shown in Figure 30.12. Essentially, each of the components of the system is analysed separately and the different values of the metric compared both with each other and, perhaps, with historical measurement data collected on previous projects. Anomalous measurements should be used to focus the quality assurance effort on components which may have quality problems.

In this section, I discuss some metrics that have been used for design, program and documentation assessment. There has been very little work done on specification quality metrics but some of the metrics for design assessment may be applied to graphical notations used in specifications. Documentation metrics such as the Fog index can be applied to natural language specifications. However, these invariably include many technical terms so it is dubious how applicable such an analysis might be.

30.6.1 Design quality metrics

Design quality was discussed in Chapter 12. There are a number of possible design attributes which are important but I suggested that the key attribute, apart from correctness, was maintainability. Quality assurance should therefore be mostly concerned with defect detection and on maintainability assessment.

As far as measurements are concerned, we cannot measure maintainability directly. It was suggested in Chapter 12 that the maintainability of a design was related to:

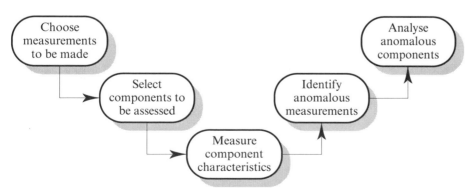

Figure 30.12
The process of
product measurement.

(1)   *Cohesion*   How closely are the parts of a component related?

(2)   *Coupling*   How independent is a component?

(3)   *Understandability*   How easy is it to understand the function of a component?

(4)   *Adaptability*   How easy is it to change a component?

Cohesion is a simple qualitative concept but it is difficult to assess it without an understanding of a component's purpose. The coupling of components can be measured by considering the number of inter-component references if an appropriate notation is used to express the design. Neither the understandability nor the adaptability of a component can be measured directly. However, a reasonable inference is that there is a relationship between these attributes and the 'complexity' of a component. Measuring the complexity may allow us to compare the understandability and adaptability of components against each other and, perhaps, against some standard.

Other factors which affect the understandability and maintainability of detailed designs are discussed later in the chapter under program quality assessment. These include the complexity of control in the design, the use of names, the nesting of conditional statements and so on.

Constantine and Yourdon (1979) have suggested that the coupling of a design can be quantified by measuring the fan-in and fan-out of design components in a structure chart (see Chapter 15). The fan-in value for a component is the number of lines entering the component's box on the structure chart. In essence, it is the number of other components which call that component. The fan-out value is the number of lines leaving a box on the structure chart; that is, it represents the number of called components (Figure 30.13).

Both fan-in and fan-out can be collected automatically if instrumented CASE tools are used to prepare design documentation. Fan-in and fan-out can also, in principle, be computed for object-oriented designs by considering the number of objects which reference a particular object and the number of objects referenced by an object. However, I don't know of any research that has applied these concepts to object-oriented designs.

A high fan-in value suggests that coupling is high because it is a measure of module dependencies. A high fan-out value suggests that the complexity of the calling component may be high because of the complexity of control logic required to coordinate the subordinate components.

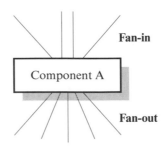

Figure 30.13
Structural fan-in and fan-out.

The problem with this simple notion of fan-in/fan-out is that it does not take into account data references such as the number of parameters passed and access to shared data structures. To address the problem of data references, Henry and Kafura (1981) identified another form of fan-in/fan-out which is informational fan-in/fan-out.

Informational fan-in/fan-out subsumes structural fan-in/fan-out. Calls to procedures are classed as fan-in to the calling procedure and fan-out from the called procedure. Informational fan-in/fan-out also takes into account the number of parameters passed from one procedure to another and the number of references made within a procedure to shared data structures.

Using informational fan-in and fan-out, Henry and Kafura suggest that the complexity of a component can be computed according to the following formula:

$$\text{Complexity} = \text{Length} \times (\text{Fan-in} \times \text{Fan-out})^2$$

Length is any measure of length such as lines of code or McCabe's cyclomatic complexity.

Henry and Kafura have validated their metric using the Unix system and suggested that the measured complexity of a component allowed potentially faulty system components to be identified. They found high values of this metric in components which had caused a disproportionate number of system problems and which had incurred high maintenance costs.

The advantage of this metric compared to structural fan-in/fan-out is that it takes into account data-driven programs. As discussed in Chapter 23 where cyclomatic complexity was explained, programs which make extensive use of tables may have a simple control structure yet the program and its tables may interact in a complex way. Structural fan-in/fan-out would not recognize this complexity as it is simply concerned with procedure calls. Informational fan-in/fan-out does measure this type of complexity as it uses data access as a parameter.

The principal disadvantage of informational fan-in/fan-out is that it can give complexity values of zero if a procedure has no external interactions. Components at the lowest level may not call other components. However, they may interact with hardware and be very complex. Similarly, components which interact with users have no fan-in but may also involve complex manipulations. Fan-in and fan-out are also hard to define in a completely unambiguous way. For example, if a record with three fields is passed to a procedure, should this be counted as one or three data elements?

Henry and Kafura's metric has been the subject of a number of independent studies (Kitchenham *et al.,* 1990; Shepherd, 1990). These checked if this metric was a better predictor of subjective complexity than other simpler metrics such as size and number of branches. They also tried to find out if structural complexity was a useful predictor of development time.

The evaluations of the metric concluded that size and the number of branches were equally valuable in predicting complexity. Fan-out on its own appeared to be a better complexity predictor than informational fan-in/fan-out. They also concluded that the informational fan-in/fan-out of a design appeared to be a useful predictor of the effort required for implementation.

Fan-in/fan-out are not completely reliable measures of design quality but both these metrics may be useful for highlighting anomalous components for further analysis. If some components have a particularly high (or low) value for these metrics, this may indicate that they are too complex. They should be studied further to assess whether or not the design should be modified.

30.6.2 Program quality metrics

Quality considerations for programs are similar to those for design assessment. Programs should be free of defects (this is easier to validate if they are simple rather than complex) and maintainable (hence they should be understandable and adaptable). Most work on software measurement has naturally focused on the analysis of programs. The reason for this is that programs are expressed in an unambiguous language and it is relatively straightforward to instrument language processing tools with facilities to collect data about the programs.

Several metrics have been suggested as predictors of the number of defects in a program. These are shown in Figure 30.14. The length of a program or program

Program metric	Description
Length of code	This is a measure of the size of a program. Generally, the larger the size of the code of a program's components, the more complex and error-prone that component is likely to be. Problems of measuring lines of code were discussed in Chapter 29.
Cyclomatic complexity	This is a measure of the control complexity of a program. This control complexity may be related to program understandability. The computation of cyclomatic complexity is covered in Chapter 23.
Length of identifiers	This is a measure of the average length of distinct identifiers in a program. The longer the identifiers, the more likely they are to be meaningful and hence the more understandable the program.
Depth of conditional nesting	This is a measure of the depth of nesting of if-statements in a program. Deeply nested if-statements are hard to understand and are potentially error-prone.

Figure 30.14
Program quality metrics.

component can be measured in different ways. The number of source code lines can be counted, with or without comment lines, the number of function points (Albrecht and Gaffney, 1983) can be estimated or the number of object-code instructions generated when the program is compiled. There are problems with all of these but, whatever measure is used, there is a relationship between the size of a component and its defect count.

Measurements of program size can be used as part of the quality assurance process. A standard may be established where some upper-limit is established for component size. Components which exceed this limit may either be redesigned or may be subjected to more detailed analysis. Although size is one of the simplest metrics and the easiest to collect, Kitchenham (1990b) claims it is as good an indicator of anomalous components as other, more sophisticated metrics.

The cyclomatic complexity of a procedure is a measure of the internal complexity of a component. Low values of this metric may correlate with understandable programs or designs. The computation of cyclomatic complexity is discussed in Chapter 23. As a measure of overall component complexity it suffers from two drawbacks:

(1) It measures the decision complexity of a program as determined by the predicates in loops and conditional statements. If a program is data-driven, it can have a very low value for the cyclomatic complexity yet still be complex and hard to understand.

(2) The same weight is placed on nested and non-nested loops. However, deeply nested conditional structures are harder to understand than non-nested conditionals.

Oviedo (1980) has developed a program complexity metric which takes data references into account. He suggests that the complexity of a component can be estimated using the following formula:

$$C = aE + bN$$

E is the number of edges in the flow graph and N is the number of references to data entities which are not declared in the component. This appears to get over some of the problems of measuring complexity but the metric has not been properly validated.

A good programming style guideline is always to use meaningful identifiers. Therefore, a reasonable hypothesis is that the comprehensibility of a program is likely to be increased if long names are used. Long names are likely to be more meaningful than short names. Of course, there are many other factors that affect program readability such as use of comments, program layout and so on. However, data on the length of identifiers is particularly easy to compute.

It would not be sensible to write requirements for identifier length into a programming standard but, again, anomalous values of this metric may suggest that the components concerned have quality problems.

Finally, measuring the depth of nesting of conditional statements may be a useful indicator of the complexity and understandability of components. Deeply nested if-statements are generally difficult to understand and normally should be avoided. Programming standards may include guidelines for depth of nesting and program analysis can check that the standards are being followed.

30.6.3 Documentation quality metrics

The quality of the documentation associated with a software product is as important as the quality of the software itself. Metrics to assess readability of documents have been developed for some time. The best known of these metrics is, perhaps, Gunning's Fog index (Gunning, 1962) which is a measure of the readability of a passage of text. The Fog index is based on the length of sentences and the number of 'difficult' words where the difficulty of a word is based on the number of syllables in the word.

The Fog index was not developed for technical documentation so it is not really clear how the use of jargon affects the metrics. The metric is simple to compute. Measuring the Fog index involves sampling text and counting words and word lengths. It would be relatively straightforward to adapt it to cope with specialized jargon terms by giving these a lower weighting than other words of equivalent length.

I don't know of any published evaluations of this or any other metric for software documentation but it might be a useful indicator of document readability. It is likely to be particularly useful where documents have multiple authors. It should be able to detect and highlight style differences between different sections of the document.

Further reading

ISO 9000 and Software Quality Assurance. This is a readable introduction to ISO 9000 and its relevance to software quality assurance. Its structure is based on the quality standard with a chapter on each topic. (D. Ince, 1994, McGraw-Hill.)

Software Metrics; A Rigorous Approach. This is an excellent book on metrics. The author does not oversell measurement. He discusses the problems of objective measurement in general before covering the specific difficulties of software measurement. Advice on setting up a metrics programme is also included. (N. E. Fenton, 1991, Chapman and Hall.)

Software Reliability Handbook. In spite of its title this book has a much broader scope than simply reliability issues. It also has excellent sections on metrics and quality assurance. (P. Rook (ed.), 1990, Elsevier.)

Software Engineering Standards Collection. A collection of various software standards covering various process activities. Not very readable but it is the most accessible way to get information about standards. (IEEE Press, 1994.)

KEY POINTS

- Software quality management is concerned with ensuring that software has a low number of defects and that it reaches the required standards of maintainability, reliability, portability and so on.

- An organizational quality manual should document a set of quality assurance procedures. This may be based on the generic model suggested in the ISO 9000 standards.

- A software quality plan should explicitly identify the quality attributes that are most significant for a particular project and should set out how these attributes can be assessed.

- Software standards are important to quality assurance as they represent an identification of 'best practice'. The quality assurance process is concerned with checking that the software process and the software being developed conforms to these standards.

- Reviews are the principal means of carrying out quality assurance. They should involve all engineers concerned with a product and its related systems.

- Software metrics can be used to gather quantitative information about the software process and software products.

- Control metrics are used to provide information to project managers about the software project. Predictor metrics allow estimates of the attributes of a software product to be made.

- The principal use of product quality metrics is to highlight anomalous components which may have quality problems. These components should then be analysed in more detail.

EXERCISES

30.1 Explain why a high-quality software process should lead to high-quality software products. Discuss possible problems with this system of quality management.

30.2 What are the stages involved in the review of a software design?

30.3 Design an electronic form which may be used to record review comments and which could be used to electronically mail comments to reviewers.

30.4 Briefly describe possible standards which might be used for:

(a) the use of control constructs in C, C++ or Ada;

(b) reports which might be submitted for a term project in a university;

(c) the process of making and approving changes to a program (see Chapter 32);

(d) the process of purchasing and installing a new computer in an organization.

30.5 Assume you work for an organization that develops database products for microcomputer systems. This organization is interested in quantifying its software development. Write a report suggesting appropriate metrics and suggest how these can be collected.

30.6 Explain why design metrics are, by themselves, an inadequate method of predicting design quality.

30.7 Consult the literature and find other design quality metrics which have been suggested apart from those discussed here. Consider these metrics in detail and assess whether they are likely to be of real value.

30.8 Do software standards stifle technological innovation?

30.9 A colleague who is a very good programmer produces software with a low number of defects but consistently ignores organizational quality standards. How should the managers in the organization react to this behaviour?

Process Improvement

Objectives

- To discuss the influence of software process factors on software quality and the productivity of software developers.

- To introduce software process improvement and factors which affect the quality of the software process.

- To describe the SEI Process Maturity Model which may be used to assess the maturity of the software process in large organizations.

- To discuss possible improvement strategies for different types of software process.

Contents

In the discussion of quality management in Chapter 30, the need for process quality assurance was covered. Process quality assurance recognizes that there is a strong relationship between the quality of the developed software product and the quality of the software process used to create that product. By assuring the quality of the software process, it is hoped that the product quality is assured.

Of course, product quality can only be achieved if the process is appropriate for the type of software that is being developed. An inappropriate software process, no matter how well it is implemented, standardized and monitored will not improve product quality. These process changes have to be made carefully. Well-intentioned process modifications which are inappropriate can actually reduce rather than improve product quality.

Over the last few years, there has been a great deal of interest in the software engineering community in *process improvement*. Process improvement means understanding existing processes and changing these processes to improve product quality and/or reduce costs and development time. Most of the literature on process improvement has focused on improving processes to reduce product defects. Once this has been achieved, cost or schedule reduction might be the principal improvement goals.

Process improvement does not simply mean adopting particular methods or tools or using some model of a process which has been used elsewhere. Although organizations which develop the same type of software clearly have much in common, there are always local organizational factors, procedures and standards which influence the process. The simple introduction of published process improvements is unlikely to be successful. Process improvement should always be seen as an activity that is specific to an organization or a part of a larger organization.

A generic model of the process improvement process is illustrated in Figure 31.1. Process improvement is a long-term, iterative process. The activities shown in Figure 31.1 might last several months. Successful process improvement requires organizational commitment and resources. It must be sanctioned by senior management and must have an associated budget to support improvements.

Figure 31.1
The process
improvement process.

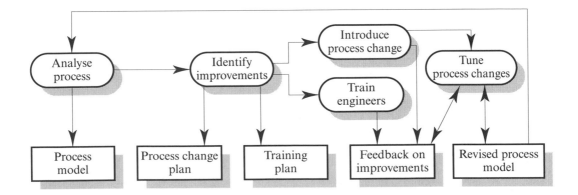

There are a number of key stages in the process improvement process:

(1)   *Process analysis*   Process analysis involves examining existing processes
      and producing a process model to document and understand the process. In
      some cases, it may be possible to analyse the process quantitatively. The
      process model may be supplemented with measurements made during the
      analysis. Quantitative analysis before and after changes have been introduced
      allows an objective assessment of the benefits (or the problems) of the
      process change.

(2)   *Improvement identification*   This stage is concerned with using the results of
      the process analysis to identify quality, schedule or cost bottlenecks where
      process factors might adversely influence the product quality. Process
      improvement should focus on loosening these bottlenecks by proposing new
      procedures, methods and tools to address the problems.

(3)   *Process change introduction*   Process change introduction means putting
      new procedures, methods and tools into place and integrating them with other
      process activities. It is important to allow enough time to introduce changes
      and to ensure that these changes are compatible with other process activities
      and more general organizational procedures and standards.

(4)   *Process change training*   Without training, process changes are almost
      certain to fail. They may be rejected by the managers and engineers respon-
      sible for development projects. If accepted, their full benefits might not be
      gained. All too commonly, process changes have been imposed without
      adequate training and the effects of these changes have been to degrade rather
      than improve product quality.

(5)   *Change tuning*   Proposed process changes will never be completely effec-
      tive as soon as they are introduced. A tuning phase is necessary where minor
      problems are discovered when the revised process is applied, modifications to
      the process are proposed and are introduced. This tuning phase should last for
      several months until the development engineers are happy with the new process.

Once a change has been introduced, the improvement process can iterate with
further analysis used to identify process problems, propose improvements and so on.
It is impractical to introduce too many changes at the same time. Apart from the
problems of training and change selection, introducing too many changes makes it
impossible to assess the effect of each change on the process.

31.1 Process and product quality

As discussed in Chapter 30, process improvement is based on the assumption that
the key factor influencing product quality is the quality of the product development
process. These ideas of process improvement stemmed from the work of an

American engineer called W. E. Deming who worked with Japanese industry after World War II to improve quality. Japanese industry has been committed to a process of continuous process improvement (the Japanese word for this is *kaizen*) for many years. This has largely contributed to the quality of Japanese manufactured goods.

Deming (and others) introduced the idea of statistical quality control. This is based on measuring the number of product defects and relating these defects to the process. The process is improved with the aim of reducing the number of product defects. The process is improved until it is repeatable. That is, the results of the process are predictable and the number of defects reduced. It is then standardized and a further improvement cycle begins.

Where manufacturing is involved, the process/product relationship is very obvious. Improving a process so that defects are avoided will lead to better products. This link is less obvious when the product is intangible and dependent, to some extent, on intellectual processes which cannot be automated. Software quality is not dependent on a manufacturing process but on a design process where the human element is significant. In some classes of product, the process used is the most significant determinant of product quality. However, for innovative applications in particular, the people involved in the process may be more important than the process used.

For software products (or any other intellectual products such as books, films, and so on where quality principally depends on the design), there are four factors that can affect product quality. These are shown in Figure 31.2.

The influence of each of these factors depends on the size and type of the project. For very large systems which are made up of separate sub-systems, developed by different teams, the principal determinant of product quality is probably the software process. The major problems with these large projects are integration, project management and communications. When teams are large, there is usually a mix of abilities and experience in the team members. As the development process usually takes place over a number of years, the development team is volatile. It may change completely over the lifetime of the project. Therefore, particularly skilled or talented individuals don't usually have a dominant effect over the lifetime of the project.

For small projects, however, where there are only a few team members, the quality of the development team is probably more important than the development process used. If the team has a high level of ability and experience, the quality of the

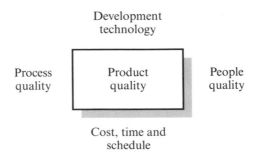

Figure 31.2
Principal product
quality factors.

product is likely to be high. If the team is inexperienced and unskilled, a good process may limit the damage but will not, in itself, lead to high-quality software.

Where teams are small, good development technology is particularly important. The team cannot devote a lot of time to tedious administrative procedures. Engineers spend much of their time in development activities so good tools can significantly affect their productivity. For large projects, a basic level of development technology is essential for information management. Paradoxically, however, sophisticated tools are less important. Team members spend a relatively small proportion of their time in development activities and more time communicating and understanding other parts of the system. This is the dominant factor affecting their productivity. Development tools make no difference to this.

The base of the rectangle in Figure 31.2 is absolutely critical. If a project, irrespective of size, is under-budgeted or planned with an unrealistic delivery schedule, the product quality will be affected. A good process requires resources for its effective implementation. If these resources are insufficient, the process cannot work effectively. If resources are inadequate, only excellent people can save a project. Even then, if the deficit is too great, the product quality will be degraded.

All too often, the real cause of software quality problems is not poor management, inadequate processes or poor quality training. Rather, it is the fact that organizations must compete to survive. Many software projects are deliberately under-budgeted in order to win a development contract. Pricing-to-win is an inevitable consequence of a competitive system. It is not surprising that product quality under such a system is variable.

31.2 Process analysis and modelling

Process analysis and modelling involve studying existing processes and developing an abstract model of these processes that captures their key characteristics. Several generic process models were introduced in Chapter 1. Throughout the book, process model fragments are used to discuss specific activities such as requirements engineering, software design and so on. Curtis *et al.* (1992) give a good overview of the general topic of process modelling. Krasner *et al.* (1992) discuss the application of process modelling and a process modelling support system.

Process analysis is concerned with studying existing processes to understand the relationships between different parts of the process. The outcome of process analysis is a process model. This should incorporate essential elements of the process which has been studied. The initial stages of process analysis are inevitably qualitative where the analyst is simply trying to discover the key features of the model. Later stages may be more quantitative. The process is analysed in more detail using various metrics that are automatically or manually collected.

The starting point for process analysis should be whatever 'formal' process model is used. Many organizations have such a formal model which may be imposed on them by the software customer. For example, contractors developing software for the US Department of Defense must follow a standard model known as MIL-STD-2167A for the software life cycle. This standard defines critical activities and life-cycle deliverables which must be produced.

Formal models can serve as a useful starting point for process analysis. However, they rarely include enough detail or reflect the real activities of software development. Formal process models are fairly abstract and only define the principal process activities and deliverables. It is usually necessary to 'look inside' the model to find the real process that is being enacted. Furthermore, the actual process which is followed often differs significantly from the formal model, although the specified deliverables will usually be produced.

Techniques of process analysis include:

(1) *Questionnaires and interviews* The engineers working on a project are questioned about what actually goes on. The answers to a formal questionnaire are refined during personal interviews with those involved in the process.

(2) *Ethnographic studies* As discussed in Chapter 5, ethnographic techniques may be used to understand the nature of software development as a human activity. Such analysis reveals subtleties and complexities which may not be discovered using other techniques.

Each of these approaches has advantages and disadvantages. Questionnaire-based analysis can be carried out in a relatively short period once the right questions have been discovered. However, if the questions are badly worded or inappropriate, an incomplete or inaccurate model of the process will be derived. Furthermore, questionnaire-based analysis appears like a form of assessment. The engineers being questioned may give the answers that they think the questioner wants to hear rather than the truth about the process used.

Ethnographic analysis is more likely to discover the true process used. However, it is a prolonged and expensive activity which can last for several months. It relies on external observation of the process. A complete analysis must continue from the initial stages of a project through to product delivery and maintenance. This will probably be impractical, when projects last several years. Ethnographic analysis, therefore, is most useful when an in-depth understanding of process fragments is required.

The output of process analysis is a process model which may be expressed at a greater or lesser level of detail. The process models used in this book are abstract, simplified models which present a generic view of the processes concerned. At this abstract level, these processes are the same in many different organizations. However, these generic models have different (sometimes radically different) instantiations which depend on the type of software being developed and the organizational environment. Detailed process models are not usually transferable from one organization to another.

Generic process models are a useful basis for discussing processes. However, they do not include enough information for process analysis and improvement. Process improvement needs information about activities, deliverables, people, communications, schedules and other organizational processes that affect the software development process. Figure 31.3 explains what might be included in a detailed process model.

There have been a number of formal notations defined for process modelling including notations based on Petri nets (Peterson, 1981) and coordination technology

Process model element	Description
Activity (represented by a round-edged rectangle with no drop shadow)	An activity has a clearly defined objective, entry and exit conditions. Examples of activities are preparing a set of test data to test a module, coding a function or a module, proofreading a document, etc. Generally, an activity is atomic i.e. it is the responsibility of one person or group. It is not decomposed into sub-activities.
Process (represented by a round-edged rectangle with drop shadow)	A process is a set of activities which have some coherence and whose objective is generally agreed within an organization. Examples of processes are requirements analysis, architectural design, test planning, etc.
Deliverable (represented by a rectangle with drop shadow)	A deliverable is a tangible output of an activity which is predicted in a project plan.
Condition (represented by a rectangle with no drop shadow)	A condition is either a pre-condition which must hold before a process or activity can start or a post-condition which holds after a process or activity has finished.
Role (represented by a circle with drop shadow)	A role is a bounded area of responsibility. Examples of roles might be configuration manager, test engineer, software designer, etc. One person may have several different roles and a single role may be associated with several different people.
Exception (not shown in examples here but may be represented as a double-edged box)	An exception is a description of how to modify the process if some anticipated or unanticipated event occurs. Exceptions are often undefined and it is left to the ingenuity of the project managers and engineers to handle the exception.
Communication (represented by an arrow)	An interchange of information between people or between people and supporting computer systems. Communications may be informal or formal. Formal communications might be the approval of a deliverable by a project manager; informal communications might be the interchange of electronic mail to resolve ambiguities in a document.

Figure 31.3
Elements of a process model.

(Winograd, 1988). These can usually be used in conjunction with a process engine which interprets the process model and advises the participants in the process. At the time of writing, there has not been a great deal of experience of using formal process models and process engines in an industrial setting.

The timing of and the dependencies between activities, deliverables and communications must also be recorded in a process model. Sometimes activities can be carried out in parallel and sometimes in sequence. They may be interleaved so that the same engineer is involved in several activities. Deliverables may be dependent on other deliverables or on some communications between engineers working on the process.

In the examples of process models in this book, I show the approximate sequence of activities from left to right. Activities that may be carried out in parallel are, as far as possible, aligned vertically.

Detailed process models are extremely complex. It is very difficult to construct a single model that incorporates all of the above elements. To illustrate the complexity of a model, consider the process fragments below. These describe the process of testing a single module in a large system which uses a strictly controlled configuration management process. The software being tested and the test data are under configuration control. Figure 31.4 shows the role responsible for the testing process, process inputs and outputs and pre- and post-conditions.

Figure 31.5 decomposes the process 'Test module' into a number of separate activities. This fragment shows only the activities in the relatively simple activity of module testing. There are four streams of activities concerned with preparing test data, writing a test harness for the module, running the tests and reporting on the tests. The activities in the preparation streams would normally be interleaved. Obviously, the preparation activities precede the execution and reporting activities.

This diagram leaves out information on pre- and post-conditions and process inputs and outputs. This information would make the model complex and very difficult to understand. For complete process modelling, it is therefore usually necessary to make several different views of the process. These are related using some common elements that are either activities or deliverables.

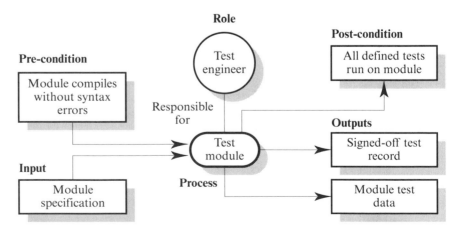

Figure 31.4
The module testing process.

Test Module

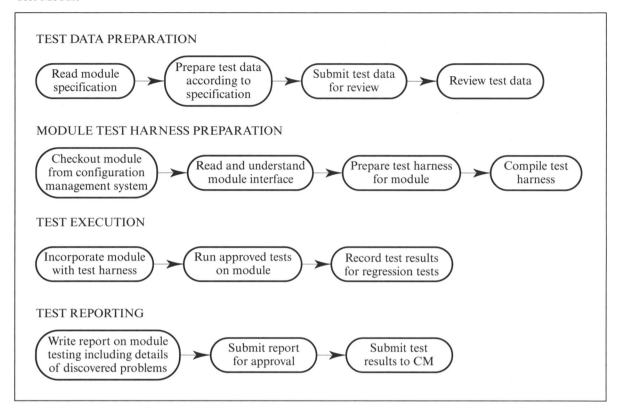

Figure 31.5
The activities involved
in module testing.

31.2.1 Process exceptions

Software processes are very complex entities. While there may be a defined process model in an organization, this can only ever represent the ideal situation where the development team is not faced with any unanticipated problems. In reality, unanticipated problems are a fact of everyday life for project managers. The 'ideal' process model must be modified dynamically as solutions to these problems are found. Examples of the kinds of exception that a project manager must deal with include:

- several key people becoming ill at the same time just before a critical project review;
- a major communications processor failure which means that electronic mail is out of action for several days;
- an organizational reorganization which means that managers have to spend much of their time working on organizational matters rather than on project management;
- an unanticipated request for new project proposals. Effort must be transferred from the project to work on a proposal.

In general, the effect of an exception is that, somehow, the resources, budgets or schedules of a project are changed. It is difficult to predict all exceptions in advance and to incorporate them into a formal process model. Many exceptions are therefore handled by managers dynamically changing the 'standard' process to cope with these unexpected circumstances.

31.3 Process measurement

Process measurements are quantitative data about the software process. Humphrey (1989), in his well-known book on process improvement, argues that the collection of process metrics is essential for process improvement. Process metrics, in their own right, can be used to assess whether or not the efficiency of a process has been improved. For example, the effort and time devoted to testing can be monitored. Effective improvements to the testing process should reduce the effort, testing time or both. However, process measurements on their own cannot be used to determine if product quality has improved. Product metrics must also be collected and related to software process activities.

Three classes of process metric can be collected:

(1)   *The time taken for a particular process to be completed*   This can be the total time devoted to the process, calendar time, the time spent on the process by particular engineers and so on.

(2)   *The resources required for a particular process*   The resources might be total effort in person-days, travel costs, computer resources and so on.

(3)   *The number of occurrences of a particular event*   Examples of events that might be monitored include the number of defects discovered during code inspection, the number of requirements changes requested, the average number of lines of code modified in response to a requirements change and so forth.

The first two types of measurement can be used to help discover if process changes have improved the efficiency of a process. Say there are fixed points in a software development process such as the acceptance of requirements, the completion of architectural design, the completion of test data generation and so on. It may be possible to measure the time and effort required to move from one of these fixed points to another. The measured values may be used to suggest areas where the process might be improved. After changes have been introduced, metric data collection can confirm or deny the benefits of process changes.

Measurements of the number of events which occur can have a more direct bearing on software quality. For example, increasing the number of defects discovered by changing the program inspection process will probably be reflected in improved product quality. However, this has to be confirmed by subsequent product measurements.

The fundamental difficulty in process measurement is knowing what to measure. Basili and Rombach (1988) have proposed what they call the GQM (Goal-Question-Metric) paradigm. This is used to help decide what measurements should be taken and how they should be used. This approach relies on the identification of:

(1) *Goals*   What the organization is trying to achieve. Examples of goals would be improved programmer productivity, shorter product development time, increased product reliability and so on.

(2) *Questions*   These are refinements of goals where specific areas of uncertainty related to the goals are identified. Examples of questions related to the above goals are:
     (a) How can the number of debugged lines of code be increased?
     (b) How can the time required to agree product requirements be reduced?
     (c) How can more effective reliability assessments be made?
          Normally, a goal will have a number of associated questions which need to be answered.

(3) *Metrics*   These are the measurements which need to be collected to help answer the questions and to confirm whether or not process improvements have achieved the desired goal. In the above examples, measurements which might be made include the productivity of individual programmers in lines of code and their level of experience, the number of formal communications between client and contractor for each requirements change, the number of tests required to cause product failure and so on.

The advantage of this approach applied to process improvement is that it separates organizational concerns (the goals) from specific process concerns (the questions). It focuses data collection and suggests that collected data should be analysed in different ways depending on the question it is intended to answer. Basili and Green (1993) describe how this approach has been used in a long-term, measurement-based process improvement programme.

31.4 The SEI process maturity model

The Software Engineering Institute (SEI) at Carnegie-Mellon University is a DoD-funded institute whose mission is software technology transfer. It was established to improve the capabilities of the US software industry and, specifically, the capabilities of those organizations that receive DoD funding for large defence projects. In the mid-1980s, the SEI initiated a study of ways of assessing the capabilities of contractors. They were particularly interested in contractors bidding for software projects funded by the US Department of Defense (DoD).

The outcome of this capability assessment work was the SEI Software Capability Maturity Model. This has been tremendously influential in convincing the software engineering community, in general, to take process improvement seriously. The SEI model classifies software processes into five different levels as shown in Figure 31.6.

These five levels are defined as follows:

(1) *Initial level*   At this level, an organization does not have effective management procedures or project plans. If formal procedures for project control exist, there are no organizational mechanisms to ensure that they are used consistently. The organization may successfully develop software but the characteristics of the software (quality and so on) and the software process (budget, schedule and so on) will be unpredictable.

(2) *Repeatable level*   At this level, an organization has formal management, quality assurance and configuration control procedures in place. It is called the repeatable level because the organization can successfully repeat projects of the same type. However, there is a lack of a formal process model. Project success is dependent on individual managers motivating a team and on organizational folklore acting as an intuitive process description.

(3) *Defined level*   At this level, an organization has defined its process and thus has a basis for qualitative process improvement. Formal procedures are in place to ensure that the defined process is followed in all software projects.

(4) *Managed level*   A level 4 organization has a defined process and a formal programme of quantitative data collection. Process and product metrics are collected and fed into the process improvement activity.

(5) *Optimizing level*   At this level, an organization is committed to continuous process improvement. Process improvement is budgeted and planned and is an integral part of the organization's process.

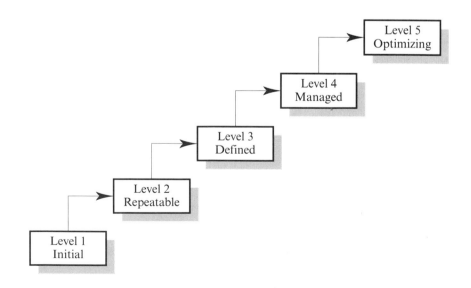

Figure 31.6
The SEI process
maturity model.

The maturity levels in the initial version of the model were criticized as being too imprecise. After experience with using the model for capability evaluation (see the next section), it was revised (Paulk *et al.,* 1993). The five levels were retained but were defined more specifically in terms of key process areas (Figure 31.7). Process improvement should be concerned with establishing these key processes and not with simply reaching some arbitrary level in the model.

The SEI work on this model has been influenced by methods of statistical quality control in manufacturing. Humphrey (1988), in the first widely published description of the model states:

> 'W. E. Deming, in his work with the Japanese industry after World War II, applied the concepts of statistical process control to industry. While there are important differences, these concepts are just as applicable to software as they are to automobiles, cameras, wristwatches and steel.'

This is a contentious statement. It is perhaps sometimes true but is certainly not a universal truth. As we have already discussed in Section 31.1, there are other factors,

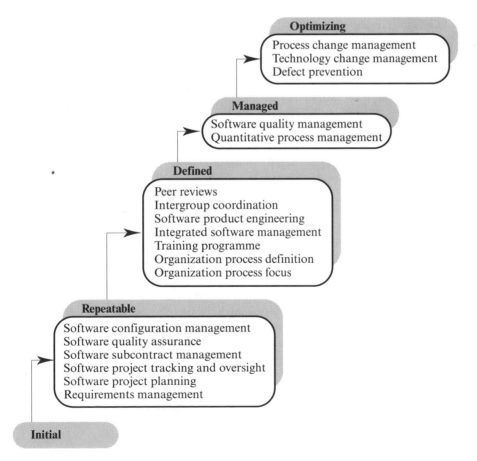

Figure 31.7
Key process areas
(© 1993, IEEE).

such as the skill and experience of the development engineers, which affect product quality. These are often as important, if not more important, than process factors.

The SEI maturity model is an important contribution but it should not be taken as a definitive capability model for all software processes. The model was developed to assess the capabilities of companies developing defence software. These are large, long-lifetime software systems which have complex interfaces with hardware and other software systems. They are developed by large teams of engineers and must follow the development standards and procedures laid down by the US Department of Defense (MIL-STD-2167A).

The first three levels of the SEI model are relatively simple to understand. The key process areas include practices which are currently used in industry. There are, however, relatively few projects (and, I suspect, even fewer organizations) which operate at levels 4 and 5. Humphrey (1989) has described practices which he considers appropriate for these levels. However, experience with these practices is so limited that it is difficult to say how effective they are.

Problems at the higher levels do not negate the usefulness of the SEI model. Most organizations are at lower levels of process maturity. There are, however, three more serious problems with the SEI model. These may mean that it is an unreliable predictor of an organization's capability to produce high-quality software. These problems are:

(1)   The model focuses exclusively on project management rather than product development. It does not take into account an organization's use of technologies such as prototyping, formal or structured methods, tools for static analysis and so on.

(2)   It excludes risk analysis and resolution as a key process technology. We have discussed the importance of risk assessment in Chapter 1. Its advantage is that it discovers problems before they seriously affect the development process. Bollinger and McGowan (1991) argue that the development paradigm assumed by the SEI model excludes risk analysis in spite of its importance in the software development process.

(3)   The domain of applicability of the model is not defined. The authors of the model clearly recognize that the model is not appropriate for all organizations. However, they do not describe the type of organizations where they think the model should and should not be used. The consequence of this is that the model has been oversold as a way to tackle software process problems. For smaller organizations, in particular, the model is too bureaucratic. Humphrey has recognized this and has recently been involved with smaller-scale process improvement strategies (Humphrey, 1995).

The authors of the SEI model admit (Humphrey and Curtis, 1991) that technology assessment was excluded because they could not find any standard way of assessing technology usage. Furthermore, they suggest that the management processes that are defined in the model are essential before technology can be effectively used.

Therefore, at the lower levels of the model, the use of particular technologies is not significant as far as product quality is concerned.

This is again an over-simplification. The effective use of technologies such as prototyping and static analysis of programs can have a significant effect on product quality. This does not depend on how these are incorporated into the software process. The routine use of tools and methods by an organization can clearly separate it from other organizations at the same level. It may mean that its product quality is superior to those products developed by products at a higher maturity level.

There are significant differences between commercial and defence software development. The problems of developing very large software systems are not necessarily shared by all organizations involved in software development. In particular, industry is able to respond much more quickly to technological change. This is evident in the way it has moved towards open systems and the widespread use of personal computers. While some of the ideas underlying the SEI model are generally relevant, the model is not completely applicable outside the domain for which it was designed.

31.4.1   Capability assessment

In discussions of process maturity and the SEI model, it is sometimes forgotten that the intention of the model was to allow the US Department of Defense to assess the capabilities of software contractors. At the time of writing, there is no published requirement for contractors to have reached a given level of maturity. However, there is an assumption in the community that organizations at the higher maturity level do have an advantage in bidding for contracts. In future, organizations will probably be expected to have reached a certain level of maturity (probably level 3) before they will be considered for DoD software contracts.

The model is intended to represent the capabilities of organizations rather than the maturity of particular projects. This makes sense from a contractual point of view but because an organization is rated at level 1 (say), this does not mean that all of its projects are at that level. Within the organization, there may be particular projects or groups working at a much higher maturity level.

Capability assessment is based on a standard questionnaire that is designed to identify the key processes in the organization. This is applied during an evaluation visit where project managers from a number of different projects are interviewed. After discussion of their responses to the questionnaire and refinement of these responses, an evaluation score is reached. A model of this assessment process is shown in Figure 31.8.

Bollinger and McGowan (1991) have criticized this evaluation process. These criticisms have been refuted by the model authors (Humphrey and Curtis, 1991). Both the criticisms and the refutations are plausible. This illustrates that the whole area of capability assessment is still immature and that further studies and research is required.

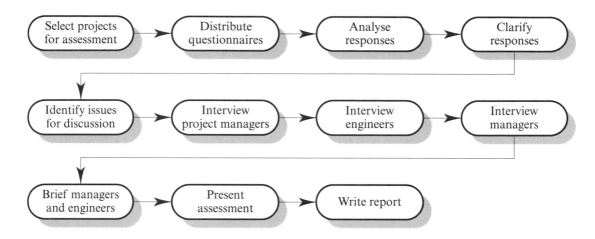

Figure 31.8
The capability
assessment process.

I think the principal problem with the current model is its stratification into levels and the judgemental association of numbers with these levels. The assessment guidelines require an organization to have all the practices at a particular level in place before it can be accredited at that level. Thus, an organization which has 80% of level 2 practices in place (say) and 70% of level 3 practices would receive a level 1 rating. A better approach would be a finer-grain capability classification in which the specific practices that are standard in an organization are identified.

31.5 Process classification

The process maturity classification proposed in the SEI model is appropriate for large, long-lifetime software projects undertaken by large organizations. There are many other types of software project and organization where this view of process maturity should not be applied directly.

Rather than attempt to classify processes into levels, with fairly arbitrary boundaries drawn between these levels, I believe a more general approach to process classification can be applied across a broader spectrum of organizations and projects. Different types of process can be identified:

(1) *Informal processes* These are processes for which there is not a strictly defined process model. The process used is chosen by the development team. Informal processes may use formal procedures such as configuration management but the choice of which procedures to use and the relationships between procedures are not predefined.

(2) *Managed processes* These are processes for which there is a defined process model in place. This is used to drive the development process. The process model defines the procedures used, their scheduling and the relationships between the procedures.

(3)   *Methodical processes*   These are processes for which some defined
      development method or methods (such as HOOD or Booch's method for
      object-oriented design) are used. These processes benefit from CASE tool
      support for design and analysis processes.

(4)   *Improving processes*   These are processes which have inherent improve-
      ment objectives. There is a specific budget for process improvements and
      procedures in place for introducing such improvements. As part of these
      improvements, quantitative process measurement may be introduced.

These classifications obviously overlap and a process may fall into several classes.
For example, the process may be informal in that it is chosen by the development
team. The team may choose to use a particular design method. They may also have
a process-improvement capability. In this case, the process would be classified as
informal, methodical and *improving*.

    These classifications are useful because they serve as a basis for multi-
dimensional process improvement. They help organizations choose an appropriate
process for different types of product development. Figure 31.9 shows different
types of product and the type of process that might be used for their development.

    The classes of system shown in Figure 31.9 may overlap. Therefore, small
systems which are re-engineered can be developed using a methodical process.
Large systems always need a managed process. However, if the domain is not well
understood, it may be difficult to choose an appropriate design method. Large
systems may therefore be developed using a managed process that is not based on
any particular design method.

    Process classification provides a basis for choosing the right process to be
used when a particular type of product is to be developed. For example, say a
program is needed to support a transition from one type of computer system to
another. This has a relatively short lifetime. Its development does not require the
standards and management procedures which are appropriate for software which
will be used for many years.

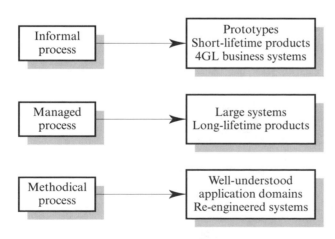

Figure 31.9
Process applicability.

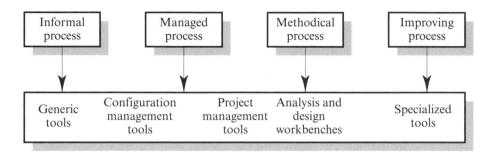

Figure 31.10
Process tool support.

Process classification recognizes that the process affects product quality. It does not assume, however, that the process is always the dominant factor. It provides a basis for improving different types of process. Different types of process improvement may be applied to the different types of process. For example, the improvements to methodical processes might be based on better method training, better integration of requirements and design, improved CASE tools and so on.

Most software processes now have some tool support so they are *supported processes*. Methodical processes are now usually supported by analysis and design workbenches. However, processes may have other kinds of tool support (for example, prototyping tools, testing tools) irrespective of whether or not a structured design method is used.

The tool support that can be effective in supporting processes depends on the process classification. For example, informal processes can use generic tools such as prototyping languages, compilers, debuggers, word processors and so on. They will not use more specialized tools in a consistent way. Figure 31.10 shows that a spectrum of different tools can be used in software development. The effectiveness of particular tools depends on the type of process that is used.

Analysis and design workbenches are only likely to be cost-effective where a methodical process is being followed. Specialized tools are developed as part of the process improvement activity to provide specific support for improving certain process activities.

Further reading

Managing the Software Process. This was the first published book on process maturity. As well as discussing the maturity model, the book provides information about what should be expected at each maturity level and what is required to move from a lower to a higher level. The tone is a bit evangelical but there is a great deal of sound software engineering wisdom in this book. (W. S. Humphrey, 1989, Addison-Wesley.)

IEEE Software, **10** (4), July 1993. This is a special issue of the journal devoted to articles on process maturity. It includes a description of version 1.1 of the capability maturity model as well as articles discussing process improvement and process modelling.

'Process modelling'. This article is an excellent overview of software process modelling. It covers various approaches to process models and identifies key issues in process model development. (B. Curtis, M. I. Kellner, J. Over, *Comm. ACM*, September 1992.)

Software Process Modelling and Technology. This book focuses particularly on process technology. It has a European rather than an American slant as it was produced as part of a large collaborative research project. (A. Finkelstein, J. Kramer and B. Nusibeh (eds), 1994, John Wiley & Sons.)

KEY POINTS

- Process improvement involves process analysis, standardization, measurement and change. Training is essential if process improvement is to be effective.

- Process models include descriptions of activities, sub-processes, roles, exceptions, communications, deliverables and other processes.

- Metrics should be collected to answer specific questions about the software process used. These questions should be based on organizational improvement goals.

- The three types of process metrics which can be collected are time metrics, resource utilization metrics and event metrics.

- The SEI process maturity model classifies software processes as initial, repeatable, defined, managed and optimizing. It identifies key processes that should be used at each of these levels.

- The SEI model is appropriate for large systems developed by large teams of engineers. It should not be applied without adaptation to local circumstances.

- Processes can be classified as informal, managed, methodical and improving. This classification can be used to identify process tool support.

EXERCISES

31.1 Describe models of the following processes:

    (a) lighting a wood fire

    (b) cooking a three-course meal (you choose the menu)

    (c) writing a small (50-line) program

31.2 Under what circumstances is product quality likely to be determined by the quality of the development team? Give examples of the types of software product that are particularly dependent on individual talent and ability.

31.3   Assume that the goal of process improvement in an organization is to increase the number of reusable components which are produced during development. Suggest three questions in the GQM paradigm which this might lead to.

31.4   Describe three types of software process metric that may be collected as part of a process improvement process. Give one example of each type of metric.

31.5   Give two advantages and two disadvantages of the approach to process assessment and improvement which is embodied in the SEI process maturity model.

31.6   Suggest two application domains where the SEI capability model is unlikely to be appropriate. Give reasons why this is the case.

31.7   Consider the type of software process used in your organization. How many of the key process areas identified in the SEI model are used? How would this model classify your level of process maturity?

31.8   Suggest three specialized software tools which might be developed to support a process improvement programme in an organization.

31.9   Explain why a methodical process is not necessarily a managed process as defined in Section 30.5.

31.10 Are process improvement programmes which involve measuring the work of people in the process and changing the process inherently dehumanizing? What resistance to a process improvement programme might arise?

Part Eight
Evolution

This final part of the book is concerned with the evolution of software systems after they have been delivered to the customer. Chapter 32 discusses general problems of software maintenance and explains why this is an expensive process. Chapter 33 discusses the configuration management procedures and tools that are essential to support managed evolution. Chapter 34 covers the increasingly important topic of re-engineering. Existing software systems are re-engineered in order that they may continue in operation and evolve to meet business needs.

Contents

32

Software Maintenance

Objectives

- To describe different types of software maintenance and explain the differences between them.

- To describe the software maintenance process.

- To explain the dynamics of program evolution as suggested by Lehman's laws.

- To describe the technical and non-technical factors, including system documentation, which affect maintenance costs.

- To explain how measures of system complexity and process metrics may be useful as maintainability predictors.

Contents

It is impossible to produce systems of any size which do not need to be changed. Over the lifetime of a system, its original requirements will be modified to reflect changing user and customer needs. The system's environment will change as new hardware is introduced. Errors, undiscovered during system validation, may emerge and require repair.

The process of changing a system after it has been delivered and is in use is called *software maintenance*. The changes may involve simple changes to correct coding errors, more extensive changes to correct design errors or significant enhancements to correct specification errors or accommodate new requirements. Maintenance therefore, in this context, really means *evolution*. It is the process of changing a system to maintain its ability to survive.

There are three different types of software maintenance with very blurred distinctions between them:

(1)   *Corrective maintenance* is concerned with fixing reported errors in the software. Coding errors are usually relatively cheap to correct; design errors are more expensive as they may involve the rewriting of several program components. Requirements errors are the most expensive to repair because of the extensive system redesign which may be necessary.

(2)   *Adaptive maintenance* means changing the software to some new environment such as a different hardware platform or for use with a different operating system. The software functionality does not radically change.

(3)   *Perfective maintenance* involves implementing new functional or non-functional system requirements. These are generated by software customers as their organization or business changes.

It is difficult to find up-to-date figures for the relative effort devoted to these different types of maintenance. A survey by Lientz and Swanson (1980) discovered that about 65% of maintenance was perfective, 18% adaptive and 17% corrective (Figure 32.1). Similar figures were reported by Nosek and Palvia (1990) 10 years later. It is therefore reasonable to assume that the current figures are about the same.

Lientz and Swanson found that large organizations devoted at least 50% of their total programming effort to maintaining existing systems. McKee (1984) found a similar distribution of maintenance effort across the different types of maintenance but suggests that the amount of effort spent on maintenance is between 65% and 75% of total available effort. Again, up-to-date figures are hard to find but maintenance almost certainly remains the single most expensive software engineering activity.

The costs of adding functionality to a system after it has been put into operation are usually much greater than providing similar functionality when software is originally developed. There are a number of reasons for this:

(1)   Maintenance staff are often relatively inexperienced and unfamiliar with the application domain. Maintenance has a poor image among software engineers. It is seen as a less skilled process than system development and is often allocated to the most junior staff.

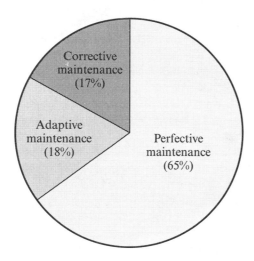

Figure 32.1
Maintenance effort distribution.

(2)   The programs being maintained may have been developed many years ago without modern software engineering techniques. They may be unstructured and optimized for efficiency rather than understandability.

(3)   Changes made to a program may introduce new faults which trigger further change requests. New faults may be introduced because the complexity of the system may make it difficult to assess the effects of a change.

(4)   As a system is changed, its structure tends to degrade. This makes the system harder to understand and makes further changes difficult as the program becomes less cohesive.

(5)   The links between a program and its associated documentation are sometimes lost during the maintenance process. The documentation may therefore be an unreliable aid to program understanding.

The first of these problems can only be tackled by organizations adopting enlightened maintenance management policies. Management must demonstrate to engineers that maintenance is of equal value and is as challenging as original software development. The best designers and programmers should be challenged and motivated by system maintenance. Boehm (1983) suggests several steps that can improve maintenance staff motivation:

(1)   Couple software objectives to organizational goals.

(2)   Couple software maintenance rewards to organizational performance.

(3)   Integrate software maintenance personnel into operational teams.

(4)   Create a discretionary, preventative maintenance budget which allows the maintenance team to decide when to re-engineer parts of the software. Preventative maintenance means making changes to the software which improve its structure so that future maintenance is simplified.

(5) Involve maintenance staff early in the software process during standards preparation, reviews and test preparation.

The second of the above problems, namely unstructured code, can be tackled using re-engineering and design recovery techniques. These are covered in Chapter 34.

The other maintenance problems are process problems. Structure naturally degrades with change. Organizations must plan to invest extra effort and resources in preventative maintenance with the aim of maintaining the structure. Good software engineering practice such as the use of information hiding or object-oriented development helps minimize the structure degradation but effort for structure maintenance is still required. These techniques also reduce the probability of fault introduction when changes are made.

The loss of traceability from code to design documents may be a consequence of poor configuration management (discussed in Chapter 33). Alternatively, it can be due to adopting a 'quick fix' approach to maintenance. A 'quick fix' means that the program is modified when a change is requested without changing other documents. Ways of avoiding this are discussed in the following section.

32.1 The maintenance process

The maintenance process is triggered by a set of change requests from system users, management or customers. The cost and impact of these changes are assessed. If the proposed changes are accepted, a new release of the system is planned. This release will usually involve elements of adaptive, corrective and perfective maintenance. The changes are implemented and validated and a new version of the system is released. The process then iterates with a new set of changes proposed for the new release. Figure 32.2, adapted from Arthur (1988), shows an overview of this process.

Change requests sometimes relate to system problems that must be tackled urgently. For example, a fault in a customer's system may have to be quickly remedied to allow normal business to continue. The natural tendency in such situations is to adopt a process as shown in Figure 32.3.

Figure 32.2
An overview of the maintenance process.

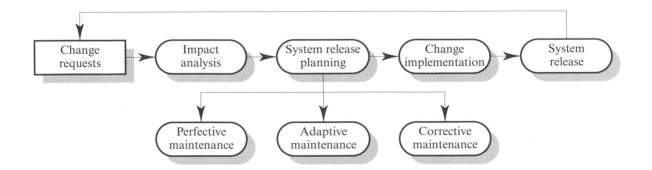

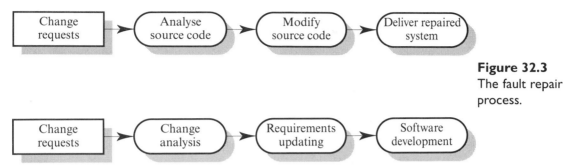

Figure 32.3
The fault repair process.

Figure 32.4
Maintenance as iterative development.

This emergency repair approach is sometimes necessary if the reported problems affect system availability. However, the danger of this approach is that design documents are not updated. The code and the design gradually become out of step. It is difficult to avoid this happening because maintenance engineers may be pressurized to deal with new emergency fixes to the software. If an engineer who made a code change leaves a team before the design is updated, it is then difficult for his or her replacement to retro-fit the necessary design changes.

A further problem with emergency system repairs is that they have to be completed as quickly as possible. A workable solution rather than the best solution as far as system structure is concerned may be chosen. This accelerates the process of software ageing so that future changes become progressively more difficult.

Rather than viewing maintenance as a separate process, it should normally be considered as an iteration of the development process. New requirements must be formulated and validated, components of the system must be redesigned and implemented and part or all of the system must be tested. This implies a process model as shown in Figure 32.4.

The development process that is used should be the normal software process used in the organization. If prototyping of the proposed changes is necessary, this should be carried out as part of the change analysis process.

This iterative development process is effective when changes are not urgent and can be batched. If emergency code repairs have to be carried out, the problems of document inconsistency and degraded structure can be avoided if the change request for the repair remains outstanding after the code faults have been fixed. It can then be reimplemented more carefully after further analysis. Of course, the code of the repair may be reused. However, an alternative, better solution to the problem may be discovered when more time is available for analysis.

32.2 System documentation

Properly produced and maintained system documentation is a tremendous aid to maintenance engineers. The system documentation includes all of the documents describing the implementation of the system from the requirements specification to the final acceptance test plan. Documents which may be produced to aid the maintenance process include:

- The requirements document and an associated rationale.

- A document describing the overall system architecture.

- For each program in the system, a description of the architecture of that program.

- For each component, a specification and design description.

- Program source code listings which should be commented. If meaningful names are used and gotos are avoided, much of the code should be self-documenting with no need for explanatory comments. Program comments need only explain complex sections of code and provide a rationale for the coding method used.

- Validation documents describing how each program is validated and how the validation information relates to the requirements.

- A system maintenance guide that describes known problems with the system and that describes which parts of the system are hardware and software dependent. The guide should also explain how evolution of the system has been taken into account in its design.

System documentation should be structured, with overviews leading the reader into more formal and detailed descriptions of each aspect of the system. It is important that documents are clear and readable otherwise they will not be used. While the standard of presentation need not match that of user manuals, it must be at such a level that readers are not discouraged by poor grammar, spelling and document layout.

Wherever possible, document production should be tool-assisted. A significant benefit of using CASE systems to support the development process is lower costs in producing system documentation. It can often be generated automatically from the CASE system repository. Even when this is impossible, a document template or outline may be produced which is then filled in by the system documenter.

32.3 Program evolution dynamics

Program evolution dynamics is the study of system change. The majority of work in this area has been carried out by Lehman and Belady (1985). From these studies, they proposed a set of 'laws' (Lehman's laws) concerning system change. They claim these 'laws' are invariant and widely applicable.

Lehman's laws are one of the few examples in software engineering of theories that have been derived from observations. It is normal practice in other sciences to base theories on observations, but objective observations in software engineering are difficult and expensive to make.

Lehman and Belady examined the growth and evolution of a number of large software systems. The proposed laws were derived from these measurements. The laws (hypotheses, really) are shown in Figure 32.5.

Law	Description
Continuing change	A program that is used in a real-world environment necessarily must change or become progressively less useful in that environment.
Increasing complexity	As an evolving program changes, its structure tends to become more complex. Extra resources must be devoted to preserving and simplifying the structure.
Large program evolution	Program evolution is a self-regulating process. System attributes such as size, time between releases and the number of reported errors are approximately invariant for each system release.
Organizational stability	Over a program's lifetime, its rate of development is approximately constant and independent of the resources devoted to system development.
Conservation of familiarity	Over the lifetime of a system, the incremental change in each release is approximately constant.

Figure 32.5
Lehman's laws.

The first law states that system maintenance is an inevitable process. Fault repair is only part of the maintenance activity. System requirements will always change so that a system must evolve if it is to remain useful. The reason for this is that the system's environment is changing with time so that the customer's requirements also change.

The second law states that, as a system is changed, its structure is degraded. Additional costs, over and above those of implementing the change, must be accepted if the structural degradation is to be reversed. The maintenance process might include explicit restructuring activities aimed at improving the adaptability of the system.

The third law is, perhaps, the most interesting and the most contentious of Lehman's laws. It suggests that large systems have a dynamic of their own that is established at an early stage in the development process. This determines the gross trends of the system maintenance process and limits the number of possible system changes. Maintenance management cannot do whatever it wants as far as changing the system is concerned. Lehman and Belady suggest that this law is a result of fundamental structural and organizational factors.

Once a system exceeds some minimal size it acts in the same way as an inertial mass. Its size inhibits major change because changes introduce new faults that degrade the functionality of the system. If a large change increment is proposed, this will introduce many new faults that will limit the useful change delivered in the new version of the system.

Large systems are usually produced by large organizations. These organizations have their own internal bureaucracies which slow down the process of change and which determine the budget allocated to a particular system. Major system changes require organizational decision making and changes to the project budget.

Such decisions take time to make. During that time, other, higher priory system changes may be proposed. It may be necessary to shelve the changes to a later date when the change approval process must be re-initiated. Thus, the rate of change of the system is partially governed by the organization's decision-making processes.

Lehman's fourth law suggests that most large programming projects work in what he terms a 'saturated' state. That is, a change to resources or staffing has imperceptible effects on the long-term evolution of the system. Of course, this is also suggested by the third law which suggests that program evolution is largely independent of management decisions. This law confirms that large software development teams are unproductive as the communication overheads dominate the work of the team. Lehman's fifth law is concerned with the change increments in each system release. I cover this in Chapter 33 which covers configuration management.

Lehman's observations seem generally sensible. They should be taken into account when planning the maintenance process. It may be that business considerations require them to be ignored at any one time. For example, for marketing reasons, it may be necessary to make several major system changes in a single release. Management should realize that the likely consequences of this are that one or more releases devoted to error repair are likely to be required.

It may appear that the radical differences which are obvious between releases of program products violate Lehman's laws. For example, over 10 years, Microsoft Word has been transformed from a simple word processor which operated in 256K of memory to a gigantic, feature-laden system. It now needs many megabytes of memory and a fast processor to operate. This seems to contradict the third and fourth of Lehman's laws. However, I suspect that this program is not really a sequence of revisions. Rather, the same name has been retained for marketing reasons but the program itself has been largely rewritten between releases.

32.4 Maintenance costs

Maintenance costs vary widely from one application domain to another. For business application systems, a study by Guimaraes (1983) showed that maintenance costs were broadly comparable with system development costs. For other classes of system, such as embedded real-time systems, maintenance costs may be up to four times higher than development costs. The high reliability and performance requirements of these systems may require modules to be tightly linked and hence difficult to change.

It is usually cost-effective to invest effort when designing and implementing a system to reduce maintenance costs. Adding functionality after delivery involves an expensive understanding and analysis activity. Therefore, any work done during development to reduce the cost of this analysis is likely to reduce maintenance costs. Good software engineering techniques such as precise specification, information hiding, loose coupling and configuration management all reduce maintenance costs.

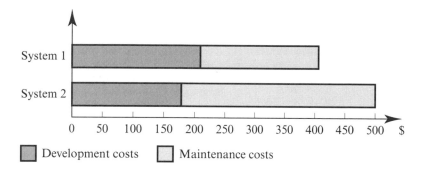

Figure 32.6
Development and
maintenance costs.

Figure 32.6 shows how overall lifetime costs may decrease as more effort is expended during system development to produce a maintainable system. Because of the potential reduction in costs in understanding, analysis and testing, there is a significant multiplier effect when the system is developed for maintainability. For System 1, extra development costs of $25,000 are invested in making the system more maintainable. This results in a saving of $100,000 in maintenance costs. This assumes that a percentage increase in development costs results in a comparable percentage decrease in overall system costs.

Maintenance costs are related to a number of product, process and organizational factors (Figure 32.7). The principal technical and non-technical factors which affect maintenance are:

(1) *Module independence*   It should be possible to modify one component of a system without affecting other system components.

(2) *Programming language*   Programs written in a high-level programming language are usually easier to understand (and hence maintain) than programs written in a low-level language.

(3) *Programming style*   The way in which a program is written contributes to its understandability and hence the ease with which it can be modified.

(4) *Program validation and testing*   Generally, the more time and effort spent on design validation and program testing, the fewer errors in the program. Consequently, corrective maintenance costs are minimized.

(5) *The quality of program documentation*   If a program is supported by clear, complete yet concise documentation, the task of understanding the program can be relatively straightforward. Program maintenance costs tend to be less for well-documented systems than for systems supplied with poor or incomplete documentation.

(6) *The configuration management techniques used*   One of the most significant costs of maintenance is keeping track of all system documents and ensuring that these are kept consistent. Effective configuration management can help control this cost.

Non-technical factors	Technical factors
Application domain	Module independence
Staff stability	Programming language
Program age	Programming style
External environment	Program validation
Hardware stability	Documentation
	Configuration
	Management

Figure 32.7
Maintenance cost
factors.

(7) *The application domain* If the application domain is clearly defined and well understood, the system requirements are likely to be complete. Relatively little perfective maintenance may be necessary. If the application is in a new domain, it is likely that the initial requirements will be modified frequently, as users gain a better understanding of their real needs.

(8) *Staff stability* Maintenance costs are reduced if system developers are responsible for maintaining their own programs. There is no need for other engineers to spend time understanding the system. In practice, however, it is very unusual for developers to maintain a program throughout its useful life.

(9) *The age of the program* As a program is maintained, its structure is degraded. The older the program, the more maintenance it receives and the more expensive this maintenance becomes.

(10) *The dependence of the program on its external environment* If a program is dependent on its external environment it must be modified as the environment changes. For example, changes in a taxation system might require payroll, accounting, and stock control programs to be modified.

(11) *Hardware stability* If a program is designed for a particular hardware configuration that does not change during the program's lifetime, no maintenance due to hardware changes will be required. However, this situation is rare. Programs must often be modified to use new hardware which replaces obsolete equipment.

As systems age, maintenance costs more. Old systems may be written in programming languages that are no longer used for new development. These systems may have been developed using design methods which have been supplanted by newer techniques. Special provision may have to be made to train staff members to maintain these programs.

This problem is becoming more severe as languages such as Ada, C++ and 4GLs take over from older languages such as FORTRAN and COBOL. Object-oriented design is increasingly replacing function-oriented development. However, object-oriented design will not replace functional approaches for many years because of the immense amount of software developed using these functional design techniques. This software will have to be maintained well into the 21st century.

32.4.1 Maintenance cost estimation

Maintenance costs are affected by many factors so it is difficult to devise systematic approaches to maintenance cost estimation. Estimates may sometimes be made using cost data from past projects. These may be reasonably accurate when previous cost information was collected for the same type of system and comparable development processes were used.

The algorithmic approach to cost estimation (COCOMO), discussed in Chapter 29, has been extended to maintenance cost estimation. Using data gathered from 63 projects in a number of application areas, Boehm (1981) established a formula for estimating maintenance costs. This uses a quantity called the Annual Change Traffic (ACT) which he defines as follows:

> The fraction of a software product's source instructions which undergo change during a (typical) year either through addition or modification

The ACT is clearly related to the number of change requests. The only way this figure can be estimated is by analogy with previous systems. Boehm's estimation method for maintenance costs uses the ACT and the estimated or actual development effort in person-months to derive the annual effort required for software maintenance. This is computed as follows:

$$AME = ACT \times SDT$$

AME and SDT are the annual maintenance effort and the software development time and the units of each are person-months (p.m.). Notice that this is a simple linear relationship. Figure 32.8 shows the computed maintenance costs for systems of various sizes assuming ACTs of 10, 20 and 30%.

Say a software project required 236 person-months of development effort and it was estimated that 15% of the code would be modified in a typical year. The basic maintenance effort estimate is:

$$AME = 0.15 \times 236 = 35.4 \text{ p.m.}$$

Boehm suggests that this rough estimate of maintenance costs should be a basis for computing a more precise figure based on the development attributes discussed in Chapter 29. The maintenance cost estimate may be refined by judging the importance of the factors affecting the cost and selecting the appropriate cost multiplier. The basic maintenance cost is then multiplied by each multiplier to give the revised cost estimate.

In my view, there are two very fundamental problems with this algorithmic approach:

(1)   In many cases, systems are completely new and there is no historic basis for estimating the ACT. The estimates or guesses made in this situation are likely to be very unreliable.

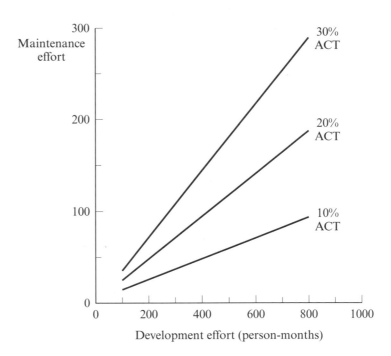

Figure 32.8
Maintenance vs
development effort.

(2) It is not clear that the development attributes are equally applicable to maintenance. Furthermore, there are many other attributes (discussed above) which affect software maintainability. It is very difficult to estimate these with any confidence.

The COCOMO model used by Boehm generated maintenance cost estimates that were reasonably close to the actual maintenance costs in his company. However, algorithmic cost modelling can only be accurate if the model is calibrated to an organization's own software development practices. If this is impossible, its results are likely to be useless.

32.5 Maintainability measurement

Managers hate surprises especially if these result in unexpectedly high costs. If the maintainability of a system can be assessed, the relative amount of effort required for maintenance can be predicted so will not come as an unexpected organizational expense. A maintainability metric can help management make an informed decision on whether a component should be maintained or completely rewritten to reduce future maintenance costs.

Maintainability metrics do not measure the cost of making a particular change to a system nor do they predict whether or not a particular component will have to be maintained. Rather, they are based on the assumption that the maintainability of a program is related to its complexity. The metrics measure some aspects of the program complexity. It is suggested that high complexity values correlate with difficulties in maintaining a system component.

McCabe (1976) devised a measure of program complexity using graph theoretic techniques. His theory maintains that program complexity is not dependent on size but on the decision structure of the program. The program flow graph and the cyclomatic complexity can be derived as discussed in Chapter 23. McCabe argues that components with a high cyclomatic complexity are likely to require more maintenance than components with a low metric value.

Halstead (1977) suggests that the complexity of a program can be measured by considering the number of unique operators, the number of unique operands, the total frequency of operators and the total frequency of operands in a program. Using these parameters, Halstead devised metrics allowing program size, programming effort, and program 'intelligence count' to be computed.

Both of these techniques may have some validity. Both suffer from the same disadvantage that they do not take into account the data structures used in the program, the program comments or the use of meaningful variable names. Shepherd *et al.* (1979) have conducted experiments using both techniques. Their results were inconclusive. Hamer and Frewin (1982) have evaluated Halstead's metrics and found them to be unreliable predictors of program understandability or maintainability.

Rather than use a single metric, Kafura and Reddy (1987) used a spectrum of seven metrics to assess the complexity of a system. They include code metrics and measures of the structural complexity of the system as discussed in Chapter 30. Their experiments showed a high correlation between the values of the metrics produced and the perceived maintainability as assessed by human maintainers.

The advantage of using a spectrum of metrics rather than a single metric is that these give a broader coverage of the factors which may affect program maintainability. Code size is a significant metric but, taken on its own, it would always imply that larger components were more expensive to maintain than smaller components. In some cases, this may be untrue. A large simple component may be easier to maintain than a smaller component with complex control logic.

Kafura and Reddy suggest that it is not the absolute values of these metrics which are important but their relative values. If some components have a much higher complexity than most others, their experiments suggested that these would cause particular problems in maintenance. Components with a high value for complexity contained a higher proportion of system faults. For example, say the average complexity value for the components in a system was X. Three components had complexity ratings which were much greater than X. The design of these complex components should be examined to see if they should be reimplemented to reduce future maintenance costs.

This spectrum of metrics gives a more accurate measure of system complexity so is more likely to be a useful maintainability predictor. However, collecting these metrics is not cheap and may require special-purpose software to be written for code analysis. This cost of this may exceed the benefits which result from maintainability estimation.

After a system has been put into service and the maintenance process is underway, data about that process can be collected. Trends in that data can give indications about the program maintainability. I don't know of any systematic experiments that have tried to relate process metrics to maintainability. However, it is reasonable to surmise that they may be useful maintainability predictors.

Examples of process metrics which may be useful for assessing maintainability are:

(1)   *Number of requests for corrective maintenance*   If the number of failure reports is increasing, this may indicate that more errors are being introduced into the program than are being repaired during the maintenance process. This may indicate a decline in maintainability.

(2)   *Average time required for impact analysis*   This reflects the number of program components that are affected by the change request. If this time increases, it implies more and more components are affected and maintainability is decreasing.

(3)   *Average time taken to implement a change request*   This is not the same as the time for impact analysis although it may correlate with it. The activities involved are making changes to the system and its documentation rather than simply assessing what components are affected. This change time depends on the difficulty of programming so that non-functional requirements such as performance are met. If the time to implement a change increases, this may indicate a decline in maintainability.

(4)   *Number of outstanding change requests*   If this number increases with time, it may imply a decline in maintainability.

Of course, as discussed in Chapter 30, any measurements must be analysed with care. It does not necessarily follow that there is a clear and unambiguous relationship between these metrics and system maintainability. Nevertheless, I suggest that their use for maintainability prediction is worth investigating.

Further reading

Reverse Engineering and Software Maintenance. The authors of this book were involved in a number of research projects investigating software maintenance. It therefore discusses state-of-the art approaches to the maintenance process. (K. Lano and H. Haughton, 1994, McGraw-Hill.)

Software Evolution. This is a readable book on the maintenance process which contains practical advice on how to tackle the maintenance problem. Its pragmatic style is a good complement to Lano and Haughton's book. (L. J. Arthur, 1988, John Wiley and Sons.)

'Viewing maintenance as reuse-oriented software development'. This is an excellent general article on maintenance. It suggests that an approach based on experience and code reuse is effective for software maintenance. (V. R Basili, *IEEE Software*, **7** (1), January 1990.)

See also the further reading recommended in Chapter 34.

KEY POINTS

- There are three principal types of software maintenance. These are perfective maintenance where new functionality is added to the system; adaptive maintenance where the system is adapted to new environments and corrective maintenance which is system repair.

- The cost of software maintenance usually exceeds the cost of software development. Typically, maintenance costs are at least 50% of lifetime system costs for business systems and even more for embedded systems.

- Investing extra effort in making a system maintainable is likely to have a significant payoff in maintenance cost reduction.

- System documentation for maintenance should include a system requirements document, design documents and validation documents. It must be kept up to date when the system is changed.

- There appear to be a number of invariant relationships (Lehman's laws) which affect the evolution of a software system. These have been derived from empirical observations and show that maintenance costs are inevitable. They provide guidelines on how to manage the maintenance process.

- Several technical and non-technical factors affect maintenance costs. These include application factors, environmental factors, personnel factors, programming language factors and documentation.

- Complexity metrics can give some hints as to components that may incur high maintenance costs. Process metrics, such as the number of outstanding change requests, may also be an indicator of system maintainability.

EXERCISES

32.1 Explain why a software system which is used in a real-world environment must change or become progressively less useful.

32.2 Software maintenance is often seen as an inferior activity to software development. Suggest five steps which software managers might take to improve the motivation of maintenance staff.

32.3 Propose a standard structure for a system maintenance document which is designed to provide guidance for system maintainers.

32.4 Explain the difficulties of measuring program maintainability. Describe why maintainability is not simply related to a single complexity metric.

32.5 Explain the rationale underlying Lehman's laws. Under what circumstances might the laws break down?

32.6 Explain why the structuring facilities offered by programming languages such as Ada are likely to lead to more maintainable programs. Suggest features of Ada or C++ which might cause maintenance problems.

32.7 Describe technical and non-technical factors which affect system maintenance costs. Explain how, as a software manager, you would attempt to minimize maintenance costs in projects which you are managing.

32.8 Given that the annual change traffic in a system is 14% per year and the initial development cost was $245,000, compute an estimate for the annual system maintenance cost. Given that the lifetime of the system is 12 years, what is the total cost of that software system?

32.9 As a software project manager in a company that specializes in the development of software for the offshore oil industry, you have been given the task of discovering those factors which affect the maintainability of the particular systems which are developed by your company. Suggest how you might set up a programme to analyse the maintenance process to discover appropriate maintainability metrics for your company.

32.10 Do software engineers have a professional responsibility to produce maintainable code even if this is not explicitly requested by their employer?

Configuration Management

Objectives

- To introduce software configuration management and its role in software product evolution.

- To describe the structure of a configuration management plan and the activities involved in configuration management planning.

- To describe critical configuration management activities. These are change control and management, version management and system building.

- To show how automated configuration management tools may be used to support the configuration management process.

Contents

Large software systems may be considered as configurations of components. During their lifetime, these systems evolve. Many different versions, made up of different component configurations, of the system are created. *Configuration management* (CM) is the process which controls the changes made to a system and manages the different versions of the evolving software product.

Configuration management involves the development and application of procedures and standards for managing an evolving system product. Procedures should be developed for building systems and releasing them to customers. Standards should be developed for recording and processing proposed system changes and identifying and storing different versions of the system.

CM may be part of a more general software quality management process. In some organizations, the same manager may share quality management and configuration management responsibilities. Software may be released by the developers to a quality assurance team who are responsible for checking that the system is of acceptable quality. It is then passed to the configuration management team who become responsible for controlling changes to the software. Controlled systems are sometimes called *baselines* as they are a starting point for controlled evolution.

There are a number of possible reasons why systems exist in different configurations. These configurations may be produced for different computers, for different operating systems, incorporating client-specific functions and so on (Figure 33.1). Configuration managers are responsible for keeping track of the differences between software versions and for ensuring that new versions are derived in a controlled way. They may also be responsible for ensuring that these new versions are released to the correct customers at the appropriate time.

The configuration management process and associated documentation should be based on a set of standards. Within an organization, these standards should be published in a configuration management handbook or as part of a quality handbook. An example of such a standard is IEEE standard 828-1983, which is a standard for configuration management plans.

These external standards may be used as a basis for more detailed organizational standards that are tailored to a specific environment. It is not particularly important which standard is taken as a starting point as all of them include comparable processes. In both the ISO 9000 quality standards (Ince, 1994) and the SEI's Capability Maturity Model (Paulk *et al.,* 1993), the existence of formal CM standards and procedures is essential for quality certification.

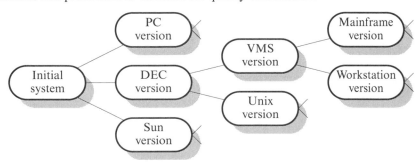

Figure 33.1
System families.

A problem with existing standards for configuration management is that they have been developed with the assumption that a waterfall model of the software process will be used for system development. This means that they cannot be readily applied to alternative development approaches such as evolutionary prototyping. The problems which arise in this case are discussed by Bersoff and Davis (1991). They propose extensions to current CM standards to handle other development process models.

In this chapter, I discuss four principal configuration management activities. These are concerned with planning for product evolution, managing changes to systems, controlling versions and releases of systems and building systems from their components. Nowadays, configuration management is almost always supported by CASE systems. Typical CASE systems for CM are therefore also covered here.

33.1 Configuration management planning

Configuration management takes over control of systems after they have been developed. However, planning this management process must start during system development. A configuration management plan should be developed as part of the overall project planning process.

The CM plan should be organized into a number of chapters and should include at least the following information:

(1)   The definition of what entities are to be managed and a formal scheme for identifying these entities.

(2)   A statement of who takes responsibility for the configuration management procedures and for submitting controlled entities to the configuration management team.

(3)   The configuration management policies which are used for change control and version management.

(4)   A description of the records of the configuration management process which should be maintained.

(5)   A description of the tools to be used for configuration management and the process to be applied when using these tools.

(6)   A definition of the configuration database which will be used to record configuration information.

Other information such as the management of software from external suppliers and the CM process auditing procedures may also be included in the CM plan.

An important part of the CM plan is the definition of responsibilities. It should define who is responsible for the delivery of each document or software component to quality assurance and configuration management. It may also define the reviewers of each document. The person responsible for document delivery need not be the same as the person responsible for producing the document. To simplify interfaces, it is often convenient to make project managers or team leaders responsible for all of the documents produced by their team.

33.1.1 Configuration item identification

In the course of developing a large software system, thousands of documents are produced. Many of these are technical working documents which present a snapshot of ideas for further development. These documents are subject to frequent and regular change. Others are inter-office memos, minutes of group meetings, outline plans and proposals and so on. These documents may be of interest to a project historian. However, they are not required for future maintenance of the system.

A key task of the configuration management planning process is to decide exactly which items (or classes of item) are to be controlled. Documents or groups of related documents under configuration control are formal documents or configuration items. Project plans, specifications, designs, programs and test data suites are normally maintained as *configuration items*. However, all documents which may be necessary for future system maintenance should be controlled.

The document naming scheme must assign a unique name to all documents under configuration control. There will be relationships between documents. For example, design documents will be associated with programs. These relationships can be recorded implicitly by organizing the naming scheme so that related documents have a common root to their name. This leads to a hierarchical naming scheme where examples of names might be:

PCL-TOOLS/EDIT/FORMS/DISPLAY/AST-INTERFACE/CODE
PCL-TOOLS/EDIT/HELP/QUERY/HELPFRAMES/FR-1

These names have a number of components. The initial part of the name is the project name, PCL-TOOLS. In this project, there are four separate tools. The tool name is used as the next part of the name. Each of these tools is made up of different named modules. This decomposition process continues until the base level formal documents are referenced (Figure 33.2).

The leaves of the documentation hierarchy are the formal project documents. Figure 33.2 shows that three formal documents are required for each managed entity. These are an object description (OBJECTS), the code of the component (CODE) and a set of tests for that code (TESTS).

The problem with naming schemes of this sort is that they are project based. Components are identified as being associated with a particular project. This may reduce the opportunities for reuse. Copies of reusable components should normally be taken out of such a scheme and renamed according to their application domain. Other problems may arise if the document naming scheme is used as a direct basis for designing a file storage structure. This may cause problems because documents may have to be retrieved and classified using attributes which are not relevant to CM.

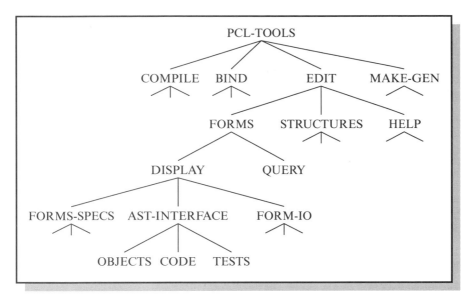

Figure 33.2
Configuration
hierarchy.

The description of this formal document identification scheme is itself a critical project document as it is used to generate unique document identifiers. Therefore, the name definition procedure should itself be placed under configuration control. It should not be changed in an arbitrary way.

33.1.2 The configuration database

As part of the configuration management plan, a database schema to record configuration information should be defined. The configuration database is used to record all relevant information relating to configurations. Its principal functions are to assist with assessing the impact of system changes and to provide management information about the CM process. As well as defining the database schema, procedures for recording and retrieving project information must also be defined as part of the CM planning process.

A configuration database must be able to provide answers to a variety of queries about system configurations. Typical queries might be:

(1)   Which customers have taken delivery of a particular version of the system?

(2)   What hardware and operating system configuration is required to run a given system version?

(3)   How many versions of a system have been created and what were their creation dates?

(4)   What versions of a system might be affected if a particular component is changed?

(5)   How many change requests are outstanding on a particular version?

(6)   How many reported faults exist in a particular version?

The CM database may be implemented as a stand-alone system or may be integrated with the version management and control system which stores the formal project documents. Software engineering database systems such as Adele (Estublier, 1985) or PCTE (Wakeman and Jowett, 1993) may be used to create this integrated repository. This allows CASE systems to be integrated with the configuration management process. Editing operations, for example, can create new versions of systems. However, as discussed in Chapter 26, most design and analysis workbenches maintain their own repository and this has limited the use of integrated systems.

More commonly, a configuration database is maintained as a separate system. The configuration items may be stored in files or in a version management system. This configuration database stores information about the configuration items and references their file names in the version management system. While this is a relatively cheap and flexible approach, its disadvantage is that the configuration items may be changed without going through the configuration database. In such cases, change information may not be recorded.

33.2 Change management

Change is a fact of life for large software systems. As discussed in earlier chapters, organizational needs and requirements change during the lifetime of a system. This requires corresponding changes to be made to the software. There is therefore a need for a system to ensure that these changes are recorded and applied to the system in a cost-effective way.

The change management process should come into effect when the software or associated documentation is put under the control of the configuration management team. Change management procedures should be designed to ensure that the costs and benefits of change are properly analysed and that changes to a system are made in a controlled way.

Change management processes involve technical change analysis, cost-benefit analysis and change tracking. The pseudo-code, shown in Figure 33.3, defines a process which may be used to manage software system changes:

The first stage in the change management process is to complete a change request form (CRF). This is a formal document where the requester sets out the change required to the system. As well as recording the change required, the CRF records the recommendations regarding the change, the estimated costs of the change and the dates when the change was requested, approved, implemented and validated. It may also include a section where the maintenance engineer outlines how the change is to be implemented.

The information provided in the change request form is recorded in the CM database. An example of a change request form, which has been partially completed, is shown in Figure 33.4. The change request form is usually defined during the CM planning process. For some contracts however, particularly government contracts, the CRF must conform to a specified client standard.

Request change by completing a change request form
Analyse change request
if change is valid **then**
     Assess how change might be implemented
     Assess change cost
     Record change request in database
     Submit request to change control board
     if change is accepted **then**
          repeat
               make changes to software
               record changes and link to associated change request
               submit changed software for quality approval
          until software quality is adequate
          create new system version
     else
          reject change request
else
     reject change request

Figure 33.3
The change
management process.

Once a change request form has been submitted, it is analysed to check that the change is valid. Some change requests may be due to user misunderstandings rather than system faults; others may refer to already known faults. If the analysis process discovers that a change request is invalid, duplicated or has already been

Change Request Form

Project: Proteus/PCL-Tools   **Number:** 23/94
Change requester: I. Sommerville   **Date:** 1/12/94
Requested change: When a component is selected from the structure, display the name of the file where it is stored.

Change analyser: G. Dean   **Analysis date:** 10/12/94
Components affected: Display-Icon.Select, Display-Icon.Display

Associated components: FileTable

Change assessment: Relatively simple to implement as a file name table is available. Requires the design and implementation of a display field. No changes to associated components are required.

Change priority: Low
Change implementation:
Estimated effort: 0.5 days
Date to CCB: 15/12/94   **CCB decision date:** 1/2/95
CCB decision: Accept change. Change to be implemented in Release 2.1.
Change implementor: **Date of change:**
Date submitted to QA: **QA decision:**
Date submitted to CM:
Comments

Figure 33.4
A partially completed
change request form.

considered, the change should be rejected. The reason for the rejection should be returned to the person who submitted the change request.

For valid changes, the next stage of the process is change assessment and costing. The impact of the change on the rest of the system must be checked. A technical analysis must be made of how to implement the change. The cost of making the change and possibly changing other system components to accommodate the change is then estimated. This should be recorded on the change request form. This assessment process may use the configuration database where component inter-relationships are recorded. The impact of the change on other components may then be assessed.

Unless the change involves simple correction of minor errors on screen displays or in documents, it should then be submitted to a change control board (CCB) who decide whether or not the change should be accepted. The change control board considers the impact of the change from a strategic and organizational rather than a technical point of view. It decides if the change is economically justified and if there are good organizational reasons to accept the change.

The term 'change control board' sounds very formal. It implies a rather grand group which makes change decisions. Formally structured change control boards which include senior client and contractor staff are a requirement of military projects. For small or medium-sized projects, however, the change control board may simply consist of a project manager plus one or two engineers who are not directly involved in the software development. In some cases, there may only be a single change reviewer who gives advice on whether or not changes are justifiable.

When a set of changes has been approved, the software is handed over to the development or maintenance team for implementation. Once these have been completed, the revised software must be revalidated to check that these changes have been correctly implemented. The CM team, rather than the system developers, is responsible for building a new version or release of the software.

Change requests are themselves configuration items. They should be registered in the configuration database. It should be possible to use this database to discover the status of change requests and the change requests which are associated with specific software components.

As software components are changed, a record of the changes made to each component should be maintained. This is sometimes called the derivation history of a component. One way to maintain such a record is in a standardized comment prologue kept at the beginning of the component. This should reference the change request associated with the software change.

If a standard prologue style is adopted, tools may be written to process the derivation histories and produce reports about component changes. An example of a standardized comment prologue incorporating change information is shown in Figure 33.5.

The change management process is very procedural. Each person involved in the process is responsible for some activity. They complete this activity then pass on the forms and associated configuration items to someone else. The procedural nature of this process means that a change process model can be designed and integrated

```
// PROTEUS project (ESPRIT 6087)
//
// PCL-TOOLS/EDIT/FORMS/DISPLAY/AST-INTERFACE
//
// Object: PCL-Tool-Desc
// Author: G. Dean
// Creation date: 10th November 1994
//
// © Lancaster University 1994
//
// Modification history
// Version      Modifier      Date       Change        Reason
// 1.0          J. Jones      1/12/94     Add header     Submitted
   to CM
// 1.1          G. Dean       9/4/95      New field      Change
   req. 07/95
```

Figure 33.5
Component header
information.

with a version management system. This model may then be interpreted so that the right documents are passed to the right people at the right time.

An example of a specialized system that has adopted this approach is Lifespan (Whitgift, 1991). This is a configuration management system which incorporates a version management system and change support system. Documents are exchanged by electronic mail. Lifespan has been designed for use in very large projects. These have formal change management procedures and may have different contractors responsible for different parts of the system. Its change management model reflects this. It is probably not cost-effective to use a system like this on smaller projects.

Comparable facilities can be implemented for smaller projects using a process modelling or workflow system (Fernström, 1993). These allow a process model to be constructed and they include 'enactment' engines to interpret this model and provide advice about process activities. I have discussed the limitations of integrated process support in Chapter 25. However, the change management process is an example of a procedural process where automation can be cost-effective.

33.3 Version and release management

Version and release management are the processes of identifying and keeping track of different versions and releases of a system. Version managers must devise procedures to ensure that different versions of a system may be retrieved when required and are not accidentally changed. They may also work with customer liaison staff to plan when new releases of a system should be distributed.

A system *version* is an instance of a system that differs, in some way, from other instances. New versions of the system may have different functionality, performance or may repair system faults. Some versions may be functionally equivalent but designed for different hardware or software configurations. If there are only small differences between versions, one of these is sometimes called a *variant* of the other.

A system *release* is a version that is distributed to customers. Each system release should either include new functionality or should be intended for a different hardware platform. Normally, there are more versions of a system than releases. Some versions may never be released to customers. For example, versions may be created within an organization for internal development or for testing.

A release is not just an executable program or set of programs. It usually also includes:

(1)   *Configuration files* defining how the release should be configured for particular installations.

(2)   *Data files* which are needed for successful system operation.

(3)   *An installation program* which is used to help install the system on target hardware.

(4)   *Electronic and paper documentation* describing the system.

All this information must be made available on some medium which can be read by customers for that software. For large systems, this may be magnetic tape. For smaller systems, floppy disks may be used. Increasingly, however, releases are distributed on CD-ROM disks because of their large storage capacity.

When a system release is produced, it is important to record the versions of the operating system, libraries, compilers and other tools used to build the software. If it has to be rebuilt at some later date, it may be necessary to reproduce the exact platform configuration. In some cases, copies of the platform software and tools may also be placed under version management.

Version management is almost always supported by some automated tool. This tool is responsible for managing the storage of each system version. When a system or component is put under the control of a version management system, its use is controlled. It may be checked out from the system to named individuals. When re-entered in the system, a new version is created and named. I discuss an example of this type of tool (RCS) in Section 33.4.3.

33.3.1 Version identification

Identifying versions of a system appears to be straightforward. The first version and release of a system is simply called 1.0, subsequent versions are 1.1, 1.2 and so on. At some stage, it is decided to create release 2.0 and the process starts again at version 2.1, 2.2 and so on. System releases normally correspond to the base versions, that is, 1.0, 2.0, 3.0 and so on. The scheme is a linear one based on the assumption that system versions are created in sequence. Version management tools such as SCCS (Rochkind, 1975) support this approach to version identification.

This scheme is simple but it has associated problems:

(1) When should a new release (that is, a new branch in the derivation graph) rather than a new version be created?

(2) If several versions are created from a single parent, how should they be numbered? For example, say a system is intended to run on a number of different computer architectures. These are all derived from a single base release numbered 1.0. Should the versions be numbered 1.1, 1.2 and so on, implying sequential derivation?

(3) If many versions of a system are created and distributed to different customers, should the version naming scheme include some customer identifier? Each customer or system user may have a unique version of the system.

These identification problems arise because the naming scheme implies a linear derivation of versions whereas the actual logical derivation structure is a network structure such as that shown in Figure 33.6.

In Figure 33.6, Version 1.0 has spawned two versions, 1.1 and 1.1a. Version 1.1 has also spawned two versions namely 1.2 and 1.1b. Version 2.0 is not derived from 1.2 but from 1.1a. Version 2.2 is not a direct descendant of version 2 as it is derived from version 1.2.

An alternative to a numeric naming structure is to use a symbolic naming scheme. For example, rather than refer to Version 1.1.2, a particular instance of a system might be referred to as V1/VMS/DBserver. This implies that this is a version of a database server for a Digital computer running the VMS operating system. This has some advantages over the linear scheme but, again, it does not truly represent the derivation structure.

The fundamental problem with both numeric and symbolic naming schemes is that they do not reflect the many different attributes which may be used to identify versions. Examples of these identifying attributes are:

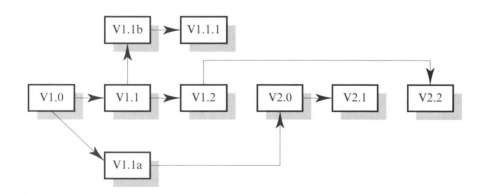

Figure 33.6
Version derivation
structure.

- customer
- development language
- development status
- hardware platform
- creation date

If each version is identified by a unique set of attributes, it is easy to add new versions that are derived from any of the existing versions. These are identified using a unique set of attribute values. They share most of these values with their parent version so relationships between versions are maintained. Versions can be retrieved by specifying the attribute values required. Functions on attributes are also support queries such as 'the most recently created version', 'the version created between given dates' and so on.

One way of providing attribute information for versions is to include it in a configuration database with a reference to the associated version name in a version management system. However, some version management systems such as Adele (Estublier, 1985) provide direct support for version identification by attributes. By specifying values for the required attributes, versions can be retrieved from the Adele database.

New system versions should always be created by the CM team rather than the system developers even when they not intended for external release. This ensures that the configuration management database is consistent. System developers should not have write access to this database.

33.3.2 Release management

New versions of a system may be created to fix reported faults or as part of the development process. In general, creating a new system version involves creating new source code and building the system. Creating a release, however, is more complex and expensive. As well as creating new source code and system building, data and configuration files may have to be prepared and new documentation written. The release must be packaged and distributed to customers.

Over the lifetime of a system, changes are likely to be proposed on a fairly regular basis. Different types of maintenance were discussed in Chapter 32. Corrective changes are intended to fix faults. Perfective changes are intended to implement new requirements or to improve system maintainability. Adaptive changes are intended to change the system to make it operate in a new environment. The configuration manager must decide how often the components affected by these changes should be rebuilt into a new version or release of the system.

Sometimes, this decision is forced on management by faults that have been discovered by customers. If these cause data corruption or system crashes customers must be provided with a fix for these problems. Sometimes, these faults are repaired by object-code patching. Object-code patching involves modifying the object code of the current version. The faulty code is replaced by an unconditional branch to the corrected code which then branches back to the end of the code being replaced.

However, this is an error-prone approach to problem repair. A better approach is to create a new system version (or interim release) which incorporates repairs to the critical faults. This interim release may be distributed without new documentation as there is no new functionality to be described.

When a new release of a system is created, the changes which have been made may introduce new faults or bring other existing faults to light. The more changes to a system, the more new faults will be introduced. Therefore, if a release incorporates a large number of changes, it is likely that there will be a correspondingly large number of new faults. These have to fixed in the next system release.

We have already looked at Lehman's laws in Chapter 32. Lehman's fifth law, the Law of Conservation of Familiarity, suggests that over the lifetime of a system, the incremental system change in each release is approximately constant. This 'law' was derived by analysing systems over many years and measuring the number of system modules which were modified in each release.

Lehman suggested that if a lot of new functionality was introduced in one release of a system, it would be necessary to issue another release fairly quickly. This would be required to correct errors that have resulted from the system changes and to improve the performance of the delivered release. Over the lifetime of a system, this was seen to be a self-regulating process. There was a limit to the rate at which new functionality could be introduced.

This suggests that it is unwise to change too much of a system's functionality at once. Otherwise an excessive number of faults may be introduced. A good change strategy is to interleave fault repair releases and releases which change the system's functionality (Figure 33.7).

If some system changes are concerned with fault repair and others with changing the system behaviour, mixing these change types could cause problems. The faults reported apply to a given version of the system code and if that code is changed to amend its behaviour, it is expensive to check if the faults still apply. All serious faults (faults which cause system corruption) should be repaired before functional or behavioural changes are applied.

Release management is complicated by the fact that customers may not actually want a new release of the system. Some system users may be happy with an existing system version. They may consider that it is not worth the cost of changing to a new release. However, as the system's functionality is enhanced, most customers will eventually decide to change.

This causes CM problems because new releases of the system cannot depend on the existence of previous releases. Consider the following scenario:

Figure 33.7
System release strategy.

(1)   Release 1 of a system is distributed and put into use.

(2)   Release 2 follows which requires the installation of new data files but some customers do not need the facilities of release 2 so remain with release 1.

(3)   Release 3 requires the data files installed in release 2 and has no new data files of its own.

The software distributor cannot assume that the files required for Release 3 have already been installed in all sites. Some sites may go directly from Release 1 to Release 3, skipping Release 2. Some sites may have modified the data files associated with Release 2 to reflect local circumstances. Therefore, the data files must be distributed and installed with Release 3 of the system.

33.3.3 Version management tools

Version management involves managing large amounts of information and ensuring that system changes are recorded and controlled. There are several CASE tools available to support this process. For Unix platforms, the most widely used version management systems are SCCS (Rochkind, 1975) and RCS (Tichy, 1985). Version management systems control a repository of configuration items where the contents of that repository are immutable (that is, cannot be changed). To work on a configuration item, it must be checked out of the repository into some working directory. After the work is complete, it is then checked into the repository. A new version is automatically created.

All version management systems provide a comparable basic set of capabilities although some have more sophisticated facilities than others. Examples of the capabilities which may be included in a version management system are:

(1)   *Version and release identification*   Managed versions may be assigned identifiers automatically when they are submitted to the system. Some systems support attribute value assignment for identification.

(2)   *Controlled change*   Versions of components must be checked out explicitly for change. The identifier of the engineer making the change is recorded. When re-submitted, a new version is created and tagged with the owner's identifier. The old version is never over-written.

(3)   *Storage management*   To reduce the storage space required by different versions which are largely the same, version management systems provide storage management facilities so that versions are described by their differences from some master version.

(4)   *Change history recording*   All of the changes made to a particular system or component may be recorded and listed.

The Unix version management systems SCCS and RCS are fundamentally similar although RCS offers more capabilities. RCS saves the source code of the most recent

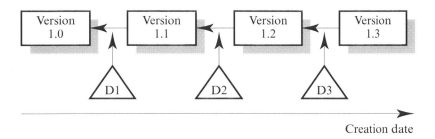

Creation date

Figure 33.8
Deltas in RCS.

version of a system as the master version. This is created from an earlier master version. When a new master is created, the previous version is deleted and replaced by a specification of the differences between it and the new master version. This difference specification is called a delta. Rather than having to store all source code of all masters, RCS need only save a single master version and a set of deltas (Figure 33.8).

Deltas are invariably much smaller than the source code of a system version. This method of storage management therefore reduces the disk space required for version management.

RCS supports the parallel development of different system releases. Release 1 can be modified after development of Release 2 is in progress by adding new level 1 deltas. In the example shown in Figure 33.9, Version 1.4 of Release 1 is created after Release 2 has been derived from Version 1.3.

As well as being associated with a particular version number, deltas are date stamped and owner stamped. If a particular version of a system is needed, the RCS user simply asks for that version either by number, by date or by owner. RCS applies the deltas in turn to create the required system.

RCS also includes a version merging capability. This may be used where independent changes have been made to a system by different people. RCS can check if the modified lines of code in each version are completely distinct. If so, it can then merge these versions so that both sets of changes are incorporated. However, this facility should be used with care. There can be subtle interactions between the merged code sections which cause system errors.

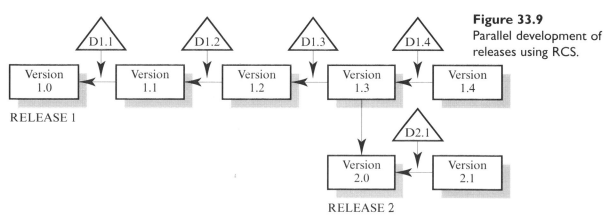

Figure 33.9
Parallel development of releases using RCS.

The main differences between RCS and SCCS are the method of storage management used and the version annotation capabilities. SCCS stores the first version of a system with further versions specified as deltas from it. It does not allow as much user-supplied information to be associated with a system version. RCS is generally more efficient for version creation. The versions that are requested most often are usually those which were created most recently.

A limitation of RCS is that it is designed to work with ASCII text. The deltas are specified as a set of edit commands to the master version. This means that it cannot be used to manage object code or any other representations which are encoded using all byte values from 0 to 255. This includes most graphics systems and documents produced by word processors. SCCS suffers from the same limitation so neither of these systems can be used to provide version management for all system documents.

33.4 System building

System building is the process of combining the components of a system into a program which executes on a particular target configuration. This may involve compilation of some components and a linking process which puts the object code together to make an executable system. For large systems, the system building process is an expensive part of the configuration management process. It may take several days to completely rebuild a system from its source code.

System building requires particular care when a host–target approach to development is used. The system is built on a host machine but executes on a separate target machine. The first sign of problems may be when the target system simply does not start. Problem diagnosis is difficult in such situations. It may be necessary to redo most of the system build to correct the fault.

Factors which the system building team must consider are:

(1)   Have all the components which make up a system been included in the build instructions?

(2)   Has the appropriate version of each required component been included in the build instructions?

(3)   Are all required data files available?

(4)   If data files are referenced within a component is the name used the same as the name of the data file on the target machine?

(5)   Is the appropriate version of the compiler and other required tools available? Current versions of software tools may be incompatible with the older versions used to develop the system.

When there are multiple source code files representing different versions, it is sometimes unclear which source files were used to derive object-code components. This can be a particular problem in Unix environments. The correspondence between source and object code files is usually maintained by giving them the same name but a different filename suffix.

The system building process is normally specified in terms of physical storage components (typically files but perhaps database entities). These are fairly large objects and each file may include several logical software components. There is rarely a one-to-one mapping between physical storage organizations and logical software structure. This can lead to confusion as mistakes are made about which logical objects are stored in which files. There is no explicit link between the logical structure of the system in terms of modules and its physical storage structure.

One way to provide such a link is to use a system modelling or module interconnection language to describe the software structure and to use this description to create the system build instructions. Module interconnection languages describe the modular structure of a system without including algorithmic or control level detail. They allow the composition structure of the system to be defined and set out the dependencies between entities in the system.

Because these languages specify dependencies, they can be used as a basis for describing system configurations. Figure 33.10 shows an example of a module

family print-server	
attributes	This attribute is set true when a printer
multiple-paper-types: **boolean** ;	has multiple paper trays.
end	
interface	The interface view sets out the names
PRINT => print-file ;	that are exported by the print server's
DISPLAY-QUEUE => show-print-queue ;	interface.
DEQUEUE => delete-print-job ;	
SELECT-PRINTER => set-printer ;	
SELECT-PAPER-TYPE =>	Notice the use of variability here. The
if multiple-paper-types **then**	interface set-input-tray is only provided
set-input-tray **endif** ;	if the attribute multiple-paper-types is true.
end	
parts	This section defines the logical compo-
PRINT => printer-controller ;	nents of the printer server.
QUEUE => queue-manager ;	
SELECT-PAPER-TYPE =>	There are a number of components slots
if multiple-paper-types **then**	which are filled in with the name of the
set-input-tray **endif** ;	logical component (also represented in
end	PCL).
physical	
SOURCE => "print_server" **repository**	This section names the files storing the
"/usr/src" ;	system or component. The name
EXECUTABLE => Print-man **binary**	following the keywords **repository** or
"/usr/utils/bin" ;	**binary** is automatically added to the file
end	name.
end	Source code is stored in the repository,
	the executable is installed on a platform
	as a binary.

Figure 33.10
A system model in PCL.

interconnection language called PCL (Sommerville and Dean, 1996) which was developed as part of a project to support software evolution. PCL was designed to model families of systems and components and to integrate descriptions of the logical system structure with its storage structure.

PCL includes constructs to define the following characteristics of a hardware or software component:

(1)   Attributes which may be used to identify different versions of the component as discussed earlier in this chapter.

(2)   The interface which it offers to other components.

(3)   The composition structure; that is, the parts of the component. Conditional composition is supported allowing components to incorporate some variability.

(4)   The physical structure; that is, the files where the source and object code of the component are maintained.

(5)   Relationships between components. There are a number of built-in relations such as 'requires'. Relations may also be user-defined.

In PCL, systems are represented as families. Several versions of a system may be denoted in a single description. Conditional expressions, based on attribute values, are used to select system versions. This approach makes it easier to maintain several system versions and shows the stable and variable parts of the system.

PCL has been designed to support the modelling of multiple versions of a system which are identified by attribute values. We can see an example of this in Figure 33.10 where two possible versions of the system are described. One version is a print-server which can manage printers with multiple paper trays; the other is designed for printers with a single paper tray.

Each system version has an associated version descriptor (also expressed in PCL) which defines the identifying attribute values for that version. It assigns values to version identification attributes named in the system description. Tools have been produced which take a version descriptor, apply this to a PCL description and create a unique system version description in PCL. This version creation tool is briefly described with other PCL tools in the following section.

33.4.1 System building tools

System building is a computationally intensive process. If all of the components of a large system have to be compiled and linked, this can take several hours or even days. There are hundreds of files involved with the consequent possibility of human error. System building tools have been developed which reduce the build time by minimizing re-compilation where no changes have been made to the component and by providing a language for specifying which files are required for system building.

For Unix systems, Make (Feldman, 1979) is a widely used system building tool. It maintains the correspondence between source code and object code versions of a system. It automatically re-compiles source code which has been modified after the creation date of the associated object code. Users write 'makefiles' which describe the dependencies between the files in which the system components are stored.

Sometimes, when you change one file, you have to re-compile the code in other files. Make provides a mechanism for specifying file dependencies. Using built-in information and user specified commands, Make can cause the object code of a system to be re-created when a change is made to part of the system source code. For example, say an object code file x.o depends on the source code files x.c and d.c. The file d.c is changed in some way. Make uses file update attributes to detect the change and re-creates x.o by re-compiling x.c and d.c. Manual re-compilation after an editing session is unnecessary.

Consider a situation where a program called comp is created out of object modules scan.o, syn.o, sem.o and cgen.o. For each object module, there exists a source code module called scan.c, syn.c, sem.c and cgen.c. A file of declarations called defs.h is shared by scan.c, syn.c and sem.c (Figure 33.11). Make represents this dependency graph as a text file and includes commands which are invoked to build the system. Modifications can be made to any of scan.c, syn.c and sem.c without requiring other files to be re-compiled. If defs.h is changed, all other files must be re-compiled.

Make re-compiles a system if the modification date of the source code is later than the modification date of the object code component with the same name. This reduces the number of unnecessary compilations of source code files which have not been modified. However, some compilations may still be carried out when they are not really necessary. For example, if comments are added to a source code component, the associated object code need not be regenerated. More dangerously, the system cannot distinguish between components which have been compiled with different compiler options. When a re-compilation with different options is requested, Make will find existing object code components unless the system builder takes some explicit action to remove them.

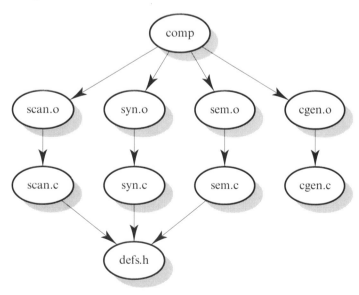

Figure 33.11
Component
dependency graph.

Make also suffers from some other limitations:

(1) It requires the dependency structure between system components to be expressed in terms of the files where these components are stored. Systems are actually structured as a set of language abstractions (procedures, functions, packages and so on). Make relies on the programmer to maintain the correspondence between files and the abstractions stored in these files.

(2) It is difficult to write and to understand makefiles for even moderately large systems as the dependency graph quickly becomes complicated. This is particularly true when the order of compilation is important, as it is in Ada. Some Ada systems provide makefile generators which process Ada component dependencies and automatically create a makefile. Unfortunately, makefile generators don't help makefile readers.

(3) It is not tightly integrated with a version management system. Although some versions of Make can be integrated with a system such as RCS, these normally only check out the most recent version of the system. They cannot deal with arbitrary versions.

These problems have been addressed by using PCL, the module interconnection language introduced earlier, as a 'front-end' to Make and a version management system. The logical system description is specified in PCL. This is processed to create a makefile as shown in Figure 33.12. The dependencies between components may be specified in an intuitive way and logical and physical component representations are explicitly linked. The phases in the process of building a system from a PCL description are:

Figure 33.12
System building from a PCL description.

(1) Variability is removed from the system description by PCL-bind. This selects the appropriate components depending on the attributes specified in the version description. The PCL code is processed and all if-statements are

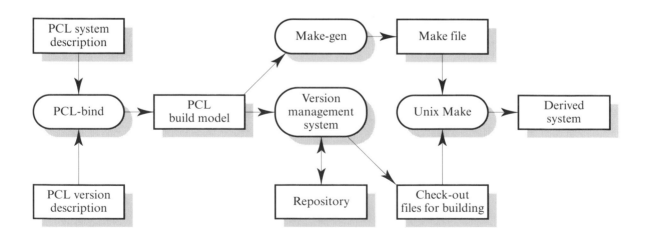

removed. This results in a 'build model' that sets out dependencies between the system components.

(2)   From the dependencies in the build model and the specified component attributes, a makefile is generated. Using file attributes, the required files are identified in the version management system and are checked out for system building.

(3)   Make is called to process the makefile and build the system.

As suggested earlier, rebuilding a system is a time-consuming process. Compiling and linking a large system requires a great deal of processing. Network-oriented system building tools are now available which can use all the computers on a workstation network for system building. These systems may be tightly integrated with a version management system so that reference may be made within the build description to system versions rather than specific filenames. Hewlett-Packard's DSEE (Leblang and Chase, 1987; Lubkin, 1991) is an example of such a system (Figure 33.13).

Features of DSEE include:

(1)   *Parallel building of different system versions*   Different versions of the same system can be built in parallel by different users.

(2)   *Parallel compilation on different network nodes*   Compilations can run in parallel by distributing build command sequences to idle nodes on the workstation network. This significantly reduces the time required for system building.

(3)   *Source code control*   Comparable facilities to those offered by RCS are provided. Thus there is a close integration between version management and system building.

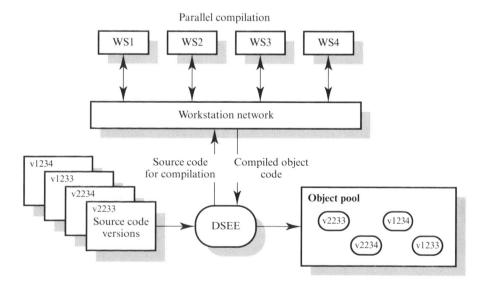

Figure 33.13
Network-oriented system building.

(4)   *Configuration identification*   A system model may be written defining which files make up each configuration. A configuration thread may be associated with this model. This thread describes which file versions and which tool options to apply when building the components in a system model.

(5)   *Derived object management*   Object code components are stored in an object pool and linked to the source code used to derive them. If a request is made to compile a source code component which has already been compiled, DSEE searches the object pool to see if the required version is available. If so, no compilation is necessary.

The developers of DSEE recognized that system building is a time-consuming process and have paid special attention to optimizing that process. This has been achieved in two ways:

(1)   *By using spare processing capacity on a workstation network*   The majority of workstations on a network are idle most of the time and may be pressed into service building a system. The build manager in DSEE checks which processors in the network are available. It automatically spawns compilations and other build activities on these processors. The results of the compilation are entered in the derived object pool as discussed below.

(2)   *By using a derived object pool*   When a version of an object is compiled, a unique descriptor is generated. It is associated with the object code of that component in a pool of derived objects. This descriptor includes a source version identifier and information about the compilation tool and its compilation options. When the component is referenced in some later build process, the derived object pool is searched to see if a compiled component is already available.

Because of the tight integration with a version management system, it is straight-forward to tag derived objects with the corresponding source code version identifier. Therefore, unlike Make, DSEE never re-compiles because of some date stamp change. Compilation of a source component only takes place when its corresponding object code is not available in the derived object pool.

Further reading

Implementing Configuration Management. This book is written from the perspective of a large system supplier. It discusses the problems of system configuration management where hardware, software and embedded firmware must all be controlled. (F. J. Buckley, 1993, IEEE Press.)

Software Configuration Management: Methods and Tools. This book focuses on software configuration management with a good summary of CM tools. (D. Whitgift, 1991, John Wiley and Sons.)

'Impacts of life cycle models on software configuration management'. As well as describing how CM policies may be adapted for different software process models, this paper also presents a good general overview of configuration management. (E. H. Bersoff and A.M. Davis, *Comm. ACM*, **34** (8), August 1991.)

'Parallel software configuration management in a network environment'. Although it is now rather old, this paper includes a good description of parallel building that may be used to speed up the system building process. (D. B. Leblang and R. P. Chase, *IEEE Software*, **4** (6), November 1987.)

KEY POINTS

- Configuration management is the management of system change. When a system is maintained, the role of the CM team is to ensure that changes are incorporated in a controlled way.

- In a large project, a formal document naming scheme should be established and used as a basis for managing the project documents.

- The CM team should be supported by a configuration database that records information about system changes and change requests which are outstanding. Projects should have some formal means of requesting system changes.

- When setting up a configuration management scheme, a consistent scheme of version identification should be established. Version attributes such as the customer name and target platform may be used to identify particular versions.

- System releases should be phased. A release which provides major new system functionality should be followed by a release which is mostly concerned with fault removal and performance enhancement.

- System building is the process of assembling system components into an executable program to run on some target computer system.

- Some tools are available to assist with the process of configuration management. **RCS** is a widely used tool for version management and **Make** is a tool for system building. Both of these are normally supplied with the Unix system.

- Integrated CM systems such as **DSEE** combine support for version management and system building. This allows for the reuse of object code that has been derived in previous system builds.

EXERCISES

33.1 Explain why the name of a document should not be used to identify the document in a configuration management system. Suggest a standard for a document identification scheme that may be used for all projects in an organization.

33.2 Using the entity-relational approach to data modelling, design a model of a configuration database which records information about system components, versions, releases and changes. Some requirements for the data model are as follows:

(a) It should be possible to retrieve all versions or a single identified version of a component.

(b) It should be possible to retrieve the 'latest' version of a component.

(c) It should be possible to find out which change requests have been implemented by a particular version of a system.

(d) It should be possible to discover which versions of components are included in a specified version of a system.

(e) It should be possible to retrieve a particular release of a system according to either the release date or the customers to whom the release was delivered.

33.3 Using a data-flow diagram, describe a change management procedure which might be used in a large organization concerned with developing software for external clients. Changes may be suggested from either external or internal sources.

33.4 Describe the difficulties which can be encountered in system building. What are the particular problems that can arise when a system is built on a host computer for some target machine?

33.5 With reference to system building, explain why it may sometimes be necessary to maintain obsolete computers on which large software systems were developed.

33.6 A common problem with system building occurs when physical file names are incorporated in system code and the file structure implied in these names differs from that of the target machine. Write a set of programmer's guidelines which help avoid this and other system building problems which you can think of.

33.7 Describe five factors which must be taken into account by engineers during the process of building a release of a large software system.

33.8 Describe two ways in which system building tools can optimize the process of building a version of a system from its components. Explain how these build optimization mechanisms are used in the DSEE environment.

34

Software Re-engineering

Objectives

- To introduce the notion of legacy systems and to explain why these systems are critical to some businesses.

- To describe different approaches to software re-engineering where legacy systems are restructured into a more maintainable form.

- To explain why data re-engineering is a particularly complex and expensive process.

- To discuss the process of reverse engineering and explain the differences between reverse engineering and re-engineering.

Contents

Since the mid-1960s, investment in software by businesses, government and other organizations has grown incredibly quickly. Software systems are used in almost all organizational activities. These systems must be maintained and evolve as new requirements emerge and new hardware is introduced into the organization.

In some businesses, it has been estimated that 80% of all software expenditure is consumed by system maintenance and evolution (Yourdon, 1989). The number of systems to be maintained is still increasing. There is a huge backlog of maintenance requests. This means that it is sometimes impossible for organizations to invest in new systems to improve organizational efficiency.

Old systems that must still be maintained are sometimes called *legacy systems*. The amount of code in these legacy systems is immense. In 1990, it was estimated (Ulrich, 1990) that there were 120 *billion* lines of source code in existence. The majority of these systems have been written in COBOL, a programming language best suited to business data processing, or FORTRAN. FORTRAN is a language for scientific or mathematical programming. These languages have limited program structuring facilities and, in the case of FORTRAN, very limited support for data structuring.

Many legacy systems are critical to the operation of the organization which uses them. They embed business knowledge and procedures which have emerged over the lifetime of the system. This knowledge may not be documented elsewhere. The risk of scrapping and rewriting these systems is very high. Much of this knowledge would have to be rediscovered by trial and error. Consequently, organizations cannot afford to make their legacy systems obsolete. They must somehow keep them in operation and continue to adapt them to new requirements.

Most legacy systems were developed before software engineering techniques were widely used. They may be poorly structured and their documentation may be either out-of-date or non-existent. The developers of these systems have long gone. There may be no one in the organization who really understands these systems in detail. The systems were often developed for mainframe computers. The need to maintain these systems may make it impossible for an organization to move to distributed workstations rather than a central computer.

The maintenance problem is compounded because these legacy systems are not simply a single program which has been developed and maintained. Most application systems are made up of a number of different programs which, in some way, share data. These programs have been developed by different people over a number of years. They may use a database management system (which may itself be obsolete) or may rely on separate files for data storage.

Figure 34.1 illustrates this situation. Different programs have been developed which use separate files. Each of these files has its own format. Often information is duplicated across files with the same information represented in different ways in different files. This duplication usually arises because information is tightly integrated with program data structures. It is not accessible as individual data items so cannot be shared by different programs.

Software re-engineering is concerned with taking existing legacy systems and reimplementing them to make them more maintainable. As part of this re-

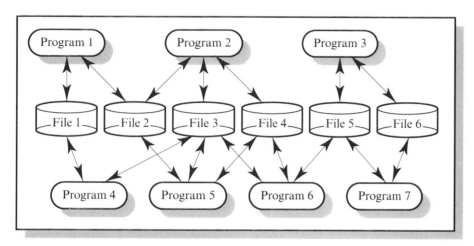

Figure 34.1
An application system composed of several different programs.

engineering process, the system may be redocumented or restructured. It may be translated to a more modern programming language, implemented on a distributed platform rather than a mainframe or its data may be migrated to a different database management system.

The critical distinction between re-engineering and new software development is the starting point for the development. Rather than start with a written specification, the old system acts as a specification for the new system. Chikofsky and Cross (1990) call conventional development *forward engineering* to distinguish it from software re-engineering. This distinction is illustrated in Figure 34.2.

Re-engineering is not the same as *reverse engineering*. The objective of reverse engineering is to derive the design or specification of a system from its source code. The objective of re-engineering is to produce a new, more maintainable system. Of course, reverse engineering to develop a better understanding of a system is often part of the re-engineering process.

The term re-engineering is also associated with business process re-engineering (Hammer, 1990). Business process re-engineering is concerned with redesigning business processes to reduce the number of redundant activities and improve process efficiency. Process re-engineering often forces software re-engineering as legacy systems may incorporate implicit dependencies on the existing processes. These have to be detected and removed before process re-engineering is possible.

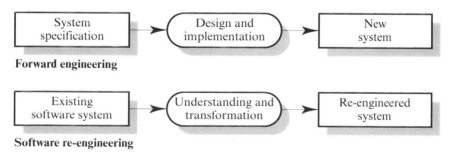

Figure 34.2
Re-engineering vs new software development.

Re-engineering a system should be considered when an organization depends on that system and when the system is regularly maintained. Re-engineering improves the system structure, creates new system documentation and makes it easier to understand. As well as maintenance cost reduction, the morale of the maintenance staff may be improved because they are working with a higher quality system.

The costs of re-engineering obviously depend on the extent of the work that is carried out. There is a spectrum of possible approaches to re-engineering as shown in Figure 34.3.

Apart from the extent of the re-engineering, the principal factors which affect re-engineering costs are:

(1)   The quality of the software to be re-engineered. The lower the quality of the software and its associated documentation (if any), the higher the re-engineering costs.

(2)   The tool support available for re-engineering. Re-engineering software is not normally cost-effective unless some automated tool support can be deployed to support the process.

(3)   The extent of data conversion required. If re-engineering requires large volumes of data to be converted, this significantly increases the process cost.

(4)   The availability of expert staff. If the staff responsible for maintaining the system cannot be involved in the re-engineering process, this will increase the costs. System re-engineers will have to spend a great deal of time understanding the system.

The alternative to re-engineering a software system is to redevelop that system using modern software engineering techniques. Where systems are very badly structured this may be the only viable option as the re-engineering costs for these systems are likely to be high. However, re-engineering has two key advantages over redeveloping software systems from scratch:

(1)   *Reduced risk*   There is a high risk in redeveloping software that is essential for an organization. Errors may be made in the system specification, there may be development problems and so on.

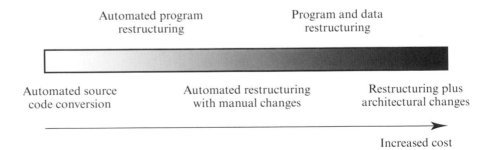

Figure 34.3
Re-engineering
approaches.

(2)   *Reduced cost*   The cost of re-engineering is significantly less than the costs of developing new software. Ulrich (1990) quotes an example of a commercial system where the reimplementation costs were estimated at $50 million. The system was successfully re-engineered for £12 million. If these figures are typical, it is about four times cheaper to re-engineer than to rewrite.

The disadvantage, of course, is that there are practical limits to the extent that a system can be improved by re-engineering. It isn't possible, for example, to convert a system written using a functional approach to an object-oriented system. It is usually impractical to make major architectural changes or to radically reorganize system data management. Although re-engineering can improve maintainability, the re-engineered system will probably not be as maintainable as a new system developed using modern software engineering methods.

34.1 Source code translation

The simplest form of software re-engineering is program translation where source code in one programming language is translated to source code in some other language. The target language may be an updated version of the original language (for example, COBOL-74 to COBOL-85) or may be a translation to a completely different language (for example, FORTRAN to C).

Source level translation may be necessary for the following reasons:

(1)   *Hardware platform update*   The organization may wish to change its standard hardware platform. Compilers for the original language may not be available on the new hardware.

(2)   *Staff skill shortages*   There may be a lack of trained maintenance staff for the original language. This is a particular problem where programs were written in some non-standard language that has now gone out of general use.

(3)   *Organizational policy changes*   An organization may decide to standardize on a particular language to minimize its support software costs. Maintaining many versions of old compilers can be very expensive.

Figure 34.4 illustrates the process of source code translation. There may be no need to understand the operation of the software in detail or to modify the system architecture. The analysis involved can focus on programming language considerations such as the equivalence of program control constructs.

Source code translation is only economically realistic if an automated translator is available to do the bulk of the translation. This may be a specially written program, a bought-in tool to convert from one language to another or a pattern matching system. In the latter case, a set of instructions how to make the translation from one representation to another has to be written. One of the most sophisticated tools available to assist this process is the REFINE system (Markosian *et al.*, 1994).

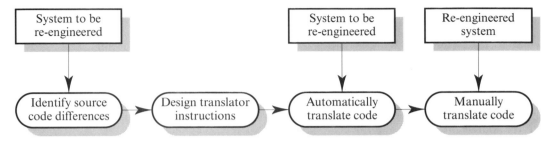

Figure 34.4
The program
translation process.

REFINE incorporates powerful pattern matching and program transformation capabilities. It is therefore possible to define patterns in the source code which should be converted. REFINE recognizes these and replaces them with the new constructs.

In many cases, completely automatic translation is impossible. Constructs in the source language may have no direct equivalent in the target language. There may be embedded conditional compilation instructions in the source code which are not supported in the target language. Some manual intervention is, therefore, almost always required to tune and improve the generated system.

34.2 Program restructuring

As I discussed in Chapter 32, maintaining programs tends to corrupt their structure. This problem is often exacerbated because the program may have been developed before programming without gotos became widely accepted. The control structure may originally have been fairly tangled with many unconditional branches and tangled control logic. When a program has the 'spaghetti' structure it is difficult to read and understand. Changes to the program may make some code unreachable but this can only be discovered after extensive analysis. Maintenance programmers often dare not remove code in case it may be accessed indirectly.

Figure 34.5 illustrates how complex control logic can make a relatively simple program difficult to understand. The program is written in a notation similar to FORTRAN which was often used to write this type of program. However, I have not made the program even more difficult to understand by using cryptic variable names.

The example in Figure 34.5 is a controller for a heating system. A panel switch may be set to On, Off or Controlled. If the system is controlled, then it is switched on and off depending on a timer setting and a thermostat. If the heating is on, Switch-heating turns it off and vice versa. Figure 34.6 shows the same example but using structured control statements so that the program may be read sequentially from top to bottom.

As well as unstructured control, complex conditions can also be simplified as part of the program restructuring process. Figure 34.7 shows how a conditional statement including 'not' logic may be replaced by a simpler, more comprehensible alternative.

```
Start:      Get (Time-on, Time-off, Time, Setting, Temp, Switch)
            if Switch = off goto off
            if Switch = on goto on
            goto Cntrld
off:        if Heating-status = on goto Sw-off
            goto loop
on:         if Heating-status = off goto Sw-on
            goto loop
Cntrld:     if Time = Time-on goto on
            if Time = Time-off goto off
            if Time < Time-on goto Start
            if Time > Time-off goto Start
            if Temp > Setting then goto off
            if Temp < Setting then goto on
Sw-off:     Heating-status := off
            goto Switch
Sw-on:      Heating-status := on
Switch:     Switch-heating
loop:       goto Start
```

Figure 34.5
A control program
with spaghetti logic.

Bohm and Jacopini (1966) proved that any program may be rewritten in terms of simple if-then-else conditionals and while loops and that unconditional goto statements were not required. This theorem is the basis for automatic program restructuring. Figure 34.8 shows how a program may be automatically restructured by converting it to a directed graph then regenerating a structured equivalent without gotos.

```
loop
    -- The Get statement finds values for the given variables from the system's
    -- environment.
    Get (Time-on, Time-off, Time, Setting, Temp, Switch) ;
    case Switch of
        when On => if Heating-status = off then
                        Switch-heating ; Heating-status := on ;
                    end if ;
        when Off => if Heating-status = on then
                        Switch-heating ; Heating-status := off ;
                    end if;
        when Controlled =>
            if Time >= Time-on and Time < = Time-off then
                if Temp > Setting and Heating-status = on then
                    Switch-heating; Heating-status = off;
                elsif Temp < Setting and Heating-status = off then
                    Switch-heating; Heating-status := on ;
                end if;
            end if ;
    end case ;
end loop ;
```

Figure 34.6
A structured control
program.

Figure 34.7
Condition
simplification.

> -- Complex condition
> **if not** (A > B **and** (C < D **or not** (E > F)))...
> -- Simplified condition
> **if** (A <= B **and** (C>= D **or** E > F))...

The directed graph that is generated is a program flow graph, as discussed in Chapter 23. Simplification and transformation techniques can be applied to this graph without changing its semantics. These detect and remove unreachable parts of the code. Once simplification has been completed, a new program is generated. While loops and simple conditional statements are substituted for goto-based control. This program may be in the original language or in a different language (for example, FORTRAN may be converted to C).

Control restructuring usually makes a program more readable and easier to understand. However, the program may still suffer from a lack of modularity whereby related components of the program may be dispersed through the code. For example, in a mathematical system there may be several functions associated with differentiation. To help identify commonality and to minimize the analysis needed when future changes are requested, these might all be grouped (perhaps in a file) as a differentiation module.

Program modularization is usually carried out manually by inspecting and editing the code. To modularize a program, relationships between components must be identified and the function of components deduced. It is therefore impossible to automate this process. However, experimental systems have been produced to provide some computer-aided assistance for modularization (Choi and Scacchi, 1990; Schwanke, 1991). These rely on an analysis of references to data and procedure call structures to infer which program components may be part of the same module.

There are, of course, problems with automatic program restructuring. These include:

(1)   *Loss of comments*   If the program has in-line comments, these are invariably lost as part of the restructuring process.

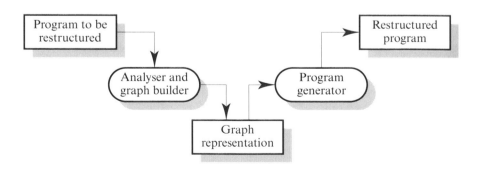

Figure 34.8
Automatic program
restructuring.

(2)   *Loss of documentation*   Similarly, the correspondence between external program documentation and the program is also lost. In many cases, however, both the comments and the documentation of a program are out-of-date so this is not an important factor.

(3)   *Heavy computational demands*   The algorithms embedded in restructuring tools are complex. A great deal of computer time is required to complete the restructuring process.

If the program is data-driven with components tightly coupled through shared data structures, restructuring the code may not give a significant improvement in under-standability. Re-engineering the data, as discussed in the following section, may also be necessary. If the program is written in a non-standard language dialect, standard restructuring tools may not work properly and significant manual intervention may be required.

In some cases, it may not be cost-effective to restructure all of the programs in a system. Some may be of better quality than others and some may not be subject to frequent change. Arthur (1988) suggests that data should be collected to help identify those programs which could benefit most from restructuring. For example, the following metrics may be used to identify the candidates for restructuring:

- failure rate
- percentage of source code changed per year
- component complexity

Other factors such as the degree to which programs or components meet current standards might also be taken into account in making restructuring decisions.

34.3 Data re-engineering

Data re-engineering is the process of analysing and reorganizing the data structures (and sometimes the data values) in a system to make it more understandable. Where a system, such as that illustrated earlier in this chapter, consists of several different programs which use different file formats, these may all have to be modified as part of the data restructuring process.

In many cases, data restructuring and reorganization take place as part of the process of converting systems to use a database management system or migrating data from one database management system to another. This situation is increasingly common as older database systems based on a hierarchical or network model are phased out to be replaced by relational or object-oriented systems.

The objective of data re-engineering is often to convert the chaotic data management situation illustrated in Figure 34.1 to a managed data environment (Figure 34.9). All data is stored in and managed by a standard database management system and a logical data model is published.

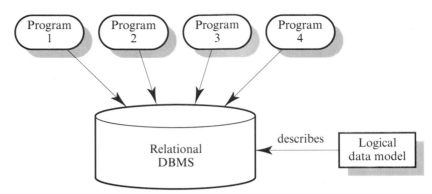

Figure 34.9
Data centralization.

End-user requirements for flexible access to information on their desktop are driving this conversion to modern database management systems. Rather than rely on report generator programs running on some mainframe to give them the information they need, end-users want raw data to be delivered to their workstation. They then use spreadsheets or other data manipulation systems to extract the information which they need from this raw data. The data required is usually retrieved by database queries written in SQL (Date and Darwen, 1993) which is a query language designed for relational database systems.

Data problems also arise because programs are now required to process much more data than was originally envisaged by their developers. Rochester and Douglass (1993) describe a funds management system, used in a finance company, that was originally designed to handle up to 99 funds. The company were managing more than 2000 funds and had to run 23 separate copies of the system. This was becoming increasingly expensive both in terms of human and computer resources. They therefore decided to re-engineer the system and its associated data.

Rickets *et al.* (1993) describe some of the problems with data which can arise in legacy systems made up of several cooperating programs:

(1) *Data naming problems*   Names may be cryptic and difficult to understand. Different names (synonyms) may be given to the same logical entity in different programs in the system. The same name may be used in different programs to mean different things (homonyms).

(2) *Field length problems*   This is a problem when field lengths in records are explicitly assigned in the program. The same item may be assigned different lengths in different programs or the field length may be too short to represent current data. To solve this problem, other fields may be re-used in some cases so that usage of a named data field across the programs in a system is inconsistent.

(3) *Record organization problems*   Records representing the same entity may be organized differently in different programs. This is a problem in languages like COBOL where the physical organization of records is set by the programmer and reflected in files. It is not a problem in languages like C++ or Ada where the physical organization of a record is the compiler's responsibility.

(4)   *Hard-coded literals*   Literal (absolute) values, such as tax rates, are included directly in the program rather than referenced using some symbolic name.

(5)   *No data dictionary*   There may be no data dictionary defining the names used, their representation and their use.

As well as inconsistent data definitions, data values may also be stored in an inconsistent way. After the data definitions have been re-engineered, the data values must also be converted to conform to the new structure. Rickets *et al.* also describe some of the data value inconsistencies which can arise:

(1)   *Inconsistent default values*   Different programs may assign different default values to the same logical data items. This may make it impossible for data to be used by any programs apart from that which created the data. The problem is compounded when missing values are assigned a default value that is valid. The missing data cannot then be discovered.

(2)   *Inconsistent validation rules*   Different programs may have applied different data validation rules. Therefore data written by one program may be rejected by another. This is a particular problem for archival data which may not have been updated in line with changes to data validation rules.

(3)   *Inconsistent units*   The same information may be represented in different units in different programs. For example, in the US or the UK, weight data may be represented in pounds in older programs but in kilograms in more recent systems.

(4)   *Inconsistent representation semantics*   Programs may have embedded some meaning in the way items are represented. For example, some programs may assume that upper-case text means an address. Programs may use different conventions and may therefore reject data which is semantically valid.

(5)   *Inconsistent handling of negative values*   Some programs may reject negative values for entities which must always be positive. Others, however, may accept these as negative values or (even worse) fail to recognize them as negative and convert them to a positive value.

Detailed analysis of the programs which use the data is essential before data re-engineering. This analysis should be aimed at discovering the function of identifiers in the program, finding the literal values which should be replaced with named constants, discovering embedded data validation rules and data representation conversions. Tools such as cross-reference analysers and pattern matchers may be used to help with this analysis. A set of tables should be created which show where data items are referenced and the changes to be made to each of these references.

Figure 34.10 illustrates the process of data re-engineering, assuming that data definitions are modified, literal values named, data formats reorganized and the data values converted.

In stage 1 of this process, the data definitions in the program are modified to improve understandability. The data itself is not affected by these modifications.

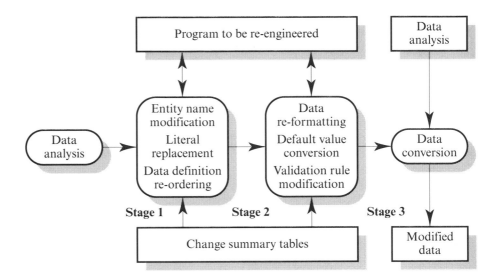

Figure 34.10
The data re-
engineering process.

It is possible to automate this process to some extent using pattern matching systems such as REFINE or awk (Aho *et al.*, 1988) to find and replace definitions. However, some manual work is almost always necessary to complete the process. The data re-engineering process may stop at this stage if the intention is simply to complete some program restructuring process. If, however, there are data value problems as discussed above, stage 2 of the process may then be entered.

If an organization decides to continue to stage 2 of the process, it is then committed to stage 3, data conversion. This is usually a very expensive process. Programs have to be written which embed knowledge of the old and the new organization. These process the old data and output the converted information. Again, pattern matching systems may be used to implement this conversion.

The change summary tables in Figure 34.10 hold details of all the changes to be made. They are therefore used at all stages of the data re-engineering process.

34.3.1 Recovering data abstractions

To save memory space, many legacy systems rely on the use of shared tables and common data areas. The information in these areas is globally accessible and may be used by different parts of the system in different ways. Making changes to these global data areas is very expensive because of the costs of analysing change impacts across all uses of the data.

The data re-engineering changes which I have described are most relevant to legacy systems made up of several programs exchanging data through files. They do not address this problem of managing global data within a program. To do so, the use of data by the program must be analysed and data abstractions re-created. These hide the data representation and provide constructor and access functions to modify and inspect the data.

There are several steps involved in converting shared global data areas to objects or abstract data types:

(1)   Analyse common data areas to identify logical data abstractions. It will often be the case that several abstractions are combined in a single shared data area. These should be identified and logically restructured.

(2)   Create an abstract data type or object for each of these abstractions. If the programming language does not have data hiding facilities, simulate an abstract data type by providing functions to update and access all fields of the data.

(3)   Use a program browsing system or cross-reference generator to find all references to the data. Replace these with calls to the appropriate functions.

This process may appear time-consuming but relatively straightforward. In practice, however, it can be very difficult because of the ways in which shared data areas are used. In languages like FORTRAN which have limited data structuring facilities, programs may have designed complex data management strategies which they implement using shared arrays. The array therefore may actually be a completely different kind of data structure. Further problems are caused by indirect addressing of shared structures and addressing by offsets from some other structure.

Further problems, which are particularly difficult to resolve, may arise because the target machine for the original program may have had a limited memory. The programmers may have used knowledge about data lifetimes and embedded this in the program. Therefore, to avoid allocating extra space, the same data area may be used to store different abstractions at different points in the program. These can only be discovered after a detailed static and dynamic analysis of the program.

34.4 Reverse engineering

Reverse engineering is the process of analysing software with the objective of recovering its design and specification. The software source code will usually be available as the input to the reverse engineering process. Sometimes, however, even this has been lost and the reverse engineering must start with the executable code.

Reverse engineering is normally part of the software re-engineering process. The design and specification are recovered to help understand a program before reorganizing its structure. However, reverse engineering need not always be followed by re-engineering.

● The design and specification of an existing system may be reverse engineered so that they can serve as an input to the requirements specification for that program's replacement.

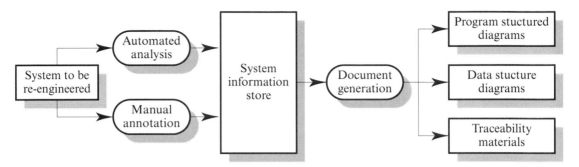

Figure 34.11
The reverse
engineering process.

- Alternatively, the design and specification may be reverse engineered so that they are available to help program maintenance. With this additional information, it may not be necessary to re-engineer the system source code.

The reverse engineering process is illustrated in Figure 34.11. The process starts with an analysis phase. During this phase, the system is analysed using automated tools to discover its structure. In itself, this is not enough to re-create the system design. Engineers then work with the system source code and its structural model. They add information to this which they have collected by understanding the system. All of this information is maintained in some information store, usually in the form of a directed graph. The program code is also stored.

Information store browsers may be available to compare the graph structure and the code. These may be used to add further information that has been inferred about the design. Documents of various types may be generated from this information. These might include program and data structure diagrams and traceability matrices. Traceability matrices show where entities in the system are defined and referenced. The process of document generation is an iterative one as the design information is used to further refine the information held in the system repository.

As part of the reverse engineering process, various tools for program understanding may be used. These usually present different kinds of system view and allow easy navigation through the source code. For example, they will allow users to select a data definition then move through the code to where that data item is used. Examples of such program browsers are discussed by Cleveland (1989), Oman and Cook (1990) and Ning *et al.* (1994).

After the system design documentation has been generated, further information may be added to the information store to help re-create the system specification. This usually involves further manual annotation to the system structure. The specification cannot be deduced automatically from the system model.

Further reading

Software Reengineering. This is an IEEE tutorial that includes most of the important papers on re-engineering which were published before 1992. Many of the papers referenced in this chapter are reprinted in it. (R. S. Arnold, IEEE Press, 1994.)

'DoD legacy systems: reverse engineering data requirements'. This is a good description of the practical problems which arise with legacy systems. The paper focuses on data re-engineering where systems managing similar but incompatible data have been combined. Other papers in this special issue on reverse engineering are also relevant. (P. Aiken, A. Muntz, R. Richards, *Comm. ACM,* **37** (5), May 1994.)

IEEE Software, **12** (1), January 1995. This special issue on legacy systems has a number of papers which are good background reading for this chapter. The paper on planning re-engineering by Sneed is a good starting point.

KEY POINTS

- Legacy systems are systems which have been in existence for some time and which are essential for the successful functioning of an organization.

- The objective of system re-engineering is to improve the system structure and make it easier to understand. The cost of future system maintenance should therefore be reduced.

- Legacy systems are often made up of suites of individual programs. These programs usually manage their own data with ad hoc arrangements made for data sharing between them.

- Program restructuring involves replacing unstructured control constructs such as gotos with while loops and simple conditional statements. This can be done automatically.

- Data re-engineering may be necessary because of inconsistent data management by the programs in a legacy system. The objective of data re-engineering may be to re-engineer all programs to use a common data-base.

- The costs of data re-engineering are significantly increased if existing data has to be converted to some new format.

- Reverse engineering is the process of deriving a system's design and specification from its source code. Tools such as program browsers may be used to assist this process.

EXERCISES

34.1 Explain why legacy systems may be critical to the successful operation of a business.

34.2 Under what circumstances do you think that software should be scrapped and rewritten?

34.3   Compare the control constructs (loops and conditionals) in any two programming languages which you know. Write a short description of how to translate the control constructs in one language to the equivalent constructs in the other.

34.4   Translate the unstructured routine shown in Figure 34.12 into its structured equivalent and work out what it is supposed to do.

34.5   Write a set of guidelines which may be used to help find modules in an unstructured program.

34.6   Suggest meaningful names for the variables used in the program shown in Figure 34.12 and construct data dictionary entries for these names.

34.7   What problems might arise when converting data from one type of database management system to another (for example, hierarchical to relational or relational to object-oriented)?

34.8   Explain why it is impossible to recover a system specification by automatically analysing system source code.

34.9   A company routinely places contractual conditions on freelance programmers working on re-engineering their applications which prevents them from taking on contracts with similar companies. The reason for this is that re-engineering inevitably reveals business information. Is this a reasonable position for a company to take given that they have no obligations to contractors after their contract has finished?

Figure 34.12
An unstructured program.

```
routine BS (K, T, S, L)
T := 1
NXT: if S >= T goto CON
L = -1
goto STP
CON: L := INTEGER (T / S)
L := INTEGER ((T+S) / 2)
if T (L) = K then return
if T(L) > K then goto GRT
S := L+1
goto NXT
GRT: S := L-1
goto NXT
STP: end
```

References

Abbott, R. (1983). Program design by informal English descriptions. *Comm. ACM,* **26** (11), 882–94 [256]

Abdel-Ghaly, A. A., Chan, P. Y. and Littlewood, B. (1986). Evaluation of competing software reliability predictions. *IEEE Trans. on Software Engineering,* **SE-12** (9), 950–67 [363]

Ackroyd, S., Harper, R., Hughes, J. A. and Shapiro, D. (1992). *Information Technology and Practical Police Work.* Milton Keynes: Open University Press [95]

Adams, E. N. (1984). Optimizing preventative service of software products. *IBM J. Res & Dev.,* **28** (1), 2–14 [351]

Agha, G. (1990). Concurrent object-oriented programming. *Comm. ACM,* **33** (9), 125–40 [269]

Aho, A. V., Kernighan, B. W. and Weinberger, P. J. (1988). *The Awk Programming Language.* Englewood Cliffs NJ: Prentice-Hall [149, 710]

Albrecht, A. J. (1979). Measuring application development productivity. In *Proc. SHARE/GUIDE IBM Application Development Symposium,* 83–92 [593]

Albrecht, A. J. and Gaffney, J. E. (1983). Software function, lines of code and development effort prediction: a software science validation. *IEEE Trans. on Software Engineering,* **SE-9** (6), 639–47 [593, 633]

Alderson, A. (1991). Meta-Case technology. In *Proc. European Symp. on Software Development Environments and CASE Technology,* Konigswinter, Germany, 81–91 [541]

Alford, M. W. (1977). A requirements engineering methodology for real time processing requirements. *IEEE Trans. on Software Engineering,* **SE-3** (1), 60–9 [123]

Alford, M. W. (1985). SREM at the age of eight: the distributed computing design system. *IEEE Computer,* **18** (4), 36–46 [73, 123]

Aron, J. D. (1974). *The Program Development Process.* Reading MA: Addison-Wesley [583]

Aron, J. D. (1983). *The Program Development Process: Part 2 – The Programming Team.* Reading MA: Addison-Wesley [47]

Arthur, L. J. (1988). *Software Evolution.* New York: John Wiley and Sons [662, 707]

Avizienis, A. (1985). The N-version approach to fault-tolerant software. *IEEE Trans. on Software Engineering,* **SE-11** (12), 1491–501 [379]

Avizienis, A. A. (1995). A methodology of N-version programming. In *Software Fault Tolerance* (Lyu, M. R., ed.). Chichester: John Wiley & Sons, 23–46 [379]

Baker, F. T. (1972). Chief programmer team management of production programming. *IBM Systems J.,* **11** (1), 56–73 [583]

Baker, T. P. and Scallon, G. M. (1986). An architecture for real-time software systems. *IEEE Software,* **3** (3), 50–8 [307]

Bansler, J. P. and Bødker, K. (1993). A reappraisal of structured analysis: design in an organizational context. *ACM Trans. on Information Systems,* **11** (2), 165–93 [213]

Barker, R. (1989). *CASE* Method: Entity Relationship Modelling.* Wokingham: Addison-Wesley [105]

Barnard, J. and Price, A. (1994). Managing code inspection information. *IEEE Computer,* **11** (2), 59–69 [488, 625]

Barnes, J. (1993). Introducing Ada 9X. *ACM Ada Letters,* **XIII** (6), 61–132 [302]

Barnes, J. G. P. (1994). *Programming in Ada,* 4th edn. Wokingham: Addison-Wesley [269, 290, 301, 393]

Basili, V. and Green, S. (1993). Software process improvement at the SEL. *IEEE Software,* **11** (4), 58–66 [647]

Basili, V. R. and Rombach, H. D. (1988). The TAME project: towards improvement-oriented software environments. *IEEE Trans. on Software Engineering,* **14** (6), 758–773 [627, 647]

Basili, V. R. and Selby, R. W. (1987). Comparing the effectiveness of software testing strategies. *IEEE Trans. on Software Engineering,* **SE-13** (12), 1278–96 [466]

Bass, B. M. and Dunteman, G. (1963). Behaviour in groups as a function of self, interaction and task orientation. *J. Abnorm. Soc. Psychology,* **66** (4), 19–28 [573]

Bass, L. and Coutaz, J. (1991). *Developing Software for the User Interface.* Reading MA: Addison-Wesley [321]

Beck, K. and Cunningham, W. (1989). A laboratory for teaching object-oriented thinking. *SIGPLAN Notices,* **24** (10), 1–6 [256]

Beer, S. J., Welland, R. C. and Sommerville, I. (1987). Describing software design methodologies. *Comp. J.,* **30** (2), 128–33 [540]

Bell, T. E., Bixler, D. C. and Dyer, M. E. (1977). An extendable approach to computer aided software requirements engineering. *IEEE Trans. on Software Engineering,* **SE-3** (1), 49–60 [123]

Bentley, R., Rodden, T., Sawyer, P., Sommerville, I., Hughes, J., Randall, D. and Shapiro, D. (1992). Ethnographically-informed systems design for air traffic control. In *Proc. CSCW'92*, Toronto, Canada, 123–29 [95]

Berlage, T. (1991). *OSF/Motif Concepts and Programming*. Wokingham: Addison-Wesley [517]

Bernstein, L. (1993). Get the design right! *IEEE Software*, **10** (5), 61–3 [140]

Bersoff, E. H. and Davis, A. M. (1991). Impact of life cycle models on software configuration management. *Comm. ACM*, **34** (8), 104–18 [677]

Bezier, B. (1990). *Software Testing Techniques*, 2nd edn. New York: Van Nostrand Rheinhold [456, 467]

Biggerstaff, T. J. and Perlis, A. J. (1989). *Software Reusability*, Vols 1–2. Reading MA: Addison-Wesley [396]

Bishop, P., Esp, D., Barnes, M., Humphreys, P., Dahll, G. and Lahti, J. (1986). PODS – a project on diverse software. *IEEE Trans. on Software Engineering*, **SE-12** (9), 929–40 [432]

Black, E. (1991). ATIS, CIS, PCTE and the software backplane. In *Proc. 4th Int. Conf. on Software Engineering and its Applications*, Toulouse, France, 601–15 [531]

Blyth, D., Boldyreff, C., Ruggles, C. and Tetteh-Lartey, N. (1990). The case for formal methods in standards. *IEEE Software*, **7** (6), 65–7 [163]

Boehm, B. W. (1979). Software engineering: R & D trends and defense needs. In *Research Directions in Software Technology* (Wegner, P., ed.). Cambridge MA: MIT Press. [717]

Boehm, B. W. (1981). *Software Engineering Economics*. Englewood Cliffs NJ: Prentice-Hall [596, 599]

Boehm, B. W. (1983). The economics of software maintenance. In *Proc. Software Maintenance Workshop*, Washington DC, 9–37 [661]

Boehm, B. W. (1988). A spiral model of software development and enhancement. *IEEE Computer*, **21** (5), 61–72 [13]

Boehm, B. W., Gray, T. E. and Seewaldt, T. (1984). Prototyping versus specifying: a multi-project experiment. *IEEE Transactions on Software Engineering*, **SE-10** (3), 290–303 [139]

Boehm, B. W., McClean, R. L., and Urfig, D. B. (1975). Some experience with automated aids to the design of large-scale reliable software. In *Proc. IEEE Trans. on Software Engineering*, **SE-1** (1), 125–33 [421]

Boehm, B. W., Penedo, M. H., Stuckle, E. D., Williams, R. D. and Pyster, A. B. (1984). A software development environment for improving productivity. *IEEE Computer*, **17** (6), 30–42 [547]

Bohm, C. and Jacopini, G. (1966). Flow diagrams, Turing machines and languages with only two formation rules. *Comm. ACM*, **9** (5), 366–71 [705]

Bollinger, T. and McGowan, C. (1991). A critical look at software capability evaluations. *IEEE Software*, **8** (4), 25–41 [650, 651]

Bolognesi, T. and Brinksma, E. (1987). Introduction to the ISO specification language LOTOS. *Computer Networks,* **14** (1), 25–59 [168]

Booch, G. (1987). *Software Components with Ada: Structures Tools and Subsystems.* Menlo Park CA: Benjamin Cummings [401]

Booch, G. (1994). *Object-oriented Analysis and Design with Applications.* Redwood City CA: Benjamin Cummings [107, 213, 215, 249, 535]

Bott, M. F. (1989). *The ECLIPSE Integrated Project Support Environment.* Stevenage: Peter Perigrinus [547]

Boudier, G., Gallo, F., Minot, R. and Thomas, I. (1988). An overview of PCTE and PCTE+. *ACM Software Engineering Notes,* **13** (5), 248–57 [560]

Braun, C. L. and Goodenough, J. B. (1985). *Ada Reusability Guidelines.* Report 3285–2–208/2 Softech [405]

Brazendale, J. and Bell, R. (1994). Safety-related control and protection systems: standards update. *IEE Computing and Control Engineering J.,* **5** (1), 6–12 [428]

Brilliant, S. S., Knight, J. C. and Leveson, N. G. (1990). Analysis of faults in an N-version software experiment. *IEEE Trans. on Software Engineering,* **16** (2), 238–47 [380, 432]

Brinch-Hansen, P. (1973). *Operating System Principles.* Englewood Cliffs NJ: Prentice-Hall [301]

Brocklehurst, S. and Littlewood, T. W. (1992). New ways to get accurate reliability measures. *IEEE Software,* **9** (4), 34–42 [364]

Brooks, F. P. (1975). *The Mythical Man Month.* Reading MA: Addison-Wesley [46, 583]

Brooks, F. P. (1987). No silver bullet: essence and accidents of software engineering. *IEEE Computer,* **20** (4), 10–20 [506]

Brown, A. W., Earl, A. N. and McDermid, J. A. (1992). Software Engineering Environments. London: McGraw-Hill. [550, 552, 556, 561]

Brown, A. W. (1993). Control integration through message-passing in a software development environment. *BCS/IEE Software Engineering J.,* **8** (3), 121–31 [518]

Browne, D. P. (1986). The formal specification of adaptive user interfaces using command language grammar. In *Proc. CHI'86,* Boston, 256–60 [152]

Budgen, D. (1993). *Software Design.* Wokingham: Addison-Wesley [213]

Burns, A. (1991). Scheduling hard real-time systems: a review. *BCS/IEE Software Engineering J.,* **6** (3), 116–28 [301]

Burns, A. and Wellings, A. (1990). *Real-time Systems and their Programming Languages.* Wokingham: Addison-Wesley [269, 290, 301]

Buxton, J. (1980). *Requirements for Ada Programming Support Environments: Stoneman.* Washington DC: US Department of Defense [119, 229, 232, 546]

Cameron, J. R. (1986). An overview of JSD. *IEEE Trans. on Software Engineering,* **SE-12** (2), 222–40 [535]

Campbell, I. (1986). PCTE proposal for a public common tool interface. In *Software Engineering Environments* (Sommerville, I., ed.). Stevenage: Peter Perigrinus Ltd, 57–72 [560]

Card, S., Moran, T. P. and Newell, A. (1983). T*he Psychology of Human–Computer Interaction.* Hillsdale NJ: Lawrence Erlbaum Associates [571]

Carroll, J. M. (1992). *The Nurnberg Funnel: Designing Minimalist Instruction for Practical Computer Skill.* Boston MA: MIT Press [340]

Checkland, P. (1981). S*ystems Thinking, Systems Practice.* Chichester: John Wiley and Sons [24, 26]

Checkland, P. and Scholes, J. (1990). *Soft Systems Methodology in Action.* Chichester: John Wiley and Sons [26]

Chen, P. (1976). The entity relationship model – towards a unified view of data. *ACM Trans. on Database Systems,* **1** (1), 9–36 [104]

Chikofsky, E. J. and Cross, J. H. (1990). Reverse engineering and design recovery: a taxonomy. *IEEE Software,* **7** (1), 13–17 [701]

Chikofsky, E. J. and Rubenstein, B. L. (1988). CASE: Reliability engineering for information systems. *IEEE Software,* **5** (2), 11–17 [536]

Choi, S. C. and Scacchi, W. (1990). Extracting and restructuring the design of large systems. *IEEE Software,* **7** (1), 66–71 [706]

Cleveland, L. (1989). A program understanding support environment. *IBM Sys. J.,* **28** (2), 324–44 [712]

Coad, P. and Yourdon, E. (1990). *Object-oriented Analysis.* Englewood Cliffs NJ: Prentice-Hall [86, 107, 249, 256]

Cobb, R. H. and Mills, H. D. (1990). Engineering software under statistical quality control. *IEEE Software,* **7** (6), 44–54 [496, 498]

Codd, E. F. (1970). A relational model of data for large shared data banks. *Comm. ACM,* **13** (6), 377–87 [103]

Codd, E. F. (1979). Extending the database relational model to capture more meaning. *ACM Trans. on Database Systems,* **4** (4), 397–434 [104]

Cohen, B., Harwood, W. T. and Jackson, M.I. (1986). *The Specification of Complex Systems.* Wokingham: Addison-Wesley [172, 174]

Colebourne, A., Sawyer, P. and Sommerville, I. (1993). MOG user interface builder: a mechanism for integrating application and user interface. *Interacting with Computers,* **5** (3), 315–32 [152, 558]

Conklin, J. (1987). Hypertext: an introduction and survey. *IEEE Software,* **20** (9), 17–42 [339]

Constantine, L. L. and Yourdon, E. (1979). *Structured Design.* Englewood Cliffs NJ: Prentice-Hall [213, 215, 218, 276, 630]

Cooling, J. E. (1991). *Software Design for Real-time Systems.* London: Chapman and Hall [307]

Cougar, J. D. (1988). Motivating IS personnel. *Datamation,* **34** (9), 59–63 [578]

Cougar, J. D. and Zawacki, R. A. (1978). What motivates DP professionals. *Datamation,* **24** (9), 27–30 [578]

Crosby, P. (1979). *Quality is Free.* New York: McGraw-Hill [612]

Curtis, B., Kellner, M. I. and Over, J. (1992). Process modeling. *Comm. ACM,* **35** (9), 75–90 [641]

Curtis, B., Krasner, H. and Iscoe, N. (1988). A field study of the software design process for large systems. *Comm. ACM,* **31** (11), 1268–87 [573]

Cusamano, M. (1989). The software factory: a historical interpretation. *IEEE Software,* **6** (2), 23–30 [8, 396]

Cutts, G. (1988). Structured systems analysis and design methodology. In *Information Technology for Organisational Systems* (H-J. Bullinger, ed.). Amsterdam: Elsevier, 363–70 [215]

Dasarthy, B. (1985). Timing constraints for real-time systems: constructs for expressing them, methods of validating them. *IEEE Trans. on Software Engineering,* **SE-11** (1), 80–6 [301]

Date, C. J. (1990). *An Introduction to Database Systems,* 5th edn. Reading MA: Addison-Wesley [103]

Date, C. J. and Darwen, H. (1993). *A Guide to the SQL Standard,* 3rd edn. Reading MA: Addison-Wesley [534, 708]

Davis, A. M. (1990). *Software Requirements: Analysis and Specification.* Englewood Cliffs NJ: Prentice-Hall [82, 123]

Davis, A. M. (1993). *Software Requirements: Objects, Functions and States.* Englewood Cliffs NJ: Prentice-Hall [64]

Dawes, J. and Davis, H. (1991). ECMA PCTE. In *Software Engineering Environments* (Long, F., ed.). Chichester: Ellis Horwood [560]

Delisle, N. and Garlan, D. (1990). A formal specification of an oscilloscope. *IEEE Software,* **7** (5), 29–36 [162]

DeMarco, T. (1978). *Structured Analysis and System Specification.* New York: Yourdon Press [86, 101]

DeMarco, T. and Lister, T. (1985). Programmer performance and the effects of the workplace. In *Proc. 8th Int. Conf. on Software Engineering,* London, 268–72 [584]

Dijkstra, E. W. (1968a). Cooperating sequential processes. In *Programming Languages* (Genuys, F., ed.). London: Academic Press, 43–112 [301]

Dijkstra, E. W. (1968b). Goto statement considered harmful. *Comm. ACM.,* **11** (3), 147–8 [372]

Dijkstra, E. W. (1976). *A Discipline of Programming.* Englewood Cliffs NJ: Prentice-Hall [488]

Diller, A. (1994). Z: *An Introduction to Formal Methods,* 2nd edn. New York: John Wiley and Sons [146, 190]

Dix, A., Finlay, J. E., Abowd, G. D. and Beale, R. (1993). *Human–Computer Interaction.* Hemel Hempstead: Prentice-Hall [320]

Dolotta, T. A., Haight, R. C. and Mashey, J. R. (1978). The programmer's workbench. *Bell Systems Tech. J.,* **57** (6), 2177–200 [533]

Donzeau-Gouge, V., Huet, G. and Kahn, G. (1984). Programming environments based on structured editors: the MENTOR experience. In *Interactive Programming Environments* (Barstow, D. R., Shrobe, H. E. and Sandewall, E., eds). New York: McGraw-Hill, 128–40 [540]

Earl, A. N., Whittington, R. P., Hitchcock, P. and Hall, A. (1986). Specifying a semantic model for use in an integrated project support environment. In *Software Engineering Environments* (Sommerville, I., ed.). Stevenage: Peter Perigrinus, 202–19 [162, 202]

Easterbrook, S. (1993). Domain modelling with hierarchies of alternative viewpoints. In *Proc. RE'93,* San Diego CA, 65–72 [74]

ECMA (1991). *A Reference Model for Frameworks of Computer-Assisted Software Engineering Environments.* ECMA TR/55, Version 2, ECMA [244, 552]

Ehrlich, W., Prasanna, B., Stampel, J. and Wu, J. (1993). Determining the cost of a stop-test decision. *IEEE Software,* **9** (4), 33–42 [365]

Ellis, C. A. and Nutt, G. J. (1980). Office information systems and computer science. *ACM Computing Surveys,* **12** (1), 27–60 [325]

Endres, A. (1975). An analysis of errors and their causes in system programs. *IEEE Trans. on Software Engineering,* **SE-1** (2), 140–9 [421]

Estublier, J. (1985). A configuration manager: the Adele data base of programs. In *Proc. Workshop on Software Engineering Environments for Programming-in-the-Large,* Harwichport, MA, 149–56 [680, 686]

Fagan, M. E. (1976). Design and code inspections to reduce errors in program development. *IBM Systems J.,* **15** (3), 182–211 [484]

Fagan, M. E. (1986). Advances in software inspections. *IEEE Trans. on Software Engineering,* **SE-12** (7), 744–51 [484]

Farchamps, D. (1994). Organisational factors and reuse. *IEEE Software,* **11** (5), 31–41 [400]

Feldman, S. I. (1979). MAKE – program for maintaining computer programs. *Software Practice and Experience,* **9** (4), 255–65 [692]

Fenton, N. E. (1991). *Software Metrics: A Rigorous Approach.* London: Chapman and Hall [132]

Fernström, C. (1993). Process Weaver: adding process support to Unix. In *Proc. 2nd Int. Conf. on the Software Process,* Berlin [521, 561, 683]

Fernström, C., Närfelt, K-H. and Ohlsson, L. (1992). Software factory principles, architectures and experiments. *IEEE Software,* **9** (2), 36–44 [521]

Fichman, R. G. and Kemerer, C. F. (1992). Object-oriented and conventional analysis and design methodologies. *IEEE Computer,* **25** (10), 22–39 [292]

Fickas, S., Van Lamsweerde, A., and Dardenne, A. (1991). Goal-directed concept acquisition in requirements elicitation. In *Proc. 6th Int. Workshop on Software Specification and Design,* Como, Italy, 14–21 [83]

Finkelstein, A., Kramer, J. and Goedicke, J. K. (1990). Viewpoint oriented software development. In *Proc. 3rd Int. Workshop on Software Engineering and its Applications,* Toulouse, France, 337–51 [83, 84]

Floyd, R. W. (1967). Assigning meanings to programs. In S*ymposium in Applied Maths* (Schwartz, J., ed.). New York: American Mathematical Society, 19–31 [488]

Forte, G. (1992). Tools fair: out of the lab, onto the shelf. *IEEE Software,* **9** (3), 70–9 [150]

Frakes, W. and Isoda, S. (1994). Success factors for systematic reuse. *IEEE Software,* **11** (5), 14–22 [400]

Fraser, M. D., Kumax, K. and Vaishnavi, V. K. (1994). Strategies for incorporating formal specifications in software development. *Comm. ACM,* **37** (10), 74–86 [160]

Frewin, G. D. (1990). Procuring and maintaining reliable software. In S*oftware Reliability Handbook* (Rook, P., ed.), 211–46 [615]

Frewin, G. D. and Hatton, B. J. (1986). Quality management – procedures and practices. *IEE/BCS Software Engineering J.,* **1** (1), 29–38 [450]

Fromme, B. and Walker, J. (1993). An open architecture for tool and process integration. In *Proc. 6th Conf. on Software Engineering Environments,* Reading, UK, 50–62 [236]

Fuggetta, A. (1993). A classification of CASE technology. *IEEE Computer,* **26** (12), 25–38 [508]

Fujiwara, E. and Pradhan, D. K. (1990). Error-control coding in computers. *IEEE Computer,* **23** (7), 63–72 [389]

Futatsugi, K., Goguen, J. A., Jouannaud, J. P. and Meseguer, J. (1985). Principles of OBJ2. In *Proc. 12th ACM Symp. on Principles of Programming Languages,* New Orleans, 52–66 [168, 172]

Gallimore, R. M., Coleman, D. and Stavridou, V. (1989). UMIST OBJ: a language for executable program specifications. *Comp. J.,* **32** (5), 413–21 [146]

Gamma, E., Helm, R., Johnson, R. and Vlissides, J. (1995). *Design Patterns: Elements of Reusable Object-Oriented Software.* Reading MA: Addison-Wesley [405, 407]

Gane, C. and Sarson, T. (1979). *Structured Systems Analysis.* Englewood Cliffs NJ: Prentice-Hall [213]

Garlan, D., Kaiser, G. E. and Notkin, D. (1992). Using tool abstraction to compose systems. *IEEE Computer,* **25** (6), 30–8 [236]

Garlan, D. and Shaw, M. (1993). An introduction to software architecture. *Advances in Software Engineering and Knowledge Engineering,* **1**, Singapore: World Scientific Publishing [227, 242]

Gautier, R. J. and Wallis, P. J. L., eds (1990). *Software Reuse with Ada.* Stevenage, UK: Peter Perigrinus [405]

Gilb, T. and Graham, D. (1993). *Software Inspection.* Wokingham: Addison-Wesley [466, 487]

Goldberg, A. and Robson, D. (1983). S*malltalk-80. The Language and its Implementation.* Reading MA: Addison-Wesley [148, 215]

Gomaa, H. (1983). The impact of rapid prototyping on specifying user requirements. *ACM Software Engineering Notes,* **8** (2), 17–28 [140]

Gomaa, H. (1993). *Software Design Methods for Concurrent and Real-time Systems.* Reading MA: Addison-Wesley [301]

Grady, R. B. (1993). Practical results from measuring software quality. *Comm. ACM,* **36** (11), 62–8 [625]

Grady, R. B. and Van Slack, T. (1994). Key lessons in achieving widespread inspection use. *IEEE Software,* **11** (4), 46–57 [485]

Graham, I. (1994). *Object-oriented methods,* 2nd edn. Wokingham: Addison-Wesley [249]

Greenbaum, J. and Kyng, M. (1991). *Design at Work: Cooperative Design of Computer Systems.* Hillsdale NJ: Lawrence Erlbaum Associates [323]

Greenspan, S. and Feblowitz, M. (1993). Requirements engineering using the SOS paradigm. In *Proc. RE'93,* San Diego CA, 260–65 [84]

Grudin, J. (1989). The case against user interface consistency. *Comm. ACM,* **32** (10), 1164–73 [322]

Guerrieri, E. (1994). Case study: Digital's application generator. *IEEE Software,* **11** (5), 95–6 [409]

Guimaraes, T. (1983). Managing application program maintenance expenditures. *Comm. ACM,* **26** (10), 739–46 [666]

Gunning, R. (1962). *Techniques of Clear Writing.* New York: McGraw-Hill [624, 634]

Guttag, J. (1977). Abstract data types and the development of data structures. *Comm. ACM,* **20** (6), 396–405 [172]

Guttag, J. V. (1980). Notes on type abstraction. *IEEE Trans. on Software Engineering,* **SE-6** (1), 13–23 [185]

Guttag, J. V., Horning, J. J. and Wing, J. M. (1985). The Larch family of specification languages. *IEEE Software,* **2** (5), 24–36 [165, 168, 172]

Habermann, A. N. and Notkin, D. (1986). Gandalf: software development environments. *IEEE Trans. on Software Engineering,* **SE-12** (12), 1117–27 [540]

Hall, A. (1990a). Seven myths of formal methods. *IEEE Software,* **7** (5), 11–20 [123, 160, 161]

Hall, J. A. (1990b). Using Z as a specification calculus for object-oriented systems. In *VDM and Z – Formal methods in Software Development* (Bjorner, D., Hoare, C. A. R. and Langmaack, H., eds). Heidelberg: Springer-Verlag, 290–318 [202]

Halstead, M. H. (1977). *Elements of Software Science.* Amsterdam: North-Holland [671]

Hamer, P. G. and Frewin, G. D. (1982). M.H. Halstead's Software Science – a critical examination. In *Proc. 6th Int. Conf. on Software Engineering,* Tokyo, 197–206 [671]

Hamlet, D. (1992). Are we testing for true reliability? *IEEE Software,* **9** (4), 21–7 [361]

Hammer, M. (1990). Reengineering work: don't automate, obliterate. *Harvard Business Review,* July–August 1990, 104–12 [701]

Hammer, M. and McLeod, D. (1981). Database descriptions with SDM: a semantic database model. *ACM Trans. on Database Sys.,* **6** (3), 351–86 [104]

Harbert, A., Lively, W. and Sheppard, S. (1990). A graphical specification system for user interface design. *IEEE Software,* **7** (4), 12–20 [152]

Harel, D. (1987). Statecharts: a visual formalism for complex systems. *Sci. Comput. Programming,* **8** (3), 231–74 [302]

Harel, D. (1988). On visual formalisms. *Comm. ACM,* **31** (5), 514–30 [302]

Harker, S. D. P., Easton, K. D. and Dobson, J. E. (1993). The change and evolution of requirements as a challenge to the practice of software engineering. In *Proc. RE'93,* San Diego CA, 266–72 [74]

Hatley, D. J. and Pirbhai, I. A. (1987). *Strategies for Real-time System Specification.* New York: Dorset House [86]

Hayes, I. J. (1986). Specification directed module testing. *IEEE Trans. on Software Engineering,* **SE-12** (1), 124–33 [161]

Hayes, I., ed. (1987). *Specification Case Studies.* London: Prentice-Hall [190]

Heath, C. and Luff, P. (1991). Collaborative activity and technological design: Task coordination in the London Underground control room. In *Proc. ECSCW'91,* Amsterdam, 65–80 [95]

Hekmatpour, S. and Ince, D. (1988). *Software Prototyping, Formal Methods and VDM.* Wokingham: Addison-Wesley [148, 163]

Henderson, P. and Minkowitz, C. (1986). The me too method of software design. *ICL Technical J.,* **5** (1), 64–95 [146]

Heninger, K. L. (1980). Specifying software requirements for complex systems. New techniques and their applications. *IEEE Trans. on Software Engineering,* **SE-6** (1), 2–13 [68, 124]

Henry, S. and Kafura, D. (1981). Software structure metrics based on information flow. *IEEE Trans. on Software Engineering,* **SE-7** (5), 510–18 [631]

Hihn, J. and Habib–agahi, H. (1991). Cost estimation of software intensive projects: a survey of current practices. In *Proc. 13th Int. Conf. on Software Engineering,* Austin TX, 276–87 [596, 597]

Hoare, C. A. R. (1969). An axiomatic basis for computer programming. *Comm. ACM,* **12** (10), 576–83 [488]

Hoare, C. A. R. (1974). Monitors: an operating system structuring concept. *Comm. ACM,* **21** (8), 666–77 [301]

Hoare, C. A. R. (1985). *Communicating Sequential Processes.* London: Prentice-Hall [149, 168]

Huff, C. C. (1992). Elements of a realistic CASE tool adoption budget. *Comm. ACM,* **35** (4), 45–54 [523]

Hughes, J. A., Randall, D. and Shapiro, D. (1992). Faltering from ethnography to design. In *Proc. CSCW'92,* Toronto, Canada, 115–22 [95]

Hull, R. and King, R. (1987). Semantic database modeling: survey, applications and research issues. *ACM Computing Surveys,* **19** (3), 201–60 [104]

Humphrey, W. S. (1988). Characterizing the software process. *IEEE Software,* **5** (2), 73–9 [649]

Humphrey, W. S. (1989). *Managing the Software Process.* Reading MA: Addison-Wesley [615, 626, 646, 650]

Humphrey, W. S. and Curtis, B. (1991). Comment on 'a critical look'. *IEEE Software,* **8** (4), 42–7 [650, 651]

Humphrey, W. S. (1995). *A Discipline for Software Engineering.* Reading MA: Addison-Wesley [649]

IEC (1995). *Draft Standards (IEC 1508) for Functional Safety-related Systems,* Parts 1, 2, 3, 4, 5, 6 and 7. International Electrotechnical Commission [435]

IEE (1989). *Software in Safety-Related Systems.* Joint BCS/IEE Report, London: Institute of Electrical Engineers [424]

IEEE (1994). *Software Engineering Standards Collection.* Los Alamitos, CA: IEEE Press [619]

Imber, M. (1991). The CASE data interchange format (CDIF) standards. In *Proc. 5th Conf. on Software Engineering Environments,* Aberystwyth, Wales, 457–74 [514]

Ince, D. (1994). *ISO 9001 and Software Quality Assurance.* London: McGraw-Hill [613, 676]

Ince, D. C. and Hekmatpour, S. (1987). Software prototyping – progress and prospects. *Information and Software Technology,* **29** (1), 8–14 [138]

Ivie, E. L. (1977). The programmers workbench – a machine for software development. *Comm. ACM,* **20** (10), 746–53 [532, 533]

Jackson, M. A. (1975). *Principles of Program Design.* London: Academic Press [215]

Jackson, M. A. (1983). *System Development.* London: Prentice-Hall [213, 215]

Jackson, M. A. (1995). *Requirements and Specifications.* Wokingham: Addison-Wesley [122]

Jacob, R. (1986). A specification language for direct-manipulation user interfaces. *ACM Trans. on Graphics,* **5** (4), 318–44 [152]

Jacobsen, I., Christerson, M., Jonsson, P. and Overgaard, G. (1993). *Object-Oriented Software Engineering.* Wokingham: Addison-Wesley [215, 249, 256]

Jahanian, F. and Mok, A. K. (1986). Safety analysis of timing properties in real-time systems. *IEEE Trans. on Software Engineering,* **SE-12** (9), 890–904 [427]

Janis, I. L. (1972). Victims of Groupthink. *A Psychological Study of Foreign Policy Decisions and Fiascos.* Boston MA: Houghton Mifflin [581]

Jelinski, Z. and Moranda, P. B. (1972). Software reliability research. In *Statistical Computer Performance Evaluation* (Frieberger, W., ed.). New York: Academic Press, 465–84 [362]

Johnson, P. L. (1993). *ISO 9000: Meeting the New International Standards*. New York: McGraw-Hill [613]

Jones, C. B. (1980). *Software Development – A Rigorous Approach*. London: Prentice-Hall [165, 168, 190]

Jones, C. B. (1986). *Systematic Software Development using VDM*. London: Prentice-Hall [190]

Joos, R. (1994). Software reuse at Motorola. *IEEE Software*, **11** (5), 42–7 [396]

Jorgensen, P. C. and Erickson, C. (1994). Object-oriented integration testing. *Comm. ACM*, **37** (9), 30–8 [450]

Kafura, D. and Reddy, G. R. (1987). The use of software complexity metrics in software maintenance. *IEEE Trans. on Software Engineering*, **SE-13** (3), 335–43 [671]

Kemerer, C. (1987). An empirical validation of software cost estimation models. *Comm. ACM*, **30** (5), 416–29 [599]

Kitchenham, B. (1990a). Software development cost models. In *Software Reliability Handbook* (Rook, P., ed.). Amsterdam: Elsevier, 487–517 [598]

Kitchenham, B. (1990b). Measuring software development. In *Software Reliability Handbook* (Rook, P., ed.). Amsterdam: Elsevier, 303–31 [624, 626, 633]

Kitchenham, B., Pickard, L. M. and Linkman, S. J. (1990). An evaluation of some design metrics. *IEE/BCS Software Engineering J.*, **5** (1), 50–8 [631]

Knight, J. C. and Leveson, N. G. (1986). An experimental evaluation of the assumption of independence in multi-version programming. *IEEE Trans. on Software Engineering*, **SE-12** (1), 96–109 [380, 432]

Kotonya, G. and Sommerville, I. (1992). Viewpoints for requirements definition. *BCS/IEE Software Engineering J.*, **7** (6), 375–87 [83, 84, 86]

Kramer, J. and Magee, J. (1985). Dynamic configuration for distributed systems. *IEEE Trans. on Software Engineering*, **SE-11** (4), 424–35 [305, 379]

Krasner, H., Terrel, J., Linehan, A., Arnold, P. and Ett, W. (1992). Lessons learned from a software process modeling system. *Comm. ACM*, **35** (9), 91–100 [641]

Kyng, M. (1988). Designing for a dollar a day. In *Proc. CSCW'88*, Portland OR, 178–88 [323]

Laprie, J.-C., Arlat, J., Béounes, C. and Kanoun, K. (1995). Architectural issues in software fault tolerance. In *Software Fault Tolerance* (Lyu, M.R., ed.). Chichester: John Wiley & Sons, 47–80 [380]

Leblang, D. B. and Chase, R. P. (1987). Parallel software configuration management in a network environment. *IEEE Software*, **4** (6), 28–35 [695]

Lee, S. and Sluizer, S. (1985). On using executable specifications for high-level prototyping. In *Proc. 3rd Int. Workshop on Software Specification and Design*, 130–4 [146]

Lehman, M. M. and Belady, L. (1985). *Program Evolution: Processes of Software Change*. London: Academic Press [664]

Leite, J. C. S. P. (1989). Viewpoint analysis: a case study. *Software Engineering Notes*, **14** (3), 111–19 [83]

Leveson, N. G. (1985). Software safety. In *Resilient Computing Systems* (Anderson, T., ed.). London: Collins, 123–43 [427]

Leveson, N. G. (1986). Software safety: why, what and how. *ACM Computing Surveys*, **18** (2), 125–63 [426]

Leveson, N. G. and Harvey, P. R. (1983). Analysing software safety. *IEEE Trans. on Software Engineering*, **SE-9** (5), 569–79 [427]

Lientz, B. P. and Swanson, E. B. (1980). *Software Maintenance Management*. Reading MA: Addison-Wesley [660]

Lim, W. C. (1994). Effects of reuse on quality, productivity and economics. *IEEE Software*, **11** (5), 23–30 [396]

Lindsay, P. A. (1988). A survey of mechanical support for formal reasoning. *IEE/BCS Software Engineering J.*, **3** (1), 3–27 [489]

Linger, R. C. (1994). Cleanroom process model. *IEEE Software*, **11** (2), 50–8 [496, 498]

Linger, R. C., Mills, H. D. and Witt, B. I. (1979). *Structured Programming – Theory and Practice*. Reading MA: Addison-Wesley [493]

Liskov, B. and Guttag, J. (1986). *Abstraction and Specification in Program Development*. Cambridge MA: MIT Press [172]

Littlewood, B. (1990). Software reliability growth models. In *Software Reliability Handbook* (Rook, P., ed.). Amsterdam: Elsevier, 401–12 [350, 364]

Littlewood, B. and Verrall, J. L. (1973). A Bayesian reliability growth model for computer software. *Applied Statistics*, **22**, 332–46 [363]

Londeix, B. (1987). *Cost Estimation for Software Development*. Wokingham: Addison-Wesley [607]

Lubkin, D. (1991). Heterogeneous configuration management with DSEE. In *Proc. 3rd Int. Workshop on Software Configuration Management*, Trondheim, Norway, 153–60 [695]

Luqi (1992). Computer-aided prototyping for a command and control system using CAPS. *IEEE Software*, **9** (1), 56–67 [146]

Lutz, R. R. (1993). Analysing software requirements errors in safety-critical embedded systems. In *Proc. RE'93*, San Diego CA, 126–33 [352, 421, 477]

MacDonell, S. G. (1994). Comparative review of functional complexity assessment methods for effort estimation. *BCS/IEE Software Engineering J.*, **9** (3), 107–17 [593]

Maguire, M. C. (1985). A review of human-factors guidelines and techniques for the design of graphical human-computer interfaces. *Computers and Graphics*, **9** (3), 221–35 [321]

Markosian, L., Newcomb, P., Brand, R., Burson, S. and Kitzmiller, T. (1994). Using an enabling technology to reengineer legacy systems. *Comm. ACM,* **37** (5), 58–71 [703]

Marshall, J. E. and Heslin, R. (1975). Boys and girls together. Sexual composition and the effect of density on group size and cohesiveness. *J. of Personality and Social Psychology,* **31** (5), 952–61 [582]

Maslow, A. A. (1954). *Motivation and Personality.* New York: Harper and Row [572]

Matsumoto, Y. (1984). Some experience in promoting reusable software: presentation in higher abstract levels. *IEEE. Trans. on Software Engineering,* **SE-10** (5), 502–12 [396]

McCabe, T. J. (1976). A complexity measure. *IEEE Trans. on Software Engineering,* **SE-2** (4), 308–20 [475, 624, 671]

McCarthy, J. (1962). Towards a mathematical science of computation. In *Proc. IFIP 62,* Munich, 21–8 [488]

McCue, G. M. (1978). IBM's Santa Teresa laboratory: architectural design for program development. *IBM Systems J.,* **17** (1), 4–25 [585]

McGuffin, R. W., Elliston, A. E., Tranter, B. R. and Westmacott, P. N. (1979). CADES – software engineering in practice. In *Proc. 4th Int. Conf. on Software Engineering,* Munich, Germany, 136–44 [229]

McKee, J. R. (1984). Maintenance as a function of design. In *Proc. AFIPS National Computer Conf.,* Las Vegas, 187–93 [660]

Meyer, B. (1988). *Object-oriented Software Construction.* Englewood Cliffs NJ: Prentice-Hall [215, 407]

Miller, G. A. (1957). The magical number 7 plus or minus two: some limits on our capacity for processing information. *Psychological Review,* **63** (1), 81–97 [569]

Mills, H. D. (1988). Stepwise refinement and verification in box-structured systems. *IEEE Computer,* **21** (6), 23–37 [493]

Mills, H. D., Dyer, M. and Linger, R. (1987). Cleanroom software engineering. *IEEE Software,* **4** (5), 19–25 [351, 484, 496]

Mills, H. D., O'Neill, D., Linger, R. C., Dyer, M., and Quinnan, R. E. (1980). The management of software engineering. *IBM Sys. J.,* **24** (2), 414–77 [144]

MOD (1995). *The Procurement of Safety Critical Software* (revised edition). Ministry of Defence UK. Interim Defence Standard 00-55 [164, 432]

Mooney, J. D. (1990). Strategies for supporting application system portability. *IEEE Computer,* **23** (11), 59–70 [410]

Moret, B. (1982). Decision trees and diagrams. *ACM Computer Surveys,* **14** (4), 593–623 [123]

Mullery, G. (1979). CORE – a method for controlled requirements specification. In *Proc. 4th Int. Conf. on Software Engineering,* Munich, 126–35 [83]

Munck, R., Oberndorf, P., Ploedereder, E. and Thall, R. (1988). An overview of DOD-STD-1838A (proposed): The common APSE interface set, Revision A. *SIGSOFT Software Engineering Notes,* **13** (5), 235–47 [560]

Murphy, G. C., Townsend, P. and Sze Wong, P. (1994). Experiences with cluster and class testing. *Comm. ACM,* **37** (9), 39–47 [450]

Musa, J. D. (1993). Operational profiles in software reliability engineering. *IEEE Software,* **10** (2), 14–32 [360]

Musa, J. D., Iannino, A. and Okumoto, K. (1987). *Software Reliability: Measurement, Prediction, Application.* New York: McGraw-Hill [363]

Myers, B. (1988). *Creating User Interfaces by Demonstration.* New York: Academic Press [152, 558]

Myers, B. (1989). User-interface tools: introduction and survey. *IEEE Software,* **6** (1), 15–23 [152]

Myers, G. J. (1975). *Reliable Software through Composite Design.* New York: Petrocelli/Charter [276]

Myers, G. J. (1979). *The Art of Software Testing.* New York: John Wiley and Sons [464]

Myers, W. (1989). Allow plenty of time for large-scale software. *IEEE Software,* **6** (4), 92–9 [596, 607]

Nakajo, T. and Kume, H. (1991). A case history analysis of software error-cause relationships. *IEEE Trans. on Software Engineering,* **18** (8), 830–8 [421]

Neighbours, J. M. (1984). The Draco approach to constructing software from reusable components. *IEEE Trans. on Software Engineering,* **SE-10** (5), 564–74 [409]

Neilson, J. (1990). *Hypertext and Hypermedia.* San Diego CA: Academic Press [339]

Nii, H. P. (1986). Blackboard systems, Parts 1 and 2. *AI Magazine,* **7** (3 and 4), 38–53 and 62–9 [230]

Ning, J. Q., Engberts, A. and Kozaczynski, W. (1994). Automated support for legacy code understanding. *IEEE Software,* **37** (5), 50–7 [712]

Nissen, J. and Wallis, P. J. L., eds (1985). *Portability and Style in Ada.* Cambridge: Cambridge University Press [410]

Norman, D. A. and Draper, S. W. (1986). *User-centered System Design.* Hillsdale NJ: Lawrence Erlbaum [152, 323]

Nosek, J. T. and Palvia, P. (1990). Software maintenance management: changes in the last decade. *Software Maintenance: Research and Practice,* **2** (3), 157–74 [660]

O'Connor, J., Mansour, C., Turner-Harris, J. and Campbell, G. H. (1994). Reuse in command and control systems. *IEEE Software,* **11** (4), 70–9 [409]

Oberndorf, P. A. (1988). The common Ada programming support environment (APSE) interface set (CAIS). *IEEE Trans. on Software Engineering,* **14** (6), 742–8 [531, 560]

Oman, P. W. and Cook, C. R. (1990). The book paradigm for improved maintenance. *IEEE Software*, **7** (1), 39–45 [712]

Orr, K. (1981). *Structured Requirements Definition*. Topeka Kansas: Ken Orr and Associates [83]

OSF (1993). *OSF/Motif Style Guide, Release 1.2*. Englewood Cliffs NJ: Prentice-Hall [416, 517, 558]

Oviedo, E. I. (1980). Control flow, data flow and program complexity. In *Proc. COMPSAC'80*, Los Alamitos CA, 146–52 [633]

Parnas, D. (1972). On the criteria to be used in decomposing systems into modules. *Comm. ACM*, **15** (2), 1053–8 [215]

Parnas, D. L., van Schouwen, J. and Shu, P. K. (1990). Evaluation of safety-critical software. *Comm. ACM*, **33** (6), 636–51 [432, 434]

Paulk, M. C., Curtis, B., Chrissis, M. B. and Weber, C. V. (1993). Capability maturity model, Version 1.1. *IEEE Software,* **10** (4), 18–27 [649, 676]

Perrow, C. (1984). *Normal Accidents: Living with High-Risk Technology*. New York: Basic Books [422]

Peterson, J. (1977). Petri nets. *ACM Computer Surveys,* **9** (3), 223–52 [123]

Peterson, J. L. (1981). *Petri Net Theory and the Modeling of Systems*. New York: McGraw-Hill [168, 427, 643]

Petschenik, N. H. (1985). Practical priorities in system testing. *IEEE Computer,* **18** (5), 18–23 [464]

Preece, J., Rogers, Y., Sharp, H., Benyon, D., Holland, S. and Carey, T. (1994). *Human–Computer Interaction.* Wokingham: Addison-Wesley [320]

Prieto-Díaz, R. and Arango, G. (1991). *Domain Analysis and Software System Modeling*. Los Alamitos CA: IEEE Press [74, 401]

Putnam, L. H. (1978). A general empirical solution to the macro software sizing and estimating problem. *IEEE Trans. on Software Engineering,* **SE-4** (3), 345–61 [599, 607]

Rader, J., Brown, A. W. and Morris, E. (1993). An investigation into the state of the practice of CASE tool integration. In *Proc. 6th Conf. on Software Engineering Environments,* Reading, UK, 209–20 [514, 521]

Randell, B. (1975). System structure for software fault tolerance. *IEEE Trans. on Software Engineering*, **SE-1** (2), 220–32 [379, 391]

Randell, B. and Xu, J. (1995). The evolution of the recovery block concept. In *Software Fault Tolerance* (Lyu, M.R., ed.). Chichester: John Wiley & Sons, 1–22 [379]

Reiss, S, P. (1990). Connecting tools using message passing in the field environment. *IEEE Software*, **7** (4), 57–66 [236]

Reps, T. and Teitlebaum, T. (1984). The synthesizer generator. In *Proc. ACM SIGSOFT/SIGPLAN Symp. on Practical Software Development Environments,* Pittsburgh PA, 42–8 [540]

Rickets, J. A., DelMonaco, J. C. and Weeks, M. W. (1993). Data reengineering for application systems. In *Software Reengineering* (Arnold, R. S., ed.). Los Alamitos: IEEE Press, 288–91 [708]

Rittel, H. and Webber, M. (1973). Dilemmas in a general theory of planning. *Policy Sciences,* **4** (3), 155–69 [31]

Robinson, P. J. (1992). *Hierarchical Object-Oriented Design.* Englewood Cliffs NJ: Prentice-Hall [213, 249, 537]

Rochester, J. B. and Douglass, D. P. (1993). Re-engineering existing systems. In *Software Reengineering* (Arnold, R. S., ed.). Los Alamitos: IEEE Press, 41–53 [708]

Rochkind, M. J. (1975). The source code control system. *IEEE Trans. on Software Engineering,* **SE-1** (4), 255–65 [684, 688]

Rockwell, R. and Gera, M. H. (1993). The Eureka software factory CoRe: A conceptual reference model for software factories. In *Proc. 6th Conf. on Software Engineering Environments,* Reading, UK, 80–95 [244]

Rombach, H. D. (1990). Design measurement: some lessons learned. *IEEE Software,* **7** (2), 17–26 [626]

Rosenberg, B. (1991). *Kornshell Script Programming.* Reading MA: Addison-Wesley [151]

Ross, D. T. (1977). Structured analysis (SA). A language for communicating ideas. *IEEE Trans. on Software Engineering,* **SE-3** (1), 16–34 [83, 123]

Royce, W. W. (1970). Managing the development of large software systems: concepts and techniques. *Proc. IEEE WESTCON,* Los Angeles, 1–9 [9]

Rubin, K. and Goldberg, A. (1992). Object behaviour analysis. *Comm. ACM,* **35** (9), 48–62 [256]

Rumbaugh, J., Blaha, M., Premerlani, W., Eddy, F. and Lorensen, W. (1991). *Object-oriented Modeling and Design.* Englewood Cliffs NJ: Prentice-Hall [86, 107]

Sackman, H., Erikson, W. J. and Grant, E. E. (1968). Exploratory experimentation studies comparing on-line and off-line programming performance. *Comm. ACM,* **11** (1), 3–11 [594]

Scheifler, R. W. and Gettys, J. (1986). The X window system. *ACM Trans. on Graphics,* **5** (2), 79–109 [416, 558]

Schneidewind, N. F. and Keller, T. W. (1992). Applying reliability models to the space shuttle. *IEEE Software,* **9** (4), 28–33 [365]

Schoman, K. and Ross, D. T. (1977). Structured analysis for requirements definition. *IEEE Trans. on Software Engineering,* **SE-3** (1), 6–15 [83, 123]

Schwanke, R. W. (1991). An intelligent tool for re-engineering software modularity. In *Proc. 13th Int. Conf. on Software Engineering,* Austin TX, 83–92 [706]

Selby, R. W., Basili, V. R. and Baker, F. T. (1987). Cleanroom software development: an empirical evaluation. *IEEE Trans. on Software Engineering,* **SE-13** (9), 1027–37 [498]

Sheldon, F. T., Kavi, K. M., Tausworthe, R. C., Yu, J. T., Brettschneider, R. and Everett, W. W. (1992). Reliability measurement: from theory to practice. *IEEE Software*, **9** (4), 13–20 [365]

Shepherd, M. (1990). Design metrics; an empirical analyis. *IEE/BCS Software Engineering J.*, **5** (1), 3–10 [631]

Shepherd, S. B., Curtis, B., Milliman, P., Borst, M. and Love, T. (1979). First year results from a research program in human factors in software engineering. In *Proc. AFIPS 79*, Arlington VA, 1021–7 [671]

Shlaer, S. and Mellor, S. (1988). *Object-Oriented Systems Analysis: Modeling the World in Data.* Englewood Cliffs NJ: Yourdon Press [256]

Shneiderman, B. (1980). *Software Psychology.* Cambridge MA: Winthrop Publishers Inc. [570]

Shneiderman, B. (1986). *Designing the User Interface.* Reading MA: Addison-Wesley [334]

Shneiderman, B. (1992). *Designing the User Interface,* 2nd edn. Reading MA: Addison-Wesley [320, 321, 334, 571]

Silberschaltz, A., Peterson, J. and Galvin, P. (1991). *Operating System Concepts,* 3rd edn. Reading MA: Addison-Wesley [301]

Smith, D. R., Kotik, G. B. and Westfold, S. J. (1985). Research on knowledge-based software environments at Kestrel Institute. *IEEE Trans. on Software Engineering*, **SE-11** (11), 1278–95 [148]

Soloway, E., Ehrlich, K., Bonar, J. and Greenspan, J. (1982). What do novices know about programming? In *Directions in Human-Computer Interaction* (A. Badre and B. Shneiderman, eds). Norwood NJ: Ablex Publishing Co, 27–54 [571]

Sommerville, I. and Dean, G. (1996). PCL: A language for modelling evolving system architectures. *BCS/IEE Software Engineering J.,* to appear. [691]

Sommerville, I., Rodden, T., Sawyer, P., Bentley, R. and Twidale, M. (1993). Integrating ethnography into the requirements engineering process. In *Proc. RE'93*, San Diego CA, 165–73 [95]

Sommerville, I., Welland, R. C., Potter, S. J. and Smart, J. D. (1989). The ECLIPSE user interface. *Software Practice and Experience,* **19** (4), 371–92 [516]

Spivey, J. M. (1990). Specifying a real-time kernel. *IEEE Software,* **7** (5), 21–8 [162, 202]

Spivey, J. M. (1992). *The Z Notation: A Reference Manual,* 2nd edn. London: Prentice-Hall [165, 168, 190]

Stefik, M. J., Bobrow, D. G. and Kahn, K. M. (1986). Integrating access-oriented programming into a multiparadigm environment. *IEEE Software,* **3** (1), 10–18 [148]

Stepney, S., Barden, R. and Cooper, D. (1992). A survey of object orientation in Z. *BCS/IEE Software Engineering J.,* **7** (2), 150–60 [202]

Stroustrup, B. (1991). *The C++ Programming Language,* 2nd edn. Reading MA: Addison-Wesley [385, 393]

Suchman, L. (1983). Office procedures as practical action. *ACM Trans. on Office Information Systems,* **1** (3), 320–8 [95]

Symons, C. R. (1988). Function point analysis: difficulties and improvements. *IEEE Trans. on Software Engineering,* **14** (1), 2–11 [594]

Tanenbaum, A. S. (1992). *Modern Operating Systems.* Englewood Cliffs NJ: Prentice-Hall [301]

Tanenbaum, A. S., Klint, P. and Bohm, W. (1978). Guidelines for software portability. *Software Practice and Experience,* **8** (5), 681–98 [410]

Taylor, R. N., Selby, R. W., Young, M., Belz, F. C., Clarke, L. A., Wileden, J. C., Osterweil, L. and Wolf, A. L. (1988). Foundations for the Arcadia environment architecture. *SIGSOFT Software Engineering Notes,* **13** (5), 1–13 [521, 547]

Tedd, M. (1989). PCTE+: the evolution of PCTE. In *Software Engineering Environments: Research and Practice* (Bennett, K., ed.). Chichester: Ellis Horwood, 143–50 [560]

Teichrow, D. and Hershey, E. A. (1977). PSL/PSA: a computer aided technique for structured documentation and analysis of information processing systems. *IEEE Trans. on Software Engineering,* **SE-3** (1), 41–8 [123]

Teitleman, W. and Masinter, L. (1984). The Interlisp programming environment. In *Interactive Programming Environments* (Barstow, D.R., Shrobe, H. E. and Sandewall, E., eds). New York: McGraw-Hill, 83–96 [532]

Thomas, I. (1989). PCTE interfaces: supporting tools in software engineering environments. *IEEE Software,* **6** (6), 15–23 [515]

Tichy, W. (1985). RCS – a system for version control. *Software Practice and Experience,* **15** (7), 637–54 [688]

Took, R. (1986). The presenter – a formal design for an autonomous display manager. In *Software Engineering Environments* (Sommerville, I., ed.). Stevenage: Peter Perigrinus, 151–69 [146]

Tracz, W., ed. (1988). *Software Reuse: Emerging Technology.* Washington DC: IEEE Computer Society Press [396]

Turner, D. A. (1985). MIRANDA: A non-strict functional language with polymorphic types. *Proc. Conf. on Functional programming and Computer Architecture,* Nancy, France, 1–16 [147]

Ulrich, W. M. (1990). The evolutionary growth of software reengineering and the decade ahead. *American Programmer,* **3** (10), 14–20 [700, 703]

Van Vliet, H. (1993). S*oftware Engineering: Principles and Methods.* Chichester: John Wiley and Sons [172]

Wakeman, L. and Jowett, J. (1993). *PCTE: The Standard for Open Repositories.* Hemel Hempstead, UK: Prentice-Hall [515, 531, 560, 680]

Wallis, P. J. L. (1982). *Portable Programming.* London: Macmillan [410]

Walston, C. E. and Felix, C. P. (1977). A method of programming measurement and estimation. *IBM Systems J.,* **16** (1), 54–73 [583]

Ward, P. and Mellor, S. (1985). *Structured Development for Real-time Systems.* Englewood Cliffs NJ: Prentice-Hall [86, 302]

Warnier, J. D. (1977). *Logical Construction of Programs.* New York: Van Nostrand [215]

Wasserman, A. I. (1990). Tool integration in software engineering environments. In *Proc. Int. Workshop on Environments,* Berlin, 137–49 [512]

Watson, D. and Earnshaw, R. A., eds (1993). *Animation and Scientific Visualisation.* London: Academic Press [333]

Weaver, P. (1993). *Practical SSADM, Version 4.* London: Pitman [215]

Weinberg, G. (1971). *The Psychology of Computer Programming.* New York: Van Nostrand [580]

Weinberg, G. (1982). *Rethinking Systems Analysis and Design.* Boston: Little, Brown and Co [96]

Whitgift, D. (1991). *Software Configuration Management: Methods and Tools.* Chichester: John Wiley and Sons [683]

Wikstrom, A. (1988). *Standard ML.* Englewood Cliffs NJ: Prentice-Hall [147]

Winograd, T. (1988). A language/action perspective on the design of cooperative work. *Human–Computer Interaction,* **3** (1), 3–30 [644]

Wirfs-Brock, R., Wilkerson, B. and Weiner, L. (1990). *Designing Object-Oriented Software.* Englewood Cliffs NJ: Prentice-Hall [256]

Wirth, N. (1971). Program development by stepwise refinement. *Comm. ACM,* **14** (4), 221–7 [215]

Wirth, N. (1976). *Systematic Programming: An Introduction.* Englewood Cliffs NJ: Prentice-Hall [215, 276]

Wordsworth, J. B. (1990). The CICS application programming interface definition. In *Proc. Z User Workshop*, Oxford, 285–94 [162, 202]

Wordsworth, J. B. (1992). *Software Development with Z.* Wokingham: Addison-Wesley [190]

Young, D. A. (1990). *X Window Systems Programming and Applications with Motif.* Englewood Cliffs NJ: Prentice-Hall [321]

Yourdon, E. (1989). RE-3: re-engineering, restructuring and reverse engineering. *American Programmer,* **2** (4), 3–10 [700]

Zave, P. (1989). A compositional approach to multiparadigm programming. *IEEE Software,* **6** (5), 15–27 [123, 148]

Zave, P. and Schell, W. (1986). Salient features of an executable specification language and its environment. *IEEE Trans. on Software Engineering,* **SE-12** (2), 312–25 [149]

Zimmermann, H. (1980). OSI reference model – the ISO model of architecture for open systems interconnection. *IEEE Transactions on Communications,* **COM-28** (4), 425–32 [232, 243]

Index

Notes

Notes

Notes

Notes

Notes

Notes

Notes

Notes

Notes